INTERNATIONAL HUMAN RIGHTS

This book provides a ... s – international human rights law, why international human rig... o world prominence, what is being done about violations of human rights, and what ...g... ... done to further promote the cause of international human rights so that everyone may one day have their rights respected regardless of who they are or where they live.

It explains:

- How the concept of international human rights has developed over time
- The variety of types of human rights (civil-political rights, economic-social rights, as well as a delineation of war crimes)
- Empirical findings from statistical research on human rights
- Institutional efforts to promote human rights
- An extensive listing of international human rights agreements
- Identification of recent prosecutions of war criminals in domestic and international tribunals
- Ongoing efforts to promote human rights through international aid programs
- The newest dimensions in the field of human rights (gay rights, animal rights, environmental rights).

Richly illustrated throughout with case studies, controversies, court cases, think points, historical examples, biographical statements, and suggestions for further reading, *International Human Rights* is the ideal introduction for all students of human rights. The book will also be useful for human rights activists to learn how and where to file human rights complaints in order to bring violators to justice.

The new edition is fully updated and includes new material on:

- The Obama presidency
- The Arab Spring and its aftermath
- Workings of the International Criminal Court
- Quantitative analyses of human rights
- War crimes.

Michael Haas is a Nobel Peace Prize nominee and the author of more than 40 books on government and politics, primarily focused on human rights. He has recently analyzed the situations in Cambodia, Korea, and Singapore as well as the major war crimes of the twenty-first century.

Haas has written the most comprehensive and detailed text on human rights to date. It provides an indispensable resource for seasoned scholars as well as students who seek an accessible entry into this complex field.

David B. Ingram, Loyola University Chicago, USA

A refreshing take on human rights, balancing depth and clarity with the richness of examples. Ideal for teaching because it both informs and encourages critical thinking and action.

Christien Van Den Anker, University of the West of England, UK

Michael Haas' *International Human Rights*, second edition is truly a "comprehensive" introduction. It covers all the major bases in this ever expanding field. As someone who has used the first edition as a textbook in introductory courses on human rights, I am delighted to find that this second edition provides even more analytical depth as it describes the various norms, treaties, histories, institutions, and debates the fall within the modern international human rights regime. I look forward to using it in the future.

J. Paul Martin is Professor and Director of Human Rights Studies at Barnard College, Columbia University, USA

This is an outstanding contribution to the study of human rights. It provides far-reaching analysis that effectively deals with the complexities of human rights, exploring essential areas other texts too often marginalise.

Richard Burchill, Wilberforce Institute for the Study of Slavery and Emancipation, University of Hull, UK

This text is remarkable – thoughtful, critical, and well-researched. It offers a truly comprehensive approach that engages the student in the challenge of human rights in the modern era.

Michael F. Cairo, Transylvania University, USA

A rare tour-de-force, this book deserves wide reading by students, scholars, and policy-makers... Through lucid writing, meticulous research and a comprehensive scope, Haas balances basic concepts with advanced analysis…A masterful contribution.

Jacqueline C. Reich, Associate Professor of Political Science, Chestnut Hill College, USA

International Human Rights is not only a comprehensive introduction to the subject of human rights and related topics, it is also a detailed, clear, thoughtful, provocative volume that will prove valuable to government policy makers, NGOs, jurists, lawyers, researchers, teachers, and students now and into the future. I highly recommend it.

Carol Rittner, RSM, Distinguished Professor of Holocaust & Genocide Studies and **Marsha Raticoff Grossman**, Professor of Holocaust Studies, The Richard Stockton College of New Jersey, USA

A comprehensive and thorough text, likely to be of relevance to the practitioner as well as the student. It is well contextualised and of relevance across jurisdictions.

Chris Gale, Director of Bradford University Law School, UK

A thorough and comprehensive survey of major theories, issues, and debates in international human rights. Written in an approachable style, it will be of use to many students and practitioners of human rights.

Jelena Subotic, Associate Professor, Political Science, Georgia State University, USA

An outstanding book providing accurate political and historical insights throughout the interdisciplinary subject of human rights. Highly recommended for students wishing to develop a broad understanding of international human rights.

Ana Beduschi, Lecturer in Law, University of Exeter, UK

Panoramic coverage of the current debates and multiple perspectives coupled with historical, religious, and philosophical underpinnings. It is scholarly yet balanced with design features today's students are seeking.

Tass Hussain, Law Lecturer, University Centre at Blackburn College, UK

An authoritative, thoughtful, and thought-provoking contribution to the interdisciplinary field of international human rights. An outstanding teaching tool surveying a wide range of theories, issues, and debates. Highly recommended.

Ekaterina Balabanova, Univeristy of Liverpool, UK

International human rights are like a friendly octopus whose many limbs reach deeply into every dimension of human life. For this we should be thankful. But this makes writing a comprehensive yet accessible text challenging, apparently except for Michael Haas, who succeeds marvelously where many others have failed.

Patrick G. Coy, Professor and Director, Center for Applied Conflict Management, Kent State University, USA

Readers interested in the intellectual basis and history of international human rights will find this book a very valuable, accessible and engaging resource.

Donn Short, Faculty of Law, University of Manitoba; Editor-in-Chief, *Canadian Journal of Human Rights*

A unique, well-written, and multi-faceted textbook on human rights in its inclusion of important issues often not found in similar human rights texts. The book is of particular value in providing numerous contrasting perspectives on contemporary human rights issues as well as developing nations' approaches to human rights.

Tamara Relis, Assistant Professor, Touro Law Center, New York, Research Fellow, London School of Economics, UK

Written in an engaging and thought provoking manner, this book provides invaluable insight into various aspects of international human rights law. It is an excellent resource for anyone studying this subject for the first time.

Shilan Shah-Davis, Senior Lecturer, University of the West of England

Haas's *International Human Rights* is the essential read for introductory courses on human rights. Important second edition updates make this an unrivaled text for students and activists interested in advancing human rights around the world.

Katy Crossley-Frolick, Denison University, USA

INTERNATIONAL HUMAN RIGHTS

A Comprehensive Introduction

Second Edition

Michael Haas

Routledge
Taylor & Francis Group

LONDON AND NEW YORK

First edition published 2008
by Routledge

Second edition published 2014
by Routledge
2 Park Square, Milton Park, Abingdon, Oxon, OX14 4RN

and by Routledge
711 Third Avenue, New York, NY 10017

Routledge is an imprint of the Taylor & Francis Group, an informa business

British Library Cataloguing in Publication Data
A catalogue record for this book is available from the British Library

Library of Congress Cataloging in Publication Data
Haas, Michael
  International human rights: a comprehensive introduction / Michael Haas. – 2nd edition.
  pages cm
  Includes bibliographical references and index.
  1. Human rights. I. Title.
  K3240.H33 2013
  341.4'8–dc23
  2013003033

ISBN: 978-0-415-53818-3 (hbk)
ISBN: 978-0-415-53820-6 (pbk)
ISBN: 978-0-203-72686-0 (ebk)

Typeset in Adobe Garamond
by Sunrise Setting Ltd, Paignton, UK

Printed in Great Britain by Bell & Bain Ltd, Glasgow

CONTENTS

TABLES

PREFACE TO THE SECOND EDITION

International human rights concerns loom much larger on the world stage today than ever before. But no comprehensive textbook on human rights has existed until now to provide a foundation for those seeking to become acquainted with the main parameters of the field of study. That's why I wrote the first edition of this book. Since then, the field of human rights studies has changed from a focus on case studies to increased theoretical speculation and hypothesis testing. A second edition seems particularly apt, not only in view of the "Arab Spring" of 2011, in which countries in the Middle East attempted to overthrow dictatorial rule, but also the first use by the United Nations in the same year of the "responsibility to protect" to justify military force in Libya and other countries.

Engaging in hitherto unavailable research, I have improved upon the first edition by providing updated information, adding new sections, and amplifying or clarifying in each chapter, aiming thereby to go beyond formalistic information to give a flavor of what is actually taking place today. As before, I focus on rights relating to culture, politics, and society. The book is intended as a scholarly contribution in itself.

Many casual observers often assume that the subject of human rights is peripheral to an understanding of contemporary world politics, yet the opposite is the case: One cannot understand world politics today without attention to human rights because of increased scrutiny of human rights violations by governments and the public, thanks to enhancements of the media provided by the Internet. The focus on human rights has shifted attention in international relations from power politics to questions of morality. Individual countries and intergovernmental organizations are now bringing perpetrators of human rights horrors to account through concerted diplomatic, economic, legal, and even military action.

The book is written by a political scientist but combines perspectives of history, law, philosophy, and sociology. At the same time, I try not to take sides in the various debates and multiple perspectives, leaving resolution of controversies for readers to determine.

I am indebted for the inspiration of the book to Professor Seth Thompson of Loyola Marymount University, who proposed that I teach a course on international human rights in 1998, though I had not previously done so. Subsequently, I taught the course at California State University campuses in Fullerton and Los Angeles as well as at Occidental College.

When I first contemplated readings for students, and I began to outline lectures, I quickly realized that books usually assigned in international human rights courses were written by authors who put together an assorted collection of their writings, some case studies, and some polemical pleas, which were more appropriate as articles in learned journals. A balanced comprehensive textbook was lacking but needed. The present volume is the result. My effort may be viewed by perspicacious readers as a critique and correction of misinterpretations and oversights by competing textbooks.

The book has a number of features. Each chapter is punctuated with boxed summaries of court cases, discussion topics, historic events, and tables that provide clarification or further details. The life spans of prominent persons are provided in each chapter to identify the eras in which they lived. Chapter notes appear at the end with details on particular points, sometimes at length. References provide opportunities for further reading on many topics that cannot be covered in depth within an introductory textbook. A Glossary provides helpful definitions, and a List of Abbreviations will assist those who may be unfamiliar with the many acronyms. Readers will also note my tendency to bullet key points throughout the text. I seek to portray a panorama of the field of international human rights, opening vistas for those who want to find broad perspectives for pursuit of the subject.

A continuing focus in the volume is on human rights activism, that is, the way in which individuals and organizations over time have heroically sought to advance human rights, whether through philosophical pleas, drafting of important legal documents, or by taking direct action. Although the volume is intended for use as a college textbook, another aim is to provide activists with a handbook to assist their efforts by providing the historical, legal, and sociopolitical context. Emphasis on complaint mechanisms will particularly serve their interests.

Two of my websites may be of interest. One (www.uswarcrimes.com) lists references from press reports. The other (www.polfilms.com) contains reviews of films focusing on human rights.

Human rights issues have been the main focus of my academic career and much of my personal life. As an adoptee and a gay person, I perhaps have a unique perspective. Throughout more than three decades of teaching at the University of Hawai'i, from 1964–1978, I enjoyed the experience of a Caucasian living in a land where Asians, Pacific Islanders, and persons of mixed ancestry constitute a numerical majority and have established a multicultural milieu that competes quite successfully with the American culture that, for the most part, non-introspectively pervades the other 49 states. I have undertaken some activism in regard to human rights issues concerning Cambodia, Korea, and within California and Hawai'i, and that is evidently why I was nominated for a Nobel Peace Prize in 2009.

Several persons have provided assistance in my efforts. I therefore want to acknowledge the following: the late Robert Benson, Loyola University School of Law; Alice Bouras, Registry of the European Court of Human Rights; Malcolm Cox, Council of Europe; Lori Galway, International Criminal Court; Barry K. Gills, University of Newcastle; Riham Hazboun, UNESCO; Kevin Johnson, University of California at Davis; Michael Kilburn, Endicott College; Henrik Kristensen, Council of Europe; Oliver Liang, International Labor Organization; Michael J. Lightfoot,

Ranjana Natarajan, and Ann Richardson, human rights attorneys in the Los Angeles area; David K. Malcolm, University of Notre Dame of Australia; Begoña Martínez Alfonso, UN Geneva office; Joao M. Nataf, Committee Against Torture; Sheena Neogi, Human Rights Committee (of the International Covenant on Civil and Political Rights); Luda Petcherina, International Labor Organization Library; Ivaylo Petrov, UN High Commissioner for Human Rights; Philip Richards, American Embassy, Belgium; Geoffrey Robinson, UCLA; Tatiana Tassoni, World Bank; Judith Yontef, Van Nuys Law Library; S. Seetaram, Caribbean Community; Jan Malinowski, Council of Europe; Auret van Heerden, President and CEO, Fair Labor Association; Kenneth R. Weiss, Los Angeles Times.

In addition, I would like to thank some of my former students, who contributed many ideas while writing term papers in my courses over the years: Muneeza Ansari, Michael Cooper, Chris De Guía, Benjamin García-Ascue, Daisy M. Jones, S. Billie Kim, Jennifer Lane, Betsy Murphy, Priscilla Palmer, Carla Riedl-Stevens, Thanapoon Rimchala, Mark Robinson, Saeko Tew, and John Walker.

I have also benefited from criticisms of earlier drafts in the preparation of the manuscript. And I wish to thank my publisher, Routledge, for providing some of the criticisms as well as suggestions that I have taken into account in the present version.

Although I seriously contemplated cutting elements in some sections to shorten the manuscript, I changed my mind on receiving the comment that those very topics were not only much needed additions to a human rights textbook but were also particularly well written. In any case, readers can judge for themselves whether any sections in the book are integral to an understanding of, or provide important perspectives on, traditional human rights concerns. For me, they provide an integrated whole and a challenge.

Michael Haas
Los Angeles

ABBREVIATIONS

ACC	Arab Cooperation Council
ACD	Asia Cooperation Dialogue
ACLU	American Civil Liberties Union
ACP	Africa, the Caribbean, and the Pacific
AFL	American Federation of Labor
AFTA	ASEAN Free Trade Area
AIDS	Acquired Immune Deficiency Syndrome
AIPU	Arab Inter-Parliamentary Union
AIU	Amnesty International USA
ALBA	Bolivarian Alliance for the Peoples of Our America
ALESCO	Arab League Educational, Scientific, and Cultural Organization
ALF	Animal Liberation Front
AMIS	African Mission on the Sudan
ANCOM	Andean Community of Nations
APEC	Asia-Pacific Economic Cooperation conference
APF	Asia Pacific Forum of National Human Rights Institutions
API	Animal Protection Institute
APRM	African Peer Review Mechanism
ARU	American Railway Union
ASA	Association of Southeast Asia
ASEAN	Association of South-East Asian Nations
ATCA	Alien Tort Claims Act
ATO	alternative trade organization
AU	African Union
BCE	before the common era
BiH	Court of Bosnia and Herzegovina
BRICS	Brazil, Russia, India, China, South Africa
BSEC	Organization of the Black Sea Economic Cooperation
BSPC	Baltic Sea Parliamentary Conference
BTO	Brussels Treaty Organization
CAAC	United Nations Security Council Working Group on Children in Armed Conflict
CACJ	Central American Court of Justice
CACM	Central American Common Market
CAEU	Council of Arab Economic Unity

CARICOM	Caribbean Community and Common Market
CARIFTA	Caribbean Free Trade Association
CAT	Committee Against Torture
CBSS	Council of the Baltic Sea States
CCPCJ	Commission on Crime Prevention and Criminal Justice
CE	common era
CED	Committee on Enforced Disappearances
CEDAW	Committee on the Elimination of Discrimination Against Women
CEFTA	Central European Free Trade Agreement
CELAC	Community of Latin American and Caribbean States
CEN–SAD	Community of Sahel-Saharan States
CERD	Committee on the Elimination of All Forms of Racial Discrimination
CESCR	Committee on Economic, Social, and Cultural Rights
CFA	Committee on Freedom of Association (of the International Labor Organization)
CIS	Commonwealth of Independent States
CITES	Convention for International Trade in Endangered Species of Wild Fauna and Flora
CM	Committee of Ministers (of the Council of Europe)
CMS	Convention on the Conservation of Migratory Species of Wild Animals
CMW	Committee on the Protection of the Rights of All Migrant Workers and Members of Their Families
CNN	Cable News Network
CoE	Council of Europe
COMESA	Common Market for Eastern and Southern Africa
Comintern	Communist International
COMSATS	Commission on Science and Technology for Sustainable Development in the South
CPD	Commission on Population and Development (of the United Nations)
CPHRFF	Convention for the Protection of Human Rights and Fundamental Freedoms
C-Plan	The Colombo Plan for Cooperative Economic and Social Development in Asia and the Pacific
CRC	Committee on the Rights of the Child
CRPD	Committee on the Rights of Persons with Disabilities
CSCE	Conference on Security and Cooperation in Europe
CSD	Commission on Sustainable Development
CSocD	Commission for Social Development (of the United Nations)
CSSDCA	Conference on Security, Stability, Development, and Cooperation in Africa
CSTO	Collective Security Treaty Organization
CSW	Commission on the Status of Women (of the United Nations)
CTBTO	Comprehensive Nuclear-Test-Ban Treaty Organization
DDT	dichloro-diphenyl-trichloroetha
DEA	US Drug Enforcement Administration
DNA	deoxyribonucleic acid (the molecule containing genetic instructions used in the development and functioning of all living organisms)
DPA	UN Department of Political Affairs
DPKO	UN Department of Peacekeeping Operations
EAC	East African Community
EAEC	Eurasian Economic Community

EAPC	Euro-Atlantic Partnership Council
EC	European Community
ECCAS	Economic Community of Central African States
ECCC	Extraordinary Chambers in the Court of Cambodia for the Prosecution of Crimes Committed during the Period of Democratic Kampuchea
ECHR	European Court of Human Rights
ECO	Economic Cooperation Organization
ECOMOG	ECOWAS Monitoring Group
ECOSOC	UN Economic and Social Council
ECOWAS	Economic Community of West African States
ECSC	European Commission for Steel and Coal
EDSA	Epifanio de los Santos Avenue (in Manila)
EEA	European Economic Area
EEC	European Economic Community
EFTA	European Fair Trade Association
EFTA	European Free Trade Association
ERA	Equal Rights Amendment (in the United States)
ESC	Economic and Social Council (of the League of Arab States)
EU	European Union
EUFOR	European Union Force
EurAsEC	Eurasian Economic Community
Euratom	European Atomic Energy Agency
Europarl	European Parliament
Europol	European Law Enforcement Organization
FAO	Food and Agricultural Organization of the United Nations
FLA	Fair Labor Association
FLO	Fairtrade Labeling Organizations International
FSIA	Foreign Sovereign Immunities Act
FTA	free trade area
FTAA	Free Trade Area of the Americas (proposed)
FTF	Fair Trade Federation
GAFTA	Greater Arab Free Trade Area
GATT	General Agreement on Tariffs and Trade
GCC	Gulf Cooperation Council
GMO	genetically modified organism
GRI	Global Reporting Initiative
GSP	generalized system of preferences
GUAM	Organization for Democracy and Economic Development (of Georgia, Ukraine, Azerbaijan, Moldova)
HIV	human immunodeficiency virus
HRC	Human Rights Committee
IACHR	Inter-American Commission on Human Rights
IACHR	Inter-American Court of Human Rights
IAEA	International Atomic Energy Agency
IBE	International Bureau of Education
IBRD	International Bank for Reconstruction and Development

ICAO	International Civil Aviation Organization
ICC	International Criminal Court
ICCPR	International Covenant on Civil and Political Rights
ICJ	International Court of Justice
ICPO	International Criminal Police Organization
ICSID	International Center for Settlement of Investment Disputes
ICTR	International Criminal Tribunal for the Prosecution of Persons Responsible for Genocide and Other Serious Violations of International Humanitarian Law Committed in the Territory of Rwanda and Rwandan Citizens Responsible for Genocide and Other Such Violations Committed in the Territory of Neighboring States, Between 1 January 1994 and 31 December 1994
ICTY	International Criminal Tribunal for the Prosecution of Persons Responsible for Serious Violations of International Humanitarian Law Committed in the Territory of the Former Yugoslavia Since 1991
IDA	International Development Association
IDP	internally displaced person
IFAD	International Fund for Agricultural Development
IFAT	International Federation of Alternative Trade
IFAW	International Fund for Animal Welfare
IFC	International Finance Corporation
IFOR	Implementation Force (in Bosnia)
IFTA	International Fair Trade Association
IFTU	International Federation of Trade Unions
IGLHRC	International Gay and Lesbian Human Rights Commission
IGO	intergovernmental organization
IIIC	International Institute of Intellectual Co-operation
ILGA	International Lesbian and Gay Association
ILO	International Labor Organization
IMCO	Intergovernmental Maritime Consultative Organization
IMF	International Monetary Fund
IMO	International Maritime Organization
INS	US Immigration and Naturalization Service
Interpol	International Criminal Police Organization
IPCC	Intergovernmental Panel on Climate Change
ITLOS	International Tribunal for the Law of the Sea
IWW	International Workers of the World
KFOR	Kosovo Force
KLA	Kosovo Liberation Army
LAS	League of Arab States
LDC	less developed country
LGBT	lesbians, gays, bisexuals, and the transgendered
LRA	Lord's Resistance Army (of Uganda)
MARPOL	International Convention for the Prevent of Pollution from Ships
MCC	Universal Fellowship of Metropolitan Community Churches
Mercosur	Mercado Común de la Sur (Common Market of South America)
MFN	most-favored-nation (treaty provision)

MIA	missing in action
MICT	Mechanism for International Criminal Tribunals
MIGA	Multilateral Investment Guarantee Association
MSF	Médecins sans Frontières
MSG	Melanesian Spearhead Group
NAACP	National Association for the Advancement of Colored People
NAFTA	North American Free Trade Area
NAM	Non-Aligned Movement
NATO	North Atlantic Treaty Organization
NED	National Endowment for Democracy
NEPAD	New Partnership for Africa's Development
NEWS!	Network of European Worldshops
NGO	nongovernmental organization
NIEO	new international economic order
NPA	NATO Parliamentary Assembly
NPT	Non-Proliferation Treaty
NTB	nontariff trade barrier
NTR	normal trade relations
OAPEC	Organization of Arab Petroleum Exporting Countries
OAS	Organization of American States
OAU	Organization of African Unity
OCAC	Organization of Central Asian Cooperation
OCHA	United Nations Office for the Coordination of Humanitarian Affairs
OECD	Organization for Economic Co-operation and Development
OECS	Organization of Eastern Caribbean States
OEEC	Organization for European Economic Cooperation
OHCHR	Office of the High Commissioner for Human Rights
OIHP	Office International d'Hygiène Publique
OILPOL	International Convention for the Prevention of Pollution of the Sea by Oil
OPCW	Organization for the Prohibition of Chemical Weapons
OPEC	Organization of Petroleum Exporting Countries
OSCE	Organization for Security and Cooperation in Europe
OSI	Office of Special Investigations, US Department of Justice
PABSEC	Parliamentary Assembly of the Black Sea Economic Cooperation
PACE	Parliamentary Assembly of the Council of Europe
PBC	Peacebuilding Commission
PCA	Permanent Court of Arbitration
PCIJ	Permanent Court of International Justice
PETA	People for the Ethical Treatment of Animals
PIF	Pacific Islands Forum
PLO	Palestine Liberation Organization
POW	prisoner of war
PQLI	Physical Quality of Life Index
PTA	preferential trade agreement
R2P	responsibility to protect
RA	Rainforest Alliance

RCD	Regional Cooperation for Development
RSS	Regional Security System (of the Eastern Caribbean)
SAARC	South Asian Association for Regional Cooperation
SACN	South American Community of Nations
SADC	Southern African Development Community
SADCC	Southern African Development Co-ordination Conference
SAFTA	South Asian Free Trade Area
SAN	Sustainable Agricultural Network
SCO	Shanghai Cooperation Organization
SCU	Serious Crimes Unit
SEALs	Sea, Air, and Land teams
SEAMCED	Ministerial Conference for the Economic Development of Southeast Asia
SEATO	South-East Asia Treaty Organization
SFOR	Stabilization Force (in Bosnia)
START	Strategic Arms Reduction Treaty
STL	Special Tribunal for Lebanon
TNC	transnational corporation
TVPA	Torture Victim Protection Act
UDAW	Universal Declaration on Animal Welfare
UMA	Union du Maghreb Árabe
UN	United Nations
UNASUR	Union of South American Nations
UNCHR	United Nations Commission on Human Rights
UNCTAD	United Nations Conference on Trade and Development
UNCTC	United Nations Center for Transnational Corporations
UNDP	United Nations Development Program
UNEF	United Nations Emergency Force
UNEP	United Nations Environmental Program
UNESCO	United Nations Educational, Scientific, and Cultural Organization
UNFPA	United Nations Population Fund
UNGASS	United Nations General Assembly
UNHABITAT	United Nations Human Settlements Program
UNHCR	United Nations High Commissioner for Refugees
UNHRC	United Nations Human Rights Council
UNICEF	United Nations Children's Fund (originally United Nations International Children's Emergency Fund)
UNIDO	United Nations Industrial Development Organization
UNIFEM	United Nations Development Fund for Women
UNMIK	United Nations Interim Administration Mission in Kosovo
Unocal	Union Oil Company of California
UNODA	United Nations Office for Disarmament Affairs
UNOSOM	United Nations Operation in Somalia
UNPFII	United Nations Permanent Forum on Indigenous Issues
UNPROFOR	United Nations Protection Force
UNRRA	United Nations Relief and Rehabilitation Administration
UNSC	United Nations Security Council

UNSG	United Nations Secretary-General
UNTC	United Nations Trusteeship Council
UN Women	UN Entity for Gender Equality and the Empowerment of Women
UPU	Universal Postal Union
USAID	US Agency for International Development
USSR	Union of Soviet Socialist Republics
WBCSD	World Business Council for Sustainable Development
WEU	Western European Union
WFP	United Nations World Food Program
WFTO	World Fair Trade Organization
WHO	World Health Organization
WRAP	Worldwide Responsible Accredited Production
WTO	World Trade Organization
WWF	World Wildlife Fund
WWF	World Wide Fund for Nature

CHAPTER 1

Introduction

A most astonishing development in world history is occurring today. Concern over the observance of human rights clearly has become such a high priority that some current and former government leaders have been brought to justice for violations of international human rights within domestic and international tribunals. One might conclude that the world community has determined that the horrors of the twentieth century, such as mass murder by governments, will not be repeated in the twenty-first century by calling to account contemporary human rights violators as states additionally confront the challenge of international terrorism. The fulfillment of the goal of universal respect for human rights has become the most prominent ethical challenge of our time.

COURT CASE 1.1 THE ARREST AND TRIAL OF AUGUSTO PINOCHET (2000–2006)

In 1998, Augusto Pinochet (1915–2006) was arrested in London for extradition to Spain to be tried for crimes against humanity committed while he was president of Chile from 1973–1990. After considerable legal maneuvering, as well as a return to Chile, Pinochet was indicted by a Chilean court in 2000 for several crimes, including kidnapping, murder, torture, and illegal burial. His trial was ongoing at the time of his death.

The world is changing dramatically in the present age of rapid communication and continual movement of goods, ideas, messages, persons, and transactions across international borders. What happens to individuals in one country often has profound implications for other countries. For example, sweatshops operating with hazardous working conditions or child labor in poorer countries may compete with businesses that respect workers' rights in industrial democracies. Human rights are not only at the forefront of concern today for prosecutors and criminal lawyers but also for businesses, consumers, trade unions, and workers in the global economy.

The present volume seeks to explain the philosophical traditions and historical forces that have brought human rights issues into the international arena as well as to identify the variety of human rights and the many concrete efforts to improve human rights observance around the world so that readers will not only appreciate that human rights have a solid intellectual and legal foundation but also will become aware of what is being done to improve human rights observance today. First, however, fundamental terms need to be clarified.

BASIC DEFINITIONS

The world today consists of states with porous borders that relate to one another economically and in many other ways. The term **international** refers to a relationship that involves or transcends two or more individual states. For human rights to be viewed in an international context, there must be reference to norms that are designed to apply on a worldwide basis. Sometimes the term "international" is contrasted with "regional," the latter referring to a smaller, contiguous geographic area of the globe.

Human refers to *homo sapiens*, those who in some accounts descended from Adam and Eve, rather than to animals, minerals, and vegetables.

The term **rights** has many possible meanings. One common dictionary meaning is "the power or privilege to which one is justly entitled," with such examples as property rights, mineral rights, stockholder rights, and film rights. But none of the four examples appears central to what is meant by human rights, and the phrases "power or privilege" and "justly entitled" suggest that a right is acquired by special means rather than possessed from birth by all persons regardless of race, color, creed, gender, and the like.

Although there is no consensus on the precise meaning of the term "human rights," nearly everyone agrees that human rights are invoked to provide the ability to demand and enjoy a minimally restrictive yet optimal quality of life with freedom from interference with legitimate behavior, equal justice before law, and an opportunity to fulfill basic cultural, economic, and social needs. At the same time, the identification of specific rights has changed over time; new rights have emerged as humans have redefined their perspectives about what is desirable and intolerable as civilized beings.

Thus, the concept of "human rights" should be perceived as a **means**, not an end. The **end** is to allow humans to enjoy the good life. Some advocates of human rights, thus, assume that the good life is effectively attained by focusing political discussions on inalienable entitlements of human beings.

Rights also presuppose **responsibilities**. Humans must be moderate in their pursuits, respecting the rights of others. Institutions of governments are responsible both for protecting against abuse and injustice and for ensuring and facilitating human development. If humans and governments act otherwise, the human rights project will end. In other words, there must be a culture and an institutional framework to support what individuals and groups claim as their rights.

A fuller understanding of the term "international human rights" requires a discussion about the different ways in which alternative conceptions have been formulated. One may find greater enlightenment by examining the presumed sources of rights, rights as legal relations, the practical effects of assuming the existence of rights, and by contrasting types of rights through an analysis of subcategories.

SOURCES OF RIGHTS

Philosophically, the term "rights" has at least two types of meanings:

- **Moral Rights**. A "right" can be viewed as an ethical justification for setting up, maintaining, and respecting protections of individuals. In other words, "rights" owe their origins to such basic values as autonomy, dignity, equality, and survival. The logical inference is that certain values should be upheld institutionally. But how can one know what is a moral right? Presumably, moral rights are established by argumentation, by appeals to something called "fairness" or "justice," or by the principle that humans should possess "freedom." According to philosopher Alan Gewirth (1912–2004), one cannot act as a moral person unless one is free from constraints on one's rights. The moral rights approach is a **rationalist** understanding of rights, in which rights are considered to be self-evidently imprescriptible.
- **Legal Rights**. Alternatively, a "right" can be defined as a type of institutional arrangement in which interests are guaranteed legal protection, choices are guaranteed legal effect, or goods and opportunities are provided to individuals on a guaranteed basis. How do we know what is a "right"? The answer is to read a law book. A focus on legal rights is a **positivist** understanding of rights in which humans gain or lose rights depending upon the current state of the law. In short, a "right" can exist only when laws or judicial opinions say so specifically.

The American Declaration of Independence of 1776 states moralistically that the rights of life, liberty, and the pursuit of happiness are inalienable and self-evident, but the meaning is vague. In contrast, specific legal rights are contained in the French National Assembly's Declaration of the Rights of Man and Citizen of 1789 and the ten constitutional amendments adopted in 1791 known as the American Bill of Rights. However, the Ninth Amendment provides for the possibility of an expansion in the number of identifiable rights. For example, there is no mention of a right to marry in the Constitution, as amended. Nevertheless, the US Supreme Court asserted that there is a right to marry in 1967 by ruling in *Loving v. Virginia*

(388US1) that no state could deny a marriage license to a man and a woman of different races. However, the same right has not been universally recognized to apply to couples of the same sex.

"RIGHTS" AS LEGAL RELATIONS

Nevertheless, conceptual clarity remains elusive, even for legal rights. Following the formulation of law professor Wesley Hohfeld (1879–1918), four different types of legal relations are often called "rights":

- **Powers** are the capabilities of a particular person to uniquely do something because of power status. For example, individuals have a right to will possessions to anyone. However, almost everyone has the power to harm another, so powers must be limited or there would be no rights.
- **Immunities** are actions that persons with higher power status cannot do to ordinary persons. For example, if someone owns property, and oil is found on the property, a rights-respecting government will not have the power to take that property away from its owner without providing reasonable compensation. Immunities are rights to which individuals are entitled.
- **Liberties**, sometimes called privileges, are actions that can be taken without the approval of anyone or any institution. However, there is a limit to the exercise of liberties – when the liberties of others are infringed. The term **civil liberties**, as used in the United States, refers to prohibitions on what government can do to individuals, as specified in the Bill of Rights, where everyone is assured of such liberties as freedom of the press. Civil liberties can also be called **civil rights**.
- **Claim-Rights** are obligations of others to us; they are the other side of the same coin as liberties. To claim a right to privacy, for example, is to tell others that they should not intrude into our personal space. The term **civil liberties**, as used in the United States, refers to the obligation of government not to infringe on various individual freedoms identified in the American Bill of Rights. **Minority rights**, on the other hand, are primarily based on three amendments (Thirteenth, Fourteenth, and Fifteenth) to the American Constitution that were passed shortly after the American Civil War (1861–1865) in order to obligate nonminorities not to discriminate against former slaves. Later constitutional amendments and laws have expanded coverage to other classes of persons, notably other minorities, women, the elderly, the disabled, and gays. Minority rights protections recognize that only governments effectively have the ultimate power to stop widespread discrimination against persons who belong to nonmainstream groups, whereas civil liberties refer to what government is not supposed to do to all persons.

Liberties and claim-rights are together understood around the world to mean "human rights." But rights are also formulated in terms of immunities and liberties to assure individuals that they have many residual powers outside the sphere both of government and of other powerful institutions. Because lawyers, political scientists, sociologists, and others approach the subject with differing perspectives, a debate is ongoing among scholars about the formal definition of "human rights."

EFFECTS OF HUMAN RIGHTS

Philosopher Isaiah Berlin (1909–1997) distinguishes between two types of liberty. **Negative liberty** exists when there are limits on adverse human behavior, whereas **positive liberty** is the power to act autonomously. Similarly, the concept of human rights has two basic effects with regard to human actions:

- Rights place **limits** on actions of others by offering a measure of protection to individuals and to specific groups. In short, certain actions are banned, and governments as well as individuals have a duty to respect those limits. In other words, there are rights claimants and correlative duty bearers. According to contemporary political scientist Henry Shue, the basic duties are threefold: (1) not to deprive individuals of rights, (2) to protect individuals against deprivation, and (3) to aid those whose rights are being violated.
- Rights also offer individuals and specific groups the **power** to seek redress and to give them a way to impose limits on those who would violate their rights. In other words, rights are "trump cards," to use the analogy of Ronald Dworkin (1931–2013), with which to annul adverse actions that might be taken by powerful groups, institutions, and persons.

DISCUSSION TOPIC 1.1 HOW SHOULD "HUMAN RIGHTS" BE DEFINED?

There are several ways of defining or approaching the subject of human rights, but no consensus. Which conception is the most useful? What are the practical consequences of defining "human rights" in different ways? Can rights exist without responsibilities?

CLASSIFICATIONS OF HUMAN RIGHTS

Another way to understand human rights is in terms of generations of rights. *The International Dimensions of Human Rights* (1982), by jurist Karel Vašák (1957–), suggests three generations based on the French trichotomy between liberty, equality, and fraternity: (1) Civil and political rights constitute the first generation, which focus on issues of liberty. (2) Economic, social, and cultural rights are the second generation, with a concern on equality. (3) The third generation, he argues, is concerned with a wide range of issues, including the rights to development, a healthy environment, group self-determination, and peace. Political scientist, David Forsythe (1941–), refers to the trichotomy respectively as negative rights, positive rights, and synthetic rights.

TABLE 1.1   **HUMAN RIGHTS GENERATIONS**

Type of rights	First recognized
Constitutional rights	13th–18th century
Civil liberties	18th century
Political rights	19th century
Minority rights	19th century
Women's rights	19th century
Rights of persons in wartime	19th century
Economic, social, and cultural rights	20th century
Right of self-determination	20th century
Group rights	20th century
Right to peace	20th century
Right to development	20th century
Right to a healthy environment	20th century
Gay rights	20th century
Responsibility to protect from genocide	21st century

A chronological approach finds more complexity than a generational classification, however (Table 1.1). The significance of the signing of the Magna Carta in 1215 was to limit the absolute authority of rulers by writing down limits to the powers of government in the form of a contract. Eventually, **constitutions** emerged as contracts between people and governments that state the boundaries of what government can and cannot do. The modern quest to protect **civil liberties** in constitutions and through legislation first emerged in the eighteenth century, when American and French citizens sought to protect personal freedoms, particularly freedom of conscience, in bills of rights.

The extension of **political rights** made headway in the nineteenth century, as requirements for those eligible to vote were reduced; instead of allowing only wealthy males to exercise the franchise, the movement toward universal suffrage gradually gained acceptance. **Minority rights**, for example, advanced as slavery was abolished worldwide. During the mid-nineteenth century, the earliest Geneva Conventions called attention to rights of civilians and soldiers in time of war; what were then identified as **war crimes** evolved into an additional concern for **crimes against humanity** and **crimes against peace** during the twentieth century. With the establishment of socialism in Russia during the early twentieth century, there was a focus on new issues; namely, **economic, social,** and **cultural rights**. The peace settlement immediately following World War I established the principle of the **self-determination of peoples**, thus extending rights from individuals to national groups. The **right to peace**, implicit in the establishment of both the League of Nations and the United Nations, was explicitly stated within a declaration adopted by the UN General Assembly in 1984. The **right to development** was declared by the UN General Assembly in 1986 so that rich countries would feel responsible to

TABLE 1.2   ALTERNATIVE CATEGORIZATIONS OF HUMAN RIGHTS

Categorizer	*Categories*
Constant	Liberty of the ancients
	Liberty of the moderns
Muskie; Vance	Freedom of violations of the human person
	Rights of fulfillment of economic needs
	Civil and political rights
Shue	Liberty
	Security rights
	Subsistence rights
Donnelly and Howard	Survival rights
	Membership rights
	Empowerment rights
	Other rights
United Nations Development Program	Equality of opportunity
	Freedom of expression
	Personal security rights
	Rights of political participation
	Rule of law

assist poor countries. The **right to a healthy environment** has become a new frontier as is the extension of rights to **gays, lesbians, bisexuals,** and the **transgendered**; both await a consensus as the twenty-first century proceeds. Perhaps the most controversial of all, the **right to be protected from genocide** (R2P), is still being debated.

Some scholars have argued that there is a **right to democracy**, by which they usually mean the free exercise of such political rights as the right to vote. However, dictatorships have elections, and many newly democratizing countries give citizens political rights but do not respect their civil rights. A country that admits political rights but not civil rights is known as an **illiberal democracy**.

Yet another way to define "human rights" is to delineate subtypes (Table 1.2). Analytical categorizations can serve to focus attention on different problem areas. Swiss philosopher Benjamin Constant (1767–1839) has contrasted the **liberty of the ancients** (freedom from government coercion) from the **liberty of the moderns** (freedom to participate in government), that is, civil rights as distinct from political rights. A few of the categories in Table 1.2 have been reviewed above, but there are some innovations as well. Edmund Muskie (1914–1996) and Cyrus Vance (1917–2002), former US Secretaries of State, identify **freedom of violations of the human persons** as the right to be personally secure, which is otherwise identified under the term "security rights." "Survival rights" and "subsistence rights" refer to the **right to life**, in particular to have food, clothing, and shelter. In some clever category schemes, **civil rights** are referred to as "membership rights" and "freedom of expression rights," whereas **political rights** have been referred to as "empowerment rights" or "political participation rights."

GLOBALISM VERSUS STATISM

This chapter began by citing breakthrough events in the development of international human rights – that is, instances when rulers of various states have been called to account for misdeeds perceived by governments, by an international organization, and even by a nongovernmental organization formed of private individuals. The concept of "international human rights" is relatively recent.

Throughout much of human history, states were either isolated from one another or governed by an imperial center. When the Roman Empire fell, national states gradually emerged in Europe that were jealous of their power and unwilling to be criticized for misconduct. Although the Catholic Church sought to impose a moral order, using the threat of excommunication, the rise of Protestantism contested the Vatican's claim to universal jurisdiction. Wars over religious preferences then convulsed Europe from the time of Martin Luther (1483–1546) until the Westphalia peace agreement of 1648, which established the principle that governments have **sovereignty**; that is, not only exercise legitimate power within the borders of their countries but ordinarily have no right to intervene in the affairs of other governments unless the lives of their own citizens are in danger. The Westphalian concept of human rights is premised on a **statist** concept of the world polity – namely, that the only legitimate units of international politics are nation-states, which cannot intervene in the affairs of other countries (the principle of **nonintervention**), though citizens of one country abroad have rights that foreign government must respect.

HISTORIC EVENT 1.1 THE PEACE OF WESTPHALIA (1648)

The Peace of Westphalia consisted of two nearly identically worded treaties – one signed by four Catholic countries at Münster, the other by two Protestant countries at Osnabrück. The practical effect was for European countries, particularly the Holy Roman Empire, to recognize the principle that leaders of countries could determine their own state religion without outside interference and that those espousing a minority religion were guaranteed freedom of worship. Boundaries of several states were redrawn, especially in German-speaking Europe, which consisted of dozens of city-states and principalities. Although many scholars date the beginning of international law and the establishment of the principle of sovereignty from the Westphalian peace agreements, the Holy Roman Empire was still allowed to depose princes of the German states, and France and Sweden reserved the right to intervene if terms of the treaty were violated. Subsequently, France upset the balance of power, seeking hegemony in the European state system, first under Louis XIV (1638–1715) and later under Napoléon Bonaparte (1769–1821).

The nation-state system began as a European idea. Membership in the system was conferred by a reciprocal exchange of diplomatic representatives. A primary role of the diplomat abroad was to look out for a country's commercial interests, including representatives of businesses while abroad. Trade agreements between states were formalized into legal contracts; that is, interstate **treaties**. As the number of commercial and noncommercial treaties increased, so did the scope of international law, which developed as the set of mutually respective limitations on state sovereignty. The Westphalian principle of nonintervention in the domestic affairs of other countries applied only to members of the state system. Enforcement of human rights and international law was left to nation-states, so the more powerful governments had more resources to impose their will on other states and to write the rules of the road.

Accordingly, colonialism and imperialism could proceed unabated in the Westphalian world. In other words, a globalized conception of the planet did exist prior to Westphalia. What changed from 1648 was a demarcation between two worlds: In Europe, limited human rights began at Westphalia and grew. In the other part of the world, European powers could violate human rights with impunity until challenged by colonists and indigenous people from 1776 to the present. Opponents of imperialism cited the principle of self-determination, a human rights principle embedded in Westphalianism, to demand independence, thereby transforming the European principle of self-government into a universal reality.

The nation-state concept also sweeps under the rug various entities that are neither colonies nor states – that is, territories that have no recognition as states and might or might not have governance structures. The Kurds, who believe that they were promised a state of their own after World War I, are now scattered across several countries in the Middle East and have only recently achieved a certain amount of autonomy within Iraq. When many African and Asian colonies achieved independence, the imperial powers had arbitrarily drawn the lines around the new countries. As a result, peoples with a coherent identity in the peripheries, who were ignored by the colonial authorities, found themselves suddenly trapped under the authority of peoples whom they did not know in the capitals of the newly independent states. Burma, for example, has had a continual civil war with Kachin, Rohingya, and many other groups living in mountainous regions. Heavily armed criminal gangs have carved out domains in México and elsewhere where their authority exceeds that of the central government. Emboldened by the Westphalian ideology of the legitimacy of the nation-state, governments have attempted to impose order in these cases, often ruthlessly.

The dominant theory of statecraft, before and after 1848, was **realism**, otherwise known as *realpolitik*. Realists argue that states should build up their power to become dominant players in the world polity. If dominant, realist-guided rulers are to increase their power even more by overwhelming other states – by force or by threat – and by grabbing colonies before other countries did so. If not dominant, states should build their power and make strategic alliances to avoid losing in wars with more powerful states. Moral principles, such as concepts of human rights, were observed only when they helped to bolster state power. A balance of power was sought to prevent intrusion by some major powers into the affairs of other countries, and the purpose of the nonintervention principle was to protect lesser European powers from being treated as colonies. But the calamities of World Wars I and II proved that such an anarchical society of states could no longer be tolerated.

The contemporary world now lives in a post-Westphalian era. All countries are members of the state system, and colonialism is mostly limited to control of a few isolated lands with small populations. State sovereignty is no longer sacrosanct. In contrast with realism and statism, the **globalist** perspective is that actions inside the borders of one country impact other countries, international organizations, or nongovernmental organizations because there is a single world economy, polity, and society. Rules written by the overwhelming majority of states for the planet can now brand domestic actions of individual states not only as illegal but can also lead to a determination that noncompliant governments are international outlaws that must be brought to justice through enforcement actions by members of the world community. Thus, state stability today is decreasingly a function of governmental power. Instead, states must observe human rights to avoid the possibility of sanctions from other countries.

The two major sources of post-Westphalian interventionist rules, as found in the corpus of international law, are multilateral agreements and international customs that are interpreted as conferring on states the power to intervene in the domestic affairs of other countries in order to enforce global norms of proper state behavior. A state's sovereignty, in other words, is now more likely to be secure when a government behaves according to norms generally respected by the world community or rules encoded in declarations and treaties adopted at international conferences on a wide range of issues, including human rights.

There are two competing forms of globalism. The **cosmopolitan** view is that humans possess rights that all governments must respect. For some cosmopolitans, state sovereignty should ideally be replaced by the authority of **supranational** organizations. **Internationalism**, in contrast, is the perspective that human rights should be defined and enforced by states, which in turn may concede some powers to intergovernmental organizations but might later decide to rescind such powers.

Human rights concerns have been central to three globalizations that have been taking place in the decades since the end of the Cold War in 1991, when the Soviet Union ceased to exist. **Economic globalization** has developed with the collapse of the barter-based socialist system headed by the Soviet Union. New competitive economic forces in the world have prompted observers to apply a **communitarian globalization** in which common norms and values must necessarily be the underpinning for a stable economic and political world order. A third trend is **informational globalization**, as individuals tune in to global media that often provide compelling images of significant human rights violations.

Some alarmists claim that globalization is leading to supranational world government, but there is no such future prospect. Governments still cling to their sovereignty, even as global forces continue to undermine the scope of their power. Meanwhile, one response to globalization is that the demand for greater respect toward human rights is emerging all over the globe. Human rights are not yet universally respected, but the overall trend is in that direction.

RELATIVISM VERSUS UNIVERSALISM

Historically, the term "human rights" is a recent notion. The human rights project is not over, as violations of the basic principles occur daily. Some argue that the concept is culture-bound, that the West is trying to impose the idea upon the rest of the world. Yet if there were a secret ballot on whether to accept specific rights, the vote would be overwhelmingly in favor of the right to life. Many of the remaining principles are derived from the right to life, so advocates of the human rights project often argue that human rights are **universal** and should be respected everywhere.

Those who dispute universalism argue for a **relativistic** approach. At one time in human history, violence was viewed as the best way to settle conflicts, but later executive authorities of governments assumed a monopoly of force to handle divisions, and even later legislative bodies emerged as supreme over the executive branch of government. Those who argue for independent courts assume that granting power to judges and juries will not undermine public order. Thus, individualistic cultures often demand rights independent of the consequences, whereas other cultures seek to balance individual rights with the needs of the community for stability. For example, the right to publish blasphemous cartoons and videos might be upheld in one country as free speech, but other cultures prefer to limit blasphemy in order to prevent the right to protest such speech from becoming dangerously violent. In other words, rights may be universal but they are interpreted and practiced in a cultural context.

DISCUSSION TOPIC 1.2 IS BLASPHEMOUS SPEECH A HUMAN RIGHT?

In 2012, a proposal was submitted to the UN General Assembly to ban blasphemy – that is, speech offensive to religious believers. Another speaker upheld the right of free speech. When printed media originating in one country only left that country by horse and buggy, speech might not have infuriated persons in other countries. Now that media are instantaneously spread worldwide, should the right to free speech be modified to ban blasphemy?

But even advocates of universalistic rights will concede that there are few **absolute rights** that can never be abridged. The right to assemble, for example, does not confer a right to demonstrate on a randomly selected private residence so that a child cannot leave home for school, thereby disrupting the right of the child to education. The right to assemble is a **qualified right** – limited by considerations of reasonable place, time, and manner of assembly. Similarly, the right to clean air does not confer an obligation on the state to provide everyone with oxygen masks for ordinary use in their daily lives. But that might change in the future.

PRIORITIES

The debate between whether civil and political rights are more fundamental than economic, social, and cultural rights was intense during the Cold War, pitting the individualist West against the collectivist Soviet bloc. Today, China argues that democratic freedoms must be postponed until citizens reach an optimal level of income and literacy. Some in the West claim that voting rights are prior to all other rights, since those who control the political system determine which rights will be enforced. However, India adopted democracy despite a population with many illiterate and poor persons, whereas majorities in illiberal democracies can restrict the rights of minorities. Arguments about which rights come first seem to be crafted to the satisfaction of those in power.

TOOLS FOR STOPPING HUMAN RIGHTS VIOLATIONS

How can individuals, states, or organizations try to stop violations of human rights? A panoply of methods has been developed over the years (Table 1.3). In later chapters of the present volume, the use of the above methods to deal with human rights violations will be analyzed.

Standard Setting. Treaties are often vague, so a more complete specification of the standards of various rights is needed. For example, many prisoners may be inhumanely crowded into a single cell for days and consider their human rights to be

TABLE 1.3 **TOOLS FOR PROMOTING INTERNATIONAL HUMAN RIGHTS**

Tool	Example
Standard setting	Agreement on provisions of the International Covenant on Economic, Social, and Cultural Rights, 1966 (see Table 6.1)
Monitoring	Establishment of a truth commission to determine facts about massacres and other human rights violations of the people of East Timor, 2002 (see Table 5.5)
Information dissemination	People power demonstrations against unjust rule in Tunisia, 2011 (see Historic Event 4.6)
Diplomatic negotiation	Adoption of a procedure to end the practice of selling diamonds for arms, 2002 (see Historic Event 10.1)
Popular pressure	Free and fair voting in Burma to replace unjust rulers, 1990 (see Historic Event 13.3)
Legal action	Nicaragua's lawsuit against the United States for mining one of its harbors, as decided by the International Court of Justice, 1986 (see Court Case 7.5)
Economic measures	The boycott of buses in Montgomery, Alabama, to protest segregation, 1955–1956 (see Historic Event 4.4)
Military action	Action to stop cross-border aggression in Korea, 1950–1953 (see Historic Event 7.1)

violated thereby. What constitutes "overcrowding" is a matter for deliberation and negotiation in order to provide a standard criterion, based on a minimum square feet of space per person. Chapters 5–7 identify some of the basic standards of contemporary human rights.

Monitoring. Several countries, nongovernmental organizations, and intergovernmental organizations collect information about compliance with international norms into reports. Human rights is no longer a private matter solely within the purview of individual states. In 1968, for example, the UN General Assembly established the Special Committee to Investigate Israeli Practices Affecting the Human Rights of the Palestinian People and Other Arabs of the Occupied Territories.

Information Dissemination. Many publications have emerged from Amnesty International, the United Nations, and other organizations, though the mass media are the major sources of information about international human rights today, including the Internet. Comments on actual conditions can take the form of verbal or other nonviolent pressures serving to humiliate violators. The most potent form of information dissemination is condemnation.

Diplomatic Negotiation. Bilateral and multilateral diplomacy, including mediation, may encourage governments to abandon unapproved practices. Many of the principal human rights treaties have been adopted at international conferences. Colonial rule has characteristically ended with negotiated agreements.

Popular Pressure. In democratic countries, voters can defeat incumbents at the polls and attempt thereby to replace unjust rulers. In undemocratic countries, "people power" mass demonstrations may bring about improvements. In both types of countries, nongovernmental interest groups can mobilize pressure, sometimes with the help of outside groups.

Legal Action. Lawyers seek to enforce laws and treaties in domestic and international courts, thereby deriving enforceable or advisory judgments. The present volume highlights many court cases that have been central to the development of international human rights, but they customarily occur after human rights violations have already occurred.

Economic Measures. Economic assistance and trade can be used on condition of compliance with international norms. Trade boycotts, as applied against South Africa, can apply economic pressure. Aid is a "carrot"; boycotts are "sticks."

Military Action. Sometimes the only way to stop atrocities is to threaten or launch a military attack that will force a country to back down or to effect regime change. The most recent case is the military effort in 2011 to stop a threatened mass murder in Libya. However, there is a danger that many human rights violations will be committed by all sides after war begins.

DESIGN OF THE VOLUME

A book on international human rights would have been very short indeed before the formation of the United Nations in 1945. Today, a textbook on the subject can only provide a foundation or introduction to a vast realm of contemporary reality.

The present volume, accordingly, seeks to identify the basic parameters of international human rights. The discussion includes how the concept of international human rights has developed over time (Chapters 2–4), the variety of types of human rights (Chapters 5–7), empirical findings from statistical research on human rights (Chapter 8), institutional efforts to promote human rights in the United States, Europe, and elsewhere (Chapters 9–13), and a discussion of some of the newest dimensions in the field of human rights as well as a discussion of problems with the rights-based approach (Chapter 14). The aim herein is to provide a comprehensive picture of why international human rights have increasingly risen to world prominence, what is being done about violations of human rights, the content of relevant international law, and what might be done to further promote the cause of international human rights.

CHAPTER 2

The Philosophical Basis for Human Rights

Scholars examine the philosophical basis of human rights for several reasons. One is to demonstrate that respect for human rights has grown over time and has a solid foundation. A second reason is to note that there are contradictions within and across various human rights traditions, both religious and secular. The present chapter provides both contexts for understanding how human rights are perceived today.

RELIGIOUS ORIGINS OF HUMAN RIGHTS

Many major religions have stressed various elements of human rights (Table 2.1). Because millions around the world are so fervently loyal to religious tenets, a review of the major faiths is an important window into understanding the varieties of perspectives about human conduct, not only across the various religions but also within competing sects. Although religious traditions tend to focus on individual duties, prohibitions, and responsibilities, they have been reinterpreted in modern times and shown to have laid a foundation for the development of human rights.

Hinduism. Perhaps the oldest surviving religion, Hinduism originated about 4,500 years ago and is so named because of its emergence along the Indus River. Its sacred texts, codified some 1,500 years ago, address the importance of duty and good conduct toward others. All human life is to be loved and respected without distinction as to friend or foe. The first and foremost ethical principle of polytheistic Hinduism is noninjury to others; no pain should be inflicted on another. As a corollary, one must practice charity and compassion to the hungry, the sick, the

TABLE 2.1   HUMAN RIGHTS ADVOCATES IN MAJOR RELIGIONS

Religions	Thinkers	Lifespan	Principal messages
Hinduism	Krisha Chaitanya	1478–1533	Legal equality
	Mahatma Gandhi	1869–1948	Self-determination; nonviolence; equality
Buddhism	Siddhārtha Gotama	c.404–484 BCE	Free speech; religious freedom; right to die
	Dalai Lama XIV	1935–	Self-determination; nonviolence
Confucianism	Confucius	c.551–479 BCE	Right to humane governance
	Mencius	371–289 BCE	Right to rebel
	Hsun-Tzu	300–230 BCE	Right to education
Judaism	Moses	c.1304–1237 BCE	Self-determination; proportional punishment
	Isaiah	fl. 8th century BCE	Right to food, shelter
	Moses Maimonides	1135–1204	Freedom from captivity; right to nonpoverty
Christianity	Jesus of Nazareth	c.4 BCE–33 CE	Freedom of thought; opposition to lynching; duty to aid the needy
	St Paul of Tarsus	3–67	Nondiscrimination
	Thomas Aquinas	1227–1274	Natural rights
	Bartolomé de las Casas	1484–1566	Indigenous peoples rights; against exploitation
	Martin Luther	1483–1546	Freedom of conscience
Islam	Mohammed	571–632	Racial equality, religious freedom, nonexploitation
	Al-Farabi	c.870–950	Self-determination; equality
	Mawlana Abu'l A`la Mawdudi	1903–1979	Many rights

homeless, and the unfortunate. Through good deeds, an individual can accumulate merit and advance toward freedom from earthly impediments. In addition, humans have no priority over the world of nature.

The basic Hindu texts contain few political prescriptions, implicitly advocating governance that does not injure individuals. However, some Hindu scholars originally upheld the traditional pre-Hindu caste system, believing that those in highest caste (the Brahmins) have derived more merit from previous incarnations and that the caste system delineates a natural order between those who do manual as opposed to mental labor. Some contemporary Hindus in India still oppose compulsory education and do not frown on child labor, believing that primary schools train children for mental labor, which is only for the brightest children whose families can afford to keep them off the labor market in their youth.

Nevertheless, in the sixteenth century Hindu philosopher **Krisha Chaitanya** (1478–1533) espoused the principle of equality before the law, and in the twentieth century the teachings of **Mahatma Gandhi** (1869–1948) brought a fresh interpretation to Hinduism, focusing on the right of self-determination of peoples, the duty of nonviolence to effect political change, and the principle of equality. (However, Gandhi was assassinated by a disciple of the Hindu nationalist ideologue, Vinayak Damodar Savarkar (1910–1949), also a nontraditional Hindu.) In 2001, a Charter on Hindu International Human Rights was published on the website of the Hindu Human Rights Group.

Buddhism. Some 2,500 years old, Buddhism has the rituals of a religion regarding the afterlife and does not recognize a supreme being. Arising within the heartland of Hinduism, Siddhattha Gotama (c.404–484 BCE), renamed **Buddha**, responded to the rise of urban societies, in which materialism and the exploitative division of labor emerged, to supersede the simpler life of self-sufficient agriculture. Born in the warrior caste, he rejected all its privileges, which he felt were illusions depriving him of the possibility of liberation from earthly suffering. After an ascetic life for six years, he divined that self-transcendence can best be achieved by altruistic service to others. To assert his philosophy in the context of a Hindu orthodoxy, Buddha was implicitly claiming the rights of free speech and freedom of religion. Buddhism stresses respect for all persons, compassion for and healing of those in pain, and opposition to the caste system; one must overcome one's selfish cravings by practicing charity and love to those in need, not only spiritually but also intellectually and materially. Accordingly, Buddhist monasticism, open to both men and women, encourages learning in order to discover new ways to relieve suffering. There is an implicit balance in Buddhism between individualism and Hindu collectivist notions. Similar to Hinduism, some Buddhists believe that one should accumulate merit by good works; having done so in the present life means a better life when reincarnated.

Outside India, Buddhism developed without competing with Hinduism, notably in Sri Lanka, Southeast Asia, and East Asia. Today's foremost contemporary Buddhist, the **Fourteenth Dalai Lama** (1935–), argues that if we understand the fundamental humanity that unites us all, we can solve problems through kindness, love, and respect for others. Explicitly, he has argued for the right of self-determination for the Tibetan people.

Confucianism. Although not a religion in the usual sense, Confucianism was founded before Buddhism by a scholar named Kong Fuzi (c.551–479 BCE), now known as **Confucius**, who was born in an era in which civil authority was precarious on account of aggression between various feudal states inside what was later unified as China. Confucianism eschews attempts to find a basis for knowledge or philosophy in otherworldly speculation, preferring to focus on empirical and practical wisdom. Confucians venerate ancestors rather than a deity. They believe that harmony and cooperation will exist when all persons honor their duties toward others, overcoming their own self-interest and egotism. Confucianism recognizes the existence of social hierarchies, so moral individuals will reciprocally follow the responsibilities of their positions in life; thus, women are supposed to be subordinate to men, the younger are to respect their elders, and all are to obey the will of just rulers. One notable quote is: "Do not impose on others what you yourself do not desire." But another is: "Women are worthless." Confucius emphasized the rectitude of the rulers, not the institutions or processes of governance, so there is no opposition between the individual and the state unless the ruler is unjust or the individual fails to carry out reciprocal obligations. Rulers and ruled, similar to members of families, coexist interdependently. The people have obligations within the context of the family and the state, not apart from the family and the state. Implicitly, dignified protests against unjust rulers aim at reminding them of their obligations.

Two later thinkers further developed Confucianism during the period of the warring states (480–221 BCE) that ultimately ended feudalism. **Mencius** (371–289 BCE) coined the term "mandate of heaven," which is not based on a notion of an afterlife but instead on the imperative of rulers to govern humanely and to advance the material well-being of the ruled, including the opportunity for education. If a ruler does nothing to rectify a decline in material conditions that cause suffering among the masses, the mandate of heaven is said to have ended, conferring an obligation on the people to overthrow the ruler in order to reestablish humane rule and, thereby, social harmony. For Mencius, governmental repression through cruel punishment results in a breakdown of the mutual trust required by a peaceful society. More broadly, when a superordinate person fails to carry out the duties prescribed in social hierarchies, the subordinate person has a right to leave the relationship. Thus, individuals can be liberated from unjust rulers as well as from cruel family elders. As a corollary, Confucians oppose most wars for squandering domestic resources.

Whereas Confucius and Mencius believed that humans are naturally good, **Hsun-Tzu** (300–230 BCE) had the opposite belief. He placed his faith in the power of education to eradicate evil tendencies. Hsun-Tzu wrote: "In order to relieve anxiety and eradicate strife, nothing is as effective as the institution of corporate life based on a clear recognition of individual rights." Hsun-Tzu, thus, has the distinction of being the first person in the world to articulate the concept of human rights. According to contemporary Confucian scholar, Hung-Chao Tai (1929–), "human rights under the traditional Chinese political culture were conceived to be part of a larger body of morally prescribed norms of collective human conduct."

Judaism. The Ten Commandments of **Moses** (c.1304–1237 BCE) is based on the principle that humans have obligations to a single God as well as to one another. The form of the principles is encoded in law, prescribed divinely. Observance of Judaic legal precepts is supposed to result in justice. Moses, of course, liberated the Hebrews from Egypt, an action that retrospectively may be said to have been based on the principle of self-determination. However, he did not argue for the broader position on the abolition of slavery for non-Hebrews. Unlike the religions of Asia, the Hebrews developed much of their political culture in Egypt with the painful knowledge that the people often have different interests from the state. The purpose of the Biblical story of Cain and Abel is to point out that all humans are indeed the keepers of our brothers and sisters. The story of the Great Flood contains the moral that God is willing to punish wickedness. Since humans are created in the image of a just God, they have the obligation to behave justly and the power to punish wickedness. The "eye for an eye" maxim suggests that there should be proportionality in punishing crime.

The moral about Sodom's destruction in the Jewish scriptures is that the residents were wicked, but the only evidence of their sins was extreme inhospitality to the angels sent to save the only just family in town. Hence, what was wrong was that the townspeople did not observe the principle of just treatment of all persons.[1]

However, God is said to have given certain land to the Hebrews, who, thus, are chosen people with special rights, committed by their historical experience and mandated by God to establish a just and wise social order second to none among the peoples of the world. After the Hebrews settled in Israel, thereby becoming Israelites, the explanation for the later loss of sovereignty over the Holy Land was wickedness – that is, failure to develop a just society.

While in exile from Israel, the prophet **Isaiah** (740–781 BCE) further described Judaic morality in a more proactive manner – allowing the oppressed to be free, sharing food with the hungry, and giving shelter to the homeless, implying the right of nonpoverty. Judaism, as later expounded by the Aristotelian-influenced physician-philosopher Rabbi Moses ben Maimon (1135–1204), known as **Moses Maimonides**, is a religion that pursues moral excellence because all humans are born with free will. Based on the principle of beneficence, he prescribed a transformative generosity to the poor based on equality and partnership rather than dependence. Maimonides, having fled his hometown, Córdoba, when non-Muslims were being persecuted, wrote in support of the use of force to stop violence, thus presenting a moral argument for what has evolved from the concept of the just war to the principle of humanitarian intervention. Today, Israel's control of occupied territories populated by Arabic-speaking Palestinians is sometimes criticized as at variance with Judaic human rights principles.

Some thinkers, notably Karl Jaspers (1883–1969), have argued that an important shift toward espousing human rights took place in what he calls the "axial age" from 900–200 BCE. During those years, Buddha, Confucius, Isaiah, and Socrates redefined ethics in terms of compassion, not dogma. Repulsed by violent means, all four sought peaceful methods of conflict resolution. According to Jaspers, they established the foundations of modern ethical philosophy.

Christianity. At a time when Romans oppressed Jews, the message of **Jesus of Nazareth** (*c.*BCE 4–33 CE), that all should be good Samaritans, caring for those in need, was that the Romans should not be dislodged by terrorism or superior force but rather by converting them to a new way of thinking in which all are treated with compassion and equality. Jesus, similarly, criticized the pursuit of wealth and was able to convince a lynch mob not to stone to death a woman accused of adultery. Christian theology developed in part from Jesus's attack on Jewish religious authorities for doctrinal intolerance and indifference to human suffering. He thereby demanded the rights of assembly and free speech to articulate unapproved views.

HISTORIC EVENT 2.1 THE LAST DAYS IN THE LIFE OF JESUS OF NAZARETH (33 CE)

Having criticized temple priests and scholars by calling them hypocrites, Jesus of Nazareth (c.4 BCE–33 CE) was arrested one night by religious authorities, detained by a religious tribunal without a charge, flogged and humiliated until morning, interrogated about his opinions without benefit of an attorney to the point of self-incrimination, and finally forwarded to secular authorities on the charges of forbidding payment of taxes to Rome and stirring up rebellion. Although secular authorities determined that he broke no law, he was sentenced to death by a king who responded to a demand from public opinion. En route to the place of execution, he was further tortured. When he arrived, he was tortured again, crucified, and died on a cross.

The circumstances surrounding Jesus's arrest, interrogation, and death indicate clearly that he was a prisoner of conscience, a man whose freedom of speech was violated. Accordingly, his mistreatment constitutes a paradigm case for the denial of human rights. It is no coincidence that London-based Amnesty International has most vigorously pursued cases of prisoners of conscience. However, many ordinary Christians today do not comprehend the human rights implications of his experience and his message, believing instead that what happened to Jesus was "God's will."

After Jesus's crucifixion, **Paul of Tarsus** (3–67 CE) began to codify such Christian principles as, "there is neither Greek nor Jew, nor slave nor free, nor man nor women, but we are all one in Christ" (Galatians 3:27–28), which can be interpreted as promoting equality among believers. However, intolerance is suggested by a statement that salvation in the afterlife comes only to those who believe in what Jesus professed (John 3:16). In short, some Christians consider Christianity to be an exclusivist religion, unlike the more syncretic Buddhist and Hindu faiths that accept a commonality to all religions.

There are several contradictions between reports about Jesus's teachings and Paul's advice to the early Christians. For example, Paul accepted slavery. Jesus associated with an apparent prostitute, whereas Paul urged Christians to have nothing to do with such people. Jesus suggested that his followers should grudgingly pay taxes to Rome, but Paul went considerably beyond in arguing that rulers are legitimate and should be obeyed because their authority comes from God. Nevertheless, other disciples refused to obey Roman law that conflicted with God's law. Some early believers, moreover, followed the principle stated in the Christian bible, "from each according to his ability, to each according to his needs," a quotation cited in *The Critique of the Gotha Program* by Karl Marx (1818–1883), during 1875, in an effort to encourage Christians to embrace the vision of an equalitarian society.

Thomas Aquinas (1227–1274), influenced by Aristotle (384–322 BCE), developed the notion that human law is legitimate to the extent that it conforms to natural law, which in turn is to be derived from divine law through the exercise of human reason. In short, he transformed the notion that God's law is superior to human law into a theory of natural rights. In choosing between God's law and human law, a Christian would have to look to the church for guidance. In 1277, however, Pope John XXI (1215–1277) condemned some of Aquinas's references to Aristotle as anti-Christian.

In 1512, **Bartolomé De Las Casas** (1484–1566) became the first bishop ordained in the "New World." Objecting that the Spanish were committing atrocities on the native peoples of the Americas, he eventually resigned his position, returned to Spain, and began to develop a concept of the rights of indigenous peoples as well as the right to live without exploitation. However, he supported the recruitment of Africans as slaves by the colonial powers.

In 1517, when **Martin Luther** (1483–1546) nailed 95 theses to the Wittenberg Church, he was primarily seeking to reform Christianity by stopping excesses and resolving contradictions. The excesses referred to such papal commands as requiring payments to the church in order to assure salvation in an afterlife. The contradictions applied to Catholic theology. After Pope Leo X (1475–1521) responded by excommunicating him in 1520, Luther asserted that all believers have freedom of conscience. The Protestant Reformation was underway when Luther's followers began to follow a different theology in which, for example, salvation was regarded entirely as a decision of God, independent of the clergy. Soon, religious wars broke out between Catholic and Protestant rulers. The Peace of Westphalia of 1648 concluded 30 years of constant warfare not only by recognizing state sovereignty but also by endorsing the practical value of religious toleration, a view propounded in the Jewish scriptures (Exodus 22:21), supported by Catholic leaders (e.g. Council of Constance, 1414), and embraced by such Protestant philosophers as John Locke (1632–1704).

Although a concern for human rights is now central to Catholic doctrine, liberation theology has not been accepted by Rome because of supposed Marxist influences. Recent popes have also condemned the right of persons of the same sex to carry on a love relationship, though same-sex partners were blessed in early church records.[2] Still, early Christian theologians failed to recognize that the ordeal of Jesus was a fundamental paradigm of human rights violations.

Islam or **Mohammedism.** Approximately 1,500 years ago, based on revelations reported over the years 610–632 from the Angel Gabriel, **Mohammed** (571–632) claimed to be the Messenger of Allah and successor to the prophets of Judaism and Christianity. He began to write the Qur'an, which was completed after his death in 651. The five pillars of Islam, according to Mohammed, are profession of faith, devotional worship or prayer, paying a religious tax, fasting, and making a pilgrimage to Mecca. Although the Qur'an explicitly argues that there should be religious toleration, non-Muslims were not considered to have equal rights. Mohammed initially sought to expel Jews from Arabia, but he relented when some of his Arabic allies proposed that Jews should instead pay tribute to remain in lands controlled by Muslims.

The Qur'ān teaches that there should be equality among the races and the sexes, though in practice they may be separated, and men may marry up to four women. The Qur'ānic principle that the witness of two women is equal to that of one man doubtless assumed that women were illiterate and could not write down their testimony. In the modern world, when Islamic women are literate, some Qur'ānic scholars advocate updating that principle. In economic matters, Mohammed preached against flaunting wealth, the tyranny of vested interests, and usury. The obligation of the tithe (religious tax) reminds everyone that they should help the poor, and the most affluent are encouraged to make voluntary contributions beyond the minimum tax. At the same time, Mohammed held slaves. Although he accepted the practice of manumission, especially for those converting to Islam, he also directed slave-owners to be kind to slaves.

An apparent paradox within the Islamic world is that Indonesia, the world's largest country in numbers of Muslims, demonstrates far more respect for human rights today than countries nearer to Saudi Arabia, the home of the holy city of Mecca. One answer is that Islamic law (shari'ah), which developed over three centuries after Mohammed died, codifies social practices and etiquette that were accepted in countries nearest Arabia but not necessarily required by Mohammed. The veil, for example, was unknown before the tenth century, and unusual practices found in some Islamic countries (cutting off hands, posses organized against infidels, harems, etc.) have little to do with the teachings of Mohammed.

Following the natural rights idea of the Aristotelian-influenced Islamic philosopher, **Al-Farabi** (c.870–950),[3] the contemporary scholar, **Mawlana Abu'l A'la Mawdudi** (1903–1979), has made a case that Mohammed actually launched the human rights movement. Among the principles contained in the Qur'ān, he argues, are the rights to life, property, inheritance, education, security, privacy, association, marriage or nonmarriage, free expression, religion, legal equality, political participation, and protest against tyranny, as well as freedom from arbitrary imprisonment, dishonor, and infanticide. However, his views have not become part of contemporary mainstream Islam.

Religious views have informed all the Secretaries-General of the United Nations. As a result, they have exhibited somewhat different styles, but all have been united in their desire for humanitarian assistance and peace.

DISCUSSION TOPIC 2.1 WHICH RELIGIOUS BASIS FOR HUMAN RIGHTS IS BEST?

Several religious traditions and alternative secular philosophies support human rights to a greater or lesser extent. Which tradition is most and least responsible for the development of human rights? Which tradition provides the best promise today for the advancement of human rights?

PHILOSOPHICAL ORIGINS OF HUMAN RIGHTS

The world's major religions are riddled with sects, each privileging different and often competing principles. Indeed, major faith-based disagreements about the scope of human rights are taking place *within* the major religious traditions more than across those divides. Accordingly, the need to bridge the diversity by finding a universal logic to support universal principles has led many important thinkers to turn to analytical and ethical philosophy (Table 2.2).

Common to the major religions is a belief that humans have duties and responsibilities as well as prohibitions ("Thou shalt not ..."). The desirable states of affairs, thus, require humans to behave a certain way in order to please a deity or to follow an important conception of how societies should be organized, as recorded in a written text. Secular philosophies, however, tend to see an opposition between

TABLE 2.2   SECULAR HUMAN RIGHTS ADVOCATES

Thinkers	*Lifespan*	*Principal contributions*
Aristotle	384–322 BCE	Liberty
Marcus Tullius Cicero	140–43 BCE	Natural law
Jean Bodin	1529–1596	Right to property; freedom of religion
Hugo Grotius	1583–1645	International law; right to security, right to justice
Thomas Hobbes	1588–1679	Social contract for security
John Locke	1632–1704	Right to life, liberty, health, property
Voltaire	1694–1778	Right to free press, speech, fair trial; against slavery
Baron de Montesquieu	1689–1755	Constitutional checks and balances; against slavery
Jean-Jacques Rousseau	1712–1778	Popular sovereignty; against slavery
Immanuel Kant	1724–1804	Self-determination
Edmund Burke	1729–1797	Rights conferred only through politics; property rights
Marquis de Condorcet	1743–1794	Women's rights; equality of political rights; against slavery
Thomas Paine	1737–1809	Right to democracy; social welfare rights
Thomas Jefferson	1743–1826	Right to pursue happiness; religious toleration
Jeremy Bentham	1748–1842	Civil and political liberties
James Madison	1751–1849	Democratic checks and balances
Johann G. Fichte	1762–1814	Self-determination; freedom of the press, speech; right to education; right to work
Georg W. F. Hegel	1770–1831	Freedom of association and thought; right to education; property rights
James Mill	1773–1836	Freedom of speech, press, religion; economic freedom
John Austin	1790–1859	Law as the only source of rights
Auguste Comte	1798–1857	Altruism as a basic principle
John Stuart Mill	1806–1873	Free speech, government to prevent harm to individuals
Karl Marx	1818–1883	Workers' rights
Friedrich Engels	1820–1895	Workers' rights

humans and governments, such that humans have rights that governments must respect. According to most secular philosophies, governments either are prohibited from acting in certain ways toward humans or are expected to provide a framework for individuals to achieve a better life. Governments, in other words, have ethical responsibilities to individuals because of human characteristics and potentials.

COURT CASE 2.1 THE TRIAL OF SOCRATES (399 BCE)

For many years Socrates (c.469–399 BCE) taught moral philosophy in Athens as a social critic, even questioning the democratic form of government then practiced. He thereby antagonized those in power. In 399 BCE, he was arrested and charged with two offenses – corrupting the youth ("failing to acknowledge the gods that the city acknowledges") and impiety ("introducing new deities"). A majority of members of a jury of 501 citizens, selected by lot, voted to convict him. In a separate vote, the jury sentenced him to death by drinking a lethal hemlock-based liquid. Although he had an opportunity to escape before the liquid was administered, he refused to do so in part because he had accepted the social contract to live under Athenian laws and would not harm the state by breaking the contract to live in another state where his social criticism would doubtless lead to the same end.

Within philosophical speculation, the concept of natural rights provided the initial basis for the development of the notion of human rights. **Aristotle** (384–322 BCE), a student of Socrates, believed that individuals should flourish, that is, develop intellectually and morally as much as possible. He concluded from his analysis of the polities of his day that the best governments acted to protect liberty by preventing encroachments upon the conditions under which humans can reach a fulfillment of their capabilities.

When Rome achieved supremacy, economic activity assured riches to many citizens, who demanded a voice in government. Accordingly, the Senate was developed as a check on executive power. Perhaps the most famous senator, **Marcus Tullius Cicero** (140–43 BCE), formulated a theory of natural law, a law superior to human laws that can be derived by rational thought and to which the executive authority should be subject. A century later, Christians who refused to obey Roman law that conflicted with God's law were therefore articulating an idea that had already gained some currency in the Mediterranean world.

The concept of natural law developed later into a theory of natural rights in which rulers should respect the rights of citizens. Indeed, Aristotle's impact on Al-Farabi, Aquinas, and Moses Maimonides was to promote the idea of natural rights, but there were limits to the scope of Aristotle's conceptions. Aristotle's influence on Aquinas may have resulted in the papal doctrine that good works are the key to salvation, but Luther disputed the notion that salvation could be purchased by good deeds. However, Aquinas was sufficiently influenced by Aristotle's concept of natural rights to assert the principle of freedom of conscience. De Las Casas, similarly, sought to turn upside down Aristotle's argument that some people are naturally born to be rulers or slaves so that he could persuade the Spanish conquistadors to stop exploiting and slaughtering the native population of the Americas.

Although the English nobles coerced King John into signing the Magna Carta in 1215, few rulers elsewhere were forced to limit their power for several centuries. Neither Aquinas nor De Las Casas challenged the legitimacy of the kings of Europe. Following Paul of Tarsus's view of the proper role of citizens, monarchs insisted that they ruled by divine right, thereby excluding the possibility that individuals might assert their rights against the state. However, if a ruler were judged to be a heretic, divine right no longer applied. Lutherans and the popes, of course, differed on which rulers were heretics, and the result was warfare between Catholic and Protestant states in the sixteenth and seventeenth centuries.

HISTORIC EVENT 2.2 THE THIRTY YEARS' WAR (1618–1648)

The Roman Empire ended in 476, when the invading Ostrogoths forced the last emperor, Romulus Augustus (c.460–?), to abdicate. In 800, Pope Leo III (750–816) decided to intrude into state affairs by crowning Charlemagne (c.742–814) as Imperator Augustus in order to reward his help for putting down a rebellion in Rome. The pope hoped to encourage Charlemagne, king of what is now known as France, and whose conquests added German and Italian territories to his realm, to reestablish the Roman Empire as the protector of the papacy, and vice versa. Although Charlemagne was not particularly interested in the pope's scheme, later popes supported the establishment of what they called the Holy Roman Empire after Charlemagne's successors split up his domain. Otto the Great (912–973), ruler of the one of the domains, is usually considered to have founded the Holy Roman Empire in 962. The emperor, understood to be a Catholic, was chosen in an election, mostly by several German-speaking kings of the Christian realm. The Thirty Years' War began in 1618, when Holy Roman Emperor Matthias (1557–1619) sought to impose Catholic Ferdinand II (1578–1637) as king of Protestant Bohemia. The Bohemians revolted, and soon many European countries took sides in a complex series of wars that lasted until the Peace of Westphalia of 1648. A major issue was whether Catholic kings could impose their religion upon Protestant subjects, but an even larger issue was which state would establish geopolitical hegemony in Europe. Eventually, Catholic France sided with Protestant states to prevent the alliance between Austria and Spain from achieving a dominant position in Europe.

During the wars of religion, French philosopher **Jean Bodin** (1529–1596) began to question the sources of sovereignty, asking who had the power to make enforceable law. While some rulers were being declared illegitimate on religious grounds, Bodin argued that governments should respect "the laws of God, and natural liberty and the natural right to property." In 1572, Bodin argued that individuals are sovereign with respect to their own property, just as states hold sovereignty over tangible real estate within their borders. He believed that rulers and states must respect private property and have no right to enslave a free person. Based on his view of natural law, Bodin said that rulers should be subject to the same laws as the ruled; otherwise, they are tyrants. However, he did not believe that subjects had a right to disobey laws or to overthrow tyrants. He also pleaded for religious toleration as a way to quell internal strife within countries. Bodin's arguments regarding sovereignty were directed in part at the Holy Roman Emperor and the pope, who were claiming that they could confer legitimacy on a state. For Bodin, neither authority had the right to intrude into state sovereignty.

One sector of the interstate conflict in the sixteenth century was between Catholic Spain and Protestant Holland, the latter a trading country that established a republic and thus had no king claiming a divine right to rule. Pondering the international chaos, Dutch scholar, **Hugo Grotius** (1583–1645), went beyond Bodin's theory of sovereignty to assert that laws of governments should neither transgress natural law nor violate natural rights. Two natural rights are the rights to justice and security; rulers should provide both, and the ruled should not place security in jeopardy by disobeying just laws or by rebelling. Regarding the instability produced by European religious wars, Grotius advocated a set of principles on which governments might agree so that a stable world order could replace the chaotic resort to force in order to solve interstate disputes. What he meant was that the customary ways in which states coexist peacefully should be codified into principles of international law. Grotius also adapted Bodin's theory of sovereignty to say that states were the sovereign authorities whose domestic laws should not be questioned by other states. He felt that governments could reciprocally accept the principle, obviously drawn from Christian theology, that they should not treat other states in a manner that they would not want to be treated. Instead of having might make right, governments should accept one another's legitimacy and move on to the task of providing the good life for their citizens.

Although Grotius was concerned that a state might violate principles of natural law in dealing with its own people, preserving a peaceful international order was a more important goal than fighting to determine whether Catholicism or Protestantism should prevail, since the prosperity resulting from trade in a world at peace would benefit all. However, Europeans could then close ranks against the rest of the world in order to give licenses to businesses for profitable colonial exploitation in parts of the nonwhite world where international law did not apply because European countries recognized no states outside Europe.

Grotian principles were endorsed after his death in the Peace of Westphalia of 1648 (see Historic Event 1.1), which settled the Thirty Years' War through two treaties that established the principle of state sovereignty. Rather than resorting to war in order to determine the state religion of a country, that matter was left to the ruler of each state. The Westphalian world of sovereign states, which existed afterward, came with a price. Rulers were free to commit unspeakable acts toward their own citizens without fear that other states would intervene to stop atrocities. French Protestants, known as Huguenots, who had been persecuted before Westphalia, soon realized that their fate hung in the balance, and they left Catholic France for many other countries, including a large-scale migration to South Africa in 1688–1689.

While the European continent was embroiled in the Thirty Years' War, yet another armed conflict was being fought in England. From 1642–1651, three civil wars pitted royalists against nobles seeking the supremacy of parliament. The civil wars ended with the execution of Charles I and the subsequent defeat of his son in battle. A republic was established, but did not last, and the monarchy was restored with the crowning of Charles II in 1660. In 1651, English philosopher, **Thomas Hobbes** (1588–1679), published an essay, *Leviathan*, that developed the concept of a "social contract" under which humans surrendered their "state of nature" rights to governmental authority in order to benefit from stable rule. Hobbes's innovation, colored by the experience of the Magna Carta as well as the civil war, was to argue that individuals existed before governments and only accepted rule by superordinate governments to the extent that the rulers would guarantee their right to security. Hobbes, however, did not entertain a broader concept of human rights in which individuals had rights that government should not abridge.

In 1685, Protestant Charles II was succeeded by his brother, James II (1633–1701), a Catholic convert. Following the birth of his son in 1688, several Protestant nobles, who feared a Catholic succession and were anxious about James's inclination to absolute monarchy, conspired to invite James's son-in-law, Prince William of Orange (1650–1702), and his wife, Mary (1662–1694), James's Protestant daughter, to sail from Holland with an army to overthrow James II. Known as the Glorious Revolution, William landed in England unopposed; James lost his nerve and abdicated by fleeing abroad. The English parliament subsequently passed the Bill of Rights Act in 1689 to disavow the concept of the divine right of kings.

After **John Locke** (1632–1704) authored an essay on the toleration of religious differences in 1667, he was asked to write a constitution by one of the proprietors of the Carolina colony just as he was formulating his political philosophy in broader terms. Although his constitution was not immediately accepted, in 1691 he published a remarkable thesis. In contrast with Hobbes, who posited the surrender of individual rights to the state in order to obtain security, Locke believed that government was set up not only to protect the natural rights of individuals against arbitrary rule by government but also to stop private citizens from jeopardizing the rights of others. Specifically, he argued that individuals instituted government to protect the rights to life, liberty, health, and property. When governments fail to do so, they violate the social contract, whereupon the people have the right to dissolve such governments and to institute new ones. He was clearly providing the philosophical basis for the English Bill of Rights.

Locke's social contract theory in turn inspired **Thomas Jefferson** (1743–1826) to formulate reasons for 13 British colonies in North America to declare themselves independent in 1776. Similar to Locke, Jefferson espoused a theory of inalienable rights endowed by a Creator, with governments deriving their powers from the consent of the governed. However, he added a new right: he replaced Locke's rights to life, liberty, health, and property with the rights to "life, liberty, and the pursuit of happiness." Jefferson justified American independence as the consequence of "a history of repeated abuses and usurpations, all having in direct object the establishment of an absolute tyranny …," as he stated in the Declaration of Independence. Jefferson objected to slavery in his first draft of the Declaration, though he retained slaves on his Virginia plantation, but delegates from other Southern states insisted on removing that passage.

Jefferson was not only influenced by Locke but also by the French-speaking philosophers of the eighteenth century, among whom perhaps the four most notable are Voltaire, Montesquieu, Rousseau, and Condorcet. All four thinkers believed in the basic principle of the Enlightenment – that science and human progress depend upon truth and are retarded by the suppression of free thought, whether by governmental or nongovernmental organizations. The project of the Enlightenment was to create a safe space for intellectuals and scientists to exchange ideas, which would ultimately benefit humanity. They opposed dogma, censorship, and intolerance of diverse beliefs in a search for universally valid principles that harmoniously govern nature, humanity, and society, believing that human reason will ultimately triumph over obscuritanism and superstition.

Voltaire (1694–1778), the nom de plume of François Marie Arouet, dared to be explicit about natural rights while exiled in England during the late 1720s. Whereas social harmony within the sovereign states of Europe was generally thought to require religious homogeneity, Voltaire learned in London that the English had social order despite diverse religious preferences, even though non-Anglicans suffered from legal restrictions and social prejudice. Why? Because economic freedom diverted their attention from religious matters. Moreover, he said, "if there were only one religion in England, there would be danger of tyranny; if there were two, they would cut each other's throats; but there are 30, and they live happily together in peace." Often jailed for his views, Voltaire's epigram about freedom of speech, religion, and of the press, "I detest what you write, but I would give my life to make it possible for you to continue to write," was later paraphrased as "I disapprove of what you say, but I will defend to the death your right to say it." Complaining bitterly that the laws of France were written in slavish response to dogmatic papal decrees without regard to natural rights, he advocated a strict separation of church and state. His public fame resulted from writing in defense of several persons accused of nothing more than attending a Protestant church service, giving shelter to a Protestant overnight, and failing to take off a cap to a member of the clergy on the street. Incensed that hearsay was accepted as definitive evidence in court, his conception of a fair trial was that it "is better to risk saving a guilty person than to condemn an innocent one." Although he considered Africans to be genetically inferior, Voltaire also opposed slavery as contrary to natural rights.

Charles-Louis de Secondat, the Baron de **Montesquieu** (1689–1755), another exponent of natural rights, further developed the concept of the separation of powers by suggesting that three branches of government should check and balance one another. His goal was to deter the abuse of power by government so that individuals could exercise their natural rights. Montesquieu also endorsed the concept of international law for resolving interstate conflict, believing that all persons were citizens of the universe and that states foolishly trying to add territory by waging war would inevitably have to defend their borders with more war. Although in principle he opposed slavery along the lines of De Las Casas's arguments, he excused the practice insofar as the conquerors of the Americas needed labor to establish their supremacy.

The eloquence of Voltaire and the logic of Montesquieu are in stark contrast with the ambiguity of Jean-Jacques **Rousseau** (1712–1778), who lived for a time in a part of Switzerland only three miles across the border from Voltaire's estate in France. Residing in a small Protestant country without a monarch, in 1752 Rousseau sought to redefine the concept of the social contract in terms of popular sovereignty. Since all humans are born free (but are "everywhere in chains"), he argued, governments are set up to implement the general will of the people, who seek to preserve their freedom while living together in communities. How can the general will of the people be determined? Scholars of Rousseau provide varying interpretations on critical passages in his writings. Some stress majoritarianism, others argue that he favors a unanimous consensus. In either case, Rousseau argued that only small countries could achieve true democracies through a deliberative process in which all have a voice. Rousseau was fundamentally opposed to slavery. When the French Revolution began, Rousseau (as well as Montesquieu and Voltaire) was dead and could not comment on what ensued. Nevertheless, Rousseau's writings were reputedly consulted to justify the Jacobin reign of terror.

The principal author of the American Constitution, **James Madison** (1751–1849), took issue with Rousseau's claim that democracy would only be possible in tiny states. In the *Federalist Paper #10*, published anonymously in 1788, he argued that a democracy would work in a larger country if the government were limited by institutional as well as regional checks and balances. Constitutions, following Montesquieu, should embody a qualified majority rule principle so that the majority would be less likely to tyrannize over the minority. However, Madison was a slave owner, and his constitution legitimated slavery, as otherwise Southerners would not ratify the Constitution. To appease Northern opponents of slavery, the Constitution banned American participation in the slave trade from 1808.

The salons of Paris, where those of a philosophical bent could converse, were often run by women. In 1787, Jean-Antoine-Nicolas de Caritat, the Marquis de **Condorcet** (1743–1794), first articulated the notion that women are entitled to equal rights. He argued that women were rational beings and therefore could be educated at the same level as men. Similarly, he felt that natural rights should be conferred on believers of all religions, and that slavery should be abolished.

Another Enlightenment thinker was the Prussian Protestant, **Immanuel Kant** (1724–1804), who rejected the notion that conferring sovereignty on enlightened despots or the people would be sufficient to ensure that justice would prevail. Instead, he wrote in 1785 that laws should be based on a universal principle, known as the categorical imperative: "Act only on that maxim through which you can at the same time will that it should become a universal law." In other words, political authorities should treat humans as ends, not means. Starting from the assumption that all humans are rational, Kant derived the principles of human dignity, individual autonomy, and political equality. Kant then argued for the superiority of representative governments whose political power is restricted by a constitution that prevents either monarchical or democratic despotism. In 1795, while French armies commanded by Napoléon Bonaparte were "liberating" European countries from absolute monarchies, Kant extended his theory to prescribe that peace could be achieved in international relations when states respect one another just as humans must respect other humans. He favored the principle of self-determination of peoples, the abolition of standing armies, noninterference by one state in the internal affairs of another state, and a world entirely composed of a federation of constitutional, representative governments.

Johann Gottlieb Fichte (1762–1814), enormously impressed with Kant, visited the latter in 1792 and published his first major work in 1796. An initial admirer of the French Revolution, he accepted the right of revolution to establish representative democracy. However, in response to the unwelcome occupation of Berlin by Napoleonic armies in 1806, he advanced the principle of national self-determination and even died as a volunteer in the war against Napoleonic France. Fichte derived the concept of human rights from the premise that all humans are rational. Concerned that individuals must be free yet restricted in some way so that order can be maintained, he echoed Jefferson in his concept of the political contract (not the social contract) as an agreement between citizens and the state wherein government is instituted to protect individual rights, particularly freedom of speech and of the press, so that philosophical and scientific inquiry would not be impeded. He also advanced the principle of the right to education and advocated state regulation of the economy to ensure the right of gainful employment. Rather than conceiving of morality as the source for law, Fichte explained that the rational basis for laws resides in the necessity for states to maintain order and to protect individual rights. Thus, for Fichte, punishment for a crime is dictated by the need to maintain order rather than to enforce morality.

HISTORIC EVENT 2.3 THE FRENCH REVOLUTION (1789–1799)

French royal extravagancy, together with financial support for the colonists in the American War of Independence, brought France to the verge of bankruptcy. In 1789, Louis XVI (1754–1793) hoped to get approval for the raising of taxes, including a land tax, by convening a meeting of the Estates General, a legislative body comprising the three estates of the clergy, nobles, and commoners that had not met since 1614. The third estate members, representing a nonaristocratic population that far outnumbered the other two estates, began to mobilize support for equal representation. By the time of the meeting, the three estates had descended into power struggle hostility. The third estate began to meet alone, adopting the title of National Constituent Assembly, and began drafting several constitutional reforms, including

Continued

the abolition of feudalism and special privileges for the clergy. Empowered by widespread unrest and popular support, in 1789 the Assembly issued the Declaration of the Rights of Man and Citizen, and in 1791 promulgated a constitution that was formally accepted by the king on September 13, shortly before the dissolution of the Assembly on September 30. It was replaced by the Legislative Assembly on October 1. That Assembly, in turn, was replaced by the National Convention on September 20, 1792, and France was declared a republic. The loose confederation of commoners originally called to represent the third estate, had consisted of representatives with a wide range of views and radical tendencies. Factions struggled against each other. One faction, the Jacobins, eventually seized control of the National Convention from the more moderate Girondists, heralding the Reign of Terror (1793–1794). The king was executed on January 21, 1793, followed by many perceived opponents of the revolution, including some of the early supporters. At each phase of the revolution, many ideas of philosophers, including the Baron de Montesquieu (1689–1755), Jean-Jacques Rousseau (1712–1778), and François-Marie Arouet (Voltaire) (1694–1778), were interpreted, or just plain hijacked, to sanction actions of those holding power. The revolution is often considered to have ended in 1799, with the coup d'état by Napoléon Bonaparte (1769–1821).

Meanwhile, the reaction in England to the French Revolution was to recast the pursuit of human rights into an evolutionary political context. **Edmund Burke (1729–1797)** was among those shocked by the violence against legitimate political institutions. Writing first in 1790, he conceived of states as organic entities that grow in accordance with their own national needs. He eschewed the toppling of monarchs or redrafting of constitutions based on the latest philosophical speculations pretending to claim universal validity. The English people had liberties, particularly those relating to property rights, because political bargains over the years conferred those rights. Burke, hence, came close to endorsing what is now called the positivistic conception of rights, namely, that rights only exist to the extent they are written down on paper as the outcome of a political process operating in a particular country. From 1793, during the Jacobin phase of the revolution, Burke condemned the purge of those who were perceived to be in disagreement with the new democratic order, including some who originally supported the revolution. He was primarily seeking a way to legitimate the English aristocracy, which feared a similar revolution in England and was therefore opposed to considering humans as having equal rights.

Thomas Paine (1737–1809) disagreed with Burke and wrote *Rights of Man: Answer to Mr Burke's Attack on the French Revolution* (1791). He argued that the Burkean position, which left rights as a political question, was wrong because political bodies could make and unmake rights, whereas rights for Paine come from nature. The purpose of government is to guarantee inherent, inalienable rights. Hereditary aristocracy and monarchy are illegitimate because they serve their own needs, not those of the nation as a whole, so they should be overthrown, even by military interventions from other countries. He also advocated what now is called the welfare state.

Shortly before Burke's first publication, in 1789 **Jeremy Bentham** (1748–1842) had tried to reformulate the logic of governance so that the rising middle class could gain power over the economically declining aristocracy. Bentham first debunked the concept of natural rights, referring to "rights" as "nonsense," and "natural rights" as "nonsense upon stilts." Previously, God was assumed to be the source of natural law and thus natural rights, but Bentham was an atheist. Instead, he grounded his hedonistic ethics on the principle of "the greatest good for the greatest number." When legislators deliberated alternatives, he would have them adopt policies that benefited more rather than fewer persons. His "felicific calculus" was designed to legitimate laws adopted by the majority party in parliament, and he condemned legislation favoring special (aristocratic) interests. He agreed in principle with Burke's anticipation of the positivist approach to human rights by saying that "from real laws come real rights." Bentham's ethics is called "utilitarianism" because he stressed the concept of "utility" as a property that brings "benefit, advantage, pleasure, good, or happiness." In practical terms, he was arguing for parliamentary supremacy and the extension of voting rights to the middle class as well as for civil and political liberties, notably freedom of speech, press, and religion.

In 1820, **James Mill** (1773–1836), Bentham's tenant and intellectual best friend, cautioned that freedom of the press does not include a license to libel. A utilitarian, Mill was also an advocate of laissez-faire economics, arguing for deregulation of the economy by the government. Although he opposed the caste system in India, he excused continued British imperialism in India as a means to bring the population greater happiness through the diffusion of European culture.

Often known as the originator of sociology, **Auguste Comte** (1798–1857) developed a three-phase theory of history in 1822. The theological phase consisted of the era in which religion dominated human thought. He equated the Enlightenment with the metaphysical phase, when the concept of individual rights was held to be at a higher plane than religious dogma. In the future positivist or scientific phase, human problems would be conceived empirically rather than theologically or theoretically, so principles of the Enlightenment would be encoded into law if they proved workable. In coining the word "altruism," he turned utilitarianism upside down, arguing that individuals should place the good of all above majoritarian self-interest. His positivism was pragmatic.

In 1832, **John Austin** (1790–1859) formulated the positivist thesis as a view that law is what has been posited (decided). In today's postmodernist discourse, he was saying that law is necessarily a political construction. Similar to Bentham, he argued that rights emerge from political deliberation and decision making, not from abstract theorizing. Human rights, in other words, are not universal; they are specific to particular countries. To distinguish Comte from Austin, the latter's theory is sometimes called "legal positivism."

James Mill's son, **John Stuart Mill** (1806–1873), felt that majoritarianism might lead to Jacobin restrictions on the minority's ability to speak freely. Writing in 1859, he argued that the need for a free society takes precedence over majority preferences, that a multiplicity of opinions is necessary so that truth can be determined in a marketplace of ideas. The main purpose of government, according to Mill, is to "prevent harm to others." Whereas Bentham would not allow the theistic concept of natural rights into the front door of the house of utilitarianism, John Stuart Mill admitted the concept of human rights into the back door. He reasoned that the freedom of speech was more important than the prerogatives of the majority because error can only be corrected if the right to free expression is guaranteed. By the same token, Mill argued that democracy should develop on its own rather than being imposed by war. He was, of course, criticizing the effort of Napoléon to topple monarchies so that the people could rule in democratic governments. Influenced by Comte that government should bring out the altruism in citizens, he was one of the first feminist philosophers, having written *The Subjection of Women* in 1869, which reiterated views of his former wife, Harriet Taylor Mill (1807–1858), whose *The Enfranchisement of Women* was published in 1851. Mill favored equality of the sexes on utilitarian grounds, namely, that half of the human race should be allowed to contribute to the betterment of civilization.

In addition to Fichte and Kant, the French Revolution had a profound effect on two other major German philosophers – Hegel and Marx. Whereas Comte sought to trichotomize history into a unilinear progression from superstition to science, in 1820 **Georg Wilhelm Friedrich Hegel** (1770–1831) conceptualized human development as a zigzag dialectical contest of ideas in which the prevailing worldview (thesis) is challenged by an alternative worldview (antithesis), thus causing tension between the two currents which provokes the development of a new idea (a synthesis) that resolves the contradiction. Whereas John Stuart Mill viewed intellectual debates among alternative policies as a marketplace with more than two possible views resulting in a convergence on what is considered "truth," Hegel believed that a single accepted worldview played a much more basic role in shaping the *Zeitgeist* (spirit of the times) within three historical eras. In the earliest era, humans are savages with freedom to think, feel, and act. In the second era, the savage accepts the tyranny of civilization and law. In the third stage, the civilized individual under the law achieves liberty. Unlike Mill's pluralistic marketplace, Hegel (as well as Burke and Rousseau) argued that in politics there must be a fundamental consensus on the principles governing the relationship between individuals and government. Hegel anticipated a gradual increase in human freedom, provided that a balance could be maintained between individualistic tendencies and the needs of the community for order. Thus, the thesis of the individual's quest for self-actualization meets the antithesis of government's need to provide order, resulting in a synthesis wherein government will respect basic human rights, notably the rights to association, education, property, religion, and speech. Whereas Locke insisted on the right to property in terms of possession, enjoyment, and distribution, Hegel focused on the way in which property can be used so that individuals will achieve their maximum potential as human beings.

Karl Marx (1818–1883) then turned Hegel on his head, claiming that what underlies history is a dialectical process that is economic and material rather than abstract and intellectual, with each later economic system prevailing over the earlier. For Marx, there was an initial dialectical contest between feudalism and primitive communism. After feudalism won, capitalism became the antithesis. In both cases, there was no synthesis; instead, the antithesis displaced the thesis because each new method of capital accumulation provided the resources for a newly emergent class to gain the political power to enforce its will. Since capitalists always strive to outcompete their rivals, monopolies will emerge under capitalism, according to Marx, when the most clever or efficient corporation is left standing, having vanquished all competitors. Then a monopolistic business in one sector will seek to control other sectors, leading perhaps ultimately to a single corporation in control of international business and world trade. Since capitalists only survive if they can accumulate capital by exploiting workers (paying them much less than the market value of the goods that they produce), monopoly corporations will seek to control governments in order to suppress workers. Then the workers, whose labor is fundamental to the economic order, will become conscious that they can withhold their labor or carry out revolutions, thereby forcing the barons of industry to surrender political power. When workers take over the government, they will establish socialism by having the state take over hitherto dominant corporations. Communism will emerge when the state is itself abolished because the governmental function of providing order will no longer be required when all accept the legitimacy of an equalitarian, interdependent economic system. For Marx, the quest for "rights" is illusory, and Marx specifically favored the abolition of property rights.

In a sense, Marx was the last great philosopher on the subject of human rights. When Marx and his collaborator, **Friedrich Engels** (1820–1895), wrote the *Manifesto of the Communist Party* in 1848, revolts arose all over Europe as the people demanded democratic rights. Even though most uprisings were suppressed, the people continued to believe that they were entitled to have governments respect their rights. Accordingly, a modest victory was achieved by the mid-nineteenth century in the long philosophical quest to raise the consciousness of humans to claim their rights. The multitude who believed in human rights was no longer interested in arcane philosophical arguments; they were increasingly determined to struggle for their rights. The resulting social movements on behalf of human rights are described in the following chapter.

METAPHILOSOPHICAL JUSTIFICATIONS FOR HUMAN RIGHTS

Although the major religions and philosophers identified various human rights concepts, several generic types of justifications for human rights were articulated in their quest. As new rights are proposed, such as the right of gays and lesbians to be accorded certificates of marriage from governments, the philosophical arguments return in public policy debates. A summary of various metaphilosophical arguments may help to clarify the disparate strands, which still vie for acceptance whenever new claims are made (Table 2.3).

Natural Law. Natural law theorists argue that there are certain self-evident principles regarding rulers and the ruled, as established either by God or by nature. Thus, rights under natural law are viewed as protections against having the state limit human freedom. For many natural law theorists, there is a private sphere where

TABLE 2.3   **HUMAN RIGHTS METATHEORIES**

Theories	Exponents	Principal arguments
Natural law	Cicero, Aquinas, Bodin, Grotius, Voltaire, Finnis, Montesquieu, Condorcet	Life should be in conformity with God or nature.
Contract theory	Hobbes, Locke, Paine, Jefferson, Rousseau	Individuals' contract with governments to provide rights in order to get a stable social order.
Communitarianism	Confucius, Aristotle, Aquinas, Etzioni	There should be a balance between individualism and the need for social order.
Rationalism	Kant, Fichte	Individuals should treat one another as ends, not means.
Utilitarianism	Bentham, Mill	The greatest good for the greatest number; free trade must be fair.
Liberal democratic theory	Madison, Lincoln	The majority rules so long as minority rights are respected.
Stages-of-growth theory	Comte, Hegel, Fukuyama, Wen	Progress is a step-by-step process.
Marxism	Marx, Engels	From each according to his ability, to each according to needs.
Social democratic theory	Lenski, Myrdal	Welfare states respect economic and social rights as well as civil and political rights.
Legal positivism	Austin	Rights are legally enacted, thus exist only when granted by governments.
Liberalism	Rawls	Individuals contract with governments to protect civil liberties, advance equal opportunities, and take care of the least fortunate.

government must not intrude. Today, there has been a revival of natural law as a wellspring for political speculation, involving such theorists as legal philosopher John Finnis (1940–). The Natural Law Party is on the ballot in Britain, Israel, and the United States.

Contract Theory. Individuals in a state of nature live an unstable existence, according to Thomas Hobbes, so they contract with government, giving up their freedom in order to have the state provide order. John Locke and most other contract theorists assume that individuals had rights before entering society, so the social or political contract is an agreement in which states respect prior individual rights. The concept of the contract, of course, starts from the premise that all humans can exercise free will autonomously, responsibly, and sensibly. Although James Madison's constitution was understood as a contract between government and those who demanded limits to the powers entrusted to various branches of government, the Constitution was nearly silent about human rights. After the American Constitution was ratified, a Bill of Rights was adopted as the first 10 amendments to the constitution.

Communitarianism. Communitarians advocate a balance between individual rights and the needs of society, since life has no meaning apart from the communities in which humans live. Communitarians argue that humans have both rights and responsibilities, and one of the responsibilities is to ensure that others are well cared for. Communitarians point out that humans are collectively responsible for the satisfaction of the basic human needs of all people, so majorities should not press their claims at the expense of those whose basic needs are unmet; no one should go to bed hungry. Most of the various religious traditions stress a need to maintain a healthy coexistence between communities and individuals. Confucianism is especially explicit about the need for a balance between society and government. Except for Hobbes and Rousseau, social contract theorists have often been accused of fostering extreme individualism, with little regard for the needs of the society as a whole. Aquinas's understanding of Aristotelian ethics is clearly communitarian. Today, communitarianism is the official philosophy of the Roman Catholic Church, which has spurned the liberation theology of Peruvian Gustavo Gutiérrez (1928–) as too "Marxist." Liberation theology exponents, who identify the need to combat injustice and poverty, do so in communitarian terms. Among the secular communitarians, the most prominent is sociologist Amitai Etzioni (1929–), who believes that there should be a balance between rights and responsibilities. He urges people to cooperate together so that government will be less necessary.

Rationalism. Rationalists believe that humans act rationally, that is, behave in accordance with self-interest. Immanuel Kant's main ethical principle, the categorical imperative, asks humans to apply a test in order to determine whether a particular behavior is ethical. The test is to assess whether one's behavior, if carried out by everyone else, would lead to morally acceptable outcomes. Kant believed that his principle went beyond the Golden Rule in Christian theology, arguing that ethics are derived neither from notions about nature nor contracts, but instead are obvious to any rational or reasonable person. Fichte followed in his tradition, believing that rights are respected because they are in the interests of individuals as well as the societies in which they live. Rationalists believe that there must be a moral basis for society in which human dignity is respected. Therefore, human rights are inalienable.

Utilitarianism. Bentham argued that what is socially desirable is that which provides the greatest good (or self-interest) for the greatest number of persons. Utilitarians generally deny that humans have any right to legal guarantees which cannot otherwise be supported by specific calculations about what is useful to large numbers of individuals in society. Of course, some economic rights might indeed emerge from such calculations, such as the protection against insider trading in the stock market and against anti-trust violations that restrain free commerce. John Stuart Mill later revised Jeremy Bentham's utilitarianism to make a careful argument for protection of individual rights, but the philosophical basis remained primarily in terms of self-interest, not religious morality. At the international level, a chaotic world can only frustrate world trade, which requires an orderly, peaceful environment. Modern-day utilitarians, sometimes called economic liberals or neoliberals or pragmatists, argue that free trade must also be fair, that is, exchanged across international boundaries without artificial trade barriers and produced by workers who are employed under humane occupational conditions. They expect that globalization will bring greater human rights by increasing middle classes around the world.

Liberal Democratic Theory. Whereas the literal definition of "democracy" is rule by the people, the concept was redefined by James Madison to mean that government should have a representative legislature and be limited by separating power into independent branches of government that can check and balance one another. Abraham Lincoln (1809–1865) reformulated the concept of democracy as "government of the people, by the people, and for the people." The American Bill of Rights, as derived from social contract theory, did not protect minorities until amendments to the Constitution were adopted after the Civil War (1861–1865) that guaranteed equal rights with particular reference to former slaves. Although "democracy" then became a Lincolnesque "majority rule with minority rights," the mainstream groups in power have the option of choosing which minority rights to protect and which to reject. During major periods of American history, the rights of ethnic minorities were not protected – the era of slavery, the abandonment of efforts to promote equality for African Americans after 1876, and today, when the civil rights struggle is not very high on the public policy agenda.[4] The rights of women, the handicapped, gays and lesbians, prisoners, and many other groups were certainly not respected when the American Bill of Rights was adopted, and they struggle today to gain respect for their rights within many of the most advanced democracies. Minorities must be vigilant and appeal to the better judgment and good sense of the majority in order to enjoy rights, so liberal democratic theory stresses prohibitions on government action by such devices as federalism and separation of powers to ensure respect for civil and political rights.

Stages-of-Growth Theory. According to Hegel, history is an endless series of challenges to the existing order, resulting in progress – Comte found an end state in the process. Locke and Adam Smith (1623–1790) envisioned the advancement of economic rights as prior to all other rights, whether in political or social development. Writing after the collapse of the Soviet Union, political economist Francis Fukuyama (1952–) has even predicted that the liberal democratic imperative, with widespread respect for human rights, had moved closer to the end of the Hegelian dialectical process – that is, the "end of history." Stages-of-growth theory, in other words, sees progress as inexorable. Marxism is a special case of stages-of-growth theory. The various left-wing ideologies inspired by Marxism point out that human rights have little meaning so long as there is a rigid class structure in society. Social equality, therefore, must come before legal equality. Many lack the funds to assert their rights in courts, and even the concept of an independent judiciary is an illusion so long as elites appoint judges. Marx thought that the abolition of feudal and bourgeois classes was necessary to produce social equality among the remaining class, the proletariat, thus finding a different end state in the stages-of-growth approach from Comte and others. Although most countries that adopted Marxian socialism failed to fulfill the promise of a good life, Marx nevertheless was shrewd in grasping the principle that differences between groups generate conflict and competition among groups, such that topdogs always enjoy more privileges than underdogs.

China under the Communist Party is perhaps the major country where the denial of human rights has been portrayed so prominently on television, as in the scene of a lone protestor trying to stop a tank that ultimately gunned down students and their supporters near Tiananmen Square during 1989. When asked to justify the slaughter of nearly two thousand persons on June 4, the government at first referred to the inherent right to keep order. But when sanctions were imposed by many Western countries, the government responded with a series of annual White Papers, articulating the view that economic rights are prior to civil and political rights. Chinese Communist leaders claimed that the need to end poverty and raise living standards trumped the right to protest. In 2007, similarly, Premier Wen Jiabao (1942–), who had visited the Tiananmen demonstrators with former Premier Zhao Ziyang (1919–2005) in 1989, argued in stages-of-growth logic that China's weak legal system had to be strengthened before democratic reforms could be enacted. A similar view, of course, was long stressed by leaders of the Soviet Union.

Social Democratic Theory. Contemporary social democracies in Scandinavia and Western Europe, however, have provided welfare state benefits for the unfortunate, thus mitigating the need for a class struggle. Social democratic theory, as developed by sociologists Gerhard Lenski (1924–) and Gunnar Myrdal (1898–1987), stresses the need for government to provide not only a liberal democratic political framework but also rights for workers, welfare benefits for those not in the workforce, full employment, universal health care, and extensive educational opportunities as guarantees of stability. The wealthiest segment of the population must support a welfare state, if only to ensure social stability.

Legal Positivism. A "right" is only what a government says is a "right," so rights are governmentally constructed, not claims with a philosophical basis. Legal positivists, thus, accept rights in particular countries during specific times and places, but they deny that rights are universal.

Liberalism. There are differences of opinion within each of the metaphilosophical approaches. Accordingly, philosopher John Rawls (1921–2002) heroically tried to synthesize several theories into a theory of liberalism. Although he has also been classified as a neo-Kantian, his principle, "greatest good of the greatest number of people" is clearly in the vocabulary of utilitarianism. He objects to the Lockean state of nature – which ends when humans agree to limited government to protect life, liberty, and property – as an inadequate formulation. Instead, he argues that individuals agree to a government that not only guarantees civil liberties but also provides equality of opportunity and the greatest benefit to the least fortunate members of society. He points out that there is no need for a comprehensive theory of human rights, whether from theology or philosophy, as those interested in human rights merely need to creatively construct governmental frameworks to protect rights. Rawls, thus, has been characterized as a "pragmatic liberal."

DISCUSSION TOPIC 2.2 WHICH PHILOSOPHICAL BASIS FOR HUMAN RIGHTS IS BEST?

Who has won the philosophical debate – proponents or opponents? If proponents have won, which philosophical tradition is most congenial to human rights? Why?

METAPHILOSOPHICAL OPPONENTS OF HUMAN RIGHTS

Not all philosophers accept the concept of human rights. A summary of metaphilosophical arguments against the idea of human rights may prove useful in understanding resistance to the extension of human rights around the world today (Table 2.4).

Traditionalism. Religious fundamentalism is one of the major barriers to human rights in the world today. When the tenets of a religion are ossified, limited to a specific set of beliefs formulated in the past with no possibility of adaptation to new circumstances, human rights are unlikely to advance. One example of traditionalism is Wahhabism, an Islamic sect dominant in Saudi Arabia that follows the precepts of Muhammad ibn Abd-Al-Wahhab (1703–1792), who believed that Islam should be practiced exactly as originally required by Mohammed. Wahhabists brand as heretics any Muslim who listens to music, watches television, takes or views photographs of humans, wears charms, and otherwise adopts any modern customs. Fundamentalists in other religions, similarly, find models of morality in an ideal past.

Elitism. Burke, though arguing in favor of tradition, subscribed to elitism. Although he believed in natural law, Burke denied that human rights could be derived from natural law. He noted that humans are unequal, so his version of natural law leaves inequality intact. He referred to the excesses of the French Revolution as motivated by the "monstrous fiction of human equality." Likewise, dictators from time immemorial have constituted themselves as the elite of society and hence have denied human rights to the masses. Instead of a democratic order, Burke favored leaving political decisions to the aristocracy, somewhat similar to the concept of the philosopher king developed by Plato (428–328 BCE).

TABLE 2.4　　**HUMAN RIGHTS OPPONENTS**

Theories	*Opponents*	*Principal arguments*
Traditionalism	Wahhab	The wisdom of the ages should be respected, not violated.
Elitism	Plato, Burke	Humans are born unequal.
Relativism	von Savigny, Maine, Lee Kuan Yew	"Human rights" are culturally defined.
Frustration-aggression theory	Freud	Industrialization requires repression, which leads to savagery.
	Hobbes Nietzsche	Human nature is savage.
Social Darwinism	Spencer, Sumner, Morgenthau	The strong should rule the weak.
Social constructionist skepticism	Foucault, Hume, Bourdieu	Elites establish orthodox views to justify denying human rights. "Rights" have no empirical basis.

Relativism. Although some traditionalists tend to conflate current cultural practices with narrow readings of religious doctrine, secular traditionalist opponents of civil and political human rights often justify their opposition in terms of relativism by invoking a cultural context. For example, jurists Friedrich Karl von Savigny (1779–1861) and Henry Maine (1822–1888) asserted that the likelihood that human rights will be respected is a function of cultural and environmental factors unique to particular communities and, thus, are culture-bound, unlikely to develop within certain cultures. Accordingly, Lee Kuan Yew (1923–), Singapore's longtime prime minister, has asserted the concept of "Asian values" to justify denial of civil and political human rights, even though many Asians disagree with Lee's view that the community is more important than the individual. Whereas the West tries to protect individuals from the oppressive state, according to Lee, the East wants to protect the state from misbehaving individuals. His view that East and West have distinct cultures, however, ignores their mutual interpenetration and cultural learning over the centuries as well as the fact that the Universal Declaration of Human Rights was coauthored by delegates from China, Europe, Lebanon, and the United States. Although Lee's concept of "Asian values" has served as a rhetorical justification to violate the civil and political rights of his democratic opponents in Singapore, after his retirement he predicted that pictures of the cruel treatment of individuals by governments appearing on television around the world would ultimately bring greater convergence between East and West on global human rights standards.

Frustration–Aggression Theory. The pessimistic writings of **Thomas Hobbes** (1588–1679), **Friedrich Nietzsche** (1855–1900), and **Sigmund Freud** (1856–1939) suggest the futility of pursuing the goal of human rights. Hobbes and Nietzsche agreed that humans can be rather nasty. For Freud, the advance of civilization requires suppression of individual personality. He felt that the division of labor associated with industrialization transforms workers into undifferentiated cogs within an economic system that has little place for the respect of individuals. Accordingly, Freud argued, humans develop frustrations in their daily lives, and from time to time the consequence is savage aggression toward scapegoats. Although Freud personally did not oppose the idea of human rights, his theory predicts that human rights campaigns will inevitably fail, since politics is a matter of groups endlessly struggling for larger and larger pieces of the pie. His thinking was obviously a reaction to the rise of Adolf Hitler (1889–1945), who came to power through democratic means. Since might makes right, according to elitists, such ideas as human rights are illusions; underlying needs for dominance are more basic. Since power is the mother tongue of politics, as Freud argued, "rights" can easily be abolished. Although Freud's psychological theories have been largely discredited as unscientific, his philosophical views in *Civilization and Its Discontents* (1930) serve as yet another explanation for the difficulty of gaining wider acceptance of a rights-based approach to world problems.

Social Darwinism. After biologist Charles Darwin (1809–1882) found evidence to support the theory of biological evolution, he applied his insight to humans. In both cases, he articulated a scientific law that the fit survive, and the weak die out. Sociologists Herbert Spencer (1820–1903) and William Graham Sumner (1840–1910) developed the Darwinian law into a social principle; namely, that there is an ongoing struggle for existence, such that the strong must dominate the weak for the human race to survive. Human rights for the weak, thus, are counter to the biological imperative. Although their extrapolation from Darwin's writings is clearly pseudoscientific, Social Darwinism even today guides much opposition to human rights. There are two variants of Social Darwinism – **libertarianism**, which advocates minimal government, and **triumphalism**, which wants to use the state to advance the fortunes of those who are successful.

In the academic study of international relations, Social Darwinism is known as **realism**. The chief exponents of realism are political scientist Hans Morgenthau (1904–1980) and former Secretary of State Henry Kissinger (1923–). According to the realists (or neo-realists, as some latter-day advocates prefer), states seek survival, so they maximize their interests, giving much priority to military power. States that fail to pursue their self-interests tend to lose out to those that do. Realists infer that human rights concerns will always be secondary and must yield to the primary aim of state self-preservation in an international system that is inherently chaotic, lacking a superordinate authority. Indeed, some realists believe that human rights issues are raised by powerful countries only to intimidate other countries. Many realists discount the notion that human rights concerns are an independent force in world politics, especially since powerful countries often violate human rights with impunity.

Social Constructionist Scepticism. According to philosophical sceptics, primacy in human thought should be given to what is real, and what is real must be observable. David Hume (1711–1776), a sceptic, believed that rights do not exist because they have no empirical basis; they cannot be seen or touched, so they are arbitrary mental constructs. When utilitarian Bentham declared that natural rights were "nonsense upon stilts," he was endorsing Hume's anti-dogma insight. But John Stuart Mill went beyond Hume and Bentham to find a utilitarian basis for human rights. Austin and the legal positivists embrace social constructionism, believing that "rights" have no philosophical basis and are only identified when governments wish to do so; governments may extend or cancel so-called rights at their whim. Social constructionists view "truth" as socially constructed, such that elites who control institutions of government and the media are able to control what nonelites believe to be true. In other words, although "rights" are conferred or denied by elites whenever they choose to do so, their primary aim in doing so is to stay in power. For example, Americans do not entirely comprehend the concept of "social class," since those in power have tried to maintain the promise of upward social mobility as a part of the "American dream." Social constructionists believe that ideas about social reality (social constructs) are often taken for granted as common sense, but, in fact, ideas about politics and society are invented within particular cultures and polities to serve the purposes of those in power. Critical legal theorists believe that judges do not base their decisions on the law or previous court precedent; instead, they make up their own mind first and then hunt for legal justifications.

Although such social constructionists as philosopher Michel Foucault (1926–1984) and sociologist Pierre Bourdieu (1930–2002) were primarily interested in deconstructing repressive orthodoxies of elites, their support for human rights is implicit, but their expectations are pessimistic. Social constructionists who are more positive about the role of human rights, such as political scientist Jack Donnelly (*c.* 1946–), are fully aware that the quest is to change minds as well as laws.

CONCLUSION

For centuries, the level of concern about human rights was limited to philosophical speculation, and most philosophers gave higher priority to other issues. Today, human rights issues fill the front pages of newspapers because there is widespread concern about violations. Philosophical speculation succeeded in inspiring action, especially the revolutions of Britain, France, and the United States, which resulted in bills of rights.

In one sense, the positivist approach appears to have won the argument, since the only human rights that are backed by the weight of authority around the world are those which have been encoded into laws and treaties that can be enforced. But advancements in human rights have emerged from social movements, not court cases. They have emerged from what political scientist David Forsythe (1941–) calls **soft law**, that is, philosophically-based principles, sometimes encoded into law, that drive nongovernmental forces to demand action from governmental institutions to respect human dignity. For critical legal theorist, Costas Douzinas (1951–), the stress on human rights has brought the ephemeral concept of justice into the forefront in the postmodern world, replacing the archaic concept of natural law. Never before, he believes, has legal theory been challenged to rid the world of horrendous violations. **Hard law**, in contrast, has enforcement provisions.

The following chapter, accordingly, traces the development of human rights by delineating historical events and movements that produced the contemporary **human rights culture** – a network of organizations and proponents that now serves as the principal spur for human rights progress.

CHAPTER 3

The Historical Basis for Human Rights

Thanks to philosophical speculation, as reviewed in the previous chapter, the view increasingly grew among the public in many countries that individuals should determine their own destinies without governmental interference. As fundamental rights were codified into national law, citizens were accorded basic rights. The historical development of human rights can be traced through certain documents that emerged over time (Tables 3.1–3.4). However, early rulers who attempted to guarantee rights were not always followed by successors with similar commitments. Rights have become more internationalized and irreversible when obtained in struggles carried on by international social movements, as indicated in the present chapter.

TABLE 3.1   EARLY DOCUMENTS OF HUMAN RIGHTS

Document	Adopted
Code of Hammurabi	1780 BCE
Torah	1280–500 BCE
Charter of Cyrus	539 BCE
Asoka's edicts	c.280 BCE
Christian Gospel	50–125
Constitution of Medina	622
Charter of Liberties	1100
Magna Carta	1215
Provisions of Oxford	1258
Provisions of Westminster	1259

EARLY DOCUMENTS OF HUMAN RIGHTS

The preamble to the constitution of Iraq, as adopted in 2005, notes that "on our land, the first law put in place by mankind was written; in our nation, the most noble era of justice in the politics of nations was laid down." The drafters of the constitution were referring to the written body of laws known as the **Code of Hammurabi**, issued by King Hammurabi (1810–1750 BCE) of ancient Babylon. The code was a systematic compilation of earlier judgments, many of which dealt with enforcement of contracts, including the marriage contract. On matters of criminal justice, those accused must be caught in the act, and unfair judges were to be fined and removed from their positions. However, some provisions among the 283 entries were harsh, for example setting the death penalty for false testimony by a witness or for a house-builder whose home collapses on a dweller.

The **Torah**, as first revealed by Moses (*c.*1304–1237 BCE), contains a legal code of 613 commandments, in which the prohibition on bearing false witness is a human rights element, as is the commandment to help the destitute and needy. However, the Torah's recognition of slavery is at variance with contemporary human rights principles, and the "eye for an eye" acceptance of capital punishment is widely opposed in Europe today.

In 539 BCE, Cyrus the Great (580–530 BCE) entered Babylon and proclaimed what is now known as the **Charter of Cyrus**, which has been claimed as the first human rights document because the word "rights" specifically appears therein. The text proclaims few rights, but the most notable are religious freedom and cultural toleration. In addition, land could be taken over only with just compensation to the owner, forced labor was banned, and slavery was abolished.

The democracy that flourished in Athens during the fifth century BCE was unprecedented in allowing male citizens to vote, participate in a legislature, and serve in executive positions, though a pragmatic aim was to provide a forum in order to enlist support from the people to pay taxes for war. The only documentary legacies are historical accounts. Plato (428–348 BCE) was clearly more unhappy with Athenian democracy than Aristotle (384–322 BCE), but neither based their evaluations on principles of human rights.

The **Edicts** of the Indian emperor, Asoka (304–232 BCE), as carved on stone pillars, provide a clue to an advocacy of human rights that focused on relief from suffering. Among the principles stated are humane treatment of prisoners, religious toleration, and impartial justice. Other edicts opposed capital punishment and torture of humans as well as animals.

The **Christian Gospels** of Matthew, Mark, Luke, and John, as recorded after the death of Jesus of Nazareth (*c.*4 BCE–34 CE), contains clear statements about the obligation to attend to the needs of the poor, a hint about opposition to capital punishment for adultery, but no condemnation of the human rights injustices associated with the arrest and interrogation of Jesus. The denial of freedom of speech, indignities after his arrest, and the crucifixion were implicitly accepted as predestined.

Perhaps the first written constitution is the **Constitution of Medina**, in which the prophet Mohammed (570–632) regulated the government of the Medina city-state, when Christians, Jews, Muslims, and pagans lived together peacefully.

No person is allowed to be left in poverty, according to the Constitution, but murder is to be avenged with murder.

The Romans were prolific in legal matters but did not recognize human rights. From the **Law of the Twelve Tables** (450 BCE) to the **Corpus Juris Civilis** (533 CE) of Emperor Justinian I (483–565), Roman law mostly codified property rights, with more privileges accorded to persons of higher status.

When the Roman Empire collapsed, the principal international entity within Europe was the Roman Catholic Church, which in turn developed canon law (church law). Because of the chaotic conditions in Europe, the church provided some rules to stabilize relations between governments. The right of asylum began in 511, when the Council of Orleans proclaimed immunity from arrest for anyone living in the confines of a church, even murderers and thieves. The laws of war, which are discussed at length in Chapter 7, began in 989, when the church banned the killing of children, clergy, merchants, peasants, and women in the conduct of war.

Several countries claim to have the world's first parliament, which allows a role for the people to formulate proposals for executives to implement. Athens, of course, had a citizen assembly, selected by lot, in the fifth century BCE, and Rome instituted an advisory Senate from 753 BCE–603 CE. Town meetings under trees, venerated by Jean-Jacques Rousseau (1712–1778), have existed for millennia and still continue in Africa and elsewhere.

The advent of a separation of power between executive and legislative branches of government is an important development in human history. The independent republic of San Marino claims that its legislature began in 301, when the state was founded, though no constitution was adopted until 1600. In 930, a parliament opened in Iceland among the Viking settlers, who founded an independent state. However, in 1262, Iceland became a colony of Norway, which in turn was ruled by Denmark from 1380, and its parliament was abolished in 1800, albeit reinstituted in 1845. The Isle of Man also claims to have the longest continually running parliament, dating from 979. Citizen assemblies were established at about that time in provinces of what is now Denmark, Germany, and Sweden. What distinguishes the development of parliaments is the separation of power between executive and legislative branches of government.

In 1066, a conquering army from Normandy took control of England and placed a French-speaking army of occupation over an English-speaking kingdom. King William (1028–1087) sought the advice of a council of Saxon nobles and church officials before making laws. In 1100, King Henry I (1068–1135) issued the **Charter of Liberties**, which granted certain freedoms to church officials (also banning both the purchase of church positions and any confiscation of church property) and to nobles (freedom from excessive taxation, right of inheritance). However, the grant was revocable, and there was no implication that the absolute authority of the monarchy was limited.

As the technology of warfare advanced during the Middle Ages, monarchs needed funds to pay for the manufacture of armaments and for mercenaries to fight battles. Spanish monarchs formed the Cortes as an advisory body of nobles in the eighth century. During the twelfth century, they expanded the Cortes to include members of the urban middle class in order to solicit money for the war to drive the Moors from Spain. When they obtained the wealth of the new world from the fifteenth century, they reduced the power of the Cortes, which was not revived until 1874.

HISTORIC EVENT 3.1 KING JOHN SIGNS THE MAGNA CARTA (1215)

The younger son of King Henry II (1133–1189), King John (1166–1216), was crowned upon the death of his elder brother, King Richard III (1157–1199), at a time when there was no fixed rule on succession to the monarchy. John's claim to legitimacy was disputed by Richard's nephew, Arthur (1187–1203), Duke of Brittany. To secure his title to the throne, John imprisoned his rival. In a series of military defeats to Philip II of France (1165–1223), England lost the territories of Anjou, Brittany, and Normandy, so John had fewer barons to tax. John also refused to accept the pope's nominee for Archbishop of Canterbury, whereupon Innocent III excommunicated him. John then submitted, accepted the papal nominee, and ceded England and Ireland as a fiefdom of the papacy, with an annual monetary tribute to be paid for the next 150 years by successive English monarchs. When King John also increased taxes on the remaining English barons to recover the three lost provinces, they rebelled and mobilized troops to take London by force. In 1215, in order to retain his throne, John signed the Magna Carta, at Runnymede meadow, which empowered a committee of barons, who could meet at any time to overrule his will.

On June 15, 1215, King John (1166–1216) signed the **Magna Carta**, under duress, which acknowledged that monarchs no longer had absolute power. The Magna Carta reiterated the Charter of Liberties, placed the king on an equal footing with the nobility, and made the powers of the monarch subject to law. One extraordinary provision was that a council of 25 barons could meet at any time to overrule any action by the king; they were entitled to seize the king's castles and possessions to enforce any disagreement. In addition to a separation of power between the institutions of the monarchy and the nobility, the Magna Carta provided that the executive authority could arrest nobles, but they had a right to defend themselves in judicial proceedings conducted in accordance with the law, including a trial with a jury consisting of fellow nobles; some 90 years later the procedure was known as the writ of *habeas corpus*. The king, under Magna Carta, could not levy taxes without the approval of the barons. The barons then took an oath to respect the king, who in turn swore to respect baronial power.

When John later disavowed the Magna Carta, civil war broke out. After John died during the war in 1216, regents of his successor, Henry III (1207–1272), ended the war by agreeing to accept the Magna Carta, which was reissued that year but without the provision for the 25-member council. Magna Carta was reissued in various watered-down forms over the years until the English barons forced Henry III to accept the **Provisions of Oxford** of 1258 (superseded in 1259 by the **Provisions of Westminster**), which established a parliament to monitor the performance of a council of 15 members that was entrusted with the responsibility to supervise ministerial appointments, local administration, and the custody of royal castles. When Henry III obtained papal approval in 1261 to disavow what he had signed under pressure, another civil war erupted. In 1265, the Earl of Leicester (1218–1265) declared that elections would be held for the council, which was to become the parliament; those eligible to vote were freeholders. In 1295, Edward I (1239–1307), Henry III's successor, finally accepted the parliament as legitimate. In 1305, he explicitly accepted the principle of *habeas corpus*. During the reign of Edward III (1312–1377), parliament became bicameral, with nobles and higher clergy sitting in the upper house, knights and burgesses in the lower house; laws and taxes required approval of both houses as well as the assent of the monarch.

In 1302, Philip IV ("Philip the Fair") (1268–1314) of France convened the Estates General, a tricameral arrangement to ask for the approval of the First Estate (clergy), the Second Estate (nobility), and the Third Estate (commoners) to levy taxes. Priests elected clergy in the First Estate, the king decided which nobles would serve in the Second Estate, and there was a limited election of Third Estate delegates within cities favored by the king. However, the Estates General were seldom summoned. Parliaments also arose in Central Europe and Scandinavia during the Middle Ages (*c.*410–1400), but with few powers exercised by the common people. Sweden's Riksdag, which can be traced to 1435, lacked significant power until 1809.

The English monarchs often sought to marginalize their parliaments by asserting executive authority, but they were resisted (Table 3.2). Charles I (1600–1649), for example, took out loans, quartered troops in houses of commoners, and imprisoned those who opposed his policies. Led by Sir Edward Coke (1552–1634), parliament issued the **Petition of Right** of 1628, intended to extend certain principles to commoners that had earlier been granted to the nobles; namely, that taxes can only be levied with parliament's consent, no person could be imprisoned without showing just cause, no soldiers could be quartered upon the citizenry, and martial law could not be used in peacetime. Although Charles I accepted the petition in principle, he ignored the provisions in practice.

As discussed in Chapter 2, in 1649, Charles I was deposed and executed. The English Commonwealth, which superseded the monarchy, began with the so-called Rump Parliament, which in turn was replaced by the Nominated Assembly. Regarded by moderates as too extreme, the council of officers for the assembly proposed a new constitution to be implemented by Oliver Cromwell (1599–1658), who chose the title of Lord Protector. Once in office, however, Cromwell proved to be just as dictatorial, provoking a successful counterrevolution following his death in September 1658, when the protectorate ended and the monarchy was restored. The new king, Charles II (r.1660–1685), was a Protestant, but he contemplated a conversion to Catholicism. His brother, the future James II (1633–1701), became a Catholic in 1671. Parliament passed the *Habeas Corpus* Act in 1679 to formalize

TABLE 3.2 HISTORICAL DOCUMENTS OF HUMAN RIGHTS IN THE SEVENTEENTH AND EIGHTEENTH CENTURIES

Document	Adopted
Petition of Right (England)	1628
Peace of Westphalia	1648
Habeas Corpus Act (England)	1679
Declaration for Liberty of Conscience (England)	1687
English Bill of Rights	1689
Act of Settlement (England)	1701
American Declaration of Rights and Grievances	1774
Virginia Declaration of Rights	1776
Declaration of Independence	1776
Catholic Relief Act (England)	1778
Constitution of the United States	1787
Declaration of the Rights of Man and Citizen	1789
Declaration of the Rights of Woman and the Female Citizen	1790
American (Federal) Bill of Rights	1791

and strengthen the Petition of Right from 1628. James II succeeded on his brother's death in 1685 and issued the Declaration for Liberty of Conscience in 1687. The declaration established a principle of freedom of religion, suspending penal laws enforcing conformity to the Church of England, allowing persons to worship where and as they saw fit and also abolished the requirement of affirming religious oaths before gaining employment in government office. Both non-Anglican Protestants and Catholics would gain from this new decree. In 1688, a group of seven Anglican nobles invited James's son-in-law, Prince William of Orange (1650–1702), to depose the king, and he sailed from Holland to England with troops. With insufficient support, James fled. Parliament voted that he had thereby abdicated and offered the crown jointly to William and his wife Mary as queen. Parliament then read its English Bill of Rights to the new monarchs, which became a statute in 1689. Parliament was to be supreme in lawmaking, especially regarding taxation and the maintenance of a standing army; parliamentary speech would be immune from prosecution; and elections would be free and fair. Other provisions in the Bill of Rights were the freedom to petition the king, the right of Protestants to bear arms, freedom from cruel and unusual punishment, freedom from excessive bail, and freedom from fines and forfeitures without trial. In 1701, the Act of Settlement provided that no Catholic could henceforth become monarch and succession would continue through the House of Hanover.

Although developments in Europe established some principles of domestic human rights, they did not contribute to the body of international law until 1648, when the Thirty Years' War ended with the **Peace of Westphalia**. The two treaties signed in Münster and Osnabrück established the current system of nation-states and advanced international law as the new basis for proper relations among governments. Three principles were established:

- The **legal equality of states** was recognized as a basic component of international law, though states differed considerably in power.
- Perhaps the most fundamental concept was the recognition of **state sovereignty**, that is, that governments should treat one another as supreme in domestic matters and would no longer depend upon papal approval to have their legitimacy respected. After 1648, thus, rulers were free to determine their own state religion, and they pledged to tolerate other religions among their subjects.
- The treaty established the principle of **noninterference** in the domestic affairs of other countries.

Under the Westphalian system, rulers respected one another's religious convictions, thus making religious toleration a principle of international affairs. Nevertheless, governments could complain about the mistreatment of their own citizens abroad and had the right to rescue them from harm.

DISCUSSION TOPIC 3.1 DOES THE WESTPHALIAN STATE SYSTEM REALLY PROMOTE HUMAN RIGHTS?

How did the Westphalian state system serve to advance human rights? What remedies were prescribed for mistreatment of individuals in 1648? Did the Westphalian nation-state system bring about an environment consistent with Grotius's expectations that international law would bring peace? Currently, most nation-states compete for power with international organizations, global corporations, and the dominant superpower, the United States, so are the philosophical principles underlying the creation of the Westphalian state system a fiction today?

MOVEMENTS TO ESTABLISH INTERNATIONAL HUMAN RIGHTS

Some observers believe that international human rights were not taken seriously until after World War II. Yet after Westphalia, several international mass movements emerged to establish an irreversible momentum toward the worldwide recognition of human rights. The first was the movement to establish democracy.

THE DEMOCRATIC MOVEMENT

Theories about democratic forms of rule leapt off the pages of philosophers' treatises onto the soil of North America when the American colonies decided to revolt against Britain. In 1774, Granville Sharp (1735–1813), grandson of the Archbishop of York, published *A Declaration of the People's Natural Rights to a Share in the Legislature*. He gave a copy to Benjamin Franklin (1706–1790), who in turn had the script republished in the colonies. Sharp's thesis inspired the formation later that year of the Continental Congress, a deliberative body composed of delegates from the 13 colonies.

Many colonists were British citizens, but they were not allowed to elect members to the parliament in London, so they could not effectively petition parliament from within. Accordingly, the Continental Congress decided not to submit its legislation to the English parliament for approval. In 1774, one of the first acts of the Continental Congress was to adopt a **Declaration of Rights and Grievances**, which primarily claimed that the colonists had the same rights as English citizens, including the right to be represented in a legislative body, trial by jury, and the right to assemble. The declaration objected to the maintenance of a standing army by England in the colonies and the quartering of troops in private homes. As the colonists were taxed to pay for the troops, they objected to taxation without representation in the English parliament.

In 1776, a **Declaration of Rights** was incorporated into the Constitution of Virginia, one of several constitutions that the colonies in rebellion adopted to replace the colonial charters under which they had been initially governed. One month later, delegates from the colonies drafted the **Declaration of Independence**, in which the principal author, Thomas Jefferson (1743–1826), substituted the right to "pursue happiness" for the right to property that had been identified by one of his favorite philosophers, John Locke (1632–1704).

In 1777, the Continental Congress adopted the **Articles of Confederation and Perpetual Union**, which were fully ratified by 1781 as a treaty among 13 states with a unicameral congress that elected a president but with no power to tax or to regulate trade. When Britain recognized American independence in 1783 under the terms of the Treaty of Paris, the newly independent country continued to hobble along under the Articles of Confederation, which many Americans perceived to be unsatisfactory. For example, each state could erect tariffs against the rest, so there was no guarantee that a national economy would ever develop.

In 1787, a new constitution was written, principally by James Madison (1751–1836), which established a stronger central government that could prevent states from impeding interstate commerce. Also included were such protections as prohibitions against *ex post facto* legislation (declaring a past action to be a crime) and bills of attainder (a law making someone guilty of a crime without a trial). But a significant human rights flaw in the Constitution was the recognition of slavery as legal throughout the country, even in states where the practice was formerly prohibited. Because leaders who wanted more civil liberties protections were against ratification of the Constitution, the framers promised on their honor to amend the constitution to establish a bill of rights after the document was ratified by the required number of nine states.

TABLE 3.3   PROVISIONS OF THE AMERICAN BILL OF RIGHTS

Article	Human rights provision
1	Freedom of religion, press, assembly, petition
2	Right to bear arms
3	Soldiers cannot be forced to live in the homes of civilians
4	Right not to be unreasonably searched; no warrants without probable cause
5	No arrest for capital or infamous crime without indictment; no double jeopardy; no self-incrimination; no loss of life, liberty, property without due process of law; no government seizure of private property for public use without just compensation
6	Right to speedy trial by impartial jury where criminal defendant is informed of the accusation, confronted by accusers, and has an attorney in defense who can subpoena witnesses
7	Right of trial by jury for civil lawsuits, using common law
8	No excessive bail or fines; no cruel or unusual punishments
9	Rights not mentioned are retained by the people
10	Powers not delegated to government are reserved by the people and the states

The **Bill of Rights**, proposed by Madison to the First Congress in 1789 and ratified in 1791, consisted of the first 10 amendments to the Constitution (Table 3.3).[1] However, the Bill of Rights originally applied to the federal government, including Washington, DC, residents; states were not covered, and the Eleventh Amendment of 1795 stripped federal courts from jurisdiction over nonconsenting state governments. The right to vote is not included because that matter was left to the individual states to determine.

Inspired in part by the American Revolution, the leaders of the French Revolution issued the **Declaration of the Rights of Man and Citizen** of 1789 and the **Declaration of the Rights of Woman and the Female Citizen** of 1790. Unlike the American Declaration of Independence, which proclaimed the right of 13 colonies to self-government, the French declarations were intended to apply universally, not just to France. The rights identified in both documents went beyond those stated in the American Bill of Rights to include the right to security and the right of resistance to oppression. The declaration regarding rights of males, but not females, was encoded into France's first constitution in 1791.

Having declared that peoples everyone should enjoy fundamental rights, France under Napoléon Bonaparte (1769–1821) conscripted citizens to overthrow the monarchs of Europe. War then ensued all over the continent. By the early nineteenth century, semi-democratic England eventually joined the despotisms of Austria, Prussia, and Russia to stop Napoléon in order to restore the balance of power in Europe. Delegates of the victorious major powers, along with a representative of the re-established French monarchy, then met in a conference, the Congress of Vienna (1814–1815), to redraw the European map in order to undo changes effected by the French armies.

Leaders of the four major powers, joined by France in 1818, agreed to call themselves the Concert of Europe, pledging collectively to organize efforts that would suppress any further democratic uprisings. However, the arrangement soon fell apart. England stopped supporting the reactionary aims and democratizing France left the Concert in 1830.[2]

As of 1815, only Britain, France, and the United States formally recognized a wide range of individual rights, though Spain had granted men the right to vote in 1812. All four countries granted the right to vote only to property owners, however, so only about 1 percent of the population were eligible to vote.

In 1832, England's Reform Act extended the right to vote to middle class males, but the common people, men and women, were still disfranchised. Accordingly, in 1838, carpenter-cum-activist William Lovett (1800–1877) issued the **People's Charter**, which began a campaign of parliamentary reform known as the Chartist Movement that made the following demands:

- Universal suffrage
- Equal electoral districts
- Abolition of the requirement that members of parliament must own property
- Payment for members of parliament
- Annual general elections
- The secret ballot.

Economist Thomas Carlyle (1795–1881) further publicized the People's Charter movement in his tract *Chartism* (1839). The suffrage proposal originally envisaged female suffrage, but the movement later dropped interest in females and demanded only universal male suffrage. Although the tenor of the Chartist Movement was radical, all the demands but an annual election eventually became law, the earliest by 1858, the latest by 1911.

HISTORIC EVENT 3.2 THE EUROPEAN REVOLUTIONS OF 1848–1849

Economic conditions in Europe deteriorated in the 1840s, including serious crop failures that resulted in high food prices. Rural residents moved to the cities in search of a better life in the new factories, where working conditions were harsh, only to find that there were few jobs because of the economic downturn. The middle class was also adversely affected by the increased cost of food. In 1848, King Louis Philippe (1773–1850) attempted to ban fundraising banquets on behalf of French workers, whereupon the people attacked the police, the king abdicated, and the new Second Republic proclaimed the right to work and universal male suffrage.

Continued

Events in Paris stimulated revolutionaries elsewhere. Provisional governments arose in Austrian-held Milan and Venice with the intention of merging into a united Italy. A Hungarian government demanded independence from Austria. The Polish in Poznań fought occupying German troops. A Polish committee demanded that Austria should cede Galicia to Poland. Czech nationalists agitated for independence from Germany. Revolts also broke out in the independent states of Bavaria and Saxony. At first, some of the rulers offered democratic concessions. Later, they used troops to quell the demonstrations and rescinded democratic reforms almost everywhere. France, meanwhile, remained in turmoil. Although Louis Bonaparte (1808–1873), nephew of Napoléon Bonaparte, was elected President of the Second Republic, he staged a coup in 1851. In 1852, he held a referendum that served to replace the Second Republic with the Second Empire. Calling himself Napoléon III, he continued in power until 1870.

The realization that states could become democratic and prosper spread to the masses throughout Europe from the early part of the nineteenth century. In 1848, there were uprisings all over Europe as the disfranchised rose in revolt against undemocratic rulers. Britain and France no longer supported the antidemocratic mood of the Congress of Vienna, and the crude suppression of the revolts by undemocratic governments in 1848 only encouraged prodemocratic forces to pressure governments even more to gain the right to vote. After 1848, male suffrage was extended by several countries in Europe, including France, though property or tax requirements for voting were still imposed.

By the turn of the twentieth century, revolutionary ferment grew stronger inside the Austro-Hungarian and Ottoman empires, where the democratic quest was manifest as nationalist movements. One hotbed was Serbia, then governed by Austria-Hungary. In 1914, a Serbian nationalist assassinated Austrian Archduke Franz Ferdinand (1863–1914). Political alliances between various groups of European nations led to hostilities, and within a few months World War I broke out. When the war was over, the Austro-Hungarian, German, and Ottoman (Turk) empires were dissolved. Nascent democratic states (Czechoslovakia, Hungary, and Poland) soon appeared in their place. The democratic imperative had been established, though the perfection of democratic principles remains a challenge today.

ANTISLAVERY MOVEMENT[3]

By 1400, slavery had already been banned in France and Scandinavia. Such philosophers as Montesquieu condemned the practice. In 1569, an English court ruled in the *Cartright* case that the common law did not recognize the status of master and slave. However, the discovery of the New World opened up vast lands for Europeans to have cleared for agriculture, including sugar production, and British and French colonies imported slaves. Some 15 million slaves from Africa were imported to the colonies in the Americas for that purpose, but in time their demeaning treatment provoked opposition. In 1700, Boston judge, Samuel Sewall (1652–1730), wrote *The Selling of Joseph* in which he developed a thesis against slavery out of his experience with a slave named Adam, who sought his freedom.

To mushroom, the antislavery movement needed a leader with a large following. When John Wesley (1703–1791) published *Thoughts upon Slavery* (1744), he had a mass base for antislavery opposition as the founder of the Methodist faith. Unitarians and members of the Society of Friends, the Quakers, also opposed slavery on moral grounds, though for centuries the Biblical "curse of Canaan" was understood by some Christians, Jews, and Muslims to be a divine statement that Africans were destined to be slaves.

Later in the eighteenth century, Granville Sharp, champion of democratic reform, also decried the practice of slavery. Espousing the cause of a slave who had been beaten almost to death by his master and abandoned, he wrote *The Injustice and Dangerous Tendency of Tolerating Slavery in England* (1769). When a slave from Virginia, who managed to escape to England, filed a writ of *habeas corpus* in 1772 to end his slave status, Sharp supported his petition, which was successful in *Somersett v. Knowles*. In 1776, Jefferson's first draft of the American Declaration of Independence objected to England's introduction of slavery into the colonies, but those from the South, where slavery was widespread, insisted that he remove that portion from the final document.

In 1787, Sharp, and his friend Thomas Clarkson (1760–1846), an Anglican deacon, formed the Society for the Abolition of the Slave Trade, which was later supported by Wesley and William Wilberforce (1759–1833), the latter an Evangelical member of parliament who was in a position to obtain support for the abolitionist cause at the highest levels of government. Formation of the society marked the first time in history when large numbers of people in one country were mobilized to protest the plight of people of another color in another part of the world. At a time when half the slaves were being transported from Africa to America on British ships, the movement threatened profits of British companies, so the appeal had to be based on morality. Clarkson was assigned to collect data about the slave trade, so he interviewed some 20,000 sailors, secured physical evidence in the form of handcuffs, leg-shackles, thumb screws, instruments for forcing open slave's jaws, and branding irons, and then published *A Summary View of the Slave Trade and of the Probable Consequences of Its Abolition* (1787), which shocked the English public.

After attending meetings of the British Society, Jacques-Pierre Brissot (1754–1793) formed a parallel Société des Amis des Noirs in France during 1788. His society attracted membership from the Marquis de Condorcet (1743–1794), the Marquis de La Fayette (1757–1834) who supported the American Revolution, and the National Constituent Assembly president, Comte de Mirabeau (1749–1791). In 1794, the assembly decreed an end to slavery in the French colonies. However, Napoléon rescinded the decree in 1802, as his wife had commercial interests in Martinique.

HISTORIC EVENT 3.3 THE HAITIAN INDEPENDENCE STRUGGLE (1790–1803)

In 1697, Spain ceded the western part of Hispaniola to France, now known as Haïti, where immensely profitable coffee and sugar plantations were established. The French colonial rulers then imported slaves from Africa to work under such harsh working conditions that in 1751–1758 they had to put down a revolt by runaway slaves. By 1778, there were some 500,000 slaves, 40,000 French, and 30,000 non-slave mulattos in Haïti. After the French Revolution began, the National Constituent Assembly requested the Haitian colonial legislature to enfranchise the mulattos, but the colonists refused. Then, in 1790, the mulattos revolted under the leadership of Vincent Ogé (1755–1791), destroying towns, burning plantations, and executing French settlers, but they did not mobilize the slaves. In 1791, former slave, François Dominique Touissaint L'Ouverture (1743–1803), who had become a slaveowner, assumed leadership of the revolt after the French executed Ogé, though his primary aim was to improve work conditions for slaves. In 1794, when slavery was abolished by the Paris government, L'Ouverture persuaded the French to accept him as the territory's governor and military commander while the colony remained under French sovereignty. L'Ouverture showed his loyalty to France by resisting efforts of Britain and Spain to attack Haïti. In 1799, Napoléon came to power in France. In 1802, after reinstituting slavery, he sent a large force to depose L'Ouverture, who accepted a peace offer from the French and went into exile in France. General Jean-Jacques Dessalines (1758–1806), L'Ouverture's military commander, agreed to the peace until word spread that Napoléon intended to reestablish slavery. Dessalines then resumed the struggle. Many French soldiers either died of yellow fever or tired of the operation. At the end of 1803, French troops surrendered to rebel forces and withdrew. Dessalines declared independence, under the name Haïti, on 1 January 1804, thereby encouraging slave revolts elsewhere around the world. In 1805, Dessalines ordered ethnic cleansing of most of the French in Haïti.

In 1787, Britain had founded the Sierra Leone colony for emancipated slaves. In 1788, petitions to end the slave trade so flooded the English parliament that a law was passed to regulate conditions on slave ships. The success of the Haitian independence movement in 1803 provided further impetus to the movement. By 1807, the last year when the US Constitution allowed the slave trade, the British parliament passed the **Abolition of the Slave Trade Act** (Table 3.4). Abolishing slavery itself was the next task.

The Society for the Abolition of the Slave Trade was renamed the Society for the Mitigation and Eventual Abolition of Slavery in 1807, and retitled again as the British Anti-Slavery Society in 1823. In each case, only men were admitted as members.

TABLE 3.4 **HISTORICAL DOCUMENTS OF HUMAN RIGHTS IN THE NINETEENTH AND EARLY TWENTIETH CENTURIES**

Document	Adopted
Abolition of the Slave Trade Act (England)	1807
Treaty of Ghent	1814
Final Act of the Congress of Vienna	1815
Catholic Emancipation Act (England)	1829
Slavery Abolition Act (England)	1833
People's Charter (England)	1838
Declaration of Sentiments (United States)	1848
Declaration of Paris	1856
Emancipation Proclamation	1862
Lieber Code	1863
Convention for the Amelioration of the Condition of the Wounded in Armies in the Field	1864
Thirteenth, Fourteenth, and Fifteenth Amendments (United States)	1866, 1868, 1870
Project of an International Declaration Concerning the Laws and Customs of War	1874
Declaration of the Rights of Women in the United States	1876
Treaty of San Stefano	1878
Manual of the Laws and Customs of War	1880
Final Act of the Congress of Berlin	1885
General Act for the Repression of the African Slave Trade	1890
Erfurt Program	1891
Rerum Novarum	1891
Treaties adopted at the First and Second Hague Conferences	1899 and 1907
Bern Conventions	1905 and 1906
Balfour Declaration	1917
Wilson's Fourteen Points	1918
Treaty of Versailles (including the Covenant of the League of Nations)	1919
Constitution of the International Labor Organization	1919
Statute of the Permanent Court of International Justice	1920
Nineteenth (Susan B. Anthony) Amendment	1920
Protocol for the Pacific Settlement of International Disputes	1924
Locarno Peace Pact	1925
Slavery, Servitude, Forced Labor and Similar Institutions and Practices Convention	1926
General Treaty for the Renunciation of War	1928
Convention Relative to the Treatment of Prisoners of War	1929
Convention Relating to the International Status of Refugees	1933

The adversaries of the War of 1812 (Britain and the United States) agreed to stop the slave trade under the terms of the **Treaty of Ghent** of 1814, which ended the war. But once again no action was taken to implement the pledge.

In 1814–1815, foreign ministers of the victorious powers (Austria, England, Prussia, Russia) over the armies of Napoléon Bonaparte met at Vienna along with a delegate from the new post-Napoleonic French government; France now restored to the House of Bourbon. Responding to the antislavery movement, they declared in the **Final Act of the Congress of Vienna** of 1815 that the slave trade was morally repugnant. Although the final act recognized the rights of the Polish minorities in Austria, Prussia, and Russia, their principal aim was to legitimate the monarchies of all five countries and to establish a five-power consultative Concert of Europe that might collaborate in suppressing democratic uprisings.

Meanwhile, women's antislavery groups formed in various English towns. Elizabeth Heyrick (1769–1831), a Unitarian who became a Quaker, forged a network of female antislavery societies, which gained momentum after publication of her *Immediate, Not Gradual Abolition* (1825). The women differed from the gradualist approach advocated by the men, and Heyrick even organized a boycott of sugar, much of which was produced by slave labor in the British colonies in the Caribbean. In 1830, after Heyrick became treasurer of the Anti-Slavery Society, she insisted that the society should call for immediate abolition. In 1833, parliament passed the **Slavery Abolition Act**, freeing more than 700,000 throughout most of the British Empire. However, the slave trade largely occurred in international waters, and no country had yet decided to enforce its ban.

Revolutions against Spain in the Americas abolished slavery, starting in the 1820s. In 1831, Nat Turner (1800–1831) led a slave revolt in which 55 whites were massacred in Virginia. As a result, there was a crackdown on slaves throughout the South, including the denial of an opportunity to receive an education. Thereafter, the American Colonization Society arose as a movement to encourage slaves to return to Africa, having founded Liberia in 1822 for emancipated slaves. The Maryland legislature, for example, provided US$200,000 for that purpose in 1833.

Then, in 1840, national abolitionist movements across the Atlantic joined together to form the Anti-Slavery International for the Protection of Human Rights, which convened the first World Anti-Slavery Conference to focus attention on the issue. By placing slavery in the larger context of human rights, the movement signaled the arrival of a wider agenda than abolition of slavery. In 1848, France abolished slavery and granted citizenship to former slaves.

Earlier, Abigail Adams (1744–1818), spouse of the second American president, John Adams (1735–1826), was among those who opposed slavery and was unhappy with the compromise that appeased Southern states so that they would ratify the Constitution. Later, Harriet Beecher Stowe (1811–1896), her brother, Henry Ward Beecher (1813–1887), William Lloyd Garrison (1805–1879), and others formed various organizations, held meetings, conducted studies, published books, and utilized the press to dramatize slavery as immoral. While Garrison printed current news events about slave conditions in his publication, *The Liberator* (1831–1865), Stowe's novel about the horrors of slavery, *Uncle Tom's Cabin* (1852), was very widely read.

From the beginning of the United States, Southern states controlled Congress by virtue of the rule that representation in the House of Representatives was constitutionally based on the number of residents in each state, with slaves counted as three-fifths of a person. As new states were admitted, the Southern states wanted to expand slavery, but prominent Northerners were adamantly opposed.

In *Dred Scott v. Sanford* (1857), the US Supreme Court (60US393) ruled that a slave named Dred Scott (1795–1858) was not automatically freed when he moved with his master to a state where slavery was outlawed. The court's decision further outraged antislavery advocates into realizing that Northern farmers could import the cheap labor of slaves, and indeed slaves existed in New Jersey, a Northern state, up to 1860. The emergence of the Republican Party, and particularly the candidacy of antislavery advocate, Abraham Lincoln (1809–1865), in 1860, was seen as a threat by entrenched Southern economic interests, so the North and the South were on a collision course. The train wreck occurred in 1861, even before President Lincoln took office, when a Southern militia fired on the federal arsenal of weaponry at Fort Sumter in the harbor of Charleston, South Carolina. Lincoln, however, conducted the resulting civil war by placing preservation of the United States as a union at a higher value than the abolition of slavery.

By 1862, while the United States was engaged in the American Civil War, 10 European countries had adopted legislation to stop ships on the high seas suspected of transporting slaves. President Abraham Lincoln issued the **Emancipation Proclamation** in 1862, to go into effect on January 1, 1863, but he only declared an end to slavery in the states that seceded, not in Delaware, Kentucky, Maryland, and Missouri, which had slaves but did not secede. In 1865, after the Civil War ended, slavery was abolished in the United States by the **Thirteenth Amendment** to the Constitution. In the next 15 years, more than 50 countries on all continents followed suit.

The **Fourteenth Amendment** to the American Constitution, ratified in 1867, applied the Bill of Rights to the states so that former slaves would receive due process and equal justice before the law to undo the badges of slavery. The **Fifteenth Amendment** of 1870 forbade the states to deny the right to vote on the basis of race. An effort to enforce racial equality continued until the Republican Party's presidential candidate pledged to withdraw troops from the Southern states in exchange for their support to win the 1876 presidential election. African Americans were subsequently discouraged from exercising the franchise by means subtle and not so subtle until passage of the Voting Rights Act of 1965. Provisions of the Bill of Rights were not enforced upon the states again until Supreme Court rulings during the twentieth century.[4]

In 1885, the **Final Act of the Congress of Berlin** declared an end to the slave trade, and in 1890 the **General Act for the Repression of the African Slave Trade** was adopted at a conference in Brussels. Brazil finally abolished slavery in 1899.

Thanks to the work of the Temporary Slavery Commission of the League of Nations, a treaty was adopted in 1926. The **Slavery, Servitude, Forced Labor and Similar Institutions and Practices Convention**, also known as the Slavery Convention of 1926, made prohibition of slavery a matter of international law.

The antislavery movement was the first worldwide mass-based movement on behalf of international human rights. However, forced labor is still a problem in the world today, affecting millions of unfortunate people.

SUFFRAGETTE MOVEMENT

In 1776, New Jersey allowed women to vote on an equal basis with men if they owned property. During the American Revolutionary War (1775–1783), Abigail Adams complained that women were not given the same rights as men. Educated at home because women were not admitted to school, she successfully campaigned for the right of girls to receive a formal education. In 1807, New Jersey rescinded female suffrage, setting back what might have developed into a trend. Nevertheless, in 1838, Britain allowed women to vote in its Pitcairn colony.

In 1792, Mary Wollstonecraft (1759–1797), a famous English writer, set forth the first feminist critique of male tyranny over females in her tract *A Vindication of the Rights of Woman*. Her most constructive proposal was for the right to education by females.

In 1840, Elizabeth Cady Stanton (1815–1902), a staunch American abolitionist and Quaker, sought to attend the World Antislavery Convention in London with her spouse, only to learn that women were not admitted. Outraged, she returned to the United States to organize the first Women's Rights Convention at Seneca Falls, New York, in 1848, when she persuaded the delegates to adopt the **Declaration of Sentiments**. In 1850, the first of several national women's rights conventions was held, advocating not only the right to vote but also liberalization of divorce laws.

In 1851, when Harriet Taylor Mill (1808–1857), spouse of John Stuart Mill (1806–1873), wrote *The Enfranchisement of Women*, feminist writer, Anne Knight (1786–1862) formed the Sheffield Female Political Association, the first women's suffrage organization for the vote in Britain. Later, similar groups emerged throughout the country. In 1866, the Isle of Man parliament became the first in the world to grant equal voting rights for men and women. In 1867, when John Stuart Mill unsuccessfully presented a petition for the female franchise as a member of parliament, the London National Society for Women's Suffrage was founded. His *The Subjection of Women* (1869) provided the philosophic basis for his petition.

After the victory of the North in the American Civil War, progressive women in the United States focused their attention on suffrage. In 1866, Stanton and fellow Quaker, Susan B. Anthony (1820–1906), founded the American Equal Rights Association to lobby for such reforms as the Fourteenth and Fifteenth Amendments. In 1868, they launched the newspaper *The Revolution* in Rochester, with the masthead "Men, their rights, and nothing more; women, their rights, and nothing less." However, Anthony and Stanton were bitterly disappointed when the Fourteenth and Fifteenth Amendments failed to establish the principle of women's equality. From 1869, Anthony appeared before Congress each year until her death to lobby for female suffrage.

In 1869, while unmarried female taxpayers in England were given the right to vote in local elections, the women's movement in the United States split. Anthony and Stanton formed the National Woman Suffrage Association, which opposed the Fifteenth Amendment because women were excluded. Then, after the Fifteenth Amendment was ratified in 1870, the group favored a constitutional amendment to grant equality to women. A rival American Woman Suffrage Association was also founded in 1869, electing antislavery leader, Henry Ward Beecher, as the first president. The latter group's strategy of getting female suffrage on a state-by-state basis bore fruit when the Territory of Wyoming granted the right to vote to women in 1869 and the Utah Territory in 1870. However, Congress revoked Utah's female suffrage in 1887.

In 1870, 44 women voted in Massachusetts, though their ballots were not counted. In 1872, Anthony and a dozen others tried to vote and were arrested. The ensuing court proceeding, in 1873, found them guilty and they were fined for violating the voting laws. They were denied the right of trial by jury. Suffragette demonstrations were then held at the centennial anniversaries of the Boston Tea Party in 1873, the Battle of Lexington in 1874, and the Declaration of Independence in Philadelphia in 1876, where Anthony read the **Declaration of the Rights of Women in the United States**.

In *Minor v. Happersett* (1874), the Supreme Court (88US162) ruled that women, though citizens, had no constitutional right to vote. However, in 1878, a constitutional amendment prohibiting the states from denying women the right to vote was first introduced in Congress.

In 1887, the two rival American suffragette organizations merged, forming the National American Woman Suffrage Association. Meanwhile, socialist parties came out for the right of women to vote throughout Europe, and in 1893 New Zealand granted the franchise to females. The state of South Australia followed suit in 1894. In 1906, 26 candidates of the Australian Labour Party were elected to parliament and formed the Parliamentary Labour Party, which in turn identified women's suffrage as a priority. In 1906, Finland voted to allow women's suffrage.

In England, in 1905, one of the first militant suffragette actions took place when Christabel Pankhurst (1880–1958) was arrested for disrupting a speech of Foreign Minister Sir Edward Grey (1862–1933). She was fined but refused to pay, resulting in a sentence of seven days imprisonment. In 1907, some 3,000 women marched from Hyde Park to the Strand, demanding the vote. American suffragettes began to adopt the tactics of their English counterparts – parades, street speakers, and pickets. In 1908, a suffragette rally in London attracted 250,000 in Hyde Park, and in 1909 women smashed the windows of government offices and department stores. A suffragette riot in 1910 resulted in 120 arrests after police attacks on female protesters at parliament.

In 1913, the year when women received the vote in Norway, suffragette violence escalated in England. Mary Richardson (1889–1961) slashed the *Rokeby Venus* in the National Gallery, and other suffragettes vandalized paintings in Manchester and Birmingham. An arson campaign was launched at racecourses, churches, and unoccupied homes of politicians. Emily Wilding Davison (1872–1913) threw herself under the king's horse at the Epsom Derby and died four days later.

During World War I, the suffragette movement was suspended. Women gained considerable recognition for working in factories while men were at war. Public opinion was more favorable to the movement after the war, and some women received a limited franchise in 1918–1920 within Austria, Britain, Czechoslovakia, Germany, Hungary, Poland, and the United States. Other countries followed around the world. When the suffragette movement quieted down, true equality between the sexes remained to be achieved throughout the world, awaiting the world feminist movement from the 1960s.

TRADE UNION MOVEMENT

By 1150, workers throughout most of Western Europe had formed craft guilds, but they declined with the arrival of capitalism and were abolished during the French Revolution, by the British parliament in 1814 and 1835, and throughout the German states. Craft guilds, however, reappeared as the Industrial Revolution progressed within burgeoning cities among journeymen shipwrights, printers, tailors, stonecutters, carpenters, and others. By the 1830s, workers met in public squares to demand higher wages and better working conditions, but employers often called troops to quell demonstrations and riots, deeming trade unions to be illegal.

Factory and living conditions of industrial workers were deplorable, as the novels of Charles Dickens (1812–1870) and others described. Welsh industrialist Robert Owen (1771–1858), who reminisced that pre-industrial society had Poor Laws and a *noblesse oblige* belief that the more fortunate should take care of the less fortunate, was upset that unregulated factories were bringing about social chaos. His *A New View of Society* (1813) advocated a utopian socialism of small industrial villages run cooperatively by worker-residents. He owned and ran such a village in Britain from 1805–1815, and in 1824 moved to New Harmony, Indiana, to set up the first of 16 model industrial villages. When Owen realized that his experiment had failed, he returned to England in 1828 to lobby for laws to protect workers from rampant exploitation. Although Owen's enterprises turned a profit, other industrialists believed that pandering to workers would place them at a competitive disadvantage, both nationally and internationally.

The British parliament slowly began to ban child labor, the objectionable practice of recruiting children for work. The Cotton Factories Regulation Act of 1819 set the minimum working age at 9 and maximum working hours at 12. The Regulation of Child Labor Law of 1833 required clean conditions of work. In 1847, the Ten Hours Bill limited working to 10 hours for children and women; the law was extended in 1867 to small factories and workshops. Collectively known as the Factory Acts, they sought to provide safety and sanitation in all workshops and regulated the hours of labor for women as well.

During the 1830s and 1840s, humanitarian industrialist Daniel Le Grand (1783–1859) in France and parliamentarian Charles Hindley (1850–1924) in England proposed an international treaty to regulate conditions of labor so that no country that provided humane conditions for workers would suffer a competitive disadvantage in the increasingly global economy. In 1843, Belgian journalist, Edouard Ducpétiaux (1804–1868), was the earliest to advocate an international labor organization, and he convened the first international conference on labor issues at Brussels in 1856.

The Chartist Movement, which began in 1838, was the first grassroots worker's movement, though the principal focus was on electoral reform. Impressed by the Chartist Movement, and further encouraged by the political discontent that was spilling over into mass uprisings in 1848, Karl Marx (1818–1883) and Friedrich Engels (1820–1895) issued the *Manifesto of the Communist Party* (1848). They interpreted the widespread unrest throughout European cities as a significant advance in a class struggle that began when capitalist elites vanquished feudal authorities, creating a bourgeois class of owners and a proletarian class of workers.

Indeed, the Industrial Revolution emerged as business owners organized workers into factories to mass produce goods for sale in an international market, thus bringing large numbers of laborers in close touch with one another. Efforts to organize workers within industrialized countries stimulated Marx and Engels to imagine a worldwide labor movement. In 1864, Marx assumed a key position in the newly formed International Workingmen's Association, later called the First International, and tried to build a socialist worker's movement out of a diverse collection of representatives of left-wing political parties.

In 1868, suffragette Susan B. Anthony advocated an eight-hour day and equal pay for equal work. Although women were excluded from most trade unions, she encouraged women in the garment and printing trades to form workingwomen's associations. In 1869, she was elected president of the Workingwomen's Central Association, but the National Labor Union Congress resisted her efforts when she urged women to replace men on strike as typesetters.

In 1869, Uriah Stephens (1821–1882), aware that union organizers and members were often shot dead, founded the Holy and Noble Order of the Knights of Labor in Philadelphia as a secret society. In 1882, the knights went public, declaring that they opposed strikes, and membership expanded as they encouraged employers to establish recreation and welfare programs. Another union with similar goals, the Brotherhood of Locomotive Firemen, was formed in 1876 by Eugene V. Debs (1855–1926).

HISTORIC EVENT 3.4 THE PARIS COMMUNE, 1871

In 1870, Prussia attacked France. By 1871, Prussian troops had defeated the French and attempted to occupy Paris. But Parisians peacefully refused to go along and restricted the Prussian military to a few city blocks. When a French authority, cooperating with the Prussians, then tried to enter Paris to collect arms from the people, the population resisted, organizing the first successful workers' revolution. They held an election with universal suffrage for an independent municipal government, known as the Paris Commune. Reforms of the new workers' government included separation of church and state and the abolition of the guillotine. Factories abandoned by industrialists were reopened and run by workers as cooperatives, and night work was abolished for bakers. Three months after the election,

Continued

a collaborationist French army returned with sufficient weapons to overthrow the Paris Commune. Some 30,000 unarmed workers were then massacred, thousands were arrested, and 7,000 were exiled.

Formation of the Paris Commune in 1871, however, frightened governments and industrialists throughout Europe. British trade unions sought to dissociate themselves from the "red terrorists of Paris." The leaders of the Paris Commune were ultimately exiled and disunited. More moderate union leaders tried to unseat Marx from leadership in the First International, whereupon he transferred the headquarters of his organization from London to New York, where his followers were predominant. However, Marx remained in England, so the leaderless movement waned and collapsed in 1876.

In 1886, a strike at the McCormick Harvester factory in Chicago for an eight-hour day led to a mass rally of strikers in Haymarket Square. After the English-speaking rally concluded, the German-speaking workers remained to hear speeches in their language, whereupon police ordered the crowd to disperse. A bomb was then lobbed toward the cops, who in turn opened fire. At least 10 died, 50 were wounded, and 8 were convicted of murder. Public sympathy for the Knights of Labor then evaporated.

After two preliminary meetings of socialist parties, the International Socialist Congress met in Paris during 1889. Attended by delegates from 20 countries, including Engels, the conference launched the Socialist International, formally adopted the principles of the International Workingmen's Association of 1864, and advocated a gradualist approach. The meeting, known as the founding of the Second (Socialist) International, declared May Day as an international working-class holiday. Nine subsequent meetings were held, adopting resolutions on various subjects, including opposition to colonialism. Lenin, who attended the early conferences, broke with the organization in 1903, as he preferred a revolutionary approach.

Workers already disappointed with the Knights of Labor had formed the Federation of Organized Trades and Labor Unions in the United States during 1881 as an umbrella organization for craft unions. In 1886, after the Haymarket Massacre, the Federation was reorganized as the American Federation of Labor (AFL), which was dedicated to worker solidarity. Rather than opposing capitalism, AFL's founder, Samuel Gompers (1850–1924), felt that workers should avoid harsh rhetoric and seek negotiations with management to improve their lot; boycotts and strikes should be used only as a last resort. He refused to ally with the Socialist Party and instead sought to support friends and oppose enemies in the Democratic and Republican parties. His first priority was union recognition; the second priority was higher wages and better working conditions. The AFL, which represented mostly white workers of the upper working class, opposed membership by African Americans as well as immigrants from Asia and Europe. The AFL sought to outlaw "yellow dog" contracts (requiring workers to pledge not to join a union), to limit the courts' power to stop strikes through injunctions, and to obtain exemption from laws that were being used to criminalize labor's use of picketing, boycotts, and strikes to support workers' demands. In 1890, Congress responded to one of the AFL's lesser concerns by including in the Trade Act a provision banning the import of goods produced abroad by prison labor.

From 1883 to 1889, Germany became the first country to adopt legislation establishing obligatory accident, disability, health, and old-age insurance programs. The aim was to wean workers away from their support of a more radical socialist agenda. Although only the top segments of the working class were covered, the reforms whetted the appetite of workers around the world to establish what later became known as the welfare state.

Perhaps the boldest assertion of the rights of workers came in 1891 from two different sources. In May, Pope Leo XIII (1810–1903) issued the encyclical *Rerum Novarum* (captioned *Rights and Duties of Capital and Labor*), which asserted, "since wage workers are numbered among the great mass of the needy, the State must include them under its special care and foresight." While firmly opposing socialism, the encyclical endorsed the right of workers to a living wage, safe and sanitary working conditions, humane work duties, reasonable hours of work, holidays and Sundays off from work, rest periods, and the right to join peaceful trade unions. The pope also opposed child labor and work too strenuous for women.

Later in 1891, the German Social Democratic Party, which was committed to socialism, issued at its convention in Erfurt a document known as the **Erfurt Program**, proclaiming opposition to "not only the exploitation and oppression of wage earners, but every kind of exploitation and oppression, whether directed against a class, a party, a sex, or a race." The Erfurt Program not only demanded rights for workers but also a broad range of civil and political rights.

In 1893, Eugene Debs formed the first industrial union, the American Railway Union (ARU), to represent railway workers more forcefully than the AFL. The following year he organized a successful strike against the Great Northern Railway for higher wages. Some 3,000 workers at the Pullman Company, which made railroad cars in Chicago, then asked for ARU support to strike for higher pay. Debs agreed. However, the company secured a court injunction to stop the strike, some 12,000 Army troops were called to the scene; 13 strikers were gunned down, 57 were wounded, Debs was imprisoned, and the ARU was disbanded.

In 1897, the International Association for the Legal Protection of Workers was formed at Basle, Switzerland, followed by a congress in Brussels later that year. In 1901, the International Association for Labor Legislation was established, also at Basle, to provide support for branches established within various countries to alleviate adverse working conditions through laws to protect safety and health on the job, to provide unemployment compensation, and to provide pensions for workers no longer able to work. Within each branch, study groups investigated labor conditions, legislatures were lobbied, and pending bills were critiqued. In 1900, Spain became the first country to adopt a worker's compensation law; in 1901, four European countries followed. Also in 1901, the International Secretariat of National Trade

Union Centres was founded among national centers of eight European countries to push for labor reforms.

Conferences were held at Bern in 1905 and 1906, where the world's first international labor standards conventions were adopted. Known as the **Bern Conventions**, they resolved an end both to night work for women and the manufacture of matches containing white phosphorus.

In 1905, the International Workers of the World (IWW) was founded in Chicago at a convention of some 200 anarchists, socialists, and radical trade unionists from all over the United States. The most famous IWW leader, Debs, had become a socialist after reading the writings of Karl Marx for the first time while in prison, and he ran as the Socialist Party's candidate for president four times from 1904 to 1920. Whereas Debs provided a democratic socialist agenda, the IWW was accused of wanting to overthrow capitalism. Successful in organizing the largely foreign-born women workers of the woolen industry in Lawrence, Massachusetts, and agricultural, longshore, and lumber workers elsewhere, the IWW became a target for government prosecution and vigilantism after the success of the communist revolution in Russia, in 1917.

When skilled workers increasingly demanded more pay, employers broke down the labor into a set of simple tasks that could be performed by unskilled workers on an assembly line, thus splitting the workforce into an upper and lower proletariat, according to the analysis of Vladimir Lenin (1870–1924). Next, the evolution of machines began to replace unskilled workers. Unions tried to organize workers to make demands, but most were still suppressed.

In 1918, Lenin organized the Third International, also known as the Communist International (Comintern), which died with the collapse of the Soviet Union in 1991. The Socialist International, however, currently continues to bring together socialist parties, which now lobby for worker protection within the global political economy rather than the former goal of world socialism.

In 1919, Gompers was a delegate within the American delegation at the Versailles Peace Conference. Together with trade union representatives from other countries, he drafted the Constitution of the International Labor Organization (ILO), which in turn has established international standards for conditions of work. The International Federation of Trade Unions, founded in 1919, originally pressured ILO to establish labor standards but was abolished in 1945, having succeeded in creating an activist ILO.

Recognition of the right to form and join trade unions remains one of the most basic rights of workers. Unions, in turn, have the power to expand workers' rights and to enforce those rights by organizing strikes. In 1864, France was the first country to recognize the right to strike, which is still not generally recognized worldwide. The right to form trade unions was first granted in the United States during 1935.

The rights of workers have increasingly been respected, thanks to the ILO and the adoption of welfare states within industrial democracies. More controversial has been the expansion of trade unions for government workers since the 1960s.

HUMANE WARFARE MOVEMENT

Another movement to recognize the universality of human rights principles emerged from the barbarity of warfare. Women took the initiative. During the Crimean War, Tchaikovsky's benefactor, Grand Duchess Elena Pavlovna (1784–1803), organized the Sisters of Mercy to help the wounded on the Russian side, and the British nurse, Florence Nightingale (1820–1910), aided the British side. On arriving home, Nightingale campaigned about the need to save lives on the battlefield.

HISTORIC EVENT 3.5 THE CRIMEAN WAR (1854–1856)

In 1852, Napoléon III persuaded the Ottoman Turks to sign treaties that recognized French sovereignty over the Holy Land, infuriating Russia. In 1853, the Turks attacked the Russian army on the Danube in Moldavia and Wallachia, but the Russians destroyed the Turkish fleet on the Black Sea. Concerned that Russian power was expanding into the Mediterranean, France and Britain issued an ultimatum, demanding that Russia relinquish control over the two Danubian principalities, allow all nations free access to the Danube, give up the right to intervene in the Ottoman Empire on behalf of Orthodox Christians, and revise a treaty dealing with the straits between the Black Sea and the Mediterranean. When Russia refused most of the terms, British and French fleets came to Turkey's defense, arriving at the Crimean peninsula to lay siege to the fortress at Sebastopol and penetrating as far as the Don River in Russia to cut off supplies to the fortress. Britain and France also attacked Russia in the Baltic Sea. In 1856, the conflict concluded with the Treaty of Paris, which ended Russia's special privileges along the Danube, demilitarized the Black Sea, and the major powers agreed to respect the territorial integrity of the Ottoman Empire from Turkey to the Middle East. Those wounded during the war suffered from poorly organized supplies and medical care, and without the attention of nurses, until Elena Pavlovna and Florence Nightingale arrived at the end of 1854. In all, 130,000 persons died in the conflict – many from disease, others on the battlefield or through inadequate medical care.

In addition to the Treaty of Paris, which ended the Crimean War in 1856, the countries involved issued the **Declaration of Paris**, which adopted principles of maritime warfare. Privateering was abolished, neutral ships were to be respected, and blockades were to be honored only if supported with sufficient force.

In 1859, Jean-Henri Dunant (1828–1910), the Swiss business executive who founded the European counterpart of the Young Men's Christian Association, witnessed the Battle of Solferino (where Italy employed French troops to detach

Italian-speaking territories from Austria) to see for himself whether Florence Nightingale was exaggerating. At the end of the 15-hour battle, there were 40,000 wounded soldiers lying on the ground without medical attention, presumably left to die. After spending three days organizing local townspeople to attend to as many of the wounded as they could, he went to Paris to persuade Napoléon III (1808–1873) to issue the following order: "Doctors and surgeons attached to the Austrian armies and captured while attending to the wounded shall be unconditionally released; those who have been attending to men wounded at the Battle of Solferino and lying in the hospital at Castiglione shall, at their request, be permitted to return to Austria."

When Dunant returned to Geneva, he published *A Memory of Solferino* (1862), which proposed an organization within each nation to aid the wounded in case of armed conflict and to help the military medical services. He sent his book to the president of Geneva's Society of Public Welfare, Gustave Moynier (1826–1910), who in turn invited Dunant to a meeting of the Society. Those present then agreed to found the Permanent International Committee of the Relief of the Wounded.

An organizing committee then formed to host the Geneva International Conference during 1863, which was attended by delegates from 16 countries. The conference created the International Committee of the Red Cross, which in 1864 was first called to action in the Danish–Prussian War. By 1874, there were 22 national Red Cross societies in European countries, and soon the Red Cross movement spread to other continents. In 1876, the Ottoman Turks founded the Red Crescent Society, a counterpart of the Red Cross within Islamic countries.

In 1864, Dunant, Moynier, and others next persuaded the Swiss government to convene a diplomatic conference at Geneva. Attended by representatives from 17 countries, the meeting adopted the **Convention for the Amelioration of the Condition of the Wounded in Armies in the Field**. Until then, war was generally thought to be beyond the bounds of international law. The Geneva Convention, as the treaty became known, detailed the rights of medical personnel and wounded soldiers.

During the nineteenth century, the Russian army was popularly known as the "army of Europe" because Russia stopped the advance of Napoléon Bonaparte in 1812. Thus, Russia played an important role at the Congress of Vienna in 1814–1815, and its army was ready to restore the balance of power when needed. Accordingly, Russian rulers and foreign ministers considered themselves to be important architects of the peace that lasted without general war during most of the nineteenth century.

In 1874, Tsar Alexander II (1818–1881), with the concurrence of Leopold II of Belgium (1835–1909), invited 15 countries to attend a conference at Brussels to examine comprehensive Russian proposals to extend the law of war beyond the 1864 Geneva Convention, which covered only the sick and wounded in time of war. Although the delegates at Brussels subscribed to a detailed statement, **Project of an International Declaration Concerning the Laws and Customs of War**, a proposed agreement in the form of a Convention on the Laws and Customs of War was never ratified. Later in 1874, the Institute of International Law set up a committee to study the Brussels declaration with a view to codifying the laws of warfare.

As a result, a **Manual of the Laws and Customs of War** was drawn up by the institute in a meeting at Oxford in 1880.

At the end of the nineteenth century, a naval arms race was being waged between Britain and Germany. There appeared to be no end in sight, as larger and larger warships were built. In 1898, believing that a military showdown was thought to be the inevitable consequence of the arms race, Russian Foreign Minister, Count Mikhail Muraviev (1845–1900), circulated a letter regarding the possibility of a disarmament conference to ambassadors in St Petersburg for transmission to their home governments. In 1899, when the response was favorable, Queen Wilhelmina of the Netherlands (1880–1962) and Tsar Nicholas II of Russia (1868–1918) invited 26 countries to The Hague to attend what was called the First International Peace Conference. The meeting was to consider disarmament, revision of existing principles governing naval and land warfare, and a procedure for peaceful settlement of international disputes.

The 10-week meeting, known as the First Hague Conference, had several positive results, though disarmament was not achieved. The most important outcome was the **Convention for the Pacific Settlement of International Disputes**, in which the countries agreed that before launching war they should submit disputes with other countries to the good offices or mediation of one or more friendly powers. A crowning achievement at the conference was the establishment of the Permanent Court of Arbitration to sit at The Hague in order to handle disputes on an ad hoc basis – that is, not necessarily bound by international legal precedents. Subsequently, arbitration treaties were negotiated by many countries around the world.

The rest of the accomplishments at The Hague dealt with humane warfare. The **Convention With Respect to the Laws and Customs of War on Land** in effect adopted the Brussels Declaration and the Oxford Manual. The **Convention for the Adaptation to Maritime Warfare of the Principles of the Geneva Convention of the 22nd August, 1864**, dealt with hospital ships and similar issues. Three separate declarations prohibited launching explosives and projectiles from balloons, disseminating poison gas, and using hollow-point bullets.

In addition, the final act of the conference expressed a desire for the 1864 Geneva Convention to be revised in accordance with the achievements at the conference. The countries also agreed to reconvene in order to draw up additional laws of humane warfare. In 1906, the Geneva Convention was then revised at a conference called by the Swiss government.

Meanwhile, the American Peace Society in Boston successfully pressured the Massachusetts legislature in 1903 to urge President Theodore Roosevelt (1858–1919) to establish a regular conference on international affairs. In 1904, the Inter-Parliamentary Union, an organization of legislators from around the world, urged a second Hague Conference to complete the unfinished business of the first. In response, Roosevelt called for the Second International Peace Conference, which was held at The Hague in 1907. Nicholas II formally opened the meeting, and the United States pressed for disarmament, limitations on the use of force to collect foreign debts, establishment of a "prize court" to settle claims regarding property and ships seized during war, and a permanent court that would develop international law through precedents developed from decisions made to resolve interstate disputes. The International Council of Women presented a petition signed by two million women in 20 countries, urging the conference to bring about world peace. The concern over humane warfare had morphed into a demand to end all wars as inhumane.

After four months of work, the Second Hague Conference added more details to the treaties adopted in 1899. The most important innovation was the assertion that war is only legal after previous and explicit warning, such as a declaration of war or an ultimatum in which war is an option. However, the 1907 treaties lacked ratifications from 17 states that had ratified the treaties signed in 1899. The prize court was never set up as a result. To the chagrin of the American delegation, the proposal for a world court was turned down. Nevertheless, American delegate Joseph Choate (1832–1917) secured a resolution for a third conference to be held by 1915 or 1916. The outbreak of World War I, the cataclysm that all the countries were trying to prevent, meant that there was no Third Hague Conference.

After World War I, more treaties were adopted to set limits and conditions on the conduct of war. In 1924, the Council agreed on the **Protocol for the Pacific Settlement of International Disputes** (Geneva Protocol), which required states to submit all interstate conflicts to arbitration, but Britain, Germany, and the United States were not signatories. More successful was the **General Treaty for the Renunciation of War** of 1928, which placed a total ban on the use of force in international affairs; all countries agreed to settle their disputes peacefully as a matter of international law. The **Convention Relative to the Treatment of Prisoners of War** of 1929 set standards for how to deal with prisoners captured during war.

However, the optimism of the 1920s was trampled upon during the 1930s, as Germany, Italy, and Japan took unilateral actions in defiance of the agreements. World War II then devastated Asia and Europe and brought war to the shores of colonial possessions in the Pacific. Although the UN, the Nuremberg War Crimes Trials, and four Geneva Conventions emerged after the carnage that claimed 62 million lives, the barbarity of war continues.

RELIGIOUS FREEDOM MOVEMENT

From the thirteenth century, after the Crusades (1095–1272), peace treaties between Christian rulers and the Ottoman Empire had provisions respecting the religious practices of conquered peoples. After the Reformation, some treaties drawn up by Christian monarchs contained guarantees for religious minorities. The Peace of Westphalia of 1648, following a series of European wars of religion, allowed the ruler in each country to designate the state religion. However, religious minorities still suffered discrimination.

Many early settlers in the 13 colonies that later became the United States were freethinkers of various kinds – that is, individuals who refused to belong to the Church of England and were therefore ineligible to serve in the British parliament. To ensure a separation of church and state, the American Constitution prohibited any religious test for public office. Following the guarantee of freedom of religious opinion provided in the Declaration of the Rights of Man and Citizen proclaimed by the French Revolution, the First Amendment to the American Bill of Rights guaranteed freedom of religion.

In 1815, the **Final Act of the Congress of Vienna** guaranteed religious equality to multiethnic Belgium and Switzerland. The delegates even made specific reference to the plight of Jews in Germany and the rights of Roman Catholics within the non-Catholic states that absorbed territories once part of Poland (Prussia and Russia). Britain, France, and Russia intervened on behalf of Greeks under Ottoman rule in 1827, which led to the independence of Greece in 1829.

A high proportion of the population of Ireland were Catholics, who were ineligible, in common with other Catholics during the reign of Henry VIII (1491–1547), to own land or to be elected to the British parliament. In 1778, the **Catholic Relief Act** permitted landownership, which meant that many Catholics in Ireland and elsewhere in the British Isles were eligible to vote but still could not sit in parliament. In 1823, barrister Daniel O'Connell (1775–1847) formed the Catholic Association to lobby for religious equality; he ran for election in 1828, won the most votes, but was not allowed to take his seat in parliament. In 1829, Britain adopted the **Catholic Emancipation Act**, which allowed the wealthiest Catholics to stand for election, though full voting rights for Catholics as well as less affluent Protestants awaited the Reform Acts of 1832, 1867, and 1884. Further restrictions on Catholics were repealed over the years, but one currently remains: a Catholic cannot become monarch of the United Kingdom of Great Britain and Northern Ireland.

Responding to an outcry regarding the persecution, and even massacres, of non-Muslims, the sultans of the Ottoman Empire issued decrees in 1839 and 1856 guaranteeing religious liberty. Nevertheless, mistreatment continued. Russia, victorious in the Russo-Turkish War in 1878, forced the Ottoman Empire to sign the **Treaty of San Stefano**, which recognized the independence of four Orthodox Catholic countries (Bulgaria, Montenegro, Romania, and Serbia) from Ottoman rule. One feature of the **Final Act of the Congress of Berlin** in 1885 was to require the four newest governments to respect the rights of Jewish minorities as a condition of their diplomatic recognition, though enforcement was left to the states themselves.

Journalist Theodor Herzl (1860–1904) was so shaken by the outpouring of anti-Semitism in France, where he covered the Dreyfus treason trial in 1894, as well as in his native Austria in 1895, that he wrote *A Jewish State* (1896). He thereby launched the Zionist movement – that is, a proposal for an independent Jewish state. In 1897, the first Jewish Congress convened in Basel. Later, Chaim Weizmann (1874–1952) spearheaded the movement, though many Jewish leaders preferred a more generic campaign to recognize minority rights. In 1898, the International League of Human Rights was formed in response to the Dreyfus affair to bring world attention to the cause of human rights; among the supporters was Albert Einstein (1879–1955).

▌ COURT CASE 3.1 THE DREYFUS TRIALS (1894 AND 1899)

In France, in 1894, Captain Alfred Dreyfus (1859–1935) was accused of pass-ing military secrets to Germany and convicted of treason. The evidence against him was a handwritten note found in a wastebasket used by a Germany military attaché by a cleaning woman who worked for French intelligence. The right-wing anti-Jewish press publicized his alleged role before the prosecutor's office deter-mined that the handwriting was not that of Dreyfus. The French High Command, however, went ahead with the prosecution rather than risk looking incompetent, a revelation that might have caused senior military officers to be fired and the government to be voted out of office. In fact, the note was revealed to have been planted by counterintelligence officer, Major Ferdinand Esterhazy (1847–1923), to confuse the Germans. Because the French were afraid to admit the ruse, Esterhazy was acquitted of charges. In 1898, novelist, Émile Zola (1840–1902), authored a strong "open letter" in the left-wing press, accusing the government of anti-Semitism and of violating Dreyfus's right to a fair trial. (Zola, in turn, was convicted of libel and went into exile in England rather than serve time in prison for his state-ment, but the following year he returned in time to see the government voted out, and he was then pardoned.) In 1899, potentially exonerating evidence surfaced, thanks to another intelligence officer, and Dreyfus was retried. However, he was again convicted. In 1904, French President Émile Loubet (1838–1929) pardoned Dreyfus, and the court reversed his second conviction. Right-wing and left-wing politicians held strong opinions, the country was bitterly divided, and Zola's letter proved the new power of intellectuals.

Atrocities committed by the Ottomans against Armenian Christians in 1894–1896 and again in 1915–1917, sometimes described as a holocaust, resulted in interna-tional disfavor toward the Ottoman Empire and its successor, the Turkish state, which was allied with the defeated Axis Powers (Austria-Hungary and Germany) in World War I. After the Ottomans were defeated by an invasion of British troops in 1917, Weizmann's efforts bore fruit when Britain issued the **Balfour Declaration**, which invited Jews to resettle in British-controlled Palestine. Efforts to establish the state of Israel did not bear fruit until after World War II.

The idea that states should consist of single nations rather than having empires with multinational populations was vigorously espoused by Woodrow Wilson (1856–1924), who made the principle of self-determination a centerpiece of his **Fourteen Points** in 1918, a declaration that shaped the Treaty of Versailles, which concluded the war with Germany. Although enforcement of rights under the trea-ties negotiated at Paris and elsewhere focused on ethnicity more than religion, one provision of the **Covenant of the League of Nations** guaranteed religious freedom, though only within overseas territories of the three defeated countries that were reas-signed to the victorious powers as mandates, as noted below.

▌HISTORIC EVENT 3.6 THE PEACE OF PARIS (1919–1920)

The Treaty of Versailles, which formally ended the war with Germany, was one of several treaties drawn up from 1919–1920, collectively known as the Peace of Paris, which redrew the territorial maps of Europe and the Middle East after World War I. Separate treaties were also drawn up for Austria (Treaty of Saint-Germain, 1919), Bulgaria (Treaty of Neuilly, 1919), Hungary (Treaty of Trianon, 1920), and the Ottoman Empire (Treaty of Sèvres, 1920). The Treaty of Saint-Germain established the new states of Czechoslovakia, Romania, and Yugoslavia (then known as the Kingdom of Croats, Serbs, and Slovenes). A seventh treaty, the Treaty of Lausanne of 1923, revised the Treaty of Sèvres. One aim in carving the various "successor states" out of the former Austro-Hungarian empire was to provide a buffer of independent states, eager to guard their sovereignty, which would thereby deter Germany from territorial expansion. Except for Armenia and the Hejaz (now part of Saudi Arabia), most states in the Middle East that were dismembered from Turkey became League of Nations Mandates.

After World War I, the principle of freedom of religion was notoriously violated as Adolf Hitler (1889–1945) came to power in Germany. News of the persecution of Jews spread, especially by refugees from Nazi rule. During World War II, the wholesale Nazi slaughter of Jews was reported, but concrete evidence did not come to light until victorious armies entered the "death camps" to see for themselves. Although the stage was set for a binding treaty on the subject, no such international agreement has ever guaranteed freedom of religion as a fundamental human right to be observed globally. Persecution and prejudice based on religious beliefs continues in the world today, as Muslims in the West and Christians in the Middle East know well.

▌DISCUSSION TOPIC 3.2 WHICH HUMAN RIGHTS MOVEMENTS HAVE BEEN MOST SUCCESSFUL?

Why did the nineteenth century, in retrospect, spawn so many human rights movements? Which among those discussed thus far have been more successful – and why? Which movements led most directly to the formation of the League of Nations?

INTERNATIONAL ORGANIZATION MOVEMENT

The final historical movement on behalf of international human rights is the effort to establish an intergovernmental organization where diplomats can be in constant touch to prevent war. Philosophers from Pierre Dubois (1250–1312) to Immanuel Kant (1724–1804) had long urged the establishment of such a body.

In 1815, the **Concert of Europe** was formed as a consultative body so that the major powers (Austria, Britain, France, Prussia, Russia) could meet in case a nationalist movement threatened to undo the balance of power. One result was intervention in minor uprisings, but the Concert also agreed to the independence of Belgium from the Netherlands in 1839.

In 1874, the first intergovernmental organization of global scope was formed. Known as the **Universal Postal Union** (UPU), the aim was to standardize mail traffic around the world. UPU proved that intergovernmental cooperation among disparate countries was feasible.

As the century progressed, England and France became more democratic and less interested in suppressing the will of the people abroad. The final meeting of the Concert of Europe was a gathering of the original five states (adding Italy and the Ottoman Turks) in the **Congress of Berlin** of 1878–1885. Once again, the feasibility of involving meetings among major powers to manage European affairs on a continuing basis was demonstrated.

Subsequently, international organizations similar to UPU were formed with more focus on human rights – the **International Sanitary Bureau** of 1902, formed entirely by governments in the Americas, and the more inclusive **Office International d'Hygiène Publique** of 1907. By then, medical science had found reliable methods for treating some communicable diseases that readily crossed international borders – namely, bubonic plague, cholera, and yellow fever.

The Hague Conferences in 1899 and 1907 involved negotiations between states that produced important results, so a framework for more permanent consultation was obviously possible. After all, a world body could reshape the world in a manner that would promote the goals of all previous movements – create an international legal order, increase democracy, abolish insidious forms of slavery, respect the rights of women and workers, and ensure the freedom of religion. And the humane warfare movement would obsolesce if no more wars occurred because of a world body that would stop war.

Proposals for an organization of all the independent governments of the world were put forward during World War I from several quarters. The Fourteenth Point of Woodrow Wilson was as follows: "A general association of nations must be formed under specific covenants for the purpose of affording mutual guarantees of political independence and territorial integrity to great and small states alike." He publicized his quest as "making the world safe for democracy." Pressure from nongovernmental organizations to establish an intergovernmental body also emerged during World War I.

Although the leaders of some countries at the Versailles conference were skeptical of Wilson's proposal, his arguments prevailed, and the **League of Nations** was born. The headquarters was in Geneva, Switzerland, a country that had been neutral throughout the war and had a long peace-loving tradition.

The United States never joined the League of Nations because Wilson would not allow the Senate to attach reservations to the treaty. Nevertheless, Washington joined both the ILO and the Permanent Court of International Justice (PCIJ). Senators feared that membership in the League might result in sending American troops abroad again, but ILO and PCIJ were viewed as consistent with the American tradition of advancing international law.

The **Covenant of the League of Nations**, as adopted in Article I of the Treaty of Versailles, committed members to "promote international co-operation and to achieve international peace and security," according to the preamble, which went on to commit the governments "not to resort to war" and to "the maintenance of justice." The words "human rights" do not appear. Nevertheless, within the provisions of the covenant, the following principles were stated or implied:

- Women may work for the League
- The right of self-determination
- Freedom of conscience and religion, subject only to the maintenance of public order and morals
- Prohibition of such abuses as the slave trade, the arms traffic and the liquor traffic
- Fair and humane conditions of labor for men, women, and children
- Supervision of treaties to suppress traffic in women and children, and the traffic in opium and other dangerous drugs
- Improvement of health, the prevention of disease and the mitigation of suffering.

However, the framers of the Treaty of Versailles rejected a pledge, sponsored by Japan, for racial equality, primarily because Americans and Europeans wanted to keep their colonial possessions.

The Covenant set up an Assembly, composed of all member states, and a Council, a smaller body designed to consist of the principal Allied and Associated Powers (Britain, France, Italy, Japan, United States) plus four countries first designated in the text and subsequently to be elected by the Assembly. Decisions of both bodies required unanimity, thereby limiting effectiveness. The United States, which did not join the League, never sat on the Council.

The **Constitution of the International Labor Organization** was drafted by the Labor Commission of the Versailles peace conference, chaired by Samuel Gompers. Article 13 of the Versailles Treaty contains the ILO Constitution, which begins with the following statement: "Whereas the League of Nations has for its object the establishment of universal peace … such a peace can be established only if it is based upon social justice [because] such injustice, hardship, and privation to large numbers of people … produce unrest so great that the peace and harmony of the world are imperiled …." ILO's Constitution, which was adopted as an independent treaty, then set the following agenda regarding "humane conditions of labor" for the organization:

- Regulation of the hours of work, including the establishment of a maximum working day and week
- Regulation of the labor supply
- Prevention of unemployment
- Provision of an adequate living wage
- Protection of the worker against sickness, disease, and injury arising out of his employment
- Protection of children and women
- Provision for old age and injury
- Protection of migrant workers
- Recognition of the principle of freedom of association
- Organization of vocational and technical education and other measures.

ILO, headquartered in Geneva, was far more committed to improving rights for individuals than was the League. Its founding document has been the basis for more than 170 international agreements over the years, such as the Convention Concerning Forced or Compulsory Labor of 1932. In 1946, the ILO became a Specialized Agency of the United Nations after amending its Constitution in 1944 to reflect the new status.

Article 14 of the Covenant asked the League to draw up a separate agreement for a world court. In 1920, the council asked 10 eminent jurists to draft such an agreement. Their proposed **Statute of the Permanent Court of International Justice**, in turn, was submitted to, and approved by, the Assembly later that year. The only specific human rights provision was for five PCIJ judges to convene in cases of labor rights unless a party to the dispute wanted a hearing by the entire 15-member court. Subsequently, decisions were rendered in 66 cases, many of which were about nationality issues. PCIJ was superseded in 1946 by the International Court of Justice (ICJ) within the UN system.

Perhaps the most important PCIJ judgment was an Advisory Opinion in the Danzig Railway Officials, or *Jurisdiction of the Courts of Danzig*, case. For the first time, international law was declared by a world court to apply not just to governments but also to individuals, provided of course that states wrote human rights provisions about individuals into treaties. Based on the precedent from the Danzig case, the PCIJ ruled in the *Rights of Minorities in Upper Silesia* case of 1928 that parents had a right to determine the language of instruction for their children in government-operated schools.

COURT CASE 3.2 THE DANZIG RAILWAY OFFICIALS CASE (1928)

The Convention of Paris, a 1920 treaty between Poland and the Free City of Danzig, contained provisions authorizing the regulation of conditions of employment for former employees of the Danzig railways, some of whom had been kept on the

Continued

job by the successor agency, the Polish Railways Administration. In 1925, four years after an implementing agreement of the treaty was adopted by both parties, some former Danzig employees sued Polish authorities in a Danzig court to receive compensation for unpaid pensions and salaries. The Polish government, however, refused to accept the jurisdiction of Danzig courts, arguing that international law only applied to states, not individuals. The League of Nation's High Commissioner for Danzig also agreed, in 1927, that the employees had no standing to sue in Danzig courts. Accordingly, the League of Nations Council asked the Permanent Court of International Justice for an Advisory Opinion on the matter. In 1928, the court held that the treaty contained "rules creating individual rights ... [that are] enforceable by the national courts," consistent with the doctrine of direct effect, which had been recognized by the Central American Court of Justice in *Diaz v. Guatemala* (1909). Instead of making a judgment about the claims, the court's Advisory Opinion informed the claimants that they could present their case before a Danzig court, and the Polish government was directed to accept whatever the court might rule. The full name of the case is the *Jurisdiction of the Courts of Danzig (Pecuniary Claims of Danzig Railway Officials Who Have Passed into the Polish Service, Against the Polish Railways Administration).*

Besides the ILO and PCIJ, the League of Nations made progress regarding human rights in several additional ways:

- Implementing the basic pledges in the seven peace treaties of the Peace of Paris after World War I
- Setting up a health organization
- Establishing a refugee organization to assist refugees and stateless persons
- Sponsoring new international agreements.

Previous international movements (for democracy, the abolition of slavery, women's rights, workers' rights, humane warfare, minority rights) became incorporated into the institutional framework of the League of Nations.

The seven treaties of the Peace of Paris addressed problems resulting from arbitrary boundaries drawn around the new states, such that religious and ethnolinguistic minorities would have been left at the mercy of the dominant nationality group in each country. In part because of pressure from Jewish advocates of minority protections at Versailles, the treaties contained six innovations – mixed arbitral tribunals, minority treaties, plebiscites, population exchanges, and mandates:

One provision authorized **mixed arbitral tribunals** to settle property claims. However, when properties of minorities were adversely affected by later agrarian reforms, the tribunals ruled that they had no jurisdiction because the reforms were domestic laws outside the terms of the peace treaties. Subsequently, the German–Polish Convention of 1922 set up a three-member Arbitral Tribunal and a five-member Upper Silesian Mixed Commission consisting of equal membership of Germany and Poland. Each country named an equal number of members to both bodies; the remaining member was chosen by the League Council.

The new states were required to have **minority treaties** to protect minority populations. The aim was to assure that ethnic identities would be protected so that minorities would be loyal members of the new states. The various minority treaties, such as the Treaty Between the Allied and Associated Powers and the Kingdom of the Serbs, Croats and Slovenes on the Protection of Minorities of 1919, left enforcement to the League of Nations Council, which set up a Minorities Question Section in the League Secretariat to hear petitions. Few petitions ever resulted in corrective action because their resolution depended on cooperation with the very states that were accused of misconduct. And the League took no action when Iraqis massacred Syrians in 1933, one year after Britain terminated its mandate in Iraq.

Plebiscites, once used by Napoléon Bonaparte to legitimize French rule over conquered territories, were authorized to determine by election the government under which a minority population preferred to live. In 1921, for example, a plebiscite was held in Upper Silesia to determine whether residents wanted to be ruled by Germany or Poland. Although the majority favored Germany, the Polish minority was unhappy with the outcome. As a result, Germany voluntarily transferred Eastern Silesia to Poland in 1922.

Population exchanges were specified in the Convention Concerning the Exchange of Greek and Turkish Populations of 1923. Orthodox Christians in Anatolia were then exchanged for Muslims in Greece. However, following that example, the Soviet Union forcibly resettled millions of Muslims in Central Asia to Russian provinces and vice versa during World War II. The practice has rarely been used ever since.

The League also created the **Permanent Mandates Commission**, since the peace settlement transferred 16 colonial possessions of the defeated Axis countries to six of the victorious countries with the stipulation that the rights of the subject populations must be protected. In general, the mandate powers agreed to consider the "well-being and development of such peoples [to] form a sacred trust of civilization ... until such time as they are able to stand alone." There were three classes of mandates. "A" mandates were close to independence. "B" mandates were to be prepared for eventual independence. "C" mandates were considered incapable of self-government for an extended period of time.[5] Mandate countries were to ensure freedom of conscience and religion and an end to the slave trade. For example, one of the "A" mandates – Palestine – was assigned to Britain in 1922. The mandate countries, in turn, reported to the Mandates Commission, but no provision was made to monitor progress toward independence of the mandated territories.

In addition, the Commission directly administered two territories – Saarland (until 1935, when the residents in a plebiscite agreed to return to German sovereignty[6]), and Danzig (until the army of Nazi Germany seized control in 1939). The Rhineland, however, was occupied by Britain, France, and the United States.[7] Except for South Africa's mandate over South West Africa (Namibia), all the League mandates were either granted independence after World War II or transferred into the UN trusteeship system.[8]

A **petition system** was also established. Members of minority groups could contact the mixed arbitral tribunals or the League with complaints about mistreatment, as in the *Upper Silesia* case mentioned above. Authorized to assess violators in order to compensate victims of mistreatment, the tribunals and the League accepted the petitions as informational only and pursued the complaints on behalf of the affected class, that is, beyond the immediate problems of the individuals lodging the complaints.

The redrawing of the European map left German minorities in several countries. Hitler exploited the self-determination principle to justify the unilateral reoccupation of the Rhineland in 1936, the annexation of Austria in 1936, the occupation of the Sudetenland part of Czechoslovakia in 1938, and the annexation of Danzig in 1939. After securing approval at the Munich Conference of 1938 to take possession of Sudetenland, Nazi troops marched in to take control of all Czechoslovakia without a shot being fired. At Munich, Britain and France had drawn a line for Hitler's irredentism at the Polish border. Therefore, Germany's attack on Poland in 1939 began World War II.

The League advanced international cooperation in other ways. In 1907, the International Office of Public Health began at Rome to promote the implementation of treaties dealing with sanitation, though later the body undertook studies of epidemics. The **League of Nations Health Organization**, formed in 1920 at Geneva, was charged with the task of combating disease around the globe; primary foci were leprosy, malaria, and typhus. Both organizations are forerunners of the World Health Organization, a UN Specialized Agency.

The League of Nations also set up a **Commission for Refugees** in 1921, headed by Fridtjof Nansen (1861–1930). After he died, the commission was renamed in 1931 as the Nansen International Office for Refugees and supplemented from 1933–1938 by the High Commission for Refugees Coming from Germany. The first major task was to provide financial, legal, and material assistance to 400,000 prisoners of war and refugees from Russia, but the scope expanded in 1922 to Armenian refugees from Turkey, refugees from Nazi Germany after 1933, Saar refugees in 1935, Austrian refugees in 1938, and Sudetenland refugees in 1938. Especially notable accomplishments were:

- The establishment of an international passport for stateless refugees
- Adoption of the Convention Relating to the International Status of Refugees in 1933
- Settlement of Saar refugees in Paraguay
- Construction of villages to house upwards of 40,000 Armenian refugees in Syria and Lebanon
- The resettlement of another 10,000 refugees in Soviet Armenia.

In 1938, the League located an office in London under the name High Commissioner for Refugees under the Protection of the League, but the number of refugees was overwhelming, especially after World War II began.

The League also set up a Temporary Slavery Commission in 1922, at first to draft a treaty on the subject. After the Slavery Convention was adopted in 1926, the body continued as the **Slavery Commission** to implement the convention's goal of ending slavery, human trafficking in prostitutes ("white slavery"), and the drug trade. The commission was charged with the responsibility of compiling records on all three issues. As a result, some 200,000 slaves were emancipated in Sierra Leone during 1927, raids in Africa stopped slave traders, and the death rate of Tanganyikan workers was lowered from about 50 percent to 4 percent.

In addition, the League sponsored several treaties. Among the most famous is the **Protocol for the Pacific Settlement of International Disputes** (1924), as discussed above. Although the 1924 Geneva Protocol and the 1925 Locarno Peace Pact were designed to provide firm guarantees against the outbreak of a new world war, the United States was not involved. Accordingly, Secretary of State Frank Kellogg (1856–1937) contacted Foreign Minister Aristide Briand, urging a wider agreement. What resulted is the **General Treaty for the Renunciation of War**, known popularly as the Pact of Paris or as the Kellogg–Briand Pact of 1928. The treaty renounced war as an instrument of national policy and pledged signatories to use only peaceful means for settling disputes except in cases of self-defense against states fulfilling responsibilities under the League.

HISTORIC EVENT 3.7 THE LOCARNO PEACE PACT (1925)

In 1924, members of the League of Nations unanimously adopted the Geneva Protocol for the Pacific Settlement of International Disputes, which outlawed international aggression. Germany, not yet a member of the League, did not sign the agreement. Because Britain refused to ratify the Geneva Protocol, provisions of the 1924 agreement were never implemented. Outside the League, five separate peace agreements, known as the Locarno Peace Pact of 1925, provided firmer guarantees than the 1924 protocol, since Germany signed the treaties and thereby was reinvited into the family of nations on an equal basis. Most important was a Treaty of Mutual Guarantee that guaranteed existing frontiers between Belgium, France, and Germany, as well as the demilitarization of the Rhineland. The countries also agreed not to make war on one another unless the terms of the agreement were flagrantly violated or unless the League authorized action against an aggressor. In addition, there were four arbitration treaties to settle disputes between Germany on the one hand and Belgium, Czechoslovakia, France, and Poland on the other hand. If one of the countries failed to observe the terms of the pact, the others were pledged to help the aggrieved country. The idea for the pact came from German Prime Minister Gustav Stresemann (1878–1929), who persuaded French Foreign Minister Aristide Briand (1862–1932).

At the same time, the Covenant suggested an alternative to war – **economic sanctions**. Although an oil embargo was discussed against Japan for its military occupation of Manchuria in 1931 and against Italy for its invasion of Abyssinia (Ethiopia) in 1935, support was insufficient among members of the League. However, the American embargo of oil exports to Japan (outside the League) on August 1, 1941, provided Tokyo with a pretext for bombing Pearl Harbor on December 7, hoping to achieve a quick victory in the Pacific.

Before World War I, the international organization movement was perhaps only a prayer. The League seemed an answer to that prayer. But the failure of the League stimulated many observers to contemplate how to construct a much better plan for an intergovernmental organization. Science fiction novelist H. G. Wells (1866–1946), a Fabian socialist who had campaigned for the League, predicted a new world war and encouraged world leaders to think seriously about a world state that would improve upon the League and place human rights at the center. After World War II, world leaders agreed that a new world assembly of nations was an imperative, as the globe might not be able to survive a World War III. And Eleanor Roosevelt (1884–1962) realized that international human rights should be in the forefront of any new organization of states.

CONCLUSION

The American and French revolutions opened the eyes of the people about their rights. The Industrial Revolution so enlarged the number of city dwellers and exploited workers that they became politically conscious. But consciousness-raising would have been impossible without the broadening of educational opportunities to provide a qualified workforce for the Industrial Revolution. As literacy increased, the idea spread that everyone is entitled to be treated equally, thereby whetting the appetite of the people for a better life. Nevertheless, human rights struggles lagged behind human suffering, awaiting leaders able to take bold steps.

The various social movements that accelerated progress in human rights provide an important lesson – that progress in human rights requires a struggle by courageous leaders with mass-based support. Each movement has left a legacy in the form of organizations that are active today. With the establishment of permanent intergovernmental organizations, institutional watchdogs can attend to immediate problems while documenting the need for even more human rights protections. Today, the task of mobilizing support on behalf of human rights has been simplified by the advent of social media that can summon demonstrators within minutes by means of cell phones and computers.

In sum, serious efforts on behalf of international human rights had already borne fruit before World War II. While the attention of the League was directed to war prevention and the fulfillment of certain human rights, the League of Nations succeeded in containing disputes involving Bulgaria and Greece but failed in its main mission to prevent World War II. But that very failure planted seeds for a more concerted effort to attend to human rights problems, as discussed in the following chapter.

CHAPTER 4

The Contemporary Basis for Human Rights

Previous eras developed international human rights incrementally, albeit in fits and starts, but a new urgency emerged after World War II. Human rights were so massively violated during the war, especially the mistreatment of civilians, that stern measures after the war seemed imperative. Otherwise, to paraphrase Supreme Court Justice Robert Jackson (1892–1954) in his opening statement at the Nuremberg war crimes trials, civilization itself would not survive.

The first postwar task was to set up a new structure of international institutions that might stop future international calamities. Later, efforts were undertaken to keep human rights issues at center stage. The current chapter focuses on how various actions taken by prominent individuals resulted in new agreements (Table 4.1), new concepts, and new institutions that have established human rights concerns as fundamental to contemporary international relations. Most agreements were treaties that came into force when ratified by a substantial number of states; the rest were declarations of policy commitments.

In addition to the progress in forging the United Nations, the following developments have been responsible for advancing the cause of human rights since the end of World War II despite the Cold War obsession with *realpolitik* – war crimes trials, Africa's quest to end colonialism and racist regimes, people power revolutions, President Jimmy Carter's initiatives, activist nongovernmental organizations, and the continuing development of international law. All these advances characterize the contemporary era of human rights.

TABLE 4.1   **SOME BASIC DOCUMENTS OF CONTEMPORARY INTERNATIONAL HUMAN RIGHTS**

Adopted	Name of instrument	In force
1941	Atlantic Charter	*
1942	Resolution on German War Crimes by Representatives of Nine Occupied Countries	*
1943	Declaration Concerning Atrocities	*
1945	Potsdam Declaration	*
1945	Charter of the United Nations	1945
1945	Agreement for the Prosecution and Punishment of the Major War Criminals of the European Axis	1945
1945	Charter of the International Military Tribunal	1945
1948	Universal Declaration of Human Rights	*
1948	American Declaration of the Rights and Duties of Man	*
1948	International Convention on the Prevention and Punishment of the Crime of Genocide	1951
1949	Geneva Conventions	1950
1950	European Convention for the Protection of Human Rights and Fundamental Freedoms	1953
1954	*Brown et al. v Board of Education of Topeka*	1954
1960	Declaration on the Granting of Independence to Colonial Countries and Peoples	*
1961	European Social Charter	1965
1967	International Covenant on Civil and Political Rights	1976
1967	International Covenant on Economic, Social, and Cultural Rights	1976
1969	American Convention on Human Rights	1978
1969	Vienna Convention on the Law of Treaties	1980
1975	Final Act of the Helsinki Conference	*
1981	African Charter on Human and Peoples' Rights	1981
1990	Cairo Declaration on Human Rights in Islam	*
1990	Charter of Paris for a New Europe	*
1993	Vienna Declaration and Program of Action	*
1998	Declaration of Human Duties and Responsibilities	*
2000	Charter of Fundamental Rights of the European Union	2009
2001	Universal Declaration on Human Diversity	*
2007	Declaration on the Rights of Indigenous Peoples	*
2008	UN Declaration on Sexual Orientation and Gender Identity	*

*Most of the documents are treaties. Asterisked items are not.

▌ THE UNITED NATIONS SYSTEM

When World War II broke out, the verdict on the effectiveness of the League of Nations was in: the League had failed. A new organization was needed to prevent war. In 1941, one of the eight points in the **Atlantic Charter** adopted by Winston

Churchill (1874–1965) and Franklin Roosevelt (1882–1945) was to establish a new association of nations. One month later, representatives of 10 additional countries agreed. Notable provisions were to prohibit the use of force in international relations except in self-defense or when authorized by that new association and to respect the "inherent dignity" and "equal and inalienable rights" of all peoples.

In 1942, accordingly, diplomats from 26 countries met in Washington to adopt the **United Nations Declaration**, a pledge that they would fight together to defeat Germany, Italy, and Japan and would not make a separate peace. Although no post-war organization was identified, the name United Nations thereby gained currency.

At the Moscow Conference in 1943, the foreign ministers of Britain, China, the Soviet Union, and the United States proposed a "general international organization, based on the principle of the sovereign equality of all peace-loving states ...." Later in 1943, Churchill, Roosevelt, and Josef Stalin (1878–1953) endorsed the idea at the Tehran Conference.

Meanwhile, several organizations were founded during 1943–1944 to be part of the proposed United Nations (UN) system – the Food and Agricultural Organization (FAO), the United Nations Relief and Rehabilitation Administration (UNRRA), and the United Nations Educational, Scientific, and Cultural Organization (UNESCO). In 1944, the International Monetary Fund (IMF) and the International Bank for Reconstruction and Development (IBRD), the latter known as the World Bank, was established in a conference at Bretton Woods, New Hampshire. Next, American, Chinese, British, and Soviet delegates met at Dumbarton Oaks in Washington, DC, during August and September 1944 to draft a charter for the new UN organization. Then, representatives of 50 countries met in San Francisco during April 1945 to hammer out a final agreement that still serves as the fundamental basis for contemporary international relations.

HISTORIC EVENT 4.1 THE UNITED NATIONS CONFERENCE ON INTERNATIONAL ORGANIZATION (1945)

After Allied troops crossed the English Channel to begin the drive to defeat Nazi Germany, plans were afoot to set up the United Nations as the successor to the League of Nations. Invitations were issued to all the Allied powers to attend a meeting in April 1945 at San Francisco to work on a draft agreement for an organization that had been conceived a half year earlier by Britain, China, the Soviet Union, and the United States at Dumbarton Oaks, a research facility in Washington, DC. The Soviet Union insisted that seats at the conference be allocated to Byelorussia and the Ukraine but opposed Argentina, which was accused of being an ally of the Axis powers (Germany, Italy, and Japan), whereas Latin American countries insisted on Argentine participation. The United States then backed all three countries as a compromise. Allied governments disputed

Continued

the composition of the delegation from Poland, seeking instead to accredit an unofficial government-in-exile in London, so the Polish seat was left vacant. Representatives of several nongovernmental organizations also assisted. With the addition of more countries than the Dumbarton Oaks four, several changes were made in the draft: (1) Regional organizations were recognized. (2) The Economic and Social Council and the Trusteeship Council, both with rotating memberships, were established. (3) Human rights, economic, and technological issues were given more emphasis. (4) A world court was to be set up independently. (5) The Security Council veto was limited to the five permanent members on substantive (nonprocedural) matters. (6) Otherwise, the Security Council could issue binding decisions. In June, the draft was finalized as the Charter of the United Nations and signed by 50 of the 51 original member countries; Poland signed later. Ratification awaited approval of the five "founding members," namely, Britain, China, France, the United States, and the Soviet Union, as well as a majority of the other signatures. On October 24, 1945, the necessary number of ratifications had been received in London, the temporary seat of the UN. October 24 thenceforth has been celebrated as United Nations Day.

The **Charter of the United Nations**, as adopted in 1945, was the first treaty of the postwar era to put human rights in the forefront. The preamble of the Charter, the first global recognition of human rights, contains the following words:

> We the peoples of the United Nations, determined to save succeeding generations from the scourge of war, which twice in our lifetime has brought untold sorrow to mankind, and to reaffirm faith in fundamental human rights, in the dignity and worth of the human person, in the equal rights of men and women of nations large and small, and to establish conditions under which justice and respect for the obligations arising from treaties and other sources of international law can be maintained, and to promote social progress and better standards of life in larger freedom …

Hence, the first priority of the UN Charter is **peace**. The second priority is **human rights**, though, of course, the concern for peace is articulated in terms of human rights. Accordingly, the world gradually changed from the Westphalian model of sovereignty and nonintervention to a Charter-based model.

Article 1 of the UN Charter lists one of the purposes as "promoting and encouraging" respect for human rights "without distinction as to race, sex, language, or religion." In Article 62, the newly created Economic and Social Council is urged to make recommendations "for the purpose of promoting respect and observance of human rights and fundamental freedoms for all."

DISCUSSION TOPIC 4.1 IS THE UN CHARTER CONTRADICTORY ABOUT HUMAN RIGHTS?

When the UN Charter was drafted in 1945, delegates to the San Francisco Peace Conference knew about the Nazi slaughter of millions of innocent civilians. The world also knew that the Soviet Union had done so during the 1930s. Was there a contradiction by placing human rights in Articles 1 and 55 and then doing nothing to institutionalize efforts to prosecute human rights violations?

However, Article 2 prohibits the UN from intervening "in matters which are essentially within the domestic jurisdiction" of any state. Thus, the goal of promoting human rights was limited by the Westphalian proscription on intervening in errant states. The UN, in other words, began as the most important contemporary institution for advancing international human rights, but the founders knew that the organization had to move cautiously. Although the League of Nations required a unanimous vote before authorizing action, the UN gave a veto only to the five major powers (Britain, China, France, the Soviet Union, and the United States) within the Security Council. The Charter states that obligations identified therein are to supersede all other treaty obligations.

The new UN had an implicit division of labor: the UN General Assembly and Security Council would handle civil and political rights issues; FAO, IBRD, IMF, UNRRA, and UNESCO would deal with economic and social problems. The adoption of a major declaration on human rights, meanwhile, was greatly influenced by a redefinition of the scope of human rights in regard to trials of war criminals.

WAR CRIMES TRIALS

German and Japanese aggression during World War II clearly was contrary to international law. In 1942, leaders of governments in exile in London adopted a **Resolution on German War Crimes by Representatives of Nine Occupied Countries**, calling for the perpetrators of "imprisonments, mass expulsions, the execution of hostages and massacres" to be brought to justice after the war. In 1943, the **Declaration Concerning Atrocities** at the Moscow Conference by Churchill, Roosevelt, and Stalin called for postwar trials of major Nazi war criminals for their "atrocities, massacres and cold-blooded mass executions." The **Potsdam Declaration** of 1945 reiterated the desire to try war criminals.

Information about the mass deportations and slaughter of millions of persons was known to many leaders of allied countries, but perhaps no person had greater knowledge than Raphael Lemkin (1900–1959), a Polish lawyer who in 1944 coined the word "**genocide**" to refer to Nazi Germany's "Final Solution" to the "Jewish problem," though of course mass murder by governments has occurred throughout history.[1]

After the war, there was a need to address the brutal treatment in the concentration camps and elsewhere that had resulted in an extermination of six million Jewish people, known as the Holocaust, as well as millions of others deemed expendable by Nazis who believed Germans to constitute the "master race."

HISTORIC EVENT 4.2 THE HOLOCAUST (1938–1945)

Adolf Hitler (1889–1945) was appointed Chancellor of Germany in 1933. Soon, political dissidents and racial minorities, especially Jews, were rounded up. In 1938, Hitler authorized a program known as *Aktion T-4* to liquidate nearly 200,000 persons with mental and physical disabilities – first children and later adults – for being biologically "unfit," as the first step in the Nazi program of "racial hygiene." The program was resisted by bureaucrats and members of the clergy, however, and was officially cancelled in 1941, but the precedent for exterminating undesirables had been established. When World War II started, Jews were first forced into ghettoes, and *Einsatzgruppen* (intervention forces) death squads were ordered to slaughter Poles, communists, and Jews in the Soviet Union, resulting in about 1.6 million deaths. After German concentration camps were constructed and opened at the end of 1941, some five million Jews and other "undesirables," including gays and members of the Roma minority, were sent to the camps to be executed by Nazi officials and their collaborators in other countries. In retreat during 1944–1945, the Nazis organized death marches, in which another 100,000 Jews died. In all, the death toll included at least six million Jews and five million non-Jews. The Holocaust, however, is usually identified solely with the extermination of Jews.

The brutal crimes committed in the conduct of war, as well as atrocities against civilians, went beyond anything ever imagined. Previously, the international community had allowed sovereign states to treat their own people however they wished, but the magnitude of slaughter could not be ignored. The international community was thus contemplating how to hold certain states accountable for actions inside their borders.

The Allied Powers considered various options in dealing with Nazi German officials who had violated the laws of warfare. Winston Churchill (1874–1965) favored summary execution. Josef Stalin (1878–1953) was keen on a show trial. But Franklin Roosevelt (1882–1945) demurred. In 1945, on becoming president, Harry Truman (1884–1972) strongly supported a proposal from Secretary of War Henry Stimson (1867–1950) to have a formal trial of Nazi officials in the best tradition of Anglo-European justice, and he secured agreement from Britain and the Soviet Union to proceed.

When allied forces liberated the various concentration camps and saw the horrific condition of the survivors, they agreed that major war criminals must be prosecuted. However, allied leaders recalled a provision in the Treaty of Versailles that required prosecution of Kaiser Wilhelm (1859–1941) of Germany for culpability in launching World War I, yet he fled to the Netherlands, which refused to surrender him for trial. In part to avoid a similar situation, postwar Germany was divided into four occupied zones – one each governed by the victorious Allied Powers (Britain, France, the Soviet Union, and the United States). Suspected war criminals were then brought under custody for trial.

In 1945, 30 articles were drawn up in the **Agreement for the Prosecution and Punishment of the Major War Criminals of the European Axis** and the **Charter of the International Military Tribunal** for trials at Nuremberg, a town in Germany where Adolf Hitler (1889–1945) held many well-publicized rallies. The major offenses included not only the customary **war crimes**, based on the Geneva and Hague conventions, but also two new crimes – **crimes against humanity** and **crimes against peace**. Although the words "genocide" and "holocaust" did not gain currency until later, the postwar war crimes trials established significant precedents by defining the two new types of international crimes, placing individuals on trial with considerable publicity, and having international panels of jurists pass sentences that were regarded as fair and measured.

On December 28, 1945, the Allied Control Council issued Control Law 10, which authorized the occupying powers to prosecute "war criminals and similar offenders." Of 91,000 Germans accused of war crimes in German courts under the framework of the postwar military occupation of Germany, some 8,000 were convicted and received punishment. But the actions of top Nazi officials had been authorized by German law, so they could not be tried in German courts. A special international tribunal was needed instead. Accordingly, there were 11 special trials (Table 4.2).

The most famous **Nuremberg War Crimes Trial** prosecution, the Ministries Case, involved Reich Ministers and other Nazi Party leaders, who, of course, did not commit specific acts on the battlefield.[2] Instead, they were charged primarily with conspiracy to wage aggressive war in defiance of international treaties. As prosecutor, Robert Jackson presented five legal grounds for their indictments:

- Hague conventions
- Treaty of Versailles of 1919 (for violating the independence of Austria, Danzig, and Czechoslovakia as well as Germany's rearmament)
- Locarno Treaty of 1925 (wherein Germany had pledged to respect the territorial status quo of Belgium, France, Great Britain, and Italy)
- General Treaty for the Renunciation of War of 1928 (the Kellogg–Briand Pact)
- United Nations Charter.

TABLE 4.2 **NUREMBERG WAR CRIMES TRIALS, 1946–1949**

Case name	Defendants	Charges	Verdicts
Doctors case	23 Nazi physicians	Inhuman experiments	16 guilty, 7 acquitted
Einsatzgruppen case	24 in mobile killing units	Mistreatment of POWs and civilians; property destruction	24 guilty
Farben case	24 industrialists	Plunder and spoliation of private property	13 guilty, 11 acquitted
Flick case	6 industrialists	Slave labor; POW labor; confiscation of Jewish property	3 guilty, 3 acquitted
Hostage case	12 army officers	War crimes	8 guilty, 2 acquitted, 2 suicides
Judges Case	16 judges	Crimes against humanity; war crimes	10 guilty, 4 acquitted, 1 died, 1 mistrial
Krupp Case	12 industrialists	Slave labor; war crimes	11 guilty, 1 acquitted
Milch Case	Field Marshall Erhard Milch	Cruel treatment of POWs; inhuman experiments; murder	guilty
Ministries Case	21 Nazi leaders	Crimes against humanity; crimes against peace; war crimes	19 guilty, 2 acquitted. 1 suicide
Pohl Case	18 members of the Economic and Administrative Office	War crimes against POWs	15 guilty, 3 acquitted
Resettlement Case	14 officials	Crimes against humanity	13 guilty, 1 acquitted

COURT CASE 4.1 TRIAL OF THE MAJOR WAR CRIMINALS AT NUREMBERG (1945–1946)

At the conclusion of World War II, the victorious allied powers rounded up important Nazi officials. Disagreements among the allied powers on what to do with the prisoners was resolved by the decision to put them on trial. German courts were inappropriate, as their actions were entirely legal under Nazi law. Accordingly, the allied powers decided, in London during 1945, to adopt the Agreement for the Prosecution and Punishment of the Major War Criminals and

Continued

of the European Axis and a second document, the Charter of the International Military Tribunal. Among some 90,000 prisoners, 24 heads of executive departments and military commanders were then scheduled for trial before a four-judge panel, including one representative each from Britain, France, the Soviet Union, and the United States. They were charged not only with war crimes, as identified in the Geneva and Hague conventions, but also for two new offenses – "crimes against peace," primarily for violating the Kellogg–Briand of 1928, and "crimes against humanity," an offense that applied to the massacres of Jews and other minorities. All four countries provided prosecutorial personnel. One defendant committed suicide before trial, another was tried *in absentia*, and a third was considered medically unfit for trial. After a stirring speech by Robert Jackson (1892–1954), an Associate Justice of the US Supreme Court at the beginning of the proceedings, he began to introduce documents and elicited testimony from witnesses, but Nazi defense attorneys effectively raised questions about the evidence. The tenor of the trial changed significantly when a film was displayed, showing horrific conditions at death camps taken at the time when they were liberated by allied soldiers. The court concluded by finding 20 of the defendants guilty and acquitting two. Hermann Göring (1893–1946) committed suicide before being sentenced. Twelve were sentenced to death by hanging, seven received prison sentences of 10–20 years or life. Five expressed some remorse. The legitimacy of the trials was questioned in Germany as well as by some allied commentators.

When the Ministries Case concluded, 12 were sentenced to be executed (though one committed suicide), 3 were given life sentences, 4 were sentenced to fixed terms (from 10 to 20 years), and 2 were acquitted. German courts, based on German law, later convicted the two who were acquitted. Although the judges in the Ministries Case consisted of a panel of jurists from the four occupying powers, United States officials carried out the proceedings in the other 10 cases.

Japanese aggression was responsible for perhaps as many deaths as the Nazis, including 23 million Chinese. The survival rate of prisoners of war (POWs) confined by the Japanese was considerably lower than in the German POW camps. In 1943, Britain, China, and the United States, pledged to "stop and punish Japanese aggression" during a conference in Cairo. One article of the **Potsdam Declaration** of 1945, which was targeted at both Germany and Japan, stated that "justice shall be meted out to all war criminals including those who have visited cruelties upon our prisoners."

The **International Military Tribunal for the Far East**, also known as the Tokyo War Crimes Tribunal, began deliberations in 1946, the year following Japan's surrender. Of 80 persons originally deemed complicit in the same three offenses defined at Nuremberg, 28 high-level Japanese leaders were put on trial. Although the United States was the sole occupying power of Japan, jurists came from 11 countries (Australia, Britain, Canada, China, France, India, New Zealand, the Netherlands, the Philippines, the Soviet Union, and the United States). Joseph Keenan (1888–1954), the sole prosecutor, was an official of the US Department of Justice who had distinguished himself in prosecuting organized crime. Seven officials were condemned to death, 16 were sentenced to life imprisonment, 2 received prison terms, 2 died during the trial, and 1 was found not guilty by reason of insanity and set free.

Whereas Hitler died before the Nuremberg trials, Emperor Hirohito (1901–1989) was not put on trial as a condition of Japan's surrender. The Emperor's support legitimized the new constitution and the postwar government.

The Tokyo trials dragged on until 1948, longer than the Ministries Case at Nuremberg. In 1948, 42 Japanese who had been considered for possible trial were released, including future Prime Minister Nobusuke Kishi (1896–1987) and microbiologist, Shirō Ishii (1892–1959), the latter having conducted experiments on humans (as did the notorious Nazi, Josef Mengele (1911–1979), who was sought as a war criminal until his death). By then, Washington's highest priority was to normalize conditions in Japan in order to fight the Cold War in Asia, where communist forces in China were approaching victory, and the Soviet Union had seized islands formerly part of Imperial Japan and was closely allied with North Korea. The impending Cold War with the Soviet Union was handled less belligerently, but Washington recruited former Nazis to develop rocketry, notably Werner von Braun (1912–1977).

Subsequently, other countries in Asia put thousands of Japanese on trial for war crimes. In 1948, for example, the Netherlands convened a military tribunal concerning the sexual abuse of women. Held in Jakarta, several Japanese military officers were convicted of forcing 35 Dutch women to serve as involuntary prostitutes in "comfort stations." Other countries in Asia put some 5,600 Japanese on trial for war crimes in their own courts, resulting in 4,400 convictions. One of the most notable, conducted in Dutch-ruled Indonesia by Australian authorities in 1946, tried 93 Japanese for the Laha Massacre of 1942, when some 300 Australian and Dutch POWs were selected at random and shot.

Although Bulgaria, France, Hungary, Romania, and Slovakia collaborated with Nazi Germany in rounding up Jews for the death camps, only France has prosecuted their own citizens as war criminals. Among the prosecutions, which began in 1979, the most famous was the trial and conviction of Klaus Barbie (1913–1991), known as the "Butcher of Lyon," who was tried in 1984 and sentenced to life in prison, where he died.

There was some controversy associated with the war crimes trials. Rather than being held accountable for the deaths of millions of civilians before and during World War II, the Soviet Union was one of the four powers sitting in judgment at Nuremberg. The February 1945 Anglo-American bombing of Dresden, including largely civilian targets, was not prosecuted as a war crime, and indeed the Soviets later vilified the Dresden overkill by the West in an effort to gain support in the East German zone that they occupied after the war. Moreover, the United States was never held accountable for the massive bombing of Tokyo from 1942–1945 or for dropping two atomic bombs on Japan in 1945, actions that produced considerable suffering among civilians despite their limited strategic value. A major reason is that the Geneva and Hague conventions did not yet apply to aerial warfare. Only in 1977, two years after the United States pulled out of Vietnam, did an additional **Protocol to the Geneva Conventions** prohibit indiscriminate aerial bombing.

Although the Nuremberg trials certainly represented a form of "victor's justice" that was resented in Germany, Nuremberg established the important precedent of accountability for major war crimes. Indeed, the United States prosecuted its own military personnel for violations of the laws of war in Vietnam,[3] and has continued to so, though accountability for torture by the US Central Intelligence Agency in handling alleged terrorists after 9/11 is still lacking.

Afterward, Lemkin's concept of genocide gained acceptance, and the **International Convention on the Prevention and Punishment of the Crime of Genocide** was adopted in 1948. When the treaty went into force in 1951, many of those supporting it anticipated that an international criminal court would be established. Instead, the focus on the Cold War was preeminent.

The Nuremberg and Tokyo proceedings brought to light many heinous offenses committed during the war. Accordingly, the Diplomatic Conference of Geneva of 1949 drafted four **Geneva Conventions**, which updated earlier agreements in order to respond to unprecedented barbarities. The treaties, which went into force in 1950, and are explained in Chapter 7, provide the major framework for contemporary assessments of the illegality of human rights practices in wartime as well as in postwar occupations.

UNITED NATIONS DECLARATION OF HUMAN RIGHTS

Eleanor Roosevelt (1884–1962), one of the delegates at the San Francisco conference in 1945, argued strongly that a major task for the UN would be to draw up a declaration stating principles of human rights. The first session of the UN Economic and Social Council (ECOSOC) in 1946 then created the Commission on Human Rights (UNCHR), charging the Commission with the initial task of preparing the following statements: (1) a universal bill of rights; (2) international declarations or conventions on civil liberties, the status of women, freedom of information and similar matters; (3) arrangements for the protection of minorities; and (4) arrangements for the prevention of discrimination on grounds of race, sex, language, or religion.

Next, French UNCHR delegate, René Cassin (1887–1976), drafted the text of the **Universal Declaration of Human Rights** in consultation with Mrs Roosevelt, Charles Malik (1906–1987) of Lebanon, and Peng-Chun Chang (1892–1957) of China. The General Assembly approved the declaration in 1948 as an international bill of rights. Although the British wanted a binding, enforceable treaty, Mrs Roosevelt knew that the US Senate would refuse to ratify any such document.

Accordingly, she insisted that the declaration should contain general principles, with a treaty to be drafted later. The most basic principles are as follows:

- Right to life, liberty, and security of the person
- Illegality of slavery
- Right to an education
- Right to employment, paid holidays, protection against unemployment, social security, and the right to a decent standard of living
- Right to equal justice before the law
- Freedom from discrimination
- Freedom of movement and asylum
- Right to full participation in cultural and political life
- Prohibition of *ex post facto* laws
- Right to privacy
- Right to a nationality
- Right to marry freely
- Right to property
- Freedom from torture or cruel, inhumane treatment or punishment
- Freedom of thought, conscience, and religion
- Freedom of assembly, expression, and opinion
- Right to redress and remedies for violations of human rights.

So resounding were the principles that 23 of the 30 articles were adopted unanimously. However, some countries were dissatisfied. Saudi Arabia objected to the provision on marriage rights. South Africa opposed the principle of racial equality. The Soviet Union wanted more respect for state sovereignty and more details regarding economic and social rights. Some progressive Western countries objected that the declaration was not a binding treaty and instead consisted of mere words with no enforcement machinery.

Nevertheless, the impact of the declaration was profound. Subsequently, 89 countries modeled human rights provisions in their constitutions on the declaration. Some scholars argue that the declaration remains important because the principles are stated in more fundamental terms than in the specifics of a treaty.

In 1948, the declaration directly inspired the Western hemisphere to adopt the **American Declaration of the Rights and Duties of Man**. The Geneva Conventions of 1949 specifically pledged to achieve the principles of the declaration. In 1950, the **European Convention for the Protection of Human Rights and Fundamental Freedoms** was adopted. The **African Charter on Human and Peoples' Rights** emerged in 1981. UNCHR drew up statements on various priorities over the years to further specify the rights stated in the declaration and has authorized work on treaties to define the principles in more concrete terms.

DELAY IN ADOPTING HUMAN RIGHTS TREATIES

After the declaration was adopted, ECOSOC asked UNCHR to put the provisions of the UN Declaration on Human Rights into the language of a single treaty.

From 1949 to 1951, the commission indeed worked on a single draft convention, but there was little progress while governments wrangled over how much attention to give to civil and political rights versus economic, social, and cultural rights.

In 1951, under pressure from Western governments, the General Assembly authorized the drafting of two separate covenants. Western countries argued that civil and political rights were **legal rights**, immediately enforceable and absolute, but economic, social, and cultural rights were **program rights** that would take more time to implement. That is, civil and political rights were regarded as rights *against* the state, whereas economic, social, and cultural rights required action *from* the state. Within the UN system, civil and political rights could be enforced through complaints and conciliation, whereas economic, social, and cultural rights would require capabilities that many countries lacked and would thus have to be monitored by annual progress reports from governments. The argument was that to achieve those capabilities, poorer countries first needed an infrastructure of hospitals, information media, roads, schools, and the like.

A major issue was how far such a treaty would authorize investigations into the internal affairs of nations. South Africa and the Soviet Union complained that the UN might intrude into internal affairs, an objection raised as well in the United States by such nongovernmental organizations as the American Bar Association. The question was whether the treaty should leave implementation and enforcement to nations themselves or should there be an international body to do so.

Under the Constitution of the United States, treaties upon ratification become the "law of the land" and thus may either conflict with or supersede federal, state, or local laws. For example, some Southern legislators feared that African Americans, using such a treaty as the legal basis for a lawsuit, could sue to end segregation. So great was the fear of the power of the UN that Senator John Bricker (1893–1986), a Republican who ran for vice president in 1948 along with unsuccessful presidential candidate Thomas Dewey (1902–1971), introduced a resolution into the Senate demanding that the United States withdraw from all conventions, covenants, and treaties emerging from the UN that had anything to do with human rights. His reasoning was that the declaration was foreign to the American tradition of constitutional rights and that under the declaration the United States would be forced to surrender its sovereignty to "UN tyranny" on such matters as immigration. The subtext of Bricker's rhetoric was to depict candidates of the opposing Democratic Party, who supported the declaration, as anti-American and, in effect, guilty of treason. In 1948, nevertheless, Truman and his running mate, Alben Barkley (1877–1956), defeated the Dewey–Bricker ticket.

The Cold War slowed progress toward adoption of a treaty. Many in the United States feared that the UN was proceeding too quickly to dismantle colonial empires that were providing stability to head off communist revolutions. The Soviet Union was displeased with the failure of the UN to seat the newly consolidated People's Republic of China in the General Assembly, as well as with Security Council action that supported South Korea in the war with communist North Korea from 1950–1953. The Soviet Union opposed any mechanism that would send investigators into countries under its control to report on the status of human rights. The Soviets even attacked civil and political rights as "bourgeois values."

The UN Commission on Human Rights was beset with contradictory pressures and lacked consensus. Some states wanted to water down provisions found in the declaration, while others wanted to add new rights. Britain and the United States insisted on moving forward only on civil and political rights, whereas the Soviet bloc wanted priority given to economic and social rights. Even though the declaration was translated into treaty language as early as 1953, there was no mood for compromise between Cold War adversaries, and the treaty languished.

Disagreements existed even within the Western bloc. Eleanor Roosevelt, the United States delegate on the commission, wanted no restrictions on freedom of speech. European countries that had been victimized by Nazi propaganda believed that the proposed treaty should prohibit any deliberate advocacy of war. European countries also wanted to ban racism, but many in the United States were opposed. In 1953, Dwight Eisenhower (1890–1961), upon becoming president, removed Eleanor Roosevelt from the commission, and his Secretary of State, John Foster Dulles (1888–1959), announced to the world that the United States would never become a party to any human rights treaty approved by the UN. The Soviet Union then condemned the United States for the action, saying that Washington had forfeited the right to lecture the world on human rights.

Nevertheless, in 1967, two human rights treaties were finally adopted by the General Assembly – the **International Covenant on Civil and Political Rights** and the **International Covenant on Economic, Social, and Cultural Rights**. The treaties were then submitted to governments for formal ratification, usually a process of approval by a legislative body in each country. Both treaties gained ratifications very slowly, as questions continued to be raised.

HUMAN RIGHTS BREAKTHROUGH: OUT OF AFRICA

In the 1950s, the human rights movement might have come to a halt except that some of the poorer countries found a clever way to advance human rights in a different way. What they stressed was the desire for prompt decolonization, a goal shared by the Soviet Union and the United States.

One of the first successful African initiatives was the UN's adoption in 1960 of the **Declaration on the Granting of Independence to Colonial Countries and Peoples**, which proclaimed that alien subjugation, domination, and exploitation constitute a denial of fundamental human rights, and demanded that immediate steps be taken to grant independence to trusteeships and other non-self-governing territories in accordance with the wishes of the people.

Accordingly, Belgium, Britain, and France were on the defensive to grant independence to their colonies, especially in Africa, and they argued that many countries were not yet ready for self-government. In 1956, France responded by granting independence to Morocco and Tunisia, and Britain did so in the Sudan. In 1957, Britain granted independence to the Gold Coast, which was renamed Ghana. In 1958, after Charles de Gaulle (1890–1970) gained power, France granted independence to Guinea and promised independence by 1960 to the Central African Republic, Congo (Brazzaville), Dahomey, Gabon, Guinea, the Ivory Coast, Malagasy, Mali,

Mauritania, and Sénégal. Belgium granted independence to the Congo (Kinshasa) in 1960 and to Rwanda and Burundi in 1962. Portugal, however, did not part with Angola, East Timor, Guinea, and Mozambique until 1974–1975.

By the mid-1960s, most African states had become independent, perhaps the greatest collective extension of human rights (by implementing the principle of self-determination of peoples) in world history. Membership in the UN swelled sufficiently to assure ratification of human rights treaties by the required number of states. That is why texts of the **International Covenant on Civil and Political Rights** and the **International Covenant on Economic, Social, and Culture Rights** were adopted during 1967, and a sufficient number of states ratified by 1976 for both treaties to go into force.

African countries also agitated to end white minority rule in Rhodesia and South Africa as well as South Africa's control of South West Africa (now Namibia). What followed were decades of diplomatic pressure and the first two cases of UN economic sanctions.

Britain treated Southern Rhodesia as a self-governing colony from 1923 and appeared to promise independence as soon as World War II ended. In 1954 London merged the territory into a federation with Northern Rhodesia and Nyasaland, whereupon leaders among white British citizens embarked on negotiations for full independence. London disagreed, the federation was dissolved in 1963, and independence was conferred on Malawi (the former Nyasaland) and Zambia (the former Northern Rhodesia). In 1965, the remaining colony, Rhodesia, declared independence of Britain under a constitution that had no intention of turning power over to the majority African population. Accordingly, Britain referred the matter to the Security Council, which, in 1966, voted an economic boycott of Rhodesia, urging countries to cease all trade and other commercial interactions with the county. Since Rhodesia relied heavily on trade with Britain, many companies in London did not want to lose business, so they evaded participation in the boycott by dealing with intermediaries. Eventually, the British government cracked down, and in 1979 the Rhodesian government yielded to a new, democratic constitution for Zimbabwe, which then joined the UN in 1980. Thirteen years of sanctions had finally paid off.

HISTORIC EVENT 4.3 THE SHARPEVILLE MASSACRE (1960)

After *apartheid* began in South Africa in 1948, black persons were required to show identification papers at checkpoints in order to leave their segregated townships to work in the nearby cities. In 1960, some 300 demonstrators peacefully began to protest the restrictive laws in Sharpeville township. Upon arriving at the scene, the police opened fire, and 69 demonstrators were killed. Four more demonstrators were gunned down in two other towns. The incident, collectively known as the Sharpeville Massacre, attracted world attention to how *apartheid* was being implemented.

Black residents of South Africa could not wait for the UN to act. After several of them protested in 1960, the government's massacre of unarmed demonstrators in what is known as the Sharpeville Massacre was quite a strategic blunder, as the event galvanized support among the new African states to bring the matter of

TABLE 4.3   THE ROLE OF THE UNITED NATIONS IN ENDING *APARTHEID*

Year	Organ	Action
1960	Security Council	Resolution demands an end to *apartheid* and racial discrimination
1962	General Assembly	Resolution calls for a boycott of South Africa, sets up a Special Committee on the Policies of *Apartheid* of the Republic of South Africa to monitor and report on developments
1963	Security Council	Resolution condemns *apartheid* and calls for a voluntary arms embargo
1963	General Assembly	Declaration on the Elimination of All Forms of Racial Discrimination
1963	General Assembly	Resolution calls for an arms embargo
1964	International Labor Organization	Declaration Concerning the Policy of Apartheid
1965	General Assembly	Adopts International Convention Against All Forms of Racial Discrimination
1966	General Assembly	Resolution condemns *apartheid* as a "crime against humanity"
1967	Economic and Social Council	Resolution authorizing the Commission on Human Rights to study and report on human rights violations
1968	General Assembly	Resolution calls for sports embargo
1969	General Assembly	Resolution condemns *apartheid* as an economic crime
1970	General Assembly	Resolution describes *apartheid* as "a crime against the conscience and dignity of mankind"
1970	General Assembly	Refuses to seat the South African delegation
1972	Security Council	Resolution condemns *apartheid*
1972	UNESCO	Declaration of Guiding Principles on the Use of Satellite Broadcasting for the Free Flow of Information of the Mass Media to Strengthening Peace and International Understanding, to the Promotion of Human Rights and to Countering Racialism, Apartheid and the Incitement to War
1973	General Assembly	Adopts International Convention on the Suppression and Punishment of the Crime of Apartheid (in force 1976)
1977	Security Council	Resolution calls for a mandatory arms embargo and for South Africa to grant Namibia independence
1983	General Assembly	Resolution calls for a boycott of any corporation trading with South Africa
1984	Security Council	Resolution declares South Africa's new constitution "null and void"
1985	General Assembly	Adopts International Convention Against Apartheid in Sports
1985	Security Council	Resolution recommends voluntary economic sanctions
1994	Security Council	Resolution lifts all sanctions

apartheid (racial segregation) to the attention of the UN General Assembly. The UN responded by setting up the Special Committee on the Policies of Apartheid, called upon member states to boycott South African goods, and, in 1963, adopted the **Declaration on the Elimination of All Forms of Racial Discrimination**. In 1965, the declaration was placed on a treaty basis in the **International Convention on the Elimination of All Forms of Racial Discrimination**. Progress in dealing with *apartheid* was slow, however (Table 4.3).

Despite the General Assembly call for a boycott in 1963, Britain, France, and the United States continued to trade with South Africa. In other words, UN resolutions were ineffective, but they kept moral pressure on the Pretoria government.

Then, in 1976, 10,000 black schoolchildren in Soweto protesting the new requirement to learn Afrikaans (the language spoken by Dutch descendants) were shot without warning, and at least 152 died. Although the requirement was rescinded in 1977, later that year the death of anti-*apartheid* leader, Steve Biko (1946–1977), while in custody made crystal clear that the South African government was defying the UN. Accordingly, the Security Council decided to get tough with South Africa, ordering more economic sanctions in 1977, though the United States vetoed resolutions to strengthen the boycott from 1979–1986.

By 1984, when the South African government drew up a new constitution establishing a tricameral legislative chamber for three races (white, Indians, coloreds), but none for blacks, the Security Council lambasted the effort. Economic sanctions finally began to work, as large corporations pulled out of the country, and South Africa was boycotted in sports following the adoption of the **International Convention Against Apartheid in Sports** in 1985. The first sign of a weakening in policy came in 1988, when Pretoria agreed to a UN peace plan to end South African rule over Namibia, which achieved independence two years later. Also, in 1990, Nelson Mandela (1918–) was released from prison, and *apartheid* laws began to be repealed. The economic boycott ended. Mandela was elected president in 1994, and a new constitution was adopted in 1996.

Clearly, the UN must assume some credit for relentlessly authorizing economic sanctions to bring pressure on countries for unacceptable human rights conditions. For the first time, the world community had acted together to end nefarious human rights abuses inside sovereign states.

PEOPLE POWER

For centuries, mass protests of the common people have demanded action from governments to attend to their needs. The French Revolution began in part when the streets of Paris were filled by people who could not afford to buy food. Democratic reforms have instituted elections so that the people, in France and elsewhere, may choose their leaders peacefully. Elections, in other words, were designed as mechanisms to obviate civil wars, demonstrations, and riots. But when phony elections are held or minorities are ignored, the people have often arisen in mass demonstrations to promote human rights.

In 1918, Mahatma Gandhi (1869–1948) urged the residents of Bihar and Gujarat to engage in nonviolent civil disobedience in light of the British insistence on taxing them despite a famine. His fame arose from the experience, and he later protested British rule over India, organizing the largest mass protests and boycotts of British goods ever held. Indian self-determination was granted in 1947.

However, mass protests in East Germany and Poland against Soviet rule were suppressed in 1953. Civil disobedience does not always work.

In 1954, the Supreme Court of the United States ruled that pupil assignment on the basis of race was illegal in *Brown et al. v. Board of Education of Topeka* (347US483). The decision applied nationwide. For many observers, the Supreme Court had taken the most sweeping action of the twentieth century to advance human rights. However, Topeka's Board of Education did nothing immediately to carry out the decision, so the Supreme Court was asked to rule on the matter again. In *Brown et al. v. Board of Education of Topeka et al.* (349US294), the court responded in 1955 by saying that implementation should be with "all deliberate speed." Once again, most school boards refused to act, and Southern politicians were determined to continue racial segregation practices indefinitely.

HISTORIC EVENT 4.4 THE MONTGOMERY BUS BOYCOTT (1955–1956)

In 1955, Rosa Parks (1913–2005), a department store worker, boarded a bus in downtown Montgomery, Alabama, and sat in the fifth row, as the first four rows were traditionally reserved for whites. After white passengers filled up the first four rows, and more boarded, the bus driver asked those in the fifth and sixth rows to move back, as was customary. Three African Americans moved, but Rosa refused. A volunteer for the National Association for the Advancement of Colored People (NAACP), which had filed the *Brown* case, she wanted to know what rights she had – and she wanted to know right then. Accordingly, she was arrested. Her arrest was then discussed by the NAACP, including African American pastors in town. They decided to ask a recent arrival in Montgomery, the Reverend Martin Luther King, Jr (1929–1958), to lead a protest boycott by African Americans of all buses in town. After 384 days, the bus company gave in. In 1956, *Browder v. Gayle* (142FSupp707) affirmed that buses could no longer segregate passengers by race.

The Montgomery bus boycott of 1955–1956 was well publicized, revealing as it did that a mass movement could lead to human rights progress. Leadership during the boycott propelled Martin Luther King, Jr (1929–1968) into world prominence. He was in demand to lead demonstrations in order to make the Supreme Court's rulings a reality and to advance the cause of human rights beyond education and transportation to voting and housing. His nonviolent approach, used by the American suffragettes as well as the followers of Gandhi, popularized the use of massive public protests to demand change when political systems were unwilling to act. Blacks and whites joined together in various protests, including "Freedom Rides" into the South, in which they sat together on buses.

In 1965, President Lyndon Johnson (1908–1973) committed thousands of American troops to intervene in Vietnam's Civil War (1954–1973), an episode known in the United States as the Vietnam War. Opponents soon began to hold rallies, both in the United States and in Europe, to persuade American leaders to withdraw. Later, mass demonstrations brought down undemocratic regimes in Thailand (1973), Portugal (1974), Iran (1979), and Nicaragua (1979).

HISTORIC EVENT 4.5 "PEOPLE POWER" IN THE PHILIPPINES OUSTS FERDINAND MARCOS (1986)

In 1972, when Ferdinand Marcos was ineligible for reelection for a third term as president of the Philippines, he declared martial law on the pretext of coping with communist insurgents. Although he lifted martial law in 1981, he continued in office on the basis of phony elections, arrest of opponents, control over the media, and transfer of assets from the economic elites to his political allies. The result was economic decline on account of increasing government mismanagement, terrorist incidents, and worker strikes. In 1983, when Marcos's health was noticeably deteriorating, his chief opponent, centrist Benigno Aquino, Jr (1932–1983), flew back to the country in order to persuade Marcos to reinstitute democracy before terrorists made the country ungovernable. But Aquino was shot dead at the airport. After a funeral procession of two million persons, Jaime Cardinal Sin (1928–2005) urged the people to use peaceful means to bring back democracy. With communist strength growing unabated, Marcos declared martial law again but yielded to American and domestic pressures to hold a snap election in 1986. Corazon Aquino (1933–2009), Benigno's widow, then ran for president, but Marcos declared that he had won. Following election fraud allegations, Catholic bishops challenged Marcos's reelection, as did Minister of Defense Juan Ponce Enrile (1924–) and Vice Chief of Staff of the Armed Forces Lt General Fidel Ramos (1928–), who barricaded themselves in military camps on opposite sides of the Epifanio de los Santos Avenue (EDSA), awaiting an attack from troops loyal to Marcos. Two hours later, Cardinal Sin, on the only independent radio station, urged citizens to express support by bringing food to soldiers in the camps. Soon, hundreds of thousands of people arrived, seemingly prepared to occupy the streets indefinitely. Members of the army began to defect, the government media was seized, and rockets attacked the presidential palace, but Marcos refused to give the order to shoot the EDSA protesters. On an American helicopter, Marcos and his wife were flown to an American military base, where they boarded a military jet for exile in Honolulu. In all, the EDSA Revolution toppled Marcos from power in only four days.

The first contemporary use of the term "people power" in connection with human rights was perhaps in connection with events in the Philippines during 1986, sometimes known as the "EDSA Revolution," when opponents of Marcos wore yellow banners. Ferdinand Marcos (1917–1989) had seized power in 1972 on

TABLE 4.4   CONTEMPORARY "PEOPLE POWER" MOBILIZATIONS

Year	Country	Nickname	Result
1974	Portugal	Carnation Revolution	Ousted dictatorship
1976	Nicaragua	Sandinista Revolution	Ousted dictatorship
1979	Iran	Khomeni Revolution	Ousted dictatorship
1986	Philippines	EDSA (Yellow) Revolution	Ousted dictatorship
1987	South Korea	June Democracy Movement	Free elections and full democracy
1989	Bulgaria		End of communist rule
1989	Czechoslovakia	Velvet Revolution	End of communist rule
1989	China	Tiananmen Square Protest	Suppressed
1989	East Germany	Fall of the Berlin Wall	End of communist rule
1989	Hungary		End of communist rule
1989	Poland		End of communist rule
1990	Mongolia		End of communist rule
1991	Iraq		Suppressed
1991	Russia		End of Soviet Union
2000	Serbia	Bulldozer Revolution	Ousted dictatorship
2001	Argentina		President resigns
2001	Philippines	EDSA II	Ousted corrupt president
2001	Philippines	EDSA III	Failed
2003	Georgia	Rose Revolution	Ousted dictatorship
2004–2005	Ukraine	Orange (Pink) Revolution	Free election
2005	Azerbaijan		Suppressed
2005	Kuwait	Blue Revolution	Women granted the vote
2005	Kyrgyzstan	Tulip Revolution	Ousted dictatorship
2005	Uzbekistan	Blood-Red Revolution	Suppressed
2006	Belarus	Denim Revolution	Suppressed
2006	Lebanon	Cedar Revolution	Syrian troops leave
2007	Burma (Myanmar)	Saffron Revolution	Suppressed
2009	Iran	Green Revolution	Suppressed
2010	Thailand	Red Shirt Movement	Suppressed
2011	Tunisia	Jasmine Revolution	Ousted dictatorship
2011	Egypt	Lotus Revolution	Ousted dictatorship
2011	Libya	Pomegranate Blossom Revolution	Ousted dictatorship with outside military help
2011	Bahrain		Suppressed
2011	Yemen		President resigns
2011	Syria		Suppressed, then a civil war
2013	Egypt		Military coup

the pretext of dealing with a communist insurgency, but that justification seemed increasingly hollow as Marcos's rule became increasingly corrupt. The EDSA, or Yellow, Revolution apparently caught the attention of Koreans, who took to the streets in Seoul during 1987 to end dictatorial rule.

In 1989, as the Berlin Wall fell, the Soviet Union no longer had the capacity or interest in maintaining dictatorships in Eastern Europe, and there was no need for the United States to support pro-West dictatorships. Human rights grew worldwide as democratic governments multiplied throughout the world, though the massacre near Tiananmen Square in Beijing during 1989 was a government statement that China would not adopt democracy. Nevertheless, the Velvet Revolution brought democracy to Czechoslovakia during 1989, the Rose Revolution toppled the corrupt government of Georgia during 2003, the Orange Revolution protested election irregularities in the Ukraine during 2004–2005 to gain a new election, the ill-fated Tulip Revolution overthrew the Kyrgyzstan government during 2005, and similar mass movements arose around the world (Table 4.4).

In 2001, an EDSA mass protest served to oust corrupt President Joseph Estrada (1937–) of the Philippines, and EDSA III occurred later that year when he was arrested as his supporters mobilized to demand his reinstatement. In the latter case, President Gloria Macapagal-Arroyo (1947–) had the support of the army and was not opposed by the Catholic leadership. The concept of human rights protests involving "people power" was thus tarnished in the Philippines.

People power movements remain an important tool in the quest to advance human rights. However, large-scale demonstrations could support violations of human rights, as happened when Benito Mussolini (1883–1945) mobilized 20,000 Black Shirts to seize power in Italy during 1922, and the Brown Shirts of Hitler attacked socialists in Germany during the 1920s. After elections in Malaysia during 1969, Malays threw stones at Chinese snake dancers in Kuala Lumpur who were celebrating the defeat of the Malay political party. When the riot was quelled, some two hundred Chinese had been massacred. Other popular mobilizations in Iraq (1991), Azerbaijan (2005), Uzbekistan (2005), Belarus (2006), Burma (2007), Iran (2009), and Thailand (2010), were also suppressed. During 2010 alone, sociologist Sun Liping (1955–) estimates that there were 180,000 local "mass incidents" in China, but they were short-lived.

HISTORIC EVENT 4.6 A TUNISIAN STREET VENDOR BURNS HIMSELF (2010)

One day in late December 2010, a Tunisian street vendor, Mohamed Bouazizi (1984–2011), had just purchased goods for resale and thus lacked bribe money for the police, who harassed him and confiscated his wheelbarrow and its contents, leaving him without a means to support his family. He then approached the local governor's office, requesting return of his means of livelihood, saying that otherwise he would

Continued

burn himself. After waiting patiently, a government official further humiliated him, whereupon he doused himself with gasoline and lit a match. Eighteen days later, despite hospital care while he was in a coma and an unfulfilled promise by President Ben Ali (1936–) to send him for treatment to France, he died. The self-immolation began a month-long mass protest against government arrogance and corruption that toppled the government by mid-January, a democratic transformation that served to stimulate other anti-government protests throughout the Middle East.

Then came the Jasmine Revolution of January 2011, when peaceful mass protests prompted the Tunisian president to flee the country, whereupon a democratic government was soon established. The events in Tunisia set an example for similar protests throughout the Middle East that year, ultimately resulting in new governments in Egypt, Libya, and Yemen, but suppression in Bahrain and Syria. The "Arab Spring" uprisings of 2011, driven by many groups and disparate motives in several countries remain incapable of monodimensional characterization.

DISCUSSION TOPIC 4.2 WHEN IS "PEOPLE POWER" MOST LIKELY TO ADVANCE HUMAN RIGHTS?

From Mussolini's Black Shirts of 1922 to the Jasmine Revolution of 2011, mass demonstrations have often produced political change. Comparing some of the "people power" examples, why did some fail? What conditions are most likely to guarantee that "people power" will advance human rights?

JIMMY CARTER'S FOREIGN POLICY

In 1977, Jimmy Carter (1924–) took office as the twenty-eighth president of the United States. In his inaugural address, he stated, "our commitment to human rights must be absolute, our laws fair, our natural beauty preserved; the powerful must not persecute the weak, and human dignity must be enhanced." Five months later, in a speech, *Humane Purposes in Foreign Policy*, he advocated a new Cold War strategy – pursuit of the goals of "justice, equity, and human rights." Although not always consistently, Carter made improvement in human rights a condition for receipt of foreign aid from the United States. Officers in American embassies around the world were assigned to keep track of human rights improvements, if any, and the State Department began to publish comprehensive annual reports on the human rights record of almost every major country in the world (except for the United States).

When the twin covenants (regarding civil-political and economic-social-cultural rights) went into force in 1976, the concept of human rights advanced beyond mere **standard setting**. Both documents empowered committees to **monitor** human rights implementation. Carter, thus, sought to lead the way though annual human rights reports.

The reorientation of American foreign policy from deterring an attack from Moscow to questioning the fundamental moral basis of the Soviet Union meant that Carter had to point out examples of what he meant in practice. In 1980, following the Soviet Union's invasion of Afghanistan, Carter announced that, in protest, no Americans would participate in the Olympic Games scheduled for Moscow. Other Western countries followed suit.

Carter is perhaps most remembered for his mediation that produced the Camp David Accords in 1978 between Israel's Menachem Begin (1913–1992) and Egypt's Anwar Al-Sadat (1918–1981), thereby establishing a practice of presidential peace-making that many succeeding presidents have tried to follow. The Accords involved Egypt's diplomatic recognition of Israel, which in turn returned the Sinai Peninsula to Egypt, and set the stage for recognition of an autonomous Palestinian Authority as a halfway house on the road to becoming a future sovereign Palestinian state.

The impact of Carter's human rights initiative was profound in raising worldwide consciousness about human rights. Scarcely covered by the press before, human rights issues were now catapulted into prominence and have never receded from world attention. However, Carter's failure to address the human rights problems of the murderous Khmer Rouge in Cambodia as well as in Iran under the dictatorial Shah, residues of a Cold War strategy that began decades earlier, underscores the difficulty that he experienced in reorienting American foreign policy from an almost exclusive concern on the Cold War imperative to contain the Soviet Union to a broad concern for human rights throughout the world. Other countries around the world also launched human rights initiatives at around the same time, but they were eclipsed by Carter's bold initiatives.

When Carter left office in 1981, the world would not have been surprised if he were content to fade into obscurity along with other former presidents, most of whom had retired to a life of leisure. Carter, however, redefined the role of a former president in 1982 by setting up an organization that has had a major impact on world affairs – the Carter Center, located at Emory University in Atlanta. Although much of Carter Center activity in the early years consisted of conferences on such subjects as arms control, health policy, human rights, and sustainable development, the former president was later notable for his efforts to build homes, eradicate disease, mediate interstate conflicts, and participate in election observer missions. In 1998, he was the first recipient of the UN Human Rights Prize, and in 2002 he received the Nobel Peace Prize.

ENDING THE COLD WAR

During the Cold War, armies and nuclear weapons were poised for a possible World War III, so efforts to defuse tensions had a high priority on both sides of the so-called Iron Curtain that separated democratic Western Europe from communist

Eastern Europe. Although the Soviet Union floated the idea of a pan-European security conference in 1950, the Western powers were not interested because they believed that Moscow's real aim was to legitimate the Soviet-dominated governments in East Germany and elsewhere in Eastern Europe, where puppet rulers and Soviet troops maintained dominance.

In October 1962, nuclear war seemed imminent when President John Kennedy (1917–1963) was determined to stop missiles, sent by the Soviet Union to Cuba, that might be launched with nuclear warheads. Diplomacy averted the crisis and then paved the way for a détente in East–West relations.

Building on the détente, the Soviet Union again proposed a European security organization. After preparatory talks in 1972, foreign ministers of Western and Eastern Europe met in 1973 to plan for a new organization. In 1975, 33 European states (all but Albania) joined Canada and the United States in signing the **Final Act of the Helsinki Conference**, which set up the Conference on Security and Cooperation in Europe (CSCE). The Soviet bloc signed to gain formal recognition of its European borders, increased trade, and a Western pledge not to oppose communism militarily and politically, while Western states wanted the Soviet bloc to accept human rights monitoring.

One of the guiding principles of CSCE in the 1975 declaration was "respect for human rights and fundamental freedoms, including the freedom of thought, conscience, religion or belief." CSCE then divided the focus into four security "baskets" – politico-military, economic, environmental, and human security. (For more on CSCE, see Chapter 12.)

The fourth basket, human security, focused on efforts to promote democratic processes, the rule of law, and respect for human rights. Thus, CSCE members had the right to question infringements of minority rights. As a result, the Public Group to Assist the Implementation of the Helsinki Accords in the USSR, known as the Moscow Helsinki Group, formed to pressure the Soviet Union. Subsequently, the group prepared more than 150 reports on various issues.

Initially, greater human rights attainments inside the Iron Curtain seemed impossible. But continued discussion of human rights problems bore increasing fruit over time. Thanks to CSCE, humanitarian cases related to family contacts, family reunification, and binational marriage were positively resolved.

Organizations similar to the Moscow Helsinki Group arose throughout various republics of the Soviet Union and Eastern European countries to monitor implementation of the Final Act and to take their leaders to task for falling short. Although such groups received reprisals inside the Iron Curtain, the content of the reports put Moscow on the defensive. The courage of members of the groups provoked citizens to defy authorities, leading to a widespread collapse of respect for dictatorial rule.

In 1984, Mikhail Gorbachëv (1931–) became General Secretary of the Communist Party of the Soviet Union. Because his country was economically bankrupt, he sought reforms to establish a Swedish-type welfare state with greater economic and political freedoms. He also permitted Eastern European countries to act independently of Moscow in liberalizing their economies, though the East German leader, Erich Honecker (1912–1994), refused. In 1989, after Hungary opened travel from the communist East to the West, the Iron Curtain became porous, the Berlin Wall was breached, and the communist experiment in Eastern Europe was over.

HISTORIC EVENT 4.7 THE DISMANTLING OF THE BERLIN WALL (1989–1991)

In 1949, when the four-power military occupation of Germany ended, the Soviet zone was transformed into the German Democratic Republic, known as East Germany, whereas the three zones of Britain, France, and the United States were combined into the Federal Republic of Germany (West Germany). Berlin, which had been divided into four zones, was now entirely surrounded by East Germany, though West Berlin was part of West Germany. Meanwhile, some 2.5 million East Berliners began to move to West Berlin in order to escape communist rule. In 1961, communist East German authorities erected a fence and later a concrete wall around West Berlin, allowing movement only through military checkpoints. Successful illegal escapes numbered only about 300 per year, though East Germany could not block radio and television broadcasts from the West. For years thereafter, communist Czechoslovakia, Hungary, and Poland also prevented East Germans from traveling to West Germany through their countries. Suddenly, in September 1989, Hungary opened its border with Austria. As a result, some 13,000 East German "tourists" began to exit through Austria to West Germany. Czechoslovakia was the conduit of travel from East Germany to Hungary. From early 1989, demonstrations demanding reforms had been held in Leipzig, East Germany, on Monday nights after services at the St Nicholas Lutheran Church. By mid-October, despite crackdowns on demonstrators, the protesters swelled to 250,000 all over East Germany. Accordingly, the Communist Party replaced Party Secretary Erich Honecker (1912–1994) – who had ordered the building of the Berlin Wall – with Egon Krenz (1937–). Krenz allowed East Germans free travel to West Germany, whereupon some East Berliners began to chip away at the Berlin Wall for souvenirs. In mid-1990, East German authorities began to dismantle the wall officially, a task that took slightly more than a year. On October 3, 1990, while the demolition was ongoing, the two parts of Germany were formally reunited.

In 1990, the **Charter of Paris for a New Europe** was adopted at a summit conference of most European countries as well as Canada, the United States, and Asian countries within the Soviet Union. The aim was to formalize CSCE in an "era of democracy, peace, and unity" by establishing permanent institutions. Considered to be the equivalent of the Congress of Vienna of 1815 and the Versailles Peace Conference of 1919, the document in effect served as the peace treaty ending the Cold War.

In 1991, Gorbachëv was ousted in a coup, and his successor, Boris Yeltsin (1931–2007), withdrew Russia from the Soviet Union. The Soviet Union was no more. With the end of the largest monolithic opposition to civil and political human rights, democracies and free markets blossomed in Eastern Europe, though communist governments remained in China, Indochina, North Korea, and Yugoslavia. In 1994, CSCE was renamed the Organization for Security and Cooperation in Europe (OSCE), to further reflect the new interest in assisting transitions from dictatorships to democracies.

With the world no longer divided between controlled and market economies, a global economy emerged. In 1994, the World Trade Organization (WTO) was established to police a world in which tariffs were to be lowered to zero so that trade could flow more freely across international borders. Human rights issues were not a part of the WTO agreement, and the lowering of trade barriers has meant that some First World corporations have increased their share of the world market by outsourcing goods to Third World countries where working conditions violate human rights standards established in treaties sponsored by the International Labor Organization (ILO). WTO, a global organization that would have been impossible during the Cold War, ironically began as a major world institution obstructing human rights progress, though the organization has more recently included human rights concerns in its programming (see Chapter 10).

NONGOVERNMENTAL ORGANIZATIONS

International nongovernmental organizations (NGOs) were crucial in the formation of the League of Nations and the United Nations as well as in the adoption of the Universal Declaration of Human Rights. They have multiplied in number and scope in the contemporary era.

Whereas governments must attend primarily to the interests of their own citizens, many NGOs have a broader perspective. NGOs are particularly active not only in presenting information to intergovernmental human rights organizations but also in providing immediate publicity to serious problems, resulting in speedy responses by the political arms of intergovernmental organizations as well as national governments. Many NGOs have Internet websites with up-to-date information on breaking news.

Humanitarian charitable organizations have operated for centuries. Christian, Jewish, Quaker, and other religious organizations continue to attend to economic and social problems, easing suffering, though their focus has rarely been oriented to the perfection of human rights. From its founding in 1948, the work of the **World Council of Churches** has been particularly prominent; composed of 349 Protestant denominations representing 600 million parishioners, its headquarters is in Geneva. Such charitable organizations have been generally **minimalist** in orientation, attending to those in need of help; in recent years they have been overshadowed by **maximalist** human rights agendas that denounce human rights violations and agitate for corrective action by governments.

Among NGOs that directly try to improve human rights, the oldest was founded in England during 1839 as the British and Foreign Anti-Slavery Society, and is now known as **Anti-Slavery International**. Originally formed to abolish the slave trade, the organization pressured the League of Nations to adopt the Slavery, Servitude,

Forced Labor and Similar Institutions and Practices Convention of 1926, and now combats debt bondage and human trafficking.

The **International Committee of the Red Cross**, perhaps the most famous human rights NGO, was formed in 1864 to provide assistance to wounded soldiers on the battlefield. In Islamic countries, the counterpart is the **Red Crescent**. In 1919, the two merged into an organization now known as the **International Federation of Red Cross and Red Crescent Societies**. Initially the aim was to assist battlefield casualties, but international agreements later empowered the Red Cross to ensure fair treatment for POWs.

As an NGO, the **Nobel Committee** had focused attention on human rights by awarding annual prizes from 1901. The last will and testament of dynamite inventor Alfred Nobel (1833–1896) set up an endowment for the Nobel Foundation to make awards – three for scientific advances, one for literature, and one for peace. (The prize in economics is conferred in his honor but is not paid from his endowment.) The peace prize is awarded to the individual or organization that advances international brotherhood/sisterhood, suppresses or reduces standing armies, or establishes or furthers peace congresses. Prizes with specific attention to civil and political or economic, social, and cultural rights have been awarded on many occasions. The Red Cross, for example, has been so honored.

An organization or person honored with a Nobel Prize has often become more effective than before. Membership in NGOs can boom after receipt of the Nobel Prize, as the enhanced level of recognition can serve to attract contributions from individuals who previously did not know that the organization existed. The next two NGOs to be described have had greatly increased contributions after receiving Nobel Peace Prizes.

Amnesty International, founded in 1961, is perhaps the first NGO to have its existence thrust onto the world stage by winning the Nobel Peace Prize (in 1977). Amnesty International's struggle on behalf of "prisoners of conscience" initially focused on victims of free speech, torture by police and prison authorities, and similar violations of civil rights. Members of the organization, who pay annual contributions, have been encouraged to write thousands of letters to governments in order to secure the release of prisoners wrongfully detained. The first three were written to the capitalist bloc, the socialist bloc, and a Third World country.

Amnesty International is also famous for publishing annual reports on the status of human rights around the world. Based on their 1969 report that the Greek military junta (1967–1974) was systematically using torture against opponents, Amnesty International began to lobby for the International Convention Against Torture and Other Cruel, Inhuman or Degrading Treatment or Punishment, which was finally adopted in 1984.

Another humanitarian aid agency, **Médecins sans Frontières** (MSF), was formed in 1971. MSF has continuing field operations to assist in disasters, epidemics, and such humanitarian crises as the establishment of makeshift refugee camps.

Another important organization today is **Human Rights Watch**, which grew out of the Helsinki Watch, the monitoring arm of the Conference on Security Cooperation in Europe, with initial support from the Ford Foundation. Founded in 1978, Human Rights Watch today has regional suborganizations including Africa, the Americas, Asia, Europe and Central Asia, the Middle East and North Africa, and the United States. The organization identifies ongoing human rights problems, publicizes their existence, and pressures governments and international organizations to act. The focus today is broad – on civil and political rights, economic, social, and cultural rights, and war crimes.

Law professor Aryeh Neier (1937–), the founding director of Human Rights Watch, became the president of the Open Society Institute in 1993. Founded by philanthropist George Soros (1930–), the agenda of the Institute is to offer grants and programs to assist the development of democracy. Current initiatives focus not only on countries, especially in Africa, but also on reforms in such areas as drugs, higher education, media development, and women's issues. The programs operate worldwide, so in 2011 the organization was renamed **Open Society Foundations**.

Many other human rights NGOs have emerged over the years. Their activities are described in detail on their websites, some as **advocacy** (maximalist) organizations goading governments in matters of civil and political rights, others as **operational** (minimalist) organizations working in the field where governments lack resources to meet goals of economic and social rights. NGOs, thus, mobilize individuals around the world to focus on human rights problems that governments might otherwise ignore. Some scholars refer to advocacy campaigns as the **mobilization of shame**, that is, the use of world public opinion to condemn violations and to demand redress for the aggrieved. NGOs push reluctant governments to act. The International Criminal Court (to be discussed in Chapter 10) could not have been established without unrelenting NGO pressure.

With the rise of informational globalization, such media as the Cable News Network (CNN) feature films focusing on human rights, and the Internet provides information about human rights issues, often with video images that galvanize action to redress injustice. One Hollywood-based NGO, the award-winning **Political Film Society**, has been giving annual awards to directors of films that raise consciousness about democracy, human rights, and peaceful methods for resolving conflicts since its formation in 1986.[4]

Initially, most NGOs have focused on specific issues. With time, such NGOs as Amnesty International have transformed themselves into new issue areas, thereby developing what is called the "new rights movement." Those initially focused on civil and political rights have embraced the cause of economic, social, and cultural rights – and vice versa.

The scenario of the "new rights movement" is for smaller national NGOs to identify victims, develop their grievances into formal claims, and then approach multinational NGOs for support. If the larger NGOs agree with the new ideas, they will approach their own governments along with the victims for redress. Once individual states adopt new norms, the larger NGOs will seek to internationalize the norms at multinational conferences. In other words, multinational NGOs serve as gatekeepers in developing human rights today. The strategy has been followed successfully in the case of caste discrimination, children's rights, female genital mutilation, gay rights, and even water rights.

NGOs constitute a major force driving the international human rights agenda in the world today. Many NGOs have consultative status with UN agencies and are represented at international conferences on human rights, pressing their agendas and often serving as transnational social movement organizations. The growth of human rights NGOs has skyrocketed over the past decades, particularly in industrial democracies. Within less developed countries, citizens have increasingly joined human rights NGOs in recent years, especially in countries that ratify human rights agreements, and the result has been increased human rights compliance. Beleaguered groups have often attracted support from NGOs abroad to press claims on their behalf. Some scholars refer to the multitude of organizations as the "global justice movement." Others suggest that NGOs, both those concerning human rights and others, have collectively become a Global Civil Society for global governance.

DISCUSSION TOPIC 4.3 WHICH NONGOVERNMENTAL ORGANIZATIONS ARE MOST EFFECTIVE?

Why are some NGOs more effective than others in dealing with human rights problems? Comparing more prominent with less prominent NGOs, what do their websites reveal about their levels of funding, membership numbers, and their scope of activities in terms of publicity and action in courts or in the field? Should Nobel prizes be awarded to some NGOs that have not yet been recognized by the Nobel Committee?

STRENGTHENING INTERNATIONAL LAW

Hugo Grotius (1583–1645), as noted in Chapter 2, hoped that relations between states could be regulated by law rather than continual armed hostility. His idea bore fruit with the adoption of **treaties** between governments. International practices that traditionally govern relations between states without being encoded in treaty form are known collectively as international **custom**. To determine what constitutes international custom in a court of law, judges refer to writings by distinguished international legal scholars, who have located historical precedents and developed **legal principles**. There is another source of international law: **judicial decisions** in international law courts, which can be cited in future cases as precedents.

Treaties have been viewed as contracts between states, with each state bound to the contract as long as other parties abide by the terms of the agreement. In short, the glue holding treaties together is the good faith of the government officials who negotiate the terms under the principle *pacta sunt servanda* (promises must be kept). Nevertheless, circumstances can change. A treaty can be considered void when unanticipated fundamental conditions change, provided that the affected parties to the treaty agree; the governing principle is *rebus sic stantibus* (things thus standing).

In practical terms, a country that violates a treaty can do so with impunity, since the unorganized world polity has no executive to enforce the terms. Although lawsuits for violations of treaties might be brought in national courts of countries adversely affected, the violating country could fail to appear in the legal proceeding and ignore the legal decision. Before World War II, countries could violate international law without fear of adverse consequences. International law was then mainly concerned with issues of **state** sovereignty – immunities of states, their diplomatic representatives, and their property.

After World War II, the collective impact of the various forces of change has been to advance international law in significant ways. What happened was the recognition that the denial of fundamental human rights to **individuals** has a profound impact on relations between states. Thus, the role of the individual, first recognized by the *Danzig Railway Officials* case, has played an increasing part within international law ever since the Nuremberg trials.

What has happened is that the principle of *jus cogens* (compelling law) has emerged, thanks to efforts by the International Law Commission. Early scholars on international law held that a treaty would be void if contrary to morality or to basic principles of international law, and could not override what was called natural law. When the theory of natural law lost favor, especially during the early years of the Cold War, *jus cogens* was forgotten. In 1969, the **Vienna Convention on the Law of Treaties** revived the concept, now based on the notion that certain principles constitute a higher law with universal validity that is recognized by the vast majority of states as having no exception, even in time of domestic disturbance or war. From 1980, when the Vienna Convention went into effect with sufficient ratifications, there appears to be some consensus based on international custom that at least 10 sets of prohibitions have achieved the status of *jus cogens* with universal jurisdiction:

* Denial of the right of self-determination
* Enforced disappearance
* Genocide, war crimes, and crimes against humanity
* Piracy and terrorism
* Slavery and the slave trade
* Traffic in narcotic drugs
* Traffic in persons for prostitution
* Racial discrimination
* Torture
* Use of force to resolve international disputes (crimes against peace).

Prolonged arbitrary detention, an additional candidate for the status of *jus cogens*, is now being debated among scholars of international law as a possible addition to the list.

The significance of *jus cogens* is that the 10 or more principles can be cited to trump all domestic and international laws throughout the world, such that there is a hierarchy of principles. Treaties stating *jus cogens* principles, thus, cannot be denounced (declared void on the basis of *rebus sic stantibus*). Countries that pass "universal jurisdiction" laws are empowered to try individuals outside their borders for offenses committed on their own citizens. The International Court of Justice may also assert a guilty finding for an infraction of international law based on *jus cogens* if a factual basis can be established. Indeed, such a verdict was reached in *Nicaragua v. United States* regarding actions of the United States to support unprovoked military operations against a Nicaraguan harbor during 1983–1984, though Washington refused to accept the decision.

A distinction can be made between soft and hard international law. **Soft international law** exists where there are no penalties for violations. **Hard international law** involves penalties for violations. Since the end of World War II, the UN has been willing to send troops to stop aggression; national and international courts have placed defendants under arrest for international crimes pending the outcome of trials; and the WTO has authorized sanctions on recalcitrant countries, including the United States. Hence, "hard" international law has clearly advanced.

Thus, as more treaties have been ratified, the international system has developed a more comprehensive constitutional-type framework. International law, in short, plays an increasingly important role in world politics. However, unless defeated in war, the most powerful states have remained largely immune from the punitive enforcement of international legal requirements.

DISCUSSION TOPIC 4.4 DOES INTERNATIONAL LAW HAVE INDEPENDENT MORAL AUTHORITY?

The development of international human rights law began with the Westphalian treaties of 1648. Many agreements since that time have added to the law. International law was originally developed to serve as a set of principles that would govern mutually beneficial relations between sovereign states. The main sources are past international custom as well as treaties and other agreements between states. As long as states are satisfied that their interests are positively affected, international law is likely to be respected. When states mutually believe that conditions have changed, they can formally denounce a treaty. Of course, states could also observe a treaty in the breach, that is, fail to carry out the terms without denouncing the treaty. To what extent are states now likely to observe human rights treaties that they have signed, even when some provisions are contrary to their interests?

TERRORISM IN THE TWENTY-FIRST CENTURY

For centuries, governments have had considerably more power than individual opponents or groups of discontented citizens that have challenged misrule. In quelling unrest, force and threats of force have been used by undemocratic rulers rather than dialogue. **Governmental terrorism**, thus, has served as the spur for the development of individual human rights principles. Studies show that terrorism is least found in strong dictatorships and democracies that respect human rights, but most often plagues weak democracies and loose authoritarian countries.

Governments have branded opponents as **terrorists** when they have employed campaigns of violence against governmental institutions and officials. Systematic assassinations of Russian government leaders in the early years of the twentieth century, for example, were undertaken by self-identified "anarchists."

Toward the end of the twentieth century, terrorist acts extended to hijackings of airplanes in which civilians were victims. In 1983, North Korean agents assassinated 17 South Korean officials while visiting Burma, a terrorist act associated with the unsettled war between the two countries.

When four airplanes were hijacked in the United States on September 11, 2001, by members of an anti-American group known as Al-Qaeda, nearly 3,000 deaths and more than 6,000 injuries were the result. Modern methods of law enforcement and surveillance have been employed by governments to prevent similar incidents, sometimes compromising principles of human rights. The terrorist acts were contrary to international law (see Chapter 7). Today, counterterrorist methods by governments appear to being rolling back established principles of human rights, and preliminary judgments on the matter have raised questions that cloud further progress in extending human rights to peoples around the globe.

DISCUSSION TOPIC 4.5 HOW MANY FREEDOMS SHOULD BE JETTISONED TO ACHIEVE SECURITY FROM TERRORISM?

Surveillance and intelligence-gathering operations are being conducted today to prevent terrorist attacks. To what extent is the right to privacy in jeopardy? How easily can efforts to monitor peaceful organizations, the Internet, and telephone traffic be abused? Is the proper approach to combating terrorism a matter for routine police work or for military officials with a larger agenda?

SUMMARY AND CONCLUSION

The contemporary spread of human rights has come from two sources – the **horizontal** trend, in which countries have been adopting constitutions with human rights provisions, and the **vertical** trend, in which international treaties have been establishing a new set of norms, institutions, and processes favorable to human rights observance. In an ideal world, there would be no international human rights problems. The first line of defense against human rights violations would be inside individual countries, which would prosecute violators at home, provided that there is a human rights infrastructure.

Human rights provisions in various treaties, as promoted by international organizations, often have been ratified by countries only in principle – that is, as mere fine-sounding goals. Thus, observance of the provisions differs from country to country, depending on the institutional framework for compliance.

A country has an adequate **human rights infrastructure** if three elements are present:

- Legal norms establish the parameters of human rights.
- Governmental institutions monitor, publicize, implement, and enforce human rights standards.
- Nongovernmental groups pressure governments to advance the cause of human rights.

The recognition of human rights lags behind human suffering, however, awaiting champions to come to the aid of the victims. In the contemporary period immediately after World War II, the victorious Western countries exercised leadership. During the height of the Cold War in the 1950s, however, the West backed away, eager to support any regime, democratic or dictatorial, which promised to fight communism. In the 1960s, Third World countries, concerned about decolonization in Africa and racism in South Africa, put human rights issues back on the world political agenda at the UN. After South Africa became a democratic country, the landscape of Africa was still littered with repressive governments, and UN agencies began to exert leadership on behalf of human rights.

Whenever the UN has become bogged down in disagreements, nongovernmental organizations have emerged as the strongest force calling for international action on a variety of human rights issues. Today, many observers believe that the most effective stimuli for action on behalf of human rights are NGOs, which provide the energy to enforce human rights treaties by public pressure more than through litigation. According to one formulation, economic globalization is **globalization from above**, which can be tamed by the **globalization from below** that NGOs provide.

The impact of the historical and contemporary forces on behalf of human rights, nevertheless, is most concretely measured by an examination of the provisions of major human rights treaties. Such an analysis appears in Chapters 5–7.

CHAPTER 5

Civil and Political Rights and Crimes Against Humanity

BASIC CIVIL AND POLITICAL RIGHTS

The **International Covenant on Civil and Political Rights** is one of the two basic documents dealing with rights relating to the relationship between people and government. The Covenant was adopted in 1967 along with two Optional Protocols. The **First Optional Protocol** provides that an individual claiming to be a victim of a violation of civil or political rights may file a complaint against a state that signs the protocol. Countries that adopt the **Second Optional Protocol** pledge to abolish the death penalty. (The other basic document, the International Covenant on Economic, Social, and Cultural Rights, is reviewed in Chapter 6.)

The Optional Protocols allow the most enthusiastic countries to go beyond the high-sounding principles in the Covenant by agreeing to specific practices and procedures. The practice of drafting an optional protocol to a human rights treaty, thus, allows for a compromise between countries that are satisfied with general commitments and those that want specific actions.

Not until 1976 were there sufficient formal ratifications for the Covenant to go into effect. Many countries were happy to adopt a mere nonbinding declaration, but the treaty also authorizes a procedure to monitor the human rights performance of any ratifying state. Because some countries took exception to some of the rights stated in the Covenant, their ratifications contained **reservations** – that is, they indicated that they did not approve of the Covenant in its entirety; instead, they would ignore or redefine a few provisions because of domestic political considerations. Most countries tolerated the reservations of other countries as a matter of courtesy, provided that they were not so numerous as to vitiate the spirit of the document.

TABLE 5.1 INTERNATIONALLY RECOGNIZED CIVIL AND POLITICAL RIGHTS

Article	Rights conferred by the International Covenant on Civil and Political Rights
1	Right to self-determination of peoples
2* and 3*	Equality; nondiscrimination
2	Access to legal remedies for rights violations
6*	Right to life; death sentence only for serious crimes meted out by a competent court
6*	Right of persons sentenced to death to seek commutations or pardons
6*	No death penalty for pregnant women or persons under 18
7*	No cruel and inhuman punishment
7*	No subjection to involuntary medical or scientific experimentation
8*	No slavery, slave trade, involuntary servitude, or (except for punishment, military service, or normal government service) forced or compulsory labor
9	Liberty and security of the person; no arbitrary arrest or detention
9	Those arrested must be informed why; right of *habeas corpus* (to be arraigned before a judge)
9	Right to a speedy arraignment and trial
9	Right of release from jail pending trial or sentence for most crimes
10	Segregation of convicted persons and minors in detention from unconvicted persons and adults
10	Right of prisoners to reformation and rehabilitation
11*	No imprisonment for nonpayment of debt
12	Right of movement and choice of residence inside one's country
12	Freedom to travel abroad and to reenter one's country
13	Right of aliens against arbitrary expulsion from a country
14	Right to a fair hearing by a competent, independent, impartial court
14	Presumption of innocence
14	Right to choose a defense attorney; right to adequate time to prepare a defense
14	Right to cross-examine witnesses
14	Protection against self-incrimination
14	Right to a language interpreter without charge
14	Right to appeal convictions and sentences
14	Right to compensation for false conviction
14	Protection against double jeopardy
15*	No *ex post facto* law (criminalizing past actions); lighter sentence after penalties are reduced for a crime
16*	Right to be treated as a person before the law
17	Right to privacy
17	Right to redress from defamation (public humiliation)
18*	Freedom of conscience, religion, thought
18*	Right of parents to provide moral and religious education for their children
19	Right to freedom of expression, ideas, information
20	No propaganda for war allowed
20	No incitement to discrimination, hostility, or violence based on racial or religious hatred
21	Right of peaceful assembly
22	Freedom of association

Continued

TABLE 5.1 (CONTINUED)

Article	Rights conferred by the International Covenant on Civil and Political Rights
23	Protection of the family; right of adults to marry voluntarily and have children
23	Equal rights for spouses
23	Protection of children when marriage is dissolved
24	Right of children to have a name, have their birth registered, and other protections as minors
25	Right to political participation; right to have access to public service
27	Right of minorities to enjoy their own culture, language, and religion

*Rights that cannot be derogated.

Article 4 provides the right of **derogation**, according to which specified rights may be abridged in case of public emergency (acute civil unrest or ongoing war). Thus,

DISCUSSION TOPIC 5.1 DOES THE INTERNATIONAL COVENANT ON CIVIL AND POLITICAL RIGHTS HAVE CONTRADICTORY PROVISIONS?

Freedom of thought is guaranteed by the International Covenant on Civil and Political Rights (Article 18), but the Covenant also bans propaganda for war (Article 20). Are the two provisions in conflict? Is the prohibition justified? Is the right of derogation really needed? Are other provisions contradictory?

some rights have priority over others, notably those dealing with discrimination, civil liberties, and life itself. A state that invokes the right of derogation is supposed to inform the UN Secretary-General of the specific rights being temporarily abridged so that other countries can then notify their citizens in that country about the source of the dangers and the suspension of certain civil and political rights. Although certain provisions cannot be suspended even then (as asterisked in Table 5.1), concern over the unpredictable threat of terrorist acts in the twenty-first century has led many democratic countries to take precautionary measures, such as 24 hour Internet and satellite surveillance that undermine expectations of privacy. Totalitarian governments, such as China and the Soviet Union, often equated civilian protests with terrorist acts to justify restricting human rights. The continuing threat of terrorist attacks challenges industrial democracies to avoid totalitarian temptations.

Among the civil and political rights enumerated in the International Covenant on Civil and Political Rights, the first to be mentioned is the right of self-determination. However, no path for self-determination is specified, so the statement can best be understood as a reiteration of the Westphalian concept of sovereignty in which every government can determine what to do vis-à-vis its people. The very identification of a "minority" people within a state may be challenged by the dominant group, as there is no right of secession. One of the most persistent demands for self-determination, which involves the peoples of Western Sahara, remains unfulfilled because Morocco insists that the "self" must include not only former Western Saharans living in Morocco but also Moroccans who moved to Western Sahara.

Kurds, who live inside the borders of Iraq, Iran, Syria, and Turkey, are the largest ethnic group in the world without a nation-state of their own. The Kurdish case is an example of **irredentism**, that is, the desire to unite peoples living in different states yet with similar cultural traditions into a single state. A future Pushtunistan, for example, would include Pushtu speakers from southern Afghanistan and western Pakistan.

VOTING RIGHTS

If there is a right of self-determination, there must be a right to vote. The establishment of voting rights enjoys a long history. After universal adult male suffrage was established by many countries during the nineteenth century, the suffragette movement agitated for female suffrage, which still lags behind in some countries. The International Covenant on Civil and Political Rights lists the right to vote in Article 25. Some observers believe that the right to vote is prior to all other rights because those elected to office by voters are empowered to extend, implement, and monitor human rights. And for voting to be meaningful, there must be freedom of assembly, association, and speech.

The **Convention on the Political Rights of Women**, adopted in 1952, urges universal female participation in politics, not just in voting. Some countries, notably India in consideration of the "untouchable" caste, reserve a certain number of seats in parliament for minorities, but there is no international agreement regarding the practice. Although the definition of "adult" varies from country to country, the **International Convention on the Rights of the Child** of 1989 defines 18 as the age of adulthood unless a country designates an earlier age. Accordingly, the international standard is that voting rights apply to those who are at least 18 years of age. In some countries (New Zealand and Uruguay), noncitizen legal residents are allowed to vote, both in their home and host countries. In Australia, voting is compulsory; nonvoters must appear before a judge to explain their absence and pay a fine.

Some persons otherwise qualified to vote, such as prisoners, encounter barriers to voting. Elections with a single candidate or party on the ballot make the right to vote meaningless. In 1996, the UN Committee on Human Rights issued **General Comments on ICCPR Article 25**, with the following guidelines:

- Restrictions on voting, such as exclusion of those with "mental incapacity," should be based on "objective and reasonable criteria."
- Government should take measures to overcome such difficulties as illiteracy, language barriers, poverty, or impediments to freedom of movement.
- Requirements about nomination dates, fees, or deposits should be reasonable and not discriminatory.

- Interference with registration or voting as well as intimidation or coercion of voters should be prohibited.
- Elections should be held at regular intervals and voting by secret ballot.

The first election observed for impartiality was the plebiscite in 1857 to determine whether Moldavia and Wallachia wanted to be united into a new country. Monitoring was done by the great powers of the day (Austria, Britain, France, Ottoman Empire, Prussia, Russia). As a result, the United Principalities of Romania was formed.

The UN first monitored elections in postwar Germany and Korea. As decolonization proceeded in the 1960s, the UN supervised elections upon the granting of independence, notably in Africa. The independence elections are known as "first generation" vote observations. Otherwise, the practice of election observation was rare until after the end of the Cold War. Today, in the "second generation" of election observation, which began with the observation of the Namibia election of 1989 and the Cambodian election of 1991, the UN and many organizations have sent observers to determine whether elections in burgeoning or weak democracies are "free and fair." They now operate in conjunction with the UN's **Declaration of Principles for International Election Observation** of 2005.

AGREEMENTS DEALING WITH THE ADMINISTRATION OF JUSTICE

Most provisions in the International Covenant on Civil and Political Rights use terms that are left undefined, so subsequent agreements have been adopted to provide clarification. Innocent persons are sometimes placed on trial on trumped-up charges. To assure that rights are uniformly respected at home and abroad, many agreements are concerned with the administration of justice (Table 5.2).

TABLE 5.2   TREATIES ON THE ADMINISTRATION OF JUSTICE

Adopted	Agreements and treaties	In force
1955	Standard Minimum Rules for the Treatment of Prisoners	
1956	ICPO-INTERPOL Constitution	1956
1963	Protocol No. 2 to the Convention for the Protection of Human Rights and Fundamental Freedoms, Conferring upon the European Court of Human Rights Competence to Give Advisory Opinions	1970
1975	Inter-American Convention on the Legal Regime of Powers of Attorney to Be Used Abroad	1976
1977	European Agreement on the Transmission of Applications for Legal Aid	1977
2001	• Additional Protocol	2002
1979	Code of Conduct for Law Enforcement Officials	
1980	Convention on International Access to Justice	1988
1982	Principles of Medical Ethics Relevant to the Role of Health Personnel, Particularly Physicians, in the Protection of Prisoners and Detainees Against Torture and Other Cruel, Inhuman or Degrading Punishment	

Continued

TABLE 5.2   (CONTINUED)

Adopted	Agreements and treaties	In force
1984	Convention Against Torture and Other Cruel, Inhuman or Degrading Treatment or Punishment	1987
2002	• Optional Protocol	2006
1983	Protocol No. 6 to the Convention for the Protection of Human Rights and Fundamental Freedoms Concerning the Abolition of the Death Penalty	1985
1984	Safeguards Guaranteeing Protection of the Rights of Those Facing the Death Penalty	
1985	Basic Principles on the Independence of the Judiciary	
1985	European Convention for the Prevention of Torture and Inhuman or Degrading Treatment or Punishment	1989
1985	Guidelines for Action on Children in the Criminal Justice System	
1985	Inter-American Convention to Prevent and Punish Torture	1987
1985	UN Standard Minimum Rules for the Administration of Juvenile Justice (Beijing Rules)	
1989	Principles on the Effective Prevention and Investigation of Extra-Legal, Arbitrary and Summary Executions	
1989	Second Optional Protocol to the International Covenant on Civil and Political Rights, Aiming at the Abolition of the Death Penalty	1991
1990	Basic Principles for the Treatment of Prisoners	
1990	Basic Principles on the Role of Lawyers	
1990	Basic Principles on the Use of Force and Firearms by Law Enforcement Officials	
1990	Guidelines for the Prevention of Juvenile Delinquency (Riyadh Rules)	
1990	Guidelines on the Role of Prosecutors	
1990	Protocol to the American Convention on Human Rights to Abolish the Death Penalty	1991
1990	Rules for the Protection of Juveniles Deprived of Their Liberty	
1990	Standard Minimum Rules for Non-Custodial Measures (Tokyo Rules)	
1996	Inter-American Convention Against Corruption	1997
1997	Declaration of Basic Principles of Justice for Victims of Crime and Abuse of Power	
1998	Body of Principles for the Protection of All Persons Under Any Form of Detention or Imprisonment	
1999	Civil Law Convention on Corruption (Council of Europe)	
1999	Criminal Law Convention on Corruption (Council of Europe)	
2000	Optional Protocol on the Sale of Children, Child Prostitution and Child Pornography	2002
2000	Principles on the Effective Investigation and Documentation of Torture and Other Cruel, Inhuman or Degrading Treatment	
2002	Protocol No. 13 to the Convention for the Protection of Human Rights and Fundamental Freedoms, Concerning the Abolition of the Death Penalty in All Circumstances	2003
2003	UN Convention Against Corruption	2005
2003	African Union Convention on Preventing and Combating Corruption	
2006	International Convention for the Protection of All Persons from Enforced Disappearance	2010

Note: Bulleted agreements, here and in subsequent tables, are additional to the treaties listed immediately above.

Perhaps the most prominent is the **Convention Against Torture and Other Cruel, Inhuman or Degrading Treatment or Punishment** of 1984, two years after principles of medical ethics were adopted to deal with the issue of torture. More stringent agreements on torture were adopted in 1985 by American and European countries. After a UN General Assembly statement of principles on investigation of torture in 2000, the convention's Optional Protocol of 2002 was drafted to authorize visits to places of detention in order to ensure that torture is not taking place, including both physical and psychological "white torture" that does not leave marks. On that basis, UN personnel have demanded to visit the prison at the US naval base at Guantánamo Bay.

Responding to the disappearances of members of the opposition in Argentina's "dirty war" (see Historic Event 5.1) and during the reign of Augusto Pinochet (1915–2006) in Chile, the **International Convention for the Protection of all Persons from Enforced Disappearance** was adopted in 2006. Other agreements deal with crime victims, detainees, disappearances, extrajudicial punishment, juvenile justice, and the death penalty. Guidelines for the role of judges, lawyers, police, prison officials, and prosecutors have also been adopted.

TABLE 5.3   **TREATIES RELATING TO UNEQUAL CIVIL AND POLITICAL RIGHTS**

Adopted	Agreements	In force
1925	Slavery, Servitude, Forced Labor and Similar Institutions and Practices Convention	1927
1953	• Protocol Amending the Slavery Convention Signed at Geneva on 25 September 1925	1953
1930	Convention Concerning Forced or Compulsory Labor	1932
1951	Convention Relating to the Status of Refugees	1954
1966	• Protocol Relating to the Status of Refugees	1967
1952	Convention on the Political Rights of Women	1954
1954	Convention Relating to the Reduction of Statelessness	1975
1954	Convention Relating to the Status of Stateless Persons	1960
1956	Convention on the Abolition of Slavery, the Slave Trade, and Institutions and Practices Similar to Slavery	1957
1957	Convention Concerning the Protection and Integration of Indigenous and Other Tribal and Semi-Tribal Populations in Independent Countries	1959
1965	International Convention on the Elimination of All Forms of Racial Discrimination	1969
1969	African Union Convention Governing the Specific Aspects of Refugee Problems in Africa	1974
1973	International Convention on the Suppression and Punishment of the Crime of Apartheid	1976
1978	Declaration on Race and Racial Prejudice	
1979	Convention on the Elimination of All Forms of Discrimination Against Women	1981
1999	• Optional Protocol	2000
1981	Declaration on the Elimination of All Forms of Intolerance and of Discrimination Based on Religion or Belief	

Continued

TABLE 5.3   (CONTINUED)

Adopted	Agreements	In force
1985	Declaration on the Human Rights of Individuals Who Are Not Nationals of the Country in Which They Live	
1990	International Convention on the Protection of the Rights of All Migrant Workers and Members of Their Families	2003
1992	Agreement Establishing the Fund for the Development of the Indigenous Peoples of Latin America and the Caribbean	1993
1992	Declaration on the Rights of Persons Belonging to National or Ethnic, Religious and Linguistic Minorities	
1993	Principles Relating to the Status of National Institutions (The Paris Principles)	
1993	Vienna Declaration and Program of Action	
1996	General Comments on ICCPR Article 25 (concerning children)	
1997	Treaty of Amsterdam	1999
1998	Declaration on the Right and Responsibility of Individuals, Groups, and Organs of Society to Promote and Protect Universally Recognized Human Rights and Fundamental Freedoms	
1999	Inter-American Convention on the Elimination of All Forms of Discrimination Against Persons with Disabilities	2001
2000	Protocol No. 12 to the Convention for the Protection of Human Rights and Fundamental Freedoms	2005
2001	Durban Declaration and Program of Action	
2005	Declaration of Principles for International Election Observation	
2006	Convention on the Rights of Persons with Disabilities	2008
2006	• Optional Protocol to the Convention on the Rights of Persons with Disabilities	2008
2007	Treaty of Lisbon	2009
2009	African Union Convention for the Protection and Assistance of Internally Displaced Persons in Africa (Kampala Convention)	

■ AGREEMENTS DEALING WITH UNEQUAL TREATMENT

Many agreements focus on unequal treatment (Table 5.3). One of the most serious problems after World War II was discrimination against refugees. Even before the International Covenant was adopted, the mistreatment of refugees was so critical that a **Convention Relating to the Status of Refugees** was adopted in 1954 and reformulated in 1960. Subsequent agreements have specified the rights of aliens, asylum seekers, and stateless persons in order to mitigate discrimination against them. Today, more than 200 millions live outside their countries of origin, including 14 million refugees; many of the rest are skilled or unskilled economic migrants, such as farm workers and nurses. What makes someone a **refugee** is a fear of suffering human rights violations if returned to the home country. What makes a person **stateless** is the denial of citizenship in the country of birth, sometimes on account of chaos in times of civil war, and failure to acquire citizenship in the country of new residence.

There is a another type of refugee, not mentioned by the treaty – **internally displaced persons** (IDPs) – who are in their native country but are unable to remain where they have previously been able to live, through natural disasters or ongoing civil war or government oppression. Today, there are 26 million IDPs, many due to climate-related disasters.

COURT CASE 5.1 *BROWN V. BOARD OF EDUCATION OF TOPEKA* (1954)

After the American Civil War (1861–1865), constitutional amendments granted citizenship, equality, and voting rights to former slaves, to be enforced by the federal occupation troops in the states that seceded. In 1877, however, federal troops were withdrawn from the states where most former slaves lived, and a system of institutionalized discrimination and segregation of the races soon emerged in those states. During World War II, those of Japanese ancestry living in the Pacific Coast states were forced to live in relocation camps in the interior of the United States. This was a use of executive power that the Supreme Court upheld in 1944 as constitutional in *Korematsu v. United States* (323US214), which argued that racial separation was only legal if a potential threat existed to national security. But the practice of segregating the use of drinking fountains, attendance at schools, and similar practices did not violate national security, so the requirement in Topeka, Kansas, that black students could only attend schools with other blacks was contested in court by lawyers on behalf of Oliver L. Brown (1918–1961) and 12 parents of 20 black children in 1951. After an appeal of the case, the US Supreme Court ruled in 1954 that racial segregation in schools was "inherently illegal." In 1955, the Supreme Court ordered all schools districts in the United States to desegregate "forthwith." The ruling was assumed by some to have applicability beyond the field of education, and a civil rights movement emerged to ban all forms of racial discrimination and segregation. A federal law to that effect finally passed in 1964, a voting rights act was adopted in 1965, and racial discrimination in housing was banned in 1968.

Although not considered refugees, some persons live confined within their own countries. Whereas the end of racial segregation in the United States came about through court and legislative action, an even more stringent form of racial separation was *apartheid*, as adopted in South Africa, where the practice was to cordon off black Africans into separate communities and require passport-type documents ("pass books") for entry into "white" South Africa. The **International Convention on the Elimination of all Forms of Racial Discrimination** of 1965, signed primarily under pressure from African states, criminalized *apartheid* so that anyone responsible for racial separation in South Africa who traveled abroad could be arrested and tried in the court of any country ratifying the treaty. In 1978, the UN Educational, Scientific, and Cultural Organization (UNESCO) adopted the **Declaration on Race and Racial Prejudice** to put further pressure on South Africa.

Upon taking office as prime minister in 1990, transformational leader, F. W. De Klerk (1936–), announced that he would ask parliament to rescind the various laws establishing racial separation. That year, Nelson Mandela (1918–), the major anti-*apartheid* leader, was released from prison after 27 years of incarceration. South Africa's *apartheid* was finally repealed in 1994. In 2001, the **Durban Declaration and Program of Action** at the World Conference Against Racism identified a post-*apartheid* agenda to combat discrimination against ethnic, linguistic, racial, and religious minorities.

Discrimination based on long-held prejudice is difficult to stop. Accordingly, the concept of **affirmative action** emerged as a way to give special attention to minorities in employment decisions. As the concept evolved, employers have been required to desegregate their employees so that members of different groups work side by side. The principle was first applied to racial segregation in the United States but later to diversification on the basis of gender or sex. Some employers at first pretended to respond to the affirmative action requirement with "tokenism" – hiring just one black or one woman on the job. The concept then developed into a formula that appeared to resemble hiring by quotas. To avoid both tokenism and quotas, a quantitative methodology developed:

- Government statistics are first compiled of percentages of all those already qualified for various occupations by race and sex in a metropolitan area.
- Employers are supposed to set goals for new hiring of qualified members of minority groups and women so that their workforce resembles the overall statistical pattern for the metropolitan region as a whole and send statistics on their actual hiring and their goals to government agencies.
- Government monitors, who have the power to recommend termination of contracts of recalcitrant employers, then check to see whether contractors are indeed diversifying their workforce.

At first, affirmative action applied to overall hiring, but later the concept was applied to specific occupations. Even later, affirmative action was extended from hiring of new workers to wages, promotion, on-the-job training, and fringe benefits of workers. Many employers resisted such regulation, but those desiring government contracts were required to comply. No court case has ever declared that affirmative action in employment is contrary to the American Constitution. Some employers did not follow the methodology carefully and were successfully sued by nonminority workers for having inept affirmative action plans. Affirmative action has succeeded in dramatically diversifying the American workforce, and other countries have taken up the concept.

The International Convention for the Elimination of Racial Discrimination of 1965 specifically recommends affirmative action, and the Convention on the Elimination of All Forms of Discrimination Against Women of 1979 supports

TABLE 5.4   CORE TREATIES ON CIVIL AND POLITICAL RIGHTS

Adopted	Treaties	In force
1965	International Convention on the Elimination of All Forms of Racial Discrimination	1969
1966	International Covenant on Civil and Political Rights	1976
1966	• Optional Protocol 1	1976
1989	• Optional Protocol 2	1991
1984	Convention Against Torture and Other Cruel, Inhuman or Degrading Treatment or Punishment	1987
2002	• Optional Protocol to the Convention …	2006
1990	International Convention on the Protection of the Rights of All Migrant Workers and Members of Their Families	2003

affirmative action on the basis of gender or sex. The question has therefore arisen when to stop affirmative action, which presumably is a temporary program until full diversification in employment is attained. That question has not yet been resolved.

Racial discrimination issues have stimulated agreements involving several classes of people. Migrants are covered by the **International Convention on the Protection of the Rights of All Migrant Workers and Members of Their Families** of 1990, which is considered by the UN Office of the High Commission for Human Rights to be one of the "core international human rights instruments" (Table 5.4).

The convention on migrant workers, which covers both their civil and political rights and their economic and social rights, raises the question whether there is a right to migrate, that is, a requirement beyond the right to travel within the International Covenant on Civil and Political Rights that confers an obligation for all countries to allow entry to citizens of other countries. Sovereign states currently claim the right to keep borders closed on the basis of criminal history and health status, but they cannot refuse persons on the basis of race or sex in view of other international agreements discussed below.

In the contemporary world of porous trade borders, a right to migrate implies a cosmopolitan claim for universal citizenship, contrary to the Westphalian lionization of national sovereignty. The European Union, for example, recognizes the right to migrate throughout member countries, but migrants have been identified in some quarters as posing security threats. The Roma of Europe, who have migrated from country to country since their arrival in Europe from Northwest India in the fourteenth century, became citizens of the European Union in 1993, when the Maastricht Treaty went into force. Nevertheless, discrimination against the Roma is pervasive.

The treaty provides no special remedy for dozens of cases of recent **forced migration** (such as the expulsion of Cuban prisoners to the United States in 1980) or the threat of forced migration (Libya's threats from 2004 to allow massive out-migration from Africa in order to get European Union sanctions lifted). Of course, the slave trade was the world's largest case of forced migration.

In an informal sense, world citizenship has been conferred upon those who use the Internet, buy products from other countries, or protest human rights injustices abroad. But many millions of persons have moved from country to country without going through proper channels. Known colloquially as "illegal aliens" or as "informal citizens," they enjoy many privileges of citizenship. Some are students, overstaying student visas. Many are desired by employers, either because they work for less pay than citizens or because there is a shortage of workers with their qualifications. An amnesty for their undocumented status might clear up the problem, but political pressures from citizens lessen that possibility. Lacking legal status, they rarely object to human rights violations on their own behalf.

Among other victims of discrimination, the **Convention on the Rights of Persons with Disabilities** of 2006 came 30 years after the UN General Assembly first adopted a declaration on the subject. However, the **Declaration on the Rights of Persons Belonging to National or Ethnic, Religious and Linguistic Minorities** of 1992 has not been followed up by a corresponding treaty.

Implementation is the key to fulfillment of human rights. The UN General Assembly has established procedural guidelines and has encouraged member states to set up their own human rights agencies in **Principles Relating to the Status of National Institutions** and in the **Declaration on the Rights and Responsibility of Individuals, Groups, and Organs of Society to Promote and Protect Universally Recognized Human Rights and Fundamental Freedoms**. The former asks member states to set up human rights monitoring agencies. The latter encourages states to cooperate with civil society organizations that seek to advance human rights.

EFFECT OF THE TREATIES

Some observers claim that human rights treaties are worthless because many countries sign and later ratify without the slightest intention of implementing provisions. The symbolic gesture of becoming a party to a human rights treaty, in short, costs nothing and may give a false impression about widespread voluntary compliance. Indeed, some of the most heinous violators have ratified human rights treaties while continuing to violate human rights. Compliant countries are usually unwilling to embarrass noncompliant countries by filing complaints so that they will not jeopardize friendly economic relations.

Research on the before–after effects of ratifying human rights treaties demonstrates that genuine progress does occur after a government ratifies.[1] Countries that become parties to human rights treaties are more likely to adopt implementing legislation and to experience a reduction in violations. The effect, as may be expected, is least pronounced in dictatorships that suppress rising democratic aspirations. There is only a modest increase in human rights observance among stable democracies, which may already have reached an asymptote in human rights observance. Dramatic effects of human rights treaties have been felt in regimes intermediate between dictatorships, on the one hand, and democracies, on the other hand. Intermediate regimes often have two more political forces, one of which is a strong supporter of human rights; once in power, the most progressive political party will seek to sign and to ratify the newest human rights treaties in order to lock in gains that otherwise might not be granted when the more conservative party takes office again. The effect is most pronounced in regard to children's rights, civil and political rights, women's rights, and the abolition of torture. In short, the adoption of human rights treaties has had a profound effect on voluntary compliance around the world.

TRANSITIONING FROM AN ERA OF HUMAN RIGHTS HORRORS

Some countries have endured horrendous eras of human rights violations by despicable regimes but have later turned the corner due to "people power" demonstrations, revolutions, transformational leaders, or other progressive political change. Victims of the former regime may justly feel that they should be compensated for their losses by those who perpetrated abuses, but the pursuit of justice may end up as an exercise in revenge that can delegitimize a new regime. For example, the philosophies that led to the guillotining of the royal family during the French Revolution morphed into a reign of terror that later adversely affected early proponents of the revolution. Similarly, Chinese and Russian revolutionary leaders proceeded to liquidate class enemies in order to eliminate opposition, but later some of the early supporters of the revolutions were also executed as rivals for political power.

HISTORIC EVENT 5.1 ARGENTINA'S "DIRTY WAR" (1976–1983)

Upon the death of Argentine President Juan Perón (1895–1974), his spouse, Isabel Martínez de Perón (1931–), took office. In 1976, she and the democratically elected government of Argentina were ousted by a military junta on the pretext of eliminating communist influence in the country. Subsequently, from 10,000 to 30,000 left-wing-leaning persons were arrested, detained in secret locations, and tortured. Their ultimate whereabouts was unknown, as some were executed and buried at sea. In 1977, mothers of those who had disappeared began to gather after mass in the Plaza de Mayo outside the Buenos Aires cathedral to protest the disappearances by wearing white scarves. As one side of the square contains the presidential palace, the weekly Thursday protests were a direct challenge to the government. Soon, Amnesty International and the United Nations applied pressure on the government to account for those who had disappeared. In 1982, the government sought to annex the nearby British-held Falkland (Malvinas) Islands, but Britain handed Argentina such a defeat that in 1983 the government granted a restoration of civil liberties, presidential elections were held, and the military leaders allowed Raúl Alfonsín (1927–2009) to take office as civilian president on condition that those in power from 1976–1983 would receive a blanket amnesty for any wrongdoing during their tenure in office. After Néstor Kirchner (1950–2010) was elected to succeed President Alfonsín, in 2003, he persuaded the legislature to revoke the amnesty laws for military officers accused of torture and assassinations. In 2005, the Argentine Supreme Court agreed that the amnesty was void. Those responsible for the "dirty war" were then brought to justice.

When serious violations are occurring inside a country, the population may be so mortified that opponents remain passive. Alternatively, dissidents can attempt to secure attention from abroad so as to obtain verbal, judicial, economic, or military pressure on their governments. Several lessons have been learned from the experience of massive human rights violations in Argentina and other countries. To bring an end to human rights abuses, the following strategy applies:

- First, victims must talk to one another and act in a subtle manner so that the repressive authorities will not be able to find a convenient way to repress the group that wants to protest.
- The loose aggregation of protesters should next form an organization to coordinate activities. Documenting individual cases is one of the most important activities for any such group, as did *Nunca Mas* during Argentina's "dirty war." Later, such documentation can be used as evidence in subsequent court actions.
- The group should seek international recognition and even backing from such organizations as Amnesty International and Human Rights Watch.
- Using public statements, the objective should be to shame those in power with facts and to have pressure exerted from the outside, hoping that the rulers will be so mortified that they will agree to pass the baton of power, as when Nelson Mandela was released from prison in 1990 and was voted president of South Africa four years later.

TRANSITIONAL JUSTICE AND TRUTH COMMISSIONS

Events of the 1980s and 1990s brought the concept of transitional justice to considered attention. Brutal dictatorships were ousted in Latin America in the 1980s, and the end of the Soviet Union ushered in new regimes in Eastern Europe in the 1990s. In both cases, the puzzle was how new leaders would deal with the horrific past, as many of those associated with past repression were still alive. How, then, should a government which succeeds a regime that grossly violated human rights temper the desire for justice with the need to build legitimacy?

There are several alternatives:

- One strategy is to **do nothing**. After the American Revolution, prosecution of Americans who sided with the British was not on the political agenda; the healing of divisions was considered of paramount importance to unify the country.
- There can be a *pro forma* **trial** of former leaders. After the Khmer Rouge regime was expelled from Cambodia in 1979, the new government put former leaders on trial *in absentia*, but the exercise was merely a formality because none of those accused of human rights violations was in custody, and there was little deliberation before a sentence was passed.
- A **show trial** of a few top leaders may also be attempted to make an example of a violator. The televised proceedings of the trial of Saddam Hussein (1937–2006) for crimes against humanity in Iraq provide a recent instance. Show trials, however, can

be shams as former leaders are railroaded without due process, as in the Moscow Trials of 1936–1938 to eliminate opponents of Josef Stalin (1878–1953).

- An **amnesty** may be granted; that is, those who committed human rights violations may be granted immunity from prosecution, as when the military regime in Argentina stepped down in 1983, allowing free elections to select a new government, provided that a blanket amnesty was granted to those who may have perpetrated human rights abuses and other crimes. Nevertheless, an amnesty might subsequently be rescinded.
- **Prosecutions** may bring human rights violators to justice, either directly in **courts** or through complaints filed with **human rights commissions** or the International Criminal Court.
- A novel approach is to organize a **truth commission**, in which evidence is compiled of the crimes of the former regime; those accused of crimes are sometimes asked to confess with or without an assurance of amnesty. A primary aim is to record an ugly period in the country's history as an example never to be repeated.

Amnesties, reparations, and trials of violators have frequently been used. Lustration, the firing of all persons associated with the former regime, was employed in Eastern European countries that overthrew Communist Party dominance. But the most pathbreaking development is the rise of truth commissions.

A **truth commission**, thus, seeks to compile an objective account of former wrongdoing on a case-by-case basis, whereas a **human rights commission** deals with individual complaints or ongoing patterns of misconduct to reach a specific remedy. Whereas human rights commissions seek **retributive justice**, truth commissions seek **restorative** or **transitional justice**. In the former case, the idea is to reset reality before the crimes occurred; the latter type uses truth commissions to build a more perfect polity and society.

In a sense, the war crimes trials at Nuremberg and Tokyo were designed to serve a transitional role between the ongoing military occupation of Germany and Japan, respectively, and the emergence of democracies in both countries. However, the domestic populations in both countries resented "victor's justice," and the effort to punish war criminals stopped in the realization that both countries would be needed as Cold War allies. The postwar occupations of both countries did, however, enable democratic institutions to rebuild themselves. Both cases have been invoked as paradigms of transitional justice, a term not used at that time, but their applicability is marred because external powers were far too dominant.

Thus far, governments have sponsored more than 50 official truth commissions (Table 5.5). The El Salvador truth commission, the first to be set up with UN assistance, documented death squad assassinations, disappearances, extrajudicial executions, and peasant massacres during the 1980s, when a right-wing government sought to suppress what they perceived to be Marxists influenced by liberation theology. Thereafter, the UN sought to set up truth commissions in peace settlements after civil wars.[2] Most truth commissions have begun without UN assistance.

Some of the bodies are called "truth and reconciliation" commissions. In the South African case, a Commission of Inquiry was set up before the Truth and Reconciliation Commission so that testimony by victims at the latter body about human rights violations under *apartheid* would deal with healing rather than fact

TABLE 5.5 OFFICIAL TRUTH COMMISSIONS

Country	Founded	Era covered	Report issued
Uganda	1974	1971–1974	1975
Bolivia	1982–1984	1967–1982	None (disbanded)
Zimbabwe	1983	1983	None
Argentina	1983–1984	1976–1983	1985
Uruguay	1985	1973–1982	1985
Uganda	1986–1995	1962–1986	None
Philippines	1986	1972–1986	None
Nepal	1990–1991	1961–1990	1994
Chile	1990–1991	1973–1990	1991
Chad	1991–1992	1982–1990	1992
Ethiopia	1992	1974–1989	1994
Germany	1992–1994	1949–1989[a]	1994
El Salvador	1992–1993	1980–1991	1993
Honduras	1992	1980–1993	1993
Rwanda	1992–1993	1990–1992	1993
Sri Lanka	1994–1997	1988–1994	1997
Burundi	1995	1993	2002
Haïti	1995–1996	1991–1994	1996
Burundi	1995–1996	1993–1995	1996
South Africa	1995–2000	1960–1994	1998–2003
Ecuador	1996–1997	1979–1996	None (disbanded)
Guatemala	1997–1999	1962–1996	1999
Nigeria	1999–2001	1966–1999	2002
Rwanda	1999	1999–[b]	Annual reports
The Ivory Coast	2000	2000	None
South Korea	2000	1975–1987	2003
Uruguay	2000–2001	1973–1985	2003
Algeria	2001	1992–1999	2005
Grenada	2001	1976–1991	2006
Perú	2001	1980–2000	2003
Panamá	2001–2002	1968–1989	2002
Yugoslavia	2002	1991–2001	None (disbanded)
Indonesia	2002	1974–1999	2005
East Timor	2002	1974–1999	2006
Sierra Leone	2002	1991–1999	2004
Ghana	2002	1966–2001	2004
Chile	2003	1973–1990	2004; 2005
Chile	2010–2011	1973–1990	Work ongoing
Central African Republic	2003	1960–2003	2003
Congo, Dem. Rep. of	2003	1960–2003	2007
Paraguay	2003	1954–1989	2008
Morocco	2004	2004–2005	2005
Indonesia	2005	1966–1998	None (disbanded)

Continued

TABLE 5.5   (CONTINUED)

Country	Founded	Era covered	Report issued
Indonesia–East Timor	2005	1999	2008
Liberia	2005	1979–2003	2009
South Korea	2005	1910–1993	2009
Ecuador	2007	1984–1998	2010
Canada	2008	1857–1996	Interim report 2012
Kenya	2008	1963–2008	Work ongoing
Mauritius	2008	1638–2010	2011
Solomon Islands	2008	1998–2003	Work ongoing
Honduras	2010	2009	2011
Sri Lanka	2010	2002	2011
Brazil	2011	1946–1988	Work ongoing
Argentina	2013	1994	Work ongoing

[a] Concerning East Germany only.

[b] Made permanent in 2002.

Principal sources: Brahm (2004), based on Hayner (1994, 2001) and Bronkhorst (1995); www.usip.org/library/truth.html.

finding. Conducted in a nonadversarial and sometimes nonpublic manner, truth and reconciliation commissions may encourage perpetrator and victim to meet each other at a session where psychological wounds can heal on all sides. Truth commissions that have been victim-centered, relying on victim narratives, have been the most successful in enabling the societies to transcend their past. Although amnesty is often a condition of setting up a commission, the South African body was empowered to grant amnesty as a reward for public testimony, whereas El Salvador passed an amnesty law after the commission's report became public.

Although national and international courts are often too adversarial to handle the task of reconciliation, truth commissions may also exist alongside tribunals that prosecute those who are named but have not come forward to confess their wrongdoing; examples are Timor-Leste and Sierra Leone. Usually, however, the commissions make recommendations for subsequent action. Evidence from the Chilean commission, including the names of those who disappeared or were killed during 1973–1990, was introduced in the investigation of former President Augusto Pinochet, who stepped down as president on condition that he would be granted amnesty for any future prosecution of offenses committed during his reign. (Pinochet pioneered the use of "disappearance" as a tool of repression.)

Truth commissions also have been created by nongovernmental organizations. In one case, the government of Brazil turned down a proposal for a truth commission, whereupon Archbishop Paulo Evaristo (1921–) of São Paulo organized one instead. The UN Commission for Historical Clarification, which worked from 1996–1999 to document 626 massacres from 1962–1996 committed in Guatemala – mostly by government forces against "internal enemies" (academics, Catholics, communists,

Mayans, and other dissenters) – was preceded by a report in 1998 by the Catholic Archdiocese of Guatemala.[3]

Some nongovernmental organizations have arisen from truth commissions. The New York-based International Center for Transitional Justice was founded in 2001 to provide consultants who can assist countries in establishing truth commissions. The Institute for Justice and Reconciliation, which arose in Capetown, South Africa, during 2000 to focus on problems in Africa, has assisted at the community level in Nigeria and Uganda. Both seek transitional justice – that is, to close a previous era of human rights suffering so that the new regime can put past violations behind and move beyond.

Post-colonial truth commissions serve the purpose of documentation. In the case of Timor-Leste, the aim was to identify those responsible for misdeeds, but Indonesia refused to prosecute them. One of South Korea's two truth commissions sought to document human rights abuses that occurred while the country was a colony of Japan. Seoul continues to be annoyed that Tokyo has never apologized or made amends for its misrule and is continually offended by what is perceived as an imperious Japanese foreign policy. The report, accordingly, has had no effect on Tokyo.

Some truth commissions have revealed more information than anticipated, resulting in pressure to prosecute those who assumed that they were being granted

HISTORIC EVENT 5.2 INDONESIA AND TIMOR-LESTE ESTABLISH A TRUTH COMMISSION (2002)

The island of Timor, colonized by Portugal in 1520, was formally divided between the Netherlands and Portugal in 1860. In 1949, the Dutch ceded their portion to Indonesia. In 1974, a war broke out in Portuguese-controlled East Timor between those favoring independence and those preferring integration into Indonesia. When Portugal withdrew in 1976, Indonesian troops aggressively moved into the vacuum, whereupon the East Timorese appealed to world opinion, particularly after film footage of a massacre of 271 persons attending a funeral during 1991 appeared on television around the world. In 1999, after more than 100,000 Timorese died in the continuing conflict, Indonesia accepted a UN plebiscite for the territory. Following a favorable vote for East Timor's independence, Indonesian military forces launched attacks on the residents, resulting in 1,400 deaths and displacing 250,000 from their homes. The UN then negotiated with Jakarta to end the violence and voted to authorize a military force in order to bring order to the territory. After the UN Transitional Authority for East Timor began operations in 1999 to prepare the territory for independence, further violence erupted in 2000 but subsided. The territory became independent as Timor-Leste in 2002. In 2005, Indonesia and Timor-Leste set up a joint Truth and Friendship Commission

Continued

to investigate perpetrators of the violence in 1999. The report, issued in 2008, concluded that the Indonesian military, police, and civilian government was responsible for widespread and systematic gross violations of human rights, including crimes against humanity. Timorese pro-independence groups were alleged to have committed some, but definitely fewer, illegal detentions. Although Timor-Leste and other countries have called for accountability in the form of prosecutions, Indonesian President Susilo Yudhoyono (1949–), accepted the report, expressed "regrets," but refused to prosecute.

amnesty. In the case of Argentina, the amnesty granted was struck down by its Supreme Court in 2005, opening the possibility that approximately 900 former officers and collaborators could be brought to trial. In 2006, the former provincial deputy police commander, Miguel Etchecolatz (1929–), was among the first to go on trial for his role in the Argentine "dirty war." He was accused of illegally arresting six persons, torturing two, and murdering four. One day after he was sentenced to life imprisonment, a key prosecution witness, Jorge Julio López (1928–2006), disappeared. Later that year, the first person involved in the "dirty war" was convicted. A 25-year sentence was handed down in the case of a former police officer responsible for the torture and disappearance of a married couple in 1978 as well as the forcible reassignment of their eight-month-old daughter to a military officer's family. The suit had been brought by close relatives of the couple. Whether such prosecutions will discourage future dictators from giving up power and allowing truth commissions to operate remains to be seen.

Truth commissions often occur in countries where governments are not equipped to handle investigative functions objectively, whether due to prejudice, tradition, or

DISCUSSION TOPIC 5.2 WHEN ARE TRUTH AND RECONCILIATION COMMISSIONS MOST USEFUL?

When massive human rights violations stop, where does justice begin? What happens to the perpetrators of violations of human rights in a former regime when a new government begins to respect human rights? What is the trade-off between giving human rights abusers amnesty versus bringing them into court? Can truth commissions play a role with terrorist groups? Among countries that have not accounted for systematic human rights violations in the past, which should organize truth commissions? Which are the most effective – truth commissions or reconciliation commissions? Why?

some other reason. Democratic countries tend to compile reports rather than set up commissions. Truth commissions are unlikely to pursue non-state terrorist groups, which are usually treated as international outlaws.

One of the campaign promises of Mexican President Vicente Fox (1942–) was to expose the "dirty war" against dissidents that was conducted by previous Mexican governments from the late 1960s to the early 1980s. However, a few days before Fox left office in 2006, a special prosecutor quietly posted on the Internet an 800-page report based on declassified documents about the Mexican "dirty war." In contrast, Congressional investigation committees in the United States and parliamentary investigations in the United Kingdom compile reports after holding hearings, and independent prosecutors sometimes compile reports based on grand jury testimony. In 2013, Argentina set up a truth commission to investigate the 1994 bombing of a Jewish site, a matter that ordinarily would be left to a police commission.

Although truth commissions seek the goals of deterrence, reconciliation, restorative and retributive or transitional justice, and social transformation, the jury is out on their ultimate benefits. Four commissions were disbanded or stopped because they were too controversial. Others have been attacked because they appear to be a form of "victor's justice." The benign effects of the El Salvador case are in contrast with the South African Truth and Reconciliation Commission, which has been accused of harming race relations. Truth commissions tend to focus on victims, who in turn may need psychological assistance more than transparency of their suffering.

In general, truth commissions have a positive effect, such as promoting democracy and deterring future human rights violations, especially when they are combined with either an amnesty or a round of prosecutions. (For prosecutions in international tribunals, see Chapter 10.) Populations truly engaged in the work of truth commissions are more likely to heal than those that proceed bureaucratically. The connection between post-conflict states and democracy, however, depends upon whether the states grow economically. If not, they may lapse into conflict again.

UNIVERSAL JURISDICTION OF CRIMES AGAINST HUMANITY

Today, lawbreakers may hop from country to country or use the Internet from any country to evade prosecution for offenses that violate basic rights of individuals in other countries. Murder is universally a crime, but a murderer may escape to another country to evade prosecution. Only when two countries have a treaty of **extradition** can an accused murderer be returned to face trial in the jurisdiction where the homicide was committed. However, a government can claim the right to demand extradition if a crime against humanity has been committed, as noted below.

Today, international crimes are increasingly being identified as having **universal jurisdiction**. To prosecute someone for an international crime, there must first be a treaty (or a relevant custom in international law) that makes the offense a crime, and, second, a court empowered to try persons for that offense. If a particular country recognizes an offense as a crime with universal jurisdiction, then its courts have primary jurisdiction when the accused and the plaintiff are present within the borders of that country, even if the alleged crime was committed in another country.

If a country harboring an accused person does not hold a trial, another country or an international tribunal may claim jurisdiction on behalf of the plaintiff. Although trial *in absentia* has little standing in international law because a valid trial under the International Covenant on Civil and Political Rights must give the accused an opportunity to present a defense, courts can appoint persons to represent defendants who are not in the country.

Which crimes have universal jurisdiction wherein prosecution is authorized in any country of the world regardless of where the offense is committed? Aside from war crimes, the subject of Chapter 7, the first such offenses are slavery and the slave trade, which were criminalized in 1926 under the **Slavery, Servitude, Forced Labor and Similar Institutions and Practices Convention**. Dehumanization, that is, forcing someone to work against their will, is a principal objection to slavery. Indeed, any form of forced labor violates civil and political rights by depriving individuals of their liberties. The **Convention Concerning Forced or Compulsory Labor** of 1930 provided more details. In 1953, a protocol to the 1926 convention was adopted. Then, in 1956, the **Convention on the Abolition of Slavery, the Slave Trade, and Institutions and Practices Similar to Slavery** was instituted, followed by the **Convention Concerning the Abolition of Forced Labor** in 1957.

The term "crimes against humanity" was first identified at the Nuremberg war crimes trials to include "murder, extermination, enslavement, deportation, and other inhumane acts committed against any civilian population, before or during the war, or persecutions on political, racial or religious grounds ..." The definition referred to such actions by Nazi Germany as mass murder, forced labor of certain groups, and wholesale removal of groups from their homelands to death camps.

Crimes against humanity have increased incrementally since the formation of the United Nations (Table 5.6) and form the corpus of **international human rights law** in peacetime. Crimes against humanity in war time, known as **international humanitarian law**, are identified in Chapter 7. The boundary between the two types of law is blurred in reference to international terrorism, however.

In 1946, while the Nuremberg war crimes trials were ongoing, the United Nations adopted the **Convention on the Prevention and Punishment of the Crime**

TABLE 5.6 TREATIES IDENTIFYING CRIMES AGAINST HUMANITY

Adopted	Agreements and treaties	In force
1925	Slavery, Servitude, Forced Labor and Similar Institutions and Practices Convention	1927
1953	• Protocol Amending the Slavery Convention Signed at Geneva on 25 September 1925	1953
1930	Convention Concerning Forced or Compulsory Labor	1932
1946	Convention on the Prevention and Punishment of the Crime of Genocide	1951
1949	Convention for the Suppression of the Traffic in Persons and of the Exploitation of the Prostitution of Others	1951
2000	• Protocol to Prevent, Suppress and Punish Trafficking in Persons, Especially Women and Children	2003

Continued

TABLE 5.6   (CONTINUED)

Adopted	Agreements and treaties	In force
1956	Convention on the Abolition of Slavery, the Slave Trade, and Institutions and Practices Similar to Slavery	1957
1957	Convention Concerning the Abolition of Forced Labor	1959
1968	Convention on the Non-Applicability of Statutory Limitations to War Crimes and Crimes Against Humanity	1968
1970	Convention on the Means of Prohibiting and Preventing the Illicit Import, Export and Transfer of Ownership of Cultural Property	1972
1973	Principles of International Cooperation in the Detection, Arrest, Extradition and Punishment of Persons Guilty of War Crimes and Crimes Against Humanity	
1973	International Convention on the Suppression and Punishment of the Crime of Apartheid	1976
1979	International Convention Against the Taking of Hostages	1983
1980	Hague Convention on the Civil Aspects of International Child Abduction (Hague Abduction Convention)	1983
1984	Convention Against Torture and Other Cruel, Inhuman or Degrading Treatment or Punishment	1987
2002	• Optional Protocol to the Convention Against Torture and Other Cruel, Inhuman or Degrading Treatment or Punishment	2006
1985	Inter-American Convention to Prevent and Punish Torture	1987
1985	European Convention for the Prevention of Torture and Inhuman or Degrading Treatment or Punishment	1989
1988	Convention Against Illicit Traffic in Narcotic Drugs and Psychotropic Substances	1990
1992	Declaration on the Rights of Persons Belonging to National or Ethnic, Religious and Linguistic Minorities	
1992	Declaration on the Protection of All Persons from Enforced Disappearance	
1995	Declaration of Principles on Tolerance	
1997	OECD Convention on Combating Bribery of Foreign Public Officials in International Business Transactions	1999
1999	Convention Concerning the Prohibition and Immediate Action for the Elimination of the Worst Forms of Child Labor	2000
2000	Convention Against Transnational Organized Crime	2003
2000	• Protocol Against the Smuggling of Migrants by Land, Sea and Air, Supplementing the United Nations Convention Against Transnational Organized Crime	2004
2000	• Protocol to Prevent, Suppress and Punish Trafficking in Persons, Especially Women and Children, Supplementing the United Nations Convention Against Transnational Organized Crime	2003
2000	• Protocol Against the Illicit Manufacturing of and Trafficking in Firearms, Their Parts and Components and Ammunition, Supplementing the UN Convention Against Transnational Organized Crime	2005
2003	Convention Against Corruption	2005
2006	International Convention for the Protection of all Persons from Enforced Disappearance	2010

of Genocide. **Genocide** is defined as "acts committed with intent to destroy, in whole or in part, a national, ethnical, racial, or religious group." Five prohibited acts are specified:

- Genocide
- Conspiracy to commit genocide
- Direct and public incitement to commit genocide
- Attempt to commit genocide
- Complicity in genocide.

More specifically, the treaty prohibits the following:

- Killing members of a group
- Causing serious bodily or mental harm to members of a group
- Deliberately inflicting on a group conditions of life calculated to bring about its physical destruction in whole or in part
- Imposing measures intended to prevent births within a group
- Forcibly transferring children of one group to another group.

Shortly after the victorious entry of Russian troops in Berlin during 1945, women were notoriously forced into prostitution. Accordingly, the **Convention for the Suppression of the Traffic in Persons and of the Exploitation of the Prostitution of Others** was adopted in 1949 as a crime against humanity with universal jurisdiction.

Government officials responsible for *apartheid* in South Africa used to travel freely around the world. That stopped with the adoption, in 1973, of the **International Convention on the Suppression and Punishment of the Crime of Apartheid**. Responsibility for enforcing *apartheid*, thus, became another crime against humanity with universal jurisdiction.

In the 1970s, criminal elements in the Philippines decided to take hostage rich Japanese business executives and tourists, demanding ransom. To classify hostage taking as an international crime, the **International Convention Against the Taking of Hostages** was adopted in 1979.

In 1984, the **Convention Against Torture and Other Cruel, Inhuman or Degrading Treatment or Punishment** identified torture by police or other governmental authorities as a crime with universal jurisdiction. Even if not practiced on a widespread basis, torture and related forms of inhumane treatment are international crimes, such that a person who tortures in one country may try to escape accountability by fleeing to another country but can be brought to justice by victims residing in the latter country.

While negotiating contracts pursuant to foreign investment, governments in some developing countries have often demanded payment from First World corporations "under the table," the functional equivalent of ransom. Accordingly, the multicontinental Organization for Economic Cooperation and Development (OECD) adopted a **Convention on Combating Bribery of Foreign Public Officials in International Business Transactions** in 1997, though the principal signatories were advanced industrial countries. A treaty with wider jurisdiction, the UN **Convention Against Corruption**, was adopted in 2003. The treaty has provisions for the recovery of sums of money paid under duress as bribes, but appropriate measures have not yet been adopted in the legal systems of all developing countries. The treaty, however, does not cover kleptocracy, when government leaders confiscate public and private assets and send them to Swiss bank accounts, as Ferdinand Marcos (1917–1989) did in the Philippines from the mid-1970s to the mid-1980s.

According to the UN Global Initiative to Fight Human Trafficking, approximately 2.5 million persons today are in forced labor, mostly aged 18–24. Each year, human trafficking affects about 60,000 persons, some 80 percent of whom are females and almost half are children. Victims go from 127 countries to 137 countries; 56 percent are in Asian and Pacific countries. En route, 95 percent report physical or sexual abuse. Of those, 43 percent end up in the commercial sex industry in developed countries, especially in countries with legalized prostitution. Some 32 percent are in debt bondage, that is, are forced to work to pay off nonexistent "debts." In some cases, they agree to relocate when promised a well-paying job, but on arrival in the new country they are told that they must pay for the cost of their passage in a job that has insufficient remuneration to pay the "debt" for many years. Young women from South Asia hired as domestic servants in the Middle East are reportedly treated as slaves. In Sri Lanka and Uganda, child soldiers are also treated as slaves. At least 80 countries ban human trafficking, but in 2006 only 3,160 were convicted of the offense out of 5,808 prosecuted.

The **Convention Against Transnational Organized Crime**, and associated protocols of 2000, also touch on crimes with universal jurisdiction, notably the smuggling of children, women, and slave laborers. The convention was adopted at the same time as the supplementary **Protocol to Prevent, Suppress, and Punish Trafficking in Persons, Especially Women and Children**. The related UN **Convention Against Illicit Traffic in Narcotic Drugs and Psychotropic Substances** was adopted in 1988 and the **Optional Protocol on the Sale of Children, Child Prostitution and Child Pornography** in 2009.

During the dictatorships of Argentina and Chile of the 1970s, many democratic opponents were arrested and never seen again. When the dictatorships ended, there was no trace of their whereabouts. They are considered to have "disappeared," possibly by being dropped into the ocean from airplanes or ships. In 1992, the UN General Assembly issued the **Declaration on the Protection of All Persons from Enforced Disappearance**, calling for a treaty. After the terrorist attack on 9/11, the United States seized suspected terrorists and located them in secret facilities for interrogation, a practice known as "extraordinary rendition," so many countries felt that the problem of disappearances had entered a new phase. The **International Convention for the Protection of all Persons from Enforced Disappearance** of 2006 provides in part that an individual can complain to an international Committee on Enforced Disappearances when a family member has been arrested but cannot be found, thereby triggering an international search for the person. In 2006, the UN reported that disappearances principally involved individuals in Colombia, Nepal, and the Russian republic of Chechnya. International forensic studies have been undertaken to ascertain locations of bodies of the disappeared. It should be noted that the dead bodies actually have rights as well – not to be trafficked, dissected, or used sexually.

There is no statute of limitations on crimes against humanity, thanks to the **Convention on the Non-Applicability of Statutory Limitations to War Crimes and Crimes Against Humanity** of 1968, and **Principles of International Cooperation in the Detection, Arrest, Extradition and Punishment of Persons Guilty of War Crimes and Crimes Against Humanity** of 1973.

In 2012, the case of three Kenyans who had allegedly been castrated, raped, or tortured by British colonial authorities in the 1950s came before Britain's High Court, which rejected the British government's claim that a statute of limitations had run out. A trial date was set, though an out-of-court settlement was likely. Another expectation of the 1968 convention is that those accused of crimes against humanity will be mandatorily extradited; indeed, the same court on the same day agreed to extradite from Britain to the United States four persons charged with complicity in the deadly bombing of American embassies in Kenya and Tanzania during 1998.

In 1998, the **Statute of the International Criminal Court** (ICC) was adopted on a treaty basis. Provisions of the Statute define the scope of crimes against humanity as follows:

- Murder
- Extermination
- Enslavement
- Deportation or forcible transfer of population
- Imprisonment or other severe deprivation of physical liberty in violation of fundamental rules of international law
- Torture
- Rape, sexual slavery, enforced prostitution, forced pregnancy, enforced sterilization, or any other form of sexual violence of comparable gravity
- Persecution against any identifiable group or collectivity on political, racial, national, ethnic, cultural, religious, gender…, or other grounds that are universally recognized as impermissible under international law
- Enforced disappearance of persons
- *Apartheid*
- Other inhumane acts of a similar character intentionally causing great suffering, or serious injury to body or to mental or physical health.

The catch-all category "other" might be interpreted to include deliberate mass starvation, though no prosecution on that basis has yet occurred. The above offenses are now considered to be so serious that they can be tried in any court within any country of the world – that is, they are crimes with universal jurisdiction. However, to give effect to that principle, national courts must first pass laws that designate which crimes have universal jurisdiction.

Not all countries accept the principle of universal jurisdiction. There is no comprehensive treaty compiling all the universal jurisdiction offenses into one document, just individual conventions for specific offenses. However, acceptance of the concept that there are offenses so horrific that all countries must bring the perpetrators to justice would be a significant milestone in the construction of a global polity as, for the first time, the world would have agreed to a common judicial code.

CIVIL AND POLITICAL RIGHTS AS "NEGATIVE" RIGHTS

Following Isaiah Berlin, as noted in Chapter 1, the argument is made that political and civil rights are **negative rights**, that is, deal with what government should **not** do, thereby preserving individual freedom. In contrast, economic, social, and cultural rights are often considered to be **positive rights** that can only advance when governments take innovative action to ensure a decent quality of life.

Within the United States, there is a similar distinction. **Civil liberties** are considered to be rights that governments cannot abridge, whereas **civil rights** are assured only when government acts aggressively to stop discrimination. Thus, civil liberties could be considered to be negative rights, with civil rights as positive rights.

There is a further distinction. **Procedural rights** are steps required of governments before courts can act. For example, a "fair trial" requires governments to provide the accused with an attorney and a hearing before an impartial tribunal. **Substantive rights** are about factual situations, such as the freedom to belong to a religion of one's choosing.

However, further analysis suggests that civil and political rights as well as civil liberties are not negative rights. They can only be attained when governments affirmatively carry out at least four tasks:

- Governments must show respect for the goals of civil and political rights by making verbal statements that raise public consciousness to end prejudice and to stop violations.
- Governments must deter violations and protect rights by setting up enforcement agencies that act, often dramatically, to stop and to redress violations.
- Governments must create institutional machinery to enforce rights, such as by using courts or establishing human rights commissions.
- Governments must spend money on goods and services to ensure rights, such as election safeguards, including tamper-proof voting machines or armed guards, to prevent fraud or voter intimidation.

Thus, civil and political rights impose both affirmative and negative obligations on governments. The affirmative obligation is to provide the infrastructure to guarantee that those who violate human rights will be held accountable in court. The negative obligation is for governments to refrain from interfering with the exercise of civil and political rights, such as the rights of free speech and privacy.

CONCLUSION

Civil and political rights are often considered to be prior to all other rights. Without a free and fair public arena, individuals cannot seek redress for violations of economic, social, and cultural rights. However, protests against violations of civil and political rights are most effective when individuals not only have the economic freedom and resources to hire lawyers on their behalf but also are seen as part of the mainstream rather than being treated as socially or culturally inferior. Thus, the two categories in practical terms deal with complementary rights, as stated in the **Vienna Declaration and Program of Action** that emerged from the World Conference on Human Rights in 1993.

An absolutist view of free speech would permit hate speech; that is, speech that incites one group to approach another group with violence. One provision of the International Covenant on Civil and Political Rights bans propaganda for war. In other words, civil and political rights may be limited to avoid serious disorder.

To further obscure the distinction between civil-political and economic-social-cultural rights, some provisions of the International Covenant on Civil and Political Rights deal with social rights. Articles 23 and 24 address issues of children, family, and marriage. Article 27 identifies the rights of minorities to their culture, language, and religion. Some of the provisions are repeated in the International Covenant on Economic, Social, and Cultural rights, which is reviewed in the following chapter.

CHAPTER 6

Economic, Social, and Cultural Rights

The first *Human Development Report* of the United Nations Development Program, published in 1990, cited the following statistics:

- Over 1 billion people, nearly 20 percent of the planet, live in absolute poverty with incomes less than US$1 per day.
- One in three children around the world suffers from serious malnutrition and is underweight.
- Half the people of the world lack primary health care, such that 3 million children die each year from immunizable diseases and 500,000 women die each year from causes related to pregnancy and childbirth.
- About 1 billion people are illiterate, and well over 100 million children of primary school age are not in school. Female illiteracy is greater than male illiteracy; nearly two-thirds of those enrolled in primary school are males.

Although the world produces enough food to feed everyone, and transportation exists to get food to those who are hungry, millions are dying of malnutrition. The structure of the international food distribution system, which governments have the power to regulate, is clearly responsible. Similarly, homeless people sometimes camp outside vacant apartments and office buildings from London to Los Angeles despite the possibility that governments could rent unused housing units from property owners and allow the homeless to use them for shelter. In short, food and shelter are available for nearly everyone, but are not allocated on the basis of need. Sociologist Johan Galtung (1930–) refers to such cruel squandering of abundant resources as involving **structural violence**. What he means is that some people are dying from lack of adequate food and shelter, albeit slowly, on account of political structures that ignore them.

The first systematic international recognition of economic and social rights appeared in 1919 within the Constitution of the International Labor Organization (ILO), which declared a desire to abolish the "injustice, hardship and privation" that workers have suffered and to guarantee "fair and humane conditions of labor." The text in part was a response by the West to the rise of Soviet Bolshevism, which threatened to advance throughout the rest of Europe. During the years between World Wars I and II, the ILO drafted treaties to promote the right to organize trade unions, a minimum working age, maximum hours of work, weekly rest periods, sickness protection, accident and old-age insurance, and freedom from discrimination in employment. During the Great Depression of the 1930s, the ILO also stressed the issue of unemployment insurance and the desirability of full employment.

In 1933, Albania abolished all private schools, thus eliminating instruction for its Greek minority. Accordingly, the Permanent Court of International Justice was asked for an advisory opinion on the matter. In 1935, the court ruled that the effect was to deprive Greeks of an essential way to maintain their identity, faith, and culture. Thus, the recognition of social and cultural rights was embedded in international law during the era of the League of Nations.

Another impetus for the development of economic and social rights is contained within the Four Freedoms identified by President Franklin Roosevelt (1882–1945) in his State of the Union address on January 6, 1941. Going beyond the constitutional principles of freedom from expression and freedom of religion, Roosevelt proclaimed that equally important norms were the freedom from want and freedom from fear. By freedom from want, he identified "economic understandings which will secure to every nation a healthy peacetime life for its inhabitants." He understood freedom from fear as disarmament and the end of dictatorships. All four freedoms were to be achieved universally.

When the Allied military campaign during World War II promised eventual victory, plans were afoot to organize the UN. Australia lobbied for a clause in the UN Charter pledging all countries to improve labor standards, provide for social security, and guarantee full employment by taking action through the General Assembly, the UN Economic and Social Council, and the ILO. The United States, however, opposed such a provision as intruding into the domestic affairs of states, so the pledge for international action was watered down to a mere principle to be implemented by individual states as they saw fit. The preamble of the UN Charter pledged governments to "promote social progress and better standards of life," but left the adoption of a bill of economic, social, and cultural rights to the future work of the UN.

In 1944, while efforts to organize the UN were underway, the American Law Institute set up a committee to draft an international bill of rights. In addition to listing the civil and political rights contained in the American Bill of Rights, the committee proposed the following economic and social rights: right to education, right to work, right to reasonable conditions of work, right to adequate food and housing, and the right to social security. The committee noted that economic and social rights had already been recognized in the constitutions of many countries – right to education (40 countries); right to work (9 countries); right to adequate housing (11 countries); and right to social security (27 countries).

A proposed bill of economic, social, and cultural rights was supported for inclusion into the Universal Declaration of Human Rights in 1948 by Eleanor Roosevelt (1884–1962) on behalf the United States. Third World countries endorsed the proposal, but there was opposition from governments in Europe, which were undergoing postwar reconstruction, so a more modest statement rather than a binding treaty was likely to emerge, if at all.

The UN Economic and Social Council (ECOSOC), created by the UN Charter, established the Commission on Human Rights to assume responsibility for translating the Declaration of Human Rights into the form of a single treaty. During the Cold War, however, the two sides in the debate between the primacy of civil and political rights versus economic and social rights were ideologically determined, as noted in the previous chapter. Yet Western countries supported anti-communist dictatorships that had no intention of supporting civil and political rights for their own people. The Soviet bloc, meanwhile, refused to support the Western bloc's text of the proposed treaty on economic and social rights, arguing that the provisions were too weak.

By 1955, consensus had been reached about the main outlines of an agreement, but the Cold War and other considerations held up final approval. The **European Social Charter** of 1961 proved that a consensus on the subject was possible, at least among Western European states. Some of the formulations in the proposed treaty were modified from 1963 to 1966. The final text of the **International Covenant on Economic, Social, and Cultural Rights**, as approved in 1966, finally entered into force in 1976 (Table 6.1).

TABLE 6.1   INTERNATIONALLY RECOGNIZED ECONOMIC, SOCIAL, AND CULTURAL RIGHTS

Article	Provisions of the International Covenant on Economic, Social, and Cultural Rights
1(1)	Right to self-determination of peoples
1(2), 24	Freedom to dispose of natural wealth and resources
1(2)	Prohibition against deprivation of means of subsistence
1(3)	Obligation of trusteeship and colonial powers to promote self-government
2(1)	Obligation to use international assistance
2(1)	Obligation to pass laws to attain economic, social, and cultural rights
2(2)	Prohibition against discrimination based on race, color, sex, language, religion, political or other opinion, national or social origin, property, birth or other status
2(3)	Obligation to adopt legislative or other measures to attain economic, social, and cultural rights
2(4)	Obligation of developing countries to guarantee economic rights to the extent possible
3	Equal economic, social, and cultural rights for men and women
4	Rights may be democratically limited only if they promote the general welfare
5(1)	No reduction in attainment of basic rights to meet Covenant obligations
5(2)	No cancellation of rights previously granted by a government

Continued

TABLE 6.1 (CONTINUED)

Article	Provisions of the International Covenant on Economic, Social, and Cultural Rights
6(1)	Right to work
6(1)	Right to choose occupation freely
6(2)	Obligation of governments to provide technical education
7a(i)	Right to fair wages
7a(i)	Equal pay for equal work regardless of sex
7a(ii)	Right to a living wage
7b	Right to safe and healthy working conditions
7c	Equal opportunity for promotion (except for seniority and competence levels)
7d	Right to rest, leisure, limited working hours, paid periodic holidays
8(1a,2)	Right to form and join trade unions for all but armed forces, police, or government bureaucrats (subject to law and public order needs)
8(1b)	Right of trade unions to join together or to join international trade unions
8(1c)	Right of unions to function freely (subject to law and public order needs)
8(1d)	Right to strike (subject to law)
9	Right to social security, including social insurance
10(1)	Obligation to protect and assist families
10(1)	Right to choose marriage partners freely
10(2)	Right of mothers of newly born children to leave from work with pay or social security benefits and other special protection
10(3)	Obligation to protect children from economic and social exploitation
10(3)	Prohibition of work of children harmful to morals or health
10(3)	Obligation to establish a minimum age for children to work
11(1)	Right to adequate and improving food, clothing, housing conditions freely chosen
11(2a)	Obligation of governments to improve and reform systems of production, conservation, distribution of food, and knowledge about nutritional principles
11(2b)	Obligation to ensure equitable distribution of world food for the needy
12(1)	Right to physical and mental health
12(2b)	Obligation to reduce stillbirths, infant mortality
12(2c)	Obligation to improve environmental and industrial hygiene
12(2c)	Obligation to prevent, treat, and control diseases, including those work-related
12(2d)	Right to medical attention for sickness
13(1)	Right to education
13(1)	Obligation of education to promote full development, sense of dignity, respect for human rights and freedom; empower democratic participation; to promote understanding, tolerance, friendship among all nations and racial, ethnic, or religious groups; promote UN activities for peace
13(2a),14	Obligation to provide free compulsory primary education either immediately or to design an implementation plan with a timetable
13(2b)	Obligation to provide secondary and technical education for all
13(2c)	Obligation to provide higher education for all who have the aptitude
13(2b,c)	Obligation to gradually provide free secondary, technical, higher education

Continued

TABLE 6.1   (CONTINUED)

Article	Provisions of the International Covenant on Economic, Social, and Cultural Rights
13(2d)	Obligation to provide education for those not completing primary grades
13(2e)	Obligation to increase schools, provide fellowships, upgrade work conditions of teachers
13(3)	Right of parents to send children to nonpublic schools, if they meet minimum standards
13(3)	Right of parents to provide moral and religious education to children
13(4)	Right to establish schools that meet minimum standards
15(1a)	Right to take part in cultural life
15(1b)	Right to enjoy benefits of science and its applications
15(2)	Obligation to develop, conserve, diffuse science and culture
15(3)	Right of scientists to free inquiry
15(4)	International scientific and cultural cooperation and contacts are encouraged
23	Pledge to furnish technical assistance to meet obligations and rights

BASIC ECONOMIC, SOCIAL, AND CULTURAL RIGHTS

The Covenant on Economic, Social, and Cultural Rights deals mostly with substantive rights. About half of the provisions in the covenant are identified as "rights," the others as "obligations." Later agreements have specified procedures to be followed in implementing the treaty, such as reporting requirements. After being fully ratified, the **Optional Protocol to the International Covenant on Economic, Social, and Cultural Rights** of 2008 established new complaint and inquiry procedures.

COURT CASE 6.1 *SOCIAL DEMOCRATIC WORKERS PARTY V. LATVIA (2001)*

The European Union requires all members to provide an efficient social security insurance system, but the specific program can vary from country to country. Latvia adopted a system in which employers contribute to a fund by paying premiums for the benefit of employees. However, some employers ignored the regulations. Alleging a breach of Articles 9 and 11 of the International Covenant on Economic, Social and Cultural Rights, because the government did not enforce the employer mandate, members of the Social Democratic Workers Party sued the government (the parliamentary majority) to ensure that the right to social security would apply to all employers without exception. The Latvian constitutional court agreed, citing principles adopted by the Committee on Economic, Social, and Cultural Rights. The case demonstrates that national courts within the European Union can apply international standards to regulate private employers.

The Covenant on Economic, Social, and Cultural Rights has encouraged the uniform extension of rights to all countries. Thus, in one case, the Latvian government was permitting some employers to escape from social security protections, but workers sued to enforce the covenant and won. In another case, the right to health governed a decision to provide treatment to those with HIV because provisions of the covenant had been written into the new constitution of the Republic of South Africa.

COURT CASE 6.2 *MINISTER OF HEALTH V. TREATMENT ACTION CAMPAIGN (2002)*

To prevent HIV infections in children, the South African government offered an anti-retroviral drug to 30,000–40,000 children of HIV-infected mothers for free for five years. Suddenly, the government announced it would offer the drug only in certain pilot sites, which would be set up in the following year, thereby denying most mothers access to treatment. The Treatment Action Campaign then sued the South African government for denial of the right to health. The High Court ruled that the drug must be offered to infected mothers giving birth in state institutions and ordered the government to present the court an outline of how it planned to extend provision of the medication to its birthing facilities in the entire country. The government appealed the decision to the Constitutional Court, which rejected the appeal and ordered the government to extend availability of the drug to hospitals and clinics, to provide counselors, and to take reasonable measures to extend the testing and counseling facilities throughout the public health sector. The decision established a framework for enforcement of the obligation to ensure economic, social, and cultural rights.

To clarify the meaning of provisions of the Covenant, several agreements have been adopted by the General Assembly and Specialized Agencies of the UN. According to the UN Office of the High Commissioner for Human Rights, three of the treaties are among the "core international human rights instruments," including the International Covenant on Economic, Social, and Cultural Rights (Table 6.2).

TABLE 6.2   CORE TREATIES ON ECONOMIC, SOCIAL, AND CULTURAL RIGHTS

Adopted	Treaties	In force
1966	International Covenant on Economic, Social, and Cultural Rights	1976
1966	• First Optional Protocol	1976
1989	• Second Optional Protocol	1991
1979	Convention on the Elimination of All Forms of Discrimination Against Women	1981
1995	• Amendment	1981
1999	• Optional Protocol	2000
1989	Convention on the Rights of the Child	1990
1995	• Amendment	
2000	• Optional Protocol to the Convention on the Rights of the Child on the Involvement of Children in Armed Combat	2002
2000	• Optional Protocol to the Convention on the Rights of the Child on the Sale of Children, Child Prostitution and Child Pornography	2002
2011	• Optional Protocol to the Convention on the Rights of the Child on a Communications Procedure	2002
1990	International Convention on the Protection of the Rights of All Migrant Workers and Members of Their Families	2003

SPECIALIZED AGENCIES OF THE UNITED NATIONS DEALING WITH HUMAN RIGHTS

While progress on adoption of the Covenant stymied on account of Cold War antagonisms, the UN established a structure to deal with economic, social, and cultural rights. The principal innovation was the framework for Specialized Agencies and Functional Commissions under ECOSOC. Most of the new bodies were created by the General Assembly, but some revived organizations that existed prior to the UN.

The **ILO**, which had been formed within the Treaty of Versailles of 1919, operated outside the League of Nations. The ILO agreed to become a Specialized Agency of the UN in 1946 and was placed under ECOSOC. The ILO has continued to sponsor treaties on issues of employment, classifying the most important as "fundamental" or "priority" treaties (Table 6.3). Basic ILO-sponsored treaties deal with such problems as child labor, collective bargaining, discrimination, equal pay, forced labor (peonage, serfdom, and slavery), the policy of full employment, and trade union rights. Those on discrimination and rights of trade unions deal with civil and political rights. The rest are economic and social rights.

In 1942, a Conference of Allied Ministers of Education met. They proposed a meeting after the war to continue the work of the International Committee of Intellectual Co-operation, which was formed in 1922, and the International Bureau of Education, that began work in 1925. In 1945, seeking a body to create a culture of peace, the UN convened a conference in London to form an educational and cultural organization. On conclusion of the meeting, the representatives adopted

TABLE 6.3   **BASIC TREATIES OF THE INTERNATIONAL LABOR ORGANIZATION**

Adopted	Treaty	Type	In force
1930	Convention Concerning Forced or Compulsory Labor	Fundamental	1932
1948	Freedom of Association and Protection of the Right to Organize Convention	Fundamental	1950
1949	Convention Concerning Freedom of Association and Protection of the Right to Organize	Fundamental	1951
1951	Convention Concerning Equal Remuneration for Men and Women Workers for Work of Equal Value	Fundamental	1953
1957	Convention Concerning the Abolition of Forced Labor	Fundamental	1959
1958	Convention Concerning Discrimination in Respect of Employment and Occupation	Fundamental	1960
1973	Convention Concerning Minimum Age for Admission to Employment	Fundamental	1976
1999	Convention Concerning the Prohibition and Immediate Action for the Elimination of the Worst Forms of Child Labor	Fundamental	2000
1947	Convention Concerning Labor Inspection in Industry and Commerce	Priority	1950
1964	Convention Concerning Employment Policy	Priority	1966
1969	Convention Concerning Labor Inspection in Agriculture	Priority	1972
1976	Convention Concerning Tripartite Consultations to Promote the Implementation of International Labor Standards	Priority	1978

the **Constitution of the United Nations Educational, Scientific, and Cultural Organization** (UNESCO), which came into force the following year.

Prior to World War II, the Office International d'Hygiène Publique (OIHP) and the League of Nations Health Organization coexisted primarily because the United States was a member of OIHP but not the League. When both organizations became moribund during World War II, the United Nations Relief and Rehabilitation Administration (UNRRA) was set up in 1943 to carry on the health functions of both organizations until ECOSOC, at its first meeting in 1946, authorized a conference to establish the **Constitution of the World Health Organization** (WHO) later that year. UNRRA was dissolved in 1947, when a WHO Interim Commission was formed to carry out work while ratifications of the WHO treaty were being registered. WHO officially began in 1948, proclaiming the right to health.

In addition to ILO, UNESCO, and WHO, ECOSOC has provided the umbrella for 15 Specialized Agencies, 10 Functional Commissions, and 5 Regional Commissions, though not all deal with human rights issues identified in the Covenant. The most salient are the Food and Agricultural Organization of the United Nations and the International Fund for Agricultural Development. The Regional Commissions for all areas of the world except Antarctica, the Arctic, and North America (Canada and the United States), assist in bringing about regional cooperation in major areas of economic, social, and cultural issues of concern to each region. The Specialized Agencies, Functional Commissions, and Regional Commissions have drafted many treaties, thereby adding to the corpus of international law.

INDIGENOUS PEOPLES' RIGHTS

International human rights developed from 1648, when the Peace of Westphalia recognized states, not peoples, as the basic units of world politics. According to the Treaty of Versailles that ended World War I, empires were to be broken up into states in which each nationality group would enjoy their own homeland. The Austro-Hungarian Empire and the Ottoman Empire in Europe were then carved up into the separates states of Austria, Bulgaria, Hungary, Czechoslovakia, Poland, Romania, and Yugoslavia in order to correspond to the principle that no people should be governed by another. The "one nation, one state" concept, a fiction embodied in the Fourteen Points of Woodrow Wilson (1856–1924), was one of the principles adopted at Versailles. Every government had minority populations, and many had indigenous peoples under their jurisdiction.

Wilson did not apply the same principle to his own country, where indigenous peoples live on 55 million acres of reservations (not their ancestral lands) in 30 states, governed by tribal governments. Although a US District Court, in 1879, ruled in United States *Ex Rel. Standing Bear v. George Crook* that native peoples living in the United States had the right to sue in American courts, many native peoples did not survive the onslaught of white settlers. Relations between the United States and 15 of the indigenous peoples are based on treaties which presuppose that both parties are sovereign, and indeed several tribal governments are now suing to regain fishing and other rights.

HISTORIC EVENT 6.1 CONGRESS PASSES THE WESTERN SHOSHONE CLAIMS DISTRIBUTION ACT (2004)

According to the terms of the Treaty of Ruby Valley of 1863, white settlers were allowed to cross Western Shoshone lands from Idaho's Snake River to the Great Salt Lake into Death Valley, California. Washington subsequently interpreted the agreement to mean that the Shoshones had given up their land. In 1979, Congress offered US$26 million to settle the land claims, but the tribes insisted on return of their lands. In 1985, the US Supreme Court ruled that the US$26 million settlement extinguished the land claims, but the tribes again refused the money. After various unsuccessful efforts to enforce the treaty in court, and Congressional legislation in 1992 and 1995, Congress passed the Western Shoshone Claims Distribution Act of 2004, awarding the Shoshones US$145 million in compensation for their land. Starting in 2011, payments have been made to members of the Western Shoshone nation.

During the League of Nations era, the rights of indigenous peoples were not included on the agenda of human rights concerns. In 1922, the Six Nations Iroquois Confederacy petitioned the League of Nations to prevent Canada from taking over Iroquois lands, but the petition was rebuffed. In 1945, a leader of the Iroquois nation sought to address the San Francisco conference that established the UN, but he was refused recognition.

During the early years of the UN, governments were eager to promote economic development, including encroachments on remote lands that had long been occupied by indigenous peoples who had preserved their way of life without joining the world capitalist system. The very existence of distinct peoples was threatened because the natural environments in which at least 350 million individuals, representing some 5,000 ethnolinguistic groups in 70 countries, were increasingly under attack. Complacently, the fate of indigenous peoples was thought to be protected by such treaties as the Convention on the Prevention and Punishment of the Crime of Genocide, the International Covenant on Civil and Political Rights, and the International Convention on the Elimination of All Forms of Racial Discrimination. The presumption was that native peoples had to assimilate (adopt the culture of the dominant group) in order to secure their rights. ILO's **Convention Concerning the Protection and Integration of Indigenous and Other Tribal and Semi-Tribal Populations in Independent Countries** of 1957 was also based on an assimilationist premise that clearly was not designed to handle the onslaught of corporations seeking to cut down rainforests and governments desiring to resettle their people from overcrowded cities to "virgin" lands.

In 1975, George Manual (1921–1989) invited 30 indigenous leaders from Canada, the United States, Australia, and New Zealand to a conference in Vancouver, Canada, where the World Council of Indigenous Peoples was formed. In 1981, the International Non-Governmental Organizations Conference on Indigenous Peoples and the Land, held at Geneva, advanced the concept of the **Fourth World** to refer to the world's indigenous peoples as contrasted with the **First World** (industrial democracies), **Second World** (non-market socialist economies), and **Third World** (developing countries). Both the Council and the Conference then pressured the UN to recognize them as distinct peoples.

In 1981 UNESCO's **Declaration of San José** responded by declaring **ethnocide** to be a form of cultural genocide that is an "extreme form of massive violation of human rights." "Ethnocide," the declaration stated, exists when a people's "right to enjoy, develop and transmit its own culture and its own language, whether collectively or individually," is denied. The term had been coined by Raphael Lemkin (1900–1959), who had also advanced the term "genocide." Nevertheless, ethnocide had been excluded from human rights protections under the Geneva Convention and other human rights agreements.

In 1982, the UN Commission on Human Rights established the Working Group on Indigenous Populations, which asked five independent experts to make a comprehensive study of indigenous peoples and to make recommendations. The working group's report concluded that the distinctive characteristic of indigenous peoples is land-rootedness, so protection of their rights must involve an end to further encroachment on ancestral territories. In 1994, the Working Group adopted a draft Declaration on the Rights of Indigenous Peoples, but the 45 articles were not accepted by governments represented on the Commission. The Working Group has continued to hold conferences, which have been attended in recent years by some 166 organizations of indigenous peoples.

In 1989, meanwhile, the ILO adopted the **Convention Concerning Indigenous and Tribal Peoples in Independent Countries** to replace the assimilationist treaty of 1971. Rejecting assimilationism, the new treaty prohibits "co-use, co-management, co-conservation, and non-removal or relocation without 'free and informed consent'." However, indigenous peoples are not empowered in the treaty with a veto over the use of their ancestral lands.

Many of the most vocal groups represent the native peoples of the Americas. In 1992, the Second Summit Meeting of Ibero-American Heads of State adopted the **Agreement Establishing the Fund for the Development of the Indigenous Peoples of Latin America and the Caribbean** to provide financial resources for the many impoverished peoples whose environments have been severely damaged.

In 2001, the Inter-American Court of Human Rights ruled in *Mayagna (Sumo) Community of Awas Tingni v. Nicaragua* that native peoples have the right to maintain communal economic systems and to have sovereign control of their homelands. The UN ECOSOC followed up that year, setting up the Permanent Forum on Indigenous Issues. The forum has issued several declarations on such subjects as communication rights, elementary education, equality issues, and women's rights, but none on whether passports for aboriginal nations should receive international recognition. In 2007, the UN General Assembly clarified many issues by issuing the **Declaration on the Rights of Indigenous Peoples**.

COURT CASE 6.3 *MAYAGNA (SUMO) COMMUNITY OF AWAS TINGNI V. NICARAGUA (2001)*

In 1993 and 1995, a Nicaraguan government province granted logging concessions to private corporations from the Dominican Republic and South Korea. The concessions, which were on the lands of the indigenous Mayagna (Sumo) Community of Awas Tingni along the Atlantic coast, were granted without any attempt to obtain consent from the aboriginal population. With legal assistance from the World Wildlife Federation, the community complained to the Inter-American Commission on Human Rights (IACHR) in 1995 and to the Nicaraguan Supreme Court in 1997. Both bodies ruled in favor of the Awas Tingni people. After further negotiations with the Nicaraguan government, in 1998 the IACHR brought the case against the Nicaraguan government before the Inter-American Court of Human Rights. In 2001, the court ruled that failure to obtain prior approval of the native population was a violation of the Inter-American Convention on Human Rights, which requires governments to demarcate boundaries of the territories where indigenous peoples can exercise sovereign control and to accord them legal protection. The court awarded the community US$30,000 for legal expenses and US$60,000 for the community to spend for the benefit of its people.

In short, indigenous peoples are under threat around the world. Their rights have been gradually identified, but often too late for them to preserve their ways of life, yet they have not been paid adequate reparations for their losses. Although they may be covered under civil rights protections as "minorities," their priorities go beyond to include land rights, self-determination, and social equality. Major international institutions, dominated as they are by states that often suppress minority peoples, have failed to recognize aboriginal rights. As individuals, they are covered by the various human rights treaties. As groups, they await fuller recognition.

AGREEMENTS AND DECLARATIONS ON SOCIAL AND CULTURAL RIGHTS

During the era of the UN, many important treaties have been adopted (Table 6.4). UNESCO, for example, sponsored the **Convention Against Discrimination in Education** followed by a protocol setting up a commission to handle complaints.

The General Assembly has fostered several agreements with special protection for children, the disabled, older persons, mentally ill persons, and women. The **Convention on Consent to Marriage, Minimum Age for Marriage and Registration for Marriage**, adopted in 1962, was designed to liberate women by requiring states to pass laws on the subject. The agreement does not specify a minimum age but, in 1965, a General Assembly resolution, **Recommendation on Consent to Marriage, Maximum Age for Marriage and Registration of Marriage**, recommended the age of 15 as the minimum. According to English law, the minimum marriage age is 18, or 16 with parental consent. Eighteen is the most common minimum age in the world. Two countries (Sudan and Tanzania) allow 12-year-olds to marry, and three countries (Brunei, Saudi Arabia, and Yemen) have no minimum legal marriage age. Common law marriages, wherein partners living together are regarded as legally married without obtaining a marriage certificate from a government agency, are recognized in Australia, Canada, New Zealand, nine states of the United States and the District of Columbia, and the English-speaking Caribbean.

The **Convention on the Rights of the Child** of 1986 codified many rights granted to those 16 and under, and the **African Charter on the Rights and Welfare of the Child** of 1990 provides additional protections, particularly those relating to social rights. However, the treaties do not agree on when a person is no longer a "child."

During World War II, Nazi officials occupying Austria, Hungary, and other countries decided to loot works of art and haul them away to Germany. Claims for return of personal and state cultural properties were made after the war, but there was no regularized procedure to handle the situation. The **Convention for the Protection of Cultural Property in the Event of Armed Conflict** of 1954, which clarifies Geneva Convention provisions on the subject, is discussed in Chapter 7.

TABLE 6.4   **TREATIES ON SOCIAL AND CULTURAL RIGHTS**

Adopted	Agreements and treaties	In force
1945	Constitution of the United Nations Education, Scientific, and Cultural Organization	1946
1946	Constitution of the World Health Organization	1948
1957	Convention Concerning the Protection and Integration of Indigenous and Other Tribal and Semi-Tribal Populations in Independent Countries	1959
1960	Convention Against Discrimination in Education	1962
1962	• Protocol Instituting a Conciliation and Good Offices Commission to Be Responsible for Seeking a Settlement of Any Disputes Which May Arise Between States Parties to the Convention Against Discrimination in Education	1968
1961	European Social Charter	1965
1962	Convention on Consent to Marriage, Minimum Age for Marriage and Registration of Marriage	1964
1970	Convention on the Means of Prohibiting and Preventing the Illicit Import, Export and Transfer of Ownership of Cultural Property	1972
1972	Convention Concerning the Protection of the World Cultural and Natural Heritage	1975
1976	Cultural Charter for Africa	1990
1981	Convention Concerning Equal Opportunities and Equal Treatment for Men and Women Workers: Workers with Family Responsibilities	1983
1981	African Charter on Human and Peoples' Rights	1986
2003	• Protocol to the African Charter on Human and Peoples' Rights and the Rights of Women in Africa	2005
1986	Convention on the Rights of the Child	1990
1989	Convention Concerning Indigenous and Tribal Peoples in Independent Countries	1991
1990	African Charter on the Rights and Welfare of the Child	1999
1992	Agreement Establishing the Fund for the Development of the Indigenous Peoples of Latin America and the Caribbean	1993
2001	Convention on the Protection of the Underwater Cultural Heritage	2006
2003	Convention for the Safeguarding of Intangible Cultural Heritage	2006
2005	Convention on the Protection and Promotion of the Diversity of Cultural Expressions	2007
2006	Convention on the Rights of Persons with Disabilities	2008
2006	• Optional Protocol to the Convention on the Rights of Persons with Disabilities	2008
2008	Optional Protocol to the International Covenant on Economic, Social, and Cultural Rights	2013

But Nazis have not been the only looters; colonial powers did so for centuries. The **Convention on the Means of Prohibiting and Preventing the Illicit Import, Export and Transfer of Ownership of Cultural Property** of 1970 stimulated lawsuits in 2005, when Greece and Italy sued the Getty Museum in Los

Angeles for illegally removing art objects from their countries, and Perú asked Yale University to return some five thousand artifacts taken from Machu Picchu. Getty was exonerated in a Greek court but returned some of the contested material to Italy, and Yale sent back thousands of artifacts to Perú. In 2006, voluntary agreements by the Boston Museum and the Metropolitan Museum of Art in New York returned 13 and 21 artifacts to Italian ownership, respectively, which in turn considered them to be out on loan. In 2012, Bolivia returned a 700-year-old mummy to Perú that had been stolen by someone who intended to sell the cultural artifact to France; the two countries then signed a treaty to stop smuggling of cultural artifacts. In 2013, the Metropolitan Museum of New York returned two tenth century statues to Cambodia.

Cultural preservation has also been forward looking. The **Convention Concerning the Protection of the World Cultural and Natural Heritage** of 1972 established the concept of World Heritage Sites. The **Cultural Charter for Africa** of 1976 articulated similar provisions to the African context, where cultural suppression is a serious problem. More recently, the **Convention on the Protection of the Underwater Cultural Heritage** of 2001, the **Convention for the Safeguarding of Intangible Cultural Heritage** of 2003, and the **Convention on the Protection and Promotion of the Diversity of Cultural Expression** of 2005 have extended the scope of cultural protection. In 2003, the **Declaration Concerning the Intentional Destruction of Cultural Heritage** came after the revelation that cultural sites in Afghanistan had been destroyed by the Taliban rulers during the last decade of the twentieth century, but the agreement was a declaration, not a treaty.

Not all international agreements on human rights have been adopted in the form of legally binding treaties. Similar to the Universal Declaration of Human Rights, many agreements have taken the form of statements of agreed-upon principles, but the path between declarations and conventions has been stony. Nevertheless, the spirit of human rights has been uplifted by several declarations regarding social and cultural rights (Table 6.5).

Some declarations have been very broad. The **Declaration of Principles of International Cultural Cooperation** of 1966 provided a framework for dealing with cultural preservation, as noted above. The **Declaration on Social Progress and Development** of 1969 specifies some of the major concerns of both human rights covenants. With respect to social rights, the declaration prioritizes protection of the family (including the welfare of children), education, equal opportunities, health, housing, poverty and illiteracy reduction, the right to freely chosen employment, scientific progress shared with the people, and welfare benefits for the poor. One element of "scientific progress" is the development of more productive agriculture that could relieve world hunger.

Several agreements focus on the frontiers of science. The **Declaration on the Use of Scientific and Technological Progress in the Interests of Peace and the Benefit of Mankind** of 1975 was concerned with the way in which scientific innovation might be put to the service of the war industry. The **Universal Declaration on the Human Genome and Human Rights** of 1998 and the **Universal Declaration on Bioethics and Human Rights** of 2005 were also motivated by a desire to establish limits to Frankensteinianism. The **Declaration on the Responsibilities of the**

TABLE 6.5   DECLARATIONS ON SOCIAL AND CULTURAL RIGHTS

Adopted	Agreements
1965	Recommendation on Consent to Marriage, Maximum Age for Marriage and Registration of Marriage
1966	Declaration of Principles of International Cultural Cooperation
1969	Declaration on Social Progress and Development
1971	Declaration on the Rights of Mentally Retarded Persons
1975	Declaration on the Rights of Disabled Persons
1975	Declaration on the Use of Scientific and Technological Progress in the Interests of Peace and the Benefit of Mankind
1978	Declaration on Race and Racial Prejudice
1981	Declaration of San José
1989	Recommendations on the Safeguarding of Traditional Culture and Folklore
1991	Principles for Older Persons
1991	Principles for the Protection of Persons with Mental Illness and the Improvement of Mental Health
1992	Declaration on the Rights of Persons Belonging to National or Ethnic, Religious and Linguistic Minorities
1993	Declaration on the Elimination of Violence Against Women
1993	Standard Rules on the Equalization of Opportunities for Persons with Disabilities
1995	Declaration of Principles on Tolerance
1996	Declaration of the Principles of Intercultural Cooperation
1997	Declaration on the Responsibilities of the Present Generation Towards Future Generations
1998	Declaration on the Right and Responsibility of Individuals, Groups and Organs of Society to Promote and Protect Universally Recognized Human Rights and Fundamental Freedoms
1998	Universal Declaration on the Human Genome and Human Rights
2001	Declaration of Commitment on HIV/AIDS
2001	Universal Declaration on Cultural Diversity
2003	Declaration Concerning the Intentional Destruction of Cultural Heritage
2003	International Declaration on Human Genetic Data
2005	Universal Declaration on Bioethics and Human Rights
2007	Declaration on the Rights of Indigenous Peoples

Present Generation Towards Future Generations, of 1997, stated the same issue but far more broadly.

Ethnic and racial discrimination were treated in Chapter 5 as violations of civil and political rights by governments. However, individuals can believe that they are entitled to their prejudices, so the cultural and social agenda is to create a climate free from negativity toward "others." The **Declaration on Race and Racial Prejudice** of 1978, the **Declaration of San José** of 1981, **Recommendations on the Safeguarding of Traditional Culture and Folklore** of 1989, the **Declaration on the Rights of Persons Belonging to National or Ethnic, Religious and**

Linguistic Minorities of 1992, and the **Declaration of Principles on Tolerance** of 1995 were adopted to encourage countries to stop demonization of minority groups.

In 1998, UNESCO decided to stress responsibilities over rights. The result was the **Declaration on the Right and Responsibility of Individuals, Groups, and Organs of Society to Promote and Protect Universally Recognized Human Rights and Fundamental Freedoms.**

In 2001, UNESCO sponsored the **Universal Declaration on Cultural Diversity**, which recommends that governments should not only respect cultural rights (notably cultural education, media pluralism, multilingualism, and the protection of artists and authors as unique developers of culture) but also foster policies of integration that promote the interaction of diverse cultural groups. The declaration was then encoded into the **Convention on the Protection of the Diversity of Cultural Expression** in 2005.

However, female genital circumcision exists in about two dozen countries and is disapproved of in even more countries. Believing that unusual cultural practices should be restricted to the private sphere, France has banned wearing of the *burka* in public despite a commitment to cultural rights.

DISCUSSION TOPIC 6.1 SHOULD MUSLIM WOMEN BE BANNED FROM WEARING HEAD OR BODY COVERINGS IN NON-MUSLIM COUNTRIES?

Although veils are not required by the Islamic faith, the custom of headscarves, veils, and *burkas* (full body coverings) is being observed increasingly by Muslims in Western European countries, where there is some concern as well that ski masks and full-face motorcycle helmets can be used as disguises for persons engaging in criminal activity. Despite the presence of significant Muslim minorities, which countries currently ban such coverings? Which non-Muslim countries accept some coverings? Do partial or total bans on distinctive coverings in the name of promoting social harmony and national security serve to infringe cultural rights? What are the limits to prohibitions and requirements regarding the wearing of certain clothing in schools?

Other declarations focus on particular groups – aboriginal peoples, the disabled, the elderly, the mentally ill and mentally retarded, persons with HIV/AIDS, and women. Appropriate treaties with binding provisions await more work by various UN bodies with member governments.

THE GAP BETWEEN RICH AND POOR COUNTRIES

While the International Covenant on Economic, Social, and Cultural Rights was being drafted, much American aid went to anti-communist regimes, Soviet aid to pro-Soviet regimes, and World Bank aid to First World contractors to build infrastructure in the Third World. In the latter case, giant corporations profited by receiving lucrative construction and consulting contracts. Some observers characterized the UN as staffed by bureaucrats who were so out of touch with the latest technological innovations that they were not dispensing useful technical assistance. While the ILO continued to design treaties to extend economic rights to workers and trade unions, the world economic order gave no rights to poor countries.

As more African countries joined the UN in the 1960s, the balance of power in the General Assembly shifted away from problems associated with the Cold War to concern for poverty within the Third World. Although many First World leaders naïvely believed that Third World governments were solely at fault for failing to improve the quality of life of their peoples, the realization increasingly dawned in developing countries that their poverty was due to policies pursued in the economically dominant First World. Accordingly, in 1964 the General Assembly convened the first UN Conference on Trade and Development (UNCTAD) to devise a coherent and effective strategy for Third World economic development.

What UNCTAD first proposed was that developing countries should adopt **import substitution** strategies; that is, develop basic industries behind tariff walls so that poor countries could become more economically self-reliant. However, the private sector in developing countries lacked the capital required to develop heavy industry, so two patterns developed. In some countries, tax revenues were used to establish government corporations, following a socialist model. In other countries, First World-based transnational corporations (TNCs) bought businesses in developing countries to gain increasingly monopolistic control of national economies, and later used their economic leverage to gain exemptions from regulations otherwise imposed on local businesses. While socialist Third World government enterprises foundered on account of lack of internal competition, First World corporations used the import substitution strategy to exploit poorer countries, failing to assist in developing their economies to the point of self-sufficiency. Even in the field of agriculture, TNCs within poor countries were sending food to rich countries while local people were starving.

In 1964, UNCTAD urged developed countries to allocate at least 0.7 percent of their gross national product for Third World aid. Half that amount was forthcoming, but with so many strings attached that developing country governments resented the aid conditions as constituting political interference on behalf of First World interests. In addition, the terms of trade declined for the Third World. They were paying increasingly more to import Western goods, while export revenues for developing countries were declining. As First World corporations found new sources of primary products within developing countries, Third World earnings from natural resources fell because of increased world supply; they were being decapitalized. By the end of the 1960s, there was a growing belief in UNCTAD that import substitution had failed to promote developing country prosperity. In response, the UN General Assembly adopted the **Declaration on Social Progress and Development** in 1969.

When the 1970s began, the North–South split between the First and Third worlds dominated discussion in the UN. Poorer countries of the south insisted that they had the right to receive considerably more aid for development, since they argued that countries in the north had become rich by exploiting them, first as colonies and later as economic neocolonies. The argument, in short, was articulated in terms of dollars and cents more than ideologies. At the same time, Marxist theories from the Second World were increasingly being accepted as valid explanations for the dismal fate of the Third World, while some former colonial powers rejected the neocolonial thesis. Nevertheless, at least four significant developments shifted the initiative to the south. First, member countries of the Organization of Petroleum Exporting Countries (OPEC) decided in 1970 that they would no longer allow Western oil corporations to determine the selling price for petroleum. They instead began to nationalize the oil industries and to set export prices, thereby showing that non-Western countries had more clout in the world economy than previously thought.

Next, French President Charles de Gaulle (1890–1970), who opposed the American involvement in the Vietnamese Civil War, decided to undermine American financing of that conflict. He was aware that Americans were buying more wine and other goods from France than the French were buying from the United States, resulting in a trade surplus in favor of France. Since the meeting at Bretton Woods, that set up the World Bank in 1944, designated the US dollar as the primary unit of international currency – which in turn was backed by gold deposits at Fort Knox and other government depositories in the United States – in 1971 France refused to accept dollars for American export purchases and instead demanded payment in gold. In response, President Richard Nixon (1913–1994) took the dollar off the gold standard, thereby forcing the price of the dollar to fluctuate in the world economy. The international economic order, which had been premised on the dollar backed by a fixed price of gold after World War II, was shattered. The world, therefore, lacked economic stability in a sea of shifting rates of exchange between national currencies.

In September 1973, the Summit Conference of Non-Aligned Nations (described below in Chapter 13), held in Algiers, called for a **new international economic order** (NIEO) that would replace the economic order which ended when the dollar was no longer backed by gold. The Third World wanted to end the exploitation and impoverishment inherent in the old order, which had consigned poor countries to ship minerals and other primary products at low prices to the First World and then to buy back goods made with the same products in Western countries at higher prices.

The coup de grace came in October 1973, after the Yom Kippur War broke out. While Israel responded to a surprise attack from Egypt and Syria, the Organization of Arab Petroleum Exporting Countries (OAPEC, not OPEC) limited shipments of

TABLE 6.6   DECLARATIONS ON ECONOMIC RIGHTS

Adopted	Agreements and treaties
1974	Universal Declaration on the Eradication of Hunger and Malnutrition
1974	Declaration and Program of Action on the Establishment of a New International Economic Order
1974	Charter of Economic Rights and Duties of States
1976	OECD Guidelines for Multinational Enterprises
1977	ILO Tripartite Declaration of Principles Concerning Multinational Enterprises and Social Policy
1986	Declaration on the Right to Development
2000	United Nations Millennium Declaration

oil to Israel's principal allies, notably the United States, Japan, and the Netherlands (the port of entry for Western Europe). To obtain sufficient petroleum, oil companies in the three countries had to buy oil on the spot market, and the selling price quadrupled through 1974. Arab countries suddenly were awash with US dollars, and a First World recession resulted as the increased cost of oil reverberated throughout their economies.

Accordingly, world economic instability prompted a call for action from the UN General Assembly, where the Third World could outvote the First World (Table 6.6). A special session of the General Assembly met in 1974 and adopted, without a formal vote, a manifesto entitled **Declaration and Program of Action on the New International Order**. Next, the General Assembly convened the World Food Conference, which issued the **Universal Declaration on the Eradication of Hunger and Malnutrition**. Later that year, the General Assembly's regular session approved the **Charter of Economic Rights and Duties of States**. Among the specifics in the NIEO proposals were the following:

- Recognition of the concept of the right to development
- National control of infrastructure on the basis of the principle of build–operate–transfer
- Relocation of First World industries to the Third World
- Joint ventures, so that First World corporations could only operate in the Third World in joint operations with local corporations
- Joint research so that patents could be filed in developing countries
- Concessional (long-term, low interest) loans with few strings attached for the Third World
- Technical assistance by developing country consultants, not by permanent staff of UN organizations, including the development of marketing capabilities
- A Third World emergency food supply program financed by food-importing countries
- Aid to increase agricultural productivity in developing countries
- First World aid at 0.7 percent of their gross domestic product

- Reduction of tariffs in developed countries
- Third World debt cancellation or rescheduling
- Buffer stocks to stabilize commodity prices – that is, stockpiles of commodities that could be bought when prices were low and sold to ease spikes in prices when supplies were low
- UN support for South–South technical assistance and other forms of cooperation, such as commodity cartels similar to OPEC
- Compensatory financing to stabilize developing country export earnings
- Indexing Third World export prices to First World exports
- A code of conduct for First World corporations operating in developing countries.

In 1975, at another special session of the General Assembly, developed countries agreed to several concrete NIEO proposals. The resulting resolution endorsed many of NIEO demands, representing a symbolic victory for the south. But the north attached reservations, and there were conflicting interpretations of the compromise. Some in the south wanted a complete restructuring of the world economy, with new institutions and new rules, but others were content with special programs and exemptions. In the end, implementation was largely left to developed countries.

In 1981, when President Ronald Reagan (1911–2004) took office, his government declared that NIEO was dead. America's experience with colonialism was primarily limited to the Philippines, so he did not share the view that past colonialism required reparations. Instead, Reagan's supporters envisioned a world economy with free trade, a concept then called **economic liberalization**, with the following components:

- Privatization, that is, the dismantling of government corporations in the Third World that had been set up during the era of import substitution
- Direct private sector loans and investment guarantees by the World Bank and related institutions to developing country corporations, thereby eliminating the middle man; that is, the former practice of making loans to governments which in turn made loans to private firms
- Deregulation: namely, phasing out governmental regulations of the economy so that market economics could operate more freely
- Export promotion, thereby replacing import substitution as the primary development strategy
- Free trade (tariff reduction) throughout the world, such that western industrial goods would enjoy access to previously protectionist developing countries, and First World corporations could increase their investment in the Third World to take advantage of the global reduction in tariffs.

However, subsidies on agricultural goods produced within developed countries were left out of the new program of economic liberalization, which focused primarily on the manufacturing sector. The intellectual architects of the new economic vision, advanced as well by the UK's prime minister, Margaret Thatcher (1925–2013), were followers of libertarian economist Milton Friedman (1912–2006), who believed that governments were inherently inefficient promoters of economic growth.

In 1986, the General Assembly adopted the **Declaration on the Right to Development**. The resolution was only symbolic, a Third World reminder to the First World that more development aid was needed.

In 1989, the Berlin Wall fell, and the Second World soon disintegrated. Insofar as the Cold War pitted Second World advocates of the priority of economic and social rights against First World exponents of civil and political rights, the latter won. Poland and other Eastern European countries soon became democracies. Economic and social rights were then "backburnered" by developed countries at the behest of transnational corporations, which advocated a world economy driven by the law of supply and demand unfettered by governmental or international regulations. The dreams of a world of free trade, as espoused by such economic philosophers as Adam Smith (1723–1790) and David Ricardo (1772–1823), seemed closer to reality than ever before in human history. Development aid used to curry favor in the Third World during the Cold War was cut.

Even before capitalism triumphed over state socialism, market economies had been developing within China, Eastern Europe, the Soviet Union, and Vietnam. During the 1990s, democratic revolutions came along with the end of state socialism in Eastern Europe, whereas China and Vietnam adopted some economic liberalization while continuing to crack down on democratic aspirations.

HISTORIC EVENT 6.2 SOLIDAMOŚĆ'S LEADER IS ELECTED PRESIDENT OF POLAND (1990)

In 1980, a strike broke out at the shipyards in Gdansk to protest poor working conditions. Lech Wałęsa (1943–), who had been arrested in 1970 for leading a strike after 80 workers were gunned down by the government, assumed leadership of the new work stoppage. Soon, his example persuaded workers throughout the country to go on a general strike, and the government decided to compromise by allowing the strikers to form a joint committee to negotiate with the government. Solidamość (Solidarity) was then formed, and the union gained legal recognition, with Wałęsa voted to chair the new body. In 1981, however, the government refused to negotiate with the union and instead declared martial law, imprisoned Wałęsa, and attempted to crush the union. Pressure, in the form of economic sanctions and Papal disapproval, continued on the Polish government to grant workers the right to strike. While under house arrest in 1983, Wałęsa was awarded the Nobel Peace Prize. After his release from house arrest in 1987, he organized a strike in 1988 to gain formal recognition for the union. Negotiations during 1989 then led to an agreement to hold free elections in Poland. Wałęsa was elected president of Poland in 1990, and left office in 1995 when he lost reelection.

The term **globalization** was increasingly used in the 1990s to describe several developments beyond economic liberalization:

- Former non-market economies entered the world capitalist system, producing a variety of low-cost consumer goods.
- Improvements in communications, especially through the Internet, made possible instantaneous shifts of capital across national boundaries, such that a country's economy could be devastated by large-scale sell-offs of its currency.
- Jet travel with relatively low-cost fuel facilitated the rapid movement of goods and people from one corner of the world to another.
- Transnational corporations bought out businesses in a wave of consolidations and mergers, such that they became global in geographic scope while many different kinds of businesses, from manufacturing to services, were vertically integrated inside the same corporate entity.
- The new demand for unskilled labor to produce goods for international markets led to internal migration of persons from the countryside to live in shantytowns within developing countries, away from their families, and without protections against unsafe conditions of work.
- Jobs in the First World were increasingly outsourced to the Third World.
- The rights of workers declined, as businesses proposed to set up shop in countries with poor labor standards and demanded concessions from unions before doing so.

The power of global corporations began to be described as **corporate imperialism** insofar as profiteering businesses trampled on human rights, particularly workers rights. Ironically, the elements of globalization had been identified by Karl Marx (1818–1893) as preconditions to the end of capitalism. For Marx, the contradictions of capitalism would not become obvious until the capitalist system spread to every nook and cranny of the globe, whereupon megamergers would lead to oligopolies and later to monopolies that exerted control over workers beyond the boundaries of an increasingly irrelevant state system. When class-conscious workers realized that they could end their exploitation by collectively taking control of monopolistic businesses, according to Marx, socialism would emerge as a more attractive economic system of peace, prosperity, and human dignity.

But the collapse of the Berlin Wall ended the socialist experiment in Eastern Europe and discredited Marxism, so opponents of globalization have decried a neglect of human rights by corporations and a failure of governments to support structural changes in the world economy in order to provide more opportunities for poorer countries. Globalization's proponents, however, have pointed out that some developing countries have benefited considerably from globalization, since there has been considerable foreign investment and job creation in some of the poorest countries, thereby bringing more wealth that may be taxed and then allocated by Third World governments to education and health, provided of course that the regimes of poor countries wanted to respond to the needs of the people. In short, globalization's supporters point to increases in the attainment of economic and social rights, while opponents focus on deficiencies in regard to civil and political rights. South Korea, poster country for emergence from Third to First World status in the early 1980s, became a democracy by the end of that decade because the middle class, created by the new wealth, demanded rule by the people.

HISTORIC EVENT 6.3 THE WORLD CONFERENCE ON HUMAN RIGHTS (1993)

In 1989, communist countries collapsed in Eastern Europe, and economic assistance to the Third World waned where East and West had formerly competed to gain supporters. Developing countries, feeling abandoned, began to demand attention in terms of economic and social rights. In 1993, the Second World Conference on Human Rights convened in Vienna to resolve a growing dissensus over human rights priorities. In preparation for the conference, Asian countries met earlier in the year at Bangkok to endorse the proposition that economic and social rights should have priority over civil and political rights, and that the major human rights covenants should be rewritten to reflect the opinions of countries that were not consulted when they were written. They championed their views under the concept of "Asian values"; that is, the importance of community and family needs over Western notions of individual rights. After considerable contention at the conference, the official position adopted by the delegates was a compromise, known as the Vienna Declaration, providing in part that the two sets of rights, civil-political and economic-social, are "universal, indivisible and interdependent and interrelated." More concretely, the conference recommended the establishment of the UN High Commissioner for Human Rights, a position approved by the UN General Assembly and established later in 1993. Thus far, there has been no Third World conference on human rights, though Riyadh hosted a human rights conference in 2003 outside the UN framework.

Responding to the end of the Cold War, the World Conference of Human Rights met at Vienna in 1993. At one extreme was the **developmentalist** view, advocated by some developing countries, that economic and social rights are superior and prior to civil and political rights. At the other extreme was the **libertarian** view, advanced by some Anglo-American democracies, that economic and social rights are not rights at all and that treating them as rights serves to justify large-scale state intervention and provides an excuse for violating civil and political rights. European welfare state advocates of a middle position somewhere between developmentalism and libertarianism, sometimes known as **social market capitalism**, were not able to bridge the gap. The social safety net of social market capitalism, meanwhile, was in jeopardy within Europe, where the rising cost of welfare programs, especially for aging populations, was confronting a shrinking in government revenues due in part to mounting unemployment. Although discussion took place on a wide variety of human rights concerns, the conference achieved little but concluded diplomatically, "all human rights are universal, indivisible and interdependent and interrelated." The one concrete achievement was the recommendation for a new position in the UN structure – the UN High Commissioner for Human Rights. The UN General Assembly endorsed the idea and established the position at the end of 1993.

One year after the Vienna conference, the World Trade Organization (WTO) was formed. The pressure to consider trade in strictly economic terms resulted in pressure to reduce tariffs as well as nontariff trade barriers (NTBs). Laws adopted by governments to boycott goods produced by child labor, for example, were now subject to possible challenge as NTBs. Under WTO rules, any country with an unacceptable NTB is subject to a potential worldwide trade boycott. The specter emerged that the WTO could authorize trade sanctions against any country in order to roll back human rights advances that had taken decades to establish.

Although globalization has brought some prosperity to many poorer countries, which benefit from the resulting increase in investment, the labor force throughout the world has been subjected to three shocks:

- Developed country unemployment has increased as factories relocate to Third World countries where the cost of labor is lower.
- Third World workers, sometimes child or prison labor, are often paid extremely low wages for more than 40 hours per week under conditions where occupational safety requirements are minimal.
- When tariff-free goods from Third World factories are imported by the First World, corporations in the latter countries face such stiff competition that they have sought to keep domestic wages static and to ask their governments not to enforce fair labor or occupational safety standards.

WTO-led globalization has been viewed as condoning violations of economic and social rights on such a scale that protests have greeted meetings of various world economic summits, the most notable of which occurred at the annual WTO meeting during 1999 in Seattle. Insofar as WTO rules continue to give priority to the free flow of trade over the rights of workers, the status of economic and social rights will be in disarray throughout much of the world. Pressure to reform WTO into a more socially conscious organization has led to some innovations in recent years, as described in Chapter 10.

Nevertheless, world poverty has declined from 52 percent of the world's people in 1981 to 21 percent in 2013. At the same time, inequality within countries has increased dramatically, and workers have responded by protesting. Economists agree that economic growth is faster in countries with a more equal distribution of income. **Globalization from above** by giant corporations may not improve human rights, but **globalization from below** holds much more promise.

MICROFINANCE

The presumption of the Millennium Development Goals, as adopted by the UN General Assembly in 2000 and discussed further below, is that those in poverty need aid and wealthier countries, private humanitarian organizations, and international organizations (which wealthy countries fund) should provide that aid, with governments of aid-receiving countries as gatekeepers. Banker-economist Muhammad Yunus (1940–) had a different idea, realizing that banks were reluctant to make small loans and would charge usurious interest rates to poor people. In 1976, he made a personal loan to 42 women to secure the wherewithal to make bamboo furniture in the village of Jobra, Bangladesh. Soon, the loan was paid back. He then decided to repeat the experiment, using money from the government bank as his starting capital. The project was so successful that he set up Grameen Bank as a Bangladesh lending facility in 1983.

Today, Grameen Bank has made loans to seven million borrowers, mostly women, for a total of about US$7 billion, and similar microfinancing banks have been established in at least 100 developing countries. Besides the economic benefits to the borrowers, microfinancing has served to empower women politically and thus fulfills many Millennium Development Goals without any public financing required. Yunus received the Nobel Peace Prize in 2006.

DISCUSSION TOPIC 6.2 WHICH HUMAN RIGHTS PRINCIPLES SHOULD GOVERN THE WORLD ECONOMY?

Proposals for a New International Economic Order (NIEO) were extinguished by the economic liberalization of the 1980s and the economic globalization following the collapse of the Berlin Wall in 1989. The possible benefits of NIEO for the Third World, in short, were viewed as costs that developed countries refused to bear. What are the human rights costs and benefits of globalization today? Should the world economy return to NIEO?

CODES OF CONDUCT

Many corporations have **corporate codes of conduct** to regulate behavior inside a business. When companies and trade unions agree on labor standards, the result is known as a **framework agreement**. The idea that **multinational codes of conduct** might be externally imposed on corporations is a new development in international relations – but they are voluntary and do not have the force of domestic or international law and might be cited in a court case.

In 1937, the International Chamber of Commerce, a nongovernmental body, established the first multinational code of conduct – the Code of Standards of Advertising Practice. The aim of the code, which has been revised several times, is to exercise "social responsibility" by ensuring that ads are "legal, decent, honest and truthful," thereby limiting unfair competition and respecting the cultures in which business is conducted around the world.

In 1971, when Reverend Leon Sullivan (1922–2001) joined the Board of Directors of General Motors, he became the first African American on the board of a major American corporation. Opposed to *apartheid* in South Africa, where General Motors was the largest employer of black Africans, he began to formulate principles to govern the auto company's trade with the country that might serve to end *apartheid*. In 1974, responding to objections to continued trade with South Africa, the British government issued a code of practice for British firms. At the urging of newly elected president, Jimmy Carter (1924–), and members of Congress, several American corporations agreed to follow the **Sullivan Principles**. Three months later, in 1977, the British code was superseded by the **European Code of Practice**, adopted by the foreign ministers of the European Economic Community to restrain trade with South Africa.

Thereafter, a step-by-step approach was taken to dismantle *apartheid*, beginning with an insistence on several fair labor practices:

- Desegregation of employment facilities
- Equal employment opportunity for all employees
- Equal pay for equal work
- A decent minimum wage and salary structure
- Increasing the number of Africans to managerial, supervisory, administrative, clerical, and technical jobs
- Measures to improve the quality of employees' lives outside work
- Fair labor practices, including allowing employees to form unions.

Later, companies were urged to break the *apartheid* law openly, challenging the government to take legal action. Meanwhile, North American and European stockholders and university students agitated to have boards of directors and regents divest their holdings of all stock in South African corporations. Then came a demand to release Nelson Mandela (1918–) from prison, followed by the requirement that black Africans must be allowed to vote. Finally, *apartheid* itself was to be abolished or businesses threatened to leave the country. Indeed, more than 100 major corporations eventually departed, so weakening South Africa's economy that the desired political change, the end of *apartheid*, occurred in 1994.

Meanwhile, consistent with the call for NIEO, the task of designing a global code of conduct was assigned by the General Assembly in 1973 to a newly created UN Center for Transnational Corporations (UNCTC). But the center failed to agree on a code of conduct during subsequent deliberations.

In 1976, the Organization for Economic Co-operation and Development (OECD) agreed upon **Guidelines for Multinational Enterprises**. And in 1977, the **ILO Tripartite Declaration of Principles Concerning Multinational Enterprises and Social Policy** was issued.

In its last stand, the UNCTC attempted to gain acceptance for environmental and labor codes at the 1992 Earth Summit in Río de Janeiro. Although agreement was reached on most of the principles, UNCTC's proposal was spurned in favor of a voluntary code of conduct proposed by the World Business Council for Sustainable Development (WBCSC), an organization of prominent transnational corporations in 34 countries formed in 1991. WBCSC's Business Charter for Sustainable Development advocates a policy of **free-market environmentalism**, that is, the development of environmental and labor standards by corporations that will be free from governmental or international regulation while not jeopardizing profits. Today, most transnational corporations and many others are members of WBCSD.

In 1990, one year after the massacre near Tiananmen Square in Beijing, Reebok left China, objecting to martial law conditions and the presence of military personnel in its plants. In 1992, Sears, Roebuck, decided to stop importing Chinese products produced by prisoners or by other forms of involuntary labor. In 1993, Levi Strauss & Co. and Timberland ended operations and investment in China. They vowed to return only when improved conditions were guaranteed.

In 1995, pickets ringed Gap clothing stores and Starbucks coffeehouses, protesting violation of human rights standards by their suppliers; as a result, both adopted codes of conduct. Also in 1995, US immigration authorities uncovered a factory in El Monte, California, where 71 Thai nationals were locked up in an apartment complex for up to 17 years to sew clothing for name brand manufacturers and retailers during 18-hour work days. In 1996, there was an outcry when news reporters found that the name of television actress Kathie Lee Gifford (1953–) was being attached to a line of clothing made by underage workers in Central America.

The events of 1995–1996 spurred US Secretary of Labor Robert Reich (1946–) to launch a "No Sweat" campaign in 1996, bringing representatives from apparel industry corporations, environmental groups, labor unions, and human rights groups together into an Apparel Industry Partnership in order to draw up a code of conduct that would restrict imports of goods produced by children, forced labor, and workers required to labor more than 60 hours per week. The following year, the President's Council on Economic Priorities issued the **Workplace Code of Conduct and Principles of Monitoring**, promoting the following conditions:

- A ban on the use of child and forced labor
- Prohibition of sexual harassment and worker abuse
- A safe and healthy workplace
- Recognition of freedom of association and collective bargaining as basic rights
- Required payment of the local minimum wage or the prevailing industry wage, with overtime hours paid at the legal rate
- Use of independent external monitors to oversee implementation.

President Bill Clinton (1946–) endorsed the workplace code that year. Not all companies accepted the recommendations, however. In 1997, Senator Edward Kennedy (1932–2009) unsuccessfully proposed a Congressional resolution to urge all American transnational corporations to adopt a code of conduct voluntarily, including a pledge to refrain from doing business in countries that violate human rights.

Rather than a universal code of conduct treaty applying to all businesses, activists have focused in more recent years on specific commodities and industries. In 1999, the Fair Labor Association (FLA) was incorporated to serve as a forum for garment manufacturers that subscribe to the Workplace Code of Conduct and Principles of Monitoring. The principles cover the issues of child labor, forced labor, nondiscrimination, fair labor standards regarding wages and hours of work, occupational health and safety, sexual harassment, and trade union rights. At least 250 corporations have adopted codes of conduct, according to the nongovernmental organization Clean

Clothes Campaign, which was formed in the Netherlands during 1990. Levi Strauss took the lead in implementing the code in 1991.[1]

Several codes of conduct have competed for acceptance. **MacBride Principles**, developed in 1984 by the Irish National Caucus and eventually adopted by most corporations in Northern Ireland, were designed to address anti-Catholic employment discrimination by Protestants in Northern Ireland; they were endorsed by the US Congress in 1998. The Coalition for Environmentally Responsible Economies, a coalition of business, labor, and public interest organizations, promote environmentally sound corporate practices that are known as the **Ceres Principles**. They were developed in 1989 following the environmentally devastating spill by the *Exxon Valdez* oil tanker in Prince William Sound, Alaska. *Caux Principles* were announced in 1994 by idealistic European and Japanese corporate leaders after deliberations at a roundtable discussion group that had met at Caux, Switzerland, from 1986; they focus on the goals of human dignity and the common good. In 1999, UN Secretary-General Kofi Annan (1938–) launched the **Global Sullivan Principles for Corporate Responsibility**. In short, there is some consensus on the need for corporate codes of conduct but not on their content.

In 1999, Secretary-General Annan proposed an organization that would bypass governments to deal directly with corporations. His proposal came into being in 2000 as the **UN Global Compact**, which now has more than 8,000 corporations in 135 countries committed to 10 principles:

- Support human rights
- Avoid human rights abuses
- Uphold collective bargaining
- End forced or compulsory labor
- Abolish child labor
- Avoid employment discrimination
- Treat the environment cautiously
- Promote environmental responsibility
- Develop and diffuse environmentally friendly technologies
- Work against bribery, corruption, and extortion.

Principles are not codes of conduct, but the Global Compact involves the development, implementation, and disclosure of responsible corporate policies and practices.

In 2000, the American Apparel Manufacturers Association launched the Worldwide Responsible Accredited Production (WRAP) to certify facilities engaged in lawful, humane, and ethical production, with headquarters in Arlington, Virginia, and offices in Dhaka and Hong Kong. Focusing on local law and workplace regulations, international workplace standards, and the environment, certification is based on 12 criteria: WRAP prohibits child labor, discrimination, forced labor, and harassment or abuse; requires health and safety conditions, freedom of association and collective bargaining; but only assures that local regulations are followed regarding compensation, benefits, customs compliance, and environmental regulations.

WRAP is supported by 25 international trade associations that represent 36 national associations and over 150,000 individual companies, but was unprepared when more than one thousands workers in Bangladesh died due to unsafe working conditions during May 2013.

Efforts to develop a universal code of conduct have continued. In 2002, after five years of joint planning by the UN Environmental Program and the Coalition for Environmentally Responsible Economies, the Global Reporting Initiative (GRI) was launched, with a headquarters in Amsterdam. GRI accepts voluntary reports from more than 20,000 firms in 80 countries on their economic, social, and environmental practices based on 57 core indicators in its Sustainability Reporting Framework.

A proposal, *Norms on the Responsibility of Transnational Corporations and Other Business Enterprises with Regard to Human Rights*, was drafted by the UN Sub-Commission on the Protection and Promotion of Human Rights. But in 2003, its parent body, the Human Rights Commission, rejected the proposal when business representatives registered strong opposition.

In 2005, the Commission on Human Rights instead adopted a recommendation, **Human Rights and Transnational Corporations and Other Business Enterprises**, asking the UN Secretary-General to appoint a special representative on the subject. As a result, political scientist John Ruggie (1944–) was named Special Representative on Business and Human Rights. His efforts to develop a framework for a code of conduct based on the responsibility of corporations as well as governments to respect human rights, with a provision for remedies ("protect, respect, and remedy"), were hotly debated when presented in 2010 as the **Guiding Principles on Business and Human Rights**, but endorsed by the Human Rights Council in 2011.

In short, codes of conduct have arisen from five sources:

- Corporations have initiated their own social audits.
- Trade associations or industries have established standards. After the Bhopal tragedy, for example, the American Chemistry Council developed standards.
- Nongovernmental organizations have launched efforts to encourage humane working conditions.
- Governments have adopted fair labor standards legislation.
- Intergovernmental organizations, notably the ILO and the UN, have played important roles.

The movement for codes of conduct demonstrates an extraordinary development, sometimes called **transnationalism**. Hitherto, advocates for human rights or other issues have assumed that the venue for action was to beg nation-states for approval. Today, thanks to the Internet and ease of world travel, intergovernmental and nongovernmental entities can meet and make decisions together. The effect is to establish **global governance** in specific issue-areas. Besides the development of codes of conduct, another example of transnational decision making is to be found in the Fair Trade movement, which is discussed next.

FAIR TRADE

Codes of conduct are relevant to large corporations. The Fair Trade movement is concerned with humane conditions of work for small-scale primary agricultural producers. In 1860, the pseudonymously authored novel, *Havelaar, or the Coffee Auctions of the Dutch Trading Company*, attacked the evils of colonial exploitation of workers, in which former communal agricultural farmers were reduced to starvation levels by being dispossessed of their lands and forced to survive by working on Dutch coffee and tea plantations. Written by Eduard Douwes Dekker (1820–1887), the novel is sometimes credited with providing inspiration to anti-colonial movements around the world.

Soon after World War II, churches in Europe and North America decided to help millions of refugees and poverty-stricken communities by selling their handicrafts through such organizations as the Mennonite Central Committee. In the 1960s, alternative trade organizations (ATOs) were formed to negotiate purchases of goods from primary producers by department stores and similar companies. The first, Oxfam, began in 1965.

In 1968, the new *Whole Earth Catalog* listed handicraft items for sale so that buyers could contact vendors directly. In 1969, the first WorldShop opened in the Netherlands with actual products for sale, whereupon WorldShops spread to adjacent countries.

In 1988, when the price of coffee nosedived, the Max Havelaar Foundation began to issue labels in the Netherlands for cans of coffee that met standards of "fair trade," such as living wages for Third World workers. The idea was to enable customers and distributors to determine whether the products really benefited producers. That event spurred the fair trade movement, and several organizations emerged.

In 1989, the International Federation of Alternative Trade (IFAT) was formed as an alliance of ATOs with a headquarters in England. Currently, 70 ATOs from 30 countries are members.

In 1989, the movement went global with the formation of the International Fair Trade Association (IFAT), now called the World Fair Trade Organization (WFTO). Members include export marketing companies, importers, national and regional fair trade networks, producer cooperatives and associations, retailers, and support organizations. In 2004, the organization issued the first FTO mark to identify registered fair trade organizations.

In 1990, several ATOs in Europe joined together to form the European Fair Trade Association (EFTA). Today, 11 ATO members import products from some 400 economically disadvantaged producer groups in 9 developing countries. The organization seeks greater efficiency in importing.

In 1994, the Network of European Worldshops (NEWS!) was established to coordinate national associations representing 2,500 shops in 13 European countries. The organization provides publicity to encourage customers to purchase fair trade commodities.

Also in 1994, American and Canadian fair trade organizations joined to form the Fair Trade Federation (FTF).

In 1997, the largest fair trade organization was formed in Bonn, Germany – the Fairtrade Labeling Organizations International (FLO). In 1998, TransFair USA joined FLO, and the following year the organization began to certify fair trade coffee, some of which has been available at Starbucks from the year 2000, as well as cocoa and tea. Other fair trade products include bananas, fresh fruits and juices, herbs, honey, rice, sports balls, sugar, vanilla, and handicraft baskets made by women in Rwanda who are seeking to bring wealth to their country. In 2002, FLO issued a standard certification mark to be applied to fair trade products. In 2009, the organization split in two. Fairtrade International (FLO International), a nonprofit organization, develops standards and licenses organizations. Profit making FLO-CERT certifies and inspects producer organizations in more than 50 developing countries. Today, the FLO-CERT label is found in 50 countries from Europe to North America to Japan.

In 1998, FLO, IFAT, NEWS!, and EFTA joined together as FINE, their alphabetical acronyms, to enhance coordination.

The main criteria for certifying fair trade products are as follows:

- **Fair price** (farmer groups receive a minimum floor price, an additional premium for "organic" products, and are eligible for pre-harvest credit)
- **Fair labor** (workers have freedom of association, safe working conditions, and a living wage)
- **Direct trade** (products are purchased in bulk by fair trade ATOs, thereby eliminating the middle man)
- **Democracy and transparency** (farmers and farm workers decide democratically how to invest profits)
- **Community development** (profits are spent on upgrading the quality of products as well as on scholarships for members of the community)
- **Gender equity** (equal pay for women and female involvement in community decision making)
- **Environmental sustainability** (harmful agrochemicals and genetically modified organisms are banned; farming is managed without adverse impacts on ecosystems).

The result is that 1.5 million primary producers in 50 countries are deriving at least US$1 billion of additional income each year. Because fair trade prices can be higher than non-fair trade products, FLO encourages producer countries to process their products before shipment, such as by roasting and packaging coffee, so that they can undersell primary products that are processed in developed countries.

The other side of the coin from fair trade is the consumer boycott, often led by nongovernmental organizations. A survey in 2000 found that about 30 percent of customers in Western countries claim to avoid purchases if they believe that the producers have harmed animals, used sweatshops, or contributed to world pollution. In contrast, the Fair Trade movement challenges economic liberals who want the market to control world trade by rewarding producers who avoid human rights violations.

▎ MILLENNIUM DECLARATION

In the year 2000, the UN General Assembly convened a special session, known as the World Summit, in order to consider goals to be achieved in the twenty-first century. The resulting **United Nations Millennium Declaration** had much to say about economic, social, and cultural rights. In addition to urging developed countries to eliminate tariffs against the Third World and to cancel their official debts, the following goals and timetables were adopted relevant to economic and social rights:

- Eradicate extreme poverty and hunger
- Achieve universal primary education
- Promote gender equality and empower women
- Reduce child mortality by two-thirds
- Improve maternal health
- Combat HIV/AIDs, malaria, and other diseases
- Ensure environmental sustainability
- Develop a global partnership for development.

In addition, all developed countries are to contribute 0.7 percent of their national income in the form of aid to the Third World.

Previously, economic growth had been the goal of development aid on the assumption that as the size of the economic pie increased, there would be more to share for everyone. The Millennium Declaration abandoned that "trickle-down" approach in favor of poverty reduction. Elimination of poverty, in turn, would be achieved by following the principles of Nobel Prize-winning economist Amartya Sen (1933–), who advocates increasing the capabilities of ordinary people through improved education and health care, better care of the environment, and women's rights. As Sen puts it, "development is freedom." The assumption that poverty is a result of exploitation was rejected in favor of the observation that poverty is a result of neglect.

The principal economic innovation of the Millennium Declaration is support for the concept of **sustainable development**. Structural changes in developing country governments, including democratic accountability, are expected to enable them to make economic gains in the global economy while respecting fundamental human rights and engaging in environmentally sound practices that enable future generations to satisfy basic human needs. The goal of economic growth, then, is to give ordinary people the capability to prosper while promoting equality and nondiscrimination.

Whereas some aid has indeed been squandered over the years, with little impact on economic growth in the poorest countries, there is a consensus today that aid for health care has been extremely effective. The eradication of smallpox and considerable reduction in the incidence of guinea worms, leprosy, and river blindness has been due to carefully organized aid efforts. Since health problems are most acute among those in poverty, aid to improve health conditions has demonstrable effects on economic growth.

Each year, the UN Statistics Division charts 16 indicators to assess progress in achieving the Millennium Development Goals within nine regions of the world. In

2012, goals had been met or were expected to do so by 2015 in 40 percent of the 144 cells of the graph, whereas 9 percent of the cases were not making progress or had deteriorated. The goal of ending poverty by 2015 will not be met, but the quest continues.

PROBLEMS OF ACHIEVING ECONOMIC, SOCIAL, AND CULTURAL RIGHTS

Economic aid to developing countries is often justified as a way to encourage greater fulfillment of economic, social, and cultural rights – or perhaps to provide preconditions for increased civil and political rights. The strategies of economic development reviewed above changed because earlier efforts did not measure up. One reason is that, on the world stage, economic, social, and cultural rights have simply been neglected in comparison with civil and political rights. There are several reasons:

First of all, treaties guaranteeing economic, social, and cultural rights concede that implementation depends upon the resources of a country. According to the International Covenant on Economic, Social and Cultural Rights, "each State Party to the present Covenant undertakes to take steps, individually and through international assistance and cooperation, especially economic and technical, to the **maximum of its available resources**, with a view to achieving progressively the full realization of the rights recognized in the present Covenant …" (my emphasis added).

Second, developing countries have the poorest attainments. Leaders of some Third World countries say that they are too poor to afford improvements in the educational and health levels of their people, though such claims are often a smokescreen for elites and dictators.

Third, leading nongovernmental organizations, such as Amnesty International, have not focused on economic, social, and cultural rights. Other organizations, such as Médecins Sans Frontières, quietly work to improve conditions, but only during crises – that is, when problems have reached mammoth proportions.

Fourth, civil and political rights are stated in absolute terms, but economic, social, and cultural rights in the various treaties are phrased in softer terms, more as goals than as duties. States are only obligated to adopt incremental programs to achieve economic and social rights and to report to the UN on what the programs are and how much progress they are making. In others words, treaties guaranteeing civil and political rights say that government should absolutely not harm people, but the treaties dealing with economic and social rights do not insist on ironclad guarantees. People have rights and governments have duties in regard to civil and political rights; in contrast, people have economic, social, and cultural rights, but treaties do not insist that governments have strong obligations to fulfill their rights.

Fifth, media can easily focus on guns pointed at protesters and similar dramas. Denials of economic, social, and cultural rights are more subtle and make headlines primarily in such circumstances as when refugee camps provide visible evidence of desperate conditions.

The sixth reason is that monitoring by the Committee on Economic, Social and Cultural Rights (CESCR), which was established by the International Covenant on

Economic, Social, and Cultural Rights, requires reports at five-year intervals and recommends action only in response to those reports. For example, in 1995 CESCR asked the Dominican Republic to provide homes to those living under bridges, on the sides of cliffs, in homes dangerously close to rivers, and to ravine dwellers. The recommendation was by way of criticism that the government's response to Hurricane David, responsible for some 2,000 deaths in 1979, was inadequate.

Boycotts of countries that deny civil and political rights often ignore the resulting adverse economic, social, and cultural consequences. When the international community adopts economic sanctions for a gross violator of civil and political rights, one consequence may be that masses are hit harder than elites. For example, sanctions in place against Iraq after the Gulf War of 1991 so deprived children of food and medicine that the UN adopted an oil-for-food program. Similarly, aid to the starving population of Somalia after 9/11 has been hobbled with restrictions in areas where a recognized terrorist group operates. In general, the more comprehensive the sanctions, the more severe are the effects on the population.

Finally, no innovative legal or concrete approaches to implementation have been developed or even proposed by countries that most strongly support economic, social, and cultural rights.

CONCLUSION

Some critics, as noted in Chapter 5, argue that economic, social, and cultural rights are fundamentally different from civil and political rights. The counterargument, that the relationship is more complex, is supported by the following observations:

The view that the cost of implementation is less for civil and political rights than for economic, social, and cultural rights lacks empirical support; nobody has yet calculated which is more expensive. Economists estimate that there is a considerable return on investment in primary education when considering such factors as reduced fertility, reduced infant mortality, lower population growth, improved family nutrition, and increased productivity.

The argument that guarantees of civil and political rights require less government action than guarantees of economic, social, and cultural rights is also wrong. Government must act to ensure fair trials and free and fair elections, just as they must manage effective educational and health care systems.

Civil and political rights are often claimed to be invariant, whereas economic, social, and cultural rights are claimed to be relative to the culture of each country. However, civil and political rights are quite variable. In Britain, officeholders can sue the press for libel, but in the United States officeholders take a lot of abuse because they are considered public figures; they must tolerate lies in the media and on the campaign trail.

Another argument is that economic, social, and cultural rights can only be extended gradually, whereas civil and political rights must be guaranteed immediately. But the right to vote was extended gradually in most Western countries, whereas the right to food requires immediate action on behalf of those who are starving.

No democracy, as Amartya Sen notes, has ever had a famine. Famines never kill the ruling class. In a country with free elections, opposing political parties, and a free press, crop failures will lead to collective action on behalf of those affected instead of stockpiling by elites while the masses starve.

Little attention has been paid above on cultural rights, which most urgently affect persecuted minorities within states. One reason is that persecution, a violation of civil and political rights, gets more attention than the byproduct, cultural suppression. Although Article 5 of the International Convention on the Elimination of All Forms of Racial Discrimination claims that the guarantee of equality before the law ensures the enjoyment of economic, social, and cultural rights, in fact many ethnic and religious groups are treated unequally on account of what mainstream groups may view as their quaint or unusual practices.

Economic, social, and cultural rights affect more persons than civil and political rights. Children, who may be too young to participate in political life, have basic needs in regard to education, health, and other elements that are at the heart of the International Covenant on Economic, Social, and Cultural Rights.

Arguments about whether civil and political rights are more important than economic, social, and cultural rights – or vice versa – can be easily deconstructed as cynical rhetoric used by governments to justify their deliberate neglect of certain basic rights.

Some observers claim that those who are poor, discriminated against, and deprived of human dignity are most likely to engage in armed insurrection against their own governments or in terrorist acts against foreign states. If so, there is a need to respect economic, social, and cultural rights in order to reduce domestic and international violence.

The following chapter, which deals with rights of individuals when systematic violence erupts, may be seen as an extension of the principles of economic, social, and cultural rights, since wars and terrorist attacks can perhaps be measured in terms of economic, social, and cultural damage (especially to children, the elderly, the infirm, and to females) even more than in terms of violations of civil and political rights. Human suffering is more likely in time of war.

DISCUSSION TOPIC 6.3 HOW CAN ECONOMIC, SOCIAL, AND CULTURAL RIGHTS BE PROMOTED MOST EFFECTIVELY?

Deprivations of economic, social, and cultural rights are often neglected in comparison with denials of civil and political rights. What has been done to increase awareness of problems relating to economic, social, and cultural rights? What kinds of actions, either by individual countries or by intergovernmental organizations, can best serve to improve economic, social, and cultural rights?

CHAPTER 7

Crimes Against Peace and War Crimes

International human rights law deals with protections of civil, political, economic, social, and cultural rights in peacetime, as discussed in Chapters 5 and 6. **International humanitarian law** deals with issues of human rights violations in wartime. The earliest philosophical recognition of international humanitarian law emerged from the doctrine of the **just war** of Saint Augustine (354–430). Subsequently, rules of warfare developed. But they were shattered during the world wars of the twentieth century. Currently, the focus has broadened to domestic and international terrorism.

DEFINING "WAR"

War must be distinguished definitionally from other violent or unfriendly acts. Otherwise, one country might perceive an unfriendly act as an act of war, mount a form of violent retaliation, and then the other side might respond, resulting in unintended war. Two forms of unfriendly behavior, accepted under international law, are retorsion and reprisal. Neither is considered an act of war.

▌ HISTORIC EVENT 7.1 THE *CAROLINE* INCIDENT (1837)

In 1837, when the American steamer *Caroline* was being leased to run supplies to rebels seeking Canadian independence, British authorities went to the American side of the Niagara River to burn the vessel, in the process killing a watchman. Whereas the British claimed the right of self-defense, Americans were outraged at what they considered to be an act of piracy. Some Americans then organized unauthorized raids into Canada for the next four years, thus responding with piracy of their own. In 1842, Secretary of State Daniel Webster (1782–1852) questioned whether the British action of 1837 was self-defense. He argued that the right of anticipatory self-defense applies only when the threat is "instant, overwhelming, and leaving no choice of means, and no moment for delibera-tion," and the responsive measures are neither "unreasonable" nor "excessive." Although Lord Ashburton (1774–1848) disputed Webster's conclusion that the British acted improperly, he admitted that his government erred because there was neither an announcement in advance nor an apology afterward about the action taken. Webster then closed the dispute on the basis of a British apology. Webster's argument has been applied ever since to determine the legality of the right of reprisal.

Retorsion is a peaceful but negative response to an unfriendly act that does not violate a treaty but is unfriendly (Table 7.1). Some examples of retorsion occurred after diplomats at the US embassy in Iran were held hostage in 1979: Washington's first response was to freeze Iranian assets and to end trade relations with Iran. Even after the release of the hostages in 1981, the United States has refused to reestablish formal diplomatic relations, a second form of retorsion.

TABLE 7.1 RETORSIONS AND REPRISALS PERMITTED UNDER INTERNATIONAL LAW

Unfriendly act	Examples
Retorsion	Currency restrictions, denunciation of treaties, expulsion of diplomats or nationals of the other state, freezing or seizing assets from another state, jamming of radio broadcasts from abroad, military maneuvers and mobilizations on the border of another state, nonrecognition of one government and recognition of a rival government, increasing trade barriers, severance or withdrawal of diplomatic relations, verbal denunciations of another country
Reprisal	Attacks on commerce, blockades, boycotts and embargoes, landing of forces to rescue nationals abroad, limited military attacks and expeditions, including bombardments, seizure of vessels

A **reprisal**, in contrast, is an act of redress for a tangible injury. Under international law reprisals may take the form of force after the injured state gives notice of displeasure, requests compensation or cessation of harmful action, yet the injuring state makes no ameliorative response. A reprisal can be acceptable under international law so long as the counteraction is proportionate to the initial injury.

The acceptance of reprisals under international law grew out of the medieval practice, now defunct, of **private reprisals** under which a person who suffered ill-treatment from another community or its members might be authorized by a government to seek redress by seizing property of a member of the errant community. The procedure was to have a government of an aggrieved person issue a "letter of marque and reprisal" to the victim, who was then authorized to take independent action. Today, such letters are not issued. Instead, governments directly take reprisals. Accordingly, the American killing of Osama Bin Laden (1957–2011) could be considered a form of reprisal for the attack on the World Trade Center in 2001 because Bin Laden greenlighted the terrorist operation, though the operation intruded into the sovereignty of Pakistan, which was not consulted beforehand.

COURT CASE 7.1 THE NAULILAA ARBITRATION (1928)

In 1914, German civilian officials and soldiers crossed over the border of Portuguese Angola one day to discuss importing food into German Southwest Africa. Following a mistranslation, a Portuguese officer seized a German official's bridle and struck him. The German then drew his pistol. Next, the Portuguese official ordered his men to fire, whereupon two German officers were killed, and the interpreter and another officer were interned. Shortly thereafter, German troops attacked and destroyed several forts and posts in Angola, though Germany and Portugal were not at war until 1916. After the war, Germany and Portugal agreed to submit the dispute, known as the Naulilaa Incident, to arbitration. In 1928, the arbitral tribunal ruled that Germany should pay for the damages because their disproportionate actions were not in response to a violation of international law by Portugal and thus were not lawful reprisals but rather resulted from a mere misunderstanding that led to imprudent behavior.

In contrast with retorsion and reprisal, **war** is usually defined as a state of armed hostility between sovereign states. However, war may technically exist if one state declares war against another without actually engaging in armed hostility. For example, Thailand declared war on the United States during World War II to appease Japan, which used Thai territory as a springboard for attacking British colonies in Southeast Asia. Thailand and the United States never fought each other and became allies in 1954 with the signing of the South-East Asia Collective Defense Treaty.

▌ DEVELOPMENT OF THE LAW OF WARFARE

For centuries, wars were considered not to violate international law, though Greek and Roman law condemned the use of poison as an instrument of war. Such philosophers as Cicero (106–43 BCE), Augustine (354–430), and Thomas Aquinas (1225–1274) agreed that war could be justified if the **aims** and the **means** were just. In other words, there has to be a good reason for going to war, and war must be fought humanely.

Over time, several principles developed in Christian theology about the concept of a **just war**. According to Augustine, "a just war is wont to be described as one that avenges wrongs, when a nation or state has to be punished, for refusing to make amends for the wrongs inflicted by its subjects, or to restore what it has seized unjustly."

For Aquinas and later theologians, the principles on which a just war could be waged are as follows:

- **Just authority** (Only rulers have the power to start a war, since they are required to maintain order; private warfare is outlawed.)
- **Just cause** or **rightful intention** (There is a right to stop gross evil and an obligation to promote good.)
- **Military necessity** (The use of force should be a response to an aggressor whose actions are certain, grave, and continuing.)
- **Last resort** (Efforts to resolve a conflict must exhaust all peaceful means before war is contemplated.).

The **means** by which a war could be fought justly were identified by just war theorists as follows:

- **Humanity** (There should be no unnecessary violence and hence prisoners should be captured, not killed, and humanely treated.)
- **Proportionality** (Violence should be only enough to stop an evil and end in peace.)
- **Chivalry** (The use of defensive force should not involve dishonorable means, expedients, or conduct. Noncombatants should not be harmed, and no war should produce evils greater than those providing the pretext to war.).

Chivalry, now known by the term "right intention," was adopted because Crusaders returning to Europe were expected to confess if they engaged in any impure action.

Among the earliest legal principles (Table 7.2), the *Cáin Adomnáin* of 697, as agreed to by several Irish notables, authorized the death penalty for anyone killing a woman in time of war and other penalties for slaying clerics, clerical students, and peasants on clerical land. In 989, six French bishops at the Synod of Charroux declared the *Pax Dei* (Peace of God), a law of warfare that was expanded and later spread throughout Europe. Among the provisions were immunity of children, clergy, merchants, peasants, and women from attack in war. In 1027, the *Treuga Dei*

TABLE 7.2   **EARLY INTERNATIONAL AGREEMENTS DEVELOPING THE LAW OF WARFARE**

Adopted	Document
697	*Cáin Adomnáin*
989	*Pax Dei*
1026	*Treuga Dei*
1139	Canon 29 (issued by the Second Lateran Council)
1675	Strasbourg Agreement
1815	Final Act of the Congress of Vienna
1856	Declaration Respecting Maritime Law (Declaration of Paris)
1864	Convention for the Amelioration of the Wounded in Armies in the Field (Geneva Convention) (in force 1865)
1868	Additional Articles Relating to the Condition of the Wounded in War
1868	Declaration to the Effect of Prohibiting the Use of Certain Projectiles in Wartime (St Petersburg Declaration)
1874	Project of an International Declaration Concerning the Laws and Customs of War (Brussels Declaration)

(Truce of God) was promulgated, declaring that war could not take place on certain days of the year – initially Sundays, but later religious holidays, including the entire period of Lent, and Fridays. The clergy could threaten violators with excommunication, a more limited sanction after the rise of Protestantism in the sixteenth century. Pope Innocent II (?–1143) urged a ban on the use of the crossbow as an overly cruel instrument of warfare in **Canon 29**, as issued by the Second Lateran Council in 1139.

Later, Dutch Protestant jurist Hugo Grotius (1583–1645) began to formulate a secular theory of the law of war. In his *The Freedom of the Seas* (1609), he argued that war should be banned in international waters. The Netherlands was trying to maintain a fleet to trade around the world, and interference by Britain and Spain was impeding the ambitions of his country.

During the Thirty Years War (1618–1648), Grotius proposed that international law should govern relations between states. His advocacy of the development of a law of warfare in his 1625 volume *De jure belli ac pacis libri tres* (*Of Laws of War and Peace*) included a theory of **just war** in which natural law binds all states. His law of justifiable war (*jus ad bellum*) was that a country should only go to war to achieve the following **goals**:

- **Defense.** Wars are just when they defend the national interest.
- **Indemnity.** Wars are just if they recover damages inflicted by another state.
- **Punishment.** Wars are just if they stop a gross ongoing injustice.
- **Last resort.** Wars are just only if peaceful methods fail to resolve an interstate conflict based on the preceding three pretexts.

In addition, Grotius's law of the conduct of war (*jus in bello*) required that the **means** used in warfare should be as follows:

- **Discrimination**. Combat should not be directed at civilians.
- **Humanity**. The sick and wounded should be cared for, and prisoners should be treated with respect.
- **Proportionality**. The scope of the war should be minimal, calibrated only to the end sought.

Presumably, government leaders had to satisfy the requirements of *jus ad bellum*, whereas military personnel in the field would have to follow the principles of *jus in bello*. If a government authorized an army to violate the principles of *jus in bello*, then both would violate the law of warfare.

DISCUSSION TOPIC 7.1 WHEN WAS THE LAST "JUST WAR"?

Using the concept of "just war," however defined, which recent war could be characterized as just? The Gulf War of 1991? The Afghan War that began in 2001? The Libyan War of 2011? Or some other recent war? Indicate why a recent war was just or unjust. If unjust, what circumstances would have to have been present to make the war just?

Consistent with Grotius's ideas, international law after the Peace of Westphalia of 1648 was recorded in the form of treaties between nation-states. Perhaps the first example of what developed as the treaty-based law concerning the conduct of warfare occurred in 1675, when France and the Holy Roman Empire signed the **Strasbourg Agreement**, which banned the use of poison and of toxic bullets.

In 1815, the **Final Act of the Congress of Vienna** identified an unjust reason for aggression – war in breach of a treaty. A government must first denounce the treaty, thereby giving notice to the other party or parties to the treaty so that there might be an opportunity to negotiate a grievance short of war. The aim was to declare retroactively that France's Napoléon Bonaparte (1769–1821) had violated international law by launching aggressive war against Russia during 1812 in violation of a peace treaty, the Treaty of Tilsit of 1807. His subsequent arrest and detention in exile made him the world's first war criminal, though he was never put on trial.

The humane warfare movement that mushroomed after the Crimean War (1853–1856) resulted in the first international recognition of a law of warfare – the **Declaration of Paris** of 1856. The agreement, which concerned maritime warfare, banned privateering (hiring private shipowners to harass and seize enemy ships), insisted that blockades must be enforced to be respected, and clarified rules regarding goods carried by neutral countries.

In 1863, President Abraham Lincoln (1809–1865) issued the Lieber Code, which covered nearly all aspects of the conduct of the war, including how to treat the property and soldiers of the enemy. Lincoln asked political scientist Francis Lieber (1799–1872) of Columbia University to codify the law of war in order to guide proper conduct of soldiers during the American Civil War (1861–1865). When the war ended, however, only one soldier was punished for violating war crimes – Henry Wirz (1823–1865).

COURT CASE 7.2 *UNITED STATES V. WIRZ* (1865)

After the American Civil War (1861–1865), Confederate Captain Henry Wirz (1822–1865), who commanded the Andersonville Prison Camp, was tried and convicted before a military commission for "conspiracy to destroy prisoners' lives in violation of the laws and customs of war" and "murder [of 12,921 persons] in violation of the laws and customs of war." He is arguably the first person ever charged, tried, and found guilty of being a war criminal. Other Confederate leaders and soldiers were pardoned, died, or left the country to avoid prosecution. As a matter of political expediency, Jefferson Davis (1808–1889), President of the Confederate States of America from 1861–1865, was never prosecuted; he retained popularity in the former secessionist Southern states.

After the Battle of Solferino in the Austro-Italian War of 1859, pressure from Henri Dunant (1828–1910) and others resulted in the **Convention for the Amelioration of the Wounded in Armies in the Field**, which was adopted in 1864, borrowing heavily from the Lieber Code. The Geneva Convention, or Red Cross Convention, as the 1864 convention is commonly known, dealt with the treatment of the sick and wounded on battlefields:

- The wounded have a right to receive medical treatment.
- Prisoners of war are to be given food and clothing and protection under the law.
- Those who carry white flags are inviolable.
- Civilians must be protected from unlimited warfare.
- The Red Cross has the right to treat wounded, to inform governments of the location of prisoners of war, to transmit mail and packets from families of prisoners, and to arrange repatriation of the seriously wounded.
- Ambulances, hospitals, their personnel, patients, and medical evacuations are to be regarded as neutral.
- Homes accommodating sick and wounded are exempt from quartering troops.
- After wounds are healed, soldiers should go home, exempt from further combat.
- Red crosses are to be used to signify medical facilities and personnel.

In 1868, the Geneva Convention was supplemented by the **Additional Articles Relating to the Condition of the Wounded in War**, which applies the same provisions to combat at sea, and requires belligerents that capture neutral medical personnel to pay them and to allow them to work normally.

In 1868, an International Military Commission of major European powers met in St Petersburg at the invitation of Tsar Alexander II (1818–1881). They agreed on the **Declaration to the Effect of Prohibiting the Use of Certain Projectiles in Wartime**, also known as the St Petersburg Declaration. The main principle enunciated was that weapons of war should be limited to making an enemy force incapable of fighting. Thus, the principle that there should be no unnecessary suffering from collateral damage entered the laws of war. A specific ban in the declaration was on explosive or flammable projectiles less than 400 grams.

The **Project of an International Declaration Concerning the Laws and Customs of War**, issued at a conference at Brussels during 1874, urged the following prohibitions:

- Poison or poisoned weapons
- Arms, projectiles, or material that would cause unnecessary suffering
- Improper uses of white flags and red crosses
- Destruction of property unless militarily necessary
- Inhumane treatment of surrendering soldiers, which were to be considered prisoners of war (POWs).

The Brussels Declaration, as the document was known, adopted the form of a proposed Convention on the Laws and Customs of War with 56 articles, but was so lengthy that adoption as a treaty required more time to consider each provision. The unfinished deliberations at the meeting encouraged Tsar Nicholas II (1868–1918) to convene a peace conference at The Hague in 1899.

THE HAGUE PEACE CONFERENCES

In 1899, when the International Peace Conference convened at The Hague, the principal item on the agenda was disarmament. Britain and Germany were locked into a naval arms race that presumably could only end in war. The main results of the conference, however, were in the development of the law of warfare; the disarmament goal was not achieved. The most significant advance was the **Convention for the Pacific Settlement of International Disputes**, which declared that all interstate disputes must be settled peacefully, that is, by good officers or mediation of a third party, by a neutral commission of inquiry, or by arbitration, and all countries should make themselves available as third parties. To help to resolve interstate disputes, a Permanent Court of Arbitration was formed at The Hague.

The remaining treaties and declarations at the Hague Conference amended and extended provisions of the 1864 Geneva Convention. Some new provisions, not obvious from the titles of the declarations, are as follows:

- Superiors are responsible for acts of subordinates.
- Soldiers cannot carry concealed weapons, engage in pillaging, or use bullets that expand or flatten inside the human body.
- Treatment of POWs was clarified to involve the same clothing, food, and shelter as the capturing country's soldiers; payment for nonstrenuous, nonmilitary work; the establishment of an information bureau to disseminate information about POWs; postage-free mail; and the right to worship.
- Neutral powers were to give safe passage to the sick and wounded and to confine captured belligerents away from the war theater, providing them with needed clothing, food, and medical attention.
- In the event that a victorious country occupies a defeated country, the occupying power is required to provide.

  o law and order
  o respect for the rights of the occupied in regard to their family, liberties, property, and religion
  o payment of damages for the destruction of nonmilitary property
  o imposition of taxes and requirement of services solely for the necessities of the occupation
  o cash payments for requisitioned services
  o a prohibition on collective punishments.

All six agreements were ratified and went into effect in 1900, though the treaty banning weapons launched from balloons expired in 1905. The final act of the Hague Conference of 1899 expressed a desire for another conference to deal with more questions.

Four years later, the Convention for the Adaptation to Maritime Warfare was amended. The **Convention for the Exemption of Hospital Ships, in Time of War, from the Payment of All Duties and Taxes Imposed for the Benefit of the State** was signed by diplomats from 25 countries at The Hague in 1904 and entered into force in 1907.

In 1906, delegates to the second conference at The Hague expanded the laws of warfare (Table 7.4), in part because of the fear of the destructive power of the

TABLE 7.3   AGREEMENTS DEVELOPING THE LAW OF WAR AT THE HAGUE CONFERENCE OF **1899**

Document	In force
Convention for the Pacific Settlement of International Disputes	1900
Convention with Respect to the Laws and Customs of War on Land	1900
Convention for the Adaptation to Maritime Warfare of the Principles of the Geneva Convention of 1864	1900
Declaration Prohibiting Launching of Projectiles and Explosives from Balloons	1900
Declaration Concerning Asphyxiating Gases	1900
Declaration Concerning Expanding Bullets	1900

TABLE 7.4   AGREEMENTS DEVELOPING THE LAW OF WAR AT THE HAGUE
CONFERENCE OF 1906

Document	In force
Convention for the Amelioration of the Condition of the Wounded and Sick in Armies in the Field	1907
Convention for the Pacific Settlement of International Disputes	1910
Convention Respecting the Limitation of the Employment of Force for the Recovery of Contract Debts	1910
Convention Relative to the Opening of Hostilities	1910
Convention Respecting the Laws and Customs of War on Land	1910
Convention Respecting the Rights and Duties of Neutral Powers and Persons in Case of War on Land	1910
Convention Relating to the Status of Enemy Merchant Ships at the Outbreak of Hostilities	1910
Convention Relating to the Conversion of Merchant Ships into War-Ships	1910
Convention Relative to the Laying of Automatic Submarine Contact Mines	1910
Convention Concerning Bombardment by Naval Forces in Time of War	1910
Convention for the Adaptation to Maritime War of the Principles of the Geneva Convention	1910
Convention Relative to Certain Restrictions with Regard to the Exercise of the Right of Capture in Naval War	1910
Convention Concerning the Rights and Duties Neutral Powers in Naval War	1910
Declaration Prohibiting Launching of Projectiles and Explosives from Balloons	1909

newest technology. Therefore, one provision was a requirement to deactivate submarine mines and torpedoes when not in use. Most of the new provisions clarified the role of neutral countries. POWs at the rank of commissioned officers were declared to be exempt from the work requirement that might be imposed on others. The final act underscored the principle of the compulsory arbitration of international disputes as the most important result of the deliberations.

One proposed treaty at the second conference at The Hague was to establish a prize court – an international court that would determine how to handle an enemy or neutral ship captured in time of war. However, only one country ratified the agreement. In 1910, an amendment to the agreement was adopted to encourage more ratifications, but the amended treaty failed as well. Without the agreement, countries that seize ships in wartime have continued to make determinations in their own courts on claims filed by shipowners from other countries.

Following up recommendations at a conference on naval warfare held at London in 1908–1909, the **Declaration Concerning the Laws of Naval War** included provisions regulating blockades, contraband, prizes, transfer to a neutral flag, naval convoys, and searches. But the agreement never entered into force.

World War I (1914–1918) shattered the expectations of the diplomats at the Hague Conferences, who had planned to meet again in 1915 but were unable to do so when the war pitted so many European countries against one another. During the war, Germany used poison gas and fired on neutral ships in international waters, so preceding conference efforts appeared to have been in vain.

LEAGUE OF NATIONS ERA

The **League of Nations Covenant**, as contained within the Treaty of Versailles, called upon states collectively to prevent and stop wars by arbitration, diplomacy, submission to the League Council, or referral to the newly formed Permanent Court of International Justice. A state was to delay going to war until three months after a decision by an international body about the validity of a pretext for war. If a state did not agree to such a procedure, other states could impose sanctions on countries that went to war.

Article 227 of the Treaty of Versailles indicted Kaiser Wilhelm (1859–1941) for violating the laws of warfare. A special tribunal, with one judge to be appointed by each of the principal Allied and Associated Powers, was authorized to try him for a "supreme offense against international morality and the sanctity of treaties." However, he fled to the Netherlands, which refused to surrender him. Article 228 provided that Germany must hand over those who committed acts "in violation of the laws and customs of war" for trials before military tribunals. In other words, individuals could be prosecuted for carrying out actions of states.

In 1920, when a list of about 1,000 persons was drawn up, the new German democratic government feared that trials in courts at local levels would adversely stir up public opinion, so they instead proposed a trial of a limited number of soldiers before the highest court in Leipzig. The Allied Powers agreed, and 12 were tried. The most famous case involved two German naval commanders who were responsible for firing on survivors in lifeboats of a torpedoed British hospital ship. Of the 12, only 6 were convicted, but given light sentences. Nevertheless, the precedent had been established that heads of state and military commanders could be tried for war crimes by a tribunal authorized by a multilateral agreement.

The Treaty of Sèvres, which made peace with the Ottoman Empire in 1920, also provided for trials of war criminals. Known as the Constantinople Trials, a special tribunal was approved by Sultan Mehmed VI (1861–1926). There were 35 trials involving some 200 soldiers, resulting in 17 death penalty verdicts. However, the occupation of Anatolia by the Allied Powers provoked resistance led by Mustafa Kamal Pasha (1881–1938) from 1919 until victory in 1922. As a result, all prisoners were released, and death sentences were never carried out.[1]

After the establishment of the League, the law of warfare expanded with the adoption of several new treaties (Table 7.5). Some treaties were proposed to further regulate various means of warfare. The first two, adopted in 1922 and 1923, dealt with chemical warfare, warfare in the air and undersea, and the use of radio broadcasts to provide valuable intelligence information, but they never went into effect. Limits on bacteriological and chemical warfare were, however, established in an agreement adopted in 1925 that went into force during 1928 – the **Protocol for the Prohibition of the Use of Asphyxiating, Poisonous or Other Gases, and of Bacteriological Methods of Warfare**.

In 1924, the **Protocol for the Pacific Settlement of International Disputes**, also known as the Geneva Protocol, sought to define "aggression," a term left undefined in the League of Nations Covenant. The agreement, adopted by the League

TABLE 7.5   AGREEMENTS DEVELOPING THE LAW OF WAR BETWEEN THE WORLD WARS

Adopted	Document	In force
1919	League of Nations Covenant	1920
1922	Treaty Relating to the Use of Submarines and Noxious Gases in Warfare (Treaty of Washington)	1923
1923	Rules Concerning the Control of Wireless Telegraphy in Time of War and Air Warfare	
1924	Protocol for the Pacific Settlement of International Disputes (Geneva Protocol)	1928
1925	Protocol for the Prohibition of the Use of Asphyxiating, Poisonous or Other Gases, and of Bacteriological Methods of Warfare	1928
1928	General Treaty for the Renunciation of War (Kellogg–Briand Pact)	1929
1928	Convention on Duties and Rights of States in the Event of Civil Strife	1929
1928	Convention on Maritime Neutrality	1931
1929	Convention for the Amelioration of the Condition of the Wounded and Sick in Armies in the Field	1931
1929	Convention Relative to the Treatment of Prisoners of War	1931
1930	Treaty for the Limitation and Reduction of Naval Armaments	1930
	• Procès-Verbal Relating to the Rules of Submarine Warfare Set Forth in Part IV of the Treaty of London of 22 April 1930	1936
1935	Treaty on the Protection of Artistic and Scientific Institutions and Historic Monuments (Roerich Pact)	1935
1937	The Nyon Agreement	1937
1937	• Agreement Supplementary to the Nyon Agreement	1937

Assembly, simply said that an "aggressor" was a country that launched war without first submitting its dispute to arbitration.

The most important treaty came in 1928, when war itself was outlawed in the **General Treaty for the Renunciation of War**, also known as the Pact of Paris or the Kellogg–Briand Pact. All interstate disputes were to be resolved peacefully thenceforth – with no exception whatsoever.

Also in 1928, two agreements focused on civil wars and neutral ships in time of war – the **Convention on Duties and Rights of States in the Event of Civil Strife** and the **Convention on Maritime Neutrality**. In 1929, two treaties amended and extended previous Geneva Conventions – the **Convention for the Amelioration of the Condition of the Wounded and Sick in Armies in the Field** and the **Convention Relative to the Treatment of Prisoners of War**. The latter had very detailed provisions regarding POWs. One important innovation was the right of monthly health inspections, which would ordinarily be handled by the Red Cross. Another is that POWs must be protected against insults, public curiosity, and violence.

In 1930, the London disarmament conference adopted the **Treaty for the Limitation and Reduction of Naval Armaments**, but only for a six-year period.

As the treaty was about to expire, the conference reconvened in 1936 to indefinitely extend Article IV, which applied the laws of warfare to submarines; the agreement was known as the **Procès-Verbal**. No agreement, however, covered aerial warfare, which was to play a substantial role during World War II.

The **Roerich Pact** of 1935, applicable only to the Americas, provided that historic monuments, museums, scientific, artistic, educational, and cultural institutions and their personnel are neutral in war. The **Nyon Agreement** of 1937, and its supplement, immediately applicable to naval warfare in the Mediterranean during the Spanish Civil War (1936–1939), provided that neutral merchant ships were permitted to defend themselves if attacked by a belligerent.

Of course, the various laws of warfare would be unnecessary if there were no wars. The main hope of the League of Nations was that gradual disarmament would limit the ability to wage war. Some arms limitation conferences were held, and a few even resulted in agreements, but they later unraveled. After World War II broke out in 1939, many of the limitations on warfare were ignored. Because of the unprecedented use of massive aerial bombing, civilian populations suffered heavy losses on an unprecedented scale.

THE NUREMBERG AND TOKYO WAR CRIMES TRIALS

During World War II, some 140 American military personnel were convicted in courts-martial of war crimes against civilians (72 for murder, 50 for rape, and 18 for both murder and rape),[2] so the prosecution of German war criminals was hardly unprecedented. In 1945, the **Agreement for the Prosecution and Punishment of the Major War Criminals of the European Axis**, and the **Charter of the International Military Tribunal** were drafted for trials at Nuremberg. The defendants were charged with one or more of three major offenses, of which two were coined for the first time – crimes against peace and crimes against humanity. The term "genocide" had not yet come into currency and thus was not used. The Charter's text defining the three offenses is as follows:

- **Crimes Against Peace**: namely, planning, preparation, initiation or waging of a war of aggression, or a war in violation of international treaties, agreements or assurances, or participation in a common plan or conspiracy for the accomplishment of any of the foregoing;
- **War Crimes**: namely, violations of the laws or customs of war. Such violations shall include, but not be limited to, murder, ill-treatment or deportation to slave labor or for any other purpose of civilian population of or in occupied territory, murder or ill-treatment of prisoners of war or persons on the seas, killing of hostages, plunder of public or private property, wanton destruction of cities, towns or villages, or devastation not justified by military necessity;
- **Crimes Against Humanity**: namely, murder, extermination, enslavement, deportation, and other inhumane acts committed against any civilian population, before or during the war, or persecutions on political, racial or religious grounds in execution of or in connection with any crime within the jurisdiction

of the Tribunal, whether or not in violation of the domestic law of the country where perpetrated.

The Charter established the foundation for current international humanitarian law in two respects:

- A government's treatment of its own citizens is a matter of international concern, thus establishing a post-Westphalian international contract.
- Individuals are accountable for their actions.

According to the Charter, the most important of the three offenses was the crime against peace. The term "crimes against humanity," as discussed in Chapter 5, was new.

Specific counts in the Nuremberg indictment charged Nazi leaders with a conspiracy to violate all three offenses and contained detailed descriptions of violations of international law. Many defendants sought exoneration on the grounds that they were merely carrying out orders (the **headquarters doctrine**) or that they were unable to control what their subordinates did, but the court rejected both arguments, ruling that they had **command responsibility**. Interestingly, Nazi Germany treated most American, British, and other allied prisoners of war according to the terms of the Geneva Convention; their reason was to ensure that allied forces would treat German POWs in an equivalent manner.

One of the terms of Japan's surrender in 1945 was the acceptance of the **Potsdam Declaration**. Article 10 of the declaration suggested two other types of war crimes:

- Violation of international laws (such as the abuse of POWs)
- Obstructing democratic tendencies and civil liberties of the Japanese people.

The latter offense was used to justify the postwar occupation by the United States that guided efforts of Japanese to reestablish their democratic institutions.

In 1945, General Douglas MacArthur II (1880–1964), Supreme Commander of Allied Forces in the Southwest Pacific Area, decided not to wait for terms of the Tokyo War Crimes Trial to be drawn up. Hastily, he arranged for an American military commission in Manila to try General Tomoyuki Yamashita (1888–1946), the Japanese commander of military operations in Southeast Asia. Yamashita was found guilty and was sentenced to death by hanging. He appealed to the US Supreme

COURT CASE 7.3 *APPLICATION OF YAMASHITA* (1946)

General Tomoyuki Yamashita (1885–1946), the Japanese commanding general in Malaya, the Philippines, and Singapore, was charged by an American military commission in Manila with two offenses:

continued

- The brutal attack on civilians known as the Manila Massacre
- Bayoneting hospital patients in Singapore.

The tribunal, hastily organized in 1945 by General Douglas MacArthur II (1880–1964), handed down a guilty verdict despite evidence that one of the units in Manila disobeyed his order to retreat, other units acted without his specific orders, and Yamashita disciplined soldiers responsible for the bayoneting incident. After his conviction, he appealed to the US Supreme Court, arguing that the documentary evidence was insufficient to link his commands with atrocities committed by his troops. In *Application of Yamashita* (327US1) the court in 1946 upheld the guilty verdict, based on the doctrine of command responsibility.

Court, which upheld the guilty verdict. He was the first general of a defeated enemy country ever tried for war crimes.

The **Charter of the International Military Tribunal for the Far East**, which operated from 1946 to 1948, defined the same offenses as those used at Nuremberg. The counts in the Tokyo indictments were stated in the following terms:

- Leading, organizing, instigating, or being accomplices in the formulation or execution of a common plan or conspiracy to wage wars of aggression
- Ordering, authorizing, and permitting inhumane treatment of POWs and others
- Deliberately and recklessly disregarding the duty to take adequate steps to prevent atrocities (mass murder, rape, pillage, brigandage, torture, and other barbaric cruelties upon the helpless civilian population)
- Plundering public and private property
- Wantonly destroying cities, towns and villages beyond any justification of military necessity
- Waging aggressive, unprovoked war.

The high-profile Nuremberg Trials overshadowed the trials in the Far East, but they both established the principle that certain offenses applied everywhere in the world. Although the tribunals were criticized at the time to be a form of "victor's justice," in 1946 the UN General Assembly accepted the principles and the judgments of the trials. Britain proposed that the Nuremberg court should be made permanent, but that goal was not fulfilled until the International Criminal Court was established in 2002.

The Nuremberg and Tokyo charters, in effect, enumerated four types of war crimes:[3]

- Aggression
- Military conduct of war

- Mistreatment of prisoners
- Misgovernment in occupying a defeated country.

Unprovoked military aggression had already been outlawed by the General Pact for the Renunciation of War of 1928. Crimes relating to the military conduct of war, mistreatment of POWs, and rules governing military occupation, which had been developed by the Geneva and the Hague Conventions, were to be elaborated more fully in the Geneva Conventions of 1949 and later treaties.

UNITED NATIONS ERA: EARLY ACCOMPLISHMENTS

A paramount objective of the **Charter of the United Nations** was to prevent future wars. In Article 2(4), unilateral **aggression** is identified as a violation of the basic principles of the UN Charter. The same provision bans even the **threat to go to war**. Article 33 reiterates provisions of previous agreements about the requirement of parties to a dispute to "seek a solution by negotiation, enquiry, mediation, conciliation, arbitration, judicial settlement" and adds "resort to regional agencies or arrangements, or other peaceful means of their own choice."

Articles 41–42 give the Security Council the power to authorize nonmilitary sanctions and, if necessary, to take military actions against recalcitrant states. Thus, all wars now require approval by the Security Council. If a country believes that legitimate self-defense requires an immediate response, the Security Council must be consulted soon after a war is in progress. The Security Council must also approve an application to launch military action in advance of hostilities. However, if the Security Council is unable to act because one of the five major powers (Britain, China, France, Russia, United States) has vetoed a resolution authorizing war on behalf of the UN, Article 33 has been interpreted by some scholars to give regional bodies the power to act instead.

During the early years of the UN, there were many advances in the development of the law of war (Table 7.6). The military excesses associated with World War II, from death camps to bombing raids, prompted efforts to expand and consolidate previous Geneva Conventions, and in 1949 four Geneva Conventions were adopted. Mindful of the horrors of the Nazis, all four conventions had three major new provisions:

- Treatment of all detainees must be on an equal basis; that is, without regard to race, color, religion or faith, sex, birth, or wealth.
- All countries must hunt for those who violate the most serious offenses; namely, deliberate killing, torture, inhuman treatment, biological experimentation, and causing serious disease or injury, so that they can be brought to justice.
- Anyone captured in wartime is entitled to a hearing before a "competent tribunal" to decide whether there is a reasonable basis for their detention.

The **First Geneva Convention** extended previous coverage to civilians on land. One requirement of the treaty, to have honorable burials of enemy dead, was violated

TABLE 7.6   EARLY AGREEMENTS DEVELOPING THE LAW OF WAR BY THE UNITED NATIONS AND SIMILAR BODIES

Adopted	Document	In force
1945	Charter of the United Nations	1945
1949	Convention for the Amelioration of the Condition of the Wounded and Sick in Armed Forces in the Field (First Geneva Convention)	1950
1949	Convention for the Amelioration of the Condition of Wounded, Sick and Shipwrecked Members of Armed Forces at Sea (Second Geneva Convention)	1950
1949	Geneva Convention Relative to the Treatment of Prisoners of War (Third Geneva Convention)	1950
1949	Convention Relative to the Protection of Civilian Persons in Time of War (Fourth Geneva Convention)	1950
1954	Convention for the Protection of Cultural Property in the Event of Armed Conflict	1956
1954	• Protocol for the Protection of Cultural Property in the Event of Armed Conflict	1956
1999	• Second Protocol to the Hague Convention of 1954 for the Protection of Cultural Property in the Event of Armed Conflict	2004
1967	Convention on the Prohibition of the Use of Nuclear Weapons (draft)	
1968	Convention on the Non-Applicability of Statutory Limitations to War Crimes and Crimes Against Humanity	1970
1973	Principles of International Cooperation in the Detection, Arrest, Extradition and Punishment of Persons Guilty of War Crimes and Crimes Against Humanity	
1974	Declaration on the Protection of Women and Children in Emergency and Armed Combat	
1977	Protocol Additional to the Geneva Conventions of 12 August 1949, and Relating to the Protection of Victims of Non-International Armed Conflicts (Protocol I)	1978
1977	Protocol Additional to the Geneva Conventions of 12 August 1949, and Relating to the Protection of Victims of International Armed Conflicts (Protocol II)	1979
2005	Protocol Additional to the Geneva Conventions of 12 August 1949, and Relating to the Adoption of an Additional Distinctive Emblem (Protocol III)	2007

in 2005, when American military personnel burned bodies of two Taliban fighters rather than providing for their burial in accordance with Afghan custom. The **Second Geneva Convention** applied the same requirements to naval combat.

The **Third Geneva Convention** focused on prisoners of war, including how to deal with those who commit criminal offenses or infractions of POW camp rules. The provision that POWs must be repatriated, even if they fear persecution after they return to their home country, complicated negotiations for an armistice to end the Korean War (1950–1953), so the UN General Assembly set up the Neutral Nations Repatriation Commission in 1953 to handle some 14,200 POWs who refused to return to their homes in China and North Korea. Despite efforts of the commission to encourage repatriation, few changed their minds. As a result of psychological torture while in detention, 23 captured Americans refused to return home.

DISCUSSION TOPIC 7.2 HAS THE UNITED STATES VIOLATED GENEVA CONVENTIONS IN GUANTÁNAMO?

About 780 persons captured during 2001 were sent to the American naval base at Guantánamo Bay. Most were rounded up by Afghan and Pakistani bounty hunters, some simply because they spoke Arabic or had Casio watches, as that was the brand of watch reportedly worn by the hijackers on September 11, 2001. Although most were later released, including at least 60 children, some have been charged with war crimes for their roles in aiding Al-Qaeda's attack on the United States on September 11. Initially denied access to attorneys, few have been tried, although the US Supreme Court ruled that they have the right to lawyers and to be tried in legislatively authorized courts. Several have complained of torture, and a few have committed suicide. To what extent has the treatment of the detainees been a violation of international law? Which specific provisions?

One of the main considerations was to cover situations similar to the Nazi German takeover of Austria and Czechoslovakia in which there was no formal declaration of war but instead armed forces of one country intruded into the territory of another country without resistance and remained as an occupying power. The **Fourth Geneva Convention**, accordingly, provided details about the administration of occupied territories. Among the most important requirements are the following:

• No individual or mass forcible transfers, as well as deportations of protected persons from occupied territory to the territory of the occupying power or to that of any other countries.
• Law and order is the responsibility of the occupying power.
• Prisoners of the occupying power who do not qualify for the full protection of POW status are entitled to humane treatment and to "the judicial guarantees which are recognized as indispensable by civilized peoples."
• The occupying power is responsible for economic reconstruction of damaged infrastructure and property.
• The occupying power should respect the sovereignty of the occupied people.
• Human rights violators should be tried and punished.

After ratifications in the 1950s, provisions of the Fourth Geneva Convention were applicable to the Four-Power occupation of Austria and Germany after World War II. Subsequent occupations that might be held to the same standard are Israel's occupation of the West Bank (1967–); Vietnam's occupation of Cambodia (1979–1989); Timor-Leste's occupation by Indonesia (1975–1999); the UN administrations of Cambodia (1991–1993), Kosovo (1999–), and Timor-Leste (1999–); as well as the American occupations of Afghanistan (2001–) and Iraq (2003–2011). The Fourth Geneva Convention could be interpreted as providing rules governing the **just peace**.

The Fourth Geneva Convention requires respect for the property of civilians and noncombatants. Because many paintings had been stolen from Jewish persons and others by the Nazis, a Conference on Jewish Material Claims Against Germany was held in 1951 at The Hague. In attendance were the governments of Israel and West Germany as well as various Jewish nongovernmental organizations. Bonn agreed at the conference to pay US$60 billion to Nazi victims in 19 countries, the first time in history when victims of human rights violations were directly compensated. Then in 1954, the **Convention for the Protection of Cultural Property in the Event of Armed Conflict** and an associated protocol were adopted, authorizing sanctions against those who would destroy, transfer, or find military uses for cultural property. A later protocol, with more details, was adopted in 1999.

DISCUSSION TOPIC 7.3 IS ISRAEL'S OCCUPATION OF THE WEST BANK IN ACCORD WITH INTERNATIONAL LAW?

After World War I, Palestine was administered by Britain as a League of Nations mandate. In 1948, while war erupted between Arab residents and Israeli independence forces, Jordan seized control of the territory west of the Jordan River, known as the West Bank, and Israel declared independence. In 1967, Israel took possession of the West Bank in the Six-Day War, though Jordan did not officially give up its claim until 1988. Meanwhile, the UN considered the West Bank to be occupied territories, and Israel put up signs accordingly. The Christian and Muslim Arabic-speaking residents of the West Bank have not been pleased with the arrangement, and Israel has allowed Jewish settlers to live in newly constructed small settlements on the West Bank. Retaliatory attacks on Israeli civilians by Palestinians have resulted in some deaths. In response, Israel has often launched counterattacks – that is, collective punishments on entire villages, aiming to deter or root out terrorists. Using an Israeli law authorizing indefinite detention, many Arabic-speaking persons have been arrested and held without trial for years, provoking some Palestinians to kidnap Israelis in order to arrange for exchanges. Despite nonratification of the Fourth Geneva Convention, is Israel violating international law? Should Israel ratify the Fourth Geneva Convention?

In 1968, the **Convention on the Non-Applicability of Statutory Limitations to War Crimes and Crimes Against Humanity** established two new principles:

- There is no statute of limitations on crimes against humanity, crimes against peace, or war crimes.
- States are obligated to extradite war criminals to countries which desire to place them on trial.

Thus, under the principle of **universal jurisdiction**, such offenders cannot escape accountability. A person guilty of the offenses identified in the four Geneva Conventions and related treaties can be captured and tried anywhere in the world, though nationals of one country are expected to be tried by their own courts. Former Nazi officials might change their names and conduct exemplary lives, but they were, and are, still subject to prosecution, as for example was Adolf Eichmann (1906–1962). The **Principles of International Cooperation in the Detection, Arrest, Extradition and Punishment of Persons Guilty of War Crimes and Crimes Against Humanity**, adopted by the General Assembly in 1973, provides more guidelines on the subject.

In 1977, two additional protocols to the Geneva Conventions were adopted. The **Protocol Relating to the Protection of Victims of International Armed Conflicts** (Protocol I) prohibits the destruction of nonmilitary targets, so indiscriminate bombing is outlawed. Two possible examples, which occurred in 2006, are the Hezbollah's firing of rockets toward Israeli civilian targets and Israel's retaliation with cluster bombs. The protocol extends Geneva Convention protections to those fighting colonial domination, alien occupation, and against racist regimes but specifically exempts mercenaries (paid soldiers) from Geneva Convention protections. Protocol I also prohibits reprisals unless they are proportional. The **Protocol Relating to the Protection of Victims of Non-International Armed Conflicts** (Protocol II) applies Geneva Convention standards to parties engaged in civil wars. In 2005, the **Protocol Additional to the Geneva Conventions of 12 August 1949, and Relating to the Adoption of an Additional Distinctive Emblem** was adopted as Protocol III.

In 1974, the General Assembly adopted the **Declaration on the Protection of Women and Children in Emergency and Armed Combat**. A follow-up came in 2002, when the **Optional Protocol to the Convention on the Rights of the Child on the Involvement of Children in Armed Conflict** was adopted. The texts serve to supplement the Geneva Conventions.

But then war criminals could only be tried in domestic courts. States tend not to confer impunity on their soldiers, though the American military has done so in recent years. In 1993, soldiers from several countries (Belgium, Canada, Italy, United States) committed various forms of abuse during their stint in Somalia, but only Italy prosecuted them. To make a reality of the Geneva Conventions, international tribunals were needed but were not set up until after the Cold War.

UNITED NATIONS ERA: IMPACT OF THE COLD WAR

Although the Soviet Union was allied with Britain and the United States during World War II, the Soviet army's advance into Germany was accompanied by an effort to strengthen communist parties so that they could take control of Eastern Europe. Western powers soon realized that the Soviet Union was spying on the

United States, developing nuclear weapons independently, and was determined to expand influence within Asia and Europe. The United States had already dropped atomic bombs in the war with Japan during 1945, so the Soviet Union sought to deter aggression from the United States by developing nuclear weapons as well. There was apprehension that any conflict might result in mutual annihilation. As long as the two countries avoided a war with each other, the conflict would continue but at a lower temperature, so a "cold war" was seen as preferable to a "hot war."

When civil war broke out between Soviet-backed North Korea and American ally South Korea during 1950, the conflict between the two economic systems was no longer hypothetical but real, with the use of nuclear weapons a feared possibility. When the Security Council met to consider the Korean War, the Soviet Union was boycotting the body to protest the failure of the UN to accredit the People's Republic of China as a member; the Republic of China, whose leaders fled to Taiwan, still occupied the China seat. The Security Council then authorized a UN Command, led by the United States, consisting of troops donated by several countries. The establishment of the UN Command in Korea, thus, became the first time when an international organization provided a collective armed response to international aggression. Angry, the Soviet Union returned to the Security Council, vowing to veto any future use of force by the body, thereby nullifying what many founders believed was the most important purpose for which the UN was established.

HISTORIC EVENT 7.2 THE UNITED NATIONS AUTHORIZES TROOPS TO DEFEND SOUTH KOREA (1950)

In 1949, the People's Army of Mao Zedong (1883–1976) was victorious in China, and a large number of Chinese under the leadership of Chiang Kai-Shek (1887–1975) fled to Taiwan. However, the latter's Republic of China retained UN membership, as the United States and many other countries refused to recognize the legitimacy of the People's Republic of China. Moscow then protested by boycotting meetings of the Security Council. In 1950, civil war broke out in Korea. When the Security Council convened to respond, the Soviet Union, still maintaining its boycott, was absent and thus unable to veto a resolution to authorize a UN force to support the South Korean army, which was being pushed to the sea by communist North Korea. The war, which continued until 1953 and was recognized as a stalemate, was concluded with an armistice and remains without a peace agreement. The United Nations Command, set up by the United States military during 1950 in accordance with the Security Council resolution, ceased to exist in 1978, when a joint American–South Korean force was established.

Accordingly, later in 1950, delegates in the UN General Assembly adopted Resolution 377, known as the **Uniting for Peace Resolution**, which declared that the General Assembly could in the future authorize the use of force to stop aggression whenever the Security Council was deadlocked. Subsequently, Resolution 377 has been used 16 times,[4] though in 1999 an American delegate to the UN argued that General Assembly authorization of force is "not legally binding." Another way to get around the veto was to rely on the implied UN Charter's acceptance of actions by regional intergovernmental organizations. Accordingly, the Organization of African Unity sent peacekeeping troops to Chad in 1981–1982, and the successor African Union has done so several times. The North Atlantic Treaty Organization (NATO), similarly, acted in Bosnia (1995) and Kosovo (1999) in the absence of UN Security Council action to relieve genocidal acts.

TABLE 7.7 **AGREEMENTS DEVELOPING THE LAW OF WAR REFLECTING COLD WAR CONCERNS**

Adopted	*Document*	*In force*
1950	UN General Assembly Resolution 377 (Uniting for Peace Resolution)	
1967	Treaty on Principles Governing the Activities of States in the Exploration and Use of Outer Space, Including the Moon and other Celestial Bodies	1967
1968	Treaty on the Non-Proliferation of Nuclear Weapons	1970
1971	Agreement on Measures to Reduce the Risk of Outbreak of Nuclear War Between the United States of America and the Union of Soviet Socialist Republics	1971
1971	Treaty on the Prohibition of the Emplacement of Nuclear Weapons and Other Weapons of Mass Destruction on the Seabed and the Ocean Floor and in the Subsoil Thereof	1972
1972	Convention on the Prohibition of the Development, Production and Stockpiling of Bacteriological (Biological) and Toxin Weapons and on Their Destruction	1975
1972	Treaty Between the United States of America and the Union of Soviet Socialist Republics on the Limitation of Anti-Ballistic Missile Systems	1972[a]
1974	• Protocol to the Treaty Between the United States of America and the Union of Soviet Socialist Republics on the Limitation of Anti-Ballistic Missile Systems	1974
1972	Interim Agreement Between the United States of America and the Union of Soviet Socialist Republics on Certain Measures with Respect to the Limitation of Strategic Offensive Arms	1972
1977	Convention on the Prohibition of Military or Any Hostile Use of Environmental Modification Techniques	1978
1977	Convention of the OAU for the Elimination of Mercenaries in Africa	1983
1980	Convention on Prohibitions or Restrictions on the Use of Certain Conventional Weapons Which May be Deemed to be Excessively Injurious or to Have Indiscriminate Effects	1983
1980	• Protocol on Non-Detectable Fragments	1983
1980	• Protocol on Prohibitions or Restrictions on the Use of Mines, Booby-Traps and Other Devices	1983

Continued

TABLE 7.7 **(CONTINUED)**

Adopted	Document	In force
1980	• Protocol on Prohibitions or Restrictions on the Use of Incendiary Weapons	1983
1980	• Protocol on Blinding Laser Weapons	1998
1996	• Protocol on Prohibitions or Restrictions on the Use of Mines, Booby-Traps and Other Devices as Amended on 3 May 1996	1998
2001	• Amendment to Article I	2004
2003	• Protocol on Explosive Remnants of War	2006
1984	Declaration on the Right of Peoples to Peace	
1987	Intermediate-Range Nuclear Forces Treaty	1988
1987	Missile Technology Control Regime	1987
1989	International Convention Against the Recruitment, Use, Financing and Training of Mercenaries	2001
1990	Conventional Armed Forces in Europe Treaty	1992[b]
1991	Strategic Arms Reductions Treaty (START I)	1994–2009

[a] Denounced by the United States in 2002.

[b] Denounced by Russia in 2007.

The Cold War revived concerns about the use of unacceptable weapons, so some earlier treaties were expanded, and new treaties were drawn up (Table 7.7), including prohibitions on weapons in the oceans and in outer space and a limitation on the use of anti-ballistic missiles. Earlier treaties concerning biological and chemical weapons were expanded to require the dismantling of all such instruments of warfare, though many countries (Russia and Syria in particular), have refused to do so.

COURT CASE 7.4 ADVISORY OPINION ON THE LEGALITY OF THE THREAT OR USE OF NUCLEAR WEAPONS (1996)

In 1994, the UN General Assembly, the World Health Organization, and six countries (Costa Rica, Egypt, Iran, Malaysia, New Zealand, and Nauru) asked the International Court of Justice whether the threat or use of nuclear weapons was legal or illegal under international law, though several governments asked the court not to decide the matter (Britain, France, Germany, Italy, Russia, and the United States). Since opposing states did not agree to have the court determine a judgment, the justices issued an Advisory Opinion. In a short statement, the court noted that international law authorizes neither threats nor uses of nuclear weapons. Divided 7–7 in ruling whether such threats or uses might be acceptable in cases of extreme self-defense wherein the survival of a state is in jeopardy, the court nevertheless unanimously urged further progress on achieving nuclear disarmament.

Possibly the most famous treaty reflecting Cold War concerns is the **Treaty on the Non-Proliferation of Nuclear Weapons** (NPT) of 1968, when the nuclear club consisted of Britain, France, the Soviet Union, and the United States. That same year, the International Court of Justice issued the *Advisory Opinion on the Legality of the Threat or Use of Nuclear Weapons*, which stated that threatening or using nuclear weapons was a violation of international law except perhaps in cases of state survival. The UN General Assembly then began to call each year for a treaty to bind countries into agreement with the world court's judgment. Although draft treaties were submitted by Costa Rica in 1997 and 2007, Britain, France, Russia, and the United States have opposed such a treaty.

Fearing nuclear war by accident, the Soviet Union and the United States signed the **Treaty Banning Nuclear Weapon Tests in the Atmosphere, in Outer Space and Under Water** in 1963 and the **Agreement on Measures to Reduce the Risk of Outbreak of Nuclear War** in 1971. The **Treaty Between the United States of America and the Union of Soviet Socialist Republicans on the Limitation of Anti-Ballistic Missile Systems** of 1972 was designed to discourage the development of more powerful nuclear weapons that might evade anti-ballistic missile installations that were being erected in both countries. A protocol to the agreement was inked two years later.

Also in 1972, the two countries adopted the **Interim Agreement Between the United States of America and the Union of Soviet Socialist Republics on Certain Measures with Respect to the Limitation of Strategic Offensive Arms**, agreeing to ban missiles launched from submarines and to stop development of long-range ballistic missiles. In 1974, the **Treaty on the Limitation of Underground Nuclear Weapon Tests**, known as the Threshold Treaty, prohibited large nuclear tests (those exceeding 150 kilotons). The agreements did not criminalize weapons but instead constituted efforts at arms control that could evaporate if one country secretly or overtly failed to abide by the agreements. In 1979, 17 countries agreed to the **Agreement Governing the Activities of States on the Moon and Other Celestial Bodies**. Negotiations for further arms control treaties were terminated abruptly when the Soviet Union invaded Afghanistan in 1979.

Although the International Court of Justice ruled that the threat or use of nuclear weapons is illegal, China, India, Israel, North Korea, and Pakistan have joined the nuclear club, and Iran is accused of wanting to gain admission. Since nuclear weapons are feared only if delivered by missiles, several countries formed the **Missile Technology Control Regime** in 1987 to discourage exports of ballistic missiles and unmanned systems with a range of at least 186 miles (300 kilometers) and a payload of more than 1,000 pounds that could include nuclear, chemical, or biological weapons. Today, the regime is supported by 34 countries, mostly advanced industrial powers, but not China. Meanwhile, regional treaties have sought to denuclearize various parts of the Third World, notably Africa, Antarctica, the Caribbean, Central Asia, Latin America, the South Atlantic, Southeast Asia, and the South Pacific (Table 7.8).

TABLE 7.8   TREATIES BANNING NUCLEAR WEAPONS

Adopted	Name of document	In force
1959	Antarctic Treaty	1961
1963	Treaty Banning Nuclear Weapon Tests in the Atmosphere, in Outer Space and under Water (Partial Test-Ban Treaty)	1963
1967	Treaty for the Prohibition of Nuclear Weapons in Latin America and the Caribbean (Treaty of Tlatelolco)	1969
1967	• Protocol I	1992
1967	• Protocol II	1979
1993	• Amendments to Treaty for the Prohibition of Nuclear Weapons in Latin America	
1967	Treaty on Principles Governing the Activities of States in the Exploration and Use of Outer Space, Including the Moon and Other Celestial Bodies	1967
1971	Treaty on the Prohibition of the Emplacement of Nuclear Weapons and Other Weapons of Mass Destruction on the Seabed and the Ocean Floor and in the Subsoil Thereof	1972
1974	Treaty on the Limitation of Underground Nuclear Weapon Tests	1974
1979	Agreement Governing the Activities of States on the Moon and Other Celestial Bodies	1984
1985	South Pacific Nuclear Free Zone Treaty (Treaty of Rarotonga)	1986
1986	• Protocols I, II, III	
1992[a]	Law of Mongolia on Its Nuclear-Weapon-Free Status	2000
1994	Declaration on the Denuclearization of the South Atlantic	
1995	Treaty on the Southeast Asian Nuclear Weapon-Free Zone (Bangkok Treaty)	1997
1995	• Protocol	
1996	African Nuclear Weapon-Free Zone Treaty (Pelindaba Treaty)	2009
1996	Comprehensive Nuclear-Test-Ban Treaty	
2005	International Convention for the Suppression of Acts of Nuclear Terrorism	2007
2006	Treaty on a Nuclear-Weapon-Free Zone in Central Asia	2009

[a] The law is a domestic law that has been recognized by the UN General Assembly. A treaty with China and Russia to guarantee Mongolia's nuclear-free status is being negotiated.

The United States used the herbicide Agent Orange to defoliate the jungles of Vietnam in support of noncommunist South Vietnam (Republic of Vietnam) in its civil war with North Vietnam (Socialist Republic of Vietnam). In response, the **Convention on the Prohibition of Military or Any Hostile Use of Environmental Modification Techniques** of 1977 was adopted to ban nonpeaceful methods that have "widespread, long-lasting or severe effects" causing "destruction, damage or injury" to the planet.

In 1980, the **Convention on Prohibitions or Restrictions on the Use of Certain Conventional Weapons Which May Be Deemed to be Excessively Injurious or to**

Have Indiscriminate Effects was adopted as a shell agreement to ban as yet unidentified new weapons. Protocols to the convention have proscribed explosive fragments, incendiary weapons, laser weapons, landmines, and weapons with fragments not detectable by X-rays. The **Comprehensive Nuclear-Test-Ban Treaty** was adopted by the UN General Assembly in 1996 but has never entered into force.

On becoming president in 1981, Ronald Reagan (1911–2004) made clear that he would work to dismantle the "evil empire" of the Soviet Union. While he persuaded Congress to make large increases in military spending, his rhetoric seemed so bellicose that the General Assembly adopted the **Declaration on the Right of Peoples to Peace** in 1984.

In 1985, when Mikhail Gorbachëv (1931–) became the General Secretary of the Communist Party of the Soviet Union, Reagan found an interlocutor who was convinced that the nuclear arms race was too costly and must end. Reagan and Gorbachëv undertook serious negotiations. They then agreed to the **Intermediate-Range Nuclear Forces Treaty** of 1987, which banned conventional and nuclear ground-launched ballistic and naval cruise missiles with intermediate ranges. Reagan's successor, George H. W. Bush (1924–), then joined Gorbachëv in signing the bilateral **Strategic Arms Reduction Treaty** (START I) of 1991 regarding nuclear weapons, that was renewed in 2010 as (under the shortened name) **Measures for the Further Reduction and Limitation of Strategic Offensive Arms** (START II). Both agreements advanced the goal of arms control but did not identify prosecutable crimes; if one country violated the provisions, the other country would no longer be bound by the treaty.

Cold War adversaries agreed not to use nuclear weapons, but that left a strategic imbalance in Europe involving conventional weapons. The **Conventional Armed Forces in Europe Treaty** of 1990 addressed that concern, setting equal limits on tanks, armored combat vehicles, attack helicopters, combat aircraft, heavy artillery, and tanks. The Soviet Union and the United States signed the treaty on behalf, respectively, of the Warsaw Pact and the North Atlantic Treaty Organization. For Western Europe, the treaty was designed as the cornerstone of its security. Although the Cold War ended in 1991, and the Warsaw Pact was superseded by the looser Commonwealth of Independent States, both Russia and the United States continued to reduce arms in compliance with treaty provisions. Although a multilateral update of the treaty was written in 1999, there have been insufficient ratifications, and in 2007 Russia denounced the 1990 treaty.

"Mercenaries," that is, foreign forces paid to intervene in a domestic conflict, were rampant in the Congo during the 1960s, prompting condemnation from many quarters. When Portugal decided to abandon its colonies in 1975, civil wars broke out in Angola and East Timor. In the latter case, Indonesian troops quickly moved to control the territory without the consent of the population. Angola's civil war became a proxy war between East and West when Cuban troops, paid by the Soviet Union, entered the country. The United States, in turn, covertly sent aid to the opposing elements in the civil war. Thirteen mercenaries were indeed captured and convicted during 1976 for violating Protocol I to the Geneva Conventions. In 1977, the **Convention of the OAU for the Elimination of Mercenaries in Africa** was adopted, but the Angolan civil war dragged on. Some Western states, however, had not ratified Protocol I, and felt that a new treaty was needed. The result is the

TABLE 7.9   POST-COLD WAR TREATIES ON THE LAW OF WARFARE

Adopted	Name of document	In force
1992	Treaty on Open Skies	2002
1993	Convention on the Prohibition of the Development, Production, Stockpiling and Use of Chemical Weapons and on Their Destruction	1997
1993	Statute of the International Criminal Tribunal for the Prosecution of Persons Responsible for Serious Violations of International Humanitarian Law Committed in the Territory of the Former Yugoslavia Since 1991	1993–2013
1994	San Remo Manual on International Law Applicable to Armed Conflicts at Sea	
1994	Statute of the International Criminal Tribunal for the Prosecution of Persons Responsible for Genocide and Other Serious Violations of International Humanitarian Law Committed in the Territory of Rwanda and Rwandan Citizens Responsible for Genocide and Other Such Violations Committed in the Territory of Neighboring States, Between 1 January 1994 and 31 December 1994	1994–2012
1998	• Amendment	1998
2002	• Amendment	2002
1997	Convention on the Prohibition of the Use, Stockpiling, Production and Transfer of Anti-Personnel Mines and on Their Destruction	1999
1997	Inter-American Convention Against the Illicit Manufacturing of and Trafficking in Firearms, Ammunition, Explosives and Other Related Materials	1998
1998	Statute of the International Criminal Court (Rome Statute)	2002
1999	Inter-American Convention on Transparency in Conventional Weapons Acquisition	2002
2000	Optional Protocol to the Convention on the Rights of the Child on the Involvement of Children in Armed Conflict	2002
2002	International Code of Conduct Against Ballistic Missile Proliferation	2002
2002	Agreement for and Statute of the Special Court for Sierra Leone	2002
2003	Statute of the Extraordinary Chambers in the Courts of Cambodia	2003
2005	Protocol Additional to the Geneva Conventions of 12 August 1949, and Relating to the Adoption of an Additional Distinctive Emblem (Protocol III)	2007
2006	International Convention for the Protection of All Persons from Enforced Disappearance	2010
2007	Statute of the Special Tribunal for Lebanon	2007
2008	Convention on Cluster Munitions	2010
2010	Statute of the International Residual Mechanism for Criminal Tribunals	2012
2010	Treaty Between the United States of America and the Russian Federation on Measures for the Further Reduction and Limitation of Strategic Offensive Arms (START II)	2011
2010	Central African Convention for the Control of Small Arms and Light Weapons, Their Ammunition and All Parts and Components That Can Be Used for Their Manufacture, Repair, and Assembly	
2013	UN Arms Trade Treaty	

International Convention Against the Recruitment, Use, Financing and Training of Mercenaries of 1989. Nevertheless, mercenaries hired by the United States were quite active in the Afghan and Iraq Wars.

While negotiating arms reduction agreements, Gorbachëv also adopted domestic reforms that ultimately led to the dismantling of the Berlin Wall, which paved the way for the reunification of Germany in 1989. Two years later, the Soviet Union collapsed, and thereby the Cold War ended.

UNITED NATIONS ERA: POST-COLD WAR ACCOMPLISHMENTS

The end of the Cold War has enabled more cooperation within the UN framework (Table 7.9). Among the advances to the law of war are prohibitions on chemical weapons, cluster bombs, landmines, and child soldiers. In the latter case, an estimated 300,000 children in at least 40 countries have been recruited to fight, often after their fathers have died or been killed.

HISTORIC EVENT 7.3 JOSEPH KONY RECRUITS CHILD SOLDIERS (1986–)

Joseph Rao Kony (1961–) was born into the Acholi clan in Uganda. When Ugandan President Tito Okello (1914–1996), an Acholi, was overthrown in 1981 by the National Resistance Army, Kony organized an opposition force, later known as the Lord's Resistance Army, as he considers himself a spokesperson for God and claims to seek a Christian theocratic state based in part on the Ten Commandments. Initially, he recruited adults to his militia, but he later decided to form an army of children. While abducting the children, Kony's army killed their family and neighbors, making the children dependent upon him. While fighting the Ugandan government, which was supporting separatists in what later became the country of South Sudan in 2011, Kony received substantial backing from the Sudan government. In 2005, Kony was indicted by the International Criminal Court for crimes against humanity. He remains at large.

In addition, arms races have been viewed as threats to peace and security. The **Treaty on Open Skies** of 1992 provided that all signatories welcome aerial surveillance to keep track of arms developments. Conventions in the Americas and Central Africa have been adopted as a counterpart to the nuclear non-proliferation treaty (Table 7.8). In 2002, the **International Code of Conduct Against Ballistic Missile Proliferation**, now endorsed by 130 countries, recognized that nuclear materials are serious threats if they can be delivered by missiles. At the time, North Korea had no such capability, but the American government believed that Iraq did and used that pretext for war in 2003.

The worldwide arms trade has long been considered a major reason for wars. In 2013, the UN secured adoption of the Arms Trade Treaty, which creates an agreed standard for transfers of any type of conventional weapon – from pistols to warplanes – and requires nations to review all cross-border arms contracts to ensure munitions will not be used in human rights abuses, terrorism, and violations of humanitarian law.

The most significant recent advance in the development of the law of warfare is the development of international criminal courts. Following the UN Security Council's establishment of war crimes tribunals for Rwanda and Yugoslavia, the **Statute of the International Criminal Court** (ICC) was adopted on a treaty basis in 1998. The ICC codifies provisions in the Geneva Conventions regarding **war crimes** (though adding some new provisions, such as a ban on conscripting those under 15), identifies (but left undefined and unprosecutable until a later agreement) the **crime of aggression**, and clarifies the meaning of the remaining Nuremberg crime, **crime against humanity**, as noted in Chapter 5. In 2010, ICC adopted a detailed definition of "aggression," which, for the first time, could be prosecuted from 2007. (More details on the Rwandan and Yugoslavian courts, as well as about ICC are provided in Chapter 10.)

FROM HUMANITARIAN MILITARY INTERVENTION TO RESPONSIBILITY TO PROTECT

Trials of war criminals come too late to resuscitate victims of their crimes. If mass slaughter is about to occur, what can the world polity do? After the Cold War ended, such a conundrum came to the fore. Competing interests of national groups arose within Yugoslavia, which soon disintegrated into Bosnia, Croatia, Kosovo, Macedonia, Serbia, and Slovenia. "Ethnic cleansing," a euphemism for genocide, occurred as leaders of some ethnic groups sought to establish majorities within independent homelands where minority ethnic groups lived. While genocidal acts were continuing, the international community looked on in horror, with no standard operating procedure to justify action that would defend those being slaughtered.

HISTORIC EVENT 7.4 THE REIGN OF THE KHMER ROUGE (1975–1979)

In 1975, Cambodia was overwhelmed by the victorious Revolutionary Army of Kampuchea, led by Pol Pot (1925–1998) and other leaders of an ideologically left-wing Maoist-oriented group known as the Khmer Rouge. Within hours of victory, the population of the capital city of Phnom Penh was evacuated, having been reassigned to work in forced labor camps. Those who objected to the new order were killed. Lacking adequate food, medicine, and shelter, at least one million of those in the work camps died of disease, exhaustion, or starvation. In addition, thousands were killed because they had been formally educated or otherwise were considered

Continued

political enemies. Many of those executed were placed in mass graves through-out the countryside, subsequently known as the "killing fields." On December 25, 1978, Vietnam's army entered Cambodia and within several months drove the Khmer Rouge to the border with Thailand. A new Cambodian government was then established.

Accordingly, the principle of **humanitarian military intervention** was advanced as a possible legitimate basis for states, individually or collectively, to dispatch military force across the borders of a country without invitation in order to prevent or end grave and widespread violations of fundamental human rights. The principle can be traced to the writings of Hugo Grotius (1583–1645), the principal founder of international law, who conceptualized "sovereignty" as limited by customary norms of international decency. As later developed by Ellery Stowell (1875–1958), the concept of humanitarian intervention was that states had a right to intervene in the affairs of other states under the following circumstances:

- Harsh governmental persecution
- Severe suppression of nationalist movements
- Inhumane and uncivilized conduct during civil and interstate wars
- Excessive cruelty and injustice in the criminal justice system
- Suppression of the slave trade
- Rescue of asylum-seekers
- Providing humanitarian relief.

Suppression of the slave trade was the most common humanitarian intervention before the twentieth century. The Monroe Doctrine of the United States, as enunciated in 1823, was in effect a threat to use American military force to prevent reimposition of colonialism in Latin American countries that gained their independence during the Napoleonic Wars. France intervened in the Syria–Lebanon conflict during 1860 to stop massacres of Christians by Muslims. Some countries entered the two world wars with humanitarian intervention in mind, but countries were cautious during the Cold War, fearing reprisals. Nevertheless, even before the Cold War ended, the Soviet leader, Leonid Brezhnev (1906–1982), justified the suppression of nationalist uprisings in Hungary (1956) and Czechoslovakia (1968) as interventions to secure the rights of workers, though he did not use the term "humanitarian intervention" to justify his Brezhnev Doctrine. Ten years after the Czech uprising was quelled with Russian tanks, Vietnam explicitly justified its military action to expel the Khmer Rouge from Cambodia as humanitarian intervention. As clarified by the International Court of Justice, humanitarian intervention must aim to prevent human suffering and "to protect life and health and to ensure the respect of persons" (*Nicaragua v. United States*, 1986).

COURT CASE 7.5 *NICARAGUA V. UNITED STATES* (1986)

In 1979, the Sandinista Party under Daniel Ortega (1945–) seized power in Nicaragua from dictator Anastasio Somoza Debayle (1925–1980) with the support of the people, elements of the Catholic Church, and other backers. Boasting that the country was building socialism, the Sandinistas established a universal literacy program and a sweeping land reform that stripped influential landowners of their property. Upon taking office in 1981, President Ronald Reagan (1911–2004) took exception to the Sandinista's socialist rhetoric and accused Nicaragua of aiding communist-supported rebels in El Salvador. Various opponents of the Sandinistas, under the umbrella term "Contras," gained clandestine financial support from the United States and other sources for a rebel army, which in turn not only destroyed bridges, crop fields, hospitals, power plants, and schools in Nicaragua but also engaged in assassinations, kidnappings, rape, and torture. The Sandinistas remained in power, nevertheless, thanks to aid from Cuba and Eastern Bloc sources. In 1986, Nicaragua submitted a complaint to the International Court of Justice that the United States not only had mined a major harbor but also attacked a fuel supply facility, a naval base, a major port, and two towns. Washington responded that the action was an example of humanitarian intervention. Rejecting the humanitarian intervention claim, the Court ruled that the United States had illegally interfered in the internal affairs of Nicaragua and violated the *jus cogens* crime against peace as well as the trade treaty between Nicaragua and the United States of 1956. The Court ordered the United States to stop all military and paramilitary activities immediately and to pay reparations. Washington rejected the decision and refused to pay the US$12 billion fine despite condemnation by the UN General Assembly for nonpayment. After Ortega lost the 1990 election, Managua dropped the complaint. However, the United States spent exactly US$12 million on the 2006 Nicaraguan presidential election for voter registration, technical assistance to the Supreme Electoral Council, and local and international election observation and civic education. Ortega then defeated the American-backed candidate to become president again.

There are two types of humanitarian intervention. One type, **rescue of nationals**, had been authorized by the Peace of Westphalia of 1648. Governments are allowed to undertake operations to rescue their own citizens who are at risk in another country, provided that three criteria are met:

- Imminent threat to life
- Unwillingness of a country to protect citizens from another country
- The rescue operation is limited.

One example of a humanitarian rescue occurred at the Entebbe airport in Uganda, when Israeli military rescued hijacked passengers. Much less successful was the attempt to rescue American diplomats held against their will in the US embassy in Iran for 444 days from 1979–1980.

HISTORIC EVENT 7.5 THE ENTEBBE RAID (1976)

One day in 1976, an Air France flight from Paris to Athens en route to Israel was hijacked by seven Palestinians and flown to Uganda with 248 passengers on board. Some 85 Israeli and Jewish passengers were then held hostage despite an Israeli demand for their release. The crew also stayed on board, prepared to take off when allowed. After Egypt unsuccessfully tried to mediate, some 200 Israeli commandos arrived at Entebbe airport, and a battle ensued. Eleven Soviet-built airplanes were destroyed on the tarmac, and all seven hijackers, four of the hostages, and about 40 Ugandan soldiers died. Afterward, the Israeli soldiers departed, and the freed hostages were flown to safety in Israel. Subsequently, Uganda convened a session of the UN Security Council, demanding condemnation of the raid for violating Ugandan sovereignty. The Security Council declined to pass any resolution on the matter, condemning neither Israel nor Uganda, though UN Secretary-General Kurt Waldheim (1918–2007) joined condemnations of Israel by Arab-speaking and Soviet bloc countries. In private conversation, National Security Adviser Henry Kissinger (1923–) criticized Israel for using American military equipment. The raid inspired the United States to develop units with similar capabilities, notably the Delta Force and later the Navy SEALs.

The other type of humanitarian intervention, **rescue of populations from gross human rights violations,** is more controversial. During the 1930s, three intervening countries claimed that they were acting in humanitarian terms – Japan's seizure of Manchuria (1931), Italy's conquest of Ethiopia (1935–1936), and Germany's annexation of the Sudetenland part of Czechoslovakia (1938). The world community, however, eventually branded all three actions as unjustified aggression. Recalling that the colonization of what is now called the "Third World" was justified by European imperialists, including Rudyard Kipling (1865–1936) and John Stuart Mill (1806–1873), as a humanitarian crusade to bring Christian civilization to the non-Christian world, there is a danger that governments might use the principle of humanitarian intervention to commit war crimes.

Presumably, humanitarian military intervention should satisfy the principles of the just war. Indeed, some scholars have developed the concept of **just intervention** as an extension of the principle of the just war to the specific problem of ongoing genocide. They argue for mandatory intervention to stop severe human rights violations involving death on a massive scale.

If there is some acceptance of the need for humanitarian intervention, the criteria are unclear. Setting the bar too high leads to inaction in the face of genocide; setting the bar too low enables states to claim the moral high ground as they engage in naked conquest under a humanitarian figleaf for the sake of geopolitical "regime change." Moreover, the right of self-determination and the principle of nonintervention are in conflict when a subnational group seeks to secede from a country, as international law recognizes the right of self-determination but no right of secession.

The concept of humanitarian intervention was discussed from 1992, as armed Serbs in Bosnia systematically began to kill Muslims (Bosniaks), whereupon the UN identified the operation as "genocide," and established the UN Protection Force (UNPROFOR), which supplied 39,000 military personnel to Bosnia and Croatia. In the latter case, the force was assigned to implement a ceasefire. In regard to Bosnia, UNPROFOR initially protected and supplied humanitarian aid to Sarajevo, sent military personnel to various cities that were declared as "save havens," and helped to create the Bosniak–Croat federation in contrast with what the Bosnian Serbs had declared in 1992 as Republika Srpska.

In 1994, genocide broke out in Rwanda. Although a small UN force was present when the mass killing began, the contingent was withdrawn at the order of the UN headquarters to avoid being overwhelmed by the genocidal mobs, though the UN commander was requesting more troops.

In 1995, the massacre of Bosniaks by Bosnian Serbs in the "safe haven" of Srebrenica defied the UN, though UNPROFOR's Dutch contingent in that town did not put up much of a defense. One month later, airplanes from NATO then began to bomb Serb positions in order to stop the genocide, and a peace accord was signed four months later, uniting the Bosniak–Croat federation with Republika Srpska into the Federation of Bosnia and Herzegovina.

In 1998, "ethnic cleansing" began again, this time within Kosovo, still a province of Yugoslavia. Belgrade, the Serbian capital of Yugoslavia, appeared to be repeating the ethnocide that had happened in Bosnia earlier in the 1990s. US Secretary of State Madeleine Albright (1937–) tried in vain to persuade the UN Security Council to undertake humanitarian intervention, but instead the body adopted a resolution that expressed "willingness" to "respond to situations of armed conflict where civilians are being targeted or where humanitarian assistance to civilians is being deliberated obstructed."

Albright was more successful in obtaining NATO support. In March 1999, NATO countries, principally the United States, started bombing Serbia. Several weeks later, Belgrade sued for peace. In June, the UN Security Council established a transitional administration to administer Kosovo toward independence.

Questions then arose whether the Bosnian and Kosovo efforts were truly a model for future humanitarian interventions. For example, there appeared to be a danger that the humanitarian intervention concept might encourage more ethnic groups to rise in protest against unjust treatment, hoping thereby to provoke outside intervention. Because the legality of the Kosovo intervention was questioned, the UN set up the Independent International Commission on Kosovo to assess the intervention. In the resulting report, published in 2000, the intervention was considered "illegal but legitimate" and concluded that the intervention was not a precedent for the future.

In October 1999, UN Secretary-General Kofi Annan (1938–), noting at the Millennium Summit that the UN had failed to stop genocide in Bosnia (1992–1994), Rwanda (1994), and Kosovo (1996–1999), specified at least three conditions for legitimate humanitarian intervention:

- Genocidal acts
- UN authorization for action
- Multilateral participation.

Nevertheless, the South Summit Declaration of the year 2000 passed a resolution firmly rejecting the concept of humanitarian intervention.

Accordingly, the Canadian Ministry of Foreign Affairs organized an International Commission on Intervention and State Sovereignty, consisting of 12 distinguished persons, to clarify the matter. Their report, issued in 2001, identified six threshold criteria to determine the legitimacy of humanitarian military intervention (or just intervention):

- Just cause (large-scale loss of life ongoing or anticipated)
- Right intention (to halt or avert human suffering)
- Right authority (authorization by the UN or regional organizations)
- Last resort (after nonmilitary measures have failed)
- Proportional means (minimal scale, duration, intensity)
- Reasonable prospects (success reasonably expected).

The latter condition would presumably include acceptance of the intervention by the people on whose behalf the intervention is launched.

The commission stressed that the world community has a responsibility to prevent serious situations before they get out of hand as well as to assist in post-intervention reconstruction. The concept of "responsibility to protect" (R2P) soon served as the justification for humanitarian intervention. Instead of allowing states to enjoy a right to conduct their own affairs as they please, R2P considers that states are only legitimately sovereign when they fulfill the responsibility to promote human rights. R2P changes the right of states to humanitarian intervention into an obligation of all states to do so. The shift was from a moral to a legal obligation.

DISCUSSION TOPIC 7.4 WHEN IS HUMANITARIAN MILITARY INTERVENTION (R2P) JUSTIFIED?

In which of the following cases was humanitarian military intervention justified? Why or why not?
- India's attack on Pakistan during 1971 as the latter waged war on East Pakistan (now Bangladesh), while ten million refugees poured into India.

Continued

- Tanzania's invasion of Uganda in 1979 to end the regime of Idi Amin (1928–2003), who was responsible for liquidating approximately 300,000 political opponents, real and imagined, over the years of his rule (1971–1979).
- Vietnam's intervention in 1978–1979 to stop massive deaths in Cambodia that occurred during the reign of the Khmer Rouge from 1975.
- In the 1990s, the NATO military interventions in Bosnia and Kosovo, which were under attack from Serbian forces that seemed intent on imposing rule by ethnic cleansing of non-Serbs in both provinces of the former Yugoslavia.
- The NATO intervention in Libya during 2011 to prevent a government massacre of the civilian population of Benghazi that ultimately toppled the rule of Muammar Gaddafi (1942–2011).

In 2003, Washington justified an attack on Iraq in various terms, some humanitarian, but without UN approval. The humanitarian claim was mostly retrospective, that is, after the claim to eradicate weapons of mass destruction proved false. Accordingly, some observers soured on the concept of humanitarian military intervention as a form of neoimperialism, particularly when the United States engaged in state building while acting as an occupying power in Iraq. R2P does not justify regime change and certainly not nation building. But after the United States and allies entered Afghanistan in 2001 and Iraq in 2003, both political systems collapsed and were only precariously reconstructed. Thus, different opinions about humanitarian intervention and R2P competed for acceptance.

In 2004, the UN High-Level Panel on Threats, Challenges and Change issued a report, *A More Secure World: Our Shared Responsibility*. The aim was to endorse R2P. Secretary-General Kofi Annan gave more support to R2P in his report *Larger Freedom* (2005).

To clarify the concept of R2P and related matters, the UN convened a World Summit in 2005. Among various outcomes, delegates agreed that the international community has a duty to intervene when governments fail to fulfill their responsibility to protect their own citizens, especially ethnic and religious minorities, from such atrocious crimes as ethnic cleansing and genocide. The World Summit also agreed that states have an obligation to stop crimes against humanity and war crimes. In 2006, the Security Council unanimously adopted Resolution 1674, which endorsed the R2P concept without providing a clarifying definition.

In 2007, the International Court of Justice tried to clarify in *Bosnia v. Serbia*, a case in which Bosnia sued Serbia for responsibility for the murder of more than 5,000 persons at Srebrenica in 1995. The court ruled that Serbia, though not directly responsible, was guilty of complicity in the massacre and thus of failure to act to prevent the massacre, saying "the obligation of States is … to employ all means reasonably available to them, so as to prevent genocide as far as possible." (The court also faulted Serbia for not bringing to justice Ratko Mladić (1942–), a resident of Serbia who was most responsible for the Srebrenica massacre, though he was captured in 2011 and extradited to The Hague to face trial by the International Criminal Tribunal for the Former Yugoslavia.)

R2P was soon invoked in four crises – in Georgia and Myanmar during 2008 and in Kenya and Guinea in 2009. In the first case, Russia identified a questionable pretext and moved unilaterally to defend secessionist South Ossetia from an attack by Georgia to retake possession of the province – clearly a military rather than a genocidal goal. When the Myanmar government clearly lacked resources to cope with the effects of the devastating cyclone, Nargis, on more than one million Burmese, France proposed an R2P intervention but arguably that threat prompted the government to accept some outside help after mediation from the Association of South-East Asian Nations. Ethnic killing, after the Kenya election, and the coup in Guinea, provoked threats to cut economic aid, whereupon the Kenyan government stopped the killing and a pro-democracy coup emerged in Guinea. In all four cases, claims about R2P were rejected, but that negative judgment served somewhat to clarify the ambiguous meaning of the concept.

In January 2009, UN Secretary-General Ban Ki-Moon (1944–) presented a report, *Implementing the Responsibility to Protect*, to provide some guidance on the concept, proposing three "pillars" of R2P:

- Protection responsibilities of states
- International assistance and capacity-building
- Decisive and timely international responses.

Later that year, the UN General Assembly adopted Resolution 63/308, taking note of his report and supporting R2P.

General Assembly discussion continued in earnest, following two more reports from the Secretary-General. *Early Warning, Assessment and the Responsibility to Protect* (2010) identified UN early warning capabilities. *The Role of Regional and Subregional Arrangements in Implementing the Responsibility to Protect* (2011) responded to the desire of regional intergovernmental organizations to act when the UN might not be able to do so. But R2P still remained a somewhat vague concept until its actual use in practice.

In 2011, the Security Council invoked R2P for the first time. The situations were in regard to the Ivory Coast, Libya, and South Sudan. In the Libyan case, NATO intervened to support an insurgent group that the government threatened to annihilate. The NATO operation in Libya began with Security Council approval and protected civilians from governmental assault, but the operation evolved from R2P to a very different outcome – regime change. The threat of mass murder ended when a new government took over.[5] But regime change by external powers is unpopular because that was what happened in the age of imperialism. Interventions in more than 100 civil wars from 1980–2005, according to one study, demonstrate that meddling brings some relief from violence, but peacekeeping operations rarely serve to improve human rights, and the verdict is not yet in on whether outside interventions help or hurt internal conflict resolution.

Noticeably absent from R2P authorization was Syria. As the Damascus government responded to peaceful protests in 2011 by killing protesters and bombing cities perceived as rebel strongholds, China and Russia became more cautious about authorizing another R2P operation, apparently fearing future applicability to government crackdowns in their rebel provinces of Xinxiang and Chechnya, respectively. If Syrian rebels expected intervention on their behalf, they were sorely disappointed. The problem remains that there is no metric to determine when R2P is applicable other than an un-vetoed majority vote in the UN Security Council.

The irony is that the great powers of the Concert of Europe felt collectively responsible to suppress democratic uprisings in the early 1800s. R2P, which turns the Concert's logic on its head, remains a contested concept.

LEGITIMATE SELF-DEFENSE

War, of course, has always been permitted in self-defense. The UN Charter recognizes the "inherent right of individual or collective self-defense" (Article 51). Under current international law, there are two types legitimate self-defense – anticipatory and in reprisal.

The UN Charter prefers **reprisal self-defense** to be temporary. States that immediately defend themselves after being attacked are required to report their actions to the Security Council, which can then authorize their actions retroactively. However, the Security Council may vote against supporting a military response because of political considerations or on account of a judgment that the action is not legitimate self-defense. To be legitimate, the following conditions must be present in the case of reprisal self-defense:

- **Second Use of Force**. There must be prior armed aggression according to UN General Assembly Resolution 3314 of 1974, which defines **aggression** as armed invasions or attacks, bombardments, blockades, armed violations of territory, allowing other states to use one's own territory to perpetrate acts of aggression, and the use of armed irregulars or mercenaries to carry out acts of aggression.
- **Preclusion**. There should be no alternative to a military response because the aggression is unabated rather than limited and neither the Security Council nor a regional organization is taking effective countermeasures.
- **Proportionality**. According to the International Court of Justice in *Nicaragua v. United States*, 1986, the response must consist only of "measures proportional to the armed aggression that has occurred."
- **Notification**. The state under attack must inform the UN Security Council whenever military action to counter aggression is undertaken. However, if the Security Council disagrees, a country's right to armed self-defense ceases.

Anticipatory Self-defense is more problematic. The example of the *Caroline* incident (Historic Event 7.1) in 1837 has served to clarify criteria to justify anticipatory self-defense before an armed attack:

- **Imminent Jeopardy**. A threat of armed attack is being carried out without delay on a state's territory, forces, or population.

- **Preclusion**. There is no alternative to self-defense because no other legitimate authority proposes to prevent or to stop the aggression.
- **Proportionality**. The self-defense is limited to stopping or preventing the aggression.
- **Notification**. Self-defense actions must be immediately reported to the UN Security Council.

The concept of anticipatory self-defense has been stretched to the doctrine of **preemptive war** on the ground that a preventive first strike is preferable to a second strike after being devastated. Israel, for example, sought in 1975 to justify a military assault on Palestinian villages in Lebanon because previous attacks on Israel had been launched from those villages. Subsequently, UN Security Council resolutions condemned Israel's attack, questioning the concept of preemptive self-defense where there had been no prior armed intervention.

In 2003, the United States invoked the preemptive war doctrine in Iraq, fearing the latter's use of weapons of mass destruction and wanting to send a signal to the nuclear ambitions of Iran and North Korea. Preemption, then, meant prevention. The following year, the UN High Level Panel for Threats, Challenges and Change recommended reinterpreting the UN Charter in order to allow the right of preemptive military or police action in cases of nonimminent but urgent threats, provided that such action is approved by the UN Security Council. However, the principles of anticipatory self-defense and preemption can be interpreted in different ways by different persons, thus providing no clear guide for what is acceptable in international law. When no weapons of mass destruction were found in Iraq, the preemption doctrine lost support.

INTERNATIONAL TERRORISM

The Latin origin of the English word "terror" means "to frighten." The term gained currency during the 1793–1794 Reign of Terror as the French Revolution morphed from a popular uprising into a new form of dictatorship. Some observers, accordingly, perceive that "one person's terrorist is another person's freedom fighter."

The nexus between war crimes and criminal acts of international terrorist groups has yet to be fully developed. Acts of terrorism are criminal acts, violations of the laws of most countries, but they are particularly heinous because innocent persons are often victims. In addition, a strict application of the principle of nonintervention might serve to protect terrorist groups in one country to plot against another country, a situation that could be a disguised act of war by the host country.

Piracy is one form of terrorism. In the late eighteenth century, pirates terrorized the high seas from the Caribbean to North Africa and beyond to loot the cargo of commercial ships. Nine of the earliest treaties of the United States, the first signed with Morocco in 1786, were aimed at ensuring bilateral cooperation to stop the Berbers from piratical attacks emanating off the North African coastline, known as the Barbary Coast. Indeed, the American government tired of paying tribute to the Barbary States and instead authorized the US Navy and US Marines to root out the pirates in a series of military campaigns from 1801–1815. Pirates, the terrorists of the day, were among the earliest international criminals, and international criminal law authorized a ship's captain to hang a pirate from the mast of a ship in international waters, that is, beyond the borders of any country. In *US v. Smith* (18US53), the US Supreme Court in 1820, allowed the prosecution of a pirate on the grounds that piracy on the high seas was a crime with universal jurisdiction.

World War I began after a chain of events following the assassination of Austrian Archduke Franz Ferdinand (1863–1914) by a member of a Serbian terrorist organization. Following the assassination in Paris of the Yugoslavian king, the French foreign minister, and two bystanders by Croatian separatists in 1934, the League of Nations took concerted efforts to adopt two treaties on terrorism in 1937. The **Convention for the Prevention and Punishment of Terrorism**, which never garnered sufficient ratifications to go into effect, defined terrorism as "criminal acts directed against a State and intended or calculated to create a state of terror in the minds of particular persons, or a group of persons or the general public." The second treaty, the **Convention for the Creation of an International Criminal Court** to try terrorists, met a similar fate.

In the 1960s, when airplanes were hijacked while en route to various destinations, terrorism reemerged as a world problem. Thereafter, several treaties dealt with terrorist acts as criminal offenses (Table 7.10). The first response was the **Convention on Offenses and Certain Other Acts Committed on Board Aircraft** of 1963. The **Convention for the Suppression of Unlawful Seizure of Aircraft** of 1970 criminalized hijackings, and the **Convention for the Suppression of Unlawful Acts Against the Safety of Civil Aviation** of 1971 (the Montréal Convention) applied to bombings aboard aircraft in flight. The same principles were applied to the problem of piracy committed on ships at sea, particularly in the Malacca Straits, in the **Convention for the Suppression of Unlawful Acts Against the Safety of Maritime Navigation** of 1988.

TABLE 7.10 **TREATIES OUTLAWING INTERNATIONAL TERRORISM**

Adopted	Document	In force
1937	Convention for the Prevention and Punishment of Terrorism	
1937	Convention for the Creation of an International Criminal Court	
1963	Convention on Offenses and Certain Other Acts Committed on Board Aircraft (Tokyo Convention)	1969
1970	Convention for the Suppression of Unlawful Seizure of Aircraft (Hijacking Convention)	1971
2010	• Protocol Supplementary to the Convention for the Suppression of Unlawful Seizure of Aircraft	
1971	Convention for the Suppression of Unlawful Acts Against the Safety of Civil Aviation (Montréal Convention)	1973
1988	• Protocol for the Suppression of Unlawful Acts of Violence at Airports Serving International Aviation	1989

Continued

TABLE 7.10 (CONTINUED)

Adopted	Document	In force
1971	Convention to Prevent and Punish Acts of Terrorism Taking the Form of Crimes Against Persons and Related Extortion That Are of International Significance [by the Organization of American States]	2003
1973	International Convention on the Prevention and Punishment of Crimes Against Internationally Protected Persons	1977
1977	European Convention on the Suppression of Terrorism	1978
2003	• Protocol Amending the European Convention on the Suppression of Terrorism	
1979	Convention Against the Taking of Hostages	1983
1980	Convention on the Physical Protection of Nuclear Material	1987
2005	• Amendment to the Convention on the Physical Protection of Nuclear Material	
1987	SAARC Regional Convention on Suppression of Terrorism [by the South Asian Association for Regional Cooperation]	1988
2004	• Additional Protocol to the SAARC Regional Convention on Suppression of Terrorism	2006
1988	Convention for the Suppression of Unlawful Acts Against the Safety of Maritime Navigation	1992
1988	• Protocol for the Suppression of Unlawful Acts Against the Safety of Fixed Platforms Located on the Continental Shelf	1992
2005	• Protocol to the Convention for the Suppression of Unlawful Acts Against the Safety of Maritime Navigation Located on the Continental Shelf	
1990	Forty Recommendations on Money-Laundering and Nine Special Recommendations on Terrorist Financing	
1991	Convention on the Making of Plastic Explosives for the Purpose of Detection	1988
1997	Convention for the Suppression of Terrorist Bombings	2001
1997	European Convention on the Suppression of Terrorism	1998
2003	• Protocol Amending the European Convention on the Suppression of Terrorism	
1998	Arab Convention for the Suppression of Terrorism	1999
1999	Convention of the Organization of the Islamic Conference on Combating International Terrorism	2002
1999	International Convention for the Suppression of the Financing of Terrorism	2002
1999	OAU Convention on the Prevention and Combating of Terrorism	2002
2004	• Protocol to the OAU Convention on the Prevention and Combating of Terrorism	
1999	Treaty on Cooperation among States Members of the Commonwealth of Independent States in Combating Terrorism	2005
2000	Convention Against Transnational Organized Crime	2003
2000	• Protocol Against the Smuggling of Migrants by Land, Sea and Air, Supplementing the United Nations Convention Against Transnational Organized Crime	2004
2000	• Protocol to Prevent, Suppress and Punish Trafficking in Persons, Especially Women and Children, Supplementing the United Nations Convention Against Transnational Organized Crime	2003

Continued

TABLE 7.10 (CONTINUED)

Adopted	Document	In force
2000	• Protocol Against the Illicit Manufacturing of and Trafficking in Firearms, Their Parts and Components and Ammunition, Supplement the UN Convention Against Transnational Organized Crime	2005
2001	Shanghai Convention on Combating Terrorism, Separatism and Extremism	2003
2002	Inter-American Convention Against Terrorism	2003
2005	Council of Europe Convention on the Prevention of Terrorism	2007
2005	Council of Europe Convention on Laundering, Search, Seizure and Confiscation of the Proceeds from Crime and on the Financing of Terrorism	2008
2005	International Convention for the Suppression of Acts of Nuclear Terrorism	2007
2006	UN Global Counter-Terrorism Strategy	
2010	Convention on the Suppression of Unlawful Acts Relating to International Civil Aviation	

To establish severe punishments for those who would try to harm high government officials, the **International Convention on the Prevention and Punishment of Crimes Against Internationally Protected Persons** was adopted in 1973. The **Convention Against the Taking of Hostages** of 1979 responded in part to a crime wave in which criminals were seizing foreign business executives, and even tourists, for ransom, notably the capture of Japanese in the Philippines. Adoption of the treaty came only one month after 52 diplomatic personnel were held hostage in the American Embassy in Tehran by a group of militants.

Terrorists have adopted the latest technology to further their aims. Fears about the seizure of nuclear materials by terrorists result in the adoption of the **Convention on the Physical Protection of Nuclear Material** in 1980, the **Convention on the Making of Plastic Explosives for the Purpose of Detection** of 1991, and the **Convention for the Suppression of Terrorist Bombings** in 1997. Such advances brought attention to how terrorists could afford new technology. Following up the **Forty Recommendations on Money-Laundering and Nine Special Recommendations on Terrorist Financing**, adopted in 1990 by the intergovernmental Financial Action Task Force, the **International Convention for the Suppression of the Financing of Terrorism** was signed in 1999.

When adopted in 1998, the Rome Statute of the International Criminal Court did not define "terrorism," leaving that task for the future while focusing on more traditional war crimes. After a debate lasting seven years, the UN General Assembly, in early 2005, adopted the **International Convention for the Suppression of Acts of Nuclear Terrorism**, which requires countries to develop protection systems for nuclear and radioactive materials and devices, as well as for nuclear installations. The treaty makes illegal the possession or use of nuclear materials by those who intend to cause death, environmental, or property damage, including those who might use nuclear materials to threaten individuals, organizations, or states. The treaty also criminalizes acts to damage a nuclear facility for the same purposes. The scope of the treaty is limited to conflicts inside the borders of states and thus is distinct from treaties banning the use of nuclear weapons in war.

Following the World Summit in 2005, UN Secretary-General Boutros Boutros-Ghali (1922–) prepared a report, *Uniting Against Terrorism: Recommendations for a Global Counter-Terrorism Strategy* (2006), with the following recommendations:

- Dissuade alienated groups from using terrorism as a means to achieve their objectives
- Ensure that terrorists lack the means to commit violent acts
- Prevent countries from supporting terrorist groups
- Develop state capacity to prevent terrorism
- Support human rights.

Four months after the report, the UN General Assembly adopted Resolution 60/288, entitled "The United Nations Global Counter-Terrorism Strategy." Although the strategy had a major focus on strengthening national efforts to prevent and combat terrorism, one practical measure was support for an international travel ban on terrorists. The strategy also urged countries to implement the **United Nations Convention Against Transnational Organized Crime** of 2000 and its three protocols. Implementation of the various proposals requires funds that have not always been forthcoming, either nationally or internationally.

Concerned over terrorist plots emanating from Pakistan, India presented a draft Comprehensive Convention on International Terrorism to the Ad Hoc Committee of the UN General Assembly on International Terrorism in 1996. The aim was to obligate countries to cooperate in preventing and punishing terrorism acts. Although there has been some agreement on provisions of a proposed treaty, adoption has been held up because governments still do not agree on a legal definition of "terrorism." One problem in securing a consensus definition is that the Organization of the Islamic Conference, an intergovernmental organization composed of 57 states with large Muslim populations, seeks to exempt acts aimed at "liberation and self-determination." Nevertheless, regional treaties banning terrorism have been adopted – in Europe (1977), South Asia (1987), Islamic countries (1998 and 1999), Central Asia (2001), and the Americas (2002). However, the China-sponsored agreement for Central Asia, the **Shanghai Convention on Combating Terrorism, Separatism and Extremism**, clearly applies to Tibet.

HISTORIC EVENT 7.6 TERRORISTS ATTACK THE WORLD TRADE CENTER AND THE PENTAGON (2001)

On September 11, 2001, four commercial airplanes were hijacked after they took off from the international airport in Boston. The hijackers, 19 in all, soon seized control of the cockpits. Two of the airplanes flew into the twin towers of the World Trade Center in lower Manhattan. One airplane plunged into a portion of the Pentagon, the headquarters of the US Department of Defense at Arlington, Virginia. A fourth hijacked airplane with an unknown destination, usually assumed to be Congress or the White House, crashed in an unpopulated field near Shanksville, Pennsylvania. The death toll consisted of 2,973 civilians and all 19 hijackers, with 24 persons missing and presumed dead. The hijackers were among a group of 27 members of Al-Qaeda, an organization of Arabic-speaking individuals led by Osama Bin Laden (1957–2011), who had, in 1996 and 1998, pronounced a "holy war" against what he considered the American occupation of the Arabian Peninsula, support for apostate Muslim governments, the devastation of the Iraqi people, humiliation of their Muslim neighbors, and Washington's support of Israel. He called upon members of his organization to engage in the killing of "Jews and the Americans." His death during an American raid in 2011 may be considered to be in reprisal for the events of that day.

The extraordinary attacks in the United States on September 11, 2001, focused world attention on the growing problem of internationally-linked terrorist organizations. Mary Robinson (1944–), while UN High Commissioner for Human Rights, condemned the September 11, 2001, attacks on the United States as a crime against humanity under international law. UN Secretary-General Annan, however, acknowledged in 2003 that provisions of the UN Charter were not articulated to the threat of globalized terrorism. Indeed, today the UN still bureaucratically assigns responsibility for dealing with problems of terrorism to its Office on Drugs and Crime, which also deals with human trafficking.

Some observers argue that a Fifth Geneva Convention is needed to take into account the peculiar situation of international terrorism. In 2006, the Supreme Court of Israel ruled that assassinations against terrorists are permitted under international law when:

- There is well-based, strong and convincing information that a targeted person is plotting a terrorist act
- Less harmful means cannot stop a terrorist plotter
- And when "the expected harm to innocent civilians is not disproportional to the military advantage to be achieved by the attack."

Not all international legal experts agree.

The latest treaty, the **Convention on the Suppression of Unlawful Acts Relating to International Civil Aviation** of 2010, supplements the Montréal Convention in light of the events of September 11. What is criminalized is the use of aircraft to cause damage, death, or injury as well as plotting to do so, including control by cyberwarfare means. Similarly, the Protocol to the Hijacking Convention, adopted in the same year, bans cyberseizure of aircraft. However, neither treaty has gone into force.

In failing to adopt a comprehensive treaty on terrorism, the international community, by default, prefers to criminalize specific acts, therefore preferring to classify "terrorism" within the scope of crimes against humanity rather than war crimes. In 2011, however, a breakthrough of sorts emerged in the quest to define "terrorism." The Special Tribunal for Lebanon, authorized by the UN Security Council in 2007 to try those accused of assassinating former Lebanese prime minister, Rafiq Hariri (1944–2005), and 22 others in 2005, identified the acts to be investigated and tried as "terrorist." The court is unusual in that the trial is supposedly in accordance with Lebanese law yet is the first special court with jurisdiction over terrorism. As a tribunal with international representation, what was notable was the court's formulation of a legal definition of "terrorism," which hitherto had not been established. Accordingly, in 2011, the Appeals Chamber declared that customary international law defines "terrorism" to consist of three additional elements:

- The perpetration of a criminal act (such as murder, kidnapping, hostage-taking, arson, and so on), or threatening such an act
- The intent to spread fear among the population (which would generally entail the creation of public danger) or directly or indirectly coerce a national or international authority to take some action, or to refrain from taking it
- When the act involves a transnational element.

Now, a generic definition exists. International lawyers have a new handle to use in prosecuting terrorists in the future, though not for approving military counterterrorism.

The emergence of globalized terrorism by a non-state international actor, Al-Qaeda, has focused attention on plotting to kill innocent civilians by nonmilitary means, as on September 11, 2001, in the United States. Although Al-Qaeda engaged in aggression, the term "war" seems inapplicable because conventional military means, such as armies and weapons, were not employed. The law of war is founded on the principle of reciprocity – that one government will refrain from barbarous acts so that the other government will not respond in kind. But terrorism is inherently an asymmetric, nonreciprocal situation.

HISTORIC EVENT 7.7 A PAKISTANI-AMERICAN TRIES TO BOMB TIMES SQUARE (2010)

American attacks on suspected terrorists in Pakistan by unmanned aerial vehicles (drones) began in 2004. Although the drones took off from military bases inside Pakistan, the Islamabad government regularly objected when civilians were injured or killed. Sometime in 2008, Pakistani relatives of a naturalized American citizen, Faisal Shahzad (1979–), were killed in a drone attack. In 2009, Shahzad went to Pakistan, where he received training in bomb making. When he returned home to Connecticut, he decided to plant a bomb at Times Square, New York City, expecting that the bomb would explode and injure or kill passersby in retaliation for the drone attack. On May 1, 2010, he purchased a sport utility vehicle, parked near Times Square with a ticking bomb inside, and fled. Observant New Yorkers noticed the unmanned motor vehicle, called the police, and the bomb never went off. Through evidence from his vehicle, he was tracked down, arrested, charged with 10 offenses, including plotting a terrorist act, pled guilty, and is now serving a life sentence. According to a Connecticut neighbor, as interviewed by a British journalist, Shahzad had repeatedly accused President George W. Bush of being a "war criminal," and once said: "They shouldn't be shooting people from the sky. You know, they should come down and fight." In his allocution in the New York court, where he admitted his guilt, he made a statement that his attack was in retaliation for American attacks in Afghanistan and Iraq.

One of the newest technological developments is the unmanned aerial vehicle, popularly known as the "drone." Thus far utilized by the United States in Afghanistan, Pakistan, Somalia, and Yemen, individuals are targeted by observational cameras in the drone, and weapons on board are fired at individuals or habitation structures. In 2012, Christof Heyns, UN Special Rapporteur on Extrajudicial, Summary or Arbitrary Executions, referred to drone attacks as "war crimes," and the subject is now before the UN Human Rights Council, which has been asked to determine which international law, if any, is violated by drones invading the airspace of other countries without permission and whether unacknowledged lethal drone attacks constitute "disappearances" under the International Convention for the Protection of All Persons from Enforced Disappearance. Although there are no treaties dealing with drones, extrajudicial executions are banned by Articles 6, 14, and 15 of the International Covenant on Civil and Political Rights as violations of crimes against humanity, not war crimes. Those who defend drone attacks in Pakistan and elsewhere claim that they hit targets on the "battlefield" of the "war on terror" or "war on Al-Qaeda." But the American military response clearly violates the Westphalian nonintervention principle in the name of self-defense. No court or treaty has yet established a legal basis for the UN Security Council to approve the use of military means against terrorists.

A further problem is that suspected terrorists, if captured, may not be convicted because the relevant international legal machinery is so weak. Indefinite detention, permitted in a military war, violates their rights in peacetime. Such a dilemma has confronted the administration of President Barack Obama (1961–), who sought to release those held in Guantánamo, while Congress limited his authority to do so. Interrogation of captured terrorists to ascertain where terrorists might strike next has often involved torture, which is prohibited both in wartime and peacetime. In other words, terrorist acts are criminal, but counterterrorism practices have been arguably criminal as well. Recent lawsuits against civilian officials authorizing torture have thus far been unsuccessful. A vicious circle is established when non-terrorists realize that legal redress is unlikely and instead decide to take revenge against drone attacks by joining the ranks of terrorists.

From 1997–2003, a UN Secretary-General Special Representative attempted to employ dialogue rather than confrontation with terrorist groups. As a result, more than 60 terrorist organizations agreed to avoid recruiting children. In the case of Al-Qaeda, the medium was cyberdialog, with the same result. Similarly, Amnesty International persuaded Basque separatists to stop attacks on civilians. Of course, such confidential negotiations have long been the hallmark of the operations of the International Committee of the Red Cross, which goes public with problems of prisoner abuse only when the abusing country is recalcitrant, refusing to change its behavior.

Most terrorist groups have been eliminated because they have either been infiltrated by local police and intelligence agencies or they make a deal with the government. Military force has worked in less than 10 percent of the groups studied by Rand Corporation.

The newest form of terrorism operates on the Internet. Known as **cyberterrorism** or **cyberwar**, an individual in one country can disrupt, damage, and frighten persons in other countries by invading e-mail addresses, programmed sets of operations, or websites. Most computer hackers annoy but are relatively harmless, but hacking that does human or material destruction can be classified as the "use of force," as defined in the UN Charter. Hacking that causes intentional death, injury, or significant destruction, thus, could fall within the scope of the law of war. In 2010, the first major cyber attack occurred when American and Israeli "cyberwarriors" disabled nearly 100 nuclear centrifuges in Iran, using the Stuxnet worm. Iran's apparent reprisal for economic sanctions in 2012 was to overload websites of Bank of America and other American companies, thereby preventing customers from using their websites. Because hackers might some day disable power grids, transportation patterns, and water filtration systems, counterterrorism planning now focuses on defenses against cyberwar or "cybergeddon."

CONCLUSION

When the first Geneva Convention was adopted in 1864, only 10 percent of the casualties were civilian. Today, civil wars, ethnic cleansing, insurgency and counter-insurgency warfare, and indiscriminate bombing have become more common and deadly than interstate wars, with civilians accounting for the overwhelming percentage of casualties. Nevertheless, widespread agreement on the illegality of warfare has not deterred decision makers from going to war.

The Geneva Conventions, which contain more than 400 articles regulating the conduct of nations involved in war, have been adopted or ratified by 186 nations. Few international treaties have been so widely accepted. The world community, therefore, implicitly recognizes that human rights issues involving international violence may be more important than all others. Although the right to life is basic within treaties regarding civil, political, economic, social, and cultural rights, superpowers have still pretended to act with impunity.

Wars of the twenty-first century do not fit the classical definition. Instead of military personnel attacking a territory abroad, there are more intrastate wars. Some are funded externally, seek population rather than territorial control, use terrorist methods, involve preemption, and are low-intensity efforts that drag on for years. One example is the Second Congo War (1998–2003), which involved 8 states and more than 25 armed groups. International law has not caught up with "new wars," as they are sometimes called.

Governments that ratify conventions and protocols dealing with the right to life and the right to peace are responsible under the Geneva Conventions and related treaties for punishing violations committed by their own military officers as well as other individuals. When governments fail to do so, the international community may be called into action. Accordingly, Chapter 8 asks why some countries respect human rights more than others, and Chapters 9–13 identify how human rights violations are being handled institutionally in the world community today.

CHAPTER 8

Quantitative and Theoretical Dimensions

Countries around the world differ substantially in their efforts to live up to human rights standards. Some countries are improving more rapidly than others. Why? What explains why some countries do better than others? To answer both questions, a comparative study is needed with quantitative measures of human rights and one or more theoretical explanations. Quantitative studies of worldwide human rights observance, to be useful, should raise five questions:

- Are there reliable and valid indicators of human rights performance?
- Is the concept of human rights unidimensional or is the concept so broad that there are empirically identifiable subsets of human rights?
- Do certain variables predict to varying degrees of human rights performance?
- How can predictors of human rights attainments be explained theoretically?
- What are the implications of the empirical evidence for policymakers?

All five questions are answered below.

HUMAN RIGHTS DATA

Empirical analysis requires data. Such United Nations Statistical Office sources as the *Demographic Yearbook* (1948–) and the *Statistical Yearbook* (1948–) report quantitative figures on economic and social attainments, as supplied by most countries around the world. Other UN agencies publish their own statistical compendia; the

UN Development Program's *Human Development Report* (1990–) provides data on a variety of socioeconomic indicators. For example, UNDP's Human Development Index is based on attainments in life expectancy, literacy, purchasing power, and school enrollment sex equality among 174 countries.

In 1958, the sociologist, Phillips Cutright (1930–), constructed two measures of social security attainments from US Social Security Administration data on countries around the world. His Social Insurance Program Experience index summed data for the years since a country adopted five types of social security programs (family allowance plans, old-age and survivor pensions, sickness and/or maternity programs, unemployment insurance, work-injury programs). Cutright's Social Insurance Program Completion index counted the number of new welfare programs adopted from the 1920s to the 1960s.

The Physical Quality of Life Index (PQLI), applied by Morris David Morris (1921–2011) to data as far back as 1960, has also been used in several studies; the index is a composite of infant mortality, life expectancy, and literacy rates. Morris discovered, for example, that PQLI has increased faster than measures of economic development.

In 1987, the Population Crisis Committee first began to issue annual reports, known as *The International Human Suffering Index*. The latter index rates 130 countries on 8 measures of economic and social attainments (clean drinking water, daily calorie supply, GNP per capita, infant immunization, life expectancy, rate of inflation, secondary school enrollment, telephones per capita).

For civil and political rights, however, the data have been qualitative, based on judgments, not precise statistical measures. Despite the difficulty, some institutions and scholars have pooled comparative judgments of different types of rights into scales, such as a three-point index from low to medium to high.

An early effort, a scale of democracy, appeared in a publication by political scientist, Russell Fitzgibbon (1902–1979), in 1956. A plethora of democracy scales has appeared ever since, some focusing on specific aspects of democratic rule, such as freedom of the press or the fairness of judicial proceedings. The *International Human Suffering Index* also has ratings on civil rights and political freedom.

Although Amnesty International has published annual reports on many countries since 1960, the organization refuses to provide qualitative or quantitative measures based on the reports despite repeated claims that the United States is the "number one abuser of human rights."[1] Not to be outdone, Human Rights Watch has published its own annual reports since 1992.

A pioneering effort to quantify judgments about human rights attainments was undertaken by Raymond Gastil (1931–) of Freedom House, which first issued the "Comparative Survey of Freedom" for 1972. With ratings claimed to be based on 17 types of civil rights and 19 political rights, Freedom House began to classify more than 100 countries along seven-point scales for both concepts. Despite first claiming that the two scales were analytically distinct, Freedom House contradictorily issued a single composite rating of each country's "status of freedom." Subsequently, Freedom House added an index of "economic freedom" that placed market economies at the top and closed economies at the bottom. Freedom House's "political torture scale" is based on the extent of incarcerations for political opinions, use of brutality and torture, disappearances after police arrest, and political executions.

In 1975, the US Department of State's annual *Country Reports on Human Rights Practices* began to provide qualitative judgments about human rights attainments across more than 150 countries, but excluding the United States. Although the reports began with a narrow scope, over time the categories of concern have risen to more than 20 distinct issues. Several European countries have followed suit.

A more ambitious undertaking was the short-lived *World Human Rights Guide*, a compilation by a former Amnesty International employee whose pseudonym is Charles Humana. Basing his ratings on Amnesty International reports and more than two dozen other sources, his first compilation was for 1982, when he rated 111 countries along four-point scales for 40 civil and political rights. In addition, he reported on 10 other aspects of human rights, using qualitative or quantitative measures, and he provided a composite rating expressed as a percentage. Humana's guidebook for 1986/87 expanded to include 121 countries, but with 45 variables. His final effort, published in 1992, covered 104 countries for 40 variables. Still seeking a composite summary scale, he employed a weighting system that gave more importance to seven of his conceptual variables.

Political terrorism scales, originally developed by political scientist Michael Stohl (1947–) in 1986, have also been used in recent studies. Stohl's original scale measures the extent to which a population is subjected to disappearance, imprisonment, torture, or execution for political views.

In 1991, the UNDP publication accepted Humana's summary percentages as its Political Freedom Index, but dropped his judgments in light of later scholarly critiques. UNDP then came up with its own composite measures, including the Gender-Related Development Index, the Gender Empowerment Measure, and the Human Poverty Index. UNDP has also published reports for geographic regions.

Funds provided by the Millennium Challenge Account, as established by the United States in 2002, have been allocated to countries on the basis of several screening criteria (Table 8.1), both civil-political and economic-social attainments. A major source of data is from the World Bank and related organizations.

One recent effort is the Gap Scale of political scientists Joe Foweraker and Todd Landman, which subtracts measures on a Rights-in-Practice Scale from a Rights-in-Principle Scale. A second, the award-winning CIRI Human Rights Data Set of political scientists David Cingranelli and David Richards, scales 13 types of human rights for 195 countries from 1981. ("CIRI" stands for the first two letters of their surnames.)

Despite the reliance on various data sources, many scholars have found inadequacies in the above compilations. Data on economic and social attainments were challenged at a conference of the International Association for Official Statistics in 2000 that was attended by 700 persons representing governments, intergovernmental and nongovernmental organizations, and scholars. Data on civil and political rights have been criticized even more.

Although Freedom House ratings have been widely used by empirical scholars, the methodology is not transparent, ratings are subjective, and the scales appear

TABLE 8.1   **PERFORMANCE CRITERIA FOR FUNDS FROM THE MILLENNIUM CHALLENGE ACCOUNT**

Performance criterion	Indicator	Source of data
Governing justly	Civil liberties	Freedom House
	Political rights	Freedom House
	Voice and accountability	World Bank Institute
	Government effectiveness	World Bank Institute
	Rule of law	World Bank Institute
	Control of corruption	World Bank Institute
Investing in people	Public primary education Spending as percent of GDP	World Bank/national sources
	Primary education completion rate	World Bank/national sources
	Public expenditures on health as percent of GDP	World Bank/national sources
	Immunization rates: DPT and measles	World Bank/national sources
Promoting economic freedom	Country credit rating	*Institutional Investor*
	Inflation	IMF
	3-year budget deficit	IMF/national sources
	Trade policy	Heritage Foundation
	Regulatory quality	World Bank Institute
	Days to start a business	World Bank

to overlap conceptually. Freedom House, which no longer employs Gastil, has nevertheless sought to improve the validity of the scales.

The State Department reports were so criticized for biased judgments that a brief critique of the 1981 report was duplicated in soft cover by the Lawyers Committee for International Human Rights; now renamed Human Rights First, the organization continued to publish annual critiques, now in hard cover. During the 1990s, however, many scholars found the State Department reports to be more objective and professional.

A data set known as Polity IV provides time-series and comparative data. Originally developed by Ted Robert Gurr (1936–), the current focus is on measuring degree of democracy and autocracy.

A fundamental problem is methodological. The scales have been developed without empirical validation – that is, the scales have not been demonstrated to be unidimensional and might instead lump disparate measures (the proverbial apples and oranges) together. Many scales measure "democracy," but fail to distinguish between procedural democracy (observance of political rights) and substantive democracy (representativeness). Consequently, higher scores on democracy scales have, unsurprisingly, been found to correlate with higher scores on scales of civil and political rights. Nevertheless, in *Improving Human Rights* (1994), I found high intercorrelations between data from six different sources. Other studies that compare alternative datasets have yielded comparable results.

HUMAN RIGHTS DIMENSIONS

According to the Vienna Conference on Human Rights of 1993, "All human rights are universal, indivisible, interdependent and interrelated" – in other words unidimensional. Alternatively, several scholars have proposed analytically but not empirically distinct categories of human rights (Table 8.2). Both claims may be incorrect and simplistic, lacking empirical foundation. Various types of human rights may be interrelated empirically in at least five ways (Table 8.2):

Unidimensionality. If a good record on civil and political rights predicts to a good record on social, economic, and cultural rights, then human rights would constitute a unidimensional phenomenon, consistent with the consensus reached at the Vienna Conference. Improvement on any one right would then provide the momentum for better observance of other human rights.

Hierarchy. The granting of some rights may unlock others; the attainment of some rights might have to wait until other rights are respected. In 1989, after the world community witnessed on television a massacre of dissidents near Tiananmen Square, the government in Beijing began to defend itself with the argument that the right of survival – the feeding of more than one billion persons – is more important than, and prior to, political rights. Although China's argument might be traced to the Jacobin desire to give priority to the welfare of the people over political freedoms, the country's dissidents appeared to agree with the contrary view that more political rights would open the door for opportunities to achieve greater prosperity. Interestingly, former premier, Wen Jiabao (1942–), has identified the ongoing development of a legal system as the last obstacle to democratic reform. In other words, if X leads to Y, then policymakers should pay most attention to improving X, whereupon Y will follow.

Inverse. Alternatively, an improvement in some rights might entail a decline in others. According to political scientist, Samuel Huntington (1927–2008), the attempt to increase democracy can retard economic development, as the masses may demand a more equitable distribution of the benefits of increased prosperity, thereby disrupting the imperatives of capital accumulation by shrewd entrepreneurs. Political chaos fomented by frustrated equalitarians, in short, might slow economic progress.

Curvilinearity. Human rights might improve under certain conditions up to an asymptote, then fluctuate randomly or decline while at intermediate levels until a

TABLE 8.2   **HYPOTHETICAL EMPIRICAL DIMENSIONS**

Type of dimensionality	*Empirical implication*
Unidimensionality	All rights cluster together
Multidimensionality	Two or more types of rights are empirically separate
Hierarchy	One right is basic, others are derivative
Inverse	As some rights are better observed, others decline
Curvilinearity	Correlation of rights fluctuates up and down

second threshold is reached, whereupon improvements might further decline or improve in a linear manner again. In one study, for example, democracy was found to vary with socioeconomic development up to a threshold, but thereafter the two variables were unrelated.[2]

Multidimensionality. When progress on civil-political rights has no effect on socioeconomic rights, there may be two or possibly more empirical dimensions. If so, efforts to improve human rights must identify separate problem areas. Nevertheless, scholars employ some of the scales mentioned above without verifying whether they are empirically distinct.

One practical implication of the multidimensional hypothesis is that instead of holding all countries to the same high standards, policymakers might better "aim ameliorative efforts at specific types of noncompliance, and recognize clusters which may be too intractable to justify attention at this time [thereby] enabl[ing] the efficient application of limited resources," as statistician David Banks (1956–) has argued. It is therefore important to determine which dimensionality assumption is correct so that potentially more effective strategies for advancing human rights can be devised.

EMPIRICAL DIMENSIONS

Are human rights unidimensional or are there empirically distinct types of human rights? One way to determine the number of empirical dimensions is to use a technique known as factor analysis. Simply stated, the procedure starts with correlations between pairs of variables and then finds out whether any such relationships hold when all other variables are held constant. What are then derived are one or more clusters of variables that are highly interrelated. If there are two or more uncorrelated clusters, then there are two or more empirically distinct dimensions. In other words, a factor analysis that derives at least two factors means that human rights are multidimensional.

The largest test of empirical dimensionality, which has been corroborated by smaller-scale studies, can be found in my *Improving Human Rights* (1994). Using 50 qualitative scales of civil and political rights from Humana's ratings and 91 quantitative measures from mostly UN sources for the years 1982 and 1986, the principal finding is that civil and political rights are empirically distinct from economic and social attainments. There was no evidence of either inverse relationships or curvilinearity between the two major types of human rights. Thus, civil and political rights neither precede nor follow increases in economic and social rights. The two sets of rights develop independently of each other.

Cluster analysis, a variant of factor analysis, identifies hierarchical relationships within superclusters. According to the cluster analysis in *Improving Human Rights*, civil and political rights are first granted to males in a country's mainstream ethnic group, then to minorities; after rights of minorities are respected, women's rights are attained. After women's rights come gay rights. The statistical pattern is indeed corroborated by the historical development of human rights described in Chapters 3 and 4. The supercluster analysis for economic and social attainments starts with quality of life in general, followed by workers' rights, then minority rights, and finally women's rights.

CORRELATIONAL EVIDENCE[3]

While some scholars have made specific predictions that may be checked through correlational analysis, others prefer to engage in case studies. Both statistical and case study analyses are valid methods for studying empirical phenomena; indeed, case studies are needed to validate statistical research.

More than 100 bivariate statistical efforts (involving correlations between predictor variable and levels of human rights observance) agree that the countries most likely to respect both civil-political and economic-social human rights have a well-educated and homogenous population with a prosperous, stable, urbanized society in which there is relative income equality, considerable media development, and competitive democratic multiparty systems. In addition, there is a consensus among empirical scholars that economic and social rights are better observed within affluent, stable democracies. Countries plagued with security problems tend to have lower attainments on civil and political rights as well as economic and social rights. Two variables consistently are demonstrated to decrease human rights violations – democracy and economic development.

Bivariate correlational studies, however, are inherently shallow. Using multivariate techniques, including cluster analysis, factor analysis, and multiple regression, both comparatively and longitudinally, the principal findings of *Improving Human Rights* regarding civil and political rights are that higher **levels of observance** are found in countries with the following characteristics:

- The parliament has many parties, with a high percentage of female legislators, the largest party has a slim plurality, and the military budget is small.
- Absence of forced labor is related to a prosperous, urban economy, with high media development and substantial education, health, and welfare budgets.

Bivariate studies overwhelmingly agree and embellish the findings with such observations as that one key to human rights observance in democracies is an independent judiciary to enforce norms. Mature democracies, in other words, observe human rights much better than all other governmental forms. Countries that are gradually democratizing often show growing pains by occasional reductions in human rights observance – and those very human rights restrictions fuel domestic unrest.

Most studies examine the impact of domestic conditions on human rights attainments, but systemic factors may play a role as well. For example, common and frequent memberships in international organizations impact states to improve human rights. Contrariwise, when countries are at war, the quest for victory tempts commanders to violate the law of war, though those very violations may prompt other countries to support the opposite side in the conflict. The data show that persistent terrorist threats in the 1980s and 1990s provoked states to engage in extrajudicial executions, but not gross restrictions on civil rights. During civil wars, on the other hand, civil rights are usually restricted, sometimes by invoking "emergency clauses," but the human rights violations emerge at the mid-crisis level rather than in the early or late stages. Countries that have a high level of human rights deficiencies tend to import a considerable amount of weapons for war and then go to war.

Variables associated with **improvements** in civil and political rights over time are as follows:

- Countries with lower taxes and lower voter turnout improve the most.
- Gender equality improves most rapidly within ethnolinguistically homogeneous, prosperous, domestically stable, urban countries that have a high degree of media development, income equality, and substantial education, health, and welfare budgets; though the same countries tend to have high death rates from cancer, heart disease, and suicide.

There are two major findings regarding economic and social rights attainments:

- Economic and social conditions improve most in ethnolinguistically homogeneous, non-Muslim, prosperous, urban countries with relative income equality and high media development as well as substantial education, health, and welfare budgets.
- Workers' rights are most respected by civilian governments where parliaments have many parties, including leftist parties, and the largest party has a slim plurality.

Perhaps the most important finding is that there are separate patterns regarding **mainstream** and **nonmainstream** groups (minorities, women, gays, and lesbians). Human rights improve in stages, beginning with mainstream groups. After a dominant ethnic group enjoys human rights, military regimes are the main barriers to the extension of human rights to nonmainstream groups. When the military steps down from power, rights are granted first to minorities, next to women, and finally to gays and lesbians. Thus, empirical evidence suggests that some forms of human rights unlock progress in other human rights.

DISCUSSION TOPIC 8.1 WHAT IS THE MOST SURPRISING CORRELATIONAL FINDING ABOUT HUMAN RIGHTS?

More than 100 statistical studies have attempted to find explanations for the incidence of human rights observance across various countries and over time. Most agree that democracies have the best human rights records, though the very term "democracy" implies a country that observes human rights. What are the most surprising findings?

The above findings report both correlational and multivariate findings. But statistical analyses mean very little until findings can be placed into a theoretical framework so that a coherent explanation can be formulated.

EMPIRICAL THEORIES

What accounts for the degree of observance of and progress in human rights? Theoretical frameworks serve the function of explaining the inner logic of socioeconomic and political processes at work. Currently, several empirical theories compete as alternative explanations for the fact that some countries have better human rights records than others (Table 8.3).

The metaphilosophical justifications for human rights identified in Chapter 2 are primarily ethical theories. However, democratic theories and Marxism are predictive theories; that is, they make predictions about which variables explain levels of human rights attainment. Some opponents of human rights, as delineated in Chapter 2, are based on ethical or ideological postulates, but other opponents believe that the steady advance in human rights is infeasible, so their predictions can also be put to the test with empirical data. Finally, some social science theories, as specified within various chapters of my *Polity and Society: Philosophical Underpinnings of Social Science Paradigms* (1992), can also be tested with empirical data. Below, the

TABLE 8.3   EMPIRICAL THEORIES OF HUMAN RIGHTS

Theory	Prediction
Liberal democratic theory	Political rights precede all other rights
Social democratic theory	Social rights precede all other rights
Stages-of-growth theory	Some rights must come before others
Marxism	Economic elites block rights of workers
Relativism	Human rights are culturally defined and follow no regular pattern
Power elite theory	Elites block rights of nonelites to stay in power
Group conflict theory	Mainstream groups block rights of nonmainstream groups
Mobilization theory	Rights are granted only after political struggles
Mass society theory	Elites block civil society to stay in power
Frustration-aggression theory	Human rights decline when economies collapse, as governments and people seek scapegoats
Freudianism	As industrialization increases, the population becomes "savage," so governments block rights to keep order
Functionalism	Governments comply with human rights norms because of favorable diplomatic experiences
Social Darwinism	Those who are productive and strong should have more rights than those who are weak

various predictive theories are evaluated in terms of the results of empirical research on human rights.

Liberal Democratic Theory. Such theorists as political scientist Robert Dahl (1915–) and sociologist Max Weber (1864–1920) stress the need for free elections, the free flow of information, a competitive economy, contending political parties, and a neutral bureaucracy as preconditions for a social order that will bring human rights for all. Since empirical evidence demonstrates that support for human rights is greater in countries with competitive multiparty systems, there is strong support for liberal democratic theory.

Social Democratic Theory. The social democratic theories of sociologists Gerhard Lenski (1924–) and Gunnar Myrdal (1898–1987), reflecting especially on the experience of Scandinavian political systems, argue that human rights are best observed when the rich in a democracy support social welfare reforms for the less wealthy. Liberal democratic theory does not insist upon the components of the welfare state, whereas social democrats conceive of social welfare programs as essential in providing human rights to the entire population. The empirical evidence indeed demonstrates that larger education, health, and welfare budgets correlate with greater attainments of human rights in general, particularly with workers' rights and women's rights.

Stages-of-Growth Theory. Some theorists stress the need for economic growth as a precondition to human rights. Political scientist Walt Rostow (1916–2003) applies the same logic to economic development, and fellow political scientist Kenneth Organski (1923–2006) finds a parallel in political development. They appear to argue that the trickle-down of capital accumulated as a country shifts from an agricultural to an industrial to a post-industrial society will bring ever-increasing democracy, human rights, and prosperity. However, Samuel Huntington has provided evidence that instability results when political rights are granted before a developing country secures solid progress in improving living standards. He cautions that the hard decisions required to transform economies often require political authoritarian rule and are hindered by premature democracy. If human rights develop in stages, we would expect to find that after countries achieve greater economic attainments, they will gradually improve civil and political rights performance. Although bivariate studies support stages-of-growth theory, multivariate analyses demonstrate that economic development goes hand in hand with improvements in civil and political rights. Since the two elements move along parallel tracks, what provokes both processes to develop in the first place? Stages-of-growth theory, in other words, does not identify what inexorability factor specifically prompts movement from one stage to another, though economist, Milton Friedman (1912–2007), suggests that the benefits of world trade in building up a country's wealth can redound to the benefit of improvements in all types of human rights.

Marxism. For Marxists, economic elites trample on human rights to preserve their economic hegemony, which ultimately rests on exploitation at home or abroad. Marxists believe that the bourgeoisie's imperative of capital accumulation is why economic elites under capitalism do not want nonelites to enjoy basic human rights, whereas worker's democracies would promote equal treatment. Workers, according to Marx, must struggle to wrest power from the bourgeoisie. Multivariate evidence supports the prediction that countries with greater income equality have more respect for human rights in general; moreover, higher welfare budgets predict to more respect for workers' rights. In short, the Marxist prediction that social equality comes before legal equality has been turned on its side: both civil-political and economic-social rights improve as a country becomes more prosperous and income distribution is more equal.

Relativism. Turning to a theory developed by opponents of human rights, relativism argues that the Western-oriented human rights conception of individualism does not fit the circumstances or outlook of non-Western peoples and hence cannot be advanced by applying foreign pressure. Relativists argue that socially constructed cultural norms determine the propensity to respect some human rights. The statistical evidence from several studies indeed finds that the percentage of Christians in a country is a much better predictor to support for civil and political rights than the percentage of Muslims. However, Turkey respects human rights more fully than other Muslim countries, and the United States lags behind other countries with large Christian populations, so there is variability with the two religious traditions. Relativism, therefore, is an inadequate explanation for variability in human rights attainments.

Power Elite Theory. Burkean elitism argues that humans are born unequal and therefore should not expect to be treated equally. The social science approach closest to Burkeanism is power elite theory. According to power elite theory, those on top seek to maintain power by setting up barriers to equal rights for nonelites. One version believes that there is something akin to an "iron law of oligarchy"; exponents are sociologists Roberto Michels (1876–1936), Gaetano Mosca (1858–1941), and Vilfredo Pareto (1948–1923). A contemporary power elite theorist, sociolinguist Noam Chomsky (1928–), argues that the rhetoric of "national security" serves as a rationale for restricting human rights. The Cold War, according to Chomsky and others, was waged by ruling elites in both the Soviet Union and the United States to justify internal and external disinterest in democratization. Social constructionists, similarly, argue that elites maintain their dominance by controlling the verbal discourse, using such arguments as "national security" to dissuade nonelites from demanding their rights. One type of power elite is the military in a country, but corporations can seek plutocratic control as well. Economist Charles Lindblom (1917–) believes that rulers must carefully weigh costs and benefits of repression; by extension, rulers are predicted to respect human rights in order to maintain their grip on power without the costly expenditures required to maintain military rule or police states. Quantitative research, as reported above, supports power elite theory insofar as military juntas stay in power by refusing to grant equal rights to civilians. However, the history of human rights is that military and civilian elites do indeed step down from power and grant rights, though they often retake power when displeased with democratic rule, so the pessimism of power elite theory is somewhat exaggerated.

Group Conflict Theory. In politics there is a perpetual struggle between groups. For Marxists, the struggle is between social classes; for power elite theory, the contending groups are elites versus nonelites. Ethnic groups struggle in heterogeneous societies, as identified by sociologist Pierre Van Den Berghe (1933–), whose concept of **herrenvolk democracy**, based in part on his analysis of South Africa, is that mainstream ethnic groups allow civil and political rights among themselves while denying them to nonmainstream groups. According to group conflict theory, thus, human rights fare better in homogeneous than in heterogeneous societies, as the latter will tend to have more internal conflict. Just as Japanese persons on the west coast of Canada, Perú, and the United States were relocated to interment camps during World War II, a current version of group conflict theory is advanced by leaders who seek to restrict human rights of Arab-appearing individuals in the name of fighting terrorist groups. Statistical findings about greater human rights in homogeneous societies support group conflict theory as an explanation for why nonmainstream groups lag behind mainstream groups. Nevertheless, group conflict theory does not explain why nonmainstream groups have advanced, especially during the twentieth century. Mobilization theory does so instead.

Mobilization Theory. Historically, elites and dominant ethnic groups have granted human rights to others. An explanation for the transformation is offered by the social science approach known as mobilization theory. Such observers as politically active Stokely Carmichael (1941–1998), later known as Kwame Ture, and political sociologist Charles Tilly (1929–2008) believe that no rights are granted without a struggle, so well organized groups can alone advance their own cause. Indeed, mobilization theory views politics in terms of the pressure group model of political scientist, Arthur Bentley (1870–1957), in which the victor in a political contest is the strongest within a parallelogram of forces. If mobilization theory is correct, human rights will be highest in countries with a vigorous civil society, including strong minority movements, trade unions, and women's organizations that can work to develop a human rights culture. Of course, mobilization efforts might invite repression, which in turn may boomerang, so there is a possible curvilinear relationship, according to political scientist Eduard Ziegenhagen (1935–). Mobilization theory clearly explains how one stage of human rights develops to another: mobilization campaigns begin because some groups want the same rights as others. The empirical evidence supports mobilization theory for the development of workers' rights but not for the increase of human rights in general.

Mass Society Theory. Human rights transformations have occurred in some countries, but not in others, so a theory is needed to explain why the masses succeed or fail to mobilize for their rights in some political systems rather than others. Since mass-based "people power" struggles are well understood by elites, the social science theory of mass society has arisen to explain why some elites are able to maintain power for long periods of time without granting human rights. There are two variants of mass society theory, which links the absence of civil society with denials of human rights. Samuel Huntington notes that political systems are often confronted with a massive social dislocation accompanying extremely rapid economic growth as the population moves from the countryside to the towns. If human rights are granted too quickly, according to mass society theory, the result will be political turmoil, so certain governments will backburner human rights as their countries develop economically. Although the evidence is that economic development can coincide with human rights progress, no scholar has yet correlated rates of economic development to test the rapid development variant. The second form of mass society theory, as explicated by sociologist William Kornhauser (1925–2004), stresses that totalitarian rule, which deprives citizens of the freedom to form a civil society, serves to build up pressures that cannot be expressed politically but are instead evident in decreasing quality of life, such as rampant alcoholism. But the second version is contrary to empirical evidence regarding women's rights, which were relatively well respected in former communist countries.

Frustration-Aggression Theory. For Sigmund Freud (1856–1939) and his followers, notably Herbert Marcuse (1898–1979), the Industrial Revolution requires individuals to repress their spontaneity in order to have the discipline to perform repetitive tasks in factories and offices. Such repression supposedly creates a longing to express savagery, whether in the form of genocide or lesser violations of human rights. Some non-Freudians believe that socioeconomic deprivation and discrimination constitute frustrations that can lead the masses to engage in violent protest, thereby inviting government repression and escalating violence. For psychiatrist Robert Lifton (1926–) and political scientist Ted Gurr, economic downswings precede human rights restrictions, whereas higher levels of economic development and prosperity predict to better human rights records. Since economic improvement has been the rule over the last several decades in most of the world, supporting empirical evidence is unavailable for anything more than temporary downswings.

Functionalism. Sociologists often assume that individuals behave in accordance with past conditioning, that is, a socialization process. Governments are more likely to observe human rights when elites and citizens are conditioned by their experience over time to appreciate the moral or pragmatic value of compliance. Frustration-aggression theorists, particularly Freudians, are pessimistic about human rights because they focus on negative socialization. The most prominent form of positive socialization theory is known as functionalism. Political theorist David Mitrany (1888–1975) predicts that governmental participation in international cooperative activities in relatively nonpolitical technical matters inevitably spills over into sensitive political issues, such as human rights. Cooperative activities, in turn, involve discussion among experts and government officials, some of whom persuade others of the virtues of human rights. Political scientist Ernst Haas (1924–2003), indeed, provided considerable support for what he called neofunctionalism in his analyses of decision making in intergovernmental institutions. Correlational research thus far reveals that countries adopting human rights treaties are much more likely to implement them in their domestic law than otherwise. Since statistical patterns do not explain why, functionalists argue that the main reason is international peer pressure.

Social Darwinism. Based on the premise that a world without a neutral international police force is so inherently dangerous that governments must maximize their power and influence in order to avoid loss of territorial control by losing wars, Social Darwinism assigns a very low priority to human rights. The theory of *realpolitik* of political scientist, Hans Morgenthau (1904–1980), sometimes referred to as "realism," is a Social Darwinist theory in which concern for human rights is viewed as a distraction from the need of every state to defend its sovereignty by being prepared militarily. Empirical data demonstrate that military rule is indeed the form of government least likely to grant human rights, but few countries are so governed, and mobilization theory appears to explain why military rule has been toppled.

Thus far, the data tentatively support democratic theories, mobilization theory, and functionalism. However, critical tests of alternative explanations are needed to determine which theory is most applicable, and thus far no simultaneous test of alternative theories has been conducted in a single study. Most empirical researchers have avoided metatheory, preferring to pile up tested hypotheses without an overall vision into which to fit the findings.

POLICY IMPLICATIONS OF EMPIRICAL RESEARCH

Several scholars have sought to determine whether foreign aid has served to encourage better human rights or instead has been used by recipient nations to suppress their people. Although findings are inconsistent, the key explanatory variable is whether the recipient countries are democracies in the first place, as foreign assistance can help existing democracies to strengthen human rights observance. But the data show that help for political parties does not necessarily promote democratization, and exposure of foreign support for a political party might cause public furor.

Looking at the other side of the coin, stable democracies with strong legal systems in developing countries attract much foreign investment, but so do stable dictatorships; investors avoid instability. Yet investors in high-tech developing companies prefer democratic governments with high educational attainments because they respect the human rights of workers. But there is a paradox: whereas post-Cold War American arms transfers tend disproportionately to go to undemocratic regimes, Chinese arms transfers are primarily to democratic countries.

Correlational and multivariate findings presented above demonstrate that human rights advance as a country develops economically, builds a communication infrastructure, and has competitive political parties. Accordingly, economic aid might be articulated specifically toward civil society and media development, whereas covert aid to political parties can easily boomerang when exposed. In view of the centrality of economic development in promoting human rights, one implication of the empirical findings presented above is that withholding economic aid will retard the advance of human rights. Although humanitarian aims justify pressuring notorious violators of human rights to release political prisoners, stop police torture of suspects, and the like, the data show that vigorous measures to promote economic development advance human rights, whereas sanctions are counterproductive. Incentives (carrots) work better than negative sanctions (sticks). Sanctions rarely dislodge single-party and military rule, but they can undermine a personalist ruler that is, one who gains support by distributing patronage (buying loyalty by dispensing favors to a small cadre).

Nongovernmental and international organizations can also use the media and publicity campaigns to shame specific violators. **Shaming** has proven moderately effective in reducing the severity of human rights abuses, especially when violators ultimately depend upon economic aid and trade. NGOs and foreign governments are better at shaming than IGOs.

A successful strategy for less developed countries with ethnolinguistic heterogeneity, which tend to be under military rule, is to support pluralism before human rights can advance on solid ground. Foreign aid, accordingly, should finance an information infrastructure, support increased educational opportunities so that a more literate population will emerge, and insist on a privatization of the economy that promotes economic pluralism. Evidence from International Monetary Fund (IMF) "structural adjustment" programs, which impose conditions on insolvent countries, demonstrates that the main benefit is in developing civil and political rights, whereas the harsh measures imposed by IMF on government spending have a negative impact on socioeconomic attainments and often result in political instability.

Another implication of empirical research is that the development of a legal system can provide many checks on the possibility of arbitrary actions by those in authority within a political system where there is a reasonable amount of consensus. The task of promoting constitutional rule ultimately falls upon leaders of loyal opposition parties to insist on multiparty elections with secret ballots. And a loyal opposition is more likely in countries that have economic pluralism.

Democracy, according to a large-scale study, can rarely be implanted in a country by bayonets. Economic sanctions imposed from outside are also unlikely incentives. A demand for "free and fair elections" as a condition of aid will not produce an increase in human rights unless the economic and social interests represented in a multiparty parliament are diverse and moderate. Too often, economically poor countries hold elections, but afterward parliamentarians represent their own personal interests. Such illiberal governments tend to be corrupt or gridlocked, thereby provoking military coups. One conception of democracy is of a form of government in which the legislature serves as an arena where lawmakers design compromises on behalf of pluralistic societal interests with an independent judiciary to mediate between groups. When aid is targeted at strengthening civil society and rule of law, recipient nations have democratized.

Foreign aid to the poorest countries should seldom be conditioned exclusively on progress in the rights of minorities, women, and workers, according to the empirical analyses reviewed herein. Since regimes are likely to provide basic human rights to the mainstream before nonmainstream groups, aid donors should apply pressure on recipient countries to establish an umbrella of general guarantees, notably observance of Bill of Rights provisions, before insisting that countries put special groups under the same umbrella. Since minority rights and workers' rights improve as economic aspects of liberal democracy emerge, the appropriate strategy is to provide aid for power grids, printing presses, telephone lines, Internet cables or wi-fi capabilities, elementary and secondary schools and textbooks, and professionalism in broadcasting, thus expanding pluralism. When states have sufficient economic

> ### DISCUSSION TOPIC 8.2 SHOULD FOREIGN AID GO TO COUNTRIES WITH POOR HUMAN RIGHTS RECORDS?
>
> The European Union and the United States screen recipients of foreign aid in accordance with human rights and other criteria. Countries with poor human rights records, in other words, are denied the very aid that might help to increase their human rights attainments. Based on case studies and quantitative studies, how can foreign assistance best improve human rights?

prosperity to extend rights to nonmainstream groups, conditional aid will no longer be needed. When progress in minority rights and women's rights is assured, gays and lesbians will be accorded more decent treatment. But case study empirical evidence also indicates that poverty can be eradicated directly by loans to the poorest members of society, especially women.

Historically, trade-union rights were respected before the establishment of welfare states. The successful efforts of such leaders as Martin Luther King, Jr (1929–1968) opened the door for advances in the rights of women and, much later, gays and lesbians. The evidence suggests that minorities and trade unionists should pursue separate but simultaneous struggles for their rights, whereas women, gays, and lesbians will derive benefit by forming coalitions that work for the success of both struggles while continuing to stress their own agendas.

CONCLUSION

Civil and political rights neither precede nor follow increases in economic and social rights. Instead, the two sets of rights are distinct and develop independently; the correlation between civil-political and social-economic rights is spurious. When the military pretends to be socially indispensable, civil and political rights are restricted. The end of autocratic rule, which tends to weaken as an information infrastructure expands, is essential before human rights can make substantial improvements. Human rights are complementary, not zero-sum, so improvements in one area do not entail a risk of lesser attainments elsewhere.

Civil and political rights, in turn, appear to be granted sequentially and thus form a hierarchy. Mainstream groups, that is, males of the dominant ethnic group, are likely to gain increased rights as arbitrary state power collapses. Later, other forms of civil and political rights emerge, such as freedom of the press and the right to vote. While mainstream groups are securing basic rights, nonmainstream groups tend to be ignored. In due course, as a government abandons military and police methods for dealing with minorities, the status of minorities improves. As a government develops a welfare state, women's rights improve. After minorities and women enjoy victories in their struggle for equal civil and political rights, gays and lesbians begin to enjoy success in achieving equal rights.

A domino effect appears to place the theory of liberal democracy as a precondition to the advancement of human rights. But liberal democracy alone can remain stagnant, without advances, until groups are mobilized to demand their own rights. Evidently liberal democratic theory explains the political climate for dominoes to stand on their own, while mobilization theory accounts for progress in extending rights. But such a scenario needs to be tested more rigorously in the years ahead.

Since the denial of basic human rights is a desperate strategy for maintaining power, advocates of human rights should urge more economic aid so that the infrastructure for a free flow of ideas and economic largesse for better social conditions can be established. Advocacy organizations that focus on particular abuses of the moment should be congratulated for successful efforts to free prisoners of conscience and similar short-term measures; but, for the long run, establishing the preconditions for a liberal and later a social democracy can best advance human rights. Current research findings and conclusions are, of course, tentative. They should be cross-checked through case studies, just as alternative theories should be put to critical tests.

Some of the empirically-based recommendations await policy decisions by individual governments. Other suggestions require concerted action in international and regional forums. Accordingly, Chapters 9–13 focus on all three levels.

CHAPTER 9

United Nations Charter-Based Organizations

In an ideal world, all human rights violations by individuals would be handled by their own governments. But when human rights are grossly violated by an errant state, other states may need to act in the name of humanity. Chapters 9–13 document the considerable extent to which members of the world community are now prepared to respond when victims of human rights seek redress beyond their borders. A continual state of mobilization on behalf of human rights exists because intergovernmental organizations (IGOs) have the power to act in the interest of the peoples of the world.

Several global organizations are relevant to human rights, constituting a form of political globalization that has become possible in an age of economic and information globalization. Most global intergovernmental organizations either are a part of the United Nations or have close relations with the UN. Perhaps the most prominent are the organs created by the UN Charter, which are reviewed in the present chapter (Table 9.1). Depending upon how "human rights" are defined, less than 3 percent of the regular UN budget is so allocated, since most organs identified below rely primarily on voluntary contributions.

The UN has four main concerns, which have developed in the following order:

- Security
- Humanitarian assistance
- Development
- Human rights.

TABLE 9.1   **MAIN UN CHARTER-BASED ORGANS FOCUSING ON HUMAN RIGHTS**

Organs	Acronym	Formed	Headquarters
Trusteeship Council	UNTC	1945	New York
General Assembly	UNGASS	1945	New York
• United Nations Children's Fund	UNICEF	1946	New York
• UN High Commissioner for Refugees	UNHCR	1945	Geneva
• UN World Food Program	WFP	1961	Rome
• UN Conference on Trade and Development	UNCTAD	1964	Geneva
• UN Development Program	UNDP	1965	New York
• UN Environmental Program	UNEP	1973	Nairobi
• UN Population Fund	UNPF	1974	New York
• United Nations Human Settlements Program	UN-HABITAT	1996	Nairobi
Security Council	UNSC	1945	New York
• International Criminal Tribunal for the Former Yugoslavia	ICTY	1993	The Hague
• International Criminal Tribunal for Rwanda	ICTR	1998	The Hague
• Peacebuilding Commission	PBC	2005	New York
• Working Group on Children in Armed Conflict	CAAC	2005	New York
Secretariat		1945	
• Secretary-General	UNSG	1945	New York
• Human Rights Council	UNHRC	1946	New York
• Office for Disarmament Affairs	ODA	1982	New York
• Office for the Coordination of Humanitarian Affairs	OCHA	1991	New York
• Department of Peacekeeping Operations	DPKO	1992	New York
• Department of Political Affairs	DPA	1992	New York
• Office of the High Commissioner for Human Rights	OHCHR	1994	Geneva
• United Nations Entity for Gender Equality and the Empowerment of Women	UN Women	2011	New York
Economic and Social Council	ECOSOC	1945	New York
• Commission on the Status of Women	CSW	1946	Vienna
• Commission on Population and Development	CPD	1946	New York
• Commission for Social Development	CsocD	1946	New York
• Commission on Sustainable Development	CSD	1992	New York
• Commission on Crime Prevention and Criminal Justice	CCPCJ	1992	Vienna
• UN Permanent Forum on Indigenous Issues	UNPFII	2000	New York
Specialized Agencies			
• International Labor Organization	ILO	1919	Geneva
• UN Educational, Scientific, and Cultural Organization	UNESCO	1945	Paris
• Food and Agriculture Organization of the United Nations	FAO	1945	Rome

Continued

TABLE 9.1 (CONTINUED)

Organs	Acronym	Formed	Headquarters
• World Health Organization	WHO	1948	Geneva
• UN Industrial Development Organization	UNIDO	1966	Vienna
• International Fund for Agricultural Development	IFAD	1977	Rome
• International Bank for Reconstruction and Development	IBRD	1944	Washington
• International Development Association	IDA	1960	Washington
• International Monetary Fund	IMF	1944	Washington
• International Court of Justice	ICJ	1946	The Hague

Human rights, however, interpenetrate the other three concerns. Accordingly, the discussion below focuses on each major UN institution and subordinate body to demonstrate how human rights concerns have become embedded within the work of the United Nations.

Both the General Assembly and the Security Council can authorize **punitive** economic and military sanctions. The rest (the former Trusteeship Council, the Secretariat, the Economic and Social Council, and the Specialized Agencies) can only engage in **proactive** measures.

TRUSTEESHIP COUNCIL (UNTC)

Under the settlement after World War II, the League of Nations **mandates** were to be converted into **trusteeships**. Former colonies of Italy and Japan's mandate in the North Pacific islands became trusteeships. The UN Charter gave explicit instructions for the Trusteeship Council to require reports from countries serving as trustees about measures taken to move the territories toward independence. But South Africa, which had the League of Nations mandate over former German South West Africa – the current Namibia – was the only mandate power that refused to accept the jurisdiction of the Trusteeship Council.

While the Cold War dominated the General Assembly and the Security Council from the late 1940s, the Trusteeship Council was the organ most in the forefront of human rights progress. In 1960, the General Assembly adopted the **Declaration on the Granting of Independence to Colonial Countries and Peoples**. Thereafter, annual reports on progress toward self-government were carefully monitored, and individuals could submit oral petitions or written complaints to the Trusteeship Council. In 1994, Palau was the last territory under the trusteeship system to be granted independence. Accordingly, the Trusteeship Council suspended operations and has not met since then.

However, recent actions by the General Assembly have created what may be called **quasi-trusteeships**. When asked to handle the administration of Cambodia, East Timor (Timor-Leste), Kosovo, Liberia, and Namibia after periods of turmoil, the UN responded in a manner that nearly constituted a trusteeship arrangement.

Most were short-term assignments, but the UN Interim Administration in Kosovo, the UN Mission in Liberia, and the United Nations Integrated Mission in Timor-Leste were still operating in 2013, albeit with much less authority than when created. Whereas the new country of Timor-Leste was admitted to the UN in 1992, Russia's veto prevents Kosovo from becoming a member.

GENERAL ASSEMBLY (UNGASS)

All members of the UN are automatically represented in the General Assembly, which begins annual sessions in September each year and can continue deliberations until the following summer. South Sudan, accepted for membership by the Security Council in 2011, became the 193rd member.

The first serious involvement of the General Assembly in human rights came in the 1960s as new African states joined the UN, eager to end *apartheid* in South Africa, racism in the British colony of Southern Rhodesia, and independence for the remaining colonies. Colonies under the jurisdiction of the Trusteeship Council were also being monitored by the General Assembly's Fourth Committee, specifically by the Subcommittee on Non-Self-Governing Territories.

The Fourth Committee, which deals with decolonization, is one of six committees:

- First Committee (Disarmament and International Security)
- Second Committee (Economic and Financial)
- Third Committee (Social, Humanitarian and Cultural)
- Fourth Committee (Special Political and Decolonization)
- Fifth Committee (Administrative and Budgetary)
- Sixth Committee (Legal).

But in 1961, the General Assembly replaced the Subcommittee on Non-Self-Governing Territories with the Special Committee on the Situation with Regard to the Implementation of the Declaration on the Granting of Independence to Colonial Countries and Peoples (known colloquially as the **Special Committee on Decolonization**) to press metropolitan countries to grant independence or self-government to all remaining colonies. Most African countries did indeed achieve independence in the 1960s. The last region to emerge from colonial status was the South Pacific, where most island states became independent during the 1970s.[1] The remaining sixteen non-self-governing territories are still being monitored by the Special Committee,[2] and steps to implement the declaration of 1960 are reviewed annually by the General Assembly.

Racism has been another major concern of the General Assembly, which exerted pressure not only on Rhodesia and South Africa but also adopted resolutions condemning Israel. Tel Aviv was considered by many states to be operating a racist government after the Six-Day War of 1967 because Israel began a military occupation of homelands of the Arabic-speaking population of Palestine. The United States opposed General Assembly resolutions on the subject, most vehemently the resolutions adopted during 1975–1991 stating that "Zionism is a form of racism and racial discrimination," and

Washington vetoed Security Council resolutions from 1973–1997 calling for an end to the Israeli occupation. At Israel's insistence, the resolutions were dropped in 1998 so that negotiations could begin with the Palestine Liberation Organization (PLO) to replace the occupation with a Palestinian state. Yet negotiations stopped in early 2001, brief summit meetings were held in 2003 and 2005, a short conference convened in 2007, and indirect talks (with mediators) were last held in 2010. Palestine has applied unsuccessfully to the Security Council for UN membership.

The General Assembly accredits delegations to represent member countries, but not always in accordance with human rights principles. During the 1980s, the Cambodian seat was held by the delegation of Democratic Kampuchea, which represented the murderous Khmer Rouge regime that the Vietnamese army ousted by 1979. The Cambodian government that succeeded the Khmer Rouge, considered by some countries to be a puppet regime of Vietnam, was not accredited by the UN. After a peace agreement in 1991, the UN organized elections in 1993 to select a new government, a key element in the peace settlement, and the newly elected government was re-admitted.

Similarly, from 1999–2001, the UNGASS refused to accredit the Taliban government as the representative of Afghanistan in view of many human rights violations, notably restrictions on the movements of females. The membership of Kosovo, which unilaterally declared independence from Yugoslavia (now Serbia) in 2008, has been blocked by Serbia's ally, Russia, despite an Advisory Opinion by the International Court of Justice in 2010 that supports the legality of Kosovo as an independent, sovereign state.

In addition to Liberia, Kosovo, and Timor-Leste, the General Assembly has authorized election monitors as well as various observer, peacekeeping, and stabilization operations. In 2012, countries under the purview of the General Assembly included the Central African Republic, Chad, Cyprus, Democratic Republic of the Congo, Eritrea and Ethiopia, Georgia, the Ivory Coast, Lebanon, South Sudan, and parts of Sudan (Abyei and Darfur). A UN Mission for the Referendum in Western Sahara is in operation, though the plebiscite has not yet been held.

HISTORIC EVENT 9.1 THE GENERAL ASSEMBLY FIRST REQUESTS A PLEBISCITE IN WESTERN SAHARA (1966)

South of Morocco, along the Atlantic coastline, lies the territory of Western Sahara, which became a Spanish protectorate in 1884 under the terms of the peace settlement reached at the Congress of Berlin. In 1965, the UN General Assembly called upon Spain to decolonize Western Sahara. The General Assembly has repeatedly asked Spain to hold a referendum on self-determination. In 1974, Spain agreed that a plebiscite would be held in early 1975, whereupon Morocco claimed sovereignty over the territory and asked the International Court of Justice to rule in its favor. One day after

Continued

the court ruled that Morocco had no legal claim to Western Sahara, some 350,000 unarmed Moroccan civilians entered Western Sahara as new residents. Subsequently, Morocco refused to accept any compromise regarding the determination of voters eligible to participate in a plebiscite for Western Sahara. In 1975, Spain relinquished administrative control to a joint Mauritanian-Moroccan administration, but the two countries then went to war. In 1979, Mauritania accepted defeat and left control of most of the territory to Morocco. However, a separate group, the Algerian-backed Polisario Front, has controlled a portion of the territory for many decades. Despite continuing efforts by the UN to achieve a settlement, the conflict remains unresolved.

Delegates to the UNGASS generally hold the rank of ambassador. In 2010–2011, 57 resolutions covering human rights issues were approximately 20 percent of a total of 295. The General Assembly is the principal arena in which international human rights declarations and treaties are adopted.

In recent years, the UNGASS chamber has been the venue for **World Summits**, that is, meetings of heads of state and government. The World Summit of 2000, which included 147 heads of state and government, adopted the Millennium Declaration to set measurable goals to be attained in seven key areas:

- Peace, security, and disarmament
- Development and poverty eradication
- Protecting the environment
- Protecting the vulnerable
- Meeting the special needs of Africa
- Strengthening the United Nations
- Human rights, democracy, and good governance.

Under the latter heading, the following goals were declared:

- To respect fully and uphold the Universal Declaration of Human Rights
- To strive for the full protection and promotion in all our countries of civil, political, economic, social, and cultural rights for all
- To strengthen the capacity of all our countries to implement the principles and practices of democracy and respect for human rights, including minority rights
- To combat all forms of violence against women and to implement the Convention on the Elimination of All Forms of Discrimination Against Women
- To take measures to ensure respect for and protection of the human rights of migrants, migrant workers, and their families
- To eliminate the increasing acts of racism and xenophobia in many societies and to promote greater harmony and tolerance in all societies
- To work collectively for more inclusive political processes, allowing genuine participation by all citizens in all our countries

- To ensure the freedom of the media to perform their essential role and the right of the public to have access to information.

Since the UN began, several bodies have been created to advance the work of the organization proactively. More than a dozen are subsidiary to the General Assembly. Some are discussed below in the chronological order of their formation (UNHCR, UNICEF, WFP, UNCTAD, UNDP, UNEP, UNFPA, UN-HABITAT). Although administratively a part of the operations of the General Assembly, the organizations discussed below operate on both UN and non-UN funds.

- **High Commissioner for Refugees** (UNHCR). A quintessential proactive UN human rights component is the relief given to refugees. After World War II, the General Assembly set up the United Nations Relief and Rehabilitation Administration from 1943–1946 and the successful International Refugee Organization from 1947–1952, both of which handled millions of displaced persons; the latter body took over the functions of the refugee organization that operated under the League of Nations. Then in 1949, the General Assembly established UNHCR in view of the continuing presence of 1.2 million displaced persons, some of whom had not been resettled after World War II and others who fled countries occupied or controlled by the Soviet Union. The Geneva-based agency, based on the founding statute and the Convention Relating to the Status of Refugees, both adopted in 1951, originally had a three-year mandate to resettle the refugees. After three years, the problem remained, and the life of UNHCR was extended for five-year intervals until 1993, when the agency was given permanent status. Thus far, the agency has helped an estimated 50 million people to restart their lives.

The term **refugee** covers those who flee their homeland to seek sanctuary in a second country. UNHCR, which recognizes the right to seek asylum and to find safe refuge, with the option to return home voluntarily, integrate locally, or to resettle in a third country, now services about 20 million refugees in 126 countries. A basic principle is that no person should be resettled in a country where there is a reasonable possibility of persecution. However, some governments have not ratified the 1951 Convention Relating to the Status of Refugees, so UNHCR often operates in an ambiguous context. In addition, UNHCR is not concerned with economic migrants, those who leave their country for a job in a new country, even if they are persecuted inside their new country of residence or would be if they returned to the country from which they came.

Originally, UNHCR's task was viewed as primarily legal – assisting refugees in securing permanent residence in a new country. Petitions for asylum, however, run afoul of disparate regulations in many countries, so those who seek asylum often have a lengthy wait before a new status is recognized. While undertaking the tedious task of filling out forms and providing representation, many refugees remained unassisted. The agency could only offer effective protection if a person's basic needs of food, medical care, sanitation, shelter, and water were met in the meanwhile, so the humanitarian task increased to the point that other UN agencies were called upon to assist, as discussed below, with the cooperation of more than 500 nongovernmental organizations.[3] The recent annual budget is US$2.5 billion. Although most countries are unwilling to accept refugees on anything more than a temporary basis, refugee camps can become nearly permanent. Sometimes, UNHCR must give food and supplies to warlords or they will not reach the refugees, so the work can be very frustrating.

Although UNHCR's mandate does not strictly apply to **internally displaced persons** (IDPs), High Commissioner for Refugees Sadako Ogata (1927–) improvised during her tenure from 1991–2000, by providing relief to some of the estimated 20–25 million persons who had left their homes but not their countries to obtain greater security from civil wars, natural disasters, or political instability. Ogata also criticized specific countries for practices causing the refugee flow. Currently, UNHCR assists approximately 15 million IDPs.

One of the most difficult UNHCR efforts occurred during 1992–1993, when the UN Operation in Somalia coordinated food aid for a starving population after law and order broke down. Efforts continue to the present, when UNHCR assists about half of the 1.5 million IDPs with shelter and relief supplies. Policing refugee camps is a major UNHCR problem.

UNHCR has also been called upon to assist countries after civil wars or major conflicts have ended, when large numbers of persons seek resettlement but resources are not immediately at hand. Since the refugees who return to their homelands usually lack the wherewithal to start anew, UNHCR provides "quick impact projects." After the Afghan War began in 2001, the High Commissioner began to handle problems relating to 2 million refugees, the largest repatriation effort in many decades.

HISTORIC EVENT 9.2 THE AFGHAN WAR (2001–2014)

On 20 September 2001, President George W. Bush (1946–) issued an ultimatum to the government of Afghanistan, which he believed was culpable in the September 11, 2001, attacks on the United States by dint of harboring members of Al-Qaeda, whom he believed plotted the attacks. Bush's principal demands were to close all terrorist training camps and to hand over every terrorist to "appropriate authorities." Afghanistan, ruled by a group known as the Taliban, reportedly offered to hand over Osama Bin Laden (1957–2011), the leader of Al-Qaeda, for trial, but Bush deemed the response insufficient. Starting on October 7, ground forces of the Afghan United Front, known as the Northern Alliance, were brought together by a special Central Intelligence Agency unit. With massive American air support, the Afghan forces engaged and defeated the Taliban and entered the capital of Kabul on November 13. A new Afghan government was soon installed, and the UN Security Council voted in December to authorize a security force, provided by NATO, to defend the new government. Meanwhile, members of Al-Qaeda and the Taliban retreated to enclaves inside Pakistan. Then by 2006, members of the Taliban returned to Afghanistan to establish increasing control in areas neglected by NATO forces while engaging in guerrilla war. In 2009, the newly elected president, Barack Obama (1961–), increased the

Continued

number of American forces in an effort to reverse the Taliban's momentum and train the Afghan government's army to take over the fight by 2014, the scheduled year of withdrawal of all foreign forces.

In addition to helping the basic needs of refugees and IDPs, the scope of UNHCR extends to stateless persons. Stateless persons, estimated at 12 million in 2012, are often trapped in refugee camps where UNHCR and other agencies assist them. In 2012, UNHCR was called upon to assist nearly 1 million refugees from the civil war in Syria despite ongoing violence.

•   **UN Children's Fund** (UNICEF). In 1946, when many refugees were orphaned children confronted with disease and famine without the benefit of family resources, the UN International Children's Emergency Fund was established to assist in China and Europe. In 1950, the scope became worldwide. In 1953, the General Assembly made UNICEF a permanent organ of the UN, dropping the words "International" and "Emergency" but retaining the UNICEF acronym. By 2012, UNICEF had field offices in 200 countries with a budget of more than US$1 billion annually, with some income derived from the sale of UNICEF holiday cards.

UNICEF's Mission Statement asserts that the primary focus of the organization is the "protection of children's rights, to help meet their basic needs and to expand their opportunities to reach their full potential." In 1989, the Convention on the Rights of the Child of 1989 began to provide a more detailed guide for UNICEF. Although the organization continues to respond to natural and wartime emergencies, from 1995–2005, when Carol Bellamy (1942–) served as UNICEF Executive Director, the emphasis shifted from child survival to children's rights. During her stewardship, priorities also shifted to the most disadvantaged children in the poorest countries, developing the "community capacity development" paradigm in which community empowerment and sustainable development were central elements. She also identified the existence of 250 million child laborers as a serious problem.

However, Bellamy's successor, Ann Veneman (1949–), returned the work of the organization to child survival when she succeeded Bellamy in 2005–2010. Veneman's successor, Anthony Lake (1939–), has identified the cause of children in armed conflict as a new child survival concern of UNICEF.

•   **World Food Program** (WFP). The World Food Program was set up in 1961 so that the Food and Agriculture Organization of the United Nations (FAO), a UN Specialized Agency discussed below, could continue as a technical organization, leaving WFP to coordinate and distribute food aid, especially during emergencies. During 2011, WFP reached about 90 million people in 73 countries on a budget of US$2.6 billion, woefully short of the resources to relieve an estimated 1 billion hungry people. FAO's Director-General, with the approval of the UN Secretary-General, appoints WFP's Executive Director.

The world has plenty of food, so the lack of proper distribution is an example of structural violence, with the death toll from hunger exceeding many prominent communicable diseases. An unresolved problem is that the food trade regime of the World Trade Organization (WTO) has been accused of nullifying WFP's food aid regime by encouraging developing countries to sell cash crops to rich countries while their own people starve. And WFP sometimes supplies food to dictatorships that can be misallocated. To overcome the various obstacles, one important program supplies nutritionally appropriate meals for schoolchildren.

• **UN Conference on Trade and Development** (UNCTAD). In 1964, a conference was held to respond to the desire of developing countries for an organization specifically designed to analyze macroeconomic reasons why developing countries were not advancing. The body, which became permanent that year, has served three functions:

- Providing an intergovernmental forum to build consensus between poor and rich countries
- Data collection, policy analysis, and research
- Technical assistance.

The first development theme stressed by UNCTAD, import substitution, did not bridge the gap. In the 1970s, UNCTAD endorsed the call for a new international economic order (NIEO), but that idea was not accepted by developed countries. In the 1980s, export promotion became the model for development. The current focus is on "sustainable development." UNCTAD is perhaps best known for conceiving the generalized system of preferences (GSP), which has enabled Third World countries to overcome tariff barriers in the First World.

UNCTAD functions to organize conferences at four-year intervals, when progress is assessed and priorities are determined. The regular annual budget is US$69 million, with US$36 million in extrabudgetary technical assistance funds.

• **UN Development Program** (UNDP). A merger of the former UN Expanded Program of Technical Assistance and the UN Special Fund, UNDP was established in 1965 to alleviate social, economic, and cultural problems in developing countries by marshalling resources for technical assistance from such UN Specialized Agencies as the UN Industrial Development Organization (UNIDO).[4] UNDP not only coordinates aid provided by other UN agencies but also serves as a clearinghouse for aid from non-UN sources to ensure that there will be no duplication of effort or funding.

Among the five Millennium Development Goals, democratic governance is at the top of UNDP's list. Accordingly, in 2002 the UNDP Democratic Governance Center opened at Oslo. UNDP annually supports an average of 26 elections.

Currently, UNDP country representatives are in 177 countries. From 1992, UNDP has issued an annual *Human Development Report*, which facilitates statistical comparisons over time as well as across countries. UNDP's proposed budget for 2010–2011 totaled approximately US$857 million.

• **United Nations Environmental Program** (UNEP). Ecological problems became an increasing concern during the 1960s, as air pollution worsened in many of the bigger cities of the world and Rachel Carson published *Silent Spring* (1962). Following the Earth Summit (UN Conference in Río de Janeiro) in 1972, UNEP was formed to apply scientific knowledge in order to solve problems of pollution in the air, land, and sea. The organization's headquarters in Nairobi, Kenya, operates on a budget of US$2.7 billion.

In 1988 UNEP and the World Meteorological Organization, a Specialized Agency of the UN established in 1950, set up the Intergovernmental Panel on Climate Change, which ultimately attributed greenhouse gasses as the culprits in a pattern of global warming. In 2009, UNEP organized an expert meeting, The New Future of Human Rights and Environment: Moving the Global Agenda Forward. More information about UNEP is available in Chapter 14.

• **United Nations Population Fund** (UNFPA). Overpopulation became a concern in the 1960s, as famines occurred in Africa because of severe droughts. In 1973, UNFPA was established initially to provide assistance to family planning programs being established, especially in the Third World. UNFPA is also concerned with reproductive health and the rights of women, including such concerns as abortion and female genital mutilation. UNFPA operates on a budget of US$783 million today. The program dealing with abortion is considered controversial in the United States, which is a large donor country.

• **United Nations Human Settlements Program** (UN-HABITAT). As developing countries developed industrial economies in urban areas, rural dwellers were attracted to migrate to the cities for work. Lacking relatives in the cities, they began to develop shantytowns with unsafe living conditions. Their plight was brought to attention at various UN conferences, especially the UN Conference on Human Settlements in 1978, which recommended formation of UN-HABITAT to establish the right to adequate housing as integral to the right to an adequate standard of living, as provided in the International Covenant on Economic, Social, and Cultural Rights. The principal focus of the organization, once known for city planning, is now sustainable urban development. The budget of approximately US$200 million is mostly derived from donations.

SECURITY COUNCIL (UNSC)

Whereas the General Assembly is an annual conclave of all UN members, the Security Council is a smaller body of 15 members that can meet at any time to handle crises. In addition to the 5 permanent members (Britain, China, France, Russia, United States), 10 non-permanent members are elected for two-year terms by the General Assembly. Decisions by the UNSC, which are supposed to bind all members, can be vetoed by any of the five permanent members; otherwise, majority rules.

Just as the General Assembly has been very effective in **standard setting** (establishing norms and principles), the UN Charter gives the UNSC the power to establish international legal principles by resolutions. Thus, as noted in Chapter 7, in 2006 the principle of "responsibility to protect" (R2P) was accepted by the UNSC as a legitimate basis for military action, though specific applicable situations were not identified in the text of the resolution. In 2011, R2P was cited for the first time as the basis for four military actions – in the Ivory Coast, Libya, South Sudan, and Yemen – though there was no consensus on how to respond to massacres taking place in Syria after 2011. R2P was one of the considerations that prompted the UNSC to authorize troops to enter Mali in 2013 to stop rebel groups from countering "violence against its civilians, notably women and children, killings, hostage-taking, pillaging, theft, destruction of cultural and religious sites, and recruitment of child soldiers."

The UNSC also has the power of **enforcement**. There are two types of enforcement actions – vertical and horizontal.

• **Vertical enforcement** involves military action. When war is imminent, breaks out, or a fragile peace exists, the UNSC has authorized member states to send peacekeeping military or police, as has occurred about 50 times thus far. Perhaps the most famous military effort was the decision to establish the UN Command in Korea, which prevented North Korean forces from annexing South Korea during 1950–1953. Although the UN Charter authorizes a Military Staff Committee to consist of a standing UN army, that provision has never been implemented. UNSC set up a **Working Group on Children and Armed Conflict** in 2005 to monitor conflicts that improperly force children into combat.

Nowadays, peacekeeping assignments do not involve the use of military force but rather seek to maintain an armistice, truce, or peace settlement. Reports on the general human rights situation have been part of recent peacekeeping assignments, and specific investigations have been authorized in several cases. Electoral assistance has also been provided by UNSC peacekeeping organs. As of 2012, there were some 110,000 UN peacekeepers (military and police) from 120 countries operating in 15 peacekeeping missions; only the United States stations more military personnel abroad. Personnel were being supplied on a voluntary basis by 116 countries. To coordinate the work, the UNSC set up the **Department of Peacekeeping Operations** in 1992. Most UNSC expenses are involved in peacekeeping. The cost since 1948 is US$69 billion, of which US$7 billion was budgeted for peacekeeping in 2012–2013.

Before peacekeeping, there must be a peace agreement. Many intractable conflicts defy resolution, so a peace settlement may be very fragile. Accordingly, in 2005 the General Assembly and the Security Council established the **Peacebuilding Commission** (PBC) as a subsidiary body, advisory to the Security Council. The mandate of the Commission is to recommend the scope of UN and non-UN operations after a peace agreement. The Commission brings together stakeholders and solicits funding not only for reconstruction from conflict and institution-building but also for developing a program of sustainable development. As of 2012, PBC was operating in Burundi, Central Africa, Guinea-Bissau, Kosovo, Liberia, Sierra Leone, and West Africa.

• **Horizontal enforcement** occurs when the UNSC authorizes pressure by governments in the form of protests, threats of economic sanctions, and the actual imposition of economic sanctions. For example, in 1985 the UNSC issued a condemnation of Israel's bombing of the headquarters of the PLO in Tunisia, which killed 75 persons, in retaliation for the PLO's role in the death of three Israelis in Cyprus. The UNSC has authorized nonmilitary sanctions at least 18 times, mostly for threats to peace during the 1990s. Among economic sanctions imposed for human rights violations, those against Rhodesia and South Africa have been judged to be successful by many observers because they were almost universally applied. The UNSC authorizes coordination by its **Sanctions Committee**.

COURT CASE 9.1 LIBYA ORDERED TO EXTRADITE TWO ACCUSED TERRORISTS (1992)

In 1988, in response to the bomb that exploded and killed all 259 persons aboard an American commercial airplane over Lockerbie, Scotland, a four-year investigation eventually revealed that the culprits were two Libyans. In 1992, the UNSC ordered Libya to hand over the Libyans accused of the act for trial in Britain and ordered all Libyan Airlines offices closed throughout the world. Libya, insisting on trying the two in Tripoli, then sued (*Libya v. Britain*; *Libya v. United States*), claiming that the home country has initial jurisdiction. Reiterating the UNSC order for Libya to send the two accused Libyans for trial in Britain, the International Court of Justice noted that decisions of UNSC are not subject to judicial review. After seven years of UNSC-approved sanctions, Libya flew the accused to Britain for trial in 1999.

Initially, the UNSC was believed to be interested solely in military threats to world peace, but the resolution of 1960 demanding an end to *apartheid* in South Africa broadened the type of threat to include butchering and humiliating members of a particular racial group. Terrorism was the basis for action against Libya, which refused to send two terrorists for trial in Britain, whereupon sanctions were authorized in 1992.

Then, in 1992, the UNSC went beyond to declare that the concept of "threat to world peace" also applied to ecological, economic, and social threats. On that basis, the UNSC not only authorized humanitarian aid to Somalia in 1992, where a famine threatened millions of lives, but also declared in 1993 that rebel interruption of that aid was a war crime under the First Geneva Convention because, in the context of military action, there can be no interference with the delivery of food and medical care to civilians.

The most complicated Security Council challenge involved the Yugoslav government in Belgrade, which undertook operations that were characterized as "ethnic cleansing" against minorities in several provinces (Table 9.2). In 1991, the UNSC voted for an arms embargo of Yugoslavia, which was strengthened in 1992 as a complete economic boycott as well as a prohibition on participation in cultural and sport events. When the Bosnian Serbs gave the name Republic Srpska to the territory that they were forming inside Bosnia, and appeared to be operating independently of Serbia, the UNSC imposed a boycott on Srpska while lifting from Serbia all but the arms embargo. In 1994, as authorized by the UNSC, airplanes under the command

TABLE 9.2   **U**N SANCTIONS IMPOSED ON THE FORMER **Y**UGOSLAVIA

Year	Organ	Action
1991	Security Council	Resolution calling for an arms boycott of Yugoslavia
1992	General Assembly	Refusal to seat the Yugoslav delegation
1992	Security Council	Resolution calling for an economic, sporting, and and travel boycott
1993	Security Council	Resolution calling for a continued arms boycott
1994	Security Council	Resolution calling for an economic boycott of Srpska, lifting the sporting and and travel boycott of Serbia
1995	Security Council	Resolution lifting all sanctions
1998	Security Council	Resolution reimposing an arms boycott of Serbia-Montenegro
2001	Security Council	Resolution lifting all sanctions

of NATO enforced a "no-fly" zone over Bosnia by shooting down Yugoslav military aircraft; Srpska-held positions were also bombed. After the Dayton Accords brought peace to Bosnia in 1995, the UNSC rescinded all sanctions.

In 1998, Serbia attempted ethnic cleansing in Kosovo, prompting a re-imposition of sanctions against Belgrade. However, China and Russia expressed concern that Western powers were using the UN for their own purposes, so they threatened to veto any proposed UN military force against Serbia. As a result of the failure of UN action, NATO forces went into Kosovo in 1999 and bombed Serbia. Although such action was deemed by some observers as contrary to international law, since the UN Charter appears to confer on the UNSC the sole power in the world to authorize the use of force in order to settle an interstate dispute, some scholars have interpreted the Charter to allow regional organizations to act when the UNSC is deadlocked.

In 1999, after Belgrade surrendered to NATO forces, the UNSC authorized the UN Interim Administration Mission in Kosovo (UNMIK). The body originally consisted of UN civilian administrators, a European Union reconstruction and economic development team, NATO peacekeepers authorized by the Security Council, and an Organization for Security and Cooperation in Europe team charged with democratic institution building, including election workers. Initially, Kosovo was considered an autonomous region within Yugoslavia. In time, the number of outside personnel has declined. Kosovo, since declaring independence in 2008, has operated as a sovereign state, though Serbia and the Serbian minority inside Kosovo do not accept the independent status of the country.

In 1999, after the bombings of two American embassies in Africa, the UNSC established what is known as the Al-Qaeda and Taliban Sanctions Committee to monitor implementation of sanctions against the Taliban regime for its support of the terrorist group that is sometimes spelled "Al-Qaida." Strengthened after September 11, 2001, the measures include an air embargo, freezing assets, stopping the sale or transfer of arms, and prohibiting members of Al-Qaeda or the Taliban from entering the borders of any UN member. In 2011, hoping to facilitate a peace agreement for Afghanistan, the Taliban was removed from the scope of the committee, which is now the **Al-Qaeda Sanctions Committee**.

In 2001, the Security Council established a separate **Counter-Terrorism Committee** to monitor implementation of a resolution that asks countries to "criminalize assistance for terrorist activities, deny financial support and safe haven to terrorists and share information about groups planning terrorist attacks." Current work involves aid to countries that builds their capacities to deal with terrorism.

A third Security Council committee dealing with terrorism is the **1540 Committee**, which was set up by Resolution 1540 in 2004. The committee is charged with the task of preventing weapons of mass destruction from getting into the hands of non-state actors, including terrorist groups.

Increasingly, the UNSC has looked at intrastate violations of human rights. In 2004, the body condemned human rights violations taking place in Darfur and called upon the government of Sudan to disarm the Janjaweed militias involved in violence against the population.

In 2006, UNSC adopted sanctions on four Sudanese officials, accusing them of war crimes and of violating the peace agreement in Darfur; they consist of a travel ban and a freeze on their assets outside Sudan. The sanctions were penalties for the massacres and displacement of largely non-Arab tribes in Darfur by Arabic-speaking militias.

The UNSC created two tribunals for serious crimes committed in Rwanda and the former Yugoslavia (Table 9.1). Although they officially report to the UNSC, they act independently. Both bodies are discussed in the following chapter.

Of the 55 UNSC resolutions passed in 2011, about half dealt with human rights, though an additional half dozen involved humanitarian aid. Thus, the percentage is much higher than in the General Assembly.

SECRETARIAT

The UN's administrative headquarters in New York consists of several units. In addition to the Office of the Secretary-General, there are 13 offices and departments. Some are programmatic, others bureaucratic. The annual budget is US$14 billion.

- **Secretary-General.** When the first Secretary-General, Trygve Lie (1896–1968), left office, he told his successor, Dag Hammskjöld (1905–1961), "You are about to take over the most impossible job on earth." Since the end of the Cold War, the Secretary-General of the United Nations (UNSG), the chief executive officer of the UN Secretariat, has become the world's secular pope. In recent years, the UNSG has undertaken personal visits on behalf of human rights and has articulated pleas for action in response to human rights violations.

Three leadership styles have been evidenced by the various Secretaries-General. Some are visionaries, who see new supranationalist roles for the UN; Hammskjöld fit that role. Others perceive themselves as managers of a sprawling bureaucracy, especially Kurt Waldheim (1918–2007). The strategist, such as Trygve Lie, reacts to situations by building coalitions to solve problems.

Secretary-General Perez de Cuellar (1920–) quietly played a supranational-ist role by injecting human rights into his role in the Central American conflicts involving El Salvador and Nicaragua in the 1980s. He was particularly active in seeking to identify death squads as perpetrators of heinous human rights violations. His successor, Boutros Boutros-Ghali (1922–), also was interested in human rights. Although one argument for the creation of the UN High Commissioner for Human Rights (discussed below) in 1994 was to divert the Secretary-General from focusing attention on human rights so that he could focus on security issues, the two issues were too intertwined for any such divorce. Indeed, his *Agenda for Peace* (1992) and *Agenda for Development* (1995) advocated democracy as essential for development and human rights as central to both democracy and peace.

While in office from 1997–2006, Secretary-General Kofi Annan (1938–) urged all UN agencies to "mainstream" human rights concerns, that is, to make human rights a part of their mandates. A strategist, he made bold pronouncements to condemn human rights abuses around the world, including, for example, Israel's treatment of Palestinians. In 2001, he brought together the Afghan factions opposing the Taliban to agree to an election for a new Afghanistan. In 2004, he condemned the

HISTORIC EVENT 9.3 THE DARFUR CONFLICT (2002–)

The western part of Sudan, known as Darfur, is inhabited by poor African Muslims. In 2001, they suffered attacks by government forces. In 2002, a group of Darfurians attacked a government outpost, revealing themselves in 2003 as the Darfur Liberation Front as they continued antigovernment attacks. Because Sudanese government troops were already deployed to cope with rebellions in the south, a decision was made in Khartoum, the Sudanese capital, to sup-ply arms to an Arabic-speaking militia known as the Janjaweed in order to pacify Darfur. The Janjaweed, however, went beyond counterattacks on the rebels and began to burn villages, rape women, and shoot unarmed men, producing an out-migration from Darfur as well as counterattacks by rival Darfurian rebel groups. At least 2.5 millions then sought refuge inside neighboring Chad; on the verge of starvation, UN humanitarian aid was sent to the region. In 2004, Chad bro-kered a ceasefire agreement between Sudan and two rebel factions, and the African Union deployed a ceasefire observation mission, but the Janjaweed failed to abide by the agreement. Later that year, when the UN Security Council asked Sudan to disarm the Janjaweed in 30 days, Khartoum refused. The Arab League and the European Union then brokered a peace agreement between Sudan and the Sudan Liberation Movement, one of the rebel groups, and the African Union sent a ceasefire monitoring unit of 7,300 persons. In 2005, the European Union and the North Atlantic Treaty Organization provided logistical support to the African Union force. Nevertheless, Janjaweed attacks continued, even killing

Continued

20 members of the African Union peace observation unit. A peace agreement was reached in 2006 with the Sudan Liberation Movement, but other rebel factions did not sign on. The Janjaweed then continued attacks, including targeting aid workers, and the Sudan government launched an offensive. Later in 2006, the UN Security Council authorized a larger force to succeed the African Union unit, pending approval by Sudan. After a temporary ceasefire in early 2007 broke down, Sudan agreed to allow the UN to do so, provided that most of the 23,000 force consisted of Africans. Peace talks continued until 2010, when the Sudan Liberation Movement withdrew from the 2006 peace agreement. Later that year, the Liberation and Justice Movement, an umbrella organization of 10 Darfur factions, was formed to negotiate a peace agreement. In 2011, the Sudan government and the Liberation and Justice Movement negotiated a peace settlement that set up a compensation fund for victims of the Darfur conflict, some power-sharing of Darfur within the Sudanese government, and established a new Darfur Regional Authority to oversee the region, with the possibility of an eventual referendum to determine its permanent status within the Republic of Sudan. In all, at least 200,000 died in the conflict, mostly from diseases.

Anglo-American intervention to topple the regime of Saddam Hussein as contrary to international law. In 2005, he began to call attention to the inadequate measures in place to deal with genocide in Darfur.

In January 2007, Annan's successor, Ban Ki-Moon (1944–), made his first overseas trip to attend the African Summit in Ethiopia so that he could declare that Darfur is the top humanitarian priority of his administration. In 2008, he successfully pleaded with the Myanmar government to open the country's airport to aid in response to the devastating cyclone, Nargis. Otherwise, he has stressed the dangers of global warming, pressed for an Israeli–Palestinian peace settlement, criticized Iran for failing to recognize the Israeli state, tried to discourage nuclear proliferation developments in Iran and North Korea, and he has popularized the Millennium Development Goals.

At the same time, Ban Ki-Moon has operated as an effective manager. Early in his first term, Mr Ban successfully reorganized several departments to separate operational from policy matters. His focus was on the Department of Peacekeeping Operations, the Office for Disarmament Affairs, and the Department of Political Affairs, which are reviewed below along with other secretariat agencies.

The position of **Under-Secretary-General** is assigned to heads of all the units in the Secretariat, field office administrators in Geneva, Nairobi, and Vienna, directors of the Regional Commissions, and heads of the various subsidiary bodies of the General Assembly (Table 9.1). **Special Representatives of the Secretary-General**, also at the Under-Secretary level, have been assigned in recent years to handle such topic areas as sexual violence in conflict and children in armed conflict.

A little noticed innovation is the **Special Rapporteur**. Identified by former Secretary-General Annan as the "crown jewel" of the UN human rights system, special rapporteurs have been assigned to handle both continuing problems and emergent situations. The first special representative, appointed in 1979, was assigned to the situation in Chile, where extrajudicial disappearances and executions were being reported. Subsequently, special rapporteurs have been appointed for other countries (Afghanistan, Bolivia, El Salvador, Equatorial Guinea, Guatemala, Iran). In 1982, the first thematic appointment was made – the Special Rapporteur on Extrajudicial, Summary and Arbitrary Executions. Special rapporteurs report not only to the Secretary-General but also to the Human Rights Council.

• **Human Rights Council** (UNHRC). By far, the most prominent human rights body within the Secretariat is the Human Rights Council. Initially established in 1946 under the Economic and Social Council (ECOSOC) as the 53-member Commission on Human Rights, the General Assembly voted in 2006 to rename the body – whose 47 members are elected annually by majority vote – and to locate the Council within the Secretariat. ECOSOC initially appointed government representatives rather than experts to the Commission, and inoffensive political posturing prevailed.

The first assignment of the former Commission, to draft the Universal Declaration of Human Rights, was completed in 1948. The second task, placing the Declaration on a treaty basis, was not completed until 1966 because of differences in approach between Cold War antagonists.

In 1967, ECOSOC first allowed the Commission to conduct a debate each year on human rights violations anywhere in the world and to appoint special committees. The first debate, held in 1979, resulted in the formation of the Special Committee to Investigate Israeli Practices Affecting the Human Rights of the Population of the Occupied Territories.

Over the years, the organ has acquired 10 functions:

- Review of annual country reports
- Studies
- Advisory services
- Technical assistance
- Field operations
- On-site investigations
- Establishment of working groups
- Debates on topical subjects
- Drafting resolutions
- Response to petitions.

Concerning the latter, in 1967 ECOSOC adopted **Resolution 1235**, which established the principle that violations of human rights could be examined in the form of a study and/or could be debated in public. **Resolution 1503**, adopted in 1970, enunciates a criterion to identify violations of states – "a consistent pattern of gross and reliably attested violations of human rights and fundamental freedoms exists." As many as 25,000 such petitions have been received in recent years. UNHRC has several possible responses to a petition – nonaction, confidential consideration, a critical statement, or public condemnation. At least 40 countries represented on UNCHR were condemned in the post-Cold War era compared with 10 before 1991; that was one reason for reorganizing the Commission, which is now called the Human Rights Council. Today, individual petitions are now deemphasized in favor of studies, advisory services, expert visits, and on-site investigations, as noted next.

In 1973, the Commission took the extraordinary step of establishing an Ad Hoc Working Group on the Situation of Human Rights in Chile. The body was created after the brutality of the coup in Chile, in which the army under Augusto Pinochet (1915–2006) deposed the duly elected president, Salvador Allende (1908–1973). The aim was to document human rights abuses. Reports of the body provided shocking evidence that many Allende supporters had been arrested but had disappeared, as their whereabouts were unknown. The UN organ has undertaken similar monitoring efforts elsewhere over the years, including one concerning the plight of Palestinians.

ECOSOC created a sensation in 2001 by failing to elect a delegate from the United States to serve on the Commission. According to the delegates who voted, the exclusion was in response to the American opposition to such innovations as the treaty banning landmines, the International Criminal Court, and the Kyoto Protocol on global warming. As a result, Congress froze a portion of the annual American assessments to the UN.

Over the years, countries elected to the Commission by the UN General Assembly were often the very countries committing serious human rights abuses. Countries deferred to the wishes of various regions, which rotated countries without regard to their human rights records.

But in 2006, when the UNHRC replaced the Commission, the body was taken out of ECOSOC and located within the Secretariat as a body considered to have equal status with ECOSOC. About 50 of the organization's 177 members pledged to vote in the future against membership for countries with unacceptable human rights records. Voting is now by secret ballot, and the Council now meets more often, requiring reports of all countries on a regular basis. Although governments are still represented, experts engage in fact-finding.

As a result, Libya, Sudan, Syria, Vietnam, and Zimbabwe did not even apply, though they formerly served on the Commission. The United States also decided not to seek a seat on the first Council, a possible admission that Washington's record might not garner majority support. China, Cuba, Russia, and Saudi Arabia, which have often been criticized for human rights issues, were nevertheless accorded seats. Although Washington applied, and was accepted for membership after Barack Obama (1961–) became president, the United States still dissents on votes in which Israel is singled out for opprobrium regarding the treatment of Palestinians.

UNHRC today maintains a field operation of 10 regional offices, 12 country missions, and 16 human rights advisers. In 2006, a **Rapid Response Unit** was created to handle fact-finding, human rights assessments, and investigations of human rights crises that have sent observers to Bolivia, the Gaza Strip and Occupied Palestinian Territories, Guinea, Kenya, Liberia, Lebanon, Madagascar, Sierra Leone, Somalia, Sudan, Timor-Leste, and Western Sahara. The main power of UNHRC is publicity – the ability to embarrass governments for human rights deficiencies.

• **Office for Disarmament Affairs** (UNODA). Some 24 treaties require disarmament, so ODA assists governments in dismantling landmines, reducing biological and chemical weapons arsenals, and assisting in regional disarmament efforts. ODA, which operates on US$10 million annually, also maintains a database of the arms trade and military expenditures to promote transparency.

• **Office for the Coordination of Humanitarian Affairs** (OCHA). Natural disasters necessarily affect the quality of life in an adverse manner, and most are handled domestically. In 1991, the General Assembly created the position of Emergency Relief Coordinator, subsequently designated as the Under-Secretary-General for Humanitarian Affairs, to coordinate assistance to victims of the most severe natural disasters. In 1998, because of the difficulty of coordinating so many agencies, OCHA was established. In recent years, agency personnel have been dispatched within 24 hours of a major natural disaster. They draw on the **Central Emergency Revolving Fund** so that the personnel will arrive on the scene with needed equipment and supplies, rather than merely engaging in needs assessment. They stay on the scene to assist in reconstruction after an emergency has ended. In 2012, OCHA coordinated aid to nine crisis sites with a budget of US$242 million.

• **Department of Peacekeeping Operations** (DPKO). As of 2012, DPKO deploys about 100,000 persons from 114 countries and spends US$7 billion annually to coordinate peacekeeping efforts in 14 countries and related efforts in an additional 10 countries. Operations, which vary from country to country, include providing security, supporting elections and other political processes, protecting civilians, helping refugees, disarming and reintegrating former combatants, and promoting human rights and the rule of law. DPKO was criticized for withdrawing peacekeepers from Rwanda in 1994 while genocide was just beginning, but the danger that peacekeepers might be massacred and the disinterest of the major powers in providing support for more troops overrode all other considerations.

• **Department of Political Affairs** (DPA). Diplomacy to prevent conflicts is the main responsibility of DPA, but one subunit deals with Palestinian rights, another with decolonization. Election monitors certify when elections are "free and fair." The first effort, in Cambodia during 1992, carried out the terms of a peace settlement. Some US$83 million are allocated to DPA out of the regular budget each year.

• **Office of the High Commissioner for Human Rights** (OHCHR). In 1993, the UN convened the World Conference on Human Rights in Vienna. Because of conflict between Western and Third World countries, the only major structural recommendation was to set up a new position, the OHCHR, so that a single person could play a more visible and active role to stop human rights violations within the Secretariat. Later that year, the General Assembly obliged. The first High Commissioner was selected in 1994.

Headquartered in Geneva, OHCHR has assumed 10 functions:

○ Secretariat assistance for several treaty-based human rights organs (discussed in Chapter 10)
○ Consciousness raising events

- ○ Studies
- ○ Field operations
- ○ Training courses
- ○ Good offices to negotiate release of prisoners and similar actions
- ○ Conflict prevention
- ○ Crisis response
- ○ Administration of the Special Committee to Investigate Israeli Practices Affecting the Human Rights of the Palestinian People and Other Arabs of the Occupied Territories, which was set up in 1968
- ○ Complaint processing at the Quick Response Desk.

As of 2012, OHCHR had established 19 special rapporteurs, two working groups, and one independent expert on a variety of human rights issues. The special rapporteurs seek to investigate human rights issues and often make public comments to protest violations.

OHCHR is also responsible for administering the **Voluntary Fund for Victims of Torture**, which the General Assembly created in 1982 to assist victims of torture and their relatives. Some 70,000 survivors of torture are assisted each year. In 2011, for example, a victim of torture formerly at Guantánamo applied for relief. OHCHR also administers the **Voluntary Fund for Technical Cooperation in the Field of Human Rights**, which was created in 1987.

OHCHR, with a budget of US$250 million, has been assuming functions that formerly burdened the Secretary-General. The result is increasing continuity and effectiveness in achieving human rights objectives, although controversy is inevitable when governments resist improvement.

- • **United Nations Entity for Gender Equality and the Empowerment of Women** (UN Women). Perhaps the most important reorganization under the administration of Secretary-General Ban Ki-Moon is the consolidation of several agencies into UN Women in 2011. They include the Division for the Advancement of Women, the International Research and Training Institute for the Advancement of Women, the Office of the Special Adviser on Gender Issues Advancement of Women, and the UN Development Fund for Women.

Rather than operating new programs, the mandate of UN Women is to ensure that all UN agencies will engage in gender mainstreaming, similar to Kofi Annan's directive to have all UN agencies focus on human rights. UN Women operates on a budget of US$500 million.

ECONOMIC AND SOCIAL COUNCIL (ECOSOC)

ECOSOC has 9 Functional Commissions, supervises 5 Regional Commissions, and has several other suborgans. Several subsidiary bodies directly relate to human rights:

- • **Commission on the Status of Women (CSW)**. In 1946, ECOSOC set up the Commission on the Status of Women as another functional commission, with administrative functions performed by the Secretariat's Division for the Advancement of Women. CSW has drafted many important declarations over the years. The most notable is the Declaration on the Elimination of Discrimination

Against Women (1967), which led in 1979 to Convention on the Elimination of All Forms of Discrimination Against Women (CEDAW) and its Optional Protocol in 1999. CSW played a role in the adoption of Security Council Resolution 1325 on Women and Peace and Security (2000), which CSW has broadened to address women's equal participation in conflict prevention, management, conflict resolution, and in post-conflict peace-building.

In the early years, the primary attention was on women's rights. In the 1960s, CSW realized that the role of women in development needed to be enhanced, as most women in the Third World were poor yet played important social, although economically inconsequential, roles. Ester Boserup's influential *Women's Role in Economic Development* (1970) furthered that focus, which broadened in the 1980s and 1990s to a campaign for gender mainstreaming and a focus on violence against women. The **Declaration for the Elimination of Violence Against Women** (1993) was one result. CSW has organized several international conferences on women. The latest, held in 1995, adopted the 362-article Beijing Resolution and Platform for Action, which forms the mandate for CSW.

Each year CSW discusses priority themes and then issues agreed **conclusions**, which indicate progress toward, and obstacles to, various goals. The Commission also adopts **resolutions** on major concerns, such as on conditions of Palestinian women and on HIV/AIDS.

From the 1980s, the Commission has handled **complaints** about patterns of "reliably attested injustice and discriminatory practices against women." The complaints, which tend to be authored by nongovernmental organizations on behalf of classes of aggrieved women, are also utilized as windows into possible areas of global focus. As a result, CSW forms working groups, which may recommend action by ECOSOC.

A major complaint, filed in 2012, was from Chinese women compelled to have abortions because of the government's strict one-child policy; some were forced to pay exorbitant fines and sterilized. For example, Feng Jianmei (1990–) was beaten by officials and forced to abort her seven-month-old foetus because her family could not afford a 40,000 Yuan (US$6,300) fine for having a second child. After pictures of Feng lying on a hospital bed with the blood-covered baby were posted online, prompting outrage, China fired the three officials responsible, apologized to the women, but has not abolished forced abortions.

UN Women, discussed above, provides secretariat functions for CSW. Because a separate, treaty-based organization coordinates progress in implementing the Convention on the Elimination of All Forms of Discrimination Against Women, CSW's focus is more general. The body created by the treaty is discussed in Chapter 10.

- **Commission on Population and Development** (CPD). Formed in 1946, the primary focus is on assisting governments in design and implementation of national population strategies. CPD compiles statistics and trends on international migration; infant, child, and maternal mortality; increased adult mortality in some regions; the impact of AIDS; fertility levels, trends and their determinants, including contraceptive use; and the relationships among population dynamics and development issues.

- **Commission for Social Development** (CSocD). Formed in 1946, CSocD reviews social components of economic development plans and action programs of other agencies. Following the World Summit for Social Development in 1995, the

Commission has been charged with responsibility for implementing the Copenhagen Declaration and Program of Action, which was a major basis for the Millennium Development Goals. Currently, CSocD is focused on poverty elimination and youth employment.

• **Commission on Sustainable Development** (CSD). In 1992, the General Assembly created a new commission focused on ecological aspects of development as a follow up to that year's Earth Summit. In 2012, at a conference in Río de Janeiro, delegates mandated CSD to work toward a global green economy as well as lifting people out of poverty.

• **Commission on Crime Prevention and Criminal Justice** (CCPCJ). In 1992, ECOSOC consolidated various units to deal with the issues of crime and justice into the CCPCJ, which focuses on combating national and transnational crime, including organized crime, economic crime, and money laundering. The Commission also promotes the role of criminal law in protecting the environment; crime prevention in urban areas, including juvenile crime and violence; and improving the efficiency and fairness of criminal justice administration systems.

• **UN Permanent Forum on Indigenous Issues** (UNPFII). Some 370 million indigenous peoples live in 70 countries but lack representation in the General Assembly. They are often threatened by activities that are carried out in the name of "development." In 1986, ECOSOC established the Working Group on Indigenous Populations, which began to prepare a declaration on indigenous peoples' rights: It is still under discussion even though the statement would not be binding on sovereign states. In 2000, ECOSOC set up UNPFII as a body with 16 experts to meet annually in New York with a mandate to provide advice on issues affecting indigenous peoples. Two years later, a secretariat was established for PFII within ECOSOC. Half of the experts are appointed by members of indigenous organizations, representing seven sociocultural regions; the other half are nominated by governments. The Partnership for Action and Dignity has the following goals:

○ Nondiscrimination and inclusion
○ Participation in decision-making
○ Social equality in development policy
○ Adopting policies for children, women, and youth
○ Monitoring respect for the rights of indigenous peoples.

Since nonindigenous peoples are not recognized as states, they cannot become members of the United Nations. Outside the UN, they have formed the intergovernmental **Unrepresented Nations and Peoples Organization**, consisting of 41 members. The most obvious is Taiwan, but the others are for ethnic groups or provinces inside existing countries.

■ SPECIALIZED AGENCIES OF THE UNITED NATIONS

The United Nations has 20 organs called Specialized Agencies, which act semiautonomously of other UN bodies. They report to the General Assembly through ECOSOC. Some of the more prominent organizations are described below.

- **International Labor Organization** (ILO). Formed after World War I outside the League of Nations, ILO was accepted as a Specialized Agency of the UN in 1946. The current Constitution, as adopted in 1944, states that the main purpose of the organization is to promote "social justice" by securing "humane conditions of labor." The main organs have a tripartite representation (one from business, one from labor, and two from government), so the tone of the organization is more communitarian than adversarial. Work is divided into four major sectors:

  - Employment (human resource development)
  - Social dialog (to build tripartite consensus)
  - Social protection (improvement in conditions of work regarding health and safety, as well as unemployment insurance)
  - Workers' rights (formulating fair labor standards).

ILO has sponsored nearly 400 treaties.

ILO uses three procedures to check on implementation of its various treaties and recommendations – country reports, compliance monitoring, and complaint processing. In 1994, with thousands of ILO-based treaty ratifications to monitor, ILO decided to require **reports** from member countries on fundamental and priority conventions biennially, whereas reports on compliance with other treaties are to be submitted every five years (formerly every four years) unless a treaty has become obsolete. A report form for every convention, ratified and unratified, asks for an identification of the appropriate domestic laws, implementing structures, measures taken toward removing obstacles to compliance, legal opinions rendered, inspector's reports, and lists of employers and trade unions notified about provisions and their comments.

Regarding **compliance monitoring**, the 20 members of the Committee of Experts on the Application of Conventions and Recommendations has met annually from 1927 to examine progress reports from governments. If the Committee finds a compliance problem, a **comment** goes to all three representatives from a country; the comment may either be an informal **direct request** or a formal **observation**. In 2012, for instance, there were 2,088 direct requests and 1,058 observations. Direct requests note discrepancies and ask for clarification; if the matter is handled satisfactorily, no written record is kept. If there is a longstanding or serious problem of noncompliance, an observation is published, and the problem is included in the annual report of the Committee, which may request a statement from an errant government on any problem and subsequently hold a public hearing on the matter. Hearings are extremely polite and nonaccusatory, focusing on difficulties of implementation. If a problem is resolved, another observation will be published. During 1964–2011, some 2,875 cases were resolved, of which 72 were in 2011 alone. From 1990, Myanmar has been repeatedly cited for violations of the Forced Labor Convention of 1930 and the Freedom of Association and Protection of the Right to Organize Convention of 1948. No other country has so consistently defied the ILO.

From 1926, the ILO has also engaged in **complaint processing**. There are four categories of complaints:

- In an **Article 24 complaint**, a workers' or employers' organization can make a **representation** about a government that fails to abide by an ILO-sponsored treaty. Up to 2012, **there have been 161** such complaints.
- An **Article 26 complaint** may be filed by governments, ILO delegates, or ILO governing bodies; in response, ILO sets up a formal commission of inquiry, which solicits written comments from both parties, conducts hearings, does on-site investigations, and makes reports. Only 13 complaints have resulted in commissions of inquiry to date.
- From 1950, **special freedom of association complaints** may be filed by workers' or employers' organizations, ILO bodies, the state concerned, or ECOSOC. In 1951, ILO set up the Committee on Freedom of Association (CFA) to handle complaints, which by 2012 numbered 2,977. Some involved murder of union officials.
- Since 1974, a panel of ILO experts can conduct **special surveys on employment discrimination** at the request of any state, employer, or worker organization. Otherwise, the ILO Conference, the plenary body, selects one subject each year for discussion.

Today, all countries are reviewed annually to determine compliance with the 1948 treaty on freedom of association. An **urgent cases** procedure permits CFA to identify the most serious cases for special attention by the ILO Secretary-General. In 2012, for example, Argentina, Cambodia, Ethiopia, Fiji, and Perú were determined to require urgent action.

ILO's scope is highly intrusive into the way governments treat people. In 1964, the ILO adopted the **Declaration Against Apartheid in South Africa**, whereupon Pretoria withdrew from the organization, effective 1966.[5] In 1981, the ILO adopted an updated Declaration on Apartheid, which involved technical assistance to liberation movements drawing from a voluntary fund. ILO actions serve to strengthen the struggles of emergent unions by exerting political and moral pressure in favor of their demands against the government, notably standards on overtime and shift work. In 1986, ILO called for the release of trade union leaders imprisoned during the 1986 state of emergency in South Africa. Post-*apartheid* South Africa rejoined in 1994.

From 1977–1980, the United States withdrew from ILO because of unhappiness that the organization was critical of Washington, which has only ratified 14 treaties and two of the core eight conventions. In particular, the World Confederation of Free Trade Unions filed a complaint against Washington regarding trade union restrictions in Puerto Rico. In 1979, after the ILO issued a statement criticizing the labor records of Czechoslovakia, Poland, and the Soviet Union, and was about to exonerate the United States regarding the complaint involving Puerto Rico, the United States decided to rejoin, believing that the organization had become more evenhanded. Subsequently, the ILO played a role in the emancipation of Poland from dictatorship by supporting the legitimacy of the Polish trade union Solidamość. One of the most significant ILO-sponsored treaties in recent years is the Maritime Labor Convention of 2006, which updated 68 previous conventions and recommendations going back to 1920 for seafaring workers; there are several binding provisions.

ILO's human rights procedures have been a model that other human rights bodies in the UN system have tried to copy. But only ILO has the tripartite system of representation that enables employers, governments, and workers to work out problems collegially.

• **United Nations Educational, Scientific, and Cultural Organization** (UNESCO). Among the agencies established at Geneva during the era of the League of Nations was the International Committee of Intellectual Co-operation, which operated from 1922 and cooperated with the International Institute of Intellectual Co-operation (IIIC) at Paris from 1925. A separate intergovernmental body, the International Bureau of Education (IBE), also began at Geneva in 1925. In 1942, European governments confronting Nazi Germany and its allies met in the United Kingdom for the Conference of Allied Ministers of Education, which in turn recommended the establishment of UNESCO. When UNESCO's Constitution was ratified in 1946, IIIC ceased operation. IBE continued until being absorbed by UNESCO in 1969.

The preamble to UNESCO's Constitution of 1945 begins with the resounding phrase "since wars begin in the minds of men, it is in the minds of men that the defenses of peace must be constructed," and declares that,

> the great and terrible war which has now ended was a war made possible by the denial of the democratic principles of the dignity, equality and mutual respect of men, and by the propagation, in their place, through ignorance and prejudice, of the doctrine of the inequality of men and races

and goes on to say,

> That the wide diffusion of culture, and the education of humanity for justice and liberty and peace are indispensable to the dignity of man and constitute a sacred duty…

Most UN members belong to UNESCO. However, Spain did not join until 1953, and the Soviet Union stayed out until 1954. In 1956, South Africa withdrew because of the organization's opposition to *apartheid*. In 1984, the United States withdrew, followed in 1985 by the departure of Britain and Singapore; all three right-wing governments objected to the proposed New International Information Order. South Africa resumed membership in 1994, Britain in 1997, and the United States in 2003. Palestine joined in 2011, whereupon Israel stopped contributing funds to UNESCO.

UNESCO, the premier intellectual UN agency, has two major functions:

- ○ To facilitate intellectual cooperation in the fields of education, science, and culture, both through conferences and by providing an information clearinghouse

- To arrange technical assistance financing, mostly consisting of seed money for research and training to assist in developing the human resource infrastructure in the fields of culture and education.

Funds for scientific endeavors are also handled by other UN agencies.

Human rights are found in all five of UNESCO's major thematic areas:

- The communication and information theme is concerned with freedom of expression, freedom of the press, gender issues, and indigenous peoples.
- The culture theme has a program on cultural diversity.
- Within the education theme, the focus is on the right to education, diversity issues in education, as well as human rights education.
- In the science theme, a major objective is to develop more female scientists.
- The social and human sciences theme specifically focuses on human rights as well as on democracy, discrimination, gender equality, racism, and xenophobia.

In 1976, UNESCO set up the World Heritage Committee to identify monuments and other cultural objects worthy of protection and recognition. As of 2012, some 745 cultural, 188 natural, and 29 mixed properties had been identified in 157 states, including the eleventh century Hindu temple, Preah Vihear, which the International Court of Justice ruled in 1962 was the property of Cambodia, though Thai troops temporarily blocked entry to the temple in 2011. UNESCO has other projects of cultural significance, including biosphere reserves, endangered languages, and geoparks.

In 1997, the annual UNESCO Guillermo Cano World Press Freedom Prize was begun in honor of a Colombian journalist who was gunned down by drug cartel assassins in front of his newspaper office. Raúl Rivero (1945–), who had been arrested in 2003 in Cuba along with 74 other dissidents, won the World Press Freedom Prize in 2004. He was then released along with several others. In 2012, Eynulla Fatullayev (1976–), an Azerbaijani journalist and human rights activist who had been jailed for a time because of his insistence in exercising the right of freedom of the press, was the winner.

UNESCO has sponsored several agreements in the form of declarations, recommendations, and treaties. The treaty most concerned with human rights is the Convention Against Discrimination in Education (1960), which was followed by a protocol (1962) that set up a Conciliation and Good Offices Commission to handle disputes under the convention. Among the various UNESCO-sponsored declarations are the Declaration on Race and Racial Prejudice (1978), the Universal Declaration on the Human Genome and Human Rights (1998), the Universal Declaration on Cultural Diversity (2001), and the International Declaration on Human Genetic Data (2003). The latter advocates keeping genetic data private.

Each member country is asked to submit **reports** on implementation of agreements on the following subjects:

- Adult, technical, and vocational education
- Discrimination in education

- ◦ Illicit import, export, and transfer of ownership of cultural property
- ◦ Peace education
- ◦ The status of teachers.

The Executive Board's Committee on Conventions and Recommendations monitors the reports.

In 2004, UNESCO launched a "Poverty as a Human Rights Violation" project. But the idea was perceived as so radical that high-profile conferences were cancelled and funding was cut. The project then toned down the rhetoric but still failed to catch the attention of the World Bank and similar agencies.

The Committee on Conventions and Recommendations also handles three **complaint procedures** to deal with violations of the right to education, the right to share in scientific advancement, the right to participate in cultural life, the right to information, freedom of thought, and freedom of association:

- ◦ When an **individual communication** goes to UNESCO, the organization will ask the government charged with the alleged violation to comment. The government's case is next argued before the Committee, which usually meets in private biannually. Since 1978, the Committee has resolved 360 of 566 communications, for a success record of 64 percent.
- ◦ Individual communications may serve to expose a **pattern of complaints**. Based on the distinction between individual **cases**, where confidentiality is often critical, and **questions**, which are broader in scope, the Committee can go public to protest systematic violations.
- ◦ In 1978, UNESCO developed a **third-party complaint** procedure, whereby human rights advocates, usually nongovernmental organizations, can complain on behalf of individuals or groups.

Generally, UNESCO does not go public with individual complaints, preferring to promote dialog between the complainants and the governments, and then recommending measures that might be taken to redress the situation.

- • **Food and Agriculture Organization of the United Nations** (FAO). After an initial conference at Hot Springs, Virginia, in 1943, FAO was formally established in 1945 to provide technical assistance in the field of agriculture. Currently, FAO operates 5 regional and 11 subregional offices, and 74 country offices. The headquarters in Rome consists of departments dealing with agriculture, consumer protection, economic and social development, fisheries and aquaculture, forestry management, human resources, and natural resource management.

An early achievement was the adoption of the International Plant Protection Convention (1952) to focus attention on the need to eradicate pests and plant diseases. In 1963, FAO issued the Codex Alimentarius, which set international food standards. The codex was developed jointly with WHO.

In 1998, FAO sponsored the Rotterdam Convention on the Prior Informed Consent Procedure for Certain Hazardous Chemicals and Pesticides in International Trade to stop the trade in harmful agricultural additives. In 2001, FAO secured the adoption of the International Treaty on Plant Genetic Resources for Food and Agriculture to support breeders and farmers.

FAO seeks to implement provisions in the Covenant on Economic, Social, and Cultural Rights (1966) that implicitly recognize the right to food, as clarified in the Covenant's Optional Protocol (2009). In 1994, FAO initiated the Special Program for Food Security, which now involves 102 countries.

In 2007, FAO adopted the Initiative on Soaring Food Prices to assist small producers through technical assistance to raise their output, thereby supporting the Fair Trade movement. With the advent of genetically-modified food crops in recent years, FAO has been working to establish a code of ethics in food and agriculture.

Accordingly, FAO has played a central role in the Millennium Development Goals, in particular the promise to halve world hunger by 2015, which FAO had already stated as a goal at the World Food Summit in 1996. In 2011, the EndingHunger campaign was launched.

- **World Health Organization** (WHO). In 1948, the WHO became a Specialized Agency, absorbing both the functions of the Rome-based International Office of Public Health, which previously promoted sanitation and later studied epidemics, and the Geneva-based League of Nations Health Organization. The preamble to the WHO Constitution, as adopted in 1946, states that "the enjoyment of the highest attainable standard of human health is one of the basic human rights of every human being."

The Director-General and nine Assistant Directors-General administer the organization. One unit under the Assistant Director-General for Sustainable Development and Health Environments is the Department of Ethics, Trade, Human Rights, and Law, which primarily assists health ministries in national governments to achieve greater awareness of human rights issues. WHO projects stress the equal treatment of females and minority populations as well as the appropriate treatment of the mentally disabled, aiming at nondiscrimination in the provision of health care. In 1977, WHO set a goal of "health for all" by the year 2000, urging each country to develop "health of the nation" plans.

In 2000, the WHO Global Water Supply and Sanitation Assessment found that 18 percent of the world's population had insufficient access to water services and about 40 percent lacked adequate sanitation. Among other reports relating to human rights in recent years, one focused on the subject of torture.

WHO takes credit for the global eradication of smallpox, continues a vaccination program in the poorer countries, and currently seeks to wipe out malaria. Mental as well as physical health are within the scope of WHO efforts. Operationally, the largest effort in recent years has been to cope with the spread of HIV-AIDS by providing programs of prevention and treatment, including efforts to reduce the cost of medicines. In 2010, WHO assisted in the recovery after a severe earthquake hit Haïti. The subsequent spread of cholera has been blamed on WHO workers brought in from other countries, but there is no definitive evidence on the source of the outbreak.

In the delivery of health care, WHO's focus has shifted from health ministries in the earlier years to the recent stress on developing networks of governmental and nongovernmental groups in local communities. WHO has enjoyed many successes as the premier agency fighting global pandemics.

• **United Nations Industrial Development Organization** (UNIDO). Consistent with UNCTAD's early stress on the need for import substitution, UNIDO was created in 1966 to support new industries in developing countries. When import substitution was rejected in the 1970s and 1980s, UNIDO refocused on export promotion.

In 2000, the UN held a special conference on the global economy. The result, as noted in Chapter 6, was agreement on the UN Global Compact, consisting of 10 principles for businesses to uphold in the world economy. The first two principles relate to human rights; worker rights account for four principles; three urge environmental responsibility; and the tenth commits businesses to fight corruption and avoid bribery and extortion. Thus far, 8,000 businesses in 135 countries around the world subscribe to the Global Compact. UNIDO is one of the seven UN agencies mandated to work toward the goals of the agreement (along with ILO, OHCHR, UNDP, UNEP, UNODC, and UN Women). In 2003, accordingly, programming was launched on productivity enhancement (improved skills, increased knowledge, upgraded technology), marketing capacity, and environmentally sound energy production.

• **International Fund for Agricultural Development** (IFAD). One of the outcomes of the World Food Conference in 1974 was the establishment of IFAD three years later as a Specialized Agency. One impetus for the formation of IFAD was widespread famine in several African countries during the 1970s. IFAD's main objective is to help poor rural populations to achieve higher incomes and improved food security though low-interest loans and grants. IFAD has invested US$13.5 billion in 913 projects and programs for some 400 million poor rural people. Although IFAD's website does not list human rights as a specific focus, the organization clearly serves several goals stated in the International Covenant on Economic, Social, and Cultural Rights.

• **World Bank Group and the International Monetary Fund**. The World Bank Group of organizations entirely raises funds from governments and on the world capital market, so they operate independently of the UN but are considered Specialized Agencies because of their origin. Two IGOs are called "the World Bank," namely, the **International Bank for Reconstruction and Development** (IBRD) and the **International Development Association** (IDA). IBRD, formed in 1944 primarily to aid European postwar reconstruction, now provides about US$27 billion, chiefly in infrastructure loans, each year to developing countries; for 2011, 132 projects were financed.

Although the first IBRD loan to a developing country was to Chile for US$2.5 million in 1948, IDA's establishment recognized that some developing countries were unable to afford loans at commercial rates, as the economic payoff might not emerge for many years. Accordingly, IDA was set up in 1960 to provide low-interest, long-term loans to developing countries. Currently, 81 countries, about half in Africa, now qualify for IDA loans, as they fall below the ceiling of US$1,175 gross national income per capita. Currently, IDA loans are as low as 1.25 percent with repayment required within 25 to 50 years. IDA annual operations, averaging US$16 billion annually, go to countries with 2.5 billion in population. Most of the 230 projects in 2011 were based on loans, but 17 percent were grants.

The remaining three members of the **World Bank Group** assist private sector investment. They are the **International Finance Corporation** (1956), the **International Center for Settlement of Investment Disputes** (1966), and the **Multilateral Investment Guarantee Association** (1988).

The **International Monetary Fund** (IMF) was also created in 1944. IMF provides capital for countries that experience such a shortfall in foreign exchange (US dollars) that they cannot pay debts owed to other countries. Although conditions are applied to any recipient, they have been administered in a controversial manner over the years. As of 2012, IMF had granted US$25 billion in concessional loans at 0 percent interest to 17 countries, while nonconcessional loans at 0.7 percent interest amounting to US$81 billion went to Greece and Portugal. Other arrangements were made with Colombia, Georgia, Kosovo, St Kitts and Nevis, and Serbia.

When the Cold War ended, so did the practice of strategic loans to encourage less developed countries to join the capitalist rather than the socialist world. Instead, IBRD and IMF subscribed to the "Washington Consensus," a term coined by economist John Williamson (1937–) that identified globalization of the world economics as the primary goal for future lending, in particular by dismantling such barriers to free trade as subsidies, government ownership of business, and tariffs.

IMF and World Bank Group legal experts argued through the years that their actions were exempt from human rights treaties because the founding Articles of Agreement clearly state that "only economic considerations shall be relevant" in all World Bank decisions. World Bank loans to developing countries often yielded more benefits to First World construction and consulting firms than to recipient countries, which remained in poverty and were unable to pay even the interest on the loans. IMF would then intervene to enable countries to pay back the loans, but the conditions for IMF loan repayment often involved cuts in government programs that increased poverty. During 1992, for example, the IMF required Mali to lift price controls and to end food subsidies during a famine, whereupon hoarders held back food, deaths from starvation increased, and what has been called an "IMF riot" toppled the government.

Accordingly, from the mid-1990s the World Bank began to stress poverty reduction as a primary focus for the poorest countries and to place a "good governance" condition on all loan recipients. **Poverty reduction**, which was initially defined in terms of per capita income, is now understood to apply to social exclusion and disenfranchisement – that is, the extent to which citizens are fragile or vulnerable. By **good governance**, the World Bank means loan implementation effectiveness, as determined by the following criteria:

- Voice and accountability (civil liberties and political stability)
- Government effectiveness (quality of policy making and public service delivery)
- Lack of regulatory burden
- Rule of law (notably, protection of property rights)
- Independence of the judiciary
- Control of corruption.

From the 1990s, the World Bank has also developed "women in development" initiatives based on data demonstrating that females are often excluded from development projects. In 2004, for example, the World Bank gave a grant to the University of Chile Law School to provide scholarships for students interested in women's rights. However, among World Bank projects in 2011–2012, a gender focus was not even categorized among 587 projects. Otherwise, the following foci were found: education (19), governance (39), health (45), indigenous peoples (2), justice and law (6), poverty reduction (10), and safety net (31); the remaining 395 projects had a strictly economic focus.

In 1994, complaints about human rights issues prompted the World Bank to establish the **Inspection Panel**, which consists of three independent experts. The panel hears **requests** for inspectors from individuals who claim to have been adversely affected by World Bank projects; a human rights violation can be one basis for a complaint. By 2012, the panel had heard 82 cases and made recommendations that prompted the World Bank to make changes.

In 1999, when the UN sought to bring peace to East Timor, Indonesia expressed adamant opposition to peacekeepers. The IMF then surprised many observers by threatening to withhold aid to Jakarta, which soon capitulated, and the UN Mission in East Timor (now Timor-Leste) began work.

The World Bank has also intervened on behalf of human rights defenders who have been attacked or jailed by recipient governments. In the case of the Chad-Cameroon Petroleum Development and Pipeline Project, the panel responded to a request from someone who had been tortured because of his opposition to the project. In 2005, the panel began to act on a complaint from the NGO Forum on Cambodia related to human rights abuses in connection with the Forest Concession Management and Control Pilot Project. Not all complaints involve human rights issues, however.

In 2005, the summit of industrial nations known as the G8,[6] urged the World Bank to waive some US$30 billion in loans to the eight poorest countries in the world. The loans were not being paid back, and the US$100 million daily interest accumulating on the loans was crushing the ability of the countries to rise from poverty. Later in the year, the World Bank Group indeed agreed to excuse debts by some poorer countries, but waivers completely stopped in 2007.

The IMF, in particular, has not overcome its use of currency devaluation and fiscal austerity that has provoked so many "IMF riots." The result is the development of regional monetary funds, which are discussed in Chapter 13.

Although the World Bank Group and IMF have recently been attempting to overcome a past in which human rights issues were neglected, the lending agencies have far to go. In 2000, Joseph Stiglitz (1943–) resigned as IMF's chief economist to protest the continuing blinders over the harm that international financial institutions have wrought for far too long.

DISCUSSION TOPIC 9.1 HOW CAN THE UN BEST HANDLE DUPLICATION OF ACTIVITIES OR SCOPE WITHIN AGENCIES THAT DEAL WITH HUMAN RIGHTS?

Human rights programming, including the issue of gender discrimination, exists within many United Nations agencies. Inevitably, underfinanced UN agencies run

Continued

into problems of duplication of effort and associated "turf battles," especially with many nongovernmental aid organizations that follow particular agendas. Identify within a particular issue-area, such as the right to health. How do the UN and non-governmental agencies involved cope with problems of mission overlap? Is overlap, which allows different approaches, really a problem?

- **Other Specialized Agencies.** The UN has also set up Specialized Agencies covering the fields of civil aviation, maritime navigation, intellectual property, meteorology, telecommunications, and tourism. Human rights elements in all these agencies do exist, but that is not their primary or secondary focus.

INTERNATIONAL COURT OF JUSTICE (ICJ)

The first world court, the Permanent Court of Arbitration (PCA), as established at The Hague in 1899, still handles disputes. However, the Permanent Court of International Justice (PCIJ), which went into existence in 1921, was superseded in 1946, by the ICJ.

ICJ, which still sits in The Hague, is composed of 15 judges elected for nine-year terms by the General Assembly and Security Council from a list of persons nominated by each country that belongs to the PCA. The legal principles applied by the court are found in treaties, international custom, precedent, legal theories propounded by widely accepted academic authorities, and *ex aequo et bono* (general principles of justice and fairness). About 20 treaties confer specific jurisdiction on the ICJ. In most cases, both parties are asked to submit formal statements. If one party does not respond, the court may proceed anyway if the statement of facts from the other party is judged to be accurate.

The court is supposed to reject political questions. When India shot down a military aircraft inside Pakistan, the court ruled in 1999 that the case (*Pakistan v. India*) was not justiciable but instead should be resolved by the UN Security Council. The Convention on the Prevention and Punishment of the Crime of Genocide had a seldom-noticed provision conferring compulsory jurisdiction on the ICJ, but that was later superseded by the Rome Statute of the International Criminal Court (see Chapter 10).

The court makes three types of decisions – binding rulings, advisory opinions, and dispute resolutions. **Binding rulings** apply when all parties to a dispute agree in advance to accept the jurisdiction of the court in a matter that is identified as a "contentious case between states." **Advisory opinions** are issued to clarify a legal issue. Three UN treaties provide for ICJ mediation and other **dispute resolution** options.[7]

If threatened action is deemed "urgent" because irreparable harm might be done to individuals, a party may request **provisional measures** to stop the action, and the court may promptly authorize interim protection in response. Among the dozen cases in which provisional measures have been authorized, the first (*United States v. Iran*, 1980) involved an order to release diplomats who were held hostage in the American Embassy in Tehran.

Of the 115 **contentious cases** before the court thus far, about half have dealt with the demarcation of borders between countries, often infuriating countries that have to give up land to a neighbor. Human rights issues have been involved in one-fourth of the cases, mostly dealing with the treatment of nationals of one country who live in another country. The next most frequent type of case, involving military actions, has occurred in about 10 percent of ICJ business. After a decision is issued in a contentious case, the Security Council may undertake enforcement measures if the rulings are not implemented.

The rights of a foreigner inside another country have been litigated on the basis of customary international law and trade treaties. In three cases involving Colombia and Perú in 1949 and 1950 (*Colombia v. Perú*), for example, an unsuccessful coup leader sought refuge at Colombia's embassy in Lima. Although the court ruled that he was not entitled to asylum and safe conduct out of the country, Colombia was not required to surrender him to Peruvian authorities to stand trial for treason.

A case involving French nationals (*France v. Egypt*) was amicably resolved in 1949, but a 1952 case involving Americans in French-occupied Morocco (*France v. USA*) was decided on narrow grounds by interpreting treaties as far back as 1836. In *Netherlands v. Sweden* (1958), the Netherlands objected to Sweden's decision to allow a Swedish guardian to bring up a child born of a Dutch father whose Swedish mother had died. ICJ ruled that there was no treaty basis to rule on the question.

In 1960, both *Ethiopia v. South West Africa* and *Liberia v. South West Africa* were filed to claim that South Africa was not administering South West Africa (Namibia) in accordance with the rules laid done by the League of Nations that established the mandate over the territory. ICJ ruled that neither plaintiff had standing to sue.

In 1973, France's nuclear weapons tests in the South Pacific were challenged by *Australia v. France* and *New Zealand v. France*. In 1974, after France decided to cease all future tests, ICJ ruled that the case was moot.

Self-determination has also been an issue. After Indonesia militarily annexed Portugal's colony of East Timor in 1975, Australia signed a treaty with Indonesia regarding the use of the continental shelf of East Timor. Since Indonesia did not accept ICJ's jurisdiction, Portugal filed suit against Australia in 1991. Rejecting the case on the ground that the proper party to the dispute was Indonesia, the court nevertheless affirmed in *Portugal v. Australia* that the East Timorese retained the right of self-determination.

The Vienna Convention on Consular Relations of 1963 was supposed to ensure consular protection for citizens abroad, but the American decentralized federal system of government, in which there are some 25,000 independent police departments around the country, often complicates compliance. Few local jurisdictions in the United States are conversant with international legal requirements, and the Eleventh Amendment to the Constitution limits Washington's power to sue state governments in court. Accordingly, Paraguay filed a case against the United States when a Paraguayan national was on death row in Virginia, as contrary to the Vienna Convention because from his arrest to his sentencing he was not afforded the right to have his embassy provide legal counsel. As a result, he was deprived of a competent defense attorney, funds to pay the attorney, and the power to have visas issued for exonerating witnesses. Although in *Paraguay v. USA* (1998) the ICJ ordered provisional measures so that the death sentence would not be carried out, pending completion of deliberations, the execution occurred anyway, whereupon Paraguay withdrew the case from ICJ's docket as moot.

In a similar case involving two Germans on death row in Arizona (*Germany v. USA*), the ICJ, in 2001, issued its first ever binding provisional measure. Washington promised not to repeat the violation, but the executions occurred anyway. An identical situation emerged in 2004, involving 51 Mexican nationals on death row in 10 states (including Arizona). The court ruling in *México v. USA* authorized reparations to México and recommended a reconsideration of the sentences. In 2005, the United States withdrew from the Vienna Convention's Optional Protocol, which empowers ICJ to rule on consular representation disputes.

Military action without UN Security Council authorization can be considered to be a crime against peace. In regard to *Nicaragua v. United States*, the ICJ, in 1984, ordered provisional measures, namely, for the United States to stop all military and paramilitary activities against Nicaragua. In ratifying the ICJ Charter, the Senate attached a reservation that excludes any prosecutions based on the UN Charter or any other multilateral treaty, so the ICJ ruling was instead based on *jus cogens* and the trade treaty between the two countries. In 1986, Nicaragua also sued Costa Rica and Honduras (*Nicaragua v. Costa Rica*; *Nicaragua v. Honduras*) for serving as staging areas for the American-backed rebels who sought to overthrow the regime in Managua, but in 1990 both cases were withdrawn in the context of a peace settlement.

Several cases relate to "ethnic cleansing," a euphemism for genocide, taking place in the former Yugoslavia. Bosnia filed the first case (*Bosnia v. Serbia*) in 1993, the first time a sovereign state ever sued another state for genocide. The first response was for the court to order provisional measures, requiring Belgrade to stop supporting genocidal actions. In 1999, *Croatia v. Serbia* filed a charge of genocide for the years 1991–1995, but Belgrade never responded, so the case remained in limbo.

Then, in 1999, Belgrade filed suit against 10 NATO countries (Belgium, Britain, Canada, France, Germany, Italy, Netherlands, Portugal, Spain, USA) for attacking Serbia. In response, ICJ rejected Belgrade's request for provisional measures and declared the complaint inadmissible against two NATO countries, Spain and the United States, because of their reservations to the Convention on the Prevention and Punishment of the Crime of Genocide. Other NATO countries were judged to be valid parties, but the case was dismissed because Serbia was not a member of the United Nations when Belgrade filed the case.

In 2007, the court ruled on the 1993 case that they could find no direct link between Serbia and the slaughter of some 8,000 Bosniaks in Srebrenica during 1995, thus rejecting the applicability of the vicarious liability principle; however, Serbia was found culpable in not acting to prevent the slaughter, which was identified as "genocide." The court assessed no damages for the offense. Although Bosnia had sued for reparations in the wholesale campaign to kill Bosniaks that had been financed by Serbia, the court narrowed the scope of the complaint to the Srebrenica

Massacre and insisted that evidence of culpability had to be incontrovertible rather than beyond a reasonable doubt.

Six cases involved the Democratic Republic of the Congo (Kinshasa), which objected to "acts of armed aggression" from three African countries. Although negotiations settled *Congo v. Burundi* and *Congo v. Rwanda*, the case of *Congo v. Uganda* was different. Ugandan authorities shot down a civilian Congo Airlines airplane in 1998, resulting in 40 deaths, seized a hydroelectric power plant, and allegedly mistreated Congolese prisoners. Although the UN Security Council ordered Uganda to refrain from further aggression in 2000, and Kampala complied, the Congo successfully requested the court to issue provisional measures that duplicated the Security Council's order. Then, in 2001, Uganda filed counterclaims with ICJ, alleging that the Democratic Republic of Congo conducted aggression against Uganda. In 2002, Congo filed a new case against Rwanda for armed aggression as well as assassinations, degrading treatment of prisoners, looting, and rapes, but provisional measures were not approved. Hearings on all claims, held in 2005, resulted in a ruling that charged Uganda with a wide variety of war crimes but also ruled that Congo should pay reparations for mistreating Ugandan diplomats.

Developments in the Congo were followed closely in Belgium and France, particularly documents reporting torture by its Ministry of Interior. Arrest warrants and witness summons were issued to Congolese officials in both European countries, which have laws that confer jurisdiction in domestic courts to human rights offenses committed abroad based on the principle of universal jurisdiction. In 2000, in *Congo v. Belgium*, the ICJ was asked to quash the legal action in Belgium, citing the principle of immunity of prosecution of government officials. Although ICJ did not immediately order Belgium to rescind the arrest warrant as a provisional measure in 2000, the ICJ's final ruling in 2002 ordered Brussels to do so. A similar case, *Congo v. France*, was filed in 2002; once again provisional measures were rejected. Congo withdrew the case in 2010 after losing many procedural challenges.

The most recent ICJ case dealing with human rights was filed in 2008. *Georgia v. Russia* was the first one filed on the basis of the International Convention on the Elimination of All Forms of Racial Discrimination. Because Russian "peacekeepers" had been systematically attacking and expelling members of various ethnic groups in the South Ossetia and Abkhazia regions of the Republic of Georgia for two decades, provisional measures were requested to stop the ongoing violent situation. ICJ agreed, asking Russia to cease military operations. In 2011, however, ICJ ruled that a country must first try to seek negotiations before filing a case with ICJ. Since Georgia had not done so, the case was dismissed on what Georgia claimed was a "technicality."

Up to 2012, there were 26 **Advisory Opinions**, mostly submitted by the General Assembly because one of the countries involved refused to agree to be a defendant in the case. Advisory Opinions enable the court to act proactively rather than punitively.

In 1966, the General Assembly terminated South Africa's League of Nations mandate over South West Africa, whereupon the Security Council, in 1970, ordered Pretoria to withdraw from the territory, declaring that any further occupation was illegal. The South African government instead continued to administer the territory and even began to impose *apartheid* restrictions. In 1971, an Advisory Opinion (*Legal Consequences for States of the Continued Presence of South Africa in Namibia*) not only stated that South Africa's control was illegal but also approved the imposition of appropriate sanctions on South Africa to force compliance. In 1988, South Africa finally agreed to depart, and Namibia became independent in 1990 after a brief period under UN administration.

COURT CASE 9.2 ADVISORY OPINION ON ISRAEL'S CONSTRUCTION OF A WALL IN THE OCCUPIED PALESTINIAN TERRITORY (2004)

In 2003, the General Assembly asked the International Court of Justice (ICJ) to comment on the legality of the "security fence" constructed by Israel that intrudes into some of the territories that are likely to become part of a separate Palestinian state. Since Palestinians do not live in a sovereign state, they could not bring the case to the court. Instead, ICJ issued an Advisory Opinion, citing several human rights treaties, that the wall violated international law, since the annexation of territory deprived Palestinians of the right of self-determination. ICJ also criticized Israel for depriving the Palestinians of specific water wells. The court asked Israel to stop building the wall, to dismantle the wall, to pay reparations for damages caused by the construction, to prosecute those involved, and called upon the General Assembly and Security Council to take actions to implement the decision. Although Israel sought to justify the fence with the claim that every state has an inherent right of self-defense, the court pointed out that Israel remains responsible to maintain order in the occupied territories as an occupying power without jeopardizing the rights of Palestinians. In addition, the court called attention to Israel's defiance of previous General Assembly resolutions and asked all states to stop any aid to Israel that might assist in continuing to build the wall. Subsequently, the General Assembly voted to support the ICJ Advisory Opinion, but Israel has refused to comply.

Another famous Advisory Opinion is the ruling in *Western Sahara* (1975), which found that the territory was a part of neither Mauritania nor Morocco. ICJ thus declared that Western Sahara is eligible for self-determination.

ICJ was also asked about the legality of nuclear weapons. The *Legality of the Use by a State of Nuclear Weapons in Armed Conflict* (1993) and the *Legality of the Threat or Use of Nuclear Weapons* (1994) determined that both the use of nuclear weapons and the threat to use nuclear weapons are contrary to international law.

In 2003, in *Legal Consequences Arising from the Construction of the Wall Being Built by Israel, the Occupying Power, in the Occupied Palestinian Territory* the court agreed with a General Assembly resolution that Israel should stop building and start dismantling the wall. But Israel was unimpressed and refused to do so.

During 2006, former Secretary of State Madeleine Albright (1937–) began to seek plaintiffs from among about 14,500 detainees in Iraq in order to sue George W. Bush (1946–) for the torture meted out to prisoners at the Abu Ghraib prison. No such case was ever filed. Heads of state are immune from prosecution while in office but not afterward. In 2011, accordingly, Bush cancelled a trip to Geneva in the likelihood that he would be arrested by Swiss authorities. Albright's action proves that a court not supposed to handle political questions can indeed become embroiled in high politics.

In 2007, the World Court made an extraordinary ruling – that Serbia did not commit genocide against Bosnia. Evidence, in other words, was insufficient to link the Belgrade government with specific actions taking place during the Bosnian Civil War. Nevertheless, cases involving individuals connected to the massacres were referred to the International Criminal Tribunal for Yugoslavia, which is discussed in Chapter 10.

In 2008, the Advisory Opinion *Accordance with International Law of the Unilateral Declaration of Independence by the Provisional Institutions of Self-Government of Kosovo* agreed that Kosovo's action was consistent with the right of self-determination. Kosovo is now recognized diplomatically by 94 of the 193 members of the UN.

COURT CASE 9.3 SERBIA EXONERATED OF RESPONSIBILITY FOR ETHNIC CLEANSING IN BOSNIA (2007)

In 2006, the case *Bosnia and Herzegovina v. Serbia and Montenegro* was submitted to the International Court of Justice (ICJ) regarding events at Srebrenica that were described in 2005 by UN Secretary-General Kofi Annan (1938–) as the worst single human rights atrocity since World War II. The accusation was that the government in Belgrade was responsible for the genocidal deaths of Bosnian Muslims (Bosniaks) during the massacre of 8,000 men and boys, including men over 65 and boys under 15, as well as the expulsion of 12,000 women and children from Srebrenica in 1995. A Serbian paramilitary unit known as the Scorpions, then officially part of the Serbian Interior Ministry, was alleged to have participated in the massacre. In 2004, the Appeals Chamber of the International Criminal Tribunal for Yugoslavia (ICTY) ruled in *Prosecutor v. Krstić* that the massacre of the male inhabitants constituted genocide, so the question before the court was whether Serbia was liable for the offense. However, respecting Serbia's claim that release of certain documents would jeopardize its national security, ICTY never subpoenaed crucial evidence that might have linked the Scorpions to the massacre. Based on the evidence presented, ICJ ruled that forces of Republika Srpska were directly responsible, but not Serbia. Belgrade, however, was found guilty of vicarious liability (failing to stop the massacre) and for failing to try or transfer Bosnian Serbs accused of genocide to the ICTY, as required by the Convention on the Prevention and Punishment of the Crime of Genocide. Later, Serbia captured the top two Srpskan officials (in 2008 and 2011) and sent them to ICTY for trial.

ICJ's decisions are not always accepted. Ideally, two countries will submit a dispute in good faith, hoping that the court will clarify the legal issues so that the matter can be resolved. The court's rulings indeed add to the body of international law, but a country's political priorities may trump legal rulings. Several other international courts have been established with the assistance of the UN. They are reviewed in the following chapter.

CONCLUSION

According to Louis Henkin (1917–2010), widely considered to be the founder of human rights law, the United Nations has grown so magnificently since its formation in 1945 that the world is now living in an entirely new era – the Era of Human Rights. Kofi Annan's mandate for all UN agencies to focus on human rights in their operations has resulted in many changes throughout the UN, some of which have been reviewed above.

The UN began as a forum to deal with international problems through diplomacy but has increasingly become an operational organization. Today, some 70 percent of the UN budget is spent on field operations, particularly in humanitarian relief and peacekeeping. Whereas interstate wars have declined since the end of the Cold War, serious human rights abuses inside countries have stimulated action in recent years. In a very real sense, the UN has come of age in regard to human rights, though proactively more than punitively.

If the UN has often responded too late or not at all to human rights problems, the reason is because the organization acts only when member governments give authorization. The UN is not a world government. Although UN agencies and leaders for it raise concerns within the world community, governments have the final say on action taken in response. Nevertheless, the UN uniquely provides legitimacy to global policies with universal applicability and relevance, thereby spearheading an unenforced global governance by serving as the premier forum for norm promotion by sponsoring declarations and treaties while acting as default coordinator of international humanitarian operations throughout the world. The UN has uniquely established moral authority throughout the world.

How, then, can such international organizations as the UN influence states to improve human rights? At least four methods are used:

- Establishment of norms
- Economic and military pressure
- Criticisms to shame violators
- Opportunities for government officials in noncompliant states to interact with their opposite numbers in compliant states through conferences, workshops, and other activities that provide peer pressure.

The United Nations is not the only IGO body that can act to improve human rights. Chapters 10, 12, and 13 review both global and regional organizations that work side by side.

DISCUSSION TOPIC 9.2 WHAT IF THE UNITED NATIONS WERE ABOLISHED?

There is no more blatant example of United Nations ineffectiveness than the withdrawal of UN peacekeepers from Rwanda in 1994, whereupon genocide proceeded unabated. Many officials in the United States have criticized the UN for following an agenda at odds with American policy, and indeed Washington has sometimes held up its payment of assessments to the UN in protest, thereby limiting the scope of UN operations. Although few seriously propose abolishing the United Nations, how should the various critics be answered? Wherein is the UN indispensable?

CHAPTER 10

Treaty-Based Global International Organizations

The United Nations has sponsored several treaties dealing with human rights, though ratifying countries are fewer in number than those represented in the UN General Assembly (which, of course, was itself established by a treaty). The non-Charter organs are presented in this chapter, followed by a discussion of several international organizations with a global scope that are outside the UN framework – principally the International Criminal Court and related judicial bodies, the International Criminal Police Organization, and the World Trade Organization.

UNITED NATIONS-SPONSORED TREATY-BASED ORGANS

Many declarations and treaties have been devoted to various aspects of human rights over the years. Independent human rights bodies have been established in the text of 10 treaties sponsored by the UN (Table 10.1). All have regular sessions in Geneva under the umbrella of the High Commissioner for Human Rights, which provides a comprehensive website, secretariat facilities, and often liaises with special rapporteurs. Members of the various committees established by the treaties, though nominated by their governments, tend to be technical experts who represent their expertise more than the priorities of their countries of origin.

Mere ratification of human rights treaties does not guarantee compliance. Instead, the primary method used by the committees to advance human rights is by requiring **initial reports** from ratifying countries on measures taken to increase the level of voluntary compliance, followed by **periodic reports**. The committees undertake a

TABLE 10.1 UN-SPONSORED TREATY-BASED ORGANS FOCUSING ON HUMAN RIGHTS

Adopted	Treaty	States ratifying	In force	Monitoring body	Acronym
1965	International Convention on the Elimination of All Forms of Racial Discrimination	175	1969	Committee on the Elimination of All Forms of Racial Discrimination	CERD
1992	• Amendment	44			
1966	International Covenant on Civil and Political Rights	167	1976	Human Rights Committee	HRC
1966	• Optional Protocol 1	114	1976		
1989	• Optional Protocol 2	75	1991		
1966	International Covenant on Economic, Social and Cultural Rights	160	1976	Committee on Economic, Social and Cultural Rights	CESCR
2008	• Optional Protocol	8			
1979	Convention on the Elimination of All Forms of Discrimination Against Women	187	1981	Committee on the Elimination of Discrimination Against Women	CEDAW
1995	• Amendment	66			
1999	• Optional Protocol	104	2000		
1984	Convention Against Torture and Other Cruel, Inhuman or Degrading Treatment or Punishment	153	1987	Committee Against Torture	CAT
1992	• Amendments	30			
2002	• Optional Protocol	64	2006		
1989	Convention on the Rights of the Child	193	1990	Committee on the Rights of the Child	CRC
1995	• Amendment	143			
2000	• Optional Protocol 1	150	2002		
2000	• Optional Protocol 2	161	2002		
2011	• Optional Protocol 3	2	2002		
1990	International Convention on the Protection of the Rights of All Migrant Workers and Members of Their Families	46	2003	Committee on the Protection of the Rights of All Migrant Workers and Members of their Families	CMW
2006	Convention on the Rights of Persons with Disabilities	126	2008	Committee on the Rights of Persons with Disabilities	CRPD
2006	• Optional Protocol	76	2008		
2006	International Convention for the Protection of	36	2010	Committee on Enforced	CED

review of the reports and make recommendations in the form of **concluding observations**. The committees can then engage in **follow-up monitoring** by evaluating responses to the recommendations. The country reports, in turn, are supposed to be submitted at regular intervals, though many countries fail to do so. To promote compliance, the treaty-based organs often engage in nonadversarial constructive dialog with countries that have not ratified the basic treaties. Nevertheless, the fact that reports are required and subject to comment has had a major impact on implementation. Countries lacking legislation on certain matters before joining one of the treaty-based organs have indeed brought their domestic law up to international standards.

The agenda for the annual plenary meetings of the committees usually consists of **discussions** on problems identified in several reports, often leading to **general comments** or **general recommendations** on thematic topics. Sometimes, a committee will make statements about problems in countries that have failed to ratify the respective treaty.

Most treaty-based committees also handle three types of **petitions** against ratifying countries:

- **Individual communications** (used by eight committees)
- **State-to-state complaints** (not used because accused countries may retaliate)
- **Inquiries** (used by three committees).

Procedures vary, as discussed below, though individuals are expected to exhaust remedies in their own countries before a complaint will be ruled admissible unless domestic procedures are unreasonably prolonged. The impact of the committees in goading states to comply is incremental compared to the more powerful Charter-based bodies.

- **Committee on the Elimination of All Forms of Racial Discrimination** (CERD). In accordance with the International Convention on the Elimination of All Forms of Racial Discrimination, CERD employs three procedures:

  - Reporting
  - Individual complaints
  - Interstate complaints.

The principal impact of CERD's review of country **reports**, which are required biennially, has been for the states to adopt legal innovations, such as constitutional provisions, laws, and enforcement agencies dealing with racial discrimination, often in response to CERD's **concluding observations** on the country reports. In 2012, 11 country reports were reviewed with detailed comments. Because a large number of countries have been unwilling to submit reports at two-year intervals, CERD has sometimes launched **investigations** to fill the gap.

According to the CERD Convention, **individual complaints** from non-self-governing territories are referred to CERD. From 1982, CERD has been able to handle petitions filed by individuals or groups, but only against countries that explicitly accept Article 14 of the CERD Convention. The Committee allows states only three months to respond to the petitions; the identity of petitioners is kept confidential until a judgment is rendered. By 2012, some 49 cases had been registered, of which 12 were ruled to violate the Convention, 16 were deemed nonviolations, 17 were inadmissible, one was dismissed, and the rest were still under consideration. In one case, 35 Danish youngsters forced their entry into the home of Iraqi refugees and terrorized the family. Although Denmark took criminal action in response, CERD considered the light penalty as a violation of Article 6 and Article 2(1)(d) of the Convention because Copenhagen failed to investigate the attack as a racial incident. The government was urged to revise criminal justice procedures accordingly and to provide adequate compensation to the family.

The Committee also holds discussions on various topics. Interpretations of provisions of the treaty, known as **general recommendations**, are published in the context of reports on thematic issues or its methods of work. In 2012, the thirty-fourth recommendation urged a variety of measures, including affirmative action, to reduce discrimination against persons of African descent throughout the world.

In 1993, CERD adopted two more implementation mechanisms. The **early-warning procedure** consists of suggesting confidence-building measures so that an ongoing problem will not escalate out of control. Criteria for determining when to employ the early-warning procedure are quite broad, including,

- Failure of a country to pass laws banning racial discrimination
- Inadequate enforcement machinery
- Escalating racial hatred and violence, especially when officeholders are appealing to racial intolerance
- Statistical evidence of a large gap between socioeconomic attainments of racial groups
- A significant exodus of refugees on account of discriminatory acts.

The **urgent procedure** is invoked when there is a serious, massive, or persistent pattern of racial discrimination. CERD then acts to stop or lower the scope of human rights violations. In 2011, for example, post-election violence in the Ivory Coast was addressed.

The early-warning and urgent action procedure has been used in response to problems in more than 20 states thus far. CERD then supported the Security Council's recommendation to send a protection force to Darfur in 2004, and, in 2005, CERD recommended an enlargement of the peacekeeping force. In 2012, CERD objected to measures taken in several countries to encroach on the homeland of aboriginal peoples – Belize (the Maya), Kenya (the Samburu), Panamá (Ngabe-Buglé), Suriname (Saramaka), Thailand (Karen), and the United States (Western Shoshone).

In 2000, CERD instituted a new procedure – **general discussions on thematic issues**. The first discussion resulted in a general recommendation on a thematic issue – problems of discrimination against the Roma (gypsy) people. In 2012, the eighth discussion was about hate speech, though no general recommendation has yet been issued on the complicated subject.

- **Human Rights Committee** (HRC). Under the authority of the International Covenant on Civil and Political Rights, ratifying countries are required to submit **compliance reports** every four years to HRC, which then makes comments in the form of **concluding observations**. In 2010, the procedure was modified: HRC now sends a list of issues to each country, asking that they respond specifically about the issues – in other words, a focused report rather than writing a general report. Then, rather than general observations, HRC will make **recommendations** on just a few issues.

HRC also receives derogation **notifications**, that is, declarations by countries that some civil and political rights are being suspended temporarily to deal with emergencies. In 2012, Guatemala, Perú, and Trinidad and Tobago did so.

The First Optional Protocol to the Covenant gives the committee competence to examine **individual communications** about countries ratifying the First Optional Protocol. Specific victims (not groups), or third parties on their behalf, can lodge complaints if they are under the jurisdiction of the country that is charged with violations of rights stated in the Covenant, but they must first exhaust national complaint procedures. Six months after allowing a country to respond to a complaint, the Committee can investigate, formulate its own views, and make a recommendation in the form of a remedy. For example, communication 2024, *Israil v. Kazakhstan*, was based on the capture of a Chinese national who fled to Kazakhstan in 2009, applied for and was granted asylum with the help of UNHCR, but in 2010 was arrested, tortured while detained, and then extradited to China despite the high probability that he would be executed there. HRC ruled that the extradition was a human rights violation. Although many communications are dismissed procedurally, mainly because the private party failed to exhaust the country's legal options, decisions on individual communications are considered by HRC to constitute case law.

An offending country is required to make **reports** on corrective measures. In 1993, for example, the Committee ruled that the 1977 law making French the official language in Québec violated the linguistic rights of English-language speakers by requiring all outdoor signs to be in French.

Remedies may include payment of compensation, repeal or amendment of legislation, or release of a detained person. In 1993, Québec agreed to revise the law to permit other languages on public signs (though they were to be half the size of the French words). Next, the Committee will organize a follow-up investigation to ensure that the remedy is adopted. If a state refuses to accept the proposed remedy, a Conciliation Commission of five persons will be established to reach a settlement.

In 1990, for example, a communication came from a Zambian robber sentenced to death after eight years of legal proceedings. He questioned the country's law imposing that penalty whenever a firearm is used in a crime, since he fired the gun without causing any injury. The Committee ruled that the mandatory death penalty may be imposed only for the most serious crimes, that the judge erred by not informing the jury that the use of the firearm had not resulted in death or injury, and that a speedy trial had been denied. The Committee ruled that his sentence should be reduced.

If a complaint is considered urgent, with irreparable harm possible to the victim, the Committee will ask a state to adopt **interim measures**. If capital punishment is involved, the government is asked to delay execution until the matter is resolved. In 2004, the case of an Uzbek officer, under sentence of death, was under consideration by the Committee. Accordingly, the Committee requested the interim measure of withholding execution. In 2005, however, the officer was executed, whereupon the Committee requested an explanation from the government in a letter that noted several similar situations in Uzbekistan's past. In 2012, HRC called for 10 interim measures of protection.

Thematic reports have been issued in the form of **general comments**, which often cover procedural matters. In 1999, a substantive general comment was issued on freedom of movement. Thirty-four general comments were made up to 2012, when freedom of expression and opinion were addressed, noting that measured limitations are allowed to protect the reputations of others (including *lese majesté*) and to maintain national security but that the penalties should not be severe. The comment criticized state monopoly control over the media and prohibitions of over-broadly defined "blasphemous" expressions.

HRC also monitors compliance with the Second Optional Protocol, which commits ratifying countries to abolish the death penalty. The United States is repeatedly criticized for excessive use of the death penalty.

• **Committee on Economic, Social and Cultural Rights** (CESCR). Based on the International Covenant on Economic, Social and Cultural Rights, **compliance reports** are required at five-year intervals though the task is perhaps too daunting for full compliance. CESCR then reviews the reports and makes **concluding observations**, which include questions and recommendations. A proposed Optional Protocol to the Covenant that would enable complaint processing has not been adopted.

The committee has devoted considerable attention to thematic discussions and has made **general comments**, consisting of extended statements interpreting various economic, social, and cultural rights. Up to 2012, 21 topics had been issued. In 2002, CESCR upheld the right to water. The latest covers the right of everyone to participate in cultural life, defined as "ways of life, language, oral and written literature, music and song, non-verbal communication, religion or belief systems, rites and ceremonies, sport and games, methods of production or technology, natural and man-made environments, food, clothing and shelter and the arts, customs and traditions through which individuals, groups of individuals and communities express their humanity" with special protection for children, the disabled, the elderly, indigenous people, migrants, minorities, those living in poverty, and women.

In 1989, 23 topics for **general discussion** have been addressed; the most recent, in 2010, was about the right to sanitation. From 1992, CESCR has also made **statements** on matters of concern. Among the 20 statements issued by 2012, the latest was on the right to development.

• **Committee on the Elimination of Discrimination Against Women** (CEDAW). Created by the Convention on the Elimination of All Forms of Discrimination Against Women of 1979, CEDAW requires **country reports** at four-year intervals, and makes concluding **observations**. Often, **follow-up reports** are requested. Among the 22 follow-up reports thus far solicited, the latest went to Fiji,

Turkey, and Ukraine. The United States is the only developed country that is not a member.

CEDAW also issues **general recommendations**. Thus far, there have been 28 general recommendations, addressing such topics as disabled women, equality in family relations, female circumcision, migrant and older women, violence against women, and women in politics.

CEDAW is greatly concerned with sex-role stereotyping. In a comment on the Belarus report of 2000, CEDAW criticized the country for reintroducing Mother's Day and Mother's Awards as encouraging traditional role perceptions. CEDAW has also asked for the decriminalization of abortion and prostitution.

Before general recommendations are adopted, a **task force** is sometimes appointed to identify parameters of an issue, followed by a working group. In 2011, CEDAW transformed a task force on gender equality in the context of asylum, statelessness and natural disasters into a working group. Otherwise, **working groups** prepare detailed agendas within preparation for the annual session. A proposed amendment, permitting CEDAW to meet more frequently than the current two weeks each year, has not yet been ratified.

The convention also gives the committee the power to request an **exceptional report**. For example, there was a pressing conflict involving women involving rapes taking place during "ethnic cleansing" in Bosnia.

CEDAW's Optional Protocol establishes procedures for **individual communications**, although gender-based complaints may also be filed with ECOSOC's Commission on the Status of Women and HRC. A working group then processes the complaint. If the communications are urgent, CEDAW may prescribe **interim measures**. In 2011, among the 66 communications, a Ugandan woman complained that Denmark planned to send her back to Uganda, where she feared that she would be forced to undergo female circumcision. As a result of her complaint to CEDAW, Denmark suspended the order.

The Protocol also creates an **inquiry** procedure whenever reliable information exists about widespread abuses in a particular country, though no complaints. CEDAW first refers complaints to the affected governments for comment, keeping names of complainants confidential. An inquiry may result in a **site visit** to a country. Within six months, the state charged with discrimination is expected to **report** on corrective measures proposed or taken to remedy any problems that have been identified. In 2011, there were three requests for inquiries.

In 2005, CEDAW issued a report on an inquiry requested by two nongovernmental organizations, Equality Now and Casa Amiga, about reported disappearances and uninvestigated murders of females working in factories at Ciudad Juarez, México. CEDAW's report, after a site visit and an exchange of information with the government in México City, led to several general recommendations, which in turn prompted the government to allocate more resources in order to ensure better treatment of the workers, though implementation has lagged behind promises.

Unlike other treaty-based organizations, CEDAW's vision is for social transformation around the world. Initial compliance often results in procedural innovations – that is, the establishment of new domestic institutions, such as commissions on the status of women. When the new bodies begin operation, they become a pressure group for substantive change.

• **Committee Against Torture** (CAT). Every four years, parties to the Convention Against Torture and Other Cruel, Inhuman or Degrading Treatment or Punishment must submit **reports** to the committee, each coordinated by a rapporteur. The committee examines each report and addresses its concerns and recommendations in the form of **concluding observations**. In 2003, CAT decided to ask for **follow-up reports**, which are now requested in most cases. In 2007, CAT began an **optional reporting procedure** in which submitted lists of concerns are sent to each country before its report is due.

In 2006, for example, CAT commented on the report of the United States, which had been due in 2001 but was instead received in 2005, with several criticisms about torture meted out by American personnel at facilities in Abu Ghraib, Iraq, and Guantánamo Bay. CAT recommended that "psychological torture" should be defined as any kind of mental suffering, secret detention facilities should be disclosed, extraordinary renditions should be terminated, imprisonment at Guantánamo should end, and those engaging in torture should be prosecuted according to American law.

In 2011, the Committee discussed the periodic report of Belarus, noting a pattern of denial of "legal safeguards, including prompt access to a lawyer and medical doctor and the right to contact family members." In CAT's concluding observations, recommendations beyond correcting that pattern included such reforms as allowing a court to make prompt reviews of detentions, instituting a complaint mechanism, and videotaping of interrogations.

CAT has made two **general comments**. The first clarifies complaint procedures; the second interprets provisions of the treaty in detail.

The committee has appointed **working groups** to review specific issues. In 2011, two groups were set up – one on health care in places of detention and the other regarding national security issues.

The CAT treaty requires automatic investigation on **individual communications, interstate complaints** (never used), or **inquiries**. (A state could specifically opt out of the complaint procedure in Article 22, but no country has.) In some cases, **interim measures** are requested. By 2011, CAT received 506 complaints concerning 31 countries. Violations were judged in 73 cases, 201 were either discontinued or inadmissible, and 102 were still under consideration. When violations occur, CAT recommends **remedies**. Many cases involve the threat of deportation of an undocumented alien to detention in a country of origin where torture is highly probable, including such countries as Kazakhstan, Sweden, and Morocco in 2010, and Spain in 2011. In the Moroccan case, CAT recommended compensation for the ill treatment received in prison. In 2012, four Canadians who had been mistreated at Guantánamo filed a complaint against Canada for failing to arrest George W. Bush during his trip to Vancouver in 2011. Thus far, CAT has made eight inquiries. In 2012, Nepal was the subject of the fifth inquiry. Evidence concerning torture in Nepal was presented in a 30-page statement with 16 recommendations, but the report was rejected by the country as "isolated instances."

Countries that ratify the Optional Protocol pledge to allow CAT's Subcommittee on Prevention to inspect detention centers. In 2006, when the Optional Protocol went into force, CAT set up the **Subcommittee on Prevention of Torture**. In 2004, an inspection had already taken place in Lithuania, which ratified early. Three visits were undertaken in 2011 (to Brazil, Mali, Ukraine). Much of the Subcommittee's work is to facilitate the establishment of national prevention mechanisms; so far 28 states of the 61 countries ratifying the Optional Protocol have done so.

The title, Subcommittee on Prevention of Torture, may give a false impression of the wide scope of concern. CAT shows considerable interest in "Other Cruel, Inhuman or Degrading Treatment or Punishment," as stated in the title of its founding treaty.

- **Committee on the Rights of the Child** (CRC). The Convention on the Rights of the Child, which established CRC, states a wide range of basic human rights of the child:

  - Civil, political, economic and social rights
  - Rights against separation from parents
  - Rights against dangers to which children are particularly vulnerable.

The First Optional Protocol pledges states to end the practice of using children as armed combatants. The Second Optional Protocol commits states to end child pornography, child prostitution, and the sale of children. The Third Optional Protocol, the only one not yet in force, would establish a complaint procedure and authorize country visits to investigate grave and systematic violations of children's rights.

CRC reviews initial and periodic **reports** at five-year intervals, and then makes **concluding observations** that thus far have asked for seven **follow-up reports**. During 2012, for example, CRC commented that Andorra should adopt legislation on child protection, while Liberia should pass laws on harmful practices, juvenile justice, and nondiscrimination.

Although CRC does not yet consider individual complaints, they may be raised before other committees, such as HRC. However, in 1996 the committee came close, asking China for permission to visit the eleventh Panchen Lama, who then was of school age but of unknown whereabouts. China refused the request, which was also made by 400 celebrities, including five Nobel Prize winners.

The Committee has made 13 **general comments**; education and health have been the main considerations. In 2011, freedom from violence was featured, going beyond an earlier discouragement of the use of corporal, cruel, and degrading punishment to a detailed examination of the adverse effects on children of mental violence (bullying, hazing) and sexual violence.

Thus far, CRC has made 10 **recommendations**; although most are procedural, substantive recommendations have been issued on children without parental care and juvenile justice. From 1993, **general discussions** have been held on various themes when CRC meets each year, including economic exploitation of children, rights of the child in families, juvenile justice, and – in 2012 – the rights of children whose parents migrate to new countries.

The Convention has been ratified by every country in the world except for Somalia, which lacks a procedure for ratification, and the United States. Although the US Senate has ratified the first two Optional Protocols, the treaty has not gone into force in part because some nonratifying states execute children under age 16 and some give life sentences to children, contrary to the Convention. The United States is the only country that sentences juveniles up to age 17 to life sentences without parole.

• **Committee on the Protection of the Rights of All Migrant Workers and Members of their Families** (CMW). The main aim of the International Convention on the Protection of the Rights of All Migrant Workers and Members of Their Families is to prevent the exploitation of more than 150 million migrants around the world who seek work and safety for their families. CMW, which first met in 2004, reviewed initial **reports** from countries ratifying the Convention; periodic reports are due every five years. CMW makes recommendations in the form of **concluding observations** on the reports. In 2012, CMW urged Bosnia to make several changes in how migrants are treated, especially by adopting laws that guarantee their full rights in employment, education, and social security. From 2014, CMW will provide lists of issues to be addressed by each country that is due for review.

The Committee will consider individual communications from those who claim that their rights under the Convention have been violated. CMW plans to publish interpretations of the content of human rights provisions, known as **general comments** on thematic issues, but has done so only once – on migrant domestic workers. The general comment followed an extensive **general discussion** on the issue.

Three **working groups** discuss major issues in preparation for general discussions at CMW meetings. They deal with criminalization of migrants, the need to separate the rights of migrants from immigration enforcement, and how to promote migrant rights through such arenas as regional organizations and the Global Forum on Migration and Development, a nongovernmental organization.

The complaint procedure included in the text of the treaty became operational when 10 countries accepted CMW's jurisdiction, which occurred in 2008. Neither the convention nor CMW deals with the problems of undocumented migrant workers.

• **Committee on the Rights of Persons with Disabilities** (CRPD). The Convention on the Rights of Persons with Disabilities set up CRPD, which requires member countries to submit initial **reports** and every four years thereafter. CRPD then analyzes the reports and makes recommendations in the form of **concluding observations**. In 2012, China's report resulted in suggestions to fight the stigmatization of children with disabilities and to revise the family planning policy, which has often resulted in their abandonment, so as to combat the root causes for the abandonment of boys and girls with disabilities. It asks the state party to provide sufficient community-based services and assistance also in rural areas.

The Optional Protocol empowers CRPD to receive. In 2013, CPRD ruled that Hungary violated the Convention by failing to provide Braille in ATM machines. CRPD has held **general discussions**. In 2013, CPRD held a half-day discussion on women and girls with disabilities.

• **Committee on Enforced Disappearances** (CED). The International Convention for the Protection of All Persons from Enforced Disappearance came into force in 2010, so CED has not yet had time to get into gear by reviewing **reports** and processing **communications** (complaints), including consideration of urgent action requests. Nevertheless, two **thematic discussions** were held during the 2012 meeting – one on non-state actors, the other on the disappearance of women and children.

TABLE 10.2   TREATY-BASED ORGANS FOCUSING ON HUMAN RIGHTS OUTSIDE THE UNITED NATIONS

Adopted	Treaty	Member states	In force	Headquarters	Acronym
1923	International Criminal Police Organization	190	1923	Lyon	Interpol
1947	General Agreement on Tariffs and Trade	NA	1948	Geneva	GATT
1956	International Atomic Energy Agency	155	1957	Vienna	IAEA
1993	International Criminal Tribunal for the Prosecution of Persons Responsible for Serious Violations of International Humanitarian Law Committed in the Territory of the Former Yugoslavia Since 1991	NA	1993	The Hague	ICTY
1994	International Criminal Tribunal for the Prosecution of Persons Responsible for Genocide and Other Serious Violations of International Humanitarian Law Committed in the Territory of Rwanda and Rwandan Citizens Responsible for Genocide and Other Such Violations Committed in the Territory of Neighboring States, Between 1 January 1994 and 31 December 1994	NA	1994	Arusha, Rwanda	ICTR
1994	World Trade Organization	157	1995	Geneva	WTO
1996	Preparatory Commission for the Comprehensive Nuclear-Test-Ban Treaty Organization	183	1996	Vienna	CTBTO
1997	Organization for the Prohibition of Chemical Weapons	188	1997	The Hague	OPCW
1998	International Criminal Court	121	2002	The Hague	ICC
1998	Victims Trust Fund	121	2002	The Hague	
1999	Serious Crimes Unit	NA	2004	Dili, Timor-Leste	SCU
2000	Special Court for Sierra Leone	NA	2002	Freetown	SCSL
2000	Regulation 64 Panels	NA	2000	Pristina	
2002	Court of Bosnia and Herzegovina	NA	2005	Sarajevo	Court of BiH
2003	Extraordinary Chambers in the Courts of Cambodia for the Prosecution of Crimes Committed during the Period of Democratic Kampuchea	NA	2006	Phnom Penh	ECCC

Continued

TABLE 10.2 (CONTINUED)

Adopted	Treaty	Member states	In force	Headquarters	Acronym
2005	War Crimes Chamber of the Court of Bosnia and Herzegovina	NA	2005	Sarajevo	WCC
2007	Special Tribunal for Lebanon	NA	2009	Leidschendam	STL
2010	International Residual Mechanism for International Criminal Tribunals	NA	2010	Arusha; The Hague	MICT

Note: NA = not applicable.

INTERNATIONAL CRIMINAL COURTS

The Security Council has established two special criminal courts to prosecute those responsible for war crimes – one for the former Yugoslavia, the other for Rwanda; both operate autonomously, though on UN funds. A successor to the Rwandan and Yugoslavian criminal courts, the International Residual Mechanism for International Criminal Tribunals, will wind up the business of both bodies. More importantly, an agreement to establish the International Criminal Court (ICC) was adopted in 1998. All four bodies are identified in Table 10.2.

• **International Criminal Tribunal for the Prosecution of Persons Responsible for Serious Violations of International Humanitarian Law Committed in the Territory of the Former Yugoslavia Since 1991** (ICTY). Massive violations of human rights law associated with "ethnic cleansing" during the wars in the former Yugoslavia led the Security Council to try conciliation in 1991, condemnation in 1992, and then adoption of a statute by the UN Security Council in 1993 to serve as terms of reference for a tribunal to punish war criminals. But a court could not negotiate peace, which was the primary goal, so a deal was made that Serbian leader, Slobodan Milošović (1941–2006), would not be prosecuted so that the Dayton Accords would bring peace in 1995.

The first indictment was issued in 1995 against Duško Tadić (1955–), who was found guilty in 1997 of merciless beatings in a prison camp and sentenced to a 25-year prison term, though he was released in 2008. He was one of 21 Serbs indicted at the same time.

HISTORIC EVENT 10.1 THE BOSNIAN CIVIL WAR (1992–1995)

In 1991, Yugoslavia's provinces of Croatia and Slovenia declared independence, and other provinces appeared interested in following suit, provoking Belgrade to military

Continued

action. The UN Security Council, to head off a bloody civil war, then authorized an arms embargo of Yugoslavia. That same year, Bosnia-Herzegovina's parliament, which had roughly equal numbers of Croats, Muslims (Bosniaks), and Serbs, voted to secede from Yugoslavia, and a referendum in 1992 agreed upon independence. However, Serbs first walked out of parliament and later boycotted the election. Serbs who had been members of the Yugoslav army soon put on uniforms of Republika Srpska, and took up arms against newly independent Bosnia, with financial and logistical support from Serbian-dominated Yugoslavia, in order to control as much territory as possible inside Bosnia. In 1992, the UN Protection Force, which had been assigned to keep Yugoslav troops from attacking Croatia, had its mandate extended to Bosnia; the mission was to secure the airport of Sarajevo, Bosnia's capital, so that relief supplies could reach the embattled population. In 1993, when the Srpskan army occupied about 70 percent of Bosnia, the Security Council declared several towns to be "safe havens" that Srpskan troops were forbidden to annex and authorized a "no-fly" zone, enforced by airplanes of NATO, to ban Yugoslav military airplanes from entering Bosnian airspace. Subsequently, four Yugoslav aircraft were shot down, and Srpska positions were shelled by NATO forces. In 1994, a truce between Bosniaks and Croats, which had been fighting from time to time inside Bosnia, was brokered in Washington. In 1995, in defiance of the UN and NATO, Srpskan troops engaged in "ethnic cleansing" of Bosniaks in Srebrenica, one of the "safe havens"; some 8,000 males were slaughtered and 12,000 women and children were expelled. After the UN Security Council authorized NATO to threaten military retribution on Belgrade, the United States brokered a peace agreement between Bosnia and Yugoslavia that was negotiated at Dayton, Ohio, and signed at Paris in late 1995. The peace agreement established a federal structure in which the Federation of Bosnia and Herzegovina occupies about an equal amount of territory with Republika Srpska. A NATO force was initially assigned to monitor the ceasefire and deter hostilities. Although the two entities are autonomous within the state of Bosnia and Herzegovina, which has a presidency that rotates every eight months between Bosniaks, Croats, and Serbs. In all, at least 100,000 deaths had occurred, and 1.8 millions were displaced as Srpskans forced Bosniaks out of their homes. In 1994, the NATO force was replaced by a small European Union force, which remains in place. The ceasefire has held.

Among the most famous cases are two Srpskan leaders of the war in Bosnia, known as the Butchers of Bosnia. Radovan Karadžić (1945–) and Ratko Mladić (1942–), who were indicted for their role in the Srebrenica massacre in 1995 and genocide. Although indicted in 1996, they were at large until the Serbian government, eager to prove itself worthy of membership in the European Union, tracked them down and turned them over to ICTY – in 2008 for Karadžić and 2011 for Mladić.

▋ COURT CASE 10.1 THE TRIAL OF SLOBODAN MILOŠEVIĆ (2001–2006)

After the disputed presidential election of 2000, Slobodan Milošević (1941–2006) resigned as president. In 2001, he was arrested by Yugoslav federal authorities on suspicion of corruption, abuse of power, and embezzlement. But when evidence appeared insufficient, Serbian Prime Minister, Zoran Đinđić (1952–2003), had Milošević flown from Belgrade to The Hague to be tried by the International Criminal Tribunal for the Former Yugoslavia. He was charged with 66 counts, including crimes against humanity, genocide, and war crimes, especially for orchestrating the "ethnic cleansing" of Muslims in Bosnia and Croats in Croatia during the 1990s while he was president of Yugoslavia. Milošević died while in detention during 2006 before a ruling was issued on his case.

In 1998, Slobodan Milošović (1941–2006) was directly responsible for forced deportation of 800,000 ethnic Albanians from Kosovo and the murder of hundreds of Kosovo Albanians. Diplomacy did not work to stop the ethnic cleansing, so in 1999 he was indicted by ICTY for a long list of offenses, and NATO bombing of Serbia forced him to stop the atrocities. Two years later, he was forced from power, and Serbian authorities surrendered him to ICTY, where the trial continued until he died in his cell at The Hague. The International Court of Justice ruling in 2007 that Serbia did not commit wholesale genocide against Bosnia may in effect have posthumously acquitted Milošović but will certainly weigh heavily in the trial of Karadžić and Mladić.

Charges have also been pressed against several Albanian Kosovars. In 2005, shortly after Kosovo Prime Minister Ramush Haradinaj (1968–) was indicted for his role in the massacre of Serbs and fellow Kosovars in Kosovo during 1998–1999, he surrendered to ICTY and was placed on trial with two of his subordinates in 2007. Although acquitted in 2008, witness intimidation was suspected, so he was rearrested and placed on trial a second time in 2010 and acquitted again in 2012.

Thus far, 147 persons have been found guilty and are serving sentences from three years to life; 22 have been found not guilty. Some appeals have caused a reduction in the years of the sentences. In 2005, the court indicted four Croatian journalists for contempt of court after they published testimony of two protected witnesses in an ongoing trial, contrary to the rules of the court.

The last indictments were issued in 2004. All trials are to end by 2012 and appeals by 2014 with the exception of the high-profile cases of Karadžić and Mladić as well as Goran Hadžić (1958–), who was arrested in 2011 and is on trial for forcible transfer and murder of hundreds of Croats and non-Serbs from Croatia as well as torture during the detention of the survivors. All three will be tried by the ICTY, but appeals will be handled by the International Residual Mechanism for International Criminal Tribunals after ICTY shuts down at the end of 2014. Other cases involving Serbian defendants will be assigned to the courts in Belgrade.

ICTY has been developing important legal principles in the field of international criminal law. For example, to find a commander guilty of crimes committed by subordinates, a prosecutor must demonstrate not only **vicarious liability** but also **subjective awareness** or **aiding and abetting**. The tribunal also identified a new war crime – rape. The decision to make rape a crime reflected a widespread practice during the Bosnian Civil War.

Although not without its critics, ICTY has forced those in the former Yugoslavia to rethink the past. The tribunal has aided in reconciliation by enabling victims to ease their suffering by coming forward to share their stories and by disqualifying from political life those who committed heinous acts.

- **International Criminal Tribunal for the Prosecution of Persons Responsible for Genocide and Other Serious Violations of International Humanitarian Law Committed in the Territory of Rwanda and Rwandan Citizens Responsible for Genocide and Other Such Violations Committed in the Territory of Neighboring States, Between 1 January 1994 and 31 December 1994 (ICTR).** In Spring 1994, approximately 800,000 persons died in a civil war involving Hutus massacring Tutsis, and vice versa. The Security Council found no interest in intervening to stop the conflict. Instead, later that year, the Security Council drafted a statute for a tribunal to hear cases involving accusations of genocide inside Rwanda as well as any actions violating international law committed by Rwandans outside the country. Although the Rwanda government initially arrested at least 120,000 persons to be tried in traditional courts for lesser offenses, they released at least 68,000 because of prison overcrowding.

In 1998, the tribunal handed down the first-ever verdict by an international court on the crime of genocide, as well as the first-ever sentence for that crime. Jean-Paul Akayesu (1953–), mayor of Taba, was convicted and given a life sentence for participating in indiscriminate beatings, murders, and sexual violence on members of the Tutsi race who fled to his town for sanctuary. His case established the precedent that systematic rape is a form of genocide.

The most celebrated case involves former Prime Minister Jean Kambanda (1955–), who pled guilty and was sentenced to life imprisonment. He is the first head of state to be convicted of the crime of genocide by an international tribunal, which clearly rejected the **state immunity doctrine** that has often been invoked by governments to shield leaders from prosecution.

An unusual case involves "hate media." Three representatives of media that incited genocide were convicted in 2003 and are serving sentences from 30 to 35 years. Two broadcast from a radio TV station, the other wrote inflammatory articles in his magazine. The provision in the International Covenant for Civil and Political Rights banning propaganda for war, accordingly, has been interpreted to apply to civil violence.

As of 2012, only 98 were indicted, of which 72 were tried and found guilty by ICTR, though 16 are on appeal. Ten have been acquitted. Two died before trial. One case is ongoing, and nine accused persons are still at large. Four cases were referred to domestic courts. Many sentences are for life imprisonment, though three are for six years. In one case, the Reverend Athanase Seromba (1963–), a Catholic priest, was convicted of ordering Hutu militiamen to padlock and then to bulldoze his church, where 2,000 Tutsis were taking shelter from the militia; those who were not crushed to death were either hacked to death or shot dead. He is serving a 15-year sentence.

- **International Residual Mechanism for International Criminal Tribunals** (MICT). Both ICTY and ICTR lasted longer than anticipated. Concerned about the cost, in 2010 the Security Council voted to establish MICT as the final resting place for any cases remaining after both tribunals close. The transfer of ICTR cases to Arusha, Rwanda, began on July 1, 2012; nine persons are still at large though indicted, so their search will continue. ICTY cases devolved to MICT in The Hague on July 1, 2013.

- **International Criminal Court** (ICC). Both ICTR and ICTY demonstrated that trials of those guilty of unspeakable acts are preferable to pretending that nothing happened worthy of attention. But the existence of the two simultaneous war crimes tribunals, engaging in some jurisprudential duplication, suggested the need for a more permanent body. Accordingly, the Rome Statute of the International Criminal Court was adopted in 1998. After workshops around the world, jointly sponsored by Amnesty International and Human Rights Watch, ratifications increased, and the statute went into force in 2002.

Although 121 countries ratified the Rome Statute by 2012, some 32 countries signed the treaty but have not ratified. According to the Vienna Convention on the Law of Treaties of 1969, which went into force in 1980, signatory countries are obliged to refrain from "acts which would defeat the object and purpose" of the treaty unless they subsequently declare they do not intend to become a party to the treaty. Later, Israel, Sudan, and the United States "un-signed" the treaty. China, India, and 39 other countries have neither signed nor ratified: the higher a country's military expenditures, the less likely that a government will join ICC. Although a declaration of the Palestine National Authority accepted the jurisdiction of the court in 2009, the ICC Prosecutor declined to honor the declaration, considering that Palestine is not yet a state.

ICC immediately had jurisdiction over crimes against humanity, genocide, and war crimes committed after July 1, 2002. In 2017, the scope will include the crime of aggression, which was defined in detail in an amendment to the Rome Statute adopted in 2010 by the ICC's plenary body, the Assembly of States. The list of war crimes was expanded in the same resolution. The Rome Statute is innovative in identifying the "joint criminal enterprise" as a concept to identify liability of those who aid or abet human rights violations, applying the idea of conspiracy from the Nuremberg war crimes lexicon to crimes against humanity.

Cases, called **situations**, may be referred not only by the Security Council, but also by individual states or the ICC Prosecutor regarding charges of genocide, war crimes, or crimes against humanity. Only the most serious crimes, therefore, are under the court's jurisdiction. In both ICTR and ICTY, accused persons were subject to the **primacy principle**; that is, the two tribunals had exclusive jurisdiction and could overrule domestic courts. In contrast, ICC primarily operates on the basis of the **complementarity principle** – that is, to be charged with violations, a government must:

- o Ratify the ICC statute
- o Be unable or unwilling to handle relevant cases.

Governments can ask ICC to prosecute cases, either within their own jurisdiction or in other countries. The UN Security Council can refer cases of nonratifying countries to ICC, and the Prosecutor can also initiate cases. ICC is a court of last resort, though with an appeal tribunal.

To avoid having the ICC handle cases by default, many states have adopted legislation and established procedures to handle the crimes under the court's jurisdiction. An example is Britain's International Criminal Court Act, under which nearly a dozen British soldiers accused of torturing prisoners in Iraq were found guilty in London during 2005.

As early as September 2005, the Prosecutor had received more than 1,500 **communications**, as complaints are called, from more than 100 countries and thus had to prioritize which **situations** to pursue and how may **cases** to prosecute within each situation. The most numerous sources of complaints were from nongovernmental organizations in France, Germany, and the United States. Not all complaints have been made public.

Under seven circumstances, communications will not result in prosecutions:

- o Acts committed before the starting date of July 1, 2002, are inadmissible.
- o Countries that ratify the statute are exempt from ICC jurisdiction during their first seven years of membership.
- o Countries that do not ratify are exempt from prosecution.
- o The UN Security Council can stop an ICC prosecution for one year, thus allowing a political approach to resolve a problem.
- o The Pre-Trial Chamber, a three-judge panel, screens recommendations from the ICC Prosecutor to place individuals on trial.
- o When alleged war criminals are tried in their own countries, ICC is prohibited from playing a role based on the principle of the exhaustion of local remedies.
- o In practice, accepted complaints are about "clearly excessive" cases in terms of casualties.

Thus, the Office of the Prosecutor plays a central role, having the power to receive complaints, conduct preliminary analyses (with or without complaints), and then launch formal investigations, thus allocating plenty of prosecutorial discretion. The Prosecutor may decide to develop a case for trial, but a three-judge panel must first approve. After given permission, the Prosecutor makes indictments and handles cases in court until completion. On some occasions, the indictments are sealed but Interpol is notified that they are wanted for trial. As a solely judicial body, the ICC does not issue arrest warrants, which are instead handled by member states; instead ICC issues "summons to appear." ICC members, thus, collectively serve as the executive branch, operationally responsible for carrying out the orders of the court. When the accused are arrested and sent to ICC, they are placed in the detention center while awaiting trial. Those who aid the prosecution by presenting evidence, though they may be complicit in violations, are immunized from subsequent prosecution. If the accused are found guilty, they may be fined, forced to forfeit assets, or sentenced to prison. ICC does not operate a prison but instead negotiates with member states that are willing to place a prisoner in one or more of their penitentiaries.

Currently, the Office of the Prosecutor is conducting preliminary analysis for situations in Afghanistan, Colombia, the Republic of Korea, Georgia, Guinea, Honduras, Nigeria, and Palestine. Investigations are ongoing regarding Sudan (for the situation in Darfur), the Democratic Republic of the Congo, Uganda, the Central African Republic, the Ivory Coast, Kenya, and Libya.

ICC members, through the Assembly of States, select 18 ICC judges, who are organized into the Pre-Trial Division, the Trial Division, and the Appeals Division. They, in turn, elect three fellow judges to serve as President, First Vice President, and Second Vice President. The president is responsible for the administration of all units except the Office of the Prosecutor. The Office of Public Counsel for Defense operates independently of other offices. The Assembly of States elects a president, who presides over the Assembly and handles public relations for ICC.

Thus far, eight situations have been accepted for prosecution, with 30 indictments thus far. Uganda, the Democratic Republic of the Congo, and the Central African Republic referred situations within their countries to the court. The Security Council referred the situations in Darfur (Sudan) and Libya, though both involve non-states parties. The Prosecutor took the initiative in the other situations. Clearly, genocide has emerged as the top priority.

○ **Situation in the Congo.** The ICC Prosecutor first acted on situations referred by the governments of the Congo (Kinshasa) and Uganda, states that were experiencing or concluding civil wars. The Ituri region of the Congo, where four million died and others suffered sexual violence or torture from 1998–2002, initially caught the eye of the Prosecutor, who, in 2003, asked the government for permission to start ICC's first investigation. The Congolese government in Kinshasa agreed, and the investigation began during 2004. In 2006, following his indictment, the first Lord's Resistance Army (LRA) prisoner arrived at an ICC detention cell: Thomas Lubanga Dyilo (1982–), of the Democratic Republic of the Congo, was charged with forced recruitment of some 30,000 child soldiers, who accounted for about 30 percent of those in his militia. The *Prosecutor v. Dyilo* trial began in 2009; he was convicted in 2012, and sentenced to 8 years imprisonment (6 years in detention have been deducted from a total sentence of 14 years). Of the four other persons charged by the Prosecutor in connection with the Situation in the Congo, one was released by the Pre-Trial Chamber; the rest have been tried and await the verdicts.

○ **Situation in Uganda.** In 2003, Uganda's president asked ICC to take up the case of the LRA, which from 1986 was conducting a civil war in the north that involved 100,000 deaths, kidnapping of some 30,000 children, and amputations of limbs of adversaries, resulting in some 1.6 million refugees. In 2005, ICC authorized its first arrest warrants – for five LRA leaders, including the leader, Joseph Kony (1962–). Kony unsuccessfully tried to negotiate an end to the civil war in exchange for amnesty from ICC and Ugandan prosecution. The case of *Prosecutor v. Kony et al.* found Kony guilty of murder, enslavement, torture, rape, and sexual violence, and he was sentenced to life imprisonment though still at large. Based on a new Ugandan law, one of the accused was tried in a domestic court and found guilty. Having established a domestic legal procedure in Uganda, therefore, the remaining LAT leaders cannot be tried by ICC.

○ **Situation in Darfur.** From 2003–2006, some 200,000 Darfurians died and two million were driven out of their homes in the western part of Sudan by the Janjaweed, a militia believed to be supported by some in the Khartoum government. In 2004, the Security Council dispatched an International Commission of Inquiry to Darfur. The resulting report in 2005 recommended that the ICC prosecute at least 51 persons for acting with "genocidal intent" but absolved the Khartoum government of collusion with the Janjaweed. The government of Sudan then attempted to negotiate a political settlement rather than submitting the accused to the court's jurisdiction. After Washington's preference for another special court, similar to ICTR and ICTY, was strongly rejected, the American delegate abstained from the 11–0 Security Council vote to refer the cases to the ICC. In response, Sudan put two members of its armed forces on trial for the torture and killing of a Darfurian, and both were found guilty by the end of 2005.

Although Sudan has not agreed to ICC jurisdiction, the court has moved forward to file cases against several persons, the most famous of which is Sudan's President Omar Al-Bashir (1944–). His indictment marks the first time in history when a sitting head of state has been summoned for prosecution. He is one of four persons who are still at large. Three of those indicted, however, voluntarily surrendered to the court. Two were placed on trial, while the third was released by the Pre-Trial Chamber. Al-Bashir's indictment appears to have resulted in a softening of Sudan's policies in Darfur and South Sudan.

COURT CASE 10.2 THE INTERNATIONAL CRIMINAL COURT INDICTS OMAR AL-BASHIR (2008)

In 1989, Omar Al-Bashir (1944–) led a coup in Sudan and assumed the position of president. Although he inherited the country's civil war in South Sudan, his government ended the war in 2005 by granting limited autonomy to South Sudan, pending a plebiscite to be held at a later time. However, when a conflict broke out in Darfur, in the western part of the country, a government-sponsored militia entered the region and was accused of burning villages and slaughtering residents up to the border with Chad, causing the displacement of at least 2.5 million Darfurians. In 2008, International Criminal Court Prosecutor Luis Moreno Ocampo (1952–) indicted Al-Bashir of genocide, crimes against humanity, and war crimes. In March 2009, the ICC issued an arrest warrant for all counts but that of genocide. When Ocampo appealed, ICC issued a second warrant for all three charges, including genocide, during July 2010. Although both warrants were to be delivered to the government of Sudan, Al-Bashir dismissed the charges as did the African Union, the Arab League, China, the Non-Aligned Movement, and Russia. The first sitting head of state indicted by ICC, he remains in office and thus far has not been taken into custody while on trips to other countries.

○ **Situation in the Central African Republic.** In 2004 the government of the Central African Republic, which was concerned over atrocities committed in the unrest of 2002–2003 (an abortive coup and revenge violence against the coup leaders) that brought a new government to power, asked ICC to investigate. In 2007, after the ICC Prosecutor completed a preliminary analysis, an investigation was launched. In 2009, two charges of crimes against humanity and three charges of war crimes were filed against Jean-Pierre Bemba Gombo (1962–). The trial began in 2010.

○ **Situation in the Ivory Coast** (Côte d'Ivoire). The Ivory Coast's civil war, which began in 1999 and was presumed to have ended with a ceasefire in mid-2003, resumed at the end of 2004 amid reports of atrocities, death squads, and racial exclusion of Muslims in the north. The government in Abidjan asked for ICC intervention in 2005, but chaos in the country continued until UN-backed intervention in 2011. In 2011, the Pre-Trial Chamber authorized the ICC Prosecutor to investigate crimes committed since 2010, and by the end of the year President Laurent Gbagbo (1945–) was indicted, sent from the Ivory Coast to the ICC, and a trial was contemplated on the four counts of crimes against humanity. He is the first sitting president ever placed in custody pending a trial for an international crime. Meanwhile, in 2012, the Pre-Trial Chamber authorized an investigation into all crimes in the Ivory Coast from 2002 to 2010, so more cases are possible in the future.

○ **Situation in Kenya.** In 2010, the ICC Prosecutor began an investigation into events in Kenya from 2007, when protests after the national election escalated into ethnic violence, including destruction of property; almost 1,000 people were killed and nearly 600,000 were displaced, forced off their land to live with relatives elsewhere in the country. Six persons, indicted in 2011, voluntarily surrendered to the court that year. Four are scheduled for trial; charges for the other two were dismissed.

○ **Situation in Libya.** The UN Security Council asked ICC on February 26, 2011, to investigate whether any actionable crimes were committed from that date during Libya's Civil War. Subsequently, ICC indicted three persons with crimes against humanity (murder and persecution). One was the head of state, Muammar Gaddafi (1942–2011), whose charges were terminated on account of his death. The second person charged, Gaddafi's second son, Saif Al-Islam Gaddafi (1972–), was detained in Libya, which annoyed ICC by refusing to send him to The Hague, and planned instead to have a trial in Tripoli, though perhaps with some ICC involvement. The third, Gaddafi's intelligence chief, Abdullah Al-Senussi (1949–), was extradited from Mauritania, also for trial in Libya in 2012. Libya insisted on trying both men, as allowed under the Rome Statute, because ICC does not allow the death penalty.

○ **Situation in Kenya.** In 2013, Uhuru Kenyata (1961–) was indicted for murders, deportations, rapes and other forms of sexual violence, persecutions, and other inhumane acts against civilians during Kenya's 2011 election. He remains at large.

○ **Colombian Situation.** In 2005, Colombia asked ICC to look into its four-decade long civil war, involving guerrilla groups, right-wing paramilitaries, and even rebel units of the Colombian government that killed 120,000 persons through massacres, targeted assassinations, and kidnappings. Currently, the prosecutor is conducting a preliminary analysis, so technically the designation "Situation in Colombia" is premature.

Pressure from the United States, which is not a member of ICC, is behind Security Council resolutions that ask ICC to refrain from investigating and prosecuting persons involved in UN peacekeeping operations from nonratifying states. The United States has threatened to withhold funds from peacekeeping operations, fearing that Americans who participate might be arrested for an ICC trial. Israel is another country that has not supported the ICC; population transfers of Israelis into the Occupied Territories appear to be a violation of the Fourth Geneva Convention, which Tel Aviv has not ratified.

○ **Victims Trust Fund.** The Rome Statute created a second institution, the Victims Trust Fund, which is managed by a board of directors, for victims of crimes against humanity, either individually or collectively. Recalling the Conference on Jewish Material Claims Against Germany of 1951, the statute confers the right of victims to compensation, rehabilitation, and restitution. The Victims Trust Fund, which is administered at The Hague, operates independently of the ICC.

With the advent of the Rome Statute, the past culture of impunity is being replaced by a culture of accountability in regard to crimes against humanity, genocide, war crimes, and crimes against peace. Although the cases may serve retributive goals, ICC's primary aim is deterrence, though they appear to critics as "show trials." Compensating victims is one form of accountability, but there is a danger that judicial action, especially the prosecution of heads of state, will constitute lawfare – that is, the use of courts by one element in a country to gain partisan political advantage, thereby hindering reconciliation in regimes transitioning from authoritarian rule to democracies. Another danger is that those who committed violations, as was the case in the Tokyo War Crimes Trials, may be needed to rebuild the country. Courts in some developing countries have begun to prosecute their own human rights violators with various forms of international backing, as reviewed next.

DISCUSSION TOPIC 10.1 IS THE WORLD COURT OBSOLETE?

Only states can sue other states before the International Court of Justice (ICJ), which is known as the World Court. However, states often sue on behalf of individuals and corporations in their countries. Meanwhile, defendants before the International Criminal Court are individuals, who are held in custody for trial after their arrest. Should the World Court be abolished or revised to guarantee justice for individuals?

INTERNATIONALIZED NATIONAL COURTS

In a few cases, technical assistance by the United Nations has assisted countries to conduct their own proceedings. Six hybrid courts have been established thus far.[1]

• **Serious Crimes Unit** (SCU). In 1999, during the UN plebiscite of Timor-Leste (East Timor), Indonesian troops slaughtered 2,000 persons and burned homes, making 250,000 homeless. The United Nations Transitional Administration in East Timor, which was assigned to handle the change from Indonesian to East Timor rule, then set up a Crimes Scene Detachment to investigate cases. Accordingly, several of those involved have been tried in the capital, Dili. In 2000, the investigation continued as the SCU, and convicted 84 persons while acquitting three defendants. Indonesia, which has refused to hand over anyone for trial, has conducted 16 trials in Jakarta, convicting only one person out of 100 named by an Indonesia inquiry commission. Because UN officials considered the Indonesian trials to be shams, in 2005 Secretary-General Annan asked a special panel to investigate why more trials had not taken place. However, because of Indonesian objections, the Security Council failed to endorse the report, which recommended an international tribunal similar to ICTR and ICTY. Instead, in 2005, Timor-Leste and Indonesia established a joint truth commission but was unable to achieve consensus and disbanded three years later. Both countries agreed that their highest bilateral priority was to improve relations rather than dwell on the past. When the UN shut down the SCU in 2005, some 600 cases were pending.

- **Special Court for Sierra Leone**. Following a 10-year civil war, in 2000 the Sierra Leone government asked the UN Secretary-General for assistance in trying those who committed serious offenses. The UN Security Council then authorized negotiations, and the result was an agreement in 2002 to pursue "serious violations of international humanitarian law and Sierra Leonean law" through the Special Court for Sierra Leone. The UN Secretary-General appointed the chief prosecutor and 7 of the 11 judges. Thus far, 21 persons have been indicted for crimes against humanity and war crimes, including rape and other forms of sexual violence. Nine were convicted, three died, one was acquitted, and the most of the rest await trial.

In 2003, one of those indicted was Charles Taylor (1948–), the former dictator of Liberia, who brought war into Sierra Leone. He was charged with such offenses as forced recruitment of child soldiers, sexual slavery, and torture. Although he was granted asylum in Nigeria during 2003, the US Congress put a US$2 million bounty on his head, and the International Criminal Police Organization (Interpol) placed him on its Most Wanted list, issuing a "red notice" on him, indicating that any country had the right to arrest him for "crimes against humanity [and] grave breaches of the 1949 Geneva Convention." In 2006, Nigeria withdrew his asylum status. He was quickly captured and then transferred to Sierra Leone for trial on 17 counts of war crimes and crimes against humanity. Later in the year, the UN Security Council authorized his removal to the ICC in The Hague, where he was tried and convicted in 2012. He is serving a 50-year sentence.

COURT CASE 10.3 CHARLES TAYLOR CONVICTED OF WAR CRIMES (2012)

Rebel forces of Charles Taylor (1948–), which were trained in Libya, fought a civil war from 1989 that ended in 1996 with the overthrow of the Liberian government.

Continued

After Taylor won an election in 1997 to become president, he employed brutal methods. A second civil war arose in 1999, when the Liberians United for Reconciliation and Democracy force entered Liberia from the north, with support from the government of neighboring Guinea, to depose Taylor. Several competing ethnic groups then began to struggle to control the natural resources of the country. In 2003, a second rebel group, the Movement for Democracy in Liberia, moved into the country from the south. Soon, the capital, Monrovia, was besieged and bombarded. After the rebels and the government reached a peace agreement, Nigerian troops of the Economic Community of West African States entered as peacekeepers, Taylor resigned and was granted asylum in Nigeria. His vice president, Moses Blah (1947–), then continued to struggle against the rebels until 2003, when peacekeeping troops authorized by the UN Security Council replaced the Nigerian troops and installed a transitional government. Taylor loyalists were finally subdued in 2004, and elections were held in 2005. After winning the election, Ellen Johnson-Sirleaf (1938–) took office as president in 2006. Taylor, meanwhile, was indicted by the UN-established Special Court for Sierra Leone in 2003 for the crime of supporting rebels in that country whose tactics included mutilations, rape, forcing children to serve as soldiers, and committing other atrocities. After Taylor's election defeat in 2005, he was granted asylum in Nigeria. In 2006, when Nigeria appeared likely to arrest him pursuant to the indictment, he fled toward Cameroon, where he was arrested at the border. He was then transferred to Liberia, which asked the Special Court for Sierra Leone to request extradition. Rather than placing him on trial in Sierra Leone amid security concerns, the UN Security Council obtained permission from the International Criminal Court to use its facilities in The Hague for his trial. The trial, which began in 2007, concluded in 2012 with a guilty verdict, and Taylor was given a 50-year sentence.

• **Regulation 64 Panels**. The United Nations Mission in Kosovo (UNMIK) was established in 1999 to operate a civilian administration after the civil war, including a judicial branch with local personnel. In 2000, UNMIK adopted Regulation 64, which set up a panel of one international prosecutor, two international judges, and one local judge within the new court system for the specific purpose of trying those accused of war crimes. Each trial then draws upon a Regulation 64 Panel. By 2007, to handle the caseload, there were eight international prosecutors and eight international judges, but they were still swamped with business. Thus far, there have been at least 35 war crimes trials. Among those indicted for genocide is Dragan Nikolić (1957–), who persecuted Muslim, Kosovo, and other non-Serb detainees at the Sušica camp within Bosnia by subjecting them to inhumane living conditions, murder, rapes, severe physical abuse, and torture during 1992.

• **Court of Bosnia and Herzegovina** (Court of BiH). In 2002, the government of Bosnia and Herzegovina established the Court of BiH as a domestic court. The court has jurisdiction over the usual offenses of any national court, including war crimes, but because of the sensitive nature of the latter offenses, a decision was made to call upon international judges to serve in cases where possible local bias based on memories of the horrific Bosnian Civil War (1992–1995) would be counterbalanced. There are 16 international judges and 42 national judges. The international judges are appointed by the Office of High Representative, a body created by the Dayton Agreement of 1995 that ended the Bosnian Civil War, and consisting of representatives of seven European countries; seven Americans serve as alternates. Whereas ICTY has jurisdiction over high-level war criminals from that war, the Court of BiH has tried lesser offenders since operations began in 2005.

For example, in 2005 Gojko Janković (1954–) surrendered to Bosnian authorities and was sent to ICTY for trial, only to be returned to Sarajevo for trial before the Court of BiH. He was accused of issuing orders, aiding and abetting, and committing the following crimes against humanity: a large-scale and systematic attack on the non-Serb population in a municipality region that involved imprisonment, killing, and sexual abuse of non-Serbs, mainly Muslim women and young girls. The verdict in *Bosnia v. Janković* was guilty, and he is now serving a 34-year sentence. Several others have been tried for similar offenses.

- **Extraordinary Chambers in the Court of Cambodia for the Prosecution of Crimes Committed during the Period of Democratic Kampuchea** (ECCC). In 1997, Cambodia asked the UN to assist in forming a special tribunal to try those implicated in the wanton loss of more than one million persons from disease, exhaustion, and starvation as well as the liquidation of the educated population, Vietnamese residents, and others during the era of the Khmer Rouge (1975–1978). An agreement was concluded in 2003 and ratified by Cambodia's legislature in 2004, authorizing four trials with 17 Cambodian and 10 UN-appointed judges. In 2007, the first indictment was issued: Kaing Guek Eav (1942–), the official operating Tuol Sleng and other prisons, had already confessed to committing torture. He was given a 35-year sentence. Four former high-ranking Khmer Rouge officials were indicted in 2010 for the second trial, which began in 2011, though one was released in 2012 for mental health reasons. The trial of Nuon Chea and Khieu Samphan began in 2011 but stopped for lack of funds. Ieng Sary died in 2013.

- **Special Tribunal for Lebanon** (STL). In 2005, Lebanese Prime Minister Rafik Hariri (1944–2006) was assassinated along with almost two dozen persons. Suspects were rounded up, but later released for lack of evidence. The UN Independent Investigation Commission alleged involvement by the Syrian government as well as by the Syrian-backed Lebanese Muslim group, Hezbollah. The multiethnic country was poised on the edge of possible civil war when a majority in parliament voted in 2006 to establish an international tribunal to try the suspects. So angered were Hezbollah officials that they sponsored people power demonstrations to bring down the government. Nevertheless, the STL opened in 2009 in Leidschendam, a small town near The Hague. The UN Secretary-General appoints the judges; some are Lebanese, but most are international jurists. Instead of a trial based on international law, the trial will be based on Lebanese law; the offense, terrorism, has been defined at length by the court (see Chapter 7). Following an indictment in 2011, the court issued arrest warrants in 2012 for four senior members of Hezbollah, which has denounced the tribunal. As they have not been rounded up, they were tried *in absentia* beginning March 2013.

INTERNATIONAL CRIMINAL POLICE ORGANIZATION (INTERPOL)

Founded in 1923, Interpol serves an important role in tracking down violators of international law and criminals who escape from jurisdictions where they face criminal charges. Originally called the International Criminal Police Commission, with a headquarters in Vienna, the organization was hijacked by the Nazi government in 1938, whereupon other countries withdrew. In 1946, the organization began a rebuilding process, headquartered temporarily in Paris, until the adoption of a new constitution in 1956, which re-titled the organization. The permanent secretariat moved to Lyon, France, in 1989.

Interpol's constitution stipulates that "mutual assistance between all criminal police authorities [are to be] within the limits of the laws existing in the different countries and in the spirit of the 'Universal Declaration of Human Rights'." The constitution forbids Interpol "activities of a political, military, religious or racial character."

Currently, police organizations cooperate with one another within the Interpol framework to bring criminals to domestic and international courts. The priority areas of cooperation are fugitives, public safety and terrorism, drugs and organized crime, trafficking in human beings, and financial as well as high-tech crime. When international arrest warrants are referred to Interpol, the organization is required to put the named individuals on a watch list around the world. In 2005, Interpol agreed for the first time to place any persons or members of organizations subject to UN sanctions on a Special Notice list, including members of Al-Qaeda and the Taliban.

Interpol is also on the lookout for the US Central Intelligence Agency agents accused of kidnapping suspected terrorists without authorization within Germany, Italy, and Spain. In 2009, Italy convicted *in absentia* 23 CIA agents who kidnapped Osama Mustafa Hassan (1963–), an Egyptian imam who had been granted asylum by Italy, on a Milan Street in 2003 and flew him to Cairo, where he was tortured. If apprehended, they would face 7–9 years in prison; the house owned by one of the agents was impounded by the court. Italy's request to extradite the CIA agents has been denied by Washington, so Interpol is prepared to arrest them and send them to Italy to serve out their sentences.

ORGANIZATIONS CONCERNED WITH DISARMAMENT

War crimes would be committed if biological, chemical, or nuclear weapons were used in combat. Accordingly, three organizations have formed to enforce treaties on the subject.

• **International Atomic Energy Agency** (IAEA). Following the Atoms for Peace address to the United Nations by President Dwight Eisenhower (1890–1969) in 1953, the UN developed the text of the **Statute of the International Atomic Energy Agency** for signature in 1956. IAEA's work is threefold:

- Nuclear verification and security
- Safety of nuclear power
- Technology transfer of peaceful uses of nuclear material.

In 1970, the Treaty on the Non-Proliferation of Nuclear Weapons went into effect, empowering IAEA to verify nuclear-weapon-free zones, the dismantling of nuclear weapon facilities and material, as well as monitor countries, by site visits and other means, which are suspected of developing nuclear weapons. Any use of nuclear weapons has been determined to be a war crime.

During 2002, when American officials were asserting that Iraq had weapons of mass destruction, IAEA findings contradicted the claim, but Washington would not listen. Mohammed El-Baradei (1942–), then IAEA Director General, has argued that members of the administration of George W. Bush (1946–) should be tried for war crimes by the ICC.

• **Comprehensive Nuclear-Test-Ban Organization**. Following up the Treaty Banning Nuclear Weapon Tests in the Atmosphere, in Outer Space and Under Water (otherwise known as the Partial Test-Ban Treaty) of 1963 and similar agreements (see Table 7.8), the **Comprehensive Nuclear-Test-Ban Treaty** was adopted by the General Assembly in 1996 with overwhelming support but still has not gone into force, needing ratification by 44 countries. Since the treaty was adopted, nuclear tests have been conducted by India, Pakistan, and North Korea.

With the signing of the treaty, a body was immediately formed: the **Preparatory Commission for the Comprehensive Nuclear-Test-Ban Treaty Organization** (CTBTO), which will be superseded by Comprehensive Nuclear-Test-Ban Organization when three more countries with nuclear facilities ratify.

In 1997, a **Provisional Technical Secretariat,** led by the CTBTO **Executive Secretary**, was established to coordinate work as three operational, if still incomplete, programs were brought on line:

- The International Monitoring System, consisting of more than 300 seismic facilities around the world
- The Global Communications Infrastructure, which transmits seismic data to Vienna
- The International Data Center, where the data are collected and analyzed.

Any release of nuclear materials into the planet is a health risk. CTBTO tracked the global dispersion of nuclear debris after the tsunami hit Fukushima in 2011. When the treaty goes into force, on-site inspections will be possible.

• **Organization for the Prohibition of Chemical Weapons** (OPCW). According to the terms of the **Convention on the Prohibition of the Development, Production, Stockpiling and Use of Chemical Weapons and on Their Destruction,** OPCW began operation when the treaty went into force in 1997.

Under the treaty, dangerous chemical weapons are not to be developed, and existing stockpiles are to be destroyed. Chemical weapons destruction facilities exist only in Russia and the United States and are monitored by OPCW.

OPCW has the power to conduct inspections to verify compliance. Where states seek to comply, OPCW can provide technical assistance. If a state is alleged to fail to comply and negotiations are tried but unsuccessful, OPCW could send an on-site inspection team but has never done so.

WORLD TRADE ORGANIZATION (WTO)

Partly in the belief that high tariffs, which worsened the Great Depression, may have been a factor in the onset of World War II, the General Agreement on Tariffs and Trade (GATT) was signed in 1947 and went into effect in 1948. GATT then became the premier international forum to encourage free trade by regulating and reducing tariffs. Several rounds of negotiation for tariff reduction culminated in the Uruguay Round (1986–1994), which drafted the Agreement Establishing the World Trade Organization. In 1995, WTO superseded GATT, thereby becoming an important engine of economic globalization.

WTO satisfies the needs of export-oriented businesses to gain access to a worldwide market. However, an exclusive focus on trade issues meant that countries with sound environmental and humane labor standards suffered a competitive disadvantage. When disagreements arose about health issues, labor conditions, and pollution, WTO's dispute resolution tribunal initially ruled that such concerns were irrelevant. Accordingly, an unusually large protest greeted WTO's third Ministerial Meeting at Seattle in 1999.

WTO adherents, however, have pointed out that human rights concerns are discussed informally during WTO meetings. Since the global trade regime requires governmental transparency, the rule of law, and a middle class associated with increased entrepreneurs in developing countries, WTO rhetoric asserts that democratization is an inevitable consequence of free trade. WTO upholds several of the Millennium Development Goals, most particularly building a global partnership for development. WTO claims that such activities as the Aid for Trade Initiative and efforts to ensure access to affordable medicines are directed to the goal of eliminating extreme poverty and hunger.

At the Fourth WTO Ministerial Council in Doha during 2001, agreement was reached that trade rules should be adjusted so that less developed countries (LDCs) are on the same playing field to compete with developed countries. The resulting Doha Development Agenda has three goals:

- Increased LDC duty-free access to first developed countries
- Tariff reduction, especially on agricultural products, textiles, and clothing
- Reduction of trade-distorting subsidies by developed countries.

Progress toward the goals has been slow, as the very countries controlling WTO votes are the ones who would have to make concessions.

According to WTO, environmental, health, and labor issues are to be included in future trade agreements. Indeed, in 2006, after the European Union filed the first environmental complaint with WTO about Brazil's ban on importing used tires, Brazil countered that non-retreadable used tires lying around a country pose a health danger to its citizens.

Human rights concerns have been used to screen new members. China's admission into WTO during 2001 was conditioned on the establishment of a "rule of law," thus for the first time invoking human rights. Cambodia's admission in 2003 occurred only after Phnom Penh addressed several concerns, including the establishment of a judicial system where individuals and corporations could obtain a fair hearing. The right of minorities to participate in the economy was a screening criterion for Macedonia, Nepal, and Saudi Arabia.

WTO members can use the procedure of **non-application** to punish WTO applicants for their human rights practices, as El Salvador, Perú, and the United States have done. In the latter case, Washington denies trade privileges to countries that sponsor international terrorism.

Members can apply **waivers** to WTO obligations in cases where trade may exacerbate human rights abuses. Because of the exchange of diamonds for guns to fight civil wars in the Congo (Kinshasa), Liberia, and Sierra Leone, in 2003 some 50 WTO members adopted the **Kimberly Waiver**, which permits countries to prohibit the import of what are known as "blood diamonds" from all three countries. The European Union's trade preferences with its former colonies under the Cotonou Agreement also operate as a waiver. In addition, WTO has granted a waiver of obligations to ensure that nations can provide affordable medicines for their citizens under the public health exception. Although there are public morals and public order exceptions in the WTO founding agreement, no country has thus far used either provision.

HISTORIC EVENT 10.2 AN INTERNATIONAL CONFERENCE ADOPTS THE KIMBERLY PROCESS (2002)

In the 1990s, a black market trade in uncut diamonds from African countries brought guns to rebels in Angola, Congo (Kinshasa), the Ivory Coast, Liberia, and Sierra Leone. The rebels committed such human rights abuses as chopping off hands, raping women, and forcing children to fight in their armies. In 2000, following a conference of diamond-producing states in Kimberly, South Africa, the UN General Assembly called for a certification scheme so that purchases of the rough diamonds would no longer finance the various civil wars. Accordingly, a conference at Ottawa in 2002 established details of the Kimberly Process Certification Scheme whereby all diamonds sold worldwide must be certified to be not a part of the illicit "blood diamond" trade. The scheme began operation in 2003. However, the Republic of the Congo was expelled from the process in 2004, as was the Ivory Coast in 2005, because of uncertainties that their certifications were valid. Liberia was placed on the approved list in 2007 after being blackballed for five years. Venezuela withdrew from the process in 2008. Many independent observers believe that the scheme, though well intentioned, is a failure because of many false certifications.

WTO has a procedure to handle disputes. Thus far, of 369 disputes filed with WTO, only 159 have been heard by an expert panel and forwarded to the **Dispute Settlement Body**, which officially authorizes a settlement, subject to review before three members of the seven-member expert Appellate Body. The rest have been negotiated outside WTO, found inadmissible on procedural grounds, or are still being processed. WTO also provides conciliation, good offices, or mediation to the parties in dispute. If a country loses a case and refuses to comply with a ruling, WTO can authorize trade sanctions by all member governments against a recalcitrant country. The only disputes relevant to human rights are concerned with violations of intellectual property rights and patent infringements.

Nevertheless, the organization often condones delays in compliance with internationally established human rights standards. WTO still has a long row to hoe.

DISCUSSION TOPIC 10.2 HOW SHOULD THE WORLD TRADE ORGANIZATION BE REFORMED?

The World Trade Organization (WTO) tends to attract protests outside its various meetings. Why? If the WTO falls short in regard to human rights, as demonstrators allege, what reform(s) of the organization would be to their liking? Are the reforms reasonable? Feasible?

CONCLUSION

Treaty-based organizations sponsored by the United Nations have encouraged countries to comply with internationally recognized human rights standards. Although they have developed a subtle jurisprudence through their response to complaints, the various international courts are fulfilling the role of prosecuting and deterring human rights violations as well as establishing precedent-setting jurisprudence. Although the WTO initially focused on economic concerns, the organization is increasingly attentive to human rights concerns. Thus, the world community is well served by UN and non-UN organizations.

Nongovernmental tribunals can also identify legal issues, acting as truth commissions. "People's tribunals" have been held over the years when national and international courts have been silent on major violations of human rights. Some of the most famous are the following: (a) After the burning of the Reichstag in Berlin during 1933, a London-based tribunal exonerated those falsely accused. (b) When Leon Trotsky (1879–1940) was put on trial in the Soviet Union for treason, a people's tribunal acquitted him. (c) In 1967, Bertrand Russell (1872–1970) sponsored a war crimes trial about the American intervention in the Vietnamese Civil War. (d) More than two dozen people's tribunals have brought out information about war crimes committed by the United States in Afghanistan, Guantánamo, and the

Iraq War. (e) The Permanent Peoples' Tribunal, founded in during 1979 in Bolgna, Italy, has examined the cases of Afghanistan, Argentina, the Armenian genocide, the Brazilian Amazon, El Salvador, Eritrea, Guatemala, Nicaragua, Tibet, Timor-Leste, and Zaïre. In 1996, after the session of Permanent Peoples' Tribunal on Industrial Hazards and Human Rights in Bhopal, 1992, the Charter on Industrial Hazards and Human Rights was adopted. (f) Environmental tribunals have also been held, namely, the First and Second International Water Tribunals (1983, 2010), the Latin American Water Tribunal (1998–). (g) The Tokyo International Women's Tribunal (2000) was concerned with Japan's use of "comfort women" during World War II.

Nevertheless, when international action either is stymied by conflicting considerations or acts in a controversial manner, national governments and regional organizations have acted instead. Accordingly, Chapters 11–13 focus on efforts by the United States, by European countries, and within the Third World regions of the Americas, the Middle East, Asia and the Pacific, and Africa.

CHAPTER 11

American Approaches to International Human Rights

The United Nations and other international organizations can act on behalf of international human rights only when there is a wide consensus, so there is a lot of unfinished business in the struggle to promote human rights. What action can one country do to promote human rights at home and to discourage violations taking place in other countries?

What happens in one country may offend a sense of decency in other countries, but other states, individually or collectively, may prefer not to get involved. Geopolitics and domestic politics often trump concerns over human rights. The fluctuation between two poles – idealistic internationalism and self-concerned nationalism – means that American foreign policy is unpredictable abroad. Thus, pressure must be mobilized by nongovernmental organizations before human rights concerns will be trumpeted.

Nevertheless, the United States has often seen its role as promoting democracy and human rights on a worldwide basis, having shed blood in order to be released from colonial tyranny and to end the crime of slavery. The vast economic and military power of the United States, which can be quickly mobilized, often leads to punitive action. But American diplomatic, economic, legal, and military efforts have a long and venerable history, too. Similar to intergovernmental organizations, the United States has used four basic tools of statecraft (diplomatic, legal, economic/humanitarian, military) to have an impact on human rights problems abroad.

DIPLOMATIC AND VERBAL ACTIONS

Human rights concerns may be expressed through public statements, asylum and immigration policies, and diplomacy. Although relatively harmless, they may have expected and unanticipated consequences and involve proactive or punitive content.

Public Statements. One example of an American proactive verbal approach occurs when the president sends a congratulatory message to the winner of a democratic election in another country. Punitive statements may include formal or informal diplomatic protests, public statements of condemnation, publication of negative reports, declarations that a diplomat is *persona non grata*, and cancellations of cultural events, diplomatic meetings, or scientific visits.

But verbal protests can backfire. In 2003, a proposed resolution decrying the "genocide" of Armenians in Turkey during 1915–1917 was placed on the Congressional agenda. In response, Ankara threatened to close air bases to American aircraft and to cancel contracts for American weapons. Despite overwhelming support for the resolution, the proposal was removed from the agenda. Turkey, the third largest recipient of American military aid, buys 80 percent of its weapons from the United States, so profits turned out to be more important.

In 2005, then Secretary of State Condoleezza Rice (1954–) mentioned the word "democracy" 37 times during a speech in Egypt, seeking to encourage the government to hold free elections. Subsequently, the banned Muslim Brotherhood took to the streets, garnered 20 percent of the vote in later elections, and the government engaged in mass arrests of opposition demonstrators. Washington did not fully anticipate the crackdown resulting from her demarche. In 2007, Rice spoke in Egypt again, but without a single mention of the word "democracy." Then, in 2009, President Barack Obama (1961–) made another speech in Cairo, this time endorsing "governments that reflect the will of the people," knowing that an election would be held in Iran the following week but unaware that subsequent protests of official results in the streets of Tehran would occur, followed by a brutal crackdown.

Publication of human rights assessments in the US State Department's annual *Country Reports on Human Rights Practices* (1975–) can exert public pressure by identifying unacceptable abuses, though reports of allies may be less critical. Many elites in countries are quite sensitive to what the *Country Reports* say. Counter-elites may gain supporters as a result. However, a backlash is also possible. In 2005, Uzbekistan responded to human rights criticisms by rescinding approval for airplanes from the United States (and other members of the North Atlantic Treaty Organization) to land and to use the country's airspace.

Asylum. A common form of proactive human rights action is to grant diplomatic asylum to individuals who have left a country or fear to return home because they fear persecution. Settlers of Massachusetts found religious freedom in the 1600s, and Jews escaped ethnic discrimination in the 1930s by leaving Nazi Germany for America and elsewhere.

In 1996, the **Human Rights Restoration Act** afforded asylum to anyone abroad forced to undergo abortion or forced sterilization because of strict population control policies. Aimed at China, few have been granted asylum on that basis. In 1999, a West Hollywood man was granted asylum when he demonstrated that a return to China might result in severe punishment because he was openly gay, though by 2013 the climate in China appeared to have changed considerably.

Mass asylum through the acceptance of **refugees** occurred after World War II, when many persons fled Eastern Europe as Communist Party governments came to power. After more than 200,000 were admitted, Congress passed the **Displaced Persons Act** of 1948, and within two years over 400,000 refugees were admitted. Subsequently, the United States accepted those fleeing communist countries during the Cold War. The **Hungarian Refugee Act** of 1956 was adopted after a Soviet crackdown of dissidents in Budapest. When the United States withdrew from Indochina in 1975, some were resettled in the United States but others left on hazardous trips by boat to any port that would accept them; the **Refugee Act** of 1980 eased restrictions on their entry. Today, nearly 100,000 refugees are admitted each year.

Immigration. Different from granting asylum, an immigrant must apply for residency and await a determination that could last months or years. Every country regulates who can enter its borders. According to the Constitution, slaves could not be imported after 1808. The first immigration act to regulate the process was adopted in 1819. Thereafter, a few restrictions of various sorts were applied in what has been called "a nation of immigrants": the **Chinese Exclusion Act** of 1882, repealed in 1943, is the most famous. The **Anarchist Exclusion Act** of 1903 kept out terrorists and extreme radicals. The **Asiatic Barred Zone Act** of 1917 disallowed all immigration from Asia except from the Philippines. Although racial exclusions were abolished by the **McCarran–Walter Immigration Act** of 1952, smaller quotas from Asian countries remained until abolished by the **Immigration Act** of 1965. An unusual form of immigration is baby adoption. Currently, more than 160,000 Korean adoptees live in the United States, a program that began in 1955 to resettle orphans. Due to China's one-child policy, a second child may be put up for adoption, and more than 60,000 have come to the United States since 1990. Currently, more than 10 million persons reside in the United States illegally, sometimes because they were recruited by employers to work at jobs for which there was a labor shortage.

Deportation. After admission to the United States, illegal and legal immigrants may be deported or extradited. In 1978, US Congress added the **Holtzman Amendment** to the Immigration and Naturalization Act, providing that anyone who had genocidally "persecuted any person on the basis of race, religion, national origin, or political opinion" should be denied entry to the United States and deported if already admitted. The Office of Special Investigations (OSI) at the US Department of Justice was then set up to locate accused Nazi war criminals living in the United States and abroad. In 1983, OSI assisted in finding Klaus Barbie (1913–1991), who had been allowed to leave Europe by the US Army at the end of World War II. Known as the "Butcher of Lyon" for his role in rounding up Jews for execution during the war, he was tracked down in Bolivia, which turned him over for US$1 billion in cash and weapons to France, where he was tried and convicted.

In 2007, Gonzalo Guevara Cerritos (1963–), who had applied for asylum in the United States after entering the country illegally, was deported to El Salvador because he was a member of the death squad that killed six Jesuit priests in his native country during 1989 even though he had been granted amnesty by the El Salvador government in 1993. He is one of several persons who have been tracked down by the Federal Bureau of Investigation, which established a unit in 2003 to locate notorious human rights violators living in the United States. In 2011, he was indicted for the same crime in Spain, which then called for his arrest and deportation to Madrid for trial.

Usually a person who is deported is sent to his country of former citizenship or residence. After 9/11, hundreds of persons who had been served orders of deportation, who had not left voluntarily, were rounded up and sent home without hearings. The **Foreign Affairs Reform and Restructuring Act** of 1998, however, bans deportation or extradition to any country that is deemed likely to torture the person.

Asylum policy and immigration policy, however, can be counterproductive from a human rights standpoint, since those who flee from persecution are no longer on the scene to struggle against the errant country. Although decisions to grant asylum and to permit immigrants fall within a complex and worthy area of domestic and international law, the pressure on offending countries is minimal.

Diplomacy. There are two forms – quiet diplomacy and public diplomacy. **Quiet diplomacy**, sometimes known as **constructive engagement**, consists of bilateral diplomatic conversations in which complaints are brought up without informing the press. Through quiet diplomacy, the United States has asked for specific persons to be released from the prisons of China and other countries. The effectiveness of quiet diplomacy, however, seldom results in major policy changes. America's "constructive engagement" with *apartheid* South Africa during the 1980s, for example, achieved nothing substantial.

Public Diplomacy uses publicity to project a country's foreign policy abroad. Highly publicized diplomatic meetings may serve to pressure countries to make positive responses, though lower-level diplomats can rarely make concessions on the spot. When America was one of the world's major powers, President Theodore Roosevelt (1858–1919), eager for a world court to settle disputes, called for the Second Hague Conference of 1907, but establishment of such a court did not occur until after World War I.

The form of public diplomacy known as the **summit conference** brings together government heads who can directly make compromises on important issues, with journalists in the wings eager to report progress. Negotiations between President Ronald Reagan (1911–2004) and Soviet Union's Party Secretary Mikhail Gorbachëv (1931–) in the 1980s eventually yielded such tangible results as the Intermediate-Range Nuclear Forces Treaty of 1987 and the Strategic Arms Reduction Treaty (START). The latter was signed by Reagan's successor George H. W. Bush (1924–) in 1991 and renewed in 2010 by President Barack Obama.

In 1982, Holocaust survivor, Tom Lantos (1928–2008), was elected to Congress. When he started work in 1983, he immediately took steps to form the bipartisan Human Rights Caucus within Congress. The Caucus, which became the Tom Lantos Commission on Human Rights upon his death, held many hearings over the years to identify human rights problems around the world. The hearings often goaded presidents to take action.

Punitive Diplomacy can range from a temporary recall of an ambassador, to an expulsion of a diplomat, to a boycott of another country's special event in order to show displeasure of a country's policies. One extreme form is suspension of diplomatic relations. The United States has had no direct diplomatic relations with Iran since personnel at the American embassy in Tehran were held hostage from 1979–1981. Perhaps the most famous cultural boycott occurred when the United States protested the Soviet invasion of Afghanistan in 1979 by refusing to send athletic teams to compete in the Moscow Olympics of 1980. President Jimmy Carter (1924–) was particularly annoyed when the invasion took place soon after he received personal assurances from Soviet leader Leonid Brezhnev (1906–1982) that Soviet troops massed on the Afghan border were not part of an invasion force. The Soviet Union reciprocated by boycotting the Olympic Games held in Los Angeles, California, in 1984.

Coercive Diplomacy, which may seem an oxymoron, occurs when a state attempts to pressure another state by threatening to impose economic or military sanctions. To be effective, the threats must be clear and severe. Otherwise, bullying may stiffen the resolve of a government to continue to violate human rights. For example, American coercive diplomacy was applied to the former Yugoslavia in the late 1990s in order to stop Serbian forces from massacring the majority Albanian population in Kosovo, then a province within Yugoslavia. When Belgrade ignored the threats, an intense bombing campaign on Serbia ensued in 1999 until President Slobodan Milošević (1941–2006) agreed to peace terms.

LEGAL ACTION

Throughout much of human history, conflicts between states have been settled by wars. The United States has used courts, legislation, and treaties to resolve international disputes.

In 1704, the Treaty of Amity, Commerce, and Navigation Between Britain and the United States set up three commissions to resolve claims arising from the Revolutionary War. In 1871, the Treaty of Washington between the two countries set up a five-member arbitration panel to resolve claims about Britain's violation of neutrality during the American Civil War. The panel had representatives from Britain, Brazil, Italy, Switzerland, and the United States. Throughout the nineteenth century, the United States tried to establish arbitration of commercial disputes in the texts of many bilateral trade treaties.

At the First Hague Conference of 1899, the United States lobbied for a world court, and the Permanent Court of Arbitration was established. American initiatives resulted in the Permanent Court of International Justice (PCIJ), created after World War I, and the International Court of Justice (ICJ) set up after World War II. Although the United States did not appear before PCIJ, Washington has been the most active defendant before ICJ, provoking conservatives in the United States to be skeptical of the value of the court. Some of the 20 cases involving the United States were reviewed in Chapter 9. The case against Iran for holding American diplomats hostage from 1979 to 1981 was won but with no effect on Tehran. Cases against the United States have often forced the federal government in Washington to ask indulgence when local authorities fail to abide by international standards in the treatment of foreigners convicted of crimes, as violations of treaty obligations by states and counties embarrass the country.

The indispensable role of Eleanor Roosevelt (1884–1962) in the adoption of the Universal Declaration of Human Rights during 1948 was a high point in the American quest to establish human rights as a major goal of foreign policy. The concept of human rights as a universal norm justified prosecution of Nazis in the Nuremberg Trials, which took place in American-occupied Germany. But the United States has refused to join the International Criminal Court (ICC).

The prosecution of domestic offenders for crimes with universal jurisdiction committed abroad can take place in national courts of the United States, thereby exercising **extraterritorial jurisdiction**. There are four ways to do so under American law:

- Some offenses are prohibited under the American Constitution.
- **Treaties** can authorize prosecution of certain crimes committed abroad.
- **International custom**, that is, long-standing practices respected by many states, constitute standards under international law that may not be contained in a specific law or treaty.
- **Legislative acts** may also establish the competence of American courts to try perpetrators of human rights violations committed abroad.

In regard to the first source, the American Constitution called upon Congress to define international crimes, particularly piracy. In 1804, the Supreme Court ruled in *Murray v. The Charming Betsy* (6US64) that American laws "ought never to be construed to violate the law of nations…" Nevertheless, in *Reid v. Covert* (1957) the court ruled (354US1) that the Constitution takes precedence over treaty obligations. In the latter case, an American citizen working for the US military was court-martialed for murder based on a treaty with Britain. However, the court ruled that the Constitution requires civilian American citizens to be tried in civilian courts.

Treaties, the second source of extraterritorial jurisdiction, are declared by the Constitution to be the "supreme law of the land" when ratified by two-thirds of the Senate. Treaties may prevail over acts of Congress, executive orders, laws of the states, and even previous court decisions, provided that the treaties are both self-executing and "last-in-time." A **self-executing treaty** specifies implementation procedures. The **last-in-time** standard means that a later treaty supersedes an earlier treaty. However, few treaties ratified by the Senate are considered self-executing, and the United States has ratified very few human rights treaties. Senators, representing states, are reluctant to concede any rights of sovereignty to the federal government, including treaties that might impinge on state laws.[1] Even when senators agree to ratify a treaty, interpretations in the form of **reservations** are often attached to the treaty.

International custom, the third basis for prosecuting human rights violations, has been cited as a back-door approach to advance human rights. Judges presented with lawsuits often find authority for their decision in common international practices. An early example of the use of international custom in deciding a case is the *Paquete Habana* (1900). The Supreme Court ruled that international custom dating from 1403 exempted civilian vessels from becoming prizes of war and went on to say that "the federal judiciary has the authority to invalidate executive action that runs counter to customary international law."

COURT CASE 11.1 THE *PAQUETE HABANA* (1900)

On March 25, 1898, a small fishing boat licensed under Spanish law named the *Paquete Habana* left Havana for 25 days of fishing with a crew of three Cubans. En route back to Havana, the Spanish–American War broke out. The vessel was seized by the American gunboat, *Castine*, as a prize of war, towed to Key West, Florida, and later sold for US$490. A second vessel was similarly captured and sold for US$800. After the owners sued to recover their lost assets, the US Supreme Court (175US677), based on customary international law, ruled that proceeds of the sales should be restored to the owners and crew of both ships.

When the United States was an international underdog, courts stressed international law and custom to establish a legal framework with an equal playing field for all governments. As international topdog, however, the Supreme Court has increasingly cited international law as just one among several reasons for rulings. Today, some Supreme Court justices strongly object to any invocation of international law, arguing that provisions in treaties are subordinate to state and national legislation.

Legislative measures are the fourth basis for claiming extraterritorial jurisdiction. About two dozen laws have been used in American courts to bring foreign human rights violators to justice (Table 11.1). Their provisions are summarized next.

Implementing the Constitutional mandate to define crimes against the laws of nations, in 1789 Congress passed a comprehensive Judiciary Act in part to provide a legal basis not only for trying pirates in American courts but also to deal with the press-ganging of American sailors by the British navy. One provision, now known as the **Alien Tort Claims Act** (ATCA), gives federal courts "original jurisdiction of any civil action by an alien for a tort … committed in violation of the law of nations or a treaty of the United States." The term "tort" refers to a deliberate act that causes injury to a person, including torture and death, although torts ordinarily involve civil suits between private individuals where monetary damages are sought from an aggrieved person. Specifically, ATCA permits aliens to file suit in federal courts for torts that either violate customary international law for which there is a universal jurisdiction or for violations of a treaty ratified by the United States.[2]

The earliest ATCA case came in *Bolchos v. Darrel* (1795), when a French privateer brought a district court suit (3FCas810No.1,607) in South Carolina to settle a dispute over the rightful ownership of African slaves seized from a British ship on the high seas. Thus, a foreigner sued a foreigner, the shipowner, utilizing ATCA. In 1820, the Supreme Court allowed the federal government to prosecute a pirate on the grounds that piracy on the high seas was an international crime in *US v. Smith* (18US53). Yet in 1812, the Supreme Court held in *The Schooner Exchange v. M'Faddon* (7Cranch116) that an American court lacked jurisdiction over a foreign armed ship that docked in an American port.

What if private persons, domestic or foreign, want to sue government officials for wrongful actions? According to the **act-of-state doctrine**, which the Supreme Court has traced to 1674, a private person cannot sue a government executive for an official act. Thus, in *Underhill v. Hernández*, the Supreme Court (168US250) ruled in 1897 that an American citizen could not sue General José Manuel Hernández, (1853–1921), the Venezuelan government head, for refusing to grant him an exit visa until he finished a construction contract. The reason for the denial of the suit was that Hernández's action was an "act of the government" as head-of-state. In effect, the **head-of-state doctrine** was advanced as having even more immunity than a simple "act-of-state."

Ordinarily, the US State Department is accorded deference by the courts when foreign policy and national security would be adversely affected by litigation, so the government as defendant will invoke "states secrets" or "national security" grounds to have a court dismiss a case. Yet an exception to the act-of-state doctrine arose during 1947. In *Bernstein v. Van Heyghen Frères Société Anonyme*, a case involved a person whose property was confiscated by the German Nazi government because he was Jewish. The Appeals Court ruled (163F2d246) that the act-of-state doctrine does not preclude litigation against a sovereign state when the US Department of State unambiguously certifies to a court that prosecution of a case can go forward without complicating the inherent ability of the executive branch to conduct foreign relations. In 1947, Germany was militarily occupied by the United States and three other victorious allied powers therefore could not object.

American courts have held insurance companies liable for payments when foreign governments have nationalized properties without just compensation; the apparent reason is that private contractual obligations (as in an insurance policy) can never be nationalized. In 1965, however, the Supreme Court (376US398) denied a legal remedy when property was nationalized by the Cuban government under Fidel Castro (1926–) in *Banco Nacional de Cuba v. Sabbatino*. Sabbatino Corporation, a company in Cuba mostly owned by American investors for wholesale sugar purchases, believed that the Cuban government offered insufficient compensation. But, according to the act-of-state doctrine, the company could not sue Cuba.

The *Sabbatino* case rankled Washington. In 1976, Congress passed the **Foreign Sovereign Immunities Act** (FSIA), replacing the act-of-state doctrine with the doctrine of **sovereign immunity**. According to the new law, most acts by foreign governments are still immune from prosecution by private persons in the United States, but two exceptions were identified beyond the *Bernstein* case:

- Insufficient compensation of the property of an American that is nationalized by a foreign government
- Commercial operations by a foreign state with direct effects on operations in the United States.

The second exception was clarified in 2000, when the Supreme Court ruled in *Dole v. Patrickson* (538US468) that a subsidiary of an American corporation did not have sovereign immunity protection even though the foreign government owned majority shares.

FSIA provides another exception – (3) when a foreign state waives immunity. The waiver can be explicit or implicit. An implicit waiver exists if a foreign state (a) agrees to arbitration in another country; (b) agrees that a contract is governed by the laws of another country; or (c) the foreign state participates in a court case without raising the immunity defense.

The ATCA of 1789 was largely forgotten for most of the nineteenth and twentieth centuries, but a landmark case in 1980 established two more exceptions to the sovereign immunity doctrine. In *Filártiga v. Peña-Irala*, an Appeals Court (630F2d876) decided (4) that a foreign government official can be prosecuted for violating a law of that government. Since torture was a violation of Paraguay's constitution, the torturer (Norberto Americo Peña-Irala) was liable as a resident of the United States. The court ordered him to pay compensation to plaintiffs who were American residents, though he was instead deported as an illegal alien. In the same ruling, the court stated (5) that there is no immunity for a crime with universal jurisdiction, since "the torturer has become like the pirate and slave trader before him … an enemy of all mankind."

From the 1970s, various nongovernmental organizations identified as many as 7,000 human rights violators and their victims living in the United States, so a hunt for other criminals ensued after *Filártiga*, which spawned more than 40 efforts to utilize ATCA in American courts. Most ATCA cases have begun as damage suits in federal trial courts; appeal courts have then been asked to clarify the scope of applicability of the law.

However, in *Argentina v. Amerada Hess Shipping Corporation* (1989), the doctrine of sovereign immunity was invoked to trump ATCA. The effect was to deny US$11.9 million in damages for Argentina's bombing of a neutral American oil tanker under Liberian registry during the Anglo-Argentine War of 1982, when Argentina took military action to annex the British-controlled Falkland Islands that Buenos Aires insisted on naming the Malvinas Islands. As a military action, Argentina was obviously committing an act-of-state.

To clear up any confusion regarding *Filártiga* and similar cases, Congress passed the **Federal Employees Liability Reform and Tort Compensation Act** in 1988, the **Anti-Terrorism** Act of 1990, the **Torture Victim Protection** Act (TVPA) of 1991, and a 1994 amendment to the Foreign Relations Authorization Act. The 1988 law stated that public employees cannot be charged on the basis of ATCA. The 1990 statute enables victims of terrorist acts to collect damages from private persons who aid or commit terrorist acts, as does the 1998 amendment, and the **Torture Victims Relief** Act of 1998.

TVPA, an amendment to the FSIA, covers acts abroad involving "severe pain or suffering" to obtain information from a person in custody, including threats to torture or to kill that person. TVPA permits a lawsuit against a torturer who resides in or is traveling throughout the United States by a victim of that torture, provided that the torture has occurred in the previous 10 years and legal remedies in the other country have been exhausted.

Filártiga found a noncitizen to be liable under ATCA. But in 1992, an appeals court, for the first time, ruled that a foreign government violated ATCA. The case is *Siderman de Blake, v. Argentina* (965F2d 699). By participating in an American court case as a plaintiff to sue Sideman de Blake, Argentina had waived its sovereign immunity for a subsequent lawsuit.

COURT CASE 11.2 *SIDERMAN DE BLAKE V. ARGENTINA* (1992)

José Siderman de Blake was arrested and tortured in 1976 during a coup in Argentina. Subsequently, his property was seized. In 1982, after fleeing to the United States and becoming an American citizen, Siderman and members of his family filed suit against Argentina for torture and illegal expropriation, whereupon Argentina countersued to obtain more of his property, thereby waiving immunity from prosecution. Although Siderman won his case in court, Argentina decided to compensate him out of court, a settlement that could be as high as US$6 million. (Specific details were not released by either party.) Significant aspects of the case are that the US Appeals Court recognized state torture as a crime with universal jurisdiction and that Argentina implicitly waived sovereign immunity by responding to Siderman's lawsuit.

In *Saudi Arabia v. Nelson* (1993), however, the Supreme Court (507US349) denied Scott Nelson, an American citizen, a remedy for being subjected to torture, a forced confession, and inhumane prison treatment (starvation) while he was detained by Saudi Arabian police for allegedly using a fake diploma to get a job. Nelson's mistreatment was a form of retaliation for his repeated complaints about defective oxygen and nitrous oxide lines as fire hazards that endangered patients at a government hospital, King Faisal Specialist Hospital in Riyadh, but the doctrine of sovereign immunity was the basis for the dismissal of the case.

The Senate ratified two important human rights treaties at this point. In 1988, following the ratification of the Convention on the Prevention and Punishment of the Crime of Genocide, Congress passed the Genocide Convention Implementation Act to criminalize acts of genocide or incitement to genocide. In 1994, following ratification of the Convention Against Torture and Other Cruel, Inhuman or Degrading Treatment or Punishment, Congress amended TVPA to permit a victim of torture to collect compensatory damages from a torturer. And, in 1996, Congress banned any extradition to countries that practice torture in the Foreign Affairs Reform and Restructuring Act.

One of the most famous cases was then litigated under ATCA and TVPA, with implications for the Genocide Convention Implementation Act. In 1995, Radovan Karadzić (1945–), the political leader of the Serbian faction during the Bosnian Civil War (1992–1995) and later President of Republika Srpska, was assessed damages for US$745 million in *Kadić v. Karadžić* (70F3d232) for having **command responsibility** in the torture of 15 Bosnian women. Although the amount has not been collected, the case was the first time a head of a government had been sued for an official act though he was tried *in absentia*.

Soon after the *Karadžić* case, the **Anti-Terrorism Act and Effective Death Penalty Act** of 1996 carved out even more exceptions to the sovereign immunity doctrine, authorizing "money damages ... against a foreign state for personal injury or death" caused by or complicit with (6) extrajudicial execution, (7) hijacking, (8) hostage taking, (9) sabotage, and (10) torture.

The Anti-Terrorism Act and Effective Death Penalty Act also banned terrorists from entering the United States. In 1987, Dr Orlando Bosch Ávila (1926–2011), responsible for the bombing of a Cuban airplane during 1976 and other criminal offenses, entered Miami while on parole from Venezuela for a minor charge. Although arrested for violating his Venezuelan parole, not for terrorism, he was pardoned in 1990 by President George H. W. Bush and lived in the United States until his death. Bush agreed with his opposition to the Cuban government.

Whereas the Anti-Terrorism Act of 1990 allowed victims to file damage lawsuits against individuals responsible for or complicit with terrorist acts, Congress amended FSIA in 1997 by passing the **Flatlow Amendment**, named after an American who was killed in an Iranian-financed terrorist attack during 1995 in the Gaza Strip, then occupied by Israel. The amendment expanded the list of exceptions to the sovereign immunity doctrine to include (11) personal acts of "an official, employee, or agent of a foreign state designated as a state sponsor of terrorism," but the government itself could be held liable. Plaintiffs then prevailed in two cases during 1997: in *Alejandre v. Cuba* (996FSupp1239), involving two civilian airplanes shot down by Cuba in international waters during 1996, and in *Flatlow v. Iran* (999FSupp1). The latter case then resulted in a judgment during 1998 for US$225 million. However, Cuban and Iranian assets, which had been confiscated on account of prior legislation, were not disbursed by the American government, which claimed that the court action hampered diplomacy by the executive branch.

What about corporations? Union Oil of California (Unocal) was also involved in an ATCA-related case. The lawsuit, *Doe v. Unocal*, was filed in 1996 by the Washington-based International Labor Rights Fund on behalf of 15 young female ethnic Karen farmers from Myanmar (formerly Burma), then living as refugees in Thailand, who claimed that they were enslaved by the Myanmar government to haul heavy loads, while cutting through thick jungle, and to grow food in connection with construction of a US$1.2 billion natural gas pipeline. The women, forced to work for free, alleged that several laborers were killed by soldiers guarding the pipeline, and two said that they were raped. In 2002, an appeals court ruled in *Doe v. Unocal* (395F3d140) that ATCA allowed foreigners to sue an American corporation in an American court for **vicarious liability**, that is, for not stopping human rights violations on the part of a subcontractor (the government of Myanmar). In 2005, Unocal settled out of court; the monetary award was not made public.

Some ATCA cases have served to discourage corporations from locating plants in countries with poor human rights records and to adopt codes of corporate conduct. In 2002, Gap, and 48 other clothing manufacturers, settled cases involving sweatshops in Saipan, Northern Marianas. Cases against other corporations under ATCA have not always had sufficient proof to go forward (e.g. *Sarei v. Rio Tinto, Presbyterian Church of Sudan v. Talisman Energy, Sinaltrainal v. Coca Cola, Bowoto v. Chevron*). More than one hundred corporations have been sued for their vicarious liability in doing business with the *apartheid* government of South Africa.

From 2001, during the presidency of George W. Bush (1946–), government lawyers sought to minimize ATCA's scope. Accordingly, a district court (346FSupp2d538) dismissed several such cases (*In re South African Apartheid Litigation*) in 2004 at the urging of the US Department of State. Although some cases were later reinstated on appeal, *Khulumani v. Barclays* and *Ntsebeza v. Daimler* remain in legal purgatory because four members of the Supreme Court have financial interests in some of the corporations, therefore denying the possibility of a quorum to decide the case.

An important test of the ability of private persons to sue government officials for damages came in 2003, when former Salvadoran Air Force Captain Alvaro Rafael Saravía was found living in Modesto, California. Reliably suspected of involvement in assassinating Archbishop Óscar Romero (1917–1980) of El Salvador, a relative of Romero filed suit against him. After, papers were served on his residence while he was not at home, but he disappeared, presumably returning to El Salvador. In 2004, in *Doe v. Saravía* (348FSupp2d1112), a judge found him liable *in absentia* and ordered to pay US$10 million in compensatory and punitive damages to the relative. The El Salvador government, not wanting to revisit El Salvador's "dirty war" of the 1980s, refused to pursue the matter.

COURT CASE 11.3 *ÁLVAREZ-MACHAÍN V. UNITED STATES* (2004)

In 1990, a federal grand jury indicted a Mexican physician, Dr Humberto Álvarez-Machaín, for his alleged role in the torture and death of a Drug Enforcement Agency (DEA) official during 1985. After the Mexican government refused to assist in arresting the physician pursuant to a warrant, the DEA's deputy director hired José Francisco Sosa (1947–), a Mexican police officer, and five bounty hunters, who kidnapped him in Guadalajara and brought him to California for trial. México then objected to the abduction, which circumvented normal extradition procedures. Although the Supreme Court (504US655) ruled in *US v. Álvarez-Machaín* that his trial could go forward despite his arbitrary arrest, the trial court exonerated him in 1992, as jurors accepted his explanation that he was merely present as a medical officer during the DEA agent's ordeal. Accordingly, in 1993 Álvarez-Machaín sued Sosa, five DEA agents, and the five bounty hunters in District Court (331F3d610), where he won US$25,000 in damages on account of the emotional distress suffered during his arrest and detention. Sosa then appealed the case, lost in Appeals Court (266F3d1045 and 331F3d641) during 2003, and went to the Supreme Court, hoping to be exonerated on the basis of the headquarters doctrine – namely, that he was not liable for what his boss ordered him to do. In 2004, the Supreme Court rejected the headquarters

Continued

doctrine defense, but nevertheless ruled in *Sosa v Álvarez-Machaín* that DEA's action in México to detain him for a single day did not constitute an offense actionable against the United States under the Federal Tort Claims Act of 1946, or the extradition treaty with México. Sosa, thus, did not have to pay damages.

In 2004, the Supreme Court (124SCt2739) noted in *Sosa v. Álvarez-Machaín* that ATCA was intended to apply to "violations of the law of nations," that is, offenses in common law, including international custom. Specifically, the court cited claims regarding commercial trade (such as prize captures) as well as "violation of safe conducts, infringement of the rights of ambassadors, and piracy" as offenses recognized under international law. Hence, the ruling took note of a very limited scope of ATCA as of 1789, left uncertain which future claims brought under ATCA would be upheld in American courts, but approvingly cited the *Filártiga* case and thus did not accept a minimalist interpretation of ATCA. The Sosa case left open the question whether the law could apply to American officials.

In 2005, *Linde v. Arab Bank* (384FSupp2d571) alleged that Arab Bank, based in Amman, Jordan, publicly advertised a fundraising appeal to support those who had been committing terrorist acts inside Israel. Defendants in *Linde* include some 700 persons in 11 countries, including American citizens. But the bank has refused an order to produce relevant records, and the case was dismissed.

Two cases were then filed against Secretary of Defense Donald Rumsfeld (1932–) before he left office at the end of 2006. In *Ali v. Rumsfeld* and *Vance v. Rumsfeld*, the contention was that Rumsfeld was responsible for their torture while under American confinement in Afghanistan and Iraq. The *Ali* case, involving Afghans and Iraqis, was rejected on appeal in 2011. *Vance*, filed by two American contractors in Iraq, was dismissed in 2012. The sovereign immunity doctrine was cited in both cases.[3]

Nevertheless, when Rumsfeld visited Paris in 2007, his arrival at Charles de Gaulle airport alerted authorities of his presence in the country. A prisoner once held at Guantánamo had filed suit with a French magistrate against him for his mistreatment. While gendarme were posted outside the place where he was breakfasting, waiting for him to depart so that they could arrest him, he was secretly whisked out of the country and flown back to the United States from Germany. Similarly, George W. Bush accepted an invitation to give a talk in Switzerland in 2011 but cancelled on learning that a court complaint was ready for filing in that country upon his arrival in Geneva. Efforts to prepare legal action against American high-level officials were also ongoing in Spain in the waning years of the Bush presidency, but they were never issued, evidently because of intervention by the new president, Barack Obama. Cases in Europe against Bush and Rumsfeld were filed on the basis of the Convention Against Torture and Other Cruel, Inhuman or Degrading Treatment or Punishment, not American law.

Nevertheless, one related case was successful. In 2007, Italy charged 22 Central Intelligence Agency (CIA) officials and five Italian collaborators with capturing Osama Moustafa Hassan Nasr (1963–) on the streets of Milan during 2003 for "extraordinary rendition" to Egypt, where he was tortured. In 2009, the court convicted the CIA officials *in absentia*. Now international fugitives, they have been ordered to pay compensation to the victim and will be imprisoned if ever extradited to Italy.

In 2006, Charles MacArthur Emmanuel (1977–), the son of Charles Taylor (1948–) who is under indictment by the ICJ, arrived at Miami airport, whereupon he was arrested for conspiracy to torture. In 2009, he was sentenced to 97 years in prison. Using ATCA, five of his victims sued him (*Kpadeh v. Emmanuel*), and in 2010 won the case. Damages, never collected, were assessed at over US$22 million.

In 2007, a case based on ATCA was filed against the Internet company, Yahoo!, which told the Chinese government in 2003 that Chinese dissidents were exchanging pro-democracy information, calling for an end to one-party rule, on their Yahoo! accounts on the Internet. Although the Bush administration tried to get the case dismissed, hoping for a ruling that no corporation would be liable under ATCA, the judge agreed to hear the case. Yahoo! then settled *Wang Xiaoning v. Yahoo!* out of court. Yahoo! not only agreed to provide an undisclosed amount to the plaintiffs but also agreed to "provide 'financial, humanitarian and legal support to these families' and create a separate 'humanitarian relief fund' for other dissidents and their families." In 2012, Wang Xiaoning (1950–), one of those convicted from Yahoo!-supplied evidence, was released from a Chinese prison after serving a 10-year sentence for "incitement to subvert state power." His co-plaintiff, Shi Tao (1968–) is still in confinement, scheduled for release in 2015.

Victims and survivors of the attacks on 9/11, filed a US$116 trillion lawsuit in *Burnett v. Al-Baraka* against Saudi Arabia and four of its princes, accusing them of financing Al-Qaeda and Afghanistan's former Taliban regime. In 2009, the Supreme Court accepted a dismissal by an appeals court, which cited the doctrine of sovereign immunity.

A lawsuit was filed against Chiquita for allowing its security firm in Colombia to torture and kill at least 40 persons in Mapiripan in July 1997 and then kill 36 persons and torture dozens in February. When a federal court agreed to hear the case in 2012, Attorney General Eric Holder (1951–) defended Chiquita in the case and won a plea bargain for them of US$25 million and five years of probation. In 2013 the Supreme Court considered whether to allow corporations operating in the United States to collect damages for human rights violations outside the United States. In *Kiobel v. Royal Dutch Petroleum*, Nigerian citizens living outside the United States claimed that from 1992 to 1995 multinational oil companies working in Nigeria aided the military dictatorship, which tortured and killed protesters who fought the environmental damage caused by the oil operations. The unanimous ruling, narrowing the scope of ATCA, held that a presumption against extraterritoriality applies to claims under ATCA, so foreigners living outside the United States could not collect damages from a foreign firm in a foreign country. The ruling, supported by the Obama administration, cast doubt on a pending case in which Kellogg, Brown and Root, a former subsidiary of Halliburton, was sued under ATCA for allegedly trafficking 13 men from Nepal to Iraq against their will to work on US military bases. The men, 12 of whom were killed, believed they were going to work at hotels in Jordan and elsewhere.

Several statutes other than ATCA and TVPA have been invoked in recent court decisions to bring alleged international human rights violators to justice (Table 11.1). Laws adopted before 9/11 have often been applied to issues other than terrorism and torture.

TABLE 11.1   AMERICAN LAWS RELATING TO HUMAN RIGHTS VIOLATIONS ABROAD

Name	Passed	Issue addressed
Alien Tort Claims Act	1789	Civil damages to compensate victims of personal injury or property damage committed outside the United States
Neutrality Act	1794	American residents cannot take part militarily in a foreign war
Foreign Sovereign Immunities Act	1976	Legal grounds for suing a foreign state are defined as "adverse commercial operations"
Holtzman Amendment to the Immigration and Naturalization Act Amendment	1978	Persecutors (on the basis of race, religion, national origin, or political opinion) ineligible to be in the USA
Genocide Convention Implementation Act	1988	Criminalizes those who commit or incite genocide
Federal Employees Liability Reform and Tort Compensation Act	1988	Federal employees are exempt from provisions of the Alien Tort Claims Act
Anti-Terrorism Act	1990	Permits victims of terrorism to sue those aiding the attacks
Torture Victim Protection Act	1991	Civil damages from a torturer
Religious Freedom Restoration Act	1993	Bans undue burdens on the exercise of religion by US government actions
Protect Act[a]	1993	Criminalizes underage sex tourism by American residents abroad
Foreign Relations Authorization Act Amendment	1994	Enables a victim of torture to sue the torturer
Human Rights Restoration Act	1996	Asylum granted for those forced abroad to have an abortion or undergo sterilization
Anti-Terrorism Act and Effective Death Penalty Act	1996	Authorizes civil damages from foreign states complicit in injury due to torture, extrajudicial execution, aircraft hijacking, hostage taking; bans entry of terrorists
War Crimes Act	1996	Criminalizes Geneva Convention war crimes
Civil Liability for State Sponsors of Terrorism Act (Flatlow Amendment)	1997	Authorizes civil damages against personal acts of officials, employees, and agents of terrorist states
Foreign Affairs Reform and Restructuring Act[b]	1998	Bans extradition to countries that practice torture
Torture Victims Relief Act	1998	Provides funds to assist torture victims
Nazi War Crimes and Japanese Imperial Government Records Disclosure Act	1998	Authorizes an investigation of hidden assets
Armenian Genocide Victims Insurance Act	2000	Authorizes a lawsuit in a California court on behalf of Armenian genocide survivors
Military Extraterritorial Jurisdiction Act	2000	Authorizes trials in the USA of defense contractors committing felonies outside the USA

Continued

TABLE 11.1 (CONTINUED)

Name	Passed	Issue addressed
Victims of Trafficking and Violence Protection Act	2000	Criminalizes human trafficking; authorizes payments to victims of terrorism
Authorization for the Use of Military Force Against Terrorists Resolution	2001	The "President is authorized to use all necessary and appropriate force against those nations, organizations, or persons he determines planned, authorized, committed, or aided the terrorist attacks that occurred on September 11, 2001, or harbored such organizations or persons …"
USA Patriot Act[c]	2001	Criminalizes international terrorism
Terrorism Risk Insurance Act	2002	Authorizes freezing private assets of terrorists to compensate victims
Detainee Treatment Act	2005	Criminalizes torturing of detainees
Military Commissions Act[d]	2006	Establishes Military Commissions to try suspected terrorists held at Guantánamo
War Crimes Act	2006	Defines "war crime" to include a "grave breach of the Geneva Conventions" or related international treaty; applies if either the victim or the perpetrator is a national of the United States
Child Soldiers Prevention Act	2008	Prohibits several categories of US military assistance to governments using child soldiers, though presidents may issue waivers to provide the aid
Human Rights Enforcement Act	2009	Creates a division of the US Department of Justice to work solely on human rights

[a] The full title is Prosecutorial Remedies and Other Tools to End the Exploitation of Children Today Act. The law was amended in 2003 to provide stiffer penalties.
[b] The full title is United States Policy with Respect to the Involuntary Return of Persons in Danger of Subjection to Torture, which is a provision in the Foreign Affairs Reform and Restructuring Act.
[c] The full name is Uniting and Strengthening America by Providing Appropriate Tools Required to Intercept and Obstruct Terrorism Act. The act was revised in 2011.
[d] Amended in 2009.

The **Religious Freedom Restoration Act** of 1993 prohibits the government from unreasonably interfering with the practice of religion, including the use of a narcotic substance in a religious ritual. Based on the law, as amended in 2000, three former inmates under American custody at Guantánamo filed suit in 2006 to collect US$10 million in damages for harassment of their Muslim religious practices – tossing the Koran into a toilet bucket and confiscation of their religious beads. But in *Rasul v. Myers* (512F3d644) an appeals court ruled in 2008 that the law did not apply to prisoners at Guantánamo. The court also ruled out ATCA as a cause of action for the same reason.

In 1993, revulsion against the practice of sex tourism, primarily in Southeast Asia, with minors led Congress to pass the **Protect Act**. In 2003, after the law was amended to provide stiffer penalties, the US Immigration and Customs Enforcement Agency formed Operation Predator, which by the end of 2005 had resulted in the arrest of more than 6,200 men. Complaints lodged with American embassies in Cambodia, Costa Rica, the Philippines, Vietnam, and elsewhere resulted in the identification of child pornography in luggage searches at airports in the United States, such that pictures of victims could be matched with minors abroad. In one such case, a violator was sentenced to 17 years in prison and fined about US$16,000 in order to provide medical, occupational, and psychological therapy to his Philippine victims in their early teens. In 2004, the American government provided US$1 million to the International Justice Mission to conduct an investigation of human trafficking in Cambodia and other countries, and End Child Prostitution in Asian Tourism asked American travel agencies to adopt the Code of Conduct to Protect Children from Sexual Exploitation in Travel and Tourism, similar to what existed in Europe.

In 1996, Congress passed the **War Crimes Act**, providing that any violation of the Geneva Conventions constitutes a felony. In 2003, 37 family members and survivors then filed *Acree v. Iraq* on behalf of 17 former Americans held as prisoners of war who were tortured in Iraq after the Gulf War of 1991. Because President Saddam Hussein (1937–2006) went into hiding after the American invasion of the country, he failed to appear for the defense. Accordingly, the district court (271FSupp2d179) awarded the plaintiffs US$959 million in damages. Although the United States had seized Iraqi assets, which could have been disbursed to the plaintiffs, the Bush administration refused to do so, arguing that the successor Iraqi regime should not be forced to pay for the wrongs committed under Saddam Hussein. When an appeals court and the Supreme Court deferred to the executive branch on the matter, plaintiffs went for relief to members of Congress, which passed a law in 2008 to allow the transfer of funds that was vetoed by President Bush. No further action on the matter has been reported.

In 1996, after the World Jewish Congress announced important discoveries about Swiss bank accounts and other assets of victims of Nazi persecution from 1933 to 1945, Swiss banks were sued for US$20 billion for not distributing funds in dormant accounts to Holocaust survivors and their heirs and otherwise collaborating with the Nazis by holding deposits from Hitler's government. In response, the American and Swiss governments launched investigations into looted assets. In early 1997, a security guard at a Swiss bank reported the shredding of relevant documents. Two weeks later, the City of New York openly considered a boycott of Swiss banks in retaliation. In 1998, a settlement of US$1.25 billion was reached between two banks, UBS AG and Credit Suisse, and lawyers representing Holocaust victims and the World Jewish Congress, resulting in the formation of the Claims Resolution Tribunal to handle individual cases. To date, more than 32,000 claims have been filed, although the tribunal has reported that the banks destroyed records of nearly 7 million accounts that had been opened in Swiss banks from 1933–1945.

Accordingly, in 1998, Congress passed the **Nazi War Crimes and Japanese Imperial Government Records Disclosure Act**, which mandated the collection of information that would facilitate survivors and their heirs to identify themselves in order to recover assets lost in World War II. Since only Jewish victims were initially to receive awards, two class-action lawsuits on behalf of non-Jewish victims of the Nazis were filed in 2000 against the Swiss National Bank and Vatican Bank, both of which were accused of laundering dental gold, gold coins, wedding rings, and other gold looted from non-Jewish Belarusian, Russian, Ukrainian, and Yugoslavian concentration camp and war victims. Disabled persons, homosexuals, Jehovah's Witnesses, and Roma gypsies have been recognized to have valid claims against the Nazis. As a result, many classes of victims of Nazi persecution were included in the US$1.25 billion judgment announced during 2000 in the ruling of *In re Holocaust Victim Assets Litigation* (105FSupp2d139). In 1998, Germany signed an agreement with the United States to return all stolen art to their rightful owners.

Similarly, in 1999, *Marootian v. New York Life Insurance Company* (CV99-10273Cas(MCx);2001USDistLexis22274) was filed on behalf of survivors of about 1.5 million Armenians who died during a forced relocation by the Turkish government from 1915 to 1923. In 2000, a California law authorized lawsuits by Armenian survivors to recover unpaid payments of US$7 million on some 2,300 life insurance policies issued from 1875–1915. As a result, Congress passed the **Armenian Genocide Victims Insurance Act** that year, and the New York company decided to settle out of court, offering survivors US$11 million and US$3 million for Armenian civic organizations.

In 2000, Congress passed the **Victims of Trafficking and Violence Protection Act**, in part to focus on human trafficking, specifically "to protect children from exploitation, abuse, or forced conscription into military or paramilitary services," a problem affecting 700,000 (mostly girls) per year, of which 50,000 then entered the United States to perform labor involuntarily, including sex slaves. The act also applied to victims of terrorism. Subsequently, some US$410 million was paid out in default judgments, including US$97 million from Cuban assets paid to heirs of those shot down in an airplane by the Cuban Air Force during 1996. The act also provided that compensation could be paid from violence resulting from a country designated as a terrorist state, thus forcing payment under the terms of the Flatlow Amendment. Accordingly, US$22 million from Iranian assets went to the Flatlow family. In 2011, there were 7,206 prosecutions (of which 508 were for labor trafficking) and 4,239 convictions; 41,210 victims were identified.

Efforts of the California legislature on behalf of victims of Japanese and Nazi slave labor, however, were dismissed during 2003 in *American Ins. Assn. v. Garamendi* (539US396) on the ground that the federal government preempts state authority in matters affecting foreign affairs. Several cases have been pursued against Japan's conduct during World War II in American courts, notably the practice of forcing women to have sex with Japanese soldiers, only to find their cases rejected on the basis that the Japanese Peace Treaty of 1951 settled all such claims. One such lawsuit, filed on behalf of former sex slaves, was rejected during 2003 in *Joo v. Japan* (332F3d649). Although some members of Congress sought to reinterpret the peace treaty through new legislation, a presidential veto was threatened on the ground that new litigation against Japan might adversely affect cooperation with Tokyo on matters of terrorism, so the proposed law did not pass.

One loophole of American law was closed in 2000 by the **Military Extraterritorial Jurisdiction Act**. Previously, serious crimes committed abroad by civilians working under contracts for the American military could only be prosecuted abroad. Under the new law, they could be tried in American courts. In 2007, a civilian interrogator for the CIA in Afghanistan, David Passaro (1966–), was the first person convicted under the law; his offense was to beat a prisoner who subsequently died.

The American approach to human rights changed significantly after some 3,000 persons died in terrorist attacks on September 11, 2001. Soon afterward, Congress passed the **Authorization for the Use of Military Force Resolution** and **the USA Patriot Act**. The resolution not only resulted in the American-led war in Afghanistan but also encouraged the roundup of suspected terrorists from around the world, sometimes paying bounties for their capture. The law criminalized "material support" for terrorist organizations and authorized a system of domestic government surveillance that continues to anger civil libertarians. In 2002, Congress adopted the **Terrorism Risk Insurance Act** to enable the president to freeze assets of terrorists and then compensate their victims.

In 2007, American citizen, José Padilla (1970–), was tried and convicted of material support for terrorism. After he was imprisoned, he sued various members of the Bush administration for damages, alleging unsuccessfully that he had been tortured in prison after his arrest in 2002. The damage suit, however, was dismissed.

COURT CASE 11.4 *UNITED STATES V. PADILLA* (2007)

In 2002, upon his return from an overseas trip, José Padilla (1970–), an American citizen, was arrested at O'Hare Airport in Chicago. A warrant had been issued in New York to hold him as a material witness in connection with the World Trade Center attacks of 2001. However, rather than extraditing him to New York, President George W. Bush (1946–) issued an executive order to transfer him to a military brig in South Carolina as an "enemy combatant," where he was to be held indefinitely without access to an attorney or any prospect of a trial on specific charges. A *habeas corpus* court ruling in 2003, *Padilla v. Rumsfeld* (352F3d695), ordered Padilla's release, a decision that was appealed to the Supreme Court. In 2004, the Supreme Court (542US426) ruled in *Rumsfeld v. Padilla* that the case was improperly filed because the case was filed in New York instead of South Carolina, the state where Padilla was being held under military authority. After refilling the case, Padilla again won his release in a district court in 2005, but an appeals court (423F3d386) instead ruled that his detention was legal, so the case went to the Supreme Court, which was expected to rule on the case later that year. Just before the ruling was to be issued, however, the US government dropped military crimes charges against him and instead filed criminal charges based on the Neutrality Act of 1794 – namely, conspiracy to "murder, kidnap and maim people overseas [in Bosnia and Chechnya]." In 2006, he was transferred from a military brig to a civilian jail in Miami. The defense moved for dismissal on the grounds that his abuse while in detention (solitary and shackled confinement, sensory deprivation, mind-altering drugs) rendered him incompetent to stand trial, but the motion was denied. After conviction by a jury in 2007 on the charge of conspiracy and material support for terrorism, he was sentenced to 17.33 years in prison, where he began using the name

Continued

Abdullah Al-Muhajir. Civil lawsuits of government officials for his abuse in confinement before trial were then dismissed. But in 2011, the government contested the sentence as too lenient, an issue that has yet to be resolved in court arguments.

Whereas, previously, terrorism was regarded in terms of the **criminal law** model, Bush framed the American struggle against terrorism as a **military** effort justified by **natural law** – as a fight to preserve civilization against modern-day barbarians. What became known as the Bush Doctrine was a claim that terrorist threats in an age of rapid communication and potential mass destruction require new measures, indeed a new paradigm beyond the framework of the Geneva Conventions and international criminal law. However, the methods are similar to those used by Britain after World War II in dealing with the communist insurgency in Malaya, Jewish terrorists in British-occupied Palestine, and unrest in Northern Ireland.

American citizen, John Walker Lindh (1981–), who was in the Afghan army at the time of his capture, was returned to the United States, where he pled guilty to "material support" to the Taliban in 2002 and was sentenced to 20 years in prison. His confession to other crimes was extracted through torture and therefore ruled inadmissible in court. He was the first of more than 200 persons convicted in civilian courts of support for terrorism. Meanwhile, several hundred suspected terrorists of various nationalities were rounded up in Afghanistan and Pakistan during 2001, and about 800 were shipped to the American Naval Base at Guantánamo Bay, Cuba.

One argument used by Bush administration officials was that terrorist groups are not protected by the Geneva Conventions because they had not ratified the Conventions. However, the Geneva Conventions apply to actions of the United States, which has ratified the Conventions, and litigation to challenge the new approach was largely successful. As commander-in-chief, Bush claimed that the president has inherent powers to act by executive orders without regard to international treaties or domestic laws in order to defend the country. When war began in Afghanistan, Central Command General Tommy Franks (1945–) at first applied Geneva Convention standards to military operations, as did the initial Guantánamo commander. But President Bush soon countermanded them, insisting that the Geneva Conventions were inapplicable. When the United States attacked and defeated Iraq in 2003, the prison at Abu Ghraib was converted into an American detention facility and was also exempted from Geneva Convention requirements.

In 2004, a military tribunal established by a presidential executive order proceeded to charge several detainees at Guantánamo with conspiracy to commit acts of terrorism, attempted murder, and aiding the enemy. The court was created without standard rules, since mistreatment of the prisoners precluded a normal trial; evidence would have been challenged as inadmissible because coerced. Litigation followed, as pro bono attorneys began to represent some of the prisoners held at Guantánamo. But, in 2004, the Supreme Court declared that no president can have a "blank check" to pursue terrorism in *Hamdi v. Rumsfeld* (547US507). As a

Red Cross report in 2005 revealed that 80 percent of those captured in Afghanistan or Iraq had been wrongfully detained, critics referred to the "new paradigm" as a justification for government terrorism, including extraordinary rendition, indefinite detention, and torture.

In 2004, photographs of Iraqis under American custody in Abu Ghraib Prison, Baghdad, revealed that unusual methods had been used, including having a vicious dog bark at a chained prisoner. Reports of extremely stressful methods of confinement and interrogation were also acknowledged by the government to have taken place in the detention facility at Guantánamo.

Public outrage prompted Congress to pass the **Detainee Treatment Act** in 2005, requiring that interrogation techniques should be limited to those allowed by the Uniform Code of Military Justice, which includes Geneva Convention protections and excludes torture. (Belief that evidence obtained by torture is meaningless was vindicated in 2007, when preposterously fanciful confessions of two detainees were made public by American prosecutors.) In signing the 2005 act into law, nevertheless, Bush issued a statement that he would not abide by the law if he felt that "protecting the American people from terrorist attacks" was a higher priority.

COURT CASE 11.5 *HAMDAN V. RUMSFELD* (2006)

In 2006, the Supreme Court of the United States ruled in a case brought by the New York-based Center for Constitutional Rights, *Hamdan v. Rumsfeld* (548US557), that Donald Rumsfeld (1932–) while Secretary of Defense violated Article 3 of the four Geneva Conventions of 1949 by refusing to allow a prisoner under the custody of the US military to be tried in a regularly constituted court but instead in a presidentially-established military commission. In so doing, the justices by implication identified George W. Bush (1946–), the author of the executive order that established the court, as a potential war criminal who might be sued. Congress, the only branch of government with the constitutional power to set up new judicial bodies, then passed the Military Commissions Act of 2006 (which was revised in 2009). In 2007, the newly constituted Military Commission dropped the initial charge of terrorism conspiracy against Salim Hamdan (1970–). In 2008, he was instead charged with providing material support to Al-Qaeda, found guilty, and then transferred to his home country, Yemen, to serve out his 5.5 year sentence. The government in Yemen released him on January 9, 2009.

The attorney representing Salim Admed Hamdan (1970–), who was one of those initially charged, objected to the court. In 2006, the Supreme Court in *Hamdan v. Rumsfeld* (126SCt2749) not only declared that Bush's tribunals were unconstitutional, because the Constitution only authorizes Congress to establish courts, but noted that the secret military courts violated Article 3 of all four Geneva Conventions. A violator of a Geneva Convention is, of course, a war criminal, so the Supreme Court was tacitly implicating Defense Secretary Rumsfeld, who implemented the executive order, and also the author of the executive order, President Bush.

Because of the Supreme Court rulings in the *Hamdi* and *Hamdan* cases, Bush recalibrated his approach. Several persons accused of major terrorist crimes were released from secret detention facilities abroad and sent to Guantánamo; a few hundred prisoners were sent to host countries, mostly in Europe; about 50 were cleared for resettlement but no countries were willing to accept them, so they became refugees; and prison conditions improved.

Congress adopted the **Military Commissions Act** of 2006 to establish the category of "illegal enemy combatant," with new procedural rules that apply neither to criminals nor to prisoners of war. Each detainee at Guantánamo was first to be screened by a Combatant Status Tribunal and then put on trial by a military commission, where the following procedures would apply:

- Coerced and hearsay testimony would be allowed.
- The prosecution could use classified testimony that the defendant would be unable to review or challenge.
- There would be no appeal from the commissions to other federal courts.
- Suspected terrorists would have no right of *habeas corpus*.
- Interrogators of the CIA and their subcontractors could continue to use severe interrogation methods.
- Provisions of the War Crimes Act that formerly criminalized anyone from violating the Geneva Conventions were repealed.

In 2007, some 240 Iraqis asked the ICC to indict members of the Bush administration as victims of war crimes. But the prosecutor considered their cases too minor to be worthy of investigation.

David Hicks (1975–), an Australian citizen, was the first person tried by the new military commission. In 2007, he pleaded guilty to providing material support to Al-Qaeda, a designated terrorist organization, although the arbitrary procedure (Executive Order 13224) for branding organizations as terrorist had been already declared unconstitutionally vague by a lower court during 2005 in *Humanitarian Law Project v. Gonzales* (380FSupp2d1134). In a plea bargain, Hicks agreed never to allege that he was tortured despite claims that he made in Afghanistan after his capture. He was sentenced to serve less than a year beyond his nearly five years of confinement. The apparent signal is that after a detainee is designated as an enemy combatant at the combatant status tribunal, they could be released only after pleading guilty; if they maintain their innocence, they could be held indefinitely.

In 2008, *Boumediene v. Bush* (553US723) overturned a provision of the Military Commissions Act of 2006. The Supreme Court accepted the principle that Guantánamo prisoners could challenge grounds for their detention by filing a writ of *habeas corpus*. The court ordered 26 prisoners released, as there were no grounds for keeping them confined.

Meanwhile, according to the principal UN investigator on torture, several countries pointed to America's lowering of standards as a justification for their own harsh methods of interrogation. Indeed, Zimbabwe cited the example of the United States to justify elements of its criminal justice system, and the treatment of prisoners from the Georgian War of 2008 was a carbon copy of what had been taking place at Guantánamo.

The election of Barack Obama as president was heralded as a clean break from the Bush Doctrine. On the second full day of his presidency, he banned the use of torture, ordered full compliance with the Geneva Conventions, replaced the term "War on Terror" with "War on Al-Qaeda," and halted all ongoing prosecutions at Guantánamo, which in turn he promised to close within a year. Concerned that the country had lost its "moral bearings," he soon released previously classified documents used in the Bush administration to justify torture to silence. Repeated criticisms on his terrorism policy direction by former Vice President Dick Cheney (1941–) then stopped, and he decided not to release torture photographs despite pressure from civil libertarians who wanted the release to create a groundswell of support for prosecuting members of the Bush administration for war crimes. No such prosecutions were undertaken, as Obama wanted to "look forward, not backward."

Instead, former Malaysian Prime Minister Mahathir Bin Mohamad (1925–) organized an unofficial Kuala Lumpur War Crimes Commission in late 2009. Seven former Abu Ghraib and Guantánamo prisoners testified with graphic accounts of almost 100 war crimes, but the American press ignored the forum. The body continued in 2012, when George W. Bush and seven members of his administration were found guilty. Similar civilian forums have been held elsewhere around the world, including in the United States.

Obama recommended a revision of the discredited Military Commissions Act of 2006 to establish many procedural safeguards for trials at Guantánamo. The restructured **Military Commissions Act**, which passed in July 2009, did not satisfy many civil libertarians, however. While court challenges to the procedures delayed prosecutions for the next four years, more detainees were nevertheless accommodated in other countries, whittling the number being held to about 160 by 2013.

In late 2009, Congress passed the **Human Rights Enforcement Act** to create the Human Rights and Special Prosecutions Section in the Criminal Division of the Department of Justice, which combined two units that had focused on discovering, deporting, and prosecuting former Nazis living in the United States. The section is also empowered to prosecute those who engage in genocide, torture, and war crimes, including the recruitment or use of child soldiers. In 2010, Peter Egner (1922–2011), a transport guard on a train bound for Auschwitz, was identified by the new unit for deportation, but he died before his case was decided.

Although Obama had hoped to resettle some of the Guantánamo detainees in the United States to set an example for other countries to do likewise, members of Congress overwhelmingly reacted negatively to the concept that "terrorists" might be imprisoned or even released in their states. So many restrictions on their movements were adopted into law that Guantánamo prisoners, in effect, became prisoners of Congress. When trials of persons responsible for the 9/11 attacks were slated to take place in New York City in November 2009, sharp reactions came from the mayor and others, so that plan was cancelled, leaving military commissions as the only tribunals for all remaining trials.

American-run prisons in Iraq were closed by 2010 in preparation for a complete American withdrawal from Iraq in 2011, as agreed upon by Bush before leaving office. An agreement to transfer prisons to the Afghanistan government was signed in 2010, but portions of the prison at Bagram Air Force Base were still being used by American authorities in 2013.

Civil litigation that started under the Bush administration rolled over to the Obama administration. One such case was the challenge to the Patriot Act of 2001 that criminalized "material support" to "terrorist organizations" and the Terrorism Risk Insurance Act of 2002 which permits seizure of bank and portfolio accounts of international terrorists. Both laws were ruled unconstitutionally vague by a lower court during 2006 in *Humanitarian Law Project v. Gonzales* (380FSupp2d1134), but the laws were upheld when the case reached the Supreme Court during 2010 in *Holder v. Humanitarian Law Project* (130SCt2705).

As more cases challenged Bush-era practices, the Obama administration surprised supporters by invoking "national security" and "states secrets" objections to cases involving human rights violations abroad and at home, whereupon judges dropped the cases. One example was *Mohamed v. Jeppesen* (539FSupp2d1128), which alleged that the defendant company was under contract from the CIA to engage in extraordinary rendition – that is, to fly suspected terrorists to secret locations where they were tortured to gain information about terrorist plots. Plaintiff Binyam Mohamed (1978–), for example, was flown to Morocco, where the exterior of his penis was sliced with a blade three times, and later sent to two other locations before ending up in Guantánamo. In 2008, the Bush Justice Department invoked "states secrets," and the case was dismissed.

Binyam Mohamed was released from Guantánamo in 2009 and sent to Britain, his country of residence. Later in 2009, a three-judge appeals court rejected the "states secrets" argument, whereupon the Justice Department appealed to the 11-judge appeals court, which reversed the appeal. In 2010, however, a court in England agreed to compensate him for £1 million because British authorities were complicit in his ordeal. In 2011, the Supreme Court refused to hear the case, thereby allowing the dismissal of the case on "states secrets" grounds. A similar case, involving 250 Iraqis suing a private contractor (*Saleh v. Titan*) was also dismissed. No monetary compensation for their torture has ever been paid by the US Treasury.

Although a court in the *Boumediene* case opened the door to habeas petitions from prisoners, the door has been shut to those who applied for habeas since 2011 even though there was no evidence of their culpability as terrorists. Others have given up trying to seek their release. Nevertheless, about 60 have been determined innocent and approved for release, and 100 have never been tried. The prison remained open while most prisoners were engaging in a hunger strike during early 2013. In a nutshell, the Obama administration has disappointed many human rights observers.

Violations of human rights are contrary to law, so the judicial approach is entirely appropriate. As the legal framework grows, the deterrent effect can be strengthened. The use of professional criminological methods, pioneered by the Federal Bureau of Investigation (FBI) in the 1920s, has set a standard that increased dramatically with the use of DNA testing since the 1990s; by 2012, some 300 persons convicted of civilian offenses, such as murder, have had previous convictions reversed. The use of DNA evidence has spread around the world.

Unfortunately, legal remedies for the misconduct of individuals rarely are effective vis-à-vis governments that have poor human rights records. Economic measures, such as foreign assistance and foreign trade, have a more systemic effect.

HISTORIC EVENT 11.1 THE MARSHALL PLAN (1947–1951)

When World War II ended, Europe's economic infrastructure had been severely damaged, and there was a lack of financial reserves for reconstruction. On account of serious food shortages and unemployment, communist parties in France, Italy, and Western Germany gained strength. In 1947, during a commencement address at Harvard University, Secretary of State George C. Marshall (1880–1959) called upon European countries to meet together to design an economic recovery plan for the United States to fund. British and French leaders then met to discuss the terms of a plan. Moscow was interested, too, but the British and French insisted that any aid program had to be preceded by an economic assessment of the economic needs of each country, a condition that the closed economy of the Soviet Union could not accept. Next, 16 Western European countries attended a conference in Paris; Spain, which was neutral during the war, was not invited. The result was the European Recovery Plan, which the press named the Marshall Plan. After providing emergency aid to Greece and Turkey in 1947, in 1948 Congress passed the Economic Recovery Act, which authorized the first US$5 billion out of an eventual US$12 billion to be provided to the Organization for European Economic Cooperation as the main recipient coordinating agency for Marshall Plan aid. European countries were to contribute matching funds. Most aid was used to purchase American goods, and 2 percent of the total was spent to advertise American products so that European consumers would be encouraged to buy them. As a result of the Marshall Plan, Western European industrial production increased by 35 percent. On gaining control of Congress in 1951, the Republican majority voted to discontinue the program as a "giveaway" that they could no longer support.

ECONOMIC MEASURES: FOREIGN ASSISTANCE

Foreign aid can be a proactive approach to improve the attainment of human rights (Table 11.2). In 1948, Congress adopted the **Economic Cooperation Act** (the "Marshall Plan") to foster European postwar economic reconstruction, though no such program was extended to war-torn Asia. Subsequently, the United States maintained aid programs with developing countries. Whereas the UN's Millennium

TABLE 11.2 PROACTIVE LAWS OF THE UNITED STATES REGARDING HUMAN RIGHTS ABROAD

Title of statute	Passed
Economic Cooperation Act	1948
Food for Peace Act	1954
Foreign Assistance Act	1961
International Development and Food Assistance Act	1975
Support for the East European Democracy (SEED) Act	1989
Freedom Support Act[a]	1992
Foreign Assistance Act Amendment	1998
Iraq Liberation Act	1998
Victims of Crime Act Amendment	2000
Zimbabwe Democracy and Economic Recovery Act	2001
Foreign Relations Authorization Act	2002
Sudan Peace Act	2002
Millennium Challenge Act	2002
International Disability and Victims of Warfare and Civil Strife Assistance Act	2003
North Korean Human Rights Act	2004
Belarus Democracy Act	2004
Iran Freedom and Support Act	2006
Democratic Republic of the Congo Relief, Security, and Democracy Promotion Act	2006
Palestinian Anti-Terrorism Act	2006
Lords's Resistance Army Disarmament and Northern Uganda Recovery Act	2010
Debt Relief for the Earthquake Recovery in Haiti Act	2010

[a] The full title is Freedom for Russia and Emerging Eurasian Democracies and Open Markets Support Act.

Development Goals encourages developed countries to devote 0.7 percent of gross national income to foreign aid, American contributions, including both public and private, are the lowest among industrialized countries – at about 0.16 percent.

The **Food for Peace Act** of 1954 originally provided a way to pay American farmers for food surpluses, which could be sent abroad to countries in need, even though the food was not always consumed for reasons of culture or spoilage en route. Later, the law was incorporated each year into the Foreign Assistance Act as the **International Development and Food Assistance Act** of 1975.

From 1961, under the **Foreign Assistance Act**, the US Agency for International Development (USAID) has been the primary foreign assistance agency, with field offices in more than 100 countries. In 2012, USAID established the Center of Excellence for Democracy, Human Rights, and Governance, which operates on a budget of US$94 million.

In *The Hard Way to Peace* (1962), sociologist Amitai Etzioni (1929–) was among the earliest to propose that foreign aid should be reserved to democracies or to countries that are in the process of democratizing. Although his suggestion fell on deaf ears at the time, the American government gradually adopted his suggestion.

In 1983, the nongovernmental **National Endowment for Democracy** (NED) was established to provide funds for the support of pro-democratic groups in other countries. Although the organization is a nongovernmental organization outside the American government, most funding comes from Congress. NED is proactive, providing technical assistance, supplies, and equipment to political groups, civic organizations, labor unions, and the media. NED also engages in election monitoring. In 2012, NED funded about 1,250 projects in 92 countries on a budget of US$27 million.

In 1984, after NED supported a candidate for office in Panamá, Congress stipulated that its funds could not be used to support office-seekers. Nevertheless, in 1990, NED used funds on behalf of candidates in Haïti and Nicaragua. In 2004, Venezuelan President Hugo Chávez (1954–2013) charged NED with providing about US$1 million to local organizations seeking to have him recalled from office. His government charged the leaders of the Venezuelan group with treason and conspiracy for receipt of NED funds, and those who signed the recall petition complained of harassment. In short, NED's meddling stirred up a hornet's nest.

After the Berlin Wall was breached, the **Support for East European Democracy Act** of 1989 and the **Freedom Support Act** of 1992 were designed to assist former satellites and republics of the Soviet Union to build democracies and market economies. The latter act superseded the former, adding the former Soviet republics of Central Asia (Kazakhstan, Kyrgyzstan, Tajikistan, Turkmenistan, and Uzbekistan).

The Human Rights and Democracy Fund was established as an amendment to the **Foreign Assistance Act** of 1998, within the Department of State, not only to address human rights emergencies but also to support such activities as election monitoring and parliamentary development. Congress authorized US$48 million in 2005, including US$4 million to stop sweatshops. In 2012, the figure was increased to US$136 million. Some aid supports human rights defenders of Internet freedom, labor rights, prison condition improvements, religious freedom, and women's rights.

Also in 1998, the **Iraq Liberation Act** officially endorsed regime change, citing human rights abuses, but prohibited the use of force to accomplish that goal. Instead, funds were distributed to seven groups opposing rule by Saddam Hussein.

Bilateral humanitarian aid for victims of natural disasters has been rushed to various countries over the years, including food, medicines, and other necessities. In 2000, Congress amended the **Victims of Crime Act** of 1984, originally focused on domestic crimes, to authorize aid for individual victims of terrorist acts outside the United States, and in 2003 the **International Disability and Victims of Warfare and Civil Strife Assistance Act** was passed in a similar vein.

Shady economic transactions with suspect businesses can be deterred through public disclosure. In 2001, for example, human rights groups persuaded the Securities and Exchange Commission to increase disclosure requirements, both for companies doing business in the United States and for those disallowed from doing business. The main purpose was to identify PetroChina as a corporation that was raising capital in order to operate in the Sudan, a country with nefarious human rights practices, but the effect was that PetroChina went to Europe to raise money instead.

In 2001, Congress passed the **Zimbabwe Democracy and Economic Recovery Act** to provide US$26 million to assist those losing their lands and to support opponents of the regime. The Harare government was then dispossessing Europeans who owned and farmed agricultural land, thereby producing serious food shortages, while also supporting civil war in the Congo (Kinshasa).

In 2003, Congress passed the **Millennium Challenge Act** to fulfill the social and economic goals and timetables of the Millennium Declaration. Congress now funds the Millennium Challenge Corporation, providing aid only to countries with "good governance," that is, countries that "root out corruption, respect human rights … adhere to the rule of law[,] … invest in better health care, better schools and broader immunization … [and] have more open markets and sustainable budget policies, nations where people can start and operate a small business without running the gauntlets of bureaucracy and bribery." President Obama continued the account, promising to help the achievement of Millennium goals, but targeted more at democracies and democratizing countries, so long as studies prove that the aid is effective. USAID administers the Millennium Challenge.

In addition, USAID provides humanitarian assistance, not only to international organizations but also bilaterally to the victims of natural disasters. Aid to victims of the Acquired Immune Deficiency Syndrome (AIDS) was a factor in reducing the incidence of new cases in the latter part of the twentieth century. AIDS cases, however, increased after the Bush administration banned the distribution of condoms; when that policy was reversed under the presidency of Barack Obama, AIDS cases declined dramatically.

In 2002, a provision in the **Foreign Relations Authorization Act** required annual reports to Congress on actions taken by the executive branch to encourage respect for human rights. Thereafter, laws focused on promoting democracy in specific countries, and aid projects targeted at specific democratic reforms showed more results than aid in general. Also in 2002, the **Sudan Peace Act** condemned the Khartoum government for engaging in genocide in the civil war with the Christian south and also for allowing a slave trade to flourish while authorizing some US$100 million to supply food to beleaguered Africans in the south.

The **North Korean Human Rights Act** of 2004 authorized US$136 million for humanitarian assistance, aid for North Korean refugees, and for nongovernmental organizations to promote human rights. That same year, the **Belarus Democracy Act** authorized aid for pro-democracy forces and funding for broadcasting to the country. As revised in 2006 and 2011, the law called for improved human rights, including the release of all political prisoners. Similarly, the **Iran Freedom and Support Act** of 2006 authorized funding to groups opposed to the current regime.

The goal of a sovereign state in Palestine, first declared by President Bush in 2001, was frustrated because elections in 2006 revealed a sharp division between West Bank voters and those of the Gaza Strip. Whereas anti-Israeli terrorism declined on the West Bank, the Gaza territory was implacably opposed to the existence of the state of Israel. Accordingly, the **Palestinian Anti-Terrorism Act** of 2006 offered aid to the West Bank alone, consisting of basic human needs and support for democracy.

Perhaps the most notable law drafted by then-Senator Barack Obama was the **Democratic Republic of the Congo Relief, Security, and Democracy Promotion Act** of 2006, which urged the UN peacekeeping force to stop arming of children and human trafficking. The later **Lord's Resistance Army Disarmament and Northern Uganda Recovery Act** of 2010 provided funds to the government of Uganda to deal with destruction wrought by the Lord's Resistance Army of Joseph Kony (1961–).

The massive earthquake that devastated Haïti occasioned economic aid to the poor country. In addition to providing aid to the country through the UN and other international channels, Congress passed the **Debt Relief for Earthquake Recovery in Haiti Act** of 2010, which asked the World Bank and IMF to cancel all debt for the country.

In disbursing aid to the world, the United States has always acted in accord with national interests, whether defined in political-strategic terms or to provide a positive image of a generous America to the world. But sometimes the aid has had strings attached, as discussed next.

TABLE 11.3 **AMERICAN LAWS ALLOWING AID SANCTIONS ON COUNTRIES VIOLATING HUMAN RIGHTS**

Title of statute	*Passed*
Mutual Security Act	1951
Foreign Assistance Act	1961
Harkin Amendment	1975
Humphrey–Cranston Amendment	1976
International Security Assistance and Arms Export Control Act	1976
International Financial Assistance Act	1977
International Security Assistance Act	1978
International Security and Development Cooperation Act	1980
Boland Amendment	1982
Specter Amendment	1983
International Financial Institutions Act	1983
International Narcotics Control Act	1989
Foreign Assistance Appropriations Act Amendment	1989
Freedom for Russia and Emerging Eurasian Democracies and Open Markets Support Act	1992
Leahy Amendment	1997
International Religious Freedom Act	1998
Victims of Trafficking and Violence Protection Act	2000
American Service-Members' Protection Act	2001
Zimbabwe Democracy and Economic Recovery Act	2001
North Korean Human Rights Act	2004

ECONOMIC AID: AID CONDITIONALITY AND SANCTIONS

Misgoverned people are often in need. More than two dozen laws authorize punitive aid sanctions, either by prescreening recipients or by terminating aid (Table 11.3).

During the Cold War, American aid went to allies and developing countries. The **Mutual Security Act** of 1951, which authorized military assistance, had a provision that aid could be terminated if the UN General Assembly or Security Council determined that a country was guilty of an unacceptable threat or breach of the peace.

In 1960, the United States banned aid to Cuba, which had become aligned with the Soviet Union. The **Foreign Assistance Act** of 1961 explicitly prohibited aid to communist countries. The ban continued right up to the end of the Cold War but continues in regard to Cuba and North Korea.

In 1971, without specifying the reason, Congress cut off aid to Greece. Congress was clearly reacting to a military coup that had just toppled a democracy.

In 1973, the Committee on Foreign Affairs of the House of Representatives held hearings for the first time on the linkage between human rights and foreign aid, which continued to be denied to Greece up to 1974. What the members learned was so disappointing that legislative proposals to make aid conditional on human rights improvement were formulated.

In 1973, Congress asked President Richard Nixon (1913–1994) to deny economic and military aid to countries with political prisoners in a clause within the **Foreign Assistance Act**. When Nixon ignored the suggestion, the 1974 version of the law broadened to suggest that security assistance (military and police) should be denied to countries that had political prisoners, practiced torture in interrogation or punishment, and otherwise had a systematic pattern of gross violations of human rights. Both were "sense of Congress" resolutions with no binding effect, but Congress explicitly stopped aid to Chile in 1974 after a military coup led by Augusto Pinochet (1915–2006) ousted democratically elected President Salvador Allende (1908–1973).

In 1975, the **Harkin Amendment** to the International Development and Food Assistance Act prohibited sending food aid to gross violators of human rights unless the food benefited those in need. If Congress objected to a country's food distribution system, the president had to submit a report within 30 days citing evidence that the food indeed went to the needy. Without such a report, the aid was required to stop. The first exclusion was imposed on Uganda because of the human rights violations of Idi Amin (1924–2003). Kampala's eligibility was restored in 1979 when he was forced out of office.

In 1976, the **Humphrey–Cranston Amendment** to the annual Foreign Assistance Act authorized the termination of economic aid to countries that massively violate human rights. In the same year, Congress overrode a veto by President Gerald Ford (1913–2006) and thereby institutionalized a human rights policy into the annual **International Security Assistance and Arms Export Control Act**. In 1977, while aid was terminated to Argentina and Zaïre (today, the Democratic Republic of the Congo), Brazil, El Salvador, Guatemala, and Uruguay refused military aid because of unfavorable State Department human rights reports in order to avoid the embarrassment of an announcement of aid cessation.

Nevertheless, there was much ambiguity in aid conditionality because of concern over the strength of communist elements in a country. The law allowed aid to some human rights violators in three situations:

- Direct aid to benefit the needy
- Extraordinary security needs
- Significant improvements in human rights.

Indonesia was exempted because of a fear of the rise of communist Vietnam without a counterweight in Southeast Asia. Iran was allowed aid under the repressive Shah Reza Pahlavi (1919–1980) because of its oil and its strategic position bordering on the Soviet Union. The United States usually ignored human rights problems in Liberia because of the country's huge Firestone Rubber investments and the fact that Liberia was the only country in Africa that granted landing and refueling privileges to American military aircraft. The Philippines received aid under President Ferdinand Marcos (1917–1989) because of the presence of US bases and the presumed need to fight communist guerrillas, who in turn capitalized on Marcos's numerous human rights violations to gain support. South Korea received aid under repressive regimes on account of the possibility of an attack from North Korea.

In 1977, the **International Financial Assistance Act** mandated the application of human rights criteria to applicants for loans from the World Bank and other multilateral financial institutions. And a new criterion was added to the prohibition to countries with widespread human rights abuses: No loans would be approved to countries that provide refuge to those engaged in aircraft hijacking. The obvious target was Uganda, which offered safe haven to Palestinians who had hijacked a commercial airplane with many Israelis on board that had landed at Entebbe in 1976.

Under the broader restrictions of the **International Security and Development Cooperation Act** of 1980, Uganda and Zimbabwe were placed on a watch list. The list grew in 1981 to include Chile, El Salvador, and Nicaragua, and in 1985 expanded to Ethiopia, Liberia, Mozambique, the Philippines, South Africa, Sudan, and Tunisia.

In 1980, several foreign aid laws were amended to add the following type of human rights violation: "causing the disappearance of persons by the abduction and clandestine detention of those persons, and other flagrant denial of the right to life, liberty, or the security of persons … ." Congress also began to limit military aid and arms sales to specific states, usually for just one year at a time, or placed countries on a watch list. Targeted over the years were Angola, Argentina, Bolivia, Brazil, Chile, El Salvador, Ethiopia, Guatemala, Haïti, Liberia, Mauritania, Morocco, Mozambique, Nicaragua, Paraguay, South Africa, South Korea, Tunisia, Uganda, Uruguay, and Zimbabwe.

Ronald Reagan, on becoming president in 1981, announced that foreign aid would focus more on stopping international terrorism. But Congress did not listen.

From 1982–1985, the **Boland Amendment** to the Defense Appropriation Act prohibited the use of covert aid to the Contras. In 1983, Congress adopted the **Specter Amendment** to the International Security and Development Cooperation Act, which required the president to certify progress in human rights conditions within El Salvador on a semiannual basis. The subtext of the amendment was to insist on the prosecution of the murderers of four American church workers in 1980 as a condition for the release of authorized American aid. The authorities in San Salvador then found scapegoats, and aid resumed. Later in 1983, Congress threatened to cut off all military aid because of evidence that death squads were operating with impunity. El Salvador then reassigned death squad leaders to postings outside the country, death squad activity was greatly reduced, and aid flowed again.

The **International Financial Institutions Act** of 1983, in superseding the International Financial Assistance Act of 1977, dropped the word "consistent" from the wording of the original act, which prohibited contributions to multilateral aid programs in countries that exhibit "a consistent pattern of gross violations of international recognized human rights." The word "consistent" had been interpreted by Reagan's subordinates as an escape clause to permit aid to El Salvador.

Under the annual Foreign Assistance Act, South Africa and Syria were denied aid in 1983. *Apartheid* was the reason for the former. Syria's military force in Lebanon was considered to be an unwelcome army of occupation, especially after the suicide massacre of 241 American marines in Beirut, Lebanon, earlier that year.

In 1989, Congress passed the **International Narcotics Control Act** with four human rights requirements aimed primarily at cocaine-producing Colombia, where the military and police operated death squads. Aid was to be denied to any country that:

- Was not a democracy
- Where military and police were engaged in a pattern of gross human rights violations
- The military exercised control over civilian authorities
- There was no improvement in human rights.

Also in 1989, an amendment to the **Foreign Assistance Appropriations Act** banned aid to any country where a democratic government was deposed. Subsequently, many countries were denied aid by presidential executive order. The first was Sudan in 1990.

The **Freedom Support Act** of 1992 banned aid to any country with a "consistent pattern of human rights violations" unless there was evidence of "significant progress toward establishing democracy and respecting human rights." Azerbaijan, in particular, was denied aid because of systematic repression of its Armenian minority. A second aid precondition was the removal of Russian troops from Estonia, Latvia, and Lithuania.

The **Leahy Amendment** to the Foreign Operations Appropriation Act of 1997 banned security aid and training to any country with an army or police force that engaged in gross human rights. The aim was to stop aid to Colombia until the government rooted out death squads from security forces.

In 1998, Congress passed the **International Religious Freedom Act** to authorize aid sanctions against countries that engage in or tolerate violations of religious freedom, such as restrictions on assembly as well as flagrant denials of the rights to life, liberty, or the security of persons, including torture. In 2011, Burma, China, Egypt, Eritrea, Iran, Iraq, Nigeria, North Korea, Pakistan, Saudi Arabia, Sudan, Tajikistan, Turkey, Turkmenistan, Uzbekistan, and Vietnam were designated by the Secretary of State as "countries of particular concern." On the "watch list" were Afghanistan, Belarus, Cuba, India, Indonesia, Laos, Russia, Somalia, and Venezuela.

In 2000, as noted above, Congress passed the **Victims of Trafficking and Violence Protection Act**, authorizing the president to deny nonhumanitarian aid to any country that condones or tolerates human trafficking. In 2005, President Bush imposed full sanctions on Cuba, Myanmar, and North Korea for failure to comply. Although Ecuador, Kuwait, and Saudi Arabia were also cited, they were allowed to receive specific aid aimed at promoting democratic reform, whereas Cambodia and Venezuela were restricted to democracy-building and humanitarian aid. Bolivia, Jamaica, Qatar, Sudan, Togo, and the United Arab Emirates were congratulated for taking positive steps toward compliance but remained on the "watch list." In 2012, countries deemed in noncompliance were Algeria, Central African Republic, Democratic Republic of the Congo, Cuba, Equatorial Guinea, Eritrea, Iran, Kuwait, Libya, Madagascar, Papua New Guinea, Saudi Arabia, Sudan, Syria, Yemen, and Zimbabwe, while 41 countries were on the "watch list."

Aid conditionality can also be contrary to human rights goals. In 2000, President Bill Clinton (1946–) signed the Treaty of Rome establishing the ICC, but he did not submit the treaty to the Senate for ratification out of concern that American armed forces operating overseas might be prosecuted by the ICC even if the United States had not ratified. His successor, President Bush, "un-signed" the treaty in 2001. Washington then carried out a campaign to undermine the ICC out of fear that Americans might be indicted as a politically-motivated form of mischief to embarrass the country.

In 2001, Congress passed the **American Service-Members' Protection Act**, which:

- Prohibited the United States from cooperating with the ICC
- Required the president to insist that American soldiers will not participate in international peacekeeping operations unless exempted from ICC jurisdiction
- Permitted the termination of American military assistance to any country ratifying the ICC treaty
- Authorized the use of military force to liberate any American or citizen of a country allied with the United States from detention by ICC at The Hague.

Opponents of the latter clause called the law the "Netherlands Invasion Act," and the Dutch government strongly protested. Based on the law, 51 countries reported that the United States threatened to terminate aid because they refused to deny themselves the possibility of referring an American citizen to ICC, though President Bush issued waivers to allow aid to 22 of those countries. Washington also signed bilateral agreements with nearly 100 countries, providing that they would not extradite

US citizens to the ICC for prosecution. By 2012, the court was so popular that 121 countries had ratified ICC's Rome Statute, and the law was ignored.

In 2001, Congress passed the **Zimbabwe Democracy and Economic Recovery Act** to oppose any loans or debt cancellations to the country. Other sanctions were travel restrictions and the seizure of the assets of President Robert Mugabe (1924–) and others responsible for the breakdown of law and order in the country following the takeover of agricultural lands from longtime Caucasian owners.

The **American Service-Members' Protection Act** of 2002 prohibited military aid to any country joining the ICC, but meanwhile the European Union actively encouraged such membership. The law, thus, was nullified.

The **North Korean Human Rights Act** of 2004 provided that aid to North Korea must be contingent on human rights improvements. Specifically, if Pyongyang made substantial progress in addressing human rights issues, nonhumanitarian aid would flow to meet the country's energy needs. Food aid could increase, provided that there was more transparency in regard to those receiving the food. In response, North Korea turned down additional aid, considering the law to be evidence of a "hostile" policy.

Aid sanctions have been leveled less obtrusively within foreign aid appropriation acts over the years. The most recent blockage of aid was to Rwanda in 2012 because that government was accused of aiding destabilizing forces in the eastern part of the Democratic Republic of Congo, where conflict has cost the lives of some five million persons from 1998, but the Obama administration was opposed, arguing that the information for the accusation was false.

Because much foreign aid tends to involve contracts from governments to private sector agencies in order to provide direct services to individuals, such as disease inoculations, the sanctions reviewed above tend to be more symbolic than punitive. Food aid, for instance, tends to respond more to agricultural surpluses in the United States than to hunger in the world. One estimate is that at least 60 percent of American foreign aid never leaves the United States. American foreign aid amounts were steadily cut over the years, especially after the end of the Cold War, though they increased after the terrorist attacks on September 11, 2001.

Foreign aid is supposed to be a temporary measure that will enable a poorer country to develop into a self-sustaining economy. If aid is successful, a country can rely on the internal market as well as derive income from foreign trade. Aid can then stop. Whereas aid sanctions tend to be microeconomic, measures related to trade can impact an entire sector or the entire country, having a macroeconomic effect.

ECONOMIC MEASURES: TRADE[4]

Foreign commerce enables a country to sell and import valuable goods and services. Governmental trade policies involve extending foreign **credit**; providing **loans** and **loan guarantees**; granting **licenses**; and making government **purchases** from other countries.

Punitive trade measures, known as **sanctions**, can limit or cancel all the various trade benefits. For example, one country might either raise a tax (a tariff) on imported goods made by child labor or establish a quota (a nontariff barrier) on the number of products estimated to be manufactured by child labor. The most severe trade sanction is an **embargo** with a particular country, that is, a ban on imports and exports; a **boycott** is only a refusal to import. Businesses eschew boycotts and embargoes if they will lose money; instead, they may engage in "sanction busting." Countries less interested in human rights might sell the same goods to the errant country, thereby nullifying the boycott. For example, when the United States suspended grain sales to the Soviet Union in the 1980s to protest the Soviet invasion of Afghanistan, Argentina sold its grain to Russia, filling the gap. Unless a restriction applies to strategic goods, where one country has a monopoly on a particular technology or spare parts, an economic boycott is unlikely to be effective.

Corporations that fail to adopt a code of conduct also risk **citizen boycotts**. While South Africa maintained *apartheid*, many nongovernmental organizations urged a boycott of Shell Oil Company, the principal supplier of petroleum to the country. Currently, the UN Human Rights Council has recommended boycotts of Hewlett-Packard, Caterpillar, and Motorola because they do business in Israel, America's ally.

Yet another way to end economic contact with a country is to engage in **divestment** – that is, for businesses to liquidate all investments from an offending state, though presumably a seller must find a buyer to liquidate an asset, and the effect may be to sell at a loss. One by one, many universities divested their endowment portfolio of companies doing business in South Africa during the 1980s.

From the founding of the United States, trade relations with other countries were initiated by negotiating treaties with **most-favored-nation** (MFN) clauses, thereby ensuring that tariffs applied to American exports would equal the lowest tariff rate applied to other countries. The first such MFN treaty was between the United States and Britain in 1794.

Washington also authorized trade restrictions from the early years of the republic (Table 11.4). In 1795, Congress passed the **National Emergencies Act** to authorize the president to take action to protect the national interest. The law, which does not specify the use of economic sanctions or identify human rights issues, provides a procedure that could be used today to single out a particular country as a gross violator of human rights.

TABLE 11.4 **AMERICAN LAWS ALLOWING TRADE SANCTIONS ON COUNTRIES VIOLATING HUMAN RIGHTS**

Title of statute	Passed
National Emergencies Act	1795
Nonimportation Act	1806
Embargo Act	1807
Nonintercourse Act	1809
Trade Act	1890

Continued

TABLE 11.4   (CONTINUED)

Title of statute	Passed
Trading With the Enemy Act	1917
Neutrality Act Amendments[a]	1935
Generalized System of Preferences Renewal Act	1974
Trade Act (Jackson–Vanik Amendment)	1974
International Security Assistance and Arms Export Control Act	1975
Arms Export Control Act	1976
Ribicoff Amendment (to the Tax Reform Act)	1976
Export Administration Amendments Act	1977
International Emergency Economic Powers Act	1977
Export Administration Act	1979
Generalized System of Preferences Renewal Act	1984
Comprehensive Anti-Apartheid Act	1986
Iraq Sanctions Act	1990
Cuban Democracy Act (Torricelli Law)	1992
Iran–Iraq Arms Non-Proliferation Act	1992
Cuban Liberty and Democratic Solidarity Act (Helms–Burton Act)	1996
Iran and Libya Sanctions Act[b]	1996
Cohen–Feinstein Amendment	1996
International Religious Freedom Act	1998
African Growth and Opportunity Act	2000
Iran Nonproliferation Act	2000
Trade Sanctions Reform and Export Enhancement Act	2000
Zimbabwe Democracy and Economic Recovery Act	2001
Burmese Freedom and Democracy Act	2003
Syria Accountability and Lebanese Sovereignty Restoration Act	2003
Clean Diamond Trade Act	2003
Iran and Syria Nonproliferation Act	2005
Iran, North Korea, and Syria Nonproliferation Act	2006
Belarus Democracy and Recovery Act	2006
Darfur Peace and Accountability Act	2006
Democratic Republic of the Congo Relief, Security, and Democracy Promotion Act	2006
Belarus Human Rights and Democracy Act	2011
Sudan Accountability and Divestment Act	2008
Congo Conflict Minerals Act	2009
Comprehensive Iran Sanctions, Accountability, and Divestment Act	2010
Iran Sanctions Act	2011
Iran Threat Reduction and Syria Human Rights Act	2012
Maritsky Act	2012

[a] Later amendments adopted in 1936, 1937, and 1939.
[b] Renewed in 2001 but superseded by several later laws.

The impressments of sailors by British ships during the Napoleonic Wars led to the passage of the **Nonimportation Act** of 1806 (as amended by the **Embargo Act** of 1807 and the **Nonintercourse Act** of 1809). The legislation, which restricted British imports, provided a pretext for Britain to launch the War of 1812. Later in the century, human rights were for the first time a consideration in regard to international trade. Goods produced by prison labor were banned by the **Trade Act** of 1890.

Trade increased dramatically during the Industrial Revolution of the late nineteenth century. European Industrial Countries seeking exclusive access to raw materials sought colonies in Africa and Asia.

China's lucrative market was coveted throughout much of the nineteenth century after Britain established a colony in Hong Kong during 1842 as a result of the Opium Wars (1839–1842 and 1846–1860); Portugal, which had been renting Macau from 1557, got approval from China in 1887 to make the territory a colony. Various countries sought exclusive trade concessions of various sorts. With China's defeat in the Sino-Japanese War of 1895, powerful trading countries scrambled for port access by partitioning the country into spheres of influence. In 1899, rather than such an imperialistic approach, McKinley's Secretary of State, John Hay (1838–1905), proclaimed the policy of the Open Door. He asked Britain, France, Germany, Italy, Japan, and Russia to make formal declarations that they would respect Chinese administrative and territorial integrity and would allow free use of Chinese ports within their spheres of influence to all countries. But Hay's efforts were for naught. China had to wait long after World War II to abolish all such encroachments and made arrangements for Britain (by 1997) and Portugal (by 1999) to give up their colonies at the end of the twentieth century.

The effort to protect domestic industries resulted in tariffs. The **Tariff Act** of 1890, sponsored by William McKinley (1843–1901), who later became president, raised import duties by an average of nearly 50 percent, though the Tariff Act was amended in 1894 to lower rates. The issue became the principal policy disagreement between the two major parties. The pro-tariff Republican Party was largely in control of Congress and the presidency until 1932.

When World War I broke out, the United States was initially neutral. Trade with Europe became imperiled by Germany's attempt to stop American shipments to Britain and France with unrestricted submarine warfare, which stopped in 1915 when President Woodrow Wilson (1856–1924) objected, but resumed in 1917, whereupon the United States entered the war. Much current legislation dealing with trade sanctions is modeled on the **Trading with the Enemy Act** of 1917, which was applied to Germany and its allies in World Wars I and II and later to the Soviet Union and its allies during the Cold War. In 1963, for example, Cuba was designated as an enemy state under the Trading with the Enemy Act. The Cuban trade embargo continues to the present, although the UN General Assembly has repeatedly voted to condemn the practice.

In 1935, the Neutrality Act of 1794 was amended (in response to Italy's invasion of Ethiopia) to prohibit American citizens from selling arms to belligerents in international wars. An amendment in 1936 (during the Spanish Civil War) banned providing credits and loans to belligerents, which in turn was applied to civil wars by an amendment in 1937. A 1939 amendment outlawed such war materials as oil and steel.

In 1944, at a meeting in Bretton Woods, New Hampshire, the post-World War II economic order determined that the US dollar would become the unit of international currency. The International Bank for Reconstruction and Development and the IMF were formed to assist European reconstruction, but their focus shifted to developing countries from the 1960s.

From the beginning of the Cold War, the United States has employed trade sanctions about 100 times. Perhaps the earliest explicit use of economic sanctions as a response to human rights violations occurred in 1967, when President Lyndon Johnson (1908–1973) issued Executive Order 11322, authorizing a boycott of Rhodesia. His action served to implement a United Nations resolution.

The United States, which long applied MFN status in foreign trade, responded to the call for a New International Economic Order in the 1970s by passing the **Trade Act** of 1974 to provide very low tariffs for certain goods imported from the Third World under the generalized system of preferences (GSP). Because labor interests in the United States were concerned that cheap products manufactured by child, forced, and prison labor would flood the market, violation of workers' rights was added as a criterion for denying GSP privileges in the **Generalized System of Preferences Renewal Act** in 1974. Currently, the United States GSP applies to about 4,650 products from 128 designated beneficiary countries and territories duty-free. Developed countries remained covered by MFN.

Congress made a stern statement in the same Trade Act of 1974 by including the **Jackson–Vanik Amendment**, cosponsored by Senator Henry Jackson (1912–1983) and Representative Charles Vanik (1913–2007), which provided that MFN status could be denied to a country with a non-market economy, especially one that either restricted emigration rights or failed to cooperate in identifying soldiers missing in action. The principal target was the Soviet Union, which was forbidding Jews from emigrating by placing onerous taxes on their exit permits. In addition, the law encouraged Cambodia, Laos, North Korea, and Vietnam to cooperate in searching for American MIAs (soldiers missing in action). When Poland was placed under martial law in 1982, Washington withdrew MFN from Warsaw in protest. Other than communist countries, MFN status over the years was denied to Afghanistan and Serbia. The amendment, which assisted Jews in migrating, is now obsolete and was repealed in 2012, thanks to the Magnitsky Act. However, that law authorizes sanctions against anyone responsible for the imprisonment, torture, and murder of Sergei Magnitsky (1972–2009), who had exposed corruption and fraud within the Russian government. In response, Russia banned the adoption in the United States of children from Russia, an example of retorsion.

The **International Security Assistance and Arms Export Control Act** of 1975 not only authorized aid cutoffs but also trade embargoes. Military weapons could not be sold to countries with unacceptable human rights records. The **Arms Export Control Act** of 1976 stipulated that military aid could be exported to countries seeking the means for legitimate self-defense. When the Arab League pressured American companies to join a boycott of Israel, Congress adopted the **Ribicoff Amendment** to the Tax Reform Act of 1976 and the **Export Administration Amendments Act** of 1977. The latter amended a 1969 law to prohibit companies from boycotting trade with Israel or any other country on friendly terms with the United States. The former, named after Senator Abraham Ribicoff (1910–1998), denied tax benefits to any country that participated in such a boycott. Both laws also banned corporate discrimination based on race, religion, sex, national origin or nationality.

The National Emergencies Act and the Trading with the Enemy Act were superseded in 1977 by the **International Emergency Economic Powers Act**, which in recent years has been interpreted to apply to human rights and terrorism issues. (The **Export Administration Act** of 1979 empowered the president to control exports for reasons of national security, foreign policy, or short supply, but it expired in 1994, whereupon President Clinton declared a national emergency and permanent applicability of the 1977 law.) As further amended by the **Trade Sanctions Reform and Export Enhancement Act** of 2000, the president was authorized to designate a country as constituting a "national emergency," whereupon the Treasury Department's Office of Foreign Assets Control could freeze assets or establish trade embargoes through a variety of means.

Based on the above framework, congressional legislation has been very selective in calling for economic sanctions. For example, when the Iranian government refused to assist in releasing diplomats who were held hostage at the American embassy in Tehran in 1980, Washington responded by freezing all Iranian assets in the United States. The assets were to be unfrozen by applications to the Iran–United States Claims Tribunal, which was set up by a bilateral treaty between the two countries in 1981 to resolve commercial disputes by 1982.

When President Reagan took office, terrorism was added to the list of serious human rights violations. In 1981, while the aforementioned claims tribunal was in operation, Iran was placed on the list of states supporting international terrorism, thus invoking sanctions that prohibited aid, loans, and weapons sales to Tehran. In 1987, the boycott was extended to imports of any goods or services from Iran. In 1997, President Clinton imposed comprehensive sanctions on Iran, prohibiting all commercial and financial transactions with Tehran, though in 2000 exceptions were allowed for imports of carpets, caviar, dried fruits, and nuts.

In 1986, after 25 of the 50 states, and 164 local governments, adopted selective purchasing laws to stop business with corporations operating in South Africa, Congress enacted, over the veto of President Reagan, the **Comprehensive Anti-Apartheid Act**, the subtext of which was a rejection of the policy of constructive engagement by Washington with Pretoria. The law stated that United States government should employ diplomatic, economic, political, and other means to encourage the South African government to end *apartheid*, to establish democracy, and to respect human rights. Among the sanctions were prohibitions on licenses and loans as well as trade (imports of armaments, coal, gold coins, petroleum, sugar, textiles, uranium, and any trade involving agencies enforcing *apartheid*). South African Airlines, for example, was not allowed to fly to the United States. The 1986 law also adopted the Sullivan Principles, as discussed in Chapter 6.

The International Emergency Economic Powers Act was applied by President Reagan in 1988 following the Libyan-sponsored terrorist attack on Pan American flight 103. As a result, Libyan assets were frozen and all trade and financial dealings were banned with Libya. Then in 1992, Libya was added to the list of terrorist states, resulting in a ban on exports of petroleum, military, or aviation equipment to Libya, commercial flights to or from Libya, and restrictions on Libyan financial activities.

In 1990, a week before American defense contractors were scheduled to fly to Iraq in order to promote the sale of advanced missile and weapons technology, Congress passed the **Iraq Sanctions Act** because of evidence that Baghdad was building biological, chemical, and nuclear weapons as well as supporting terrorism and engaging in gross violations of human rights against the Kurdish minority. The law was the first time Congress ever approved a comprehensive sanctions package, including a total ban on all commercial transactions. As a result, defense contractors were stopped from completing their sales. Iraq invaded Kuwait five months later, and sanctions remained until the Iraq War of 2003.

In 1994, the Marrakesh Agreement Establishing the World Trade Organization established MFN, now known as **normal trade relations** (NTR), as the basis for world trade. From 1994, presidents have given annual waivers to most countries formerly considered ineligible for MFN. Currently, the United States has permanent NTR with all countries but Cuba and North Korea.

In 1989, following the brutal crackdown on demonstrators near Beijing's Tiananmen Square, many Anglo-European countries, including the United States, began a boycott of Chinese goods. Meanwhile, as China developed a market economy in the 1980s, Beijing had been seeking NTR status. In 1990, President George H. W. Bush (1924–), onetime ambassador to Beijing, granted China a waiver to the MFN prohibition, and a majority in Congress did not vote down the waiver. Bush, of course, hoped that China would not oppose the Gulf War of 1991, but interests supporting MFN for China inside the United States included the National Association of Wheat Growers, some 100 trade associations and companies in the Business Coalition for US–China Trade, as well as the law firm of Jones, Day, Reavis & Pogue, which was paid by China to lobby for its interests. Congressional efforts to impose sanctions on China in response to human rights issues were twice vetoed by President Bush. However, when Chinese goods produced by forced laborers were disallowed by customs authorities in accordance with the Slavery Convention of 1926, the result was a backlash from Beijing. Subsequently, China was less cooperative in diplomacy with the United States whenever trade sanction threats were issued and more cooperative when threats were not a part of the diplomatic environment.

In 1992, the **Cuban Democracy Act** further restricted trade with Cuba, including trade of foreign subsidiaries of American corporations, with the exception of medical supplies. In short, the United States established a secondary boycott. The law provides that the embargo may be lifted when Habana holds free elections and establishes a market economy.

Also in 1992, the **Iran–Iraq Arms Nonproliferation Act** banned trade with any business that contributes to the development of advanced conventional, biological, chemical, or nuclear weapons. About a dozen companies, mostly Chinese, were then disallowed from doing business with the United States government for periods of two to three years until they were deemed compliant. Later laws strengthened trade sanctions.

In 1995, President Clinton announced his intention to impose punitive tariffs on more than US$1 billion of Chinese goods, the largest trade sanction in American history, because of piracy of American films, music, and software. Within three weeks Beijing caved in to forestall the imposition of tariffs. On the same date that China agreed to combat piracy, Clinton announced in an apparent *quid pro quo* that he would separate American trade policy toward China from human rights concerns. Later in the same year, the United States lobbied to have the UN Commission on Human Rights stop issuing condemnations of Beijing's human rights record. The lobbying produced a 21–20 vote favorable to China. In 2001, President George W. Bush made the NTR waiver permanent.

The year 1996 was a banner year for passage of legislation authorizing economic sanctions. **The Cuban Liberty and Democratic Solidarity Act**, cosponsored by Senator Jesse Helms, Jr (1921–2008) and Representative Dan Burton (1938–) and sometimes called the Libertad Act, prohibits trade with any company doing business with Cuba; European firms were the principal targets. Although restrictions on trade with Cuba began in opposition to communist rule, human rights issues continued to be stressed after the end of the Cold War.

The second 1996 law, the **Iran and Libya Sanctions Act**, authorized sanctions against non-American companies that provided new investments worth over US$40 million for the development of petroleum resources in Iran or Libya and violated a UN trade boycott of Libya in arms, certain oil equipment, and civil aviation services. Sanctions consisted of a denial of Export-Import Bank assistance, trade licenses, bank loans or credits, government contracts, and some or all imports from the violating company. The act, which was to expire in five years, was renewed in 2001, though a separate **Iran Nonproliferation Act** passed in 2000. When Tripoli decided to abandon a nuclear weapons program in 2004, sanctions were lifted from Libya.

In 1996, six years after the Burmese government annulled election results won by the National League for Democracy, some 250 members of that political party were arrested by the government. The following month, the Massachusetts legislature imposed a 10 percent fine on contractors with the state government that did business with Myanmar in a law that was modeled on similar legislation at the state and local level in the 1980s regarding South Africa. Three months later, Senators William Cohen (1940–) and Dianne Feinstein (1933–) proposed an amendment to the Foreign Operations Appropriations Act, known as the **Cohen–Feinstein Amendment**, which authorized the president to have the power to prohibit new private investment with Myanmar as long as that government continued to engage in large-scale political repression, including the house arrest of Aung San Suu Kyi (1945–). In 1998, the Massachusetts law and similar laws in various cities were declared unconstitutional in *National Foreign Trade Council v. Baker* (26FSupp2d287) for interfering with executive prerogatives to be the exclusive branch involved in making foreign policy, a ruling affirmed by the Supreme Court during 1999 in *Crosby v. National Foreign Trade Council* (530US363). The court also cited the Cohen–Feinstein Amendment as a basis for declaring that national laws preempt state laws in matters of foreign affairs. In any case, Apple Computer, Eastman Kodak, Philips Electronics, and Hewlett-Packard were among the companies that withdrew their businesses from Myanmar.

As early as 1993, the UN General Assembly denounced Sudan for the brutal civil war in the south of the country. Sudan's support for international terrorism, efforts to destabilize neighboring governments, and human rights violations, including slavery and the denial of religious freedom to Christians, rankled many members of Congress, which contemplated a strong Sudan sanctions law involving a ban on all trade and freezing of Sudanese assets. In 1997, President Clinton then preempted the legislation by an executive order authorizing a more selective ban on trade. He was reacting to corporations that noted that Sudan accounted for 80 percent of the world supply of gum arabic, an indispensable ingredient in candy, ink, and other products.

In addition to aid restrictions, the **International Religious Freedom Act** of 1998 authorized trade embargoes on countries that persecute religious minorities. The principal offender, China, was given a waiver.

In 2000, Congress passed the **African Growth and Opportunity Act**. Although primarily aimed at promoting economic development through duty-free trade, eligibility is based on human rights considerations. Initially, 34 of the 48 countries in sub-Saharan Africa were eligible; today, 40 qualify. Those ineligible are Central African Republic, Democratic Republic of Congo, Equatorial Guinea, Eritrea, Madagascar, Somalia, Sudan, and Zimbabwe.

Because of economic "mismanagement, undemocratic practices, and the costly deployment of troops to the Democratic Republic of Congo," the IMF and the World Bank suspended all assistance to Zimbabwe by the end of the twentieth century. In 2001, Congress passed the **Zimbabwe Democracy and Economic Recovery Act** to provide American assistance in debt relief and financial assistance provided that the government would take steps to increase democracy. The United States, according to the law, would only support World Bank aid projects to the country if they served to increase democracy and human rights. Sanctions were also imposed on individuals, corporations, and organizations that participated in activities that undermine human rights. In recent years, bills have been introduced in Congress to repeal the law, which remains in effect.

An important provision of the **US Trade Act** of 2002 was the requirement that future preferential trade agreements (PTAs) concluded with other countries must require a minimum in environmental and labor standards. At the time, Washington had concluded trade agreements with Canada, Israel, Jordan, and México. Subsequently, when bilateral PTAs were negotiated with seven more countries and those in the Caribbean Free Trade Agreement, the requirement had no effect. Instead, each country sought to improve their domestic legislation on the subject in order to qualify for PTA status.

The year 2003, when the United States invaded Iraq, brought another wave of economic sanctions. Further repression in Myanmar led to the passage of the **Burmese Freedom and Democracy Act**, which required comprehensive economic sanctions, including a ban of all imports, freezing assets, voting against all loans to the government of Myanmar as well as calling for the release from arrest of all political prisoners. The law was renewed annually until 2012, when the government decided to hold a limited free election.

In 2003, Congress also adopted the **Clean Diamond Trade Act** to implement provisions of a multilateral agreement to stop serious human rights violations in Liberia and Sierra Leone, in which paramilitary rebels had been using uncut diamonds to purchase military armaments. The law prohibited the importation of rough diamonds from either country, whereupon the illicit trade shifted from diamonds to logs and timber. The same law put a US$2 million bounty on the capture of Charles Taylor, Liberia's president, who left the country and was granted asylum in Nigeria, although the Liberian civil war continued with Taylor loyalists. In 2004, accordingly, sanctions were imposed on the Taylorites. The **Congo Conflict Minerals Act** of 2009 extended similar provisions in the law to the Democratic Republic of the Congo and adjoining countries, where minerals were being traded for arms.

Under the **Syria Accountability and Lebanese Sovereignty Restoration Act** of 2003, Damascus was cited for undermining the stability of Iraq and Lebanon. The law specifically objected to the presence of Syrian troops in Lebanon since 1976, Syria's development of chemical weapons, money laundering, and shipments of military items to insurgent forces in Iraq. Banned were all exports to Syria except for food and medicines and transactions with the Commercial Bank of Syria. Syrian troops left Lebanon in 2005 with little effect on the sanctions.

Suspicions continued about Iran's nuclear ambitions and Syria's chemical weapons development, and in 2005 North Korea withdrew from the Nonproliferation Treaty after contentious negotiations. Sanctions legislation became the order of the day. The Iran Nonproliferation Act of 2000 was revised in 2005 as the Iran Nonproliferation Amendments Act but was extended to Syria, so the revised law was also called the **Iran and Syria Nonproliferation Act**. And in 2006, Congress passed the **Iran, North Korea, and Syria Nonproliferation Act** to extend sanctions on all three countries in order to stop any shipments that would advance further weapons development. Stiffer sanctions against Iran were adopted by legislation in 2010, 2011, and 2012. The latter law, the **Iran Threat Reduction and Syria Human Rights Act**, reacted as well to the massacres by the Syrian government in its civil war.

Continued anti-democratic measures by the government prompted passage of the **Belarus Democracy Reauthorization Act** of 2006 and the **Belarus Human Rights and Democracy Act** of 2011, which not only continued to authorize sanctions in the form of blocking assets and trade to the country until human rights conditions improved but also urged the International Ice Hockey Federation to cancel plans to hold the 2014 World Ice Hockey Championship in Minsk.

In 2003, Sudan began to attack villages in Darfur, prompting further condemnation. The 2006 **Darfur Peace and Accountability Act** amended the 1997 bill to exempt sanctions from Darfur, South Sudan, and some other areas of the country while continuing the ban on all Sudanese petroleum. The **Sudan Accountability and Divestment Act** of 2007 went farther, prohibiting debt financing for companies that do business in Sudan, requiring companies seeking contracts with the federal government to certify that they are not doing business in Sudan, and encouraging state and local government to divest from any company with commercial ties to the country.

The **Democratic Republic of the Congo Relief, Security, and Democracy Promotion Act** of 2006 urged the UN peacekeeping force to stop arming of children and human trafficking, and supported the arms embargo of the country. Chaotic conditions continue.

Many skeptics, pointing for example to the survival of the Cuban government, argue that economic sanctions do not work. Nevertheless, multilateral sanctions imposed on South Africa played an important role in ending *apartheid* in South Africa. Sanctions reportedly convinced Serbia to turn over President Slobodan Milošević to The Hague in 2001 for trial at the international court on war crimes in the former Yugoslavia. Sanctions on Libya led the country to surrender two terrorists to a Scottish court in 1999 and to abandon a nuclear weapons program in 2004.

DISCUSSION TOPIC 11.1 CAN NONMILITARY SANCTIONS EVER BE EFFECTIVE?

Reviewing examples of diplomatic, legal, and economic sanctions, when are they most and least likely to be effective? To stop serious human rights abuses, why not threaten or employ military sanctions instead?

Nevertheless, economic sanctions work slowly, and many corporations get around sanctions by using third parties. Companies will often relocate their assets to Swiss bank accounts while decisions to impose sanctions are being discussed. Because many observers are understandably impatient whenever millions of lives are in imminent jeopardy, the tendency for sanctions to fail in bringing about the desired behavior will provoke some countries to contemplate military action.

MILITARY AND VIOLENT ACTION

In his "Farewell Address," a letter of 1796, President George Washington (1732–1799) urged his country to avoid "entangling alliances." He was aware that Alexander Hamilton (1755–1804) proposed that the United States intervene on the side of Britain while Thomas Jefferson (1743–1826) sought the support of the government to aid France in the continental war fought by Napoléon Bonaparte (1769–1821). He warned against wars abroad as contrary to the interest of a young country amid major powers that could inflict material damage on the country, and he had seen enough dead bodies as the commander of the revolution. With his support, the **Neutrality Act** was passed in 1794 to prohibit American residents from participating militarily in foreign wars.

The United States began without a standing army, preferring state militias to keep the peace. Nevertheless, there was need for a navy, which was formed in 1794 to cope with the threat of piracy along the North African Coast, experienced up to 1816.

Throughout American history, military force has been used on several occasions. Massacres of the native peoples of North America in pursuit of the "manifest destiny" to have territorial boundaries on the Atlantic and Pacific are an embarrassment today. Declaration of war on Britain in 1812, though justified as a response to British seizure of sailors aboard American ships, was also in apparent pursuit of annexing Canada. At the end of the Napoleonic Wars (1803–1815), Spain considered recolonizing territories in the Americas that had declared independence. The Monroe Doctrine, as declared in 1823, threatened that the United States was prepared to use military force to stop any such recolonization, a goal central to human rights concerns.

The next war started as a minor dispute over the border between México and Texas. The end in 1848 saw American troops marching into México City and detaching areas beyond Texas into the territory of the United States.

Victory of the United States in the Spanish–American War of 1898, which began on a phony pretext, resulted in annexation of Guam, the Philippines (before Germany could do so), and Puerto Rico. The Congressional resolution in 1898 formalized the annexation of Hawai'i because there were insufficient votes to ratify a treaty on the matter. Indeed, the previous president, Grover Cleveland (1837–1908), did not approve, calling annexation contrary to international law. The Native Hawaiians did not dare resist because a formidable number of American troops were docked on ships in the ports of Honolulu.

President Woodrow Wilson (1856–1924) famously led the United States into World War I in 1917 to "make the world safe for democracy." Less remembered is Wilson's occasional dispatch of American troops to Central American countries whenever American commercial interests appeared in jeopardy.

HISTORIC EVENT 11.2 JAPANESE ARE RELOCATED TO INTERNMENT CAMPS (1942–1945)

On December 7, 1941, Japanese airplanes bombed the naval base at Pearl Harbor, Hawai'i. Soon, Japanese submarines surfaced and shelled locations on the West Coast of the United States. Fearing that residents of Japanese ancestry might cooperate with an invasion force, the US Army requested President Franklin Roosevelt (1882–1945) to take drastic measures. In 1942, after a nighttime curfew was imposed on Japanese residents of the West Coast, an order came for all persons of Japanese ancestry on the West Coast, 65 percent of whom were American citizens, to report to temporary locations. Although 11,000 were allowed to move to other parts of the United States, some 110,000 were sent to war relocation camps in the interior, where most remained until 1945, though some young Japanese males

Continued

were able to leave the camps if they volunteered to serve in the US Army. Those of Japanese ancestry living in other parts of the United States, including Hawai'i, were not affected by the internment order unless specific evidence warranted their detention. In 1944, the Supreme Court ruled in *Korematsu v. United States* (323US214) that the relocation was lawful because national security trumped Bill of Rights protections. Some American residents of Austrian, German, and Italian ancestry were also detained until the war ended in 1945. Some 23,000 Japanese on the West Coast of Canada were also relocated, and Perú sent about 2,000 persons of Japanese ancestry to relocation camps in Texas. After the war, some compensation was provided to those who had been detained.

The Pact of Paris in 1928, negotiated by American Secretary of State Frank Kellogg (1856–1937) with French Foreign Minister Aristide Briand (1862–1832), declared that any use of force was illegal under international law. More than 50 countries signed on.

In 1941, Japan bombed Pearl Harbor, Nazi Germany declared war on the United States, and Americans were at war again. Because American military officials were nervous about the role of Japanese nationals and Japanese Americans living on the Pacific Coast, they pretended that they had evidence sufficient to warrant their removal to the interior of the United States for most of the war, though no such action was taken in Hawai'i, where the Japanese accounted for 37 percent of the population.

After the war, Kellogg–Briand Pact principles were incorporated into the United Nations Charter, but the United States and its allies soon were opposed by the Soviet Union and its allies in a Cold War. Under the UN Charter, the United States and other countries found that they could use six types of military action in response to human rights problems. The principal proactive methods were:

- To finance and participate in international **peacekeeping forces**, which in time have had human rights components
- To enforce (much later) **no-fly zones** that serve to prevent a country from attacking its own people.

The punitive methods have been:

- The **threat of force**
- The **use of force**.

Intermediate are:

- Supplying **nonlethal aid** to one side in a conflict
- Furnishing **military aid** to allies.

Both punitive methods, if used unilaterally, violate the UN Charter, which declares that the United Nations has the exclusive right to authorize the use of force in order to settle interstate disputes, although military reprisals and retorsions remain exceptions. Insofar as military and nonlethal aid involve taking sides in a civil war, they violate the custom of neutrality in time of war or the Convention on Duties and Rights of States in the Event of Civil Strife of 1928.

As a country that initially fought for the right of self-determination, presidents have justified American entry into war on the basis of that right. Foreign policy "doctrines," beginning with the Monroe Doctrine of 1823, which applied to Latin America, have been proclaimed to justify support for military action abroad.

With the advent of the Cold War, the Truman Doctrine of 1947 justified American involvement in providing economic and military aid to back the Greek and Turkish governments from possible takeovers led by external Communist Party forces, again relying on the principle of self-determination. According to President Harry Truman (1884–1972), "the policy of the United States [is] to support free peoples who are resisting attempted subjugation by armed minorities or by outside pressures."

Peacekeeping. The United States has supplied peacekeeping forces for the United Nations on several occasions, supporting the principle of self-determination. The first occasion was in 1953, when the UN authorized a peacekeeping force along the border between North and South Korea after the armistice ending the Korean War (1950–1953). Americans remained in the UN Command until 1967, when North Korea demanded its removal, whereupon American troops took over.

HISTORIC EVENT 11.3 THE UNITED STATES OBJECTS TO SUEZ CANAL SEIZURE (1956)

After a coup, Muhammad Naguib (1901–1984) seized power in Egypt during 1952. One grievance of his government was about the continued British control over the Suez Canal. When he became president, Naguib quarreled with other members of the coup and eventually resigned in 1954. His successor was Gamal Abdel Nasser (1918–1970). On July 26, 1956, Nasser nationalized the Suez Canal and blocked Israeli shipping through it. Although the United States urged Britain and France to resolve the crisis through negotiations, London and Paris instead secretly coordinated action with Israel, which launched an attack on Egypt's Sinai Peninsula on October 29. One day later, the United States summoned the UN Security Council to demand Israel's withdrawal, and the Soviet Union presented a similar motion. Both proposals were vetoed by Britain and France, which proceeded to bomb Egypt on October 31. In an emergency session on November 2, the General Assembly relied on the Uniting for Peace Resolution to call for an immediate ceasefire, withdrawal of all forces behind armistice lines, an arms embargo, and the reopening of the Suez Canal.

Continued

On November 5, Britain and France landed troops, heading for Port Said. Then Britain and France agreed to a cease fire on November 6. On November 7, the General Assembly authorized the establishment of the UN Emergency Force (UNEF) to land between the opposing forces, thereby enforcing a ceasefire. Although Britain and France agreed, and withdrew troops by the end of the year when UNEF forces arrived, Israel at first refused to allow UNEF into areas under its control but finally left the Sinai in March 1957. The Suez Canal was then left under Egyptian control and was cleared for passage by all countries. A major result was that Britain and France had to reconsider their role as junior partners of an alliance headed by the United States, and Egypt welcomed the Soviet Union as a new friend.

In 1956, objecting to the Anglo–French–Israeli attack on Egypt, the United States joined the Soviet Union in calling for a ceasefire. Washington sent peacekeepers to separate the adversaries. In 1957, President Dwight Eisenhower (1890–1969) proclaimed a policy "to secure and protect the territorial integrity and political independence of such nations, requesting such aid against overt armed aggression from any nation controlled by international communism." Known as the Eisenhower Doctrine, one aim was retroactive justification of his Suez policy. The major purpose was to isolate Egypt's Gamal Abdel Nasser (1918–1970), who was seeking to unite all Arabic-speaking countries into a single state. Again, Eisenhower phrased his doctrine in terms of self-determination.

American personnel have been assigned to various peacekeeping forces over the years, but opinion in Washington soured over the practice after 28,000 American peacekeepers, including 160 military personnel, went to Somalia in 1992 to assist in feeding the starving population suffering from to a severe drought amid chaotic conditions. In 1993, as starvation conditions subsided, the military sought to keep the peace by shooting at looters and others causing disorder. During October, American forces were attacked, two helicopters were shot down, 80 were wounded, 1 was captured and later released, but 18 were killed. Some of the American dead bodies were dragged through the streets, a spectacle broadcast on television.

In 2010, the United States contributed US$2.6 billion to the US$7 billion UN peacekeeping budget. Peacekeeping operations are rarely launched or expanded without American financial commitments. In 2012, the United States contributed 17 soldiers and 111 police to UN peacekeeping operations.

No-fly zones. First established over Iraq between the two Gulf Wars from 1991–2003, the UN had authorized "no-fly" zones over the northern and southern parts of Iraq to deter genocidal aerial massacres against Kurds and Shiites. The UN-approved no-fly zone in Bosnia (1993–1995) sought to prevent violations of the ceasefire that ended the civil war. However, ground attacks continued, and in 1995 the UN authorized a bombing campaign against rebel forces of Republika Srpska. (The bombers were supplied by the United States as part of a force of NATO, the first time NATO ever launched a military operation.)

In 2011, the UN Security Council authorized a no-fly zone over Libya because the government threatened to massacre rebels in the eastern town of Benghazi. NATO forces, including the United States, maintained the no-fly zone on the basis of the R2P principle. However, other NATO countries went beyond the mandate to support rebel forces in the overthrow of the Libyan government.

Threat of force. The United States Navy demonstrated readiness to defend the Republic of China in 1955 while the islands of Quemoy and Matsu were being bombarded by the People's Republic of China. Secretary of State John Foster Dulles (1888–1959) warned China that the United States was prepared to use nuclear weapons to stop the attacks. After the conflict died down, a defense treaty was signed between Taipei and Washington. In 1958, Mainland China again fired artillery shells, but stopped after American aircraft fired air-to-air missiles, demonstrating a willingness to support the alliance with reprisals. Thereafter, American threats of force were rare.

Use of force. American coercive diplomacy, as noted above, has used force, though only occasionally in regard to human rights issues. In 1950, when the UN Security Council authorized the defense of South Korea from North Korean military aggression, Washington supplied troops. The right of self-determination was at issue.

But Eisenhower, through the CIA, aided small forces that toppled the democratic government in Guatemala during 1953. In 1960, when Belgium abandoned its colony in the Congo, civil war broke out. Patrice Lumumba (1925–1961), duly elected prime minister of the new government, decided to accept Soviet assistance in restoring order, whereupon Eisenhower asked the CIA to aid the other side. Lumumba was assassinated, President Joseph Kasa-Vubu (1910–1969) assumed control, and Joseph-Désiré Mobutu (1930–1997) organized a coup that brought him to power from 1965 until his death. The Cold War trumped self-determination.

The Kennedy Doctrine, in response to the success of Fidel Castro's successful revolution in Cuba, extended the Truman Doctrine to Latin America. President John Kennedy (1917–1963) was reacting to the fear that Cuban communism would be exported. Support for Latin American dictators was one element of that policy. The unsuccessful secret Bay of Pigs invasion in 1961, however, led him to be cautious about using military force again.

President Lyndon Johnson (1908–1973) did more than offer secret aid to counter the spread of communism. The Johnson Doctrine, at first applied to the Dominican Republic in 1965 and later that year directed to Vietnam, was that American troops would be sent whenever communists were likely to overthrow a "free" government. Johnson escalated troop levels dramatically to assist one side in a civil war that Americans call the Vietnam War. American troops did topple the democratically elected government in the Dominican Republic but were mired in defense of an undemocratic South Vietnam for eight years.

The Nixon Doctrine, announced in mid-1969, qualified the Johnson Doctrine to require any country requesting American aid to bear primary responsibility for its own defense. President Richard Nixon (1913–1994) wanted to withdraw American troops, so he hoped that the war would gradually be "Vietnamized." A lesser known element of the Nixon Doctrine was the promise to provide a "shield" if a nuclear power threatened an ally or a country that an American president decided was vital to its national security.

In 1976, President Gerald Ford (1913–2006) declared that the United States would take "appropriate action" if Cuba intervened anywhere in the Western Hemisphere. Known as the Ford Doctrine, his speech was a response to the dispatch of Cuban troops to Angola in 1975, while he supplied covert CIA funding to the other side in the Angolan civil war. A proxy war ensued until a ceasefire in 1991 brokered by Moscow and Washington. The two Cold War adversaries tired of their proxy war, but the country remained at civil war until 2002, when there was no superpower to challenge the role of the United States.

Not until 1980, three years after taking office, did President Jimmy Carter (1924–) enunciate a policy known as the Carter Doctrine: "An attempt by any outside force to gain control of the Persian Gulf region will be regarded as an assault on the vital interests of the United States of America, and such an assault will be repelled by any means necessary, including military force." Carter, reacting to the Soviet invasion of Afghanistan that year, was concerned that its aggression would be a stepping stone toward Soviet control of Gulf oil.

In 1983, President Reagan authorized a small force to invade the island of Grenada, presumably to rescue American students from danger; if true, the action would be consistent with international law. In 1985, he clarified his approach to foreign policy when he sought to justify American support for rebels in Honduras who were trying to topple the government of Nicaragua. Known as the Reagan Doctrine, he argued that democracies have the right to aid in the overthrow of left-leaning governments; the subtext was fear that the Soviet Union might gain a beachhead in Central America. The policy, phrased to appear supportive of self-determination, ignored the fact that Nicaragua was a democracy and that American hostility to the regime could only be counterbalanced by Soviet support.

In 1989, American troops invaded Panamá to capture President Manuel Noriega (1934–) and install a new government after the parliament declared that a state of war existed with the United States, Americans reportedly were harassed, and an American marine was killed. President George H. W. Bush gave four reasons but not a "doctrine":

- To protect the Panamá Canal
- To safeguard potential threats against American citizens
- To defend democracy and human rights in Panamá
- To eradicate a major center of drug trafficking.

Then came the Gulf War of 1991, when the United States returned to a clear self-determination justification for military force. After Iraq attacked and occupied Kuwait, the United States sought and received UN approval for a multinational force to launch a counterattack that pushed Iraq back to the border between the two countries.

President Bill Clinton was primarily interested in domestic affairs. Under his presidency, the United States did nothing initially to stop ethnic cleansing in Bosnia by Serbs. But the United States enforced the UN-authorized no-fly zone over Bosnia from 1993 to 1995. In 1994–1995, when Republika Srpska violated the Bosnian ceasefire, American bombing with UN approval caused the violations to cease. Clinton then brokered a peace accord and sent peacekeeping troops to Bosnia to maintain the ceasefire.

In 1994, meanwhile, Clinton sent American troops to Haïti to stop unrest due to repression that was provoking an outpouring of refugees. In 1999, Clinton ordered the bombing of Serbia to stop a potential genocide in Kosovo by the Serbian government. Since the UN Security Council did not authorize the bombing, the Clinton Doctrine was unveiled as a policy that Washington had a responsibility to intervene militarily to prevent gross human rights abuses, with or without UN authority. He was adopting the R2P principle even before the UN did so.

On a few occasions, the United States has engaged in reprisal attacks. Terrorist attacks occasioned American aerial counterattacks against Libya (for bombing a Pan American airplane) during 1988 and against locations reputed to be Al-Qaeda training camps in Afghanistan (for bombing American embassies in Kenya and Tanzania) during 1998.

When the attacks on the World Trade Center and Pentagon occurred on September 11, 2001, the United States could have undertaken a reprisal similar to the bombardments of 1988 and 1998. Instead, President George W. Bush declared that the United States had the right of reprisal – to root out terrorist groups. Congress obliged with a resolution, the Authorization for the Use of Military Force of 2001, but the Bush Doctrine went far beyond reprisal to justify war against a country that harbored or aided terrorist groups. Ergo, the war in Afghanistan to root out terrorists, including the roundup of alleged terrorists for interrogation and later imprisonment but without any international legal precedent.

The Bush Doctrine soon contemplated preemptive war in Iraq. In 2002, Congress adopted the Authorization for Use of Military Force Against Iraq Resolution, giving Bush authority, "to use all necessary and appropriate force … to prevent any future acts of international terrorism against the United States … ." As later disclosed, the American objectives in Iraq were as follows:

- Eliminate weapons of mass destruction
- Prevent Iraq from threatening the Middle East and beyond
- Maintain Iraq's territorial integrity
- Cut links between the Iraq government and international terrorism
- Deter Iran and Syria from aiding Iraq
- Minimize disruption in oil markets
- Change from tyrannical rule to pluralistic democratic governance
- Effect punishment of the Iraqi government for defying UN resolutions.

In 2003, an Anglo-American coalition attacked and toppled Saddam Hussein from power.

Both the Afghan War and the Iraq War failed to meet the requirements of international law, as military operations were not approved by the UN Security Council beforehand. In 2003, some American soldiers filed *Doe v. Bush*, questioning whether the Iraq War was legal, but the case (323F3d133) was dismissed because of the "political question" doctrine; that is, the court deferred to the executive in a matter of foreign policy and national security. In 2006, First Lieutenant Ehren Watada (1978–) refused to report for duty in Iraq because he believed that the war was illegal and that under the doctrine of command responsibility he potentially could be charged with war crimes. He was court-martialed in 2007, but a mistrial was declared after the military judge stated that he lacked the power to determine whether the order to deploy to Iraq was lawful. In 2009, before a retrial, the Obama administration asked the army to dismiss the case, and he was discharged from the army. In a similar case in Germany, a judge ruled in 2005 that the Iraq War was illegal, so German soldiers could refuse to serve there.

Some battlefield misconduct, contrary to the First Geneva Convention, occurred in Afghanistan and Iraq. The American military conscientiously sought to discipline those who misbehaved on the battlefield and to compensate civilians for unintended losses of life and property.

While war was ongoing in both countries, prisoners were detained, but the Third Geneva Convention was not applied while they were confined. About 100 violations of the standards set forth in the Third Geneva Convention have reportedly occurred,[5] on orders from President Bush and Secretary of Defense Rumsfeld, at Bagram Prison in Afghanistan, Abu Ghraib in Iraq, and the Guantánamo Bay Naval Base. A few military prosecutions have been reported of lower-level personnel for misconduct at Abu Ghraib, but nothing more.

When objections were raised that the Bush Doctrine was allowing the sweeping use of force to go to war or to arrest anyone anywhere on the pretext of stopping terrorism, Bush tempered his policy in his State of the Union address in 2006 by taking a leaf out of the Wilson Doctrine, arguing that the United States had a special responsibility to spread democracy. Retroactively, he was taking credit for replacing the dictatorships in Afghanistan and Iraq with democratic states. What remains to be seen was whether both fragile democracies will be able to support human rights.

However, after the invasion in Afghanistan during 2001, Al-Qaeda leaders and the Taliban insurgency regrouped across the border in Pakistan. By 2006, the Taliban posed a serious threat to the unity of the country inside Afghanistan. Because Pakistani territory provided safe havens to terrorists in remote areas where the Islamabad government has little control, Bush decided to use unmanned aerial vehicles ("drones") to kill suspected Al-Qaeda terrorists rather than arresting suspects on the ground for trial. While leaders in Washington believed that they were killing enemies on the battlefield, Pakistanis were outraged that the United States was attacking and killing citizens of their country instead of engaging in a police operation. Although a formal justification for drone attacks to kill civilian members of a criminal gang was released by the Obama administration in early 2013, no compensation has ever been paid to innocent civilians killed by drone attacks.

One reason for the sweeping victory of Barack Obama in the presidential election of 2008 was an expectation that, as president, be would bring an increased respect for human rights. But he preferred to do so with speeches rather than dramatic policy reversals. In his Nobel Peace Prize acceptance speech, during 2009, he became the first president to endorse the concept of "just peace," namely, that peace should not be considered merely the absence of war but the absence of structural violence. The Obama Doctrine claimed that the world would continue in turmoil as long as some governments failed to grant basic civil, political, economic, social, and cultural rights to their people. That, he suggested, was why the United States had gone to war in the past. But was that what would guide him as president?

In 2009, his first year in office, military forces increased in Afghanistan, drone attacks multiplied, and he dispatched a military unit to rescue Americans held hostage by terrorists off the coast of Somalia. In 2010, he sent military troops on a new assignment, implementing the Lord's Resistance Army Disarmament and Northern Uganda Recovery Act of 2010, to assist the Uganda government in bringing Lord's Resistance Army commander, Joseph Kony, to justice. A secret order in 2009 to locate Osama Bin Laden (1957–2011) resulted in an operation within Pakistan during 2011 that ended in the death of the top Al-Qaeda leader. And in 2011, when American troops left Iraq on a timetable set up by Bush, Obama supported the UN-authorized no-fly zone over Libya.

Obama's military moves sent mixed signals. Increased military troops in Afghanistan could be justified by the UN mandate to keep order, the rescue of hostages has support in international law, R2P justified the no-fly zone, and the operation against Osama Bin Laden could be considered as a reprisal for the 9/11 massacres. But drone attacks have continued without a consensus that they have firm legal support, despite some evidence that more innocent civilians have been killed than terrorists and that populations haunted by drones are radicalized thereby.

Military occupation. Such American multilateral military occupations as those of Austria, Germany, and Japan after World War II, can boast more success in promoting human rights than the American and Russian occupations of the two parts of Korea after World War II. When the Fourth Geneva Convention was adopted, rules for military occupation were codified, but the United States no longer engaged in military occupation after Okinawa reverted to Japan in 1971.

Accordingly, the UN had reason to be concerned as the victorious army quickly installed a new government in Afghanistan during 2001. With military operations winding down, the UN Security Council authorized the International Security Assistance Force, led by NATO, to provide stability for the new government. And that stability has been elusive, resulting in displacement of the civilian population.

However, the American victory in Iraq during 2003 did not result in a new government. After the UN authorized an Anglo-American occupation authority, insurgents mounted a challenge to the occupation even before a new government was elected. The outcome was a turbulent Iraq, with continuing American civilian, military, and police operations that ignored the Fourth Geneva Convention, committing about 50 violations.[6] In 2005, a new Iraqi government was finally elected. With an Iraqi army and police force presumably trained to defend the country, the foreign occupation of Iraq ended in 2011.

CONCLUSION

As the world's sole superpower in the twenty-first century, the role of the United States in regard to international human rights is ambivalent. The tradition of proactive support for human rights clashes with the power to impose punitive measures, and disagreements on appropriate measures fill the political discourse today. American leaders rely on coercive diplomacy now more than in the past. Although the strong legal tradition presumably provides victims of human rights abuse with an opportunity to have their day in court, judges have often dismissed their cases. American foreign aid is greater than any other country in the world in dollar terms, but the ratio of aid to national income is far below the UN Millennium goal of 0.7 percent. Congress has passed a maze of aid and trade legislation over the years, some proactive and some punitive, but geopolitical ambitions of presidents have often backburnered human rights issues. Finally, although the UN authorizes military action in regard to human rights primarily in peacekeeping, Washington sometimes embarks on unauthorized military action anyway to maintain its power position in the world. Criticisms of the United States abound because a refusal of the UN to back American military adventures deprives them of legitimacy in the eyes of many countries in the world.

DISCUSSION TOPIC 11.2 DOES WASHINGTON HAVE AN EXEMPLARY RECORD IN PROMOTING HUMAN RIGHTS?

International law was in the forefront of concern when the United States Constitution was written. A Bill of Rights was written as the first ten amendments to the American federal constitution. Subsequently, the United States played a constructive role in the development of the original Geneva Convention, the Hague Conferences, the League of Nations, and the United Nations. Since the United States became a superpower, some observers believe that Washington has preferred geopolitics to exercising moral leadership. Do you agree? What are the plusses and minuses of American foreign policy in regard to human rights? What about American domestic policies and practices regarding human rights?

CHAPTER 12

European Approaches to International Human Rights

Although European countries employ the four basic tools of diplomatic, judicial, economic, and military methods to cope with human rights problems around the world, an historical comparison of the policies of individual countries is beyond the scope of the present volume. Instead, the chapter focuses on European intergovernmental organizations, which have made so many extraordinary contributions to human rights and have brought about an increasing convergence in human rights practices across the region.

COUNCIL OF EUROPE (CoE)

In September 1946, 14 months after stepping down as Britain's wartime prime minister, Winston Churchill (1874–1965) gave a speech at the University of Zürich calling for "a United States of Europe" that would be as free and peaceful as multiethnic Switzerland. Three years later, 10 Western European countries founded the CoE by adopting the **Statute of the Council of Europe**, sometimes known as the Treaty of London, which was ratified within only three months. The purpose of the organization, as proclaimed in the statute, is "to achieve a greater unity between its members for the purpose of safeguarding and realizing the ideals and principles which are their common heritage and facilitating their economic and social progress."

In 1950, CoE members adopted the **European Convention for the Protection of Human Rights and Fundamental Freedoms** (Table 12.1). The impetus was fourfold:

TABLE 12.1 **BASIC TREATIES OF THE COUNCIL OF EUROPE**

Adopted	Title	In force
1946	Statute of the Council of Europe	1946
1950	European Convention for the Protection of Human Rights and Fundamental Freedoms	1953
1952	• Protocol 1 (adds rights to property, education, secret ballot)	1954
1963	• Protocol 2 (advisory opinions of ECHR allowed)	1970
1963	• Protocol 3 (legal procedures)	1970
1963	• Protocol 4 (freedom of movement, residence, etc.)	1968
1966	• Protocol 5 (judge selection, legal procedures)	1971
1983	• Protocol 6 (death penalty abolished)	1985
1984	• Protocol 7 (right of appeal, equality in marriage, etc.)	1988
1985	• Protocol 8 (petition procedures)	1990
1990	• Protocol 9 (petition procedures)	1994
1992	• Protocol 10 (majority vote by Committee of Ministers)	
1994	• Protocol 11 (restructure control machinery)[a]	1998
2000	• Protocol 12 (discrimination banned)	2005
2002	• Protocol 13 (death penalty abolished)	2003
2004	• Protocol 14 (judicial review)	2010
1955	European Social Charter	1956
1988	• Additional Protocol	1992
1991	• Amending Protocol	
1995	• Additional Protocol	1998
1996	• revised European Social Charter	1999
1987	European Convention for the Prevention of Torture and Inhuman or Degrading Treatment of Punishment	1989
1993	• Protocol No. 1	2002
1993	• Protocol No. 2	2002
1995	Framework Convention for the Protection of National Minorities	1998

[a] Supersedes Protocols 2, 3, 5, 8, 9, and 10.

- Response to the atrocities of World War II
- Support for European integration
- Prevention of another general European war
- An effort to show the human rights superiority of Western Europe over Soviet-controlled Eastern Europe.

However, unlike the Universal Declaration of Human Rights adopted by the United Nations in 1948, the European Convention initially had no reference to self-determination or the protection of minority peoples, and there is a reference to responsibilities as well as rights. Fourteen protocols have been adopted, dealing with such issues as the right to education and property, free elections and freedom of movement, prohibitions of the death penalty and discrimination, and various criminal justice procedures, including compensation for wrongful conviction. Under the aegis of the CoE, some 200 other treaties have been adopted, as discussed below. Most are aimed at harmonizing national laws, a necessity for increased transborder migration, tourism, and trade.

Although CoE originally was conceived to promote economic integration, that function became the *sine qua non* for the European Economic Community (EEC). What was left for CoE was a focus on human rights. From the standpoint of complaint processing, there are now four basic treaties (Table 12.1).

Thanks primarily to the end of the Cold War, membership increased more than fourfold to the current 47, including countries as far away as Iceland, Turkey, and states in the Caucasus (Armenia, Azerbaijan, Georgia). The principal membership requirement is that a state must have a genuine democracy that is committed to the rule of law and human rights; members must adopt the European Convention for the Protection of Human Rights and Fundamental Freedoms of 1950, though not necessarily its protocols. Although CoE has been criticized for expanding membership to countries with many human rights deficiencies, the reason for a low bar to new members is the experience that countries are more likely to improve inside the organization than outside. Indeed, many of the most recent countries are currently being monitored very closely. Some 800 million persons are represented in CoE.

Undemocratic Belarus is the only sizeable European country that is not a member. Spain was considered ineligible for membership while governed by fascist Francisco Franco (1892–1975). Observer status has been granted to Canada, the Holy See, Israel, Japan, México, and the United States. With 4 percent of its land west of the Urals, Kazakhstan is interested in CoE membership and applied for Special Guest status in 1999 and Observer status in 2006, but CoE awaits democratic improvements before granting either status. In 2011, Morocco and Palestine were granted Partner for Democracy status, a relationship available to countries neighboring Europe that have free elections.

The main organs of the CoE are the Secretariat, Committee of Ministers (CM), European Court of Human Rights (ECHR), Parliamentary Assembly (PACE), Congress of Local and Regional Authorities, and the Conference of Non-Governmental Organizations. In addition, heads of government have held three **summits** over the years.

Secretariat. Located in Strasbourg, France, near the German border, the Secretariat handles administrative tasks for the Council. Within the Secretariat's **Directorate General of Human Rights**, the **Human Rights Co-operation and Awareness Division** handles the functions of documentation, information compilation and dissemination, organizing meetings, research, training, and coordinating work with other international organizations, including the European Union.

Committee of Ministers (CM). All CoE foreign ministers, their deputies, or permanent representatives meet in the CM to conduct **discussions** on current political issues and to negotiate **treaties**. So far, more than 200 treaties have been adopted, many of which deal with human rights (Tables 12.1–12.7). They also issue **resolutions** to assist in implementing ECHR judgments during four sessions annually. **Rapporteurs** and **working parties** are appointed for specific issues; of the 13 operating in 2013, one is devoted to social and health questions.

Over time, CoE has received an increasing number of complaints. **Intrastate complaints**, which are more numerous, involve individuals, groups, or nongovernmental organizations claiming denials of their rights by the states in which they reside. **Interstate complaints** are by one state against another.

Initially, CM relied on a body known as the European Commission on Human Rights. When human rights complaints were addressed to CoE, the Secretariat handed them over to the Commission, which could either make an **award** based on the principle of **just satisfaction** to the victim or refer the case to CoE's ECHR if the defendant state accepted the court's jurisdiction. After the court made a ruling, CM would monitor implementation of the decision.

Up to the mid-1990s, the Commission handled more complaints than ECHR. As CoE membership increased dramatically after the end of the Cold War, the number rose exponentially – from 404 in 1981 to 4,750 in 1997, while cases annually submitted to ECHR rose from 7 to 119 over the same years. Since not all cases are decided during the year when they are filed, the backlog in 1997 was over 12,000.

Accordingly, a decision was made, effective 1998 when Protocol 9 was ratified, to abolish the Commission and have ECHR handle all complaints and to become a fulltime body. CM, through the **Steering Committee for Human Rights**, then restricted itself to its original powers of supervising implementation of the court's decisions and making specific recommendations to member states. (CoE's Secretary-General may also direct questions about implementation to an errant state.)

European Court of Human Rights (ECHR). The world's longest-standing human rights tribunal, ECHR was set up in 1959. Unlike the former Commission, ECHR is supranational; that is, its decisions are legally binding and can override domestic law.

Complainants must file an **application** to ECHR, alleging a violation of one of CoE's treaties. Many applications are inadmissible for technical reasons or because there is no treaty basis for their complaint. After an application is ruled **admissible**, negotiations may ensue for a **friendly settlement** or there may be a **hearing** in court. If a plaintiff prevails, there are two possible outcomes. In the most common outcome, **individual measure**, the victim is compensated (called **just satisfaction**). The court has ordered more than 40 governments thus far to provide financial restitution to injured parties. Alternatively, a **general measure** asks governments to change their laws or administrative procedures, though the affected state may take its time to comply. ECHR has also issued two **advisory opinions** (about the selection of judges).

Thus far, among 16 **interstate applications**, five countries complained about Turkey's use of torture in the early 1980s, to which there was a resolution involving a friendly settlement procedure in 1985. One interstate complaint involved torture allegations in Greece, and another was over British interrogation techniques in Northern Ireland. The three most recent complaints were filed by Georgia against Russia. Seeking to build support, the court has been hesitant to rule against states, so most cases have been decided in favor of complainants through the issuance of **decisions** in the form of reports; only three cases have resulted in formal **judgments**. The term "margin of appreciation" is used when the court finds ambiguity in a treaty and gives some latitude in interpreting a provision vis-à-vis the state involved.

From 1998, the court has received an increasing number of **individual applications**, particularly from Russia and Turkey. From 1958 to 2009, there were nearly 643,000 applications, of which only 39 percent were admissible; violations were found in over 83 percent of the 12,340 judgments. Almost half of the cases have involved denial of the right to a fair or speedy trial. By 2012, the court had made decisions or judgments on more than 17,000 cases. Because of the large volume of cases, settling individual matters rather than building jurisprudence with landmark rulings, similar cases are now being consolidated, resulting in wider scope of applicability.

COURT CASE 12.1 *SÖRING V. UK* (1989)

Jens Söring, a German national, sought to marry fellow University of Virginia student, Elizabeth Haysom, a Canadian. When her parents disapproved, he killed them with her approval. They flew six months later to England, where they were arrested. Virginian authorities then indicted them for murder and sought to extradite them to the United States. Söring (but not Haysom) objected on the ground that the mistreatment of prisoners on death row in the United States amounted to cruel and unusual punishment. After exhausting British legal channels, he appealed to the European Court of Human Rights, which agreed that the extradition would violate the European Convention on Human Rights. However, based on Britain's bilateral extradition treaty with the United States, authorities in London then obtained a commitment from the United States that neither person would be subjected to the death penalty. Accordingly, they were extradited to Virginia, where he is serving a life sentence, and she was given a 45-year sentence. The case has served to expand coverage of the European treaty outside Europe and establishes the principle that the multilateral European treaty has precedence over bilateral treaties.

ECHR has issued many landmark rulings. In 1989, the court ruled that the treatment of American prisoners on death row was inhumane in *Söring v. UK*. In 2012, the Grand Chamber ruled that Khaled El-Masry (1963–), a German citizen, was illegally tortured by American authorities and is due €60,000 (US$88,000) as compensation from Macedonia for mistreatment in confinement while Macedonia agreed to cooperate with a covert operation run by US Central Intelligence Agency.

COURT CASE 12.2 *EL-MASRY V. MACEDONIA* (2012)

In December 2003, when the pseudonymous name "Khalid Al-Masry" was on a list issued by the US Central Intelligence Agency (CIA) as a suspected terrorist, auto

Continued

sales executive Khaled El-Masry (1963–), was vacationing in Macedonia. Suddenly arrested by Macedonian authorities, police forced him into a locked room in a Skopje hotel, where he was questioned for 23 days in English, a language with which he had limited proficiency, while he was denied a request to contact the German Embassy. Questioned about alleged ties with terrorist organizations amid a death threat, he was handed over the following month to the CIA at Skopje airport, where, during further questioning, he was hooded, severely beaten, shackled, sodomized, and subjected to sensory deprivation in the presence of Macedonian officials. He was then flown to Afghanistan, where, for more than four months he was locked in a dark, dirty, tiny concrete cell in a brick factory near Kabul. Again, while interrogated and denied access to the German Consulate, he was repeatedly beaten, kicked, and threatened. Finally realizing that they had the wrong man, the CIA flew him to Albania, where he was dropped in a desolate wilderness road without funds, food, or water. When he finally reached Albanian authorities, they flew him home to Germany, where he brought suit. In 2007, Germany issued arrest warrants for the CIA officers involved, but they were not around, so the case could not go forward. His next legal action suit, *Khaled v. Tenet* (2007), was dismissed by an American court under the Alien Tort Claims Act when the administration of George W. Bush (1946–), on behalf of CIA Director George Tenet (1953–), invoked the "state secrets" doctrine to get the case dismissed. He then sought relief from the European Court of Human Rights. In 2012, the Grand Chamber unanimously found Macedonia culpable for its role in the premeditated abuse, torture, and secret imprisonment and was ordered to compensate El-Masry for €60,000 (US$88,000).

Because of ECHR, several state practices have changed. Austria revised its criminal code and amount of payments for legal aid attorneys. Belgium gave rights to illegitimate children and dropped its vagrancy law. Britain changed laws dealing with compensation for wrongful arrest, freedom of information, prison rules, privacy, and voting rights for convicted inmates. France had to guarantee privacy of telephone calls after two cases about illegal wiretapping. Germany modified pre-trial detention procedures and had to provide interpreters free of charge. In Ireland, civil legal aid was instituted. Italy was ordered to revise regulations governing detention on remand and to shorten the length of criminal proceedings. In the Netherlands, the law on detention of mental patients was modified. Switzerland amended its military penal code and regulations governing reformatories. In 2005, the court ordered Turkey to retry Abdullah Öcalan (1948–), the alleged leader of Kurdish dissidents, because he did not receive a fair trial.

The success rate of petitioners is over 50 percent, and state compliance with decisions is very high. However, some governments have taken years rather than days to implement ECHR decisions. Aside from ostracizing a government by suspending membership or voting rights, the CoE can withhold technical assistance to member countries, a sanction that would particularly harm less prosperous countries.

In some cases, countries brought before ECHR have refused to accept jurisdiction, claiming that emergency conditions (the right of derogation) precluded the extension of full human rights. An example of the latter, in which the court accepted Britain's explanation, is *Brogan v. United Kingdom*, a 1988 case in which the police, without judicial action, detained a Northern Ireland resident. Some observers claim that judges are pressured by their countries of appointment. Nevertheless, ECHR decisions have had a worldwide impact, since they are cited by national courts in countries inside and outside Europe. Indeed, ECHR has been considered by some scholars as a world human rights court.

Parliamentary Assembly of the Council of Europe (PACE). Each legislature of the member countries sends delegates to PACE, a 318-member body, in rough proportion to the size of each political party in its legislature. The size of each country's delegation is weighted by population, with a minimum of 2 and a maximum of 18. So that delegates will think in terms of Europe rather than their own country, delegates are seated ideologically, with five major groupings – Socialists, People's Parties, Liberal Democrats, Democrats, and the Unified European Left. PACE members select the body's president, who convenes a committee with one representative from each party grouping, and its secretary-general, who handles administrative matters.

PACE has eight committees:

- Political Affairs and Democracy
- Legal Affairs and Human Rights
- Social Affairs, Health, and Sustainable Development
- Migration, Refugees, and Displaced Persons
- Culture, Science, Education, and Media
- Equality and Non-Discrimination
- A procedural committee
- The monitoring committee.

The latter committee decides whether members and applicants for membership operate in accord with CoE's basic treaties.

PACE elects judges of the ECHR. After its committees issue **reports**, PACE issues **opinions**, makes **recommendations**, or passes **resolutions**. Up to 2012, PACE had issued 282 opinions, 2,005 recommendations, and 1,907 resolutions, mostly relating to human rights. Resolution 1902, for example, urged action on the Syrian Civil War refugee crisis.

CM and PACE can suspend countries for gross violations of human rights. From 1967–1974, Greece was suspended while under military rule. From 1981 to 1985, Turkey was suspended because of torture of prisoners. Although Belarus was granted Special Guest in 1992, in 1997 that status was suspended for its persecution of opposition leaders and has not been restored. In 2000 and 2001, PACE suspended the voting rights of Russia because of the crackdown in Chechnya and appointed a special committee to investigate whether Russian officials should be tried for war crimes.

TABLE 12.2 **CoE HUMAN RIGHTS TREATIES DEALING WITH LOCAL GOVERNMENT**

Adopted	*Title*	*In force*
1980	European Outline Convention on Transfrontier Co-operation Between Territorial Communities or Authorities	1981
1995	• Additional Protocol	1998
1998	• Protocol No. 2 … Concerning Interterritorial Co-operation	2001
2009	• Protocol No. 3 … Concerning Euroregional Co-operation Groups	2013
1985	European Charter of Local Self-Government	1988
2009	• Additional Protocol … on the Right to Participate in the Affairs of a Local Authority	2012
1992	Convention on the Participation of Foreigners in Public Life at the Local Level	1997

In 2003, PACE passed a resolution providing that a country could be stripped of voting rights if the delegation from that country contained no women. In 2004, Ireland and Malta were cited, pending the appointment of a woman to their delegations. In 2004, PACE threatened to suspend Ukraine over proposed extraconstitutional changes, but the issue was resolved when voters elected a new government in 2005. PACE threatened to suspend Armenia (in 2008), Azerbaijan (2009), and Bosnia (2010) because of undemocratic developments in their countries.

Since 1999, PACE has elected a **Commissioner for Human Rights**, who is charged with four tasks:

- Promoting human rights awareness
- Facilitating national human rights bodies
- Identifying gaps in human rights law and practice
- Promoting the full enjoyment of human rights in member countries.

In 2010, the Commissioner was authorized to engage in **third-party intervention** in proceedings before the ECHR. The first third-party intervention occurred in 2011, when the commissioner intervened on behalf of a disabled Romanian. In all, four third-party interventions have occurred so far.

The Commissioner has made 5 formal **recommendations** – the latest (in 2009) on the right to housing – and 14 **opinions**. An opinion issued in 2011 questioned recently passed legislative restrictions on the media.

Congress of Local and Regional Authorities. CoE members must be democracies. However, the term "democracy" is vague, and democratic processes can be thick or thin, especially at the subnational level. In 1984, a decision was made to form a political assembly of 636 members who hold elective office (regional or municipal councilors, mayors, presidents of regional authorities) representing over 200,000 authorities. The Congress, which meets in Strasbourg, is primarily committed to maintaining the administrative, financial, and political independence of local governments. The Congress also encourages devolution and regionalization, the independence of local governments, and transfrontier cooperation between

TABLE 12.3   COE HUMAN RIGHTS TREATIES DEALING WITH CRIMINAL JUSTICE

Adopted	Title	In force
1957	European Convention on Extradition	1960
1975	• Additional Protocol	1979
1978	• Second Additional Protocol	1983
2010	• Third Additional Protocol	2012
2012	• Fourth Additional Protocol	
1959	European Convention on Mutual Assistance in Criminal Matters	1962
1978	• Additional Protocol	1982
2001	• Second Additional Protocol	2004
1964	European Convention on the Supervision of Conditionally Sentenced or Conditionally Released Offenders	1975
1966	European Convention Providing a Uniform Law on Arbitration	
1968	European Convention on Information on Foreign Law	1969
1978	• Additional Protocol	1979
1969	European Agreement Relating to Persons Participating in Proceedings of the European Commission and Court of Human Rights	1971
1970	European Convention on the International Validity of Criminal Judgments	1974
1972	European Convention on the Transfer of Proceedings in Criminal Matters	1978
1972	European Convention on State Immunity	1976
1972	• Additional Protocol	1985
1974	European Convention on the Non-Applicability of Statutory Limitation to Crimes Against Humanity and War Crimes	2003
1977	European Convention on Products Liability in Regard to Personal Injury and Death	
1977	European Agreement on the Transmission of Applications for Legal Aid	1977
2001	• Additional Protocol	2002
1983	Convention on the Transfer of Sentenced Persons	1985
1997	• Additional Protocol	2000
1983	European Convention on the Compensation of Victims of Violent Crimes	1988
1985	European Convention on Offences Relating to Cultural Property	
1987	European Convention for the Prevention of Torture and Inhuman or Degrading Treatment or Punishment	1989
1993	• Protocol No. 1	2002
1993	• Protocol No. 2	2002
1998	European Agreement Relating to Persons Participating in Proceedings of the European Court of Human Rights	1999
2001	Convention on Cybercrime	2004
2003	• Additional Protocol … Concerning the Criminalization of Acts of a Racist and Xenophobic Nature Committed through Computer Systems	2006
2005	Convention on Action Against Trafficking in Human Beings	2008
2011	Convention on Preventing and Combating Violence Against Women and Domestic Violence	
2011	Convention on the Counterfeiting of Medical Products and Similar Crimes Involving Threats to Public Health	2011

local authorities. Delegates have adopted treaties (Table 12.2), the most notable of which is the Charter of Local Self-Government of 1985. The protocol to the Charter, adopted in 2009, provides that citizens have a right to participate in the political affairs of their local and regional governments. The main work of the congress between sessions is to make **monitoring visits**, followed by **reports**. As a result, the Congress has issued more than 300 **recommendations** to local authorities. The Congress established a Group of Independent Experts to assist in drafting reports; at least one of the group goes on each site visit.

Conference of International Non-Government Organizations (INGOs). In 1952, the CoE began to grant Consultative status to nongovernmental organizations and upgraded this to the level of Participatory status in 2003. Accordingly, in

TABLE 12.4 **COE HUMAN RIGHTS TREATIES DEALING WITH SOCIAL RIGHTS**[a]

Adopted	Title	In force
1953	European Interim Agreement on Social Security Schemes Relating to Old Age, Invalidity and Survivors	1954
1953	European Interim Agreement on Social Security Other than Schemes for Old Age, Invalidity and Survivors	1954
1953	• Protocol … Relating to Old Age, Invalidity and Survivors	1954
1953	European Convention on Social and Medical Assistance	1954
1953	• Protocol	1955
1955	Agreement on the Exchange of War Cripples Between Member Countries of the Council of Europe with a View to Medical Treatment	1956
1962	Agreement Between the Member States of the Council of Europe on the Issue to Military and Civilian War-Disabled of an International Book of Vouchers for the Repair of Prosthetic and Orthopaedic Appliances	1963
1964	European Code of Social Security	1968
1964	• Protocol to the European Code of Social Security	1968
1990	• European Code of Social Security (Revised)	
1972	European Convention on Social Security	1977
1972	• Supplementary Agreement	1977
1994	• Protocol to the European Convention on Social Security	
1974	European Convention on the Social Protection of Farmers	1977
1997	Convention for the Protection of Human Rights and Dignity of the Human Being with Regard to the Application of Biology and Medicine	1999
1998	• Additional Protocol … on the Prohibition of Cloning Human Beings	2001
2002	• Additional Protocol … Concerning Transplantation of Organs and Tissues of Human Origin	2006
2005	• Additional Protocol … Concerning Biomedical Research	2007
2008	• Additional Protocol … Concerning Genetic Testing for Health Purposes	

[a] See also Table 12.1. Not included: conventions dealing with archaeology, medical technology standards, and university standards.

2005, the Conference of INGOs was launched to facilitate input from some 400 groups into PACE deliberations.

Expert Bodies. The CoE also has several expert advisory bodies. More than a dozen have been created "topsylike" over the years by the CM, PACE, or by treaties. Some have subsidiary expert advisory bodies. Their work is taken into account when the CM, PACE, and ECHR deliberate.

Perhaps the earliest is the **European Committee on Crime Problems**. Set up by the CM in 1958, the body has been useful in identifying crime-related treaties and activities regarding criminal law, judicial and procedure, criminology, and penology. Thus far, the body has issued 48 reports, 40 resolutions, and 72 recommendations.

A related body focusing on public and private law was created in 1963 – the **European Committee on Legal Cooperation**. In addition to treaty development, the body has issued hundreds of opinions in the form of recommendations. The two bodies are an integral part of CoE's focus on criminal justice (Table 12.3).

Although Article 3 of the European Convention for Human Rights bans the use of torture, specific machinery was thought necessary to ensure compliance.

TABLE 12.5   **CoE HUMAN RIGHTS TREATIES DEALING WITH DIVERSITY**[a]

Adopted	Title	In force
1954	European Cultural Convention	1955
1955	European Convention on Establishment	1965
1957	European Agreement on Regulations Governing the Movement of Persons Between Member States of the Council of Europe	1958
1959	European Agreement on the Abolition of Visas for Refugees	1960
1963	Convention on the Reduction of Cases of Multiple Nationality and Military Obligations in Cases of Multiple Nationality	1968
1977	• Protocol	1978
1977	• Additional Protocol	1983
1993	• Second Protocol	1995
1967	European Convention on Consular Functions	2011
1967	• Protocol … Concerning the Protection of Refugees	
1977	European Convention on the Legal Status of Migrant Workers	1983
1980	European Agreement on Transfer of Responsibility for Refugees	1980
1988	Arrangement for the Application of the European Agreement of 17 October 1980 Concerning the Provision of Medical Care to Persons During Temporary Residence	
1992	European Charter for Regional or Minority Languages	1998
1995	Framework Convention for the Protection of National Minorities	1998
1997	European Convention on Nationality	2000
2005	Framework Convention on the Value of Cultural Heritage for Society	2011
2006	Convention on the Avoidance of Statelessness in Relation to State Succession	2009

[a] Does not include conventions regarding audiovisual heritage.

Accordingly, the European Convention for the Prevention of Torture and Inhuman or Degrading Treatment or Punishment was adopted in 1987. When the treaty went into force in 1989, the Committee for the Prevention of Torture and Inhuman or Degrading Treatment or Punishment, now the **European Committee for the Prevention of Torture**, went into operation. Composed of independent experts appointed from each country by the Council of Ministers, they have the power to make scheduled and unscheduled checks on prisons, police cells, psychiatric hospitals, and compounds for asylum seekers, except for places already visited by the Red Cross. Prisoners can be interviewed in private. Reports to the governments after site visits are confidential unless, as is usually the case, the country agrees to make them public. By 2012, some 198 periodic visits, 131 ad hoc visits, and 276 public reports had been undertaken. Russia and Turkey have been charged with the most violations. Many other treaties have been adopted in the field of criminal justice over the years. They are monitored by PACE.

In 1990, after the Berlin Wall collapsed and Eastern European governments were in constitutional disarray, the **European Commission for Democracy Through Law** was formed. Known popularly as the Venice Commission for its founding and meeting venue, the aim was to advise member countries how to restructure constitutions and cope with other legal matters.

The goal of "economic and social progress" in CoE's founding statute was given substance in 1956 within the European Social Charter, one of the two fundamental treaties adopted by the Council of Europe (Table 12.1). The Charter contains many rights, including protection against poverty and social exclusion, right to housing, right to protection in cases of harassment or termination of employment, and rights of workers with family responsibilities. Member countries were required to file biennial **reports** on compliance. Initially, the reports were reviewed by a Committee of Experts, which was renamed the Independent Committee of Experts in the 1991

TABLE 12.6 CoE HUMAN RIGHTS TREATIES DEALING WITH RIGHTS OF CHILDREN

Adopted	Title	In force
1961	European Agreement on Travel by Young Persons on Collective Passports Between the Member Countries of the Council of Europe	1962
1967	European Convention on the Adoption of Children	1968
2008	• European Convention on the Adoption of Children (Revised)	2011
1969	European Agreement on Au Pair Placement	1971
1970	European Convention on the Repatriation of Minors	
1975	European Convention on the Legal Status of Children Born out of Wedlock	1978
1980	European Convention on Recognition and Enforcement of Decisions Concerning Custody of Children and on Restoration of Custody of Children	1983
1996	European Convention on the Exercise of Children's Rights	2000
2003	Convention on Contact Concerning Children	2005
2007	Convention on the Protection of Children Against Sexual Exploitation and Sexual Abuse	2010

Protocol and the European Committee of Social Rights in 1998. From 1993, CM made **recommendations** to states regarding implementation of the European Social Charter (before then, they were adopted as resolutions). The CoE, CM, and PACE, all of which initially had jurisdiction to act on complaints concerning economic and social issues, have deferred to the European Committee of Social Rights in matters of social rights since the 1991 Protocol, which allows **complaints** for decisions from the committee by parties directly affected. The 1995 Protocol allowed **collective complaints**, that is, third-party petitions by trade unions and nongovernmental organizations accepted by the expert committee. In 1996, the Charter and existing protocols were consolidated into the Revised Charter.

So far, more than 18,000 complaints based on the Social Charter have been filed, either with the European Committee of Social Rights or the Council of Ministers. Recently, Greece has been a major focus. In 2011, among 747 complaints, one involved two trade unions objecting to the Committee about several matters, including a Greek law that allowed employers to hire workers aged 25 and below at a pay rate below the country's minimum wage.

By 2012, some 87 collective complaints were received, of which less than 10 percent were inadmissible on procedural grounds; most were decided "on the merits" as violations. The Committee ruled in 2012 that the law constituted illegal age discrimination. Among the 87 collective complaints filed thus far, one was filed by the Federation of Employed Pensioners of Greece in which the Committee ruled in 2012 that a Greek law reducing pension payments was illegal.

TABLE 12.7　**CoE HUMAN RIGHTS TREATIES DEALING WITH CIVIL AND POLITICAL RIGHTS**[a]

Adopted	Title	In force
1955	European Convention on Establishment	1965
1976	European Convention on the International Effects of Deprivation of the Right to Drive a Motor Vehicle	1983
1978	Convention on the Control of the Acquisition and Possession of Firearms by Individuals	1982
1981	Convention for the Protection of Individuals with Regard to Automatic Processing of Personal Data	1985
2001	• Additional Protocol … Regarding Supervisory Authorities and Transborder Data Flows	
1999	Civil Law Convention on Corruption	2003
1999	Criminal Law Convention on Corruption	2002
2003	• Additional Protocol	2005
2001	Convention on Information and Legal Co-operation Concerning "Information Society Services"	
2001	European Convention on the Legal Protection of Services Based on, or Consisting of, Conditional Access	2003
2009	Convention on Access to Official Documents	

[a] Does not list treaties regarding broadcasting and copyrights.

In 1995, the Framework Convention for the Protection of National Minorities was adopted. Site visits are conducted by the **Advisory Committee** of Independent Experts, which is appointed by the CM. The Convention requires states to make **reports** on the status of minorities, to which the Advisory Committee makes **comments**. Diversity issues are now among the most important sources of CoE treaties on human rights (Table 12.5).

Rather than consider social rights as guarantees without larger societal consequences, CoE's Second Summit, in 1997, adopted a much larger view, using the term "social cohesion" to mean "the capacity of a society to ensure the well-being of all its members, minimizing disparities and avoiding marginalization." In 1998, accordingly, the **European Committee for Social Cohesion** was set up by the CM to promote "standards, policies, practices and tools in the social, disability, health, bioethical, migration and Roma fields, and to support nondiscrimination and equal opportunities as well as ethnic and cultural diversity, with a view to reducing inequality and building confidence in a common and secure future for all." Thus far, the body has established subordinate expert committees in several fields of interest. Whereas the European Committee of Social Rights monitors compliance with the European Social Charter, the European Committee for Social Cohesion provides proactive programs to facilitate compliance. Among the groups most marginalized are children, and the CoE has responded accordingly (Table 12.6).

In 2002, the CM adopted the statute for an expert group, **European Commission Against Racism and Intolerance**, to combat "racism, racial discrimination, xenophobia, anti-Semitism and intolerance." A general framework is provided by Protocol 11 to the European Convention for the Protection of Human Rights and Fundamental Freedoms, which prohibits discrimination "on any ground such as sex, race, color, language, religion, political or other opinion, national or social origin, association with a national minority, property, birth or other status." The Commission reviews whether member states' legislation, policies, and other measures are effective in reducing racism, xenophobia, anti-Semitism and intolerance, and then formulates general policy recommendations in the form of **declarations** or **statements**. Thus far, three declarations (on political discourse and terrorism) and six statements (about conditions in Armenia, Azerbaijan, France, Italy, Russia, and Switzerland) have been issued.

Also in 2002, the CM established the **European Commission for the Efficiency of Justice**. Experts from all member countries seek to promote the rule of law. A recent study focused on protection of crime victims and divorce procedures.

The Warsaw Declaration and Action Plan adopted at the Third CoE Summit, held in 2005, established the **Forum for the Future of Democracy**. Experts meet annually to identify governance problems and solutions. Many important CoE treaties deal with the civil and political rights basic to a fully functioning democracy (Table 12.7).

Although gender equality is included in many CoE agreements, no specific treaty on gender equality has emerged thus far. In 1979, the CM established the Committee for Equality between Women and Men, which was superseded in 1988 by the **Committee of Ministers on Equality of Women and Men**. In 1997, the **Steering Committee for Equality Between Women and Men**, to which each country appoints an expert, embarked on a program of gender mainstreaming, preventing and combating violence against women, and stopping the trafficking in women. Then in 2012 the first meeting of the **Gender Equality Commission** was held. Activities are now being developed.

In 1989, PACE set up the **North–South Center** in conjunction with the European Union to provide technical assistance outside Europe. Located in Lisbon, the center focuses most of its attention on Africa and the Middle East with conferences and seminars on global education, issues relating to migration, and on problems of youth. Twenty-one European countries belong, plus Cape Verde Islands and Morocco.

The CoE may appear rather formalistic if summarized only in terms of commit-tees, complaints, statistics, treaties, and the like. In fact, a multitude of activities involving technical assistance to member countries serves to increase compliance with human rights standards, including conferences, country visits, task forces, and workshops. Technical experts predominate in the various working groups, where they soften the views of countries by applying their knowledge to achieve consen-sus. Nevertheless, the organization has not been reluctant to identify violations of human rights, including criticism of Russia's actions in Chechnya.

TABLE 12.8   EUROPEAN UNION AGREEMENTS WITH HUMAN RIGHTS PROVISIONS

Adopted	Title	In force
1985	Agreement Between the Governments of the States of the Benelux Economic Union, the Federal Republic of Germany and the French Republic on the Gradual Abolition of Checks at Their Common Borders (Schengen Agreement)	1993
1986	Single European Act	1987
1989	Community Charter of the Fundamental Social Rights of Workers	1998
1992	Treaty Establishing the European Union (Maastricht Treaty)	1993
	• Protocol on Social Policy	
	• Agreement on Social Policy	
	• Protocol on Economic and Social Cohesion	
1995	Europol Convention	1998
1997	Treaty of Amsterdam Amending the Treaty of the European Union, the Treaties Establishing the European Communities and Certain Related Acts	1999
2000	Partnership Agreement Between the Members of the African, Caribbean and Pacific Group of States of the One Part and the European Community and Its Member States of the Other Part (Cotonou Agreement)	2003
2005	• First revision	2008
2010	• Second revision	
2000	Charter of Fundamental Rights of the European Union	2009
2001	Treaty of Nice Amending the Treaty on European Union, the Treaties Establishing the European Communities and Certain Related Acts	2003
2004	Treaty Establishing a Constitution for Europe	
2007	Treaty on the Functioning of the European Union (Treaty of Lisbon)	2009

EUROPEAN UNION (EU)

Whereas the CoE is mostly an **intergovernmental organization**, serving at the pleasure of its member countries, the EU is a **supranational organization**, empowered to make binding laws affecting governments and individuals. The evolution of cooperation leading to the EU, which now has 27 members, has been complex.

The impetus for the EU came from three sources. One was an agreement in 1944, formalized by 1948, to form **Benelux**, a customs union among Belgium, Luxembourg, and the Netherlands. The second development was the formation of the Organization for European Economic Cooperation (OEEC) to distribute Marshall Plan aid.[1] The most dramatic event was a speech on May 9, 1950, now celebrated as Europe Day, in which French Foreign Minister Robert Schuman (1886–1963) proposed economic integration of the coal and steel industry, which was largely concentrated in the Saarland, a German province along the Rhine River that was under French postwar occupation until 1935.

In 1951, France, Germany, Italy, and the Benelux countries formed the **European Commission for Steel and Coal** (ECSC). In 1957, the six set up the **European Economic Community** (EEC) and the **European Atomic Energy Agency** (Euratom). The **European Economic and Social Committee**, established in 1958, is an advisory body consisting of representatives from employer organizations, trade unions, and other interests. In 1958, the Benelux Economic Union Treaty was signed, forming the **Benelux Economic Union**. In 1960, seven EEC non-members organized the Geneva-based **European Free Trade Association** (EFTA), though over the years, most countries left EFTA.[2] In 1965, some structures of the ECSC, EEC, and Euratom were combined into the **European Communities** by the Treaty Establishing a Single Council and Single Commission of the European Communities, which went into effect in 1967.

In 1973, Britain, Denmark, and Ireland joined. Greece became a member in 1981. Greenland, when granted home rule by Denmark in 1985, decided not to become a part of the EEC. Portugal and Spain joined in 1986.

In 1985, human rights were brought into the picture by the Schengen Agreement, which unified the territories of the European Communities so that labor and tourists could pass freely from country to country; Britain and Ireland have still not ratified, however. In 1986, the European Communities were fully merged into the **European Community** by the Single European Act, the preamble of which referred for the first time to promoting democracy and fundamental rights. The text also established four internal market freedoms – free movement of capital, goods, people, and services. In 1989, the **Community Charter of the Fundamental Social Rights of Workers** ensured that the economic unification would respect workers' rights.

After the Berlin Wall came tumbling down in 1989, and the Soviet Union evaporated in 1991, dreams of a European-wide economic market became plans. In 1992, when ECSC was about to expire, the three EC organizations and the Benelux Economic Union were consolidated into the EU by the **Treaty on European Union**, known as the Maastricht Treaty, which went into force in 1993. Maastricht not only recognized CoE's founding European Convention for the Protection of Human Rights and Fundamental Freedoms of 1950 as guiding principles but also incorporated provisions relating to social policy. Treaty provisions encouraged cooperation in regard to the following matters of concern to human rights:

- Employment
- Labor law and working conditions
- Occupational safety and hygiene
- Social security
- The right of collective bargaining
- The right to work
- The right to travel.

The Maastricht Treaty created the **Committee of the Regions** to represent local governments and regions (Basque, Flanders, etc.), as nominated by member countries, which are consulted before regulations are adopted, thereby ensuring smooth implementation.

In 1992, Czechoslovakia, Hungary, and Poland formed the **Central European Free Trade Agreement** (CEFTA). Some adjacent countries joined in the next few years (Bulgaria, Croatia, Romania, Slovenia), but when peace returned to the Balkans, Macedonia joined in 2006, and all but Bulgaria and Slovenia dropped out as they joined the EU. At the South East Europe Prime Ministers Summit, in 2006, a new CEFTA agreement was drawn up. Then in 2007, Albania, Bosnia, Moldova, Montenegro, Serbia, and the UN Mission in Kosovo signed on, whereupon Bulgaria and Slovenia pulled out to become EU members, followed in 2013 by Croatia. CEFTA, in other words, served as a preparatory body for eventual EU membership.

There was no longer any reason for Austria, Finland, and Sweden to pretend neutrality between a Western European bloc and a Soviet bloc. Accordingly, they joined EU in 1995.

The Maastricht Treaty was revised in 1997 by the **Treaty of Amsterdam**, which identified the founding human rights principles of the EU as:

- Liberty
- Democracy
- Human rights
- Fundamental freedoms
- The rule of law.

After 1999, when the Amsterdam Treaty went into effect, the EU human rights mandate was broadened to ban discrimination based on sex, race, color, ethnic or social origin, genetic features, language, religion, political beliefs or any other opinion, membership in a national minority, property, birth legitimacy, disability, age, sexual orientation, and nationality. In addition, EU citizens have a right of residence throughout member countries, and any citizen can vote and run for office. Maastricht also authorized a monetary union, so finance ministers met to create the

Frankfurt-based European Central Bank in 1998 and the Eurozone in 1999, though coins and notes were not circulated until 2002.

Maastricht was amended by the **Treaty of Nice** of 2001, which went into force in 2003. The Nice Treaty was a compromise, so from 2002 negotiations proceeded to develop a Constitution on the Future of Europe. In 2004, 10 Eastern European countries joined (Cyprus, Czech Republic, Estonia, Hungary, Latvia, Lithuania, Malta, Poland, Slovenia, Slovakia). When the constitution was completed in 2005, a referendum was considered to be the mode of adoption, but the effort went up in smoke when voters in France and the Netherlands rejected the constitution. A reworked version, the Treaty on the Functioning of the EU, known as the **Treaty of Lisbon**, was adopted by governments (not voters) in 2007 as an amendment both to Maastricht/Amsterdam/Nice and to the Single European Act. That same year, Bulgaria and Romania joined, and Croatia became the 28th member in 2013, bringing the total membership to the present 28.

Whereas the Nice Treaty contained some procedural changes, the Lisbon Treaty, which went into force in 2009, consolidated the various supranational economic elements, the intergovernmental noneconomic policy framework, and what has been developing as a separate foreign policy structure. From a legal perspective, EU now combines supranational elements (customs union, common market, monetary union) with certain issue-areas where EU policies preclude or can be separate from national policies. EU policies supersede national policies in the areas of freedom, justice, security, and social cohesion. The Lisbon Treaty has clarified that the Eurogroup consists of countries that use the Euro currency.

The **Charter of Fundamental Rights of the European Union**, which had been proclaimed by the Commission, the EU Council, and the EU Parliament in 2000, was incorporated into the Lisbon Treaty. The Charter generally incorporates provision of the CoE's basic documents (European Convention for Human Rights plus European Social Charter), previous EU treaties, as well as case law derived from previous EU law and court cases. Perhaps the most important element of the Lisbon Treaty is that the EU can now speak with a single voice in matters of foreign policy.

The EU's organizational structure is less complex. The headquarters in Brussels is the **European Commission**. The **European Council** is the collective executive, consisting of all EU government heads. There is a bicameral legislature consisting of the **Council of the European Union**, also known as the **Consilium**, and the **European Parliament** (Europarl). Citizens in EU countries elect Europarl delegates every five years. The **Court of Justice of the European Union** and the **European Central Bank** are the remaining major institutions. Other bodies are noted below.

The Maastricht Treaty established the position of **European Ombudsman** (or Euro-Ombudsman). An independent organ located in Strasbourg, the European Ombudsman can receive complaints from citizens that allege improper functioning by any EU body except for the Court of Justice of the European Union. The Ombudsman is appointed by Europarl. Complaint processing is in accordance with the Code of Good Administrative Behavior adopted by Europarl in 2001. In 2011, the Ombudsman office received 177 complaints, decided 157 cases, and initiated 26 inquiries on its own; most were about the Commission. In a recent case filed against the European Commission, for example, a job applicant was turned down for a job by the Commission for not wanting to travel by air, a case classified as one of discrimination. Possible responses are a **friendly settlement, transfer** of the complaint to another competent body, a **finding of no maladministration**, a critical **remark**, or a **recommendation** to another body. In 2011, 25 recommendations were made; overall, some 82 percent of all recommendations are adopted. If an EC body makes an unsatisfactory response to a recommendation, the Ombudsman can send Europarl a Special Report with recommendations; no such report was issued in 2011.

Within the Maastricht Treaty, EU members also agreed to establish the **European Law Enforcement Organization** (Europol). The Europol Convention, drafted the following year, was ratified in 1998. The headquarters, known as the European Police Office, are in The Hague. Europol not only covers all EU members but also works closely with law enforcement agencies of non-EU countries throughout Europe (Albania, Bosnia, Croatia, Macedonia, Moldova, Norway, Russia, Serbia, Switzerland, Turkey) as well as with Canada, Colombia, Iceland, and the United States. The International Criminal Police Organization (Interpol) defers to Europol in making arrests inside European countries. In 2005, when Italy issued arrest warrants for CIA suspects in the abduction of an Egyptian cleric from Milan to Egypt, Europol was authorized to make the arrests. Originally a semi-independent organization, Europol was brought into the umbrella of the EU by the Lisbon Treaty.

European Commission. The EU chief executive is the **Commission President**, who is nominated by the Consilium and elected by Europarl. Increasingly, the president has exercised leadership powers, transforming the EU from past formalism into a more consensus-building model of decision making. In agreement with the president, the Consilium selects one commissioner from the nominee of each of the EU member countries to serve as the collective executive, known as the **College of Commissioners**. Each commissioner holds a ministerial-type portfolio, similar to a cabinet position. The Commissioner for External Relations deals with human rights issues, though there is no separate department on the subject. Commissioners work with the 23,000 Eurocrats at the Brussels headquarters or office in Luxembourg to implement EU laws and policies. The Commission has the sole power of proposing legislation (except in foreign affairs) to the bicameral body, though either body might request a proposal, and they may initiate nonbinding resolutions. From 2009, the EU has recognized the right of initiative: A petition of one million citizens in EU countries may request the Commission to submit a proposed law to the legislative bodies. In 2006, the Commission, for the first time, proposed criminal laws: some were about terrorist incidents, recruitment, and training; others identified environmental crimes.

Large numbers of refugees fled from conflicts in the former Yugoslavia. In response, several EU innovations emerged. Uniform procedures were adopted for applicants for political asylum, known as the Common European Asylum System. A **European Refugee Fund**, set up in 2002 within the Commission, supports the reception, integration, and voluntary repatriation of refugees, and for up to three years provides displaced persons with residency, work permits, living accommodations, access to social and medical services, and schooling for their children.

European Council. Composed of heads of all EU governments, the European Council sets policy for the other bodies. A major responsibility is to admit new members. Countries that wish to become members of the EU must first apply to the Commission, which after an investigation will refer the matter to the European Council. The investigation first determines whether a candidate fulfills the "Copenhagen criteria" – that is, the country has:

- A democracy
- A free market
- Rule of law
- Associated freedoms and institutions.

Although there is a procedure for withdrawal, no country has done so.

In 1993, EU revamped criteria for membership, as follows:

- Stable institutions
- A functioning democracy
- Rule of law
- Respect for human rights
- Respect for and protection of minorities
- A functioning market economy
- The *acquis*; that is, both the ability to assume membership obligations and an adherence to the aims of the economic, monetary, and political union.

In 2004, the European Neighborhood Policy, also known as Wider Europe, made overtures to Belarus, Moldova, Russia, and the Ukraine and later to Armenia, Azerbaijan, and Georgia. In 2008, the EU launched an Eastern Partnership to attract participation by Central Asian countries formerly in the Soviet Union, but Russia had already organized a Eurasian Economic Community and opted out of the Partnership (see Chapter 13).

Several CoE countries have decided to remain outside the EU – Albania, Andorra, Liechtenstein, Iceland, Norway, San Marino, and Switzerland. Croatia joined in 2013. Iceland, Macedonia, Montenegro, Serbia, and Turkey are candidate members who have applied but must fulfill certain conditions before being allowed to join.

Serbia's desire to join the EU prompted Belgrade to turn over additional persons charged with war crimes to the International Criminal Tribunal for the Former Yugoslavia in 2005, whereupon the membership application of Serbia was formally opened. In 2006, the application was suspended because Belgrade had not arrested the Serbians who led the Bosnia War; namely, Radovan Karadžić (1945–) and Ratko Mladić (1943–). They were arrested and turned over to the International Criminal Tribunal for the Former Yugoslavia in 2011.

The poorer European countries are so eager to gain the economic advantages of membership that they generally take actions to meet the stiff preconditions. Turkey, which began negotiations for membership in 2005, has adopted dozens of amendments dealing with women's rights to meet the required conditions. However, Ankara must resolve several more problems – allowing the Kurdish minority to educate and broadcast in their native language and ending torture in the criminal justice system. Although France wants Turkey to acknowledge guilt for genocide against Armenians from 1915–1923 as a condition of membership, that condition is not among the official preconditions. Nevertheless, Prime Minister Recep Tayyip Erdogan (1954–) called for an impartial study of the matter in 2005. Although some EU countries are skeptical that Turkey will ever be admitted, Ankara's efforts to qualify for membership clearly are applauded by Europeans who want human rights to advance as far as possible around the world as well as by Kurds inside the country who are enjoying greater freedoms.

The Maastricht Treaty permitted the EU to respond to persistent and serious human rights violations or other violations by its members through two procedures. **Preventive procedures** are various forms of technical assistance – education and cooperation, and information. **Sanctions** can be limited or involve suspension of economic privileges but not expulsion. Grounds for suspension require unanimous votes; limited sanctions need majorities. The Treaty of Nice provides a procedure whereby the errant country is notified that sanctions might be imposed and is given an opportunity for corrective action to avoid suspension.

EU member countries that are deemed to persistently violate human rights in a serious manner may have their voting rights or membership suspended. Such action requires a two-thirds vote of the European Parliament, followed by a unanimous European Council decision (excluding the country concerned). During about half of 2000, after the neo-Nazi party of Jörg Haider (1950–2008) joined the ruling coalition in the Austrian parliament, the remaining EU members voted to impose a freeze on bilateral relations with Vienna. The main concern was that his Freedom Party, which garnered 27 percent of the vote, would encourage other neo-Nazi groups to run for office elsewhere throughout Europe.

Council of the EU (Consilium). The upper chamber of the EU legislative body is the Council, or Consilium. Each country supplies a ministerial-level official to the Council. The ministers present at a particular meeting depend upon the issue being discussed, so on a given day the agricultural or foreign ministers might meet. Foreign ministers meet about once a month in the **Foreign Affairs Council**. Economics and finance ministers comprise the **Ecofin Council**. As a lawmaking body, the Consilium passes laws, negotiates treaties, and adopts the annual budget subject to approval by the lower chamber, Europarl. Nonlegislative discussions are conducted in private.

In 1972, the Consilium issued the **Paris Declaration**, admitting that the economic advances of the organization had not "trickled down" to the social level – that is, had not promoted the well-being of ordinary citizens. Accordingly, the Social Action Program was launched with poverty reduction as a focus for future aid. From 1975 to 1980, some 66 projects and studies dealt with poverty in Europe. Anti-Poverty Action Programs continued up to 1990. Evaluation of the results of the economic focus on poverty led to the conclusion that social exclusion was the real source of poverty, thus identifying the need to focus on social rights and projects for social inclusion.

In 1991, the Consilium adopted the **Resolution on Human Rights, Democracy, and Development**, which provided equal stress on civil-political and economic-social rights. From 1992, all EC agreements on trade or cooperation with Third World countries must contain a clause stipulating that human rights are an essential element in the relations between the parties. The 1991 resolution provides for reduction in, or suspension of, aid programs or trade concessions to any country that fails to respect human rights in two circumstances: "grave and persistent" human rights violations or "serious interruption of democratic processes." An exception is allowed for emergency humanitarian assistance, where natural disasters or oppressive governments produce large-scale human suffering.

Sanctions, called **restricted measures**, can be imposed by the Consilium on non-members for human rights or other reasons. They can take the form of freezing of assets, trade embargoes, and visa denials to specific individuals. EU economic sanctions, which can affect both member and nonmember countries, are not to be taken lightly; they are far more effective than CoE aid sanctions.

The first non-EU country to be sanctioned was Uganda in 1977 because of the excesses of Idi Amin (1923–2003). In 1989, after the massacre near Tiananmen Square, the EU imposed an arms embargo on China. In 1990, the EU banned arms exports to Myanmar, and in 1997 the EU withdrew its trade privileges under the organization's generalized system of preferences, citing the widespread use of forced labor. In 2000, the organization condemned Russian military action in Chechnya, where about 100,000 civilians lost their lives, though no embargo was ordered. In 2005, the EU was divided on imposing sanctions on the Sudan, regarding the Darfur genocide, preferring to refer the matter to the International Criminal Court, which then indicted President Omar Al-Bashir (1944–).

Today, 32 countries are currently under EU-imposed sanctions. In 2012, fresh sanctions were imposed on supporters of the coup in Guinea-Bissau. Others on the EU blacklist, which is imposed by individual EU states, include Afghanistan, Belarus, Bosnia, Democratic Republic of the Congo, Egypt, Eritrea, Guinea, Iran, Iraq, the Ivory Coast, Lebanon, Liberia, Libya, Mauritius, Moldova, Myanmar, North Korea, Serbia, Somalia, Sudan, Syria, Tunisia, as well as Al-Qaeda and the Taliban. EU suspended sanctions against Zimbabwe following adoption in 2013 of a constitution.

In 1997, the Council set up the European Monitoring Centre on Racism and Xenophobia as an expert body. Five years later, the focus was clarified as the areas of employment, education, legislation, and racist violence and crimes, including ethnic disparities in education, attitude surveys, and statistics on hate crimes. In 2003, the Consilium upgraded the center to become the Fundamental Rights Agency, which was superseded in 2007 by the **European Agency for Fundamental Rights**. The agency promotes human rights through public events and research reports; a recent report was on victims of crime.

European Parliament (Europarl). Whereas debates in the Consilium enable governments to defend national interests against proposals for Europeanization, Europarl delegates often vote along party lines to form left–right caucuses that scrutinize proposals ideologically. Although Europarl has less power than the consilium, popular voting for Europarl seats links the EU directly with citizen preferences, which, on account of the failure of the proposed European Constitution, have increasingly been taken into account. Europarl can refuse to support the budget submitted by the Commission's president, in effect a vote of no confidence, and did so in 1999.

When Europarl is in session in Strasbourg, the Committee on Foreign Affairs has a **Subcommittee on Human Rights**. Two other committees relating to human rights are the **Committee on Civil Liberties, Justice, and Home Affairs** and the **Committee on Women's Rights and Gender Equality**. From 2000, Europarl has published the *Annual Report on Human Rights*, which has a worldwide focus. In 2012, Europarl voted to establish a single high-level official on human rights and awaits concurrence from other EU bodies.

Europarl has spoken out about human rights abuses abroad as well as within EU, sometimes in the form of published **opinions**. Revelations about the role of European countries in extraordinary renditions by the CIA prompted Europarl to initiate investigations. In 2006, an investigator reported allegations that 14 CE member countries provided secret prisons and airfields for secret flights to other countries where suspected terrorists were tortured. Poland, for example, has undertaken further investigation to determine who was responsible.

Any EU citizen may file a petition with Europarl's **Committee on Petitions**, which may include human rights complaints. About 1,500 petitions are filed each year. Europarl then attempts to mediate. If unsuccessful in mediation, and a violation is found, Europarl may ask the EU Commission to bring action against the offending state to the EU Court of Justice. In 2009, for example, a person with a French degree in pharmacy sought to live and work in the UK, which refused to recognize his degree as valid, so he appealed to the Committee on Petitions on grounds of discrimination based on nationality. The committee then successfully asked the UK to change the law. Accordingly, the petitioner filed suit with the UK High Court for income lost by the initial refusal. When the appeal was denied because the original refusal was in accordance with the law before the law changed, he went back to the Committee in 2012, which classified the problem as lack of "access to justice," and began to mediate on his behalf.

HISTORIC EVENT 12.1 THE EUROPEAN UNION ADOPTS THE COTONOU AGREEMENT (2000)

When European countries recovered from the devastation of World War II, they began to pay attention to struggling countries that had been British, Dutch, and French colonies. In 1963, the European Economic Community adopted the Yaoundé Convention to coordinate aid with 18 Associated African States and Madagascar, mostly former French colonies. The agreement, as revised in 1969, was extended to 1974. When the United Kingdom joined the European Community in 1973, an arrangement to include

Continued

20 developing countries within the British Commonwealth was discussed. One result was the adoption, in 1975, of the first of four Lomé Conventions, which were aimed initially at allowing agricultural and mineral exports from African, Caribbean, and Pacific states to enter the cooperating European countries free of duty and later at coordinating aid and investment. Lomé IV, adopted in 1989 to cover a 10-year period, was the first to introduce aid conditionality – that is, the possibility of canceling or withholding privileges based on an assessment of human rights, democracy, good governance (absence of corruption), and environmental protection. A revision in 1995 made respect for human rights and the rule of law conditions of aid, and failure to respect human rights could result in aid suspension. However, in 1999, the United States complained that Lomé subsidies were a violation of World Trade Organization (WTO) regulations. WTO's Dispute Settlement Body agreed, so the European Union negotiated an agreement with the United States to settle the matter. Then, in 2000, consistent with the Charter of Fundamental Rights of the European Union adopted that year, aid policies were redesigned under the Cotonou Agreement to pay particular attention to human rights, especially support for democracy as a precondition for reducing poverty. Under Cotonou, sanctions have been imposed on Myanmar and Zimbabwe. In addition, Cotonou includes a provision on the International Criminal Court and refers to cooperation in countering proliferation of weapons of mass destruction as well as terrorism. Cotonou also has a provision relating to the prevention of mercenary activities. Cotonou was revised in 2005 and 2010.

One of the most important EU agreements is the **Lomé Convention** of 1989, which was revised several times and replaced by the **Cotonou Agreement**, linking the EU with 79 developing countries in Africa, the Caribbean, and the Pacific (the ACP group). To be renewed every five years, Cotonou provides trade and aid (EuropeAid) and has a human rights clause.

Whereas the EU urged ACP countries to join the International Criminal Court (ICC) during the years from its beginning in 2002, the United States threatened to cut off aid to any country that joined, thereby cross-pressuring many vulnerable countries. Nevertheless, only six ACP countries have failed to join ICC, and American pressure ceased after the election of President Barack Obama (1961–).

EuropeAid policy is mostly premised on a **proactive** rather than a **punitive** approach to human rights, reasoning that negative measures do not address the root causes of human rights abuses but instead punish peoples for inadequacies of governments. EU policy is that poverty reduction, the main objective of its overseas development policy, is only possible in a democracy, and aid is generally distributed at the local level rather than to a bureaucracy for redistribution. In addition to aid for economic development projects, much aid is provided with the specific aim of promoting democracy through institution-building, such as the funding of an election and legal training.

On the proactive side, Europarl launched the **European Initiative for Democracy and Human Rights**, providing EuropeAid funds primarily for macro-level projects developed by intergovernmental organizations, such as the African Union and the UN High Commissioner for Human Rights. Critiques of the initiative led to adoption of the **European Instrument for Democracy and Human Rights** in 2006, providing about €1 billion in funds designed to encourage democratization "from below." The objectives are as follows:

- Enhancing respect for human rights in "at risk" countries
- Strengthening civil society groups promoting reforms in democracy and human rights
- Supporting actions consistent with EU guidelines on human rights
- Supporting regional and international frameworks that protect human rights and advance the rule of law
- Electoral observer missions.

In addition to publicity, seminars, support for human rights attorneys, and training in human rights around the world, the program provides an annual statistical index of press freedom and of gay-lesbian freedom.

EuropeAid programs for nonmember countries, particularly those within the African, Caribbean, and Pacific countries, are designed to promote the following priority areas:

- Strengthening democracy, good governance, the rule of law
- Cooperating with civil society to promote political pluralism, a free media and sound justice system
- Abolishing the death penalty
- Combating repression and torture (through better police training and creating criminal courts)
- Fighting racism and discrimination
- Gender equality
- The protection of children.

From 1988, Europarl's Human Rights Subcommittee has been in part responsible for the awarding of the **Sakharov Prize for Freedom of Thought** to an individual or group that has advanced human rights anywhere in the world. In 2005, Ladies in White won – for their efforts to free some 75 dissidents in Cuba who had been imprisoned in 2003. Later in 2005, Cuba freed 15 of the dissidents for medical reasons. The award in 2012 went to two imprisoned Iranian dissidents – attorney Nasrin Sotoudeh (1963–) and film director Jafar Panahi (1960–).

Court of Justice of the European Community. To ensure compliance with EU regulations, the Court of Justice was created in 1952 at Luxembourg. To gain respect for impartiality and professionalism, the court established human rights principles in its proceedings – namely, the rights to a fair trial, for an appeal, for privacy, to free association and expression, to acquire and hold property, and to professional secrecy.

There are three tribunals. One judge from each EU member serves on the **Grand Chamber of the Court of Justice**, though judges usually sit on three- and five-judge chambers. The **General Court**, established in 1988, has a composition similar to the Court of Justice. The Grand Chamber determines points of law, whereas the General Court handles cases involving torts. There is also a **Civil Service Tribunal**, created in 2004 for employees of the EU. Combined, all three courts have handled some 15,000 cases over the years. In 2011, human rights issues before the Grand Chamber accounted for 110 of 688 new cases, 74 of 638 cases settled, and there were 849 pending cases not yet classified. The General Court, which has a similar total caseload, generally resolves contract disputes and rarely human rights issues. In general, rulings have supported cases filed against national governments based on EU standards. Complaints involving neither EC law nor EC institutions go to the CoE's ECHR.

Member states can appeal cases in national courts to the EU court in order to clarify questions of EU law. Decisions are implemented by the individual states. Usually, the court hears cases filed against EU institutions. In 1997, the court began to hear criminal cases. From 2003, specialized chambers on particular subjects have been organized to hear initial cases. All decisions are required to be unanimous.

COURT CASE 12.3 THE *BOSMAN* CASE (1995)

In some European countries, a football (soccer) team could prohibit their players from moving to another team even after their contracts expired. The contract of one such player, Jean-Marc Bosman (1964–), expired with the team in Liège, so he tried to move to the team in Dunkerque. But the Liège team not only refused but retaliated by lowering his pay and rank. He then took his case and similar disputes to the Court of Justice of the European Union, suing for restraint of trade. The court not only ruled that workers had a right to transfer to another employer but also that quotas could not restrict the number of European Union nationals allowed on member teams. The ruling is similar to a case in the United States during 1976 that established the principle of "free agency" (409FSupp233,261;532F2d615).

From 1969, the Court of Justice referred to human rights issues in its rulings regarding commercial litigants but without the power to do so against governments. Later, the court began to rule that fundamental rights must be respected not only by EC institutions but also by member governments in implementing EC law. In 1977, Europarl, the European Commission, and the Council of Ministers signed a joint declaration vowing to respect fundamental rights, as defined by the Court of Justice. Nevertheless, the bifurcation of courts between CoE and EU is only informally coordinated, as the Court of Justice tends to restrict its cases to economic issues.

High Representative of the Union for Foreign Affairs and Security Policy. For many years, the EU lacked a single voice in foreign policy. In 1997, the Treaty of Amsterdam established the separate position of High Representative for Common Foreign and Security Policy. The Lisbon Treaty retitled the position as High Representative of the Union for Foreign Affairs and Security Policy, and also placed the position as President of the European Council with responsibility to implement policies adopted therein by the foreign ministers. The Lisbon Treaty also authorized the establishment of the European External Action Service, which serves as the EU foreign ministry and employs ambassadors and professional diplomats to assist the High Representative.

When Yugoslavia began to disintegrate in the 1990s through secession by several states, the EU played an unprecedented role in several respects. In 2003, the European Union Force (EUFOR) was used in Macedonia to prevent Serbia from expanding war to the country. Then EUFOR replaced NATO peacekeepers in Bosnia in 2004. During 2005, logistical cooperation between the EU and NATO was provided in Darfur at the request of the African Union. EUFOR peacekeeping units also were assigned in 2006 to the Democratic Republic of the Congo. In 2007, EUFOR went to the Central African Republic and Chad. Only the Bosnia EUFOR is still operational.

In 1998, as Serbia began to invade Kosovo, High Representative Javier Solana (1942–) tried to mediate and sent monitors to Kosovo, but Belgrade was not initially interested in compromise. In 1999, the EU voted economic sanctions against Serbia, and NATO began to bomb Serbia. After the bombing ended, the UN Interim Administration in Kosovo included an EU unit to provide economic recovery. When the conflict between Serbs and Kosovars (ethnic Albanians) heated up in Kosovo during 2001, Solana again attempted to mediate.

In 2002, High Representative Solana criticized the United States for failing to treat those detained at Guantánamo as prisoners of war. He also opposed the Iraq War, though EU countries in Eastern Europe expressed support for the Anglo-American invasion. In 2004, he mediated in the dispute between presidential candidates following the election in the Ukraine. Involved in establishing the Road Map for Peace between Israel and the Palestinian authorities, he criticized the former for obstructing elections of the latter in 2005. In 2010, when Solana's term was up, he was replaced by the Baroness Catherine Ashton (1956–).

The High Representative is also Vice President of the European Commission, and the President of the **European Defense Agency**. The latter body, set up in 2004, mindful of American aggression in Iraq during 2003, reports to the European Council and has the same EU members except Denmark. Although some countries have proposed that the European Defense Agency become an instrument to compete with NATO, Britain consistently has vetoed the suggestion, relying for security as it does on what George VI (1895–1952) in 1941 called its "special relationship" with the United States.

Currently, the EU is undergoing an economic and financial crisis because some countries have accumulated a large amount of debt in using the Euro currency.

Although a financial restructuring is in progress, human rights will remain a high priority within the EU. Nevertheless, EU officials had a reason to feel elated: the Nobel Peace Prize was awarded to the European Union in 2012.

ORGANIZATION FOR SECURITY AND COOPERATION IN EUROPE (OSCE)

The idea to link Western Europe with Eastern Europe in a security organization emerged from a meeting of foreign ministers at Helsinki in 1973 and was accepted at a summit of government heads two years later. The Conference on Security and Cooperation in Europe (CSCE) was formed in 1975 by the **Helsinki Final Act** as a bargain between the Western and Soviet blocs: the West recognized Soviet hegemony in Eastern Europe, while the Soviets allowed human rights monitoring. The founding agreement committed the organization to three basic principles or "baskets":

1   Military security
2   Economic security (economics, science, technology, and environment)
3   Human security (information, education, culture, and human rights).

Over time, CSCE third-basket reports on human rights abuses inside the Iron Curtain chipped away at the legitimacy of communist regimes.

In 1989, the Berlin Wall was breached, so the organization sought a new role. The transitions from communism to capitalism in Eastern Europe provided unique opportunities. Accordingly, CSCE members met at the Second Summit in 1990 to sign the **Charter of Paris for a New Europe**, which codified guiding principles governing the "human dimension," and refocused the human security basket as:

•   Promoting tolerance
•   Strengthening democratic processes
•   Combating racism, xenophobia, and discrimination.

In 1995, CSCE was retitled the OSCE as agreed at the Fourth Summit the preceding year.

CSCE and OSCE have distinguished themselves from CoE and EU by following a process approach in which conferences are held on specific topics, discussion is wide-ranging, a consensus is sought on particular goals and plans of action, and a document is issued. **Action plans** involve reports, site visits, workshops, and similar vehicles. The Helsinki Final Act, the founding instrument, is thus supplemented by many documents that enunciate binding commitments, norms, principles, and standards; together, the documentary basis is known as *acquis* OSCE. The organization has grown by accretion rather than by a systematic design and is result-oriented rather than legalistic.

The organization began as a cooperative venture among states of Eastern and Western Europe. In July 1992, following the Third Summit, Yugoslavia's membership was suspended for its support of ethnic cleansing in Bosnia. A fact-finding mission was dispatched in September, and in December a report condemned Yugoslavia. Belgrade finally regained membership in 2000. By 2007, membership had increased to 57, with 12 partner states. Members now include those who have joined CoE plus Belarus, the Holy See, Monaco, Central Asian states (Kazakhstan, Kyrgyzstan, Tajikistan, Turkmenistan, Uzbekistan), and North American states (Canada, United States). The partner states are Afghanistan, Algeria, Australia, Egypt, Israel, Japan, Jordan, Mongolia, Morocco, South Korea, Thailand, and Tunisia.

In 1991, CSCE set up a **Secretariat** in Prague, but in 1994 the Secretariat moved to Vienna, leaving a small public information office in Prague. Within the Vienna office, there are eight units:

- Action Against Terrorism Unit
- Borders Team
- Office of the Special Representative and Coordinator for Combating Trafficking in Human Beings
- Conflict Prevention Center
- Economic and Environmental Activities Unit
- External Cooperation Unit
- Gender Section
- Strategic Police Matters Unit.

In 1990, the Charter of Paris for a New Europe created the annual **Parliamentary Assembly**, whose members from national legislatures agreed at their first meeting in 1992 to locate the headquarters in Copenhagen, separate from the Secretariat. There are three General Committees, one of which is the **Democracy, Human Rights and Humanitarian Questions Committee**. The parliamentarians not only debate and recommend policies but ask questions of OSCE leaders, similar to the question period in the British House of Commons. A major operational task is election monitoring.

At the summit meeting in 1992, two new bodies were created. The **Forum for Security Cooperation** was established as a body of defense ministry officials that would meet weekly in Vienna to cope with ongoing challenges and to negotiate agreements on arms control, disarmament, and confidence- and security-building measures. The **High Commissioner on National Minorities**, located at The Hague, was set up to promote ethnic dialog and to recommend prompt action to deescalate tensions that might lead to large-scale violence against minorities. One month after its creation, High Commissioner missions were dispatched to Kosovo, Sandjak, and Vojvodina, though Belgrade did not cooperate. The High Commissioner has actively sought to defuse tensions within many of the newest members. In a mission to Latvia in 2005, problems of the Russian minority were reviewed, thereby pacifying Moscow's anger over frequent OSCE criticisms regarding such matters as Russian troops in Georgia and Moldova and the suppression of the democratic process in Chechnya. In the latter case, Russia first asked OSCE officials to monitor elections and later asked them to leave when their report was unfavorable.

The Convention on Conciliation and Arbitration of 1995 established the **Court of Conciliation and Arbitration**, located in Geneva; 33 of the 57 OSCE members have ratified the treaty. The court may organize conciliation commissions and arbitration tribunals when requested to handle disputes involving territorial integrity, maritime delimitation, and environmental and economic issues.

Another body, the **Representative on Freedom of the Media**, was set up in 1997. The main task is to monitor press restrictions and to intervene on behalf of news media and journalists who are under threat.

OSCE has many field operations, consisting of centers, missions, offices, or projects in member countries, accounting for a large portion of the organization's budget. The first field office opened in Skopje during 1992, to ensure that the ongoing conflict in Yugoslavia would not spill over into Macedonia. Later in 1992, an OSCE office was set up in Georgia to play a peacekeeping role; the office has remained to provide assistance in matters of human rights. In 1997, when a pyramid scheme impoverished many Albanians, OSCE established an office in Tirana to assist the country's democratization process. Currently, six field operations are in the Balkans, two in the Caucasus, five in Central Asia, and three in former republics of the Soviet Union. Fifteen other field offices existed over the years. The purpose is to assist in transitioning from areas of conflict to peaceful democratic operations. In some cases, assistance has been given to national war crimes prosecutions.

In 1989, CSCE decided to launch the **Human Dimension Mechanism**, the initial element of which was a formal complaint process, known as the **Vienna Mechanism**, in which one member government may complain about another, triggering an investigation and, in the event that a problem is uncovered, an effort to conciliate. During the first year of operation, the mechanism attracted about 100 complaints, dealing with such matters as the imprisonment of Václav Havel (1936–2011) in Czechoslovakia and Turkey's treatment of its Kurdish minority.

In 1991, a second element was added to the Human Dimension Mechanism. Known as the **Moscow Mechanism**, OSCE authorized ad hoc missions of independent experts to assist in resolving a specific problem. The latter has been used seven times – to investigate atrocities and attacks on unarmed civilians in Croatia and Bosnia-Herzegovina, Estonian legislation in regard to human rights, implementation of Moldova's legislation on minority rights and interethnic relations, human rights violations in Yugoslavia (in which the latter refused to cooperate), military operations in the former Yugoslavia, the attempted assassination of Turkmenistan President Saparmurat Niyazov (1940–2006) in 2002, and irregularities in the 2010 Belarus election.

In 1991, the Office for Free Elections was established to administer the Human Dimension Mechanism. In 1997, the structure became the **Office for Democratic Institutions and Human Rights**, charged primarily with the function of providing technical assistance and monitoring member and partner states. The office, located in Warsaw, consists of five units:

- The Democratization Department holds workshops to strengthen the rule of law, promote leadership skills for females, and combat violence against women.

- The Elections Department dispatches observers to elections. OSCE was on the scene in the Ukraine during 2005 to condemn election fraud in the first election and then returned to certify that the rescheduled election was free and fair.
- The Human Rights Department monitors trials, visits prisons, and holds workshops on nondiscrimination and tolerance.
- The Contact Point on Roma and Sinti Issues seeks to end the social exclusion of Roma and related groups by raising policy issues with governments and mediating conflicts.
- In 2004, the Tolerance and Non-discrimination Department, set up primarily to combat hate crimes, publishes an annual incident report and encourages governments to strengthen hate crime laws.

Among efforts at conflict resolution, one was the dispute over Nagorno-Karabakh, a territory populated mostly by Armenians that is located entirely inside Azerbaijan. In 1988, the two countries began an undeclared war over the issue. The council had hoped in 1992 to prepare for a conference to launch a peace process, but nothing happened until 1994, when Armenia prevailed and the war ended. The **Minsk Group**, consisting of three persons from France, Russia, and the United States, was then formed to negotiate a settlement. Although the issue remains unresolved, the territory is a de facto but unrecognized independent, self-proclaimed Republic of Nagorno-Karabakh.

OSCE ultimately was given responsibility for implementing provisions of the Dayton Peace Agreement of 1995 regarding Bosnia, including military disengagement, holding elections, and monitoring human rights compliance. OSCE personnel replaced the UN mission in Bosnia after 1995. OSCE's experience, which continues to the present, provides a model of how a regional organization can serve to improve human rights after peace is negotiated among parties to a war which had genocidal aspects.

When Kosovo flared up in 1998, OSCE dispatched observers, but they pulled out in 1999 because of Serbian obstruction. War then ensued. After the war stopped, OSCE returned to organize elections in Kosovo.

During the twenty-first century, Russia has repeatedly accused OSCE of being a tool of the West. Vladimir Putin (1952–) objected to OSCE for characterizing the Belarus election of 2001 as unfair and for appearing to take sides in the Ukraine's Orange Revolution of 2004. Rather than OSCE's loose structure, Putin is calling for reform that would make for a more centralized structure in which action could be stopped by objections from countries of the former Soviet Union.

Two non-OSCE bodies meet in Vienna, where OSCE is located: after five years of negotiations within the organizations, the Treaty on Conventional Armed Forces in Europe was signed in 1990. Regarded as the cornerstone of conventional stability and security from the Atlantic to the Urals, the treaty established the **Joint Consultative Group** (though officially outside OSCE) in Vienna to monitor compliance. A related body is the monthly **Open Skies Consultative Commission**, which meets at OSCE headquarters. The purpose is to monitor the Open Skies Treaty of 1992 that entered into force in January 2002. Covering territory of 34 countries from Vancouver to Vladivostok, the body coordinates unarmed aerial observation flights to ensure that military preparations are spotted before they are utilized. More than 500 overflights have already occurred.

OSCE, thus, is now involved in conflict prevention, post-conflict rehabilitation, and democracy building. The organization plays an important role in the diplomatic and political aspects of the human dimension of security, leaving military operations to NATO and other bodies.

NORTH ATLANTIC TREATY ORGANIZATION (NATO)

One basic human right is the right to personal security. In 1948, to deter a possible invasion of Western Europe by the Soviet Union that might unleash a nuclear holocaust, five countries (Belgium, France, Luxembourg, the Netherlands, and the United Kingdom) signed a defense agreement at Brussels, the Treaty of Economic, Social and Cultural Collaboration and Collective Self-Defense, forming the Brussels Treaty Organization (BTO).

In 1949, 10 countries of Western Europe (BTO countries plus Denmark, Iceland, Italy, Norway, and Portugal), Canada, and the United States signed the Treaty of Washington to form NATO as a collective security agreement. The preamble to the treaty states that NATO is "founded on the principles of democracy, individual liberty and the rule of law." BTO military responsibilities were then transferred to NATO.[3] A summit in 1999 adopted the **Strategic Concept**, which acknowledged "new risks to Euro-Atlantic peace and stability, including [1] oppression, [2] ethnic conflict, [3] economic distress, [4] the collapse of political order, and [5] the proliferation of weapons of mass destruction."

From 1952 to 1982, four more Western European countries joined (Greece, Spain, Turkey, and West Germany). To develop liaison with Eastern European countries, the 1991 summit set up the North Atlantic Cooperation Council, which in 1997 became the Euro-Atlantic Partnership Council (EAPC) through which Eastern European countries joined NATO in 1999 (Czech Republic, Hungary, Poland), in 2004 (Bulgaria, Estonia Latvia, Lithuania, Romania, Slovakia, Slovenia), and in 2009 (Albania, Croatia). Today, several European countries west of the former Soviet Union remain nonmembers – Austria, Bosnia, Finland, Ireland, Kosovo, Macedonia, Malta, Montenegro, Serbia, Sweden, Switzerland, and the ministates of Andorra, Liechtenstein, Monaco, and San Marino. Although Russia and former states of the Soviet Union contemplated NATO membership, they remained in EAPC, and Moscow instead forged alliances with countries of the Caucasus and Central Asia. Today, all the countries listed above not in NATO are members of EAPC.

In 1994, NATO began the Mediterranean Dialogue with Algeria, Egypt, Israel, Jordan, Mauritania, Morocco, and Tunisia. In 1998, a decision was made to designate countries with which cooperative arrangements were established outside Europe as Contact Countries, as they were invited to participate in its activities, conferences, exercises, and workshops. But that designation later split into three categories. Gulf Cooperation Council countries Bahrain, Kuwait, Qatar, and the United Arab Emirates are members of the Istanbul Cooperation Initiative, launched in 2004.

Thereafter, NATO decided to develop a relationship with others countries, called Partners Across the Globe; they are Afghanistan, Australia, Iraq, Japan, Mongolia, New Zealand, Pakistan, and South Korea. Also from 2011, Colombia, Malaysia, Mongolia, Singapore, and Tonga are designated as Operational Partners.

In order to ease tensions between NATO and Russia, the NATO–Russia Permanent Joint Council was set up in 1997 as a consultative body. However, Russia withdrew temporarily in 1999 while NATO was bombing Serbia. In 2002, the body was renamed the NATO–Russia Council, with a broader scope, including all NATO countries, with the possibility of joint action. When Russia intervened in Georgia during 2008, the body stopped meeting temporarily. One activity emerging from closer relations with Russia occurred later that year, when NATO's Office of Information and Press sponsored a conference in Moscow on the human rights responsibilities of the military in armed domestic conflicts.

Administratively, NATO headquarters has a dual structure – civilian and military. The civilian side has a staff of 1,200. The military component comprises 400 military and 100 civilian personnel. On the civilian side, there are some 2,000 members of national delegations and supporting staff members of national military representatives. On the military side, about 300 also work at missions of partner countries outside Brussels.

Originally in London, the headquarters moved to Paris in 1952. When French President Charles de Gaulle (1890–1970) expressed considerable displeasure over America's intervention into the civil war in Vietnam, the headquarters moved to Brussels in 1967. He also withdrew French troops from the integrated military command, though they were restored in 1993 when he was out of office. Within the headquarters, the Secretary-General heads the International Staff, which is organized into Divisions plus some independent offices. The top person on the military side is the Supreme Allied Commander Europe.

The main human rights issue within NATO has been women's rights. In 1996, NATO formed the Committee on Women in the NATO Forces. Twice renamed, the body is now the **NATO Committee on Gender Perspectives**, which is advisory to the **Military Committee**. In 2003, the **Equal Opportunities and Diversity Policy** was adopted with the aim of combating discrimination within the civilian employees. In the field, Gender Advisers are assigned to military commands. The **Special Representative for Women, Peace and Security** was established in 2012 within the International Staff.

In 2004, concern over human trafficking was assigned to the military structure. NATO military personnel in the field are on the lookout and are responsible for taking measures to stop the practice. Naval vessels patrolling the Mediterranean under the NATO flag are among the ways in which the policy is implemented. The **Senior Coordinator on Combating Trafficking in Human Beings** is in charge.

The first significant human rights role for NATO was in regard to what subsequently has been called the Responsibility to Protect (R2P). In 1995, the UN Security Council authorized NATO air strikes to stop genocide and to force the Bosnian Serbs to negotiate a peace agreement. The resulting Dayton Peace Agreement set up the multinational peacekeeping Implementation Force (IFOR) under NATO command, with a grant of authority from the UN. The General Framework Agreement establishing IFOR had a human rights clause. In 1996, the Security Council authorized NATO to operate the Stabilization Force (SFOR) as IFOR's successor. In 1998, when the UN mandate expired, NATO operated SFOR, primarily for civilian reconstruction. One of SFOR's assignments, to cooperate with the International Criminal Tribunal for the Former Yugoslavia in arresting the two top Bosnian Serb leaders, was never accomplished. NATO still supports a small contingent in Bosnia, though in 2004 SFOR responsibility was passed on to the European Union under the acronym EUFOR.

◼ HISTORIC EVENT 12.2 KOSOVO'S QUEST FOR INDEPENDENCE

In 1389, in the Battle of Kosovo, Serbia fought to prevent the armies of the Ottoman Empire from bringing Islam into Europe. Serbia lost and was an Ottoman province until 1815. After World War I, Kosovo and Serbia became part of the same country, first known as the Kingdom of Serbs, Croats, and Slovenes, and after 1929 as Yugoslavia. Serbia, the dominant province in Yugoslavia, split Kosovo administratively into several counties. Ethnic Albanians, who comprised a majority within Kosovo, protested to the League of Nations in 1921 that they were denied self-determination, but the League rejected their complaint. After World War II, as the Kosovar population increased to about 80 percent of Kosovo, efforts to achieve more autonomy within Yugoslavia were also frustrated. Street protests led to Serbian repression and, in 1990, to the cancellation of what little autonomy Kosovo enjoyed within Yugoslavia. Protesters then declared Kosovo an independent country, but no other country recognized the declaration. In 1995, the Kosovo Liberation Army (KLA) was formed, and its attacks on Serbian police led to the intervention of the Serbian army. In 1998, as violence escalated, airplanes of NATO bombed Serbia, which then agreed to an armistice, under which representatives of the Organization for Security and Cooperation in Europe sent observers to monitor the truce. When the KLA broke the ceasefire in 1999, Serbian troops went into Kosovo with the apparent intention of killing as many Kosovars as possible, or so it seemed when 45 Kosovars were massacred in Račak. As a result, the European Union imposed economic sanctions on Serbia. Belgrade then rejected terms of a proposed peace agreement, which would have given NATO unlimited access within Kosovo as well as Serbia. In 1999, without UN Security Council authorization, NATO forces bombed Serb military targets in Kosovo and ultimately civilian and military targets in Serbia. After 78 days, Serbia sued for peace. The Security Council then placed Kosovo under a temporary UN civilian administration, pending possible reintegration into Yugoslavia as an autonomous province, and authorized a NATO-led force of 50,000 troops from 39 countries to maintain order. However, Kosovo leaders wanted the UN to grant independence, something that Russia was determined to block in the Security Council. In 2008, Kosovo declared independence anyway, whereupon the UN General Assembly referred the declaration

Continued

to the International Court of Justice for an advisory opinion about its legality. In 2010, the court ruled that the independence was legal. In 2011, clashes between Serb-populated North Kosovo and the Kosovo government occurred. By 2012, when some 90 countries had recognized Kosovo as an independent state, a referendum in the Serb-majority area of North Kosovo rejected independence. Because of continuing Russian opposition, Kosovo has not been voted a member of the UN. The UN civilian authority still maintains a police force, though other functions have been transferred to the Kosovo government. The UN-authorized military Stabilization Force also remains in the country.

A similar pattern was repeated in regard to Kosovo, though without UN authorization. In 1998, EAPC began to provide humanitarian relief to ethnic Kosovar refugees fleeing from Kosovo into Albania and Macedonia. After a military exercise in Albania, NATO bombed Serbia. In response, Serbia stopped harassing Kosovars, so NATO ceased military operations. But, in 1999, Serbia resumed ethnic cleansing in Kosovo, whereupon NATO launched Operation Allied Force, which engaged in an 11-week bombing of Serbia to stop genocide against Albanians in Kosovo. After the war ended, the UN Security Council authorized NATO troops to organize the peacekeeping force, the Kosovo Force (KFOR). In 2001, NATO began operating missions in Albania and Macedonia to prevent a Kosovar insurgent group from using the border areas for staging operations to unleash raids into Kosovo. EU replaced NATO's mission in 2003.

NATO's bombing of Serbia in 1999 hit more than 500 civilians and many civilian targets, prompting an outcry in some quarters that NATO was violating human rights while invoking the principle of humanitarian intervention. UN Secretary-General Kofi Annan (1938–) expressed reservations over NATO's military operation without Security Council authorization. The following year, Human Rights Watch submitted a complaint on behalf of some of the civilian victims of the NATO bombing to the International Criminal Tribunal for the Former Yugoslavia, which ruled in 2001 that the case, *Bankovic v. Belgium et al.*, was not within its mandate.

In 2003, NATO took over command of the International Security Assistance Force in Afghanistan, which had been established by the United Nations in 2001 after the Afghan War. The aim was to provide a secure environment conducive to free and fair elections, the spread of the rule of law, and the reconstruction of the country. In 2004, NATO provided security for the election in Afghanistan, and in 2005 the force began to fight a Taliban-led insurgency in the south.

Also in 2003, some NATO members, notably France and Germany, blocked possible NATO military action in Iraq because they perceived that insufficient evidence backed Washington's claim that the regime headed by President Saddam Hussein (1937–2006) was hiding weapons of mass destruction. After the war, NATO forces arrived to equip and to train the Iraq security forces.

DISCUSSION TOPIC 12.1 WHICH FOREIGN POLICY DOES NATO PRIMARILY SERVE?

Among human rights problems around the world, NATO has operated as an effective instrument on a few occasions. Which human rights concerns have galvanized NATO? Do NATO's actions show a pattern in which American foreign policy is in reality the top priority?

EU and NATO have cooperated with independent missions in Darfur from 2005. The Darfur operation, which involved airlifting African Union peacekeeping forces, is NATO's first effort in Africa. In 2005, NATO also provided humanitarian relief to the victims of a severe earthquake in Pakistan.

In 2011, after street protests arose in Libya, its leader, Muammar Gaddafi (1942–2011), threatened to massacre the residents of Benghazi, a town supportive of the movement, whereupon the Arab League called for action to stop the violence. A no-fly zone was authorized by the UN Security Council, citing R2P. NATO countries then provided aerial support. The government was toppled in a few months, though the Security Council did not authorize regime change. NATO made that outcome inevitable.

NORDIC COUNCILS

In 1952, parliamentarians of Denmark, Iceland, Norway, and Sweden decided to meet together on a regular basis in an organization known as the **Nordic Council**. Finland joined in 1955. The organization was formalized by the Treaty of Cooperation Between Denmark, Finland, Iceland, Norway, and Sweden in 1962. In 1970, the autonomous regions of Åland and the Faroe Islands were given Associate Member status within the Danish and Finnish delegations, respectively. Self-governing Greenland became an associate member and was added to the Danish delegation in 1984. The Sámi minority (Laplanders living in the northernmost countries) has de facto observer status. Estonia, Latvia, and Lithuania are also formally recognized as observer states.

The headquarters for the Nordic Council is in Copenhagen. In 1971, foreign ministers of Nordic countries agreed to form the Council of Ministers, which is discussed below. Both councils are headquartered in Copenhagen with separate secretariats that share the same office building.

The Nordic Council of Parliamentarians has seven committees. The **Citizens' and Consumer Rights Committee** deals with civil and political rights, the **Culture and Education Committee** promotes educational competence and language cooperation, and the **Welfare Committee** focuses on social rights. The agenda each year consists of about 10 questions, of which at least one deals with human rights; in recent years, gender equality and human trafficking were discussed.

The Council of Ministers, in contrast, consists of 11 separate ministerial-level meetings that meet together once per year, including the Nordic Council of Ministers for Education and Research, Nordic Council of Ministers for Health and Social Affairs, Nordic Council of Ministers for Labor, Ministers for Gender Equality, and Nordic Ministers for Culture. Under the Council of Ministers are about 10 institutes and 20 advisory bodies, including the Nordic Center for Welfare and Social Issues, Nordic Council on Disability, the Nordic Culture Fund, the Nordic Development Fund, the Nordic Joint Committee for Agriculture and Food Research, and the Nordic Sámi College.

Scandinavian countries achieved some limited economic integration in a manner that anticipated the EU. In 1952, visa-free travel among the countries was established, and the legislators agreed in 1954 to the free movement of labor. In 1955, a citizen of one country working in another country was eligible for the same social and welfare benefits while in the latter country. The same applies to political rights: A citizen of one country residing in another can vote or run for office in the country of residence.

From 1995, the comprehensive Nordic Model of gender equality and mainstreaming has inspired feminists around the world. The exemplary Nordic Model also applies to labor relations and welfare systems.

Except for Norway, Nordic countries now belong to the EU. Accordingly, the councils play supportive roles within the EU.

BALTIC COOPERATION

Prior to the advance of the Soviet Union after World War II, the Baltic countries of Estonia, Latvia, and Lithuania were independent states. Under the Soviet Union they were republics but sought increased autonomy. In 1989, the Baltic Parliamentary Group and Baltic Council of government heads were formed even before the Berlin Wall fell. When the Soviet Union collapsed in 1991, the legislators set up the Republic of Estonia, the Republic of Latvia and the Republic of Lithuania Interparliamentary Assembly, known for short as the Baltic Assembly, as the successor to the Baltic Parliamentary Group. Also in 1991, government heads of the three countries formed the Council of the Baltic States, and in 1993 renamed the body the Baltic Council and agreed to a free trade area. In 1994, the government heads adopted the Agreement on Baltic Parliamentary and Governmental Cooperation and set up three bodies – the **Baltic Assembly** (of parliamentarians), the **Baltic Council of Ministers**, and the **Baltic Presidents' Council** (government heads). All three bodies continue to deepen the relationship between the three countries and since 2008 have focused on three issue-areas:

- Energy and infrastructure
- Human resources, social security, and living standards
- Science, research, and education.

Their Secretariat is in Riga, Latvia.

The initial trilateral organizations sparked interest elsewhere in the region, both within the Scandinavian states and in Germany, Poland, and Russia. In 1991, at the initiative of the legislature of Finland, the **Baltic Sea Parliamentary Conference** (BSPC) began as an informal organization among members of parliaments along the Baltic, with the Baltic Assembly as a member from 1992. The **Working Group on Labor Market and Social Welfare** and the **Working Group on Trafficking in Human Beings** are two of BSPC's seven working groups that have been formed over the years.

In 1992, meanwhile, the **Council of the Baltic Sea States** (CBSS) was launched by a Terms of Reference agreement in which two among six "subjects for cooperation" are "assistance to new democratic institutions" and "humanitarian matters and health." In addition to the original 10 members of CBSS bordering on the Baltic Sea, Iceland joined in 1995. The European Commission is also considered as a member. There are now 10 observer countries (Belarus, Britain, France, Italy, Netherlands, Romania, Slovakia, Spain, Ukraine, United States). In 1998, Stockholm was selected as the site of the CBSS **Secretariat**.

In 1999, the organization drew praise from UN Secretary-General Annan for achieving progress on improving the status of Russian minorities in Estonia, Latvia, and Lithuania. At the CBSS **Summit** in 2000, the basic principles referenced were "democracy, rule of law, [and] human rights." The Council's **Working Group on Democratic Institutions** sponsors expert conferences on a wide range of issues, most recently freedom of the press, trafficking in minors and women, civil society, and women's rights. A working group on democratic institutions existed from 1992 to 2009.

At the 2005 CBSS meeting, Russia discussed possible compensation with Poland over the Katyń Massacre of some 20,000 Polish citizens in 1940. But Moscow also continued to criticize Estonia, Latvia, and Lithuania for mistreatment of their Russian minority populations. In 2008, CBSS decided to become project-oriented and now has four expert bodies – the **Task Force Against Trafficking in Human Beings**, the **Expert Group for Cooperation on Children at Risk**, the **Expert Group on Sustainable Development**, and the **Policy Forum on Climate Change Adaptation**.

CBSS cooperates with related organizations. From 1989, the Central European Initiative and the Baltic Development Forum have brought together government officials and private sector representatives to discuss economic issues. The **Northern Dimension Partnership in Public Health and Social Well-Being**, which began in 2003, has the same membership plus Canada, and focuses on AIDS/HIV, drug dependence, mental health issues, occupational safety, primary health, and prison health.

BLACK SEA COOPERATION

In 1992, at the initiative of Turkey, government heads of 11 countries (Albania, Armenia, Azerbaijan, Bulgaria, Georgia, Greece, Moldova, Romania, Russia, Turkey, and the Ukraine) bordering on or near the Black Sea signed the Bosporus Statement to form the **Organization of the Black Sea Economic Cooperation** (BSEC) to promote economic cooperation as well as "human rights and fundamental freedoms, prosperity through economic liberty, social justice, and equal security." In 1994, Serbia joined, but Greece vetoed any new memberships after Turkey vetoed Athens' later candidacy of Cyprus. Nine of the larger European countries plus Egypt, Israel, Tunisia, and the United States, attend meetings as observers.

In 1993, the **Declaration on the Establishment of the Parliamentary Assembly of the Black Sea Economic Cooperation** (PABSEC) was signed among Speakers of legislatures of Albania, Armenia, Azerbaijan, Georgia, Moldova, Romania, Russia, and Turkey as a separate body; Greece joined in 1995, Bulgaria in 1997, Serbia in 2007. PABSEC's aim is to facilitate implementation of BSEC decisions into national laws; the **Cultural, Educational and Social Affairs Committee** is one of three specialized bodies. From 1994, both bodies have been headquartered in Istanbul. BSEC adopted a charter in 1994 that came into force in 1997. Human rights considerations have focused on matters of culture, displaced persons, good governance, refugees, and the social protection of pensioners, but the primary focus is on economic, environmental, and energy projects.

In 1997, as an offshoot of BSEC, the Agreement Establishing the Black Sea Trade and Development Bank was adopted by the same 11 initial countries with an authorized capital of US$1.325 billion to provide funds for entrepreneurial efforts in the region. Headquarters is in Thessalonica, Greece.

The Joint Declaration of the **Black Sea Forum for Dialogue and Partnership** was adopted in 2006 as a result of a Romanian initiative. Government heads of Armenia, Azerbaijan, Bulgaria, Georgia, Greece, Moldova, Romania, Turkey, and Ukraine adopted the declaration. All but Bulgaria, Greece, and Turkey have continued as full members in a loose consultative framework "designed primarily to define a common vision of democratic and sustainable development." Among the four goals, most are economic, but one is to promote,

> good governance, strengthening of tolerance and non-discrimination, civil society capacity-building, empowerment of the youth through provision of better education and research opportunities, with a view to creating a regional environment conducive to the promotion of democracy and fundamental rights and freedoms.

SOUTH-EAST EUROPEAN COOPERATION

In 1996, one year after the Dayton Accords appeared to herald a new era in the Balkans, Bulgaria initiated a loose cooperative body, consisting of annual meetings of government heads, foreign ministers, and political directors to promote security, democracy, justice, and wage the battle against international crime. Founding members of the **South-East European Cooperation Process** are Albania, Bosnia, Bulgaria, Greece, Macedonia, Romania, Serbia, and Turkey. They were joined by Croatia (2005), Moldova (2006), Montenegro (2007), and Slovenia (2007).[4]

Although separate from other international organizations, the EU set up a different arrangement in the region, as discussed next.

Europarl provided the leadership for the **Stability Pact for South-Eastern Europe** of 1999, amid the chaos of the Kosovo War, which provided for projects in the Balkans to achieve free trade agreements, the free movement of people across the region, eradication of corruption and organized crime, and the creation of conditions for the voluntary return of refugees. Over time, the focus shifted toward promotion of democracy, economic prosperity, human rights, and peace. The pact was first administered outside the EU and involved several EU nonmembers, including some outside Europe, as well as more than 10 international organizations. The headquarters was within the European Commission in Brussels. Then, in 2008, a statute for the Regional Cooperation Council was adopted to supersede the pact. With a secretariat in Sarajevo, the primary aim is to promote economic and social development. In 2011, the organization secured over US$40 million for regional programs and projects in South-East Europe. A hybrid organization, membership has been granted to all the Balkan states minus Kosovo (which is instead represented by the UN Interim Administration Mission in Kosovo). Additional members include several countries and intergovernmental organizations.[5]

ORGANIZATIONS RELATED TO THE COMMONWEALTH OF INDEPENDENT STATES (CIS)

Russia, once the center of an empire and later a union of socialist republics, has exercised leadership in Europe for centuries. When the Soviet Union ended, the former common economy and security evaporated, so leaders of the new Russian Federation felt responsibility to construct a new grouping of former republics. The result was the adoption in 1991 of the **Agreement Establishing the Commonwealth of Independent States**, known as the Creation Agreement, at a summit of government heads of Belarus, Russia, and the Ukraine. The document also officially dissolved the Union of Soviet Socialist Republics.

At a summit meeting in Alma Ata, Kazakhstan, a few weeks later, eight former republics (Armenia, Azerbaijan, Kazakhstan, Kyrgyzstan, Moldova, Turkmenistan, Tajikistan, Uzbekistan) joined CIS by signing onto the **Alma Ata Protocols**, which stated the purposes of the organization as:

[1] "seeking to build democratic law-governed states ... [2] recognition and respect for state sovereignty and sovereign equality, [3] the inalienable right to self-determination, [4] principles of equality and noninterference in the internal affairs, [5] the rejection of the use of force, the threat of force and economic and any other methods of pressure, [6] a peaceful settlement of disputes, [7] respect for human rights and freedoms, including the rights of national minorities, [8] a conscientious fulfillment of commitments and other generally recognized principles and standards of international law.

The three Baltic republics and Moldova, former Soviet republics, refused CIS membership. Georgia joined in 1993 but left in 2008 in the aftermath of the Georgian

War to gain NATO protection. In 1993, the **Charter of the Commonwealth of Independent States** was adopted. All but Turkmenistan and the Ukraine ratified the Charter. Since Charter ratification is a condition of CIS membership, they decided to continue to attend CIS meetings as nonmembers.

A secretariat was established at Minsk, Belarus, in 1991. The secretary-general position has been held by four Russians and two Belarusians. The Charter created the CIS Council of Ministers of Defense as a successor to the Warsaw Pact, the former military cooperation agreement of the Soviet Union with Eastern European countries.

In 2002, CIS heads of state negotiated the Convention on the Standards of Democratic Elections, Electoral Rights, and Freedoms in the Member States of the Commonwealth of Independent States. The **CIS Election Monitoring Organization**, established thereby, has monitored and approved several elections in all CIS countries, but independent observers have not always agreed that the elections have been free and fair. CIS-related organizations exclusively are also discussed in Chapter 13 under the heading "Central Asia."

Organization for Democracy and Economic Development (GUAM). Several countries were reluctant to accept Russian leadership in a regional organization. In 1997, government heads of four countries agreed to form the Organization for Democracy and Economic Development and signed the charter for the organization in 2001. As an acronym, the group adopted GUAM, standing for the original four members (Georgia, Ukraine, Azerbaijan, Moldova). Uzbekistan joined in 1999 but withdrew in 2005. Latvia and Turkey are observer countries. The secretariat in Kiev opened its office in 2009. Among the eight working groups, one is on culture, science and education, and another on drug trafficking, organized crime, and terrorism.

Not to be outdone, legislators of the four countries met in 2004 to adopt the Declaration on Establishment of the GUAM Parliamentary Assembly. Also headquartered in Kiev, the organization gives parliamentary support to measures for strengthening democracy, stability, and security in the region.

Community for Democracy and Peoples' Rights. Sometimes called CIS-2, the Community for Democracy and Peoples' Rights was launched in 2001 by four unrecognized states within the CIS orbit. They are Abkhazia and South Ossetia, two territories that broke away from Armenia but have not been recognized as independent states; Nagorno-Karabakh, a territory surrounded by Azerbaijan with a majority Armenian population; and Transnistria, a territory inside Moldova on the border of the Ukraine. In 2007, they adopted a declaration that calls for peaceful settlement of their respective conflicts. The organization has also been called the Community for Democracy and Human Rights.

Community of Democratic Choice. Another organization of former Soviet republics, the Community of Democratic Choice, was formed in 2005 to link the Baltic and Black Sea countries with the aim of promoting democracy, human rights, and the rule of law outside the Russian orbit. Founding members are Baltic countries Estonia, Latvia, Lithuania; Black Sea countries Moldova, Romania, Ukraine; and Georgia, Macedonia, and Slovenia. Bulgaria, a Black Sea country, is an official observer country along with Azerbaijan, Czech Republic, Hungary, Poland, the United States, the EU, and the OSCE.

COMMUNITY OF DEMOCRACIES

Immanuel Kant's vision of a union of representative governments came to fruition with the formation of the Community of Democracies, a transregional organization of 25 democracies. The idea for the grouping came from American Secretary of State Madeleine Albright (1937–), who was frustrated when Russia vetoed action regarding Serbia's apparent resumption of Balkan ethnic cleansing in Kosovo during 1999. Although approval for the bombing of Serbia to stop Serbia's attack on Kosovo was obtained from NATO instead, she felt that a new organization was needed so that future R2P-based decisions could bypass the Security Council veto, and she found a sponsor, Polish Minister of Foreign Affairs Bronisław Geremek (1932–2008), who convened a meeting at Warsaw in 2000.

To become a member of the governing council, a government must satisfy criteria identified in the **Warsaw Declaration** issued at the first meeting in 2000 that launched the organization – to uphold "core democratic principles and practices," including free and fair elections, freedom of speech and expression, equal access to education, rule of law, and freedom of peaceful assembly.

In 2004, the group established a Democracy Caucus within the UN General Assembly. A Permanent Secretariat was established in Warsaw in 2007.

Within Europe, only Finland, Hungary, Italy, Lithuania, Poland, Portugal, Romania, and Sweden are members. Others are from Africa (Cape Verde, Mali, Morocco, Nigeria, South Africa), Asia (India, Japan, Mongolia, Philippines, South Korea), Central America (Costa Rica, El Salvador), North America (Canada, México, United States), and South America (Chile, Uruguay). The executive committee consists of a representative from the Permanent Secretariat plus one member from each continent (Africa, the Americas, Asia, Europe).

The organ began with two pillars – the governmental pillar (Ministerial Conference of foreign ministers plus Parliamentary Forum for Democracy), and the civil society pillar (leaders of nongovernmental organizations organized as the International Steering Committee). In 2010, a third pillar was added – a Corporate Democracy Forum, representing the private economic sector, with a mission to promote the rule of law and the role of women in business as well as to identify threats to democracy from a business perspective.

In 2005, working groups were first established, with experts from among the pillars, to develop project initiatives. The host country for each biennial meeting identifies the working groups. An **Academic Advisory Board** consists of experts from member and nonmember countries on democratization studies, political change, modernization and development, comparative politics, good governances, rule of law, economic prosperity and gender politics, and response to national and transnational threats and challenges to democracy.

Among the projects are workshops on democratic education and democratic transition held in nonmember countries. In 2010, the **Youth Dimension** was launched: The Young Diplomats for Democracy project brings young diplomats and activists together for discussion and training related to democracy promotion and support, and the Young Leaders Forum unites young civil society democracy activities. In

2012, in response to the democratization wave in the Middle East, the **Democracy Partnership Challenge** was established to solicit donors for proposals that would advance reform in countries emerging from authoritarian rule. The **Leaders Engaged in New Democracies** initiative facilitates efforts of leaders from past transitions to democracy to assist those currently engaged. The annual **Geremek Award**, named in honor of the co-founder of the Community of Democracies, was first conferred in 2009. The 2011 winner was the entire Belarusian opposition.

ARCTIC COUNCIL

In 1996, foreign ministers of the six European states bordering on the Arctic Ocean (Denmark, Finland, Iceland, Norway, Russia, Sweden) plus Canada and the United States met together in Ottawa to form the Arctic Council of foreign ministers as a forum for cooperation between national governments and indigenous peoples. The body is informal, having been set up by the Ottawa Declaration at the end of the 1996 meeting. The secretariat was designated at Tromsø, Norway, effective 2013.

A unique feature is that six nongovernmental international organizations representing indigenous communities are permanent participants in the Arctic Council – the Aleuts, Athabaskans, Gwich'ins, Inuits, Sámis, and the Russian Association of the Indigenous Peoples of the North. Observer status has been granted to Britain, France, Germany, Netherlands, Poland, Spain, and nine intergovernmental organizations, including three UN bodies. The **Arctic Council Indigenous Peoples' Secretariat** was established in 1994 in Copenhagen to assist organizations of the six native peoples, especially their cooperation in the Arctic Council.

The principal goal of the Arctic Council is sustainable development. Living conditions of the indigenous peoples are a central focus of six working groups. The **Sustainable Development Working Group** has projects on children, education, health, and youth. In 2011, the Council concluded the first binding treaty, the Arctic Search and Rescue Agreement.

CONCLUSION

At one time, peaceful relations in Europe were thought to be promoted by intermarriage among the royal families. Today, the complex web of intergovernmental organizations is playing that role despite apparent rivalries between them.

The larger European regional organizations reviewed above have complementary responsibilities. CoE has a promotional and judicial role. EU can apply economic sanctions to egregious cases but hopes one day to be able to refer less serious matters to CoE's overloaded judicial process. OSCE is particularly adept at diplomatic and political negotiations as well as monitoring elections. NATO's military capabilities are both in the areas of enforcement and logistics. Overlapping organizational interests can serve to ensure that a human rights problem will receive condign attention. Nevertheless, relations between CoE and OSCE have not always been friendly, while France has sought to persuade other European governments that an EU military force might be desirable as an alternative to NATO. Similar overlapping responsibilities at a pan-regional level have been emerging from organizations in the Arctic, the Balkans, the Baltic, around the Black Sea, and in Scandinavia.

Europeans clearly prefer proactive methods in approaching human rights issues around the world. The labyrinthine array of institutions means that care must be exercised to avoid rivalry or duplication of one another's efforts. The comprehensive scope of European human rights programming attests to the ability of countries with similar cultural backgrounds to cooperate in depth. Other regions, as indicated in the following chapter, have not always been so successful.

DISCUSSION TOPIC 12.2 IS EUROPE'S HUMAN RIGHTS RECORD SUPERIOR TO THE UNITED STATES?

Have the European Union, the Council of Europe, and the Organization for Security and Cooperation in Europe advanced human rights beyond the accomplishments of the United States? In which respects?

CHAPTER 13

Developing Country Approaches to International Human Rights

The present chapter delineates efforts to deal with human rights problems within countries in Africa, the Americas, Asia, the Middle East, and the Pacific – mostly developing or Third World countries.[1] A comparison of approaches followed by each of more than 100 countries in those regions is beyond the scope of the present volume. Since regional intergovernmental organizations are quite prominent in handling human rights, they serve as the focus of attention.

THE AMERICAS

What is most noteworthy in the American hemisphere is a long tradition of regional cooperation, which began when Simón Bolívar (1783–1830) convened the Congress of Panamá in 1826. After several more inter-American conferences, the **Union of American Republics** was formed in 1890, with a headquarters, the Pan American Union, in Washington, DC, by 1910. But dramatic world events in Europe overshadowed the region, which feared that the continent might become involved in World War I. Some Inter-American Conferences for the Maintenance of Peace were held, after 1919, while Pan American Union activities laid the foundation for cooperation in nonmilitary matters.

   • **Organization of American States** (OAS). After the two world wars, countries in the Americas signed the **Inter-American Treaty of Reciprocal Assistance** (the Rio Treaty) in 1947, a military pact, as the Cold War began. Next, members of the Union of American Republics attended the Bogotá Conference of American States of 1948, which produced the **Charter of the Organization of American States**

(OAS) to supersede the former Union and adopted the **American Declaration on the Rights and Duties of Man** several months before the Universal Declaration of Human Rights. In contrast with European intergovernmental organizations, which for decades have worked with governments trying to improve and to harmonize human rights practices, many governments in the Americas were hostile to human rights until more democracies began to emerge in the 1990s. Subsequent growth has been remarkable.

The OAS Charter states that member states are committed to "democratic institutions, [and] a system of individual liberty and social justice based on respect for the essential rights of man" and further says that "all human beings, without distinction as to race, nationality, sex, creed or social condition, have the right to attain material well-being and spiritual growth under circumstances of liberty, dignity, equality of opportunity, and economic security." The American Declaration on the Rights and Duties of Man lists specific rights, including the rights to education, to a family, and to protection of children, mothers, and personal reputation. Many agreements in the area of human rights have been adopted over the years (Table 13.1). Those dealing with asylum, cultural relations, and women's rights came earliest.

TABLE 13.1 **HUMAN RIGHTS AGREEMENTS OF THE ORGANIZATION OF AMERICAN STATES**

Adopted	Title of the declaration or treaty	In force
1948	Charter of the Organization of American States	1951
1967	• Protocol of Buenos Aires	1970
1985	• Protocol of Cartagena de Indias	1988
1992	• Protocol of Washington	1997
1993	• Protocol of Managua	1996
1948	Inter-American Convention on the Granting of Civil Rights to Women	1949
1948	Inter-American Convention on the Granting of Political Rights to Women	1954
1954	Convention on Diplomatic Asylum	1954
1954	Convention on Territorial Asylum	1954
1954	Convention for the Promotion of Inter-American Cultural Relations[a]	
1957	Protocol to the Convention on Duties and Rights of States in the Event of Civil Strife[b]	
1969	American Convention on Human Rights (Pact of San José)	1978
1988	• Additional Protocol … in the Area of Economic, Social and Cultural Rights (Protocol of San Salvador)	1999
1990	• Protocol … to Abolish the Death Penalty	1991
1971	Convention to Prevent and Punish the Acts of Terrorism Taking the Form of Crimes Against Persons and Related Extortion That Are of International Significance	2003
1981	Inter-American Convention on Extradition	1992

Continued

TABLE 13.1 **(CONTINUED)**

Adopted	Title of the declaration or treaty	In force
1984	Inter-American Convention on Conflict of Laws Concerning the Adoption of Minors	1988
1985	Inter-American Convention to Prevent and Punish Torture	1987
1989	Inter-American Convention on Support Obligations	1996
1989	Inter-American Convention on International Return of Children	1994
1991	Resolution 1080 (Santiago Declaration)	
1992	Protocol of Washington	
1994	Convention on the Prevention, Punishment and Eradication of Violence Against Women	1995
1994	Inter-American Convention on International Traffic in Minors	1997
1994	Inter-American Convention on Forced Disappearances of Persons	1996
1996	Inter-American Convention Against Corruption	1997
1999	Inter-American Convention on the Elimination of All Forms of Discrimination Against Persons with Disabilities	2001
2001	Inter-American Democratic Charter	
2002	Inter-American Convention Against Terrorism	2003

[a] Revises the Convention for the Promotion of Inter-American Cultural Relations of 1936.

[b] Protocol to the Convention on Duties and Rights of States in the Event of Civil Strife of 1928.

The **American Convention on Human Rights** was adopted in 1969. Some rights were granted that were not in the original European Convention for the Protection of Human Rights and Fundamental Freedoms – the right of reply, rights of children, the right to a name and a nationality, and the right of asylum.

All 21 independent states in the Western Hemisphere joined the OAS in 1948; today, in 2013, there are 35 members, with six new Caribbean countries in line for membership.[2] Three years after the Cuban revolution of 1959, Havana was charged with subversion in the region and formally expelled, though six countries abstained in the vote.

In 1979, the OAS General Assembly called for President Anastasio Somoza (1925–1980) to resign after being cited for human rights violations of the National Guard and mediation efforts failed. Soon after Somoza stepped down, power was seized by the Sandinista National Liberation Front (named after Augusto César Sandino (1895–1934)) who was assassinated after leading Nicaragua's resistance against the American occupation of the country from 1927 to 1933 that installed Somoza). With Washington's assistance, a Nicaraguan insurgent group then formed inside the border of Honduras to launch a civil war, which ended in 1989 through the mediation of Óscar Árias (1940–). One provision of the ceasefire was to have OAS and UN agencies monitor the demobilization of the insurgents, an operation that lasted from 1990 to 1993, involving relocation and humanitarian assistance for some 120,000 displaced persons within demobilization areas. As a result, OAS was transformed into an operational organization, aiding refugees.

In 1991, the OAS General Assembly adopted the **Santiago Declaration**, sometimes known as Resolution 1080, which requires the OAS Secretary-General to convene the Permanent Council and the Meeting of Consultation within 10 days after a coup or other interruption of a legitimate, elected government. In 1992, the **Protocol of Washington** provided that a government which overthrows a democracy can be expelled from OAS. Resolution 1080 has been invoked several times: Haïti (1991, 2002), Perú (1992, 2000), Guatemala (1993), Paraguay (1996, 1999), Venezuela (twice in 2002), and Honduras (2009–2011). Cuba's suspension in 1962 was revoked in 2009, though Havana has not yet decided to participate.

The supreme organ, established in 1970, is the annual General Assembly. A member state may request a meeting of the Consultation of the Ministers of Foreign Affairs to consider urgent situations that threaten peace. A Secretary-General heads the General Secretariat (the Pan American Union up to 1970) – located in Washington, DC – which has several subunits. In 1990, the **Unit for Promotion of Democracy** was established; the current mission is to coordinate election supervision missions and to administer country programs to improve democratic institutions. In 1999, the **Justice Studies Center** of the Americas was located at Santiago, Chile, to provide technical assistance to countries for improving their criminal justice systems.

In 2001, the OAS adopted the **Inter-American Democratic Charter**, which broadened the focus on civil and political rights in the Santiago Declaration by defining essential elements of a "democracy." In addition, OAS **Secretary-General visits** to countries are held to advance human rights. In 2005, for example, the Secretary-General visited Nicaragua regarding the forthcoming general election, in which an opposition political party expressed concern about the fairness of the electoral process.

OAS also has some specialized organs related to human rights, a few of which date before World War II. In 1902, the Pan American Sanitary Bureau was established to fight the spread of disease from ships; the name was changed in 1947 to Pan American Sanitary Organization and again in 1949 to the **Pan American Health Organization**. The **Inter-American Children's Institute**, founded in 1927, engages in research and social action on problems of minors and families, including trafficking, child labor, commercial sexual exploitation, international abduction, and war-affected children. The **Inter-American Commission of Women**, set up in 1928, and the world's first intergovernmental organization focusing on the civil, political, economic, social, and cultural rights of women, requires periodic reporting. The **Inter-American Indian Institute**, which dates from 1940, coordinates programs on the needs and rights of indigenous peoples.

The Inter-American Economic and Social Council, created in 1967 to advance social and economics rights, was superseded in 1983 by the **Inter-American Council for Integral Development**. The **Inter-American Cultural Council**, also set up in 1967, promotes cultural exchanges though the **Committee for Cultural Action**.

In recent years, OAS has been attacked by the Bolivarian Alliance for the Peoples of Our America (ALBA) about the domination of the United States over the organization. In 2012, ALBA countries (Bolivia, Ecuador, Nicaragua, Venezuela) withdrew from the Rio Pact, in part based on human rights concerns, openly questioning whether Washington wants to be an equal partner in the organization. That question has long crippled enthusiasm for OAS.

• **Inter-American Commission on Human Rights** (IACHR). In 1959, OAS established the autonomous IACHR, with a headquarters in Washington, DC. The commission performs several functions:

  o Drafting declarations and treaties
  o Holding conferences and seminars to raise consciousness about the need to advance human rights
  o Monitoring situations
  o Publishing country and thematic reports
  o Responding to complaints
  o Making visits
  o Issuing recommendations
  o Issuing precautionary measures.

The Commission was first authorized to handle complaints in 1965, though only 10 countries (Argentina, Chile, Colombia, Costa Rica, Ecuador, Jamaica, Nicaragua, Perú, Uruguay, Venezuela) recognize the competence of the Commission. Today, nearly 1,000 **petitions** are received each year. When ruled admissible as possible violations of the treaties ratified by the members, the petitions are considered **cases** and are first referred to the states for a response. Compared with other human rights bodies around the world, the Commission imposes few technical requirements for individual complaints, so the complaints can be used as pretexts for wide-ranging surveys of the entire country of the complainant.

In response to a petition, the Commission may hold **hearings**, make **recommendations** to states, issue **precautionary measures** (for immediate action in urgent cases), undertake **friendly settlements**, or make a **decision on the merits**. In the latter case, the Commission may either publish a **report** or **refer** the matter to the jurisdiction of the IACHR, described below, as **advisory opinions** or as **contentious cases** for judgments. When a complaint is about a dangerous situation, the Commission can ask IACHR to issue **provisional measures** to states so that individuals can be placed out of harm's way before cases are tried. Since the Commission prefers informal settlements, they can be determined with great speed, but implementation may often drag on for years.

Authorization for onsite inspections (**in *loco* visits**), which often involve observing the human rights situation in a country in response to petitions from member states, expanded in 1965 to involve investigation of complaints from individuals, and again in 1969 to nonmember states. From 1961, the Commission has carried out 69 onsite inspections (**in *loco* visits**) to 23 countries to investigate member states. Some 44 **country reports** have been published as a result. In 2000, for example, OAS representatives were present in Perú to monitor national elections.

From 1965, the Commission has received thousands of **petitions**, and has processed some 12,000 **cases** based on alleged violations of the Convention, the Declaration, or another human rights instrument. In 2010, for example, the Commission received

1,598 petitions; Colombia topped the list. Of the 1,676 petitions evaluated from that year and previous years, Perú was the largest source with 1,584 cases and 88 **hearings**. In addition, there were 375 **requests for precautionary measures** in 2010; of the 68 granted, Colombia came in first. There were 11 **friendly settlements**.

The Commission's approach to human rights can be illustrated by the handling of Chile. In 1973, the Commission's executive secretary went to Chile after the coup led by General Augusto Pinochet (1915–2006) that toppled the democratically elected government of President Salvador Allende (1906–1973). After the Commission's visit, the report of 1974 lambasted the new Chilean government for human rights violations based on a thorough inspection of courts, legislation, and prisons. In 1975, the Commission received complaints from almost 1,000 Chileans regarding disappearances and torture. Annual reports on the situation in Chile kept up the pressure until the government agreed to hold elections in 1989.

In 2008, the United States was found in violation of the American Declaration by imposing the death penalty on José Ernesto Medellín (1975–2008), Rubén Ramírez Cárdenas (1970–), and Humberto Leal García (1973–2011) of Colombia. Precautionary measures, including new trials, to stop the executions were ignored when Medellín was executed in 2008 and García was executed in 2011 with the approval of the governor of Texas over the objections of President George W. Bush (1946–). In 2009, the Commission cited the United States for bringing up unadjudicated crimes during sentencing, as well as failing to provide right to counsel, notification of consular authorities, right to request a fair commutation hearing, and reparations to the Medellín family. To date, the United States has failed to respond to the recommendations, so the Commission continues to monitor the situation.

In 2009, the Commission found that the three Peirano Basso brothers, alleged to have caused the collapse of the banking system in Uruguay, were judged to have been illegally held in prison for two and a half years without being charged or put on trial. Uruguay then complied with the recommendation to release them.

The Commission has appointed eight experts as **special rapporteurs**, both to report on particular countries and on topical areas. The human rights addressed are those of Afro-descendants, children, gays/lesbians/bisexuals/transgendered, human rights defenders, indigenous peoples, migrants, prisoners, and women.

In 1997, the commission established the **Office of the Special Rapporteur for Freedom of Expression** to monitor press freedom, including the safety of human rights advocates. The office has the following authority:

- Handle individual cases of violations
- Issue precautionary measures
- Hold hearings
- Make official visits
- Hold seminars and workshops to acquaint government officials with legal requirements
- Make declarations
- Publish annual reports on member countries.

Five criteria are applied to determine which countries require special attention from the Commission each year:

- Absence of free elections
- Uses of states of emergency to suppress rights
- Frequent extrajudicial executions, torture, and forced disappearances
- Countries transitioning from the first three situations to human rights compliance
- Grave situations and institutional crises.

In 2010, for example, a precautionary measure was issued, asking Suriname to protect the indigenous Mahos, whose territory was, and is, being invaded by a commercial organization that burned the community's crops and threatened to kill them.

In the annual report for 2010, there was an extensive report on human rights in Haïti after the hurricane, in particular discrimination and violence against females. The report also cited positive developments in Colombia, but negative conditions in Cuba, Honduras, and Venezuela. In the case of Honduras, the Special Rapporteur condemned Tegucigalpa for the death of nine journalists after the coup d'état in early 2010, some after receiving death threats in which the state failed to provide protection and whose murderers remained unpunished.

In 1994, Belize was cited for allowing logging and oil drilling operations that jeopardized ancestral lands of the Mayan people. The Commission recommended that the government more carefully delineate the ancestral lands, thus following precedent in *Awas Tingni v. Nicaragua* (2001), as noted in Chapter 6.

Commission **recommendations** need not await complaints. In 2002, when reports emerged of possible mistreatment of detainees at the Guantánamo Naval Base in Cuba, the Commission recommended that the United States hold hearings required by the Geneva Conventions to determine which persons were prisoners of war. Washington rejected the request, so American membership on the Commission was suspended in 2003.

In 2002, the Commission also criticized Perú for lack of judicial due process in the celebrated trial of Lori Berenson, whereupon Lima withdrew from the IACHR.

COURT CASE 13.1 THE TRIALS OF LORI BERENSON (1996 AND 2001)

In 1995, an American citizen, journalist Lori Berenson (1969–), was arrested on a bus in Lima, Perú, amid a mass arrest of suspected terrorists for aiding a contemplated attack on Perú's Congress by leftist rebels. Her press photographer husband was second-in-command of the Túpac Amaru Revolutionary Movement, though she claimed that she was unaware of the connection while renting an apartment used as a safe house by members of the terrorist organization. In 1996, she was

Continued

tried by a hooded military tribunal without the benefit of cross-examination under an anti-terrorism law decreed during a state of emergency. She was found guilty and sentenced to life imprisonment without parole for "reason against the fatherland." The trial was later condemned by the UN Commission on Human Rights. In 1998, the Committee on Arbitrary Detentions of the UN High Commissioner for Human Rights visited her in prison, and then in 1999 condemned her detention as arbitrary and a violation of the International Covenant on Civil and Political Rights. In 2000, the Inter-American Court of Human Rights ruled that she and four other prisoners should be retried in civilian courts. Perú's Supreme Military Justice Commission then vacated her military trial and ordered a new civilian trial. In 2001, she was again found guilty and sentenced to a 20-year term. She then appealed to the Inter-American Commission of Human Rights, which ruled in 2002 that she was denied due process, subjected to inhumane detention, and that Perú should bring its anti-terrorism law up to the standards of the Covenant. When Perú refused to revise the law, the Commission referred the case to the Inter-American Court of Human Rights, which in turn reversed the Commission's decision. Berenson was released after 15 years but must remain on parole in Perú until 2015.

In 2003, Trinidad and Tobago was informed that its use of the death penalty was inconsistent with the 1990 **Protocol to Abolish the Death Penalty** of the American Convention on Human Rights to Abolish the Death Penalty, whereupon the country withdrew from the Protocol.

- **Inter-American Court of Human Rights** (IACHR). In 1978, 60 years after the Central American Court of Justice (CACJ) suspended operations, the American Convention on Human Rights came into force, creating the IACHR, a body independent of OAS. Of the 25 OAS members that have ratified the American Convention on Human Rights thus far, only Dominica, Grenada, and Jamaica have not ratified the Optional Clause to the Convention and thus do not accept the jurisdiction of the court. Trinidad and Tobago agreed to the Optional Clause in 1991 but withdrew effective 1999, when the Protocol to the American Convention on Human Rights to Abolish the Death Penalty went into effect. Perú tried to withdraw from the jurisdiction from 1999 to 2001 but did not follow the proper procedure to do so. The United States signed but did not ratify the agreement to set up the court. OAS members who have not ratified are Antigua and Barbuda, Bahamas, Belize, Canada, Guyana, St Kitts-Nevis, St Lucia, and St Vincent and the Grenadines. If a state has not accepted the Optional Clause of the Convention on Human Rights, the court instead invokes the American Declaration of the Rights and Duties of Man of 1948 as the basis for decisions involving its country.

Cases may be filed with the court either by the Commission on Human Rights or by a ratifying government, but not by individuals. However, an individual can submit a complaint to the Commission, which usually issues recommendations to errant states. If recommendations are not followed, the Commission may refer the case to the court. In 2012, for example, 12 cases were referred by the Commission to the court. Litigation before the court must be about specific violations rather than general patterns, as the Commission handles the latter type of question.

The court may award **compensatory damages**, including attorney's costs and amounts for emotional harm, but not punitive damages. In November 2001, for example, the court ordered payments in *Barrios Altos v. Perú* involving the massacre of 15 persons by a state-sponsored death squad in Lima. Some US$175,000 was authorized for four survivors and 11 next-of-kin of the murdered victims and a payment of US$250,000 for the family of one of the victims. The government of Perú was also ordered to grant the victims' families free health care and educational support, to repeal two amnesty laws, to establish the crime of extrajudicial execution, to ratify the International Convention on the Non-Applicability of Statutory Limitations to War Crimes and Crimes Against Humanity, to make a public apology, and to erect a memorial monument to the victims of the massacre. If a state fails to abide by a decision of the court, the matter may be referred to the OAS General Assembly.

Any OAS member country may ask the court for an advisory opinion. Thus far, the court has issued 20 **advisory opinions**, mostly in the early years of the court. In 2000, because the United States has not ratified the Optional Clause, the court issued an advisory opinion that 17 Mexicans on death row in Texas, who had not been afforded the opportunity to seek consular representation, were being denied due process.

From fall 2004, the court has processed some 552 cases, including 154 **contentious cases**, 95 **provisional measures** (similar to the Commission's precautionary measures), and 303 **friendly settlements**. Perú accounts for more contentious cases (23) than any other country but also more friendly settlements (68). Venezuela's provisional measures (21) exceed all other countries. In contrast, the CoE and EU courts have handled many more cases.

In 2009, the court (*Gonzalez v. México*) ordered reparations to relatives of more than 300 female workers aged 15–25 who had disappeared in Ciudad Juárez, presumably after their rape and murder. In another landmark case, in 2012, *Riffo v. Chile*, the court heard an appeal from a case in which the divorced father sought the award of a child instead of the mother because the latter came out as a lesbian. IACHR ruled that the mother's rights had been violated, thus that sexual orientation was an impermissible premise for court action.

- **Central American Integration System**. After independence from Spain, five Central American countries (Costa Rica, El Salvador, Guatemala, Honduras, Nicaragua) tried to form a Federal Republic of Central America in Guatemala City in 1823. They set up the capital to San Salvador in 1834, and then abandoned the effort because of civil war from 1838 to 1841 as countries pulled out, declaring their independence. After five abortive attempts at reunion by various leaders, they signed a peace treaty in 1907 providing for a **Central American Court of Justice**, headquartered in Costa Rica, which lasted until 1918. Of the 10 cases decided during the 11 years of the court's existence, all five human rights cases were dismissed.

In 1951, they signed the Charter of San Salvador, forming the Organization of Central American States, and amended the Charter to establish a new **Central American Court of Justice** the following year, though the court in Managua heard its first case in 1994. In 2012, the court took up a dispute between two branches of the El Salvador government – whether the Constitutional Court or the National Assembly has the power to elect justices.

In 1955, foreign ministers met, issuing the Declaration of Antigua Guatemala, which pledged that they would work toward an "integral union." In 1960, they agreed to start the Central American Bank for Economic Integration, but the idea was suspended in 1973 on account of conflicts within several members. Then, in 1991, six Central American countries (the original five plus Panamá) agreed in the Protocol of Tegucigalpa to form the **Central American Integration System**, pledging regional peace, political freedom, democracy and economic development, with the General Secretariat in San Salvador, El Salvador. Belize joined in 2000. Two Associated States have been admitted – Dominican Republic (2004) and Haïti (2013).

In 1992, the six signed the General Treaty for Economic Integration to establish the **Central American Common Market** backed by the **Central American Bank for Economic Integration**. The bank has five non-regional members: Argentina, Colombia, México, Taiwan, and Spain.

Guatemala, El Salvador, Honduras, and Nicaragua have formed a group called **The Central America Four**, which is on a faster track of cultural, migratory, and political integration with common internal borders and a similar passport. Belize, Costa Rica, the Dominican Republic, and Panamá are only involved in matters of economic integration.

- **Andean Community of Nations** (ANCOM). Bolivia, Chile, Colombia, Ecuador, and Perú agreed to form the Andean Pact in an agreement signed in the **Cartagena Agreement** of 1969, which pledged members to a common market dedicated to "the principles of equality, justice, peace, solidarity, and democracy," with a headquarters in Lima. In 1973, Venezuela joined, but Chile withdrew in 1976. In 1996, the common market was renamed Andean Community of Nations.

In 1980, the countries agreed to the **Riobamba Code of Conduct** as a pledge to observe human rights. The **Andean Health Organization** was launched in 1998.

In 1993, the Free Trade Zone entered into full operation for Bolivia, Colombia, Ecuador, and Venezuela, and the following year the Common External Tariff went into effect. Visa-free travel was approved in 2005.

In 2000, the five Andean countries formalized the Presidential Declaration on the Andean Community Commitment to Democracy of 1998 into the **Andean Community Commitment to Democracy** as an Additional Protocol to the founding Cartagena Agreement of 1969 that would have the effect of suspending the benefits of membership to any country that might have a "disruption of the democratic order." In 2001, the **Machu Picchu Declaration on Democracy**, the **Rights of Indigenous Peoples**, and the **War Against Poverty** provided further evidence of a strong human rights commitment.

After the Southern Common Market (known as Mercosur) emerged in 1997, Andean countries sought to unite with them. An agreement was drawn up for a free trade area to combine both blocs by 1998. Currently, Bolivia and Chile, had free trade agreements with Mercosur, accepting what is known as the "**democratic clause**," which could be invoked to withdraw economic cooperation from a country that becomes undemocratic. Negotiations for a merger between the two blocs languished until 2004, when the **Constitutive Treaty of the Union of South American Nations** was drawn up, and signed in 2008 (see below). In 2005, the five Mercosur members then became Associate Members of ANCOM.

• **Mercado Común de la Sur** (Mercosur). In 1985, the presidents of Argentina and Brazil signed the Argentina–Brazil Integration and Economics Cooperation Program, foundation for the formation in 1991 of the Mercado Común de la Sur (Mercado Común de la Sul in Portuguese) by the Treaty of Asunción. Mercosur first demonstrated a concern for human rights during an attempted coup in Paraguay during 1997, when Argentina, Brazil, and the United States so warned the military in Asunción that they backed down and restored civilian rule. The founding agreement was then amended to have a clause requiring all members to be democracies. The treaty was further updated in 1994 by the Treaty of Ouro Preto with the addition of Paraguay and Uruguay. In 2005, the four ANCOM members became Associate Members of Mercosur.

Although Venezuela sought to join in 2006, Paraguay vetoed the application. But Asunción's membership was itself suspended on account of the "**democracy clause**" in 2012, when its president was removed from office in a legislative coup d'état, whereupon Venezuela was welcomed into Mercosur the following month. Bolivia is now an "accessing member," with full membership expected when approved by the other five members.

Mercosur's Common Market Council (economic and foreign ministers) and the executive body, the Common Market Group (of foreign ministry officials from each country), are serviced by 10 subsidiary bodies, one of which is the **Labor, Employment and Social Security Matters Working Group**. Intra-Mercosur trade grew from US$10 billion in 1991 to US$88 billion in 2010; Brazil and Argentina accounted for nearly half. A Joint Parliamentary Committee submits proposals to, and seeks to implement, Mercosur decisions.

Mercosur has signed free trade agreements with several countries – Colombia (2005), Israel (2007), Egypt (2010), and the State of Palestine (2011). In 2008, Mercosur countries signed the Constitutive Treaty of the Union of South American Nations, as discussed next.

• **Union of South American Nations** (UNASUR). Modeled on the European Union, UNASUR is a merger between ANCOM and Mercosur, created at a Summit of government heads in 2008 by the Constitutive Treaty of the Union of South American Nations. Headquartered in Brasilia, UNASUR has 12 member countries covering all South America except for French Guiana, with provisions for Associate Membership for that country as well as for the Caribbean states. In 2010, the upheaval in Ecuador prompted an Optional Clause containing the "democratic provision." The treaty and protocol came into force in 2011, and the difficult task of uniting two economic blocs began.

In 2012, when Wikileaks founder, Julian Assange (1971–), went into the Ecuadorian embassy in London to apply for diplomatic asylum, the British government threatened to extract him with violence. In response, UNASUR foreign ministers met to condemn Britain for respecting neither the right of asylum nor the inviolability of embassies, whereas the OAS failed to do so. As of 2013, Assange remained at the embassy despite warrants for his arrest and extradition to Sweden for trial.

- **Caribbean Community and Common Market** (CARICOM). In 1965, the Caribbean Free Trade Association (CARIFTA) was formed by the Agreement at Dickenson Bay between Antigua and Barbuda, Barbados, and the future renamed Guyana as English-speaking former colonies seeking free trade. Shortly afterward, a supplementary agreement in 1968 opened the door to new members, and Dominica, Grenada, Jamaica, Montserrat, St Kitts and Nevis, St Lucia, St Vincent and the Grenadines, and Trinidad and Tobago joined. British Honduras (Belize) became a member in May 1971.

In 1973, the Treaty of Chaguaramas established CARICOM as the successor to CARIFTA, with a goal of a Caribbean Single Market and Economy, and Barbados, Guyana, Jamaica, and Trinidad and Tobago signed the agreement. In 1974, several more countries joined – Antigua and Barbuda, Belize, Dominica, Grenada, Montserrat, St Kitts and Nevis, St Lucia, and St Vincent and the Grenadines. Later members are Bahamas (1983), Haïti (2002), and Suriname (1995). Associate Members are Anguilla, Bermuda, British Virgin Islands, Cayman Islands, and Turks and Caicos.

In 1997, the organization adopted the **Charter for Civil Society**, enunciating the following principles:

[1] fair and open democratic process; [2] the effective functioning of the parliamentary system; [3] morality in public affairs; [4] respect for fundamental civil, political, economic, social and cultural rights; [5] the rights of women and children; [6] respect for religious diversity; and [7] greater accountability and transparency in government.

The secretariat is in Georgetown, Guyana.

To promote the goals of the Charter, the **Council for Human and Social Development** was established in 1998. Priorities are on cultural preservation and women's rights.

The founding treaty was revised in 2001, providing for the **Council for Human and Social Development** as one of five Ministerial Councils. The common market treaty went into effect in 2006 for all CARICOM members but Bahamas, Montserrat, and Haïti, which have not yet entered.

- **Organization of Eastern Caribbean States** (OECS). In 1981, OECS was formed under the Treaty of Basseterre – with a secretariat in Castries, Saint Lucia – as the successor to the West Indies Associated States that existed from 1967 as a pre-independence arrangement to phase out direct British colonial rule. Dedicated to economic harmonization and integration, OECS emphasizes human rights and good governance. Members are Antigua and Barbuda, Dominica, Grenada, Montserrat, St Kitts and Nevis, St Lucia, and St Vincent and the Grenadines.

In 2008, Trinidad and Tobago, Grenada, St Lucia, and St Vincent and the Grenadines agreed to form an economic union within OECS. The Eastern Caribbean Supreme Court, created under the West Indies Associated States, continues to function.

- **Regional Security System** (RSS). At the suggestion of the United States, OECS members (Antigua and Barbuda, Barbados, Dominica, St Lucia, and St Vincent and the Grenadines) in 1982 signed a military security memorandum, known as the RSS, with the aim of preventing communist coups. In 1983, the United States invaded Grenada to install a new government after a military coup. St Kitts and Nevis joined in 1983, Grenada in 1985. In 1996, RSS was placed on a treaty basis. Based in Barbados, the organization has been active in combating organized crime in the region and providing disaster relief after hurricanes. In 2010, RSS aided Haïti after its devastating earthquake.

- **North American Free Trade Agreement** (NAFTA). In 1988, the Canada–United States Free Trade Agreement was formed by a bilateral treaty. The arrangement was superseded by NAFTA in 1994 with the addition of México. Tariffs on most goods have now been removed.

NAFTA's formation was controversial because observers felt that cheap Mexican products would be traded without strict environmental standards and under unsatisfactory working conditions. Accordingly, two supplementary agreements were adopted the same year – the **North American Agreement on Environmental Cooperation** and the **North American Agreement on Labor Cooperation**.

The latter treaty, enforced by a separate **Commission for Labor Cooperation**, merely provides that each country's "labor laws and regulations provide for high labor standards, consistent with high quality and productivity workplaces, and shall continue to strive to improve those standards in that light." The Council, which governs the Commission, has the power to collect annual reports on labor conditions, including occupational safety and health, child labor, or minimum wage technical labor standards, but may only hear disputes if national labor laws are being violated. Disputes, in turn, are to be resolved after expert investigations by arbitration or by issuance of Council recommendations. One result of NAFTA has been an influx of workers from México into the United States for work without first obtaining visas or other legal documentation, often bringing small children that are technically illegal aliens but know no other country as home.

One reaction south of the American border came even before NAFTA was signed. In early 1994, residents of Chiapas reacted with a declaration of "war" against México in anticipation of efforts of the government to convert ancestral lands of indigenous peoples into commercial developments. The group, known as Zapatista Army of National Liberation, backed up demands for local autonomy with armed occupation of seven towns, where prisoners were freed and military and police barracks were set on fire. Although the Mexican government sent troops to quell the uprising within a week, the movement continues, as municipalities operate autonomously of the government. In 2001, the Zapatistas presented demands to the Mexican legislature for a law protecting indigenous peoples, but their initiative was rejected. In 2007, the Zapatistas convened the first of three Intercontinental Indigenous Encounters, the latest in 2009. Subcomandante Marcos (1957–), as the leader is known, continues today to add more autonomous villages with Good Government Councils to the movement, a "third way" that seeks to build participatory democracy at the local level as opposed to the intergovernmental approach of the organization discussed next.

▌ HISTORIC EVENT 13.1 THE CASE OF LUIS POSADA CARRILES (2005)

Luis Posada Carriles (1928–) has been accused of bombing a Cuban civilian airplane in 1976 and of financing the bombing of six hotels in Cuba during 1997. Cuban born, he relocated to the United States in 1961 and was later recruited as a CIA operative. In 1968, the CIA dropped him because of his association with criminal elements, so he moved to Venezuela, where he became a citizen, though he was later imprisoned there on criminal charges; he eventually escaped from prison. While in Panamá in 2000, he was convicted and imprisoned for plotting to kill Fidel Castro (1926–) at a summit conference. Pardoned by the Panamanian president in 2005, he sneaked into the United States to seek asylum and was soon jailed for making false statements on his naturalization application. When his whereabouts became known, the Venezuelan government requested his extradition to serve out his prison sentence, and Cuba sought him on charges of terrorism, though Havana decided to defer the case to Venezuela. Although Cuba and Venezuela sought to put him on trial, a federal judge accepted the American government's prediction that he might be tortured upon arrival in Venezuela, whereupon Caracas attacked the United States for hypocrisy in the "war on terrorism" by not allowing him to be extradited. In 2007, American immigration charges were dropped on the basis that statements on his application were mistranslated, and he was released on bail. Subsequently, he was indicted in an American federal court for lying about his role in the 1997 incident, but a jury found him not guilty in a trial during 2011. He lives in Miami as a hero to some in the Cuban-American community, while Havana refers to him as "Osama Bin Laden of Latin America."

• **Community of Latin American and Caribbean States** (CELAC). In 1986, Caribbean and Latin American countries formed the Río Group, an annual summit conference that excluded Canada, Cuba, the United States, and the remaining colonies of European countries. The grouping was reacting to the American support for rebels opposing the government of Nicaragua. In 2008, Cuba was accepted for membership after Raúl Castro (1931–) replaced his brother Fidel (1926–) as president. Then, in 2010, the Río Group (set up in 1986 to hold annual summits) was superseded by CELAC; both were formed as alternatives to OAS in order to avoid domination by the United States. In 2013, Raúl Castro was voted CELAC president, the organization agreed to draw up a development and reconstruction plan for Haïti, and it began to draw up a constitution.

• **Bolivarian Alliance for the Peoples of Our America** (ALBA). In 2004, Venezuelan President Hugo Chávez (1954–2013) signed an agreement with Cuban President Fidel Castro (1926–) to exchange Venezuelan oil for Cuban educational resources and medical supplies. The agreement established ALBA as a bilateral organization, offering a People's Trade Agreement as an alternative paradigm for trade agreements that focus on big business. Caracas and Havana, with reasons for wanting to avoid American domination in the region, wanted to go their own way, and leaders of other countries took notice.

ALBA became trilateral when Evo Morales (1959–) of Bolivia joined in 2006, and expanded to Nicaragua under Daniel Ortega (1945–) in 2007, and Ecuador under Rafael Correa (1963–) in 2009. Under José Manuel Zelaya (1952–), Honduras became a member in 2008, but withdrew after Zelaya was ousted in a coup the following year. Dominica joined in 2008, and Antigua and Barbuda and St Vincent and the Grenadines signed on in 2009. Suriname and St Lucia are "special guest members," intending to become full members. Haïti joined ALBA in 2012.

In 2010, the leaders signed an agreement for a common currency, the sucre. The organization is considered a breakthrough in international legal theory by forging a Third World perspective on how relations between countries should be governed, focusing on providing adequate housing, gender equity, and worker safety while eradicating poverty and racism, thus rekindling the New International Economic Order project of the 1970s.

- **Summit of the Americas**. In 1994, heads of hemispheric governments met, except for Cuba, with the aim of building a consensus on a wide range of issues, most notably the possibility of a Free Trade Area of the Americas (FTAA) that might merge the CARICOM, NAFTA, and UNASUR (ANCOM plus Mercosur). Six subsequent summits have been held, but many governments are skeptical, given the World Trade Organization's perceived bias toward developed countries. Negotiations for the FTAA collapsed in 2005.

Clearly, regional organizations in the Americas have been leaders in the quest to improve human rights. Instead of Europe's overlapping organizations, the Americas have the advantage of somewhat more coherence.

THE MIDDLE EAST

Most countries in the Middle East are united in opposition to the way in which Israel deals with the Gaza Strip and the West Bank of the Jordan River, where a sovereign Palestinian state might come into existence. The military approach failed when Israel defeated enemies in 1948, 1967, and 1973. Saudi Arabia has attempted diplomacy to resolve the issue without success. In 2006, broadcasts of the trial of Saddam Hussein (1937–2006) throughout the Arab media brought recognition to Nurembergian jurisprudence for the first time within the region. While regional organizations hold some promise for improved human rights in the region, the "Arab Spring" of 2011 – in which revolts against authoritarian rule toppled governments in Egypt, Libya, Tunisia, and Yemen – with a prospect of greater democracy, contrasts with the crackdowns in Bahrain and Syria. Iran and Israel, at odds with each other, remain outliers to the region.

- **League of Arab States** (LAS). Founded in 1944, the Arab League has 22 members,[3] including the Palestine Authority, which was admitted in 1974 as the Palestine Liberation Authority (PLO). The Pact of the League of Arab States, signed in 1945, established the organization with the following purpose:

to draw closer the relations between member States and co-ordinate their political activities with the aim of realizing a close collaboration between them, to safeguard their independence and sovereignty, and to consider in a general way the affairs and interests of the Arab countries.

Specific areas of cooperation identified in the pact are:

- Economic and financial
- Communications
- Culture
- Nationality
- Social welfare
- Health.

The original, unstated purpose was to pressure colonial powers to grant independence to Arab states and to prevent the establishment of the state of Israel. In 1949, LAS agreed that citizenship should not be given throughout the Arabic-speaking world to Palestinians forced out of their homelands, thus ensuring that there would be a refugee problem. Arab countries also began expelling Jewish residents, many of whom then resettled in Israel with bitter anti-Arab attitudes. In 1954, LAS called for a comprehensive economic boycott of Israel that was even extended in 1967 to a ban on films with pro-Israeli American actors. But, in 1994, the Gulf Cooperation Council (discussed below) ended the secondary and tertiary boycotts of Israel, provoking condemnation from LAS, which claimed to be the sole body with the power to make foreign policy for the region.

The supreme body is the Council, with committees for each of the six issue-areas. Any state under attack or threat of attack may summon the Council, which is empowered to repel the attack. In 1950, to strengthen defense elements, the Treaty of Joint Defense and Economic Co-operation of the League of Arab States was inked by all members of LAS, creating two subsidiary bodies: the Joint Defense Council and the Economic Council, which was renamed the **Economic and Social Council** (ESC) in 1980. Two committees of the LAS Council are relevant to human rights – the **Arab Women's Committee** and the **Human Rights Committee**. In 1970, an **Arab Health Organization** was founded.

In 1968, LAS decided to create the **Permanent Arab Commission on Human Rights**. Among the promotional activities of the commission was the offer to assist Iraq in writing its new constitution in 2003, but the main focus has been on the rights of Arabic-speaking residents inside Israel. In 1983, the **Arab Declaration on the Rights of the Child** was adopted. In 1994, LAS adopted the **Arab Charter on Human Rights**, which reaffirmed principles in both International Covenants (see Chapters 5 and 6). A Women's Summit was held in 2001. As revised in 2004, the Charter's scope expanded to include children's rights, rights of the handicapped, and women's rights, but neither version went into force.

In 1964, meanwhile, LAS held a meeting at which the PLO was founded. Ten years later, the League recognized the PLO as the sole representative of the Palestinian peoples over the objections of Jordan, which then occupied the West

Bank as a result of the peace settlement with Israel, brokered by the UN after the war in 1948 to establish the Jewish state, though Jordan renounced sovereignty over the area in 1988. Council meetings regularly condemn Israel, ask for the immediate return of the Golan Heights to Syria, and back Palestinian rights in accordance with UN General Assembly resolutions.

In 1979, Egypt's membership was suspended from the League because President Anwar Sadat (1918–1981) signed a peace treaty with Israel, whereupon the League's secretariat moved from Cairo to Tunis. In 1989, the headquarters returned to Cairo, and Egypt was readmitted in 1990. Although LAS condemned Iraq's attack on Kuwait in 1990, by a 12–8 margin, both countries remained members. No punitive action was taken when Jordan signed a peace treaty with Israel in 1994.

In 2011, Libyan leader, Muammar Gaddafi (1942–2011), faced opposition as large numbers of demonstrators demanded his removal from office. When he threatened to massacre his opponents, LAS convened, expelled Tripoli from League membership, and favored a no-fly zone over the country in order to promote a peaceful outcome. After he was ousted, Libya was readmitted that year. LAS also suspended Syria from membership in 2011, but took no action until December 2011, when an Arab League commission was sent to monitor the massacres. In 2013, the Syrian seat at the Arab League was occupied by Syrian National Coalition.

HISTORIC EVENT 13.2 THE ARAB LEAGUE SUPPORTS A NO-FLY ZONE OVER LIBYA (2011)

During early 2011 uprisings of citizens occurred in several Arabic-speaking countries, including Libya. Although some countries negotiated with the protesters, other countries used police and military force to stop the protests. Libya, ruled by Muammar Gaddafi (1942–2011) from 1969, mobilized its army, used deadly force, and even threatened to level the rebel town of Benghazi, which had a population of some 700,000. The rebels, who formed a counter force, had established a National Transitional Council. Because Gaddafi was refusing to negotiate a peaceful solution, the UN Security Council adopted two resolutions. The first, adopted on February 26, condemned Libya for using violence, proposed economic sanctions, and invited the International Criminal Court to investigate. Meanwhile, the Gulf Cooperation Council, meeting on March 8, called upon the Security Council to impose a no-fly zone. Four days later, foreign ministers of the League of Arab States, in an unprecedented action, also asked the Security Council to authorize a no-fly zone over Libya. The Security Council then voted on March 17 to authorize a no-fly zone. Soon, the air forces of some members of the North Atlantic Treaty Organization, complying with the request, destroyed the Libyan air force and bombed other targets to facilitate victory by the rebels. The government tried to defend itself but ultimately collapsed when Gaddafi was killed on October 20. The rebels then formed a new Libyan government.

In 1946, the organization adopted the **Cultural Treaty of the Arab League**. To implement their goals, the League Council, in 1952, set up the **Institute of Arab Research and Studies**, which in turn was brought under the autonomous **Arab League Educational, Scientific, and Cultural Organization** (ALESCO) by the **Arab Cultural Unity Charter** of 1970. ALESCO, which has the same 22 members as the League, is based in Tunis. In 1989, the **Arab Centre for Arabization, Translation, Authorship and Publication** was set up in Damascus.

Over the years, LAS has addressed cultural issues, economic goals, and problems of emigrant laborers, and has pledged to advance the role of women. LAS has attempted to mediate several regional conflicts, not always successfully. In 1976, the Arab League Summit authorized the formation and deployment of an Arab peacekeeping force, mainly Syrian, in Lebanon and in 1989 drew up an agreement to end the civil war in Lebanon. An Arab peace plan for Israel was developed in 2002, and a delegation presented the proposal on a trip to Israel five years later; instead, Israel began construction of a security wall in 2002 to fence in the territories of Palestinian Authority. Accordingly, to determine whether Tel Aviv had the power to divide farming and residential communities of Palestinian residents, the League submitted a legal request to the International Court of Justice, which agreed with LAS in opposing the fence. In 2003, the League opposed the American intervention of Iraq.

In 1990, LAS adopted the **Cairo Declaration on Human Rights in Islam**. The Council adopted, in 1994, the **Arab Charter on Human Rights**, which recognizes the "right to a life of dignity based on freedom, justice and peace" and also rejects Zionism and racism for violating human rights and threatening peace. In 2004, the Charter was slightly revised, after approval by the **Permanent Arab Commission on Human Rights**, and sufficient ratifications were received by 2008 to go into effect. Among the rights recognized are the right to liberty and security, equality before the law, protection from torture, the right to own private property, freedom to practice religious observance, and freedom of peaceful assembly and association. According to one clause,

> all forms of racism, Zionism and foreign occupation and domination constitute an impediment to human dignity and a major barrier to the exercise of the fundamental rights of peoples; all such practices must be condemned and efforts must be deployed for their elimination.

In 2004, LAS sent a fact-finding mission to Darfur. According to the report, "gross human rights violations" were committed by government forces and pro-government militias. Accordingly, the scheduled Arab Summit meeting was postponed for two months because Sudan, a LAS member, objected to the statement. Soon, a new press release promised relief for the human suffering in Darfur, and Sudan not only welcomed that relief but also pledged to make peace with rebels in Darfur. The League, thus, engaged in quiet diplomacy in an effort to stop the imposition of threatened external sanctions on Khartoum. LAS then joined the European Union in negotiations to reach a settlement of the dispute in Darfur. Although neither the Summit nor the Council condemned Sudan's human rights violations, they urged member governments to improve their implementation of the concepts of democracy and human rights, notably the rights of children and women. Never before had LAS adopted a measure that would involve significant changes in internal governance of a member country.

Also in 2004, after some 8,000 Palestinian prisoners began a hunger strike, the LAS Secretary-General called for a UN investigation of charges of inhumane prison conditions in Israel, contrary to the Geneva Conventions. After American abuse of prisoners in Iraq was exposed in 2005, Arab governments began to pay closer attention to their own prison conditions. In 2005, LAS called upon the United States to apologize for abuses committed against the Qur`ān within the Guantánamo detention center.

In 2011, the Arab League sponsored Palestine for a seat in the UN General Assembly as a state. Although the state was first proclaimed in 1988 and is now recognized by more than 100 countries, Israel granted the Gaza Strip autonomy in 2005, but the West Bank remains under Israeli occupation. In 1974, the General Assembly granted observer status to the PLO, which renamed itself "Palestine" in 1998. In 2012, the General Assembly overwhelmingly agreed to recognize Palestine as a nonmember state. Israel then cut off funding to the Authority, whereupon the Arab League voted to provide the same amount to sustain the Authority.

Although security issues have often trumped other issues, human rights are of increasing priority. Because consensus is sometimes difficult within the League, several subregional organizations are discussed next.

- **Council of Arab Economic Union** (CAEU). In 1957, 13 members of the Arab League signed the Joint Arab Economic Action Charter to create the Council of Arab Economic Union, seeking a customs union and associated economic entities. One goal was to draft common legislation on labor and social security. The first step was adoption of the Agreement to Facilitate and Develop Trade Among Arab Countries in 1981 by the Arab League's Economic and Social Council, and approval by 17 Arab League member countries. The Greater Arab Free Trade Area (GAFTA) was launched in 1997 by 14 countries (Bahrain, Egypt, Iraq, Kuwait, Lebanon, Libya, Morocco, Oman, Qatar, Saudi Arabia, Sudan, Syria, Tunisia, United Arab Emirates). Algeria, Dijbouti, Jordan, and Yemen joined later; the Comoros, Mauritania, and Somalia have applied for membership. GAFTA is supervised and run by CAEU. The next step was the signing by Egypt, Jordan, Morocco, and Tunisia of the Agadir Agreement for the Establishment of a Free Trade Zone Between the Arabic Mediterranean Nations in 2004. All members of the Agadir Agreement are (Egypt, Jordan, Morocco, Tunisia) members of GAFTA.

- **Cooperation Council for the Arab States of the Gulf** (GCC). Six Arab-speaking monarchies bordering on the Persian Gulf, under the leadership of Saudi Arabia, formed an organization – known for short as the Gulf Cooperation Council – by adopting a charter in 1981. The members are Bahrain, Kuwait, Oman, Qatar, Saudi Arabia, and the United Arab Emirates; all belong to CAEU and GAFTA. Jordan and Morocco have been invited to join, and Yemen has applied for membership. In 2012, Saudi Arabia revived an earlier proposal for a confederation of states as a response to fears that the Arab Spring might topple the smaller governments.

In 1984, the GCC Council set up the Joint Defense Council to manage the Peninsula Shield Force. Military units based in Saudi Arabia, with a maximum total of 10,000 persons, are contributed by the six countries. When Iraq's invasion of Kuwait occurred in 1991, the Peninsula Shield Force sat on the sidelines. In 2011,

GCC called for a no-fly zone over Libya before the Arab League, and a GCC force with soldiers from all six countries, was sent to assist the Bahraini armed forces in quelling an uprising without engaging in direct confrontation with protesters. GCC continues to object to Iran's nuclear development program and occupation of three islands (the Greater and the Lesser Tunbs and Abu Musa) that belong to the United Arab Emirates, but several countries still maintain relations with Tehran to create a platform for negotiation.

The primary initial objective was economic. A customs union was declared in 2003, but Bahrain made a separate free trade agreement with the United States that year, torpedoing the group. A common market was planned for 2008, but implementation has lagged. Although Bahrain, Kuwait, Qatar, and Saudi Arabia agreed to a Monetary Council in 2009, preparatory to a monetary union by 2020 with a common currency, Oman declined to join in 2006, and the United Arab Emirates balked in 2009.

The founding charter vaguely mentions cultural and educational goals. The human rights focus is on social aid, social care, social development, and social security. To coordinate social rights projects, there are several bodies, most prominently the **Executive Bureau of the Ministers of Labor and Social Affairs Council**, a technical commission under the Council of Labor and Social Affairs. Other coordination committees exist for problems of children and the handicapped, one aim of which is to draft model legislation for rehabilitation and employment of the handicapped, as well as to promote the quality of the services to children. The major human rights interest in foreign policy is over the treatment of Palestinians by Israel. GCC also has a **Council of Health Ministers** and an **Education and Training Bureau**.

• **Arab Inter-Parliamentary Union** (AIPU). In 1974, Bahrain, Egypt, Jordan, Kuwait, Lebanon, Mauritania, Palestine, Sudan, Syria, and Tunisia met to launch AIPU. Although the organization serves as a caucus within the worldwide Inter-Parliamentary Union, one of AIPU's human rights goals is to strengthen democratic concepts and values. Membership consists of the same 22 members in the League. The principal activities have been forums or seminars on a variety of topics, two of which were on problems of the handicapped and the role of women. In 2004, the LAS attempted to set up a competing Arab Parliament at the League headquarters in Cairo, eventually to occupy a building in Damascus, but the latter body has been much less active.

• **Arab Cooperation Council** (ACC). In 1989, riots broke out in Jordan from a population demanding political liberalization, whereupon Amman forged the ACC with Egypt, Iraq, and Yemen. The organization collapsed after Iraqi military forces attempted to annex Kuwait in 1990.

• **Union du Maghreb Árabe** (UMA). One day after ACC was formed, five North African government heads (Algeria, Libya, Mauritania, Morocco, Tunisia) met to form the Arab Maghreb Union through a Declaration and Constitutive Act. They pledged "to work together with the international community for establishing a world order where justice, dignity, freedom and human rights prevail … ." The organization has been hamstrung by the dispute between Algeria and Morocco over a territory that the former calls Western Sahara, the latter Moroccan Sahara. The name of the organization is itself a problem. "Maghreb" means "Western," but

"Arab" excludes at least 25 million of the indigenous Berbers, who represent a tribal tradition that speaks a different language.

Although regional intergovernmental organizations in the Middle East have a potential to address human rights issues, traditional views continue to prevail. Progressive groups have instead formed nongovernmental organizations in the region.

EAST ASIA AND SOUTHEAST ASIA

Asia is a much larger region compared to Europe and the Middle East, stretching as it does from the Urals to Japan and the Philippines. Subregional intergovernmental efforts predominate. Because of the Cold War divide, regional organizations emerged much more slowly in Asia, some with the encouragement of the UN Economic and Social Commission for Asia and the Pacific. Civil and political rights issues were not prominent until very recently. Many technical bodies address social issues, such as education, but offer assistance without identifying gaps in human rights standards.

• **The Colombo Plan for Cooperative Economic and Social Development in Asia and the Pacific** (C-Plan). Beginning as a British initiative at a meeting of the Commonwealth in 1950, London asked India, Pakistan, and Sri Lanka to present economic development plans for possible funding, vaguely similar to the Marshall Plan for Europe, to foreign aid agencies of Australia, Britain, Canada, and New Zealand. The organization was officially launched at the 1951 conference, where plans of Cambodia, Laos, and Vietnam were also presented, and the United States became a member of the new Colombo Plan for Cooperative Economic Development in South and South-East Asia. In 1997, the name changed to the present long title, reflecting an expansion to 27 countries beyond the original 7. Rather than having ample resources, however, C-Plan became an annual shopping fair in which fund-seeking countries sought support from the six donor countries. Some of the projects developed human resources in developing countries, but the effort lacked focus. Nevertheless, C-Plan continues.

• **Ministerial Conference for the Economic Development of Southeast Asia** (SEAMCED). By 1966, Japan had recovered economically from the devastation of World War II and sought to make amends for the destruction during the war in Southeast Asia by convening a ministerial body, somewhat similar to C-Plan, which would ask countries for proposals for regional intergovernmental organizations to develop the economic capabilities of the region. But Tokyo's thinking soon became clear: the desire was to develop new markets of raw materials in the region and improve skill levels within corporations in Southeast Asia subsidiary to those headquartered in Japan, so the effort collapsed in 1975. In the meantime, regional organizations were created in family planning, fisheries development, infrastructure, tax policy, and tourism, creating disparate, uncoordinated subregional bodies, some of which continue to the present.[4] East Asia, divided by the different policies of China, Japan, and the Koreas, has never been able to develop leadership for regional bodies.

• **Southeast Asian Ministers of Education Organization** (SEAMEO). The United States decided to offer similar assistance for Southeast Asian intergovernmental bodies without a convening institution. The result was some fleeting support for bodies created by SEAMCED as well as the financing of the Southeast Asian Ministers of Education Organization, which has continued to revitalize public education in the region, even though initial American support dwindled.

- **Association of Southeast Asia** (ASA). In 1961, Malaysia, the Philippines, and Thailand formed ASA with economic objectives in mind. But Britain's attempt to transform Malaya into Malaysia by annexing Sabah (claimed by the Philippines) and Sarawak (claimed by Indonesia) provoked tension from 1962 to 1966, and British and Indonesian troops occasionally clashed along the border.

- **Association of South-East Asian Nations** (ASEAN). From 1965, the United States sent thousands of troops to intervene in the civil war in Vietnam, going against Indonesia's loyalty to NAM. Accordingly, Indonesia took the initiative to supersede ASA by forming ASEAN with Malaysia, the Philippines, Singapore, and Thailand in 1967, and in 1971 obtained approval for a **Declaration on the Neutralization of Southeast Asia**. The **Bangkok Declaration**, which launched ASEAN, references the goals of "freedom, social justice, and economic well-being" and "respect for justice and the rule of law." The meaning of "social justice" was then understood as the "elimination of poverty, hunger, disease and illiteracy."

But as long as civil war continued in Vietnam, with communist insurgencies active in other countries of Southeast Asia, ASEAN countries were without resources to achieve their goals. After the United States withdrew from Vietnam in 1975, the first ASEAN Summit of 1976 adopted a peace treaty, the Treaty of Amity and Cooperation in Southeast Asia, which pledged close diplomatic and economic cooperation. In 1977, the organization established a secretariat at Jakarta and embarked on annual meetings of ASEAN Economic Ministers, seeking prosperity through increased intraregional trade. ASEAN's annual meetings of foreign ministers then became the ASEAN Ministerial Meeting, and 25 more ministerial bodies were established over the years, including such issue-areas as education (1977), labor (1979), health (1980), poverty elimination (1998), and culture (2003), to sponsor aid projects.

Rule in Southeast Asia was illiberal and undemocratic in the early years, and ASEAN was called a "dictator's club." And any expansion of membership to all Southeast Asian countries would have brought in some of the world's worst violators of human rights – Burma (later called Myanmar) and the three Indochinese countries (Cambodia, Laos, Vietnam). Oil-rich Brunei, a sultanate, was admitted in 1984 upon achieving independence from Britain.

Then a dramatic change occurred in 1986, when the streets of Manila were filled with citizens demanding the fall of the government of President Ferdinand Marcos (1917–1989). Although he had imposed dictatorial rule over a democratic system in 1972, promising to eradicate insurgents, 14 years later the insurgencies remained and the quest to return to democracy was overwhelming. Thereafter, reforms in ASEAN countries gradually responded to desires of the growing middle classes, created by economic progress – but slowly. Singapore, for example, continued to impose one-party rule. But Manila expelled American military bases from the Philippines in 1991.

COURT CASE 13.2 *SEOW V. SINGAPORE* (1990)

As Singapore became a prosperous country, many wealthy residents sought maids. Some employers, however, molested the maids, mostly Filipinas, prompting several Catholic organizations to assist them. In 1987, the Singapore government arrested 22 Catholics, mostly lay workers, accusing them of engaging in a "Marxist conspiracy" to overthrow the government because the group allegedly had ties to a dissident living in London. On the basis of an indefinite detention law, they were detained without charges, attorneys, or trial in a prison noted for torturing dissidents. A few weeks later, after odd-sounding television confessions, they were released. When Lee Hsien Loong (1952–), the son of Prime Minister Lee Kuan Yew (1923–), later goaded them into claiming that their confessions were obtained through physical and psychological torture, they were rearrested, and the government shut down Catholic organizations with whom they were associated. Their attorney, Francis Seow (1928–), was also arrested, indefinitely detained, and tortured that year. He was released, though he repeatedly refused to admit complicity in any anti-government conspiracy. In 1990, when Seow sued the prime minister for his arbitrary confinement and torture, the latter admitted under oath that the Christian social workers were just "do gooders." Nevertheless, Seow lost the case before a judge appointed by the government of Lee Kuan Yew. The case illustrates why Singapore, a major advocate of the "Asian Values" opposition to civil and political rights, has been resistant to human rights progress within Asia.

In 1994, ASEAN's concern over the growing economic and military power of China also led to an extraordinary development: The innovation was the establishment of an annual conference with a security focus – the **ASEAN Regional Forum** with Australia, Canada, China, the European Union, Japan, Laos, Papua New Guinea, Russia, South Korea, New Zealand, the United States, and Vietnam. In due course, Bangladesh, Cambodia, India, North Korea, Pakistan, and Timor-Leste joined. Thereby, ASEAN became the linchpin of regional intergovernmental organization in East and Southeast Asia.

However, in 1993, Bangkok was the site of an international conference of Asian countries preparatory to the World Conference on Human Rights later that year in Vienna. The declaration from the meeting, however, supported the concept of "Asian values," that is, the notion that civil and political rights should be subordinated to economic and social rights. First World participants in Vienna regarded the declaration as reactionary.

Having cast aspersions on civil and political rights concerns, ASEAN admitted Vietnam in 1995, and Laos and Myanmar (Burma) were admitted in 1997. Myanmar's admission so rankled many European Union countries that they called off an Asia–Europe Meeting in 1998 and began to insist on the exclusion of Myanmar from any future meetings with ASEAN because that government not only refused to recognize election results of 1990 but also had been suppressing supporters of democracy ever since. In 1997, ASEAN was scheduled to admit Cambodia, but a coup in Phnom Penh prompted the organization to delay membership until 1999, when rival factions became reconciled, suggesting that a constitutional government was a precondition to ASEAN membership.

HISTORIC EVENT 13.3 BURMA'S ELECTION RESULTS ARE IGNORED (1990)

In 1962, a military coup ended democratic rule in Burma. In 1988, the streets of the capital, Rangoon, were filled with protesters, including Aung San Suu Kyi (1945–), daughter of Aung San (1915–1947), who had negotiated Burma's independence from Britain in 1947. With the country on the verge of civil war, another military coup was launched to squelch the protests. However, the new military leaders agreed to hold free elections in 1990. Overwhelmingly, Aung San Suu Kyi's political party (the National League for Democracy) won, but the military leaders refused to respect the results of the election. Aung San Suu Kyi was then placed under house arrest in 1990 but released and rearrested several times thereafter. The military government, which changed the name of the country to Myanmar in 1989, arrested many other members of the opposition and steadfastly refused to hold elections. Pressure from Western countries then ensued in the form of economic boycotts. The Association of South-East Asian Nations, which admitted Myanmar as a member in 1997, applied more subtle pressure and is credited by some observers with the decision of the government to hold elections in 2012. Although Aung San Suu Kyi won a seat in those parliamentary elections, along with other members of her political party, only 46 seats in two houses of parliament were contested. Most seats are still held by the Myanmar military.

In 1998, Indonesian President Suharto (1921–2008) was ousted by a democracy-seeking public. Led by Jakarta, ASEAN began a transformation into an organization looking for ways to promote human rights. Also in 1998, Philippine President Joseph Estrada (1937–) openly criticized Malaysia for imprisoning Deputy Prime Minister Anwar Ibrahim (1947–), whose increasing popularity was a threat to Prime Minister Mahathir's continuation in power. His remark was the first time one ASEAN leader had publicly criticized another.

As democracy emerged in Indonesia, the **Plan of Action** adopted at the ASEAN Summit in 1998 focused on economic issues, including human resource development. But there was a section pledging that ASEAN would "promote and protect all human rights and fundamental freedoms of all peoples" and delineating such problems as the plight of children, the disabled, the elderly, and women.

Initially, ASEAN's efforts to employ quiet diplomacy to encourage Myanmar to become more democratic produced almost no results. In 2003, Malaysian Prime Minister Mahathir bin Mohamad (1925–) even suggested Myanmar's expulsion from ASEAN if the military regime remained obstinate. A multicountry civil society organization, the ASEAN People's Assembly, was formed in 2006, with Myanmar's lack of democracy identified as an important problem. When the brutal crackdown of the Saffron Revolution came in 2007, with mass arrests of tens of thousands of protesting monks, hundreds of whom were beaten severely, Indonesian President Susilo Bambang Yudhoyono (1949–) felt that ASEAN had lost credibility and needed dramatic changes.

In 2008, the **ASEAN Charter** was adopted, pledging "adherence to the rule of law, good governance, the principles of democracy and constitutional government, "respect for fundamental freedoms, the promotion and protection of human rights, and the promotion of social justice," and "upholding … international humanitarian law … ." Human rights had become a central concern of ASEAN.

In 2009, the **ASEAN Intergovernmental Commission on Human Rights** was formed, with membership from all 10 ASEAN countries. Also in 2009, the **ASEAN Commission on the Promotion and Protection of the Rights of Women** was formed.

Quiet diplomacy at ASEAN meetings eventually paid off in 2010, when Myanmar's dissident leader Aung Sang Suu Kyi (1945–) was released from prison along with many members of the National League for Democracy. Free elections in 2012 enabled her party to win some of the seats in the parliament.

Then in 2012, ASEAN adopted an **ASEAN Human Rights Declaration** containing 38 articles that summarized the two International Covenants and add the rights to development and peace. The framework now exists to develop an effective human rights mechanism, though complaint processing is not among the powers of the commission.

From the start, ASEAN was eager to increase multilateral economic cooperation. An **ASEAN Free Trade Area** (AFTA) agreement was signed in 1992, producing a procedure to develop a list of items for lowering tariffs. By 2011, more than 99 percent of the items on the list had been accepted by the first six ASEAN countries (Brunei, Indonesia, Malaysia, Philippines, Singapore, Thailand) at the 0.5 percent tariff range. The late-joining Indochinese countries and Myanmar have even lowered 80 percent of the products to the 0.5 percent level. AFTA, thus, now exists, shattering the expectations of those who were skeptical when planning began.

From the start, ASEAN asserted its presence in the UN by means of an ASEAN voting bloc. ASEAN has continued to remain in the center of Asian regional cooperation, where nearly 100 technical intergovernmental bodies operate.[5] Thailand was also central in the formation of the **Bay of Bengal Initiative** in 1997, seeking economic cooperation with Bangladesh, India, and Sri Lanka. In 2001, the ASEAN foreign ministers proposed an **Asia Cooperation Dialogue** (ACD) among ASEAN, GCC, and SAARC member countries, and Thailand hosted the first ACD meeting in 2002. Central Asian countries and China are now represented for a total of 32 states from the original 18.

• **Asia-Pacific Economic Cooperation** (APEC). In 1980, APEC arose. Australia, Japan, and the United States were seeking a free trade area among countries bordering on both sides of the Pacific that might threaten ASEAN's goal of a free trade area. In response, Malaysian Prime Minister Mahathir developed the concept of an East Asian Caucus in 1992, dividing Asian countries from Western countries, and an eventual **East Asian Summit** emerged in 2005 with ASEAN joining the three economic giants of China, Japan, and South Korea in a common economic forum. Nevertheless, APEC set up a headquarters in Singapore for the 21 members[6] and thus became geographically linked to the heartland of ASEAN.

One goal in APEC's founding Canberra Agreement was "to study, formulate and recommend measures for the development of, and where necessary the coordination of services affecting, the economic and social rights and welfare" of the peoples of the region. Services identified in the agreement are education, health, housing, and social welfare. Although the subject of human rights is not formally discussed, the project work of the organization serves to alleviate economic and social inequality. Formation of the WTO in 1995, however, slowed APEC's momentum, as the world was becoming a free trade area.

• **Asia Pacific Forum of National Human Rights Institutions** (APF). One important human rights organization is transregional and deserves separate attention. In 1996, the UN High Commissioner for Human Rights hosted four national human rights bodies (Australia, India, Indonesia, New Zealand) in Darwin, Australia. Believing that matters of human rights had been left out of regional organizations, the four countries decided to form APF, with headquarters in Sydney. Eleven new human rights bodies have now joined (Afghanistan, Jordan, Malaysia, Mongolia, Nepal, Palestine, Philippines, Qatar, South Korea, Thailand, Timor-Leste). Three country institutions (Bangladesh, Maldives, Sri Lanka) are associate members. To become a full member, a national human rights body must conform to the Paris Principles, guidelines developed at the UN conference in Paris during 1991 that established minimum standards for national human rights bodies.

APF holds annual meetings to determine priorities for the region, sometimes attended by almost 100 civil society and governmental bodies. The major objective is to assist countries in the region to establish national human rights institutions. One success of APF is the formation of the ASEAN Intergovernmental Commission on Human Rights, as mentioned above.

SOUTH ASIA

The **South Asian Association for Regional Cooperation** (SAARC), consisting of the countries bordering India except for China (Bangladesh, Bhutan, Nepal, Pakistan, and Sri Lanka), plus the Maldive Islands, was formed as an initiative by Bangladesh. The founding **SAARC Charter** of 1985, adopted by government heads of all six countries, establishes such goals as "social justice" and "promoting the welfare and improving the quality of life of the peoples of the region." Although some countries have populations of millions in the region, next to India they felt that something was needed to balance relations diplomatically and economically, and ASEAN left them out. The Secretariat was located at Kathmandu in 1987. Afghanistan joined in 2007. The continuing division of Kashmir between India and Pakistan, however, remains a cloud over the organization.

Human rights issues emerged quite early in SAARC, with a focus on women due in part to the fact that female prime ministers have headed governments in India and Sri Lanka. One of the technical committees is entitled **Women, Youth, and Children**; another is the **Human Resource Development Committee**. The 1993 summit adopted a declaration that places the goal of relieving poverty as a high priority. In 1998, the SAARC **Human Resource Development Center** was set up at Islamabad to sponsor conferences and studies. Kathmandu hosts the **Tuberculosis Center**, and the **Cultural Center** is in Colombo. There are nine other regional centers, mostly focused on economic development issues.

In 2002, the foreign ministers, which constitute the annual SAARC Council of Ministers, adopted two human rights treaties. The **Convention on Preventing and Combating Trafficking in Women and Children for Prostitution** provides for a regional task force to compile information and undertake periodic reviews of efforts to stop the practices and authorizes repatriation and rehabilitation of those rescued. The **Convention on Regional Arrangements for the Promotion of Child Welfare in South Asia** set up a nutrition initiative.

The **Social Charter** was adopted by SAARC in 2004. Targets with national action plans are authorized for:

- Alleviating poverty
- Empowering women
- Mobilizing youth
- Developing human resources
- Promoting health and nutrition
- Protecting children.

Civil society organizations in each country have goaded progress.

From the beginning, an economic cooperation arrangement was a SAARC goal. The **South Asian Free Trade Area** (SAFTA) agreement was signed in 2004 and entered into force in 2006, from whence the Trade Liberalization Program immediately began under the SAFTA Ministerial Council of commerce ministers. Trade barriers were to be reduced, but progress has not occurred on schedule. Article 11 of the SAFTA Agreement provides special consideration for the least developed countries, in particular to ensure that sustainable development will be respected.

The **Charter of Democracy**, adopted by the SAARC Council in 2011, pledges that member countries will advance equality of opportunity, gender mainstreaming, and participatory democracy. A "democracy clause" unites SAARC against "any unconstitutional change in government in any South Asian country, and work towards the restoration of democracy … ." However, government heads at the SAARC Summit in 2012 failed to sign the document.

CENTRAL ASIA

Five Soviet Republics (Kazakhstan, Kyrgyzstan, Tajikistan, Turkmenistan, Uzbekistan) were suddenly given independence in 1991, when the Soviet Union ceased to exist. So shattered was the common economic and security system provided until then by Moscow, new arrangements were sought to provide continuity and stability, though progress has been difficult, and China and Russia vie for influence in the region. The Commonwealth of Independent States, discussed in Chapter 12, was an initial effort to regroup under a single tent, but other organizations have arisen with relevance to Central Asia.

- **Economic Cooperation Organization** (ECO). Established initially as Regional Cooperation for Development (RCD) from 1964 to 1979, ECO began in 1980. In 1992, membership expanded from the original three RCD countries (Iran, Pakistan, Turkey) to include Afghanistan, Azerbaijan, and four "stan" countries of Central Asia. Uzbekistan, the fifth "stan," joined in 2005.

The basic agreement, the **Treaty of Izmir** of 1977, as amended (in 1990, 1992, and 1996), provides two human rights goals – raising "the standard of living and quality of life" and "mutual assistance in economic, social, cultural, technical and scientific fields." In addition, the **Istanbul Declaration** from the summit in 1992 called attention to a desire to enhance the "empowerment of women and their full participation in the economic development activities in the ECO region." One project is the establishment, in 2002, of a special fund to rebuild war-torn Afghanistan.

In 2003, members signed the **ECO Trade Agreement**, the most important goal of which is the elimination of trade barriers in the region. The highest body, the Council of Ministers, has established six directorates within the ECO Secretariat in Tehran. The **Directorate of Human Resources and Sustainable Development**, set up in 2005, focuses on achieving the Millennium Development Goals, especially improved health conditions. An ECO Health Ministerial Meeting was first held in 2010.

ECO has two specialized agencies relating to human rights. In 1995, the Summit of ECO countries revived an earlier RCD body as the **ECO Cultural Institute** based on a charter signed by Afghanistan, Iran, Pakistan, and Tajikistan. Among the projects was a Diplomatic Art Gallery on display at the ECO Secretariat in 2011. In 1998, four countries (Iran, Kyrgyzstan, Tajikistan, Turkey) agreed to the charter for the **ECO Educational Institute**. (A parliamentary assembly was set up in 2012.)

- **Eurasian Economic Community** (EAEC or EurAsEC). In 1991, the five "stans" formed the Central Asian Commonwealth, but the grouping has been renamed several times – Central Asian Economic Union (without Tajikistan and Turkmenistan) in 1994, Central Asian Economic Cooperation in 1998, and the Organization of Central Asian Cooperation (OCAC) in 2002 with the return of Tajikistan. In 2003, a Common Economic Space proposal emerged to link CIS and OCAC countries, but the EU attracted interest from the Ukraine, a key CIS country. In 2009, most CIS members agreed in principle to establish a free trade area, but Azerbaijan, Uzbekistan, and Turkmenistan decided to delay consideration.

Meanwhile, Belarus, Kazakhstan, and Russia formed a customs union in 1996, and the "stans" formed the Eurasian Economic Community with Belarus and Russia in 2000. The split between OCAC and EAEC ended when the former merged into the latter in 2005. In 2008, however, Uzbekistan dropped out. Apart from seeking an eventual common market, the organization is committed to equal rights in education and health care. One of the proposed goals of EAEC is to protect migrant workers, who face problems of criminality, employer discrimination, and over taxation.

• **Collective Security Treaty Organization** (CSTO). Security issues in Central Asia were approached early. In 1992, when NATO sought to expand in scope toward Central Asia, Armenia, Russia, and four Central Asian countries agreed to establish the non-CIS CSTO for a five-year period. When the organization officially began in 1994, Azerbaijan, Belarus, and Georgia had already joined. In 1999, six countries agreed to CSTO's renewal (Armenia, Belarus, Russia, Kazakhstan, Kyrgyzstan, Tajikistan). In 2006, Uzbekistan joined CSTO. The Secretariat is in Moscow. Although CSTO has held peacekeeping exercises, they mostly involve Russian forces.

• **Shanghai Cooperation Organization** (SCO). Concerned about Russia's CSTO sponsorship involving countries on its border, and seeking to counterbalance NATO, China saw an opportunity to befriend Central Asian countries that formerly had been part of the Soviet Union. In 1996, China's foreign ministry hosted a meeting to enhance border security, and foreign ministers from Kazakhstan, Kyrgyzstan, Russia, and Tajikistan signed the Treaty on Deepening Military Trust in Border Regions. Annual meetings, called the Shanghai Five, were formalized during mid-2001 by a declaration that identified three "evil forces" – extremism, separatism, and terrorism. When Uzbekistan joined the five in 2001, the grouping was renamed the Shanghai Cooperation Organization.

A charter, signed in 2002, states the aim of SCO as the "promotion of a new democratic, fair and rational political and economic international order." A declaration about extremism refers to radical Islamic elements that have been suppressed, at times brutally, in several member countries. China, in targeting separatism, had Xinxiang province in mind, since Uyghur Muslim dissidents have often sought support within the "stans" for their aim of creating an East Turkestan or a Uyghurstan.

Thus far, SCO has sponsored about two dozen projects related mostly to economic and defense matters, though Russia has blocked China's aim of making SCO more relevant to economic development issues. In 2002, SCO members agreed to increase cultural cooperation. Joint military exercises have been held. SCO and CSTO signed an agreement in 2007 to enhance cooperation in crime and drug trafficking.

Washington applied for observer status in SCO in 2006 and was turned down, a clear sign of the geopolitical significance of both organizations vis-à-vis the United States. Although SCO pledges to respect human rights, crackdowns on dissident minority populations within member countries continue, though Russia denounces inhumane conditions at Guantánamo.

PACIFIC ISLANDS COUNTRIES

Whereas British colonies of the Pacific Islands were the latest countries to reach independence, French colonial possessions remain. All have enjoyed the advantage of being democratic, with pride in their indigenous Micronesian, Melanesian, and Polynesian cultures, but lacking in resources to be on a par with modern states. Two intergovernmental bodies have served the region well, though several dozen coexist.[7] The countries were at peace when the two organs began, but subsequently have encountered troublesome internal conflicts.

- **Pacific Community**. In 1947, Australia sponsored the formation of the South Pacific Commission, which then had as full members the six colonial powers of the region – Australia, Britain, France, the Netherlands, New Zealand, and the United States. In 1997, after the independence and admission of many independent countries in Micronesia, north of the equator, the organization was renamed Pacific Community. Today, along with all the founding countries except the Netherlands, 22 island states are members, though some are still not yet sovereign.[8] The Secretariat is in Nouméa, New Caledonia, a territory whose inhabitants are French citizens who will vote on self-governance in 2018.

The aim, as stated in the original **Canberra Agreement** of 1947, is to provide economic assistance for the peoples of the South Pacific, one purpose of which is to "study, formulate and recommend measures for the development of … the economic and social rights and welfare of the inhabitants … ." A wide variety of projects has been launched. Within the **Social Resources Division**, there are three programs – Cultural Affairs (cultural conservations), Human Development (education, gender equality), and Public Health.

- **Pacific Islands Forum**. In 1971, Fiji hosted a conference of the leaders of four other newly independent island states (Nauru, Papua New Guinea, Samoa, Tonga) plus Australia and New Zealand; the result was the establishment of the South Pacific Forum. In 1999, the organization changed its name from South Pacific Forum in recognition of the presence of the North Pacific island states of Micronesia among the newest members. Today, all 16 independent states in the region are members.[9]

The Forum initially encouraged self-determination for the remaining territories. Accordingly, the Forum still exerts pressure on France to grant independence to French Polynesia and New Caledonia. New Caledonia attends as an observer, since France promises to grant independence to the territory by 2018. The Forum also welcomed East Timor's participation while the country was spurned by ASEAN. When a dissident group in West Papua, which Indonesia governs as the province of Irian Jaya, petitioned the Forum for observer status, in 2001, the Forum responded by asking Indonesia to respect human rights in the province.

Whereas most discussions focus on economic development, the third summit in 1973 mentioned the goal of promoting the "social and economic well-being" of the island peoples. Several subsequent declarations have supported human rights. The **Vision Statement** of 1995 pledged the Forum to work toward "improvement in the quality of people's lives, including human development, equality between women and men, and protection of children." The 2004 Forum declaration committed members to the "full observance of democratic values" and for the "defense and promotion of human rights." Since the region contains several indigenous peoples, including those in Australia and New Zealand, the Forum's policies are always mindful of cultural rights.

Most Pacific island countries have experienced stable, democratic rule. Fiji, however, has experienced coups in 1987, 2000, and 2006 because a major issue has been how power should be shared between the native Fijians and descendants of the sugarcane workers who were recruited from India by colonial Britain to live in the country. From 1999, there was a breakdown of law and order on the Solomon Islands, as longtime residents of the main island began to forcibly expel newcomers of another ethnic group from neighboring islands.

Up to 2000, the supreme Forum body was a summit of government heads. That year, the first official meeting of foreign ministers adopted the **Biketawa Declaration** in response to both the Fiji and Solomon Islands situations, giving unequivocal support to the principles of democracy and human rights, specifically:

- "good governance"
- "liberty of the individual under the law, in equal rights for all citizens regardless of gender, race, color, creed or political belief and in the individual's inalienable right to participate by means of free and democratic political process"
- "peaceful transfer of power, the rule of law and the independence of the judiciary, just and honest government"
- "equitable economic, social and cultural development to satisfy the basic needs and aspirations"
- respect for and protection of "indigenous rights and cultural values, traditions and customs."

The Biketawa Declaration also adopted a process of conflict resolution for the region under which the Forum dispatched its first election monitoring team to the Solomons in 2001. Two years later, responding to urgent pleas from the Solomon Island government, 10 forum members sent the **Regional Assistance Mission** to the Solomon Islands, a peacekeeping force to assist law enforcement officers in rounding up lawbreakers and in handling the burgeoning prison population, with 2013 as the final year of operation.

Insolvent Nauru was the second beneficiary of the Biketawa Resolution, but for economic reasons. From 2004 to 2009, the Forum established a program to recapitalize the bankrupt country, which relied primarily on exports of fertilizers from sea birds rich in phosphates until their exhaustion.

In 2005, the Forum departed from its customary informality to adopt the **Agreement Establishing the Pacific Islands Forum**, which states the four pillars of the **Pacific Plan for Regional Integration and Cooperation**:

- Economic growth
- Sustainable development
- Good governance
- Security.

The good governance objective is support for "a safe, enabling, inclusive and sustainable environment for economic growth and personal development and human rights," including "participatory decision-making mechanisms" that include "nongovernment groups, women and youth" and "the maintenance of strong Pacific cultural identities … ." Although the agreement has not yet gone into force because several countries have not yet ratified, programming consistent with the Pacific Plan proceeds.

In 2009, the Forum suspended Fiji from membership because Suva's government was determined to be unacceptably undemocratic. But of course, the action was consistent with the Forum's longstanding objection to French colonial rule in New Caledonia and Tahiti.

Forum-sponsored conferences have addressed the need for cultural sensitivity and on the role of women in economic development. In 2005, the Regional Workshop on National Human Rights Mechanisms was held under the auspices of the Forum Secretariat. Many programs on education and health have been pursued over the years to meet the Millennium Development Goals.

In 2012, the **Pacific Leaders Gender Equality Declaration** stressed gender mainstreaming. Efforts to implement the Pacific Islands' Pacific Island Countries Trade Agreement, as adopted in 2001, continue.

- **Melanesian Spearhead Group** (MSG). In 1986, government heads of Papua New Guinea, Solomon Islands, and Vanuatu met together before a Pacific Islands Forum summit. Concerned that the main beneficiaries of the organization appeared to be Polynesian countries, from 1987 they declared their caucus to be the Melanesian Spearhead Group, at first only as a mini-summit. Later, MSG established an annual meeting of foreign ministers. A Secretariat in Vanuatu parallels activities of the Forum Secretariat in some respects.

- **Polynesian Leaders Group**. MSG, an entirely independent intergovernmental organization, stimulated an initial meeting in 2011 of a Polynesian Leaders Group which was formally launched in a meeting in 2012 at Apia, Samoa, by American Samoa, Cook Islands, French Polynesia, Niue, Samoa, Tokelau, Tonga, and Tuvalu. Disruption in the comprehensive work of the Pacific Islands Forum is unlikely.

AFRICA

While Europe experienced world wars in the first half of the twentieth century, and Latin America was largely at peace, wars in Asia arose midcentury and were resolved by the end of the century. But Africa is now the arena for the world's most intractable violent conflicts. As in the case of other continents, intergovernmental organizations tell the most important story about human rights in Africa, where independence began to dawn in the early 1960s.

- **African Union** (AU). The Organization of African Unity (OAU) was launched with the adoption of a charter in 1963 that proclaimed the aims of:

  ○ Ending colonization and *apartheid*
  ○ Promoting solidarity among African states

○ Providing a forum for cooperation in development
○ Ensuring the sovereignty and territorial integrity of independent states in Africa.

Unlike other regional organizations, OAU began with human rights at the forefront, notably the white-dominated regimes of Southern Africa.

In 1981, OAU adopted the **African Charter on Human and People's Rights** and the **Grand Bay Declaration and Plan of Action on Human Rights**. A severe drought and famine that engulfed the continent, with a crippling effect on Africa's external indebtedness, prompted adoption in 1985 of **Africa's Priority Program for Economic Recovery**. In 1990, the OAU **Declaration on the Political and Socio-Economic Situation in Africa and the Fundamental Changes Taking Place in the World** committed the organization to address challenges to peace, democracy, and security. Also in 1990, the **Charter on Popular Participation** placed African citizens at the center of development and decision-making.

The treaty establishing the African Economic Community in 1991, known as the Abuja Treaty, sought to create an African common market through six stages. The practical method is to first develop subregional economic communities, described below, as building blocks.

Over the years, the organization's peacekeeping forces have been sent on many occasions. The first force was assigned to Chad from 1981 to 1982. The **Mechanism for Conflict Prevention, Management and Resolution** of 1993 provided an institutional means for solving conflicts to promote peace, security, and stability – the **Peace and Security Council** – which monitors threats to peace as well as human rights violations and can deploy an African Standby Force. The **Cairo Agenda for Action** of 1995 re-launched OAU's political, economic, and social development program. In 1998, OAU then assisted in negotiating a ceasefire in the Democratic Republic of the Congo (Kinshasa).

In 1997, the African Common Position on Africa's External Debt Crisis demanded relief from crushing loan payments. In 1999, OAU developed a common position on unconstitutional government changes and in 2000 adopted the **Lomé Declaration** on a framework for OAU response to unconstitutional changes.

In 1999, member states agreed to form a new organization, to be known as the African Union. Then, in 2000, the annual assembly adopted the **Constitutive Act of the African Union**, which provides for "non-indifference" (instead of "noninterference") regarding the internal affairs of member countries when human rights violations and security issues emerge, as well as respect for the following:

[1] democratic principles, [2] human rights, [3] the rule of law … [4] good governance and [5] respect for the sanctity of human life.

Today, AU has 54 members, all continental and major island countries except for the Îles Éparses, Réunion, Mayotte, Saint Helena, Ascensión and Tristan da Cunha, Madeira, Canary Islands, Spanish North Africa, and Morocco. The latter, a member of AOU until Western Sahara was admitted in 1984, otherwise participates in the organization. From time to time, members are suspended for the overthrow of democratic governments.

The AU secretariat, known as the **Commission**, is in Addis Ababa, Ethiopia, headed by a Secretary-General who administers eight portfolios, including **Peace and Security** (conflict prevention, management and resolution; combating terrorism); **Political Affairs** (human rights, democracy, good governance, electoral bodies, civil society bodies, humanitarian affairs, refugees, returnees, internally displaced persons); and **Social Affairs** (health, children, drug control, population, migration, labor and employment, sports and culture).

The Constitutive Act authorized a continent-wide parliament, which was created in 2000 at Addis Ababa by the **Protocol Establishing the Pan-African Parliament**. Pending sufficient ratifications to go into force, the body began anyway and moved for its first session to Midrand, South Africa, in 2004. The aim of the body is to debate AU policies, including the budget, with representatives from AU countries. Thus far, 47 legislatures of the 54 member countries have sent delegates. There are 10 permanent committees, including **Health, Labor, and Social Affairs; Education, Cultural, Tourism, and Human Resources; Gender, Family, Youths, and People with Disabilities; and Justice and Human Rights**. In 2005, a motion to create the **Pan-African Parliament Trust Fund** included the goal as promoting "good governance, transparency and democracy, peace security and stability, gender equality and development in the integration of African people within Africa and other nations." HIV/AIDS, hunger, and poverty on the continent were also mentioned as appropriate uses of the fund.

AU's Executive Council, composed of foreign ministers, has several advisory technical bodies. The **Economic, Social, and Cultural Council** is an expert body that sponsors studies on thematic issues, including human rights, while encouraging an African-wide civil society. There are seven expert committees, including one on **Health, Labor, and Social Affairs** and on **Education, Culture, and Human Resources**. The other committees focus on economic matters. Other expert bodies are discussed next.

In 2000, the leaders made the **Solemn Declaration on the Conference on Security, Stability, Development and Cooperation**, establishing fundamental principles for the promotion of democracy and good governance for the **Conference on Security, Stability, Development and Cooperation in Africa** (CSSDCA), which was established in principle at the AU summit and then formalized in 2002 by a **Memorandum of Understanding**, which states commitments on all four goals contained in the title of the conference, and also contains deadlines for adopting various measures to advance democracy, human rights, and the rule of law, including such issues as refugee protection; principles of good governance; term limits for officeholders; dismantling political parties formed on the basis of ethnic, religious, or other divisions; and establishing independent electoral commissions. CSSDCA commitments and monitoring mechanisms are binding on and accepted by all AU member states. Monitoring is done by the CSSDCA unit within the AU Commission. CSSDCA visitation panels of eminent persons make biennial reviews, which are submitted to the Conference on Security, Stability, Development and Cooperation in Africa at AU summits.

Regarding issues of economic and social rights, members at the AU summit in 2001 adopted a program known as the **New Partnership for Africa's Development**

(NEPAD), which has an explicit human rights focus. The primary aim is to end poverty in Africa by achieving the 7 percent growth rate set by the United Nations Millennium Development Goals. NEPAD emphasizes the concept of "mutual accountability," so that both Africans and those who trade with or give aid to Africa have responsibilities to promote "[1] peace, [2] security, [3] democracy, [4] good governance, [5] human rights and [6] sound economic management" as conditions for sustainable development.

In 2002, AU countries supporting NEPAD issued the **Declaration on Democracy, Political, Economic and Corporate Governance**, subsequently endorsed by a summit of African leaders, which sets out an action plan to support democratic institutions of government, good governance (including strengthening the civil service and judicial system), and human rights. Under human rights, the states pledged to develop civil society institutions; support the African Charter on Human and Peoples' Rights, the African Commission, and the African Court; and ensure "responsible free expression," including freedom of the press. The declaration also contains pledges on economic and corporate governance and socioeconomic development.

Implementation of NEPAD, which has a coordinating office in Midrand, South Africa, was originally guided by the **African Peer Review Mechanism** (APRM), a team of African "eminent persons." After making an APRM report, the team first discusses problem areas with each government and, within six months, puts the report on the agenda of the African Commission on Human Rights and the appropriate subregional body. If a government fails to rectify the problems, NEPAD can engage in "constructive dialogue" or even recommend sanctions. In early 2003, a Memorandum of Understanding on the APRM was adopted by the NEPAD heads of state implementation committee meeting and went into force within two months. States can opt out of APRM by not ratifying the memorandum. Currently, NEPAD has six programs. Although most focus on economic issues, education, gender mainstreaming, and health issues are within the scope. The aim is to achieve Millennium Development Goals.

NEPAD was set up autonomously at first, with its own secretariat. In 2010, the secretariat was superseded by the NEPAD Planning and Coordinating Agency, thereby integrating NEPAD into AU as a technical expert body. CSSDCA and NEPAD overlap. CSSDCA's requirements are more detailed and specific than those of NEPAD, which is a voluntary program. AU coordinates both processes.

In 2002, shortly after the first AU summit that adopted the **Declaration on the Principles Governing Democratic Elections in Africa**, the organization sent election observers to Togo. AU also held up Madagascar's membership application until verifying that legislative elections were in accordance with the wishes of the people. Similar visits by the **African Union Election Observers Mission** have taken place over the years at almost every election, from 2007 based on principles in the **African Charter on Democracy, Elections and Governance**. In 2012, for example, election visits went to Burkina Faso, Ghana, and Sierra Leone.

From the first major UN force in Africa that was sent to the Congo in 1960, African countries noticed that non-African troops were less effective because they did not understand cultural sensitivities in the continent. That was one important consideration for the formation of another expert body, the **Peace and Security Council** in 2002. Based on a protocol, the body has 15 country members, elected by the assembly, which can meet at any time and at any diplomatic level at Addis Ababa headquarters. The mandate is for peacemaking, peacebuilding, as well as peacekeeping. Intervention can be recommended for "grave circumstances, namely war crimes, genocide and crimes against humanity." Sanctions can be authorized "whenever an unconstitutional change of government takes place in a member state." The Peace and Security Council can also "facilitate humanitarian action in situations of armed conflicts." All decisions are subject to approval by the Executive Council of foreign ministers.

In 2003, the Executive Council reviewed the security and human rights situations in several African countries – Angola, Burundi, Central African Republic, Comoros, Congo (Kinshasa), the Ivory Coast, Liberia, Somalia, and the Sudan. AU then sent a peacekeeping force to Burundi in 2003; the UN later took over the operation. In Somalia, AU provided a military observer mission. In Sudan, there was an AU verification and monitoring team.

HISTORIC EVENT 13.4 SUDAN'S CIVIL WAR (1955–1972, 1983–2005)

Before World War II, Sudan was a British colony administratively separated into the Arabic-speaking Muslim north and the African animist and Christian south. When Britain promised independence to Sudan as a unitary state, effective 1956, those in the south were displeased that the arrangement did not grant them autonomy. Accordingly, a few army officers loyal to the south mutinied in 1955. After the mutiny was suppressed, small-scale insurgencies began. By 1971, the various anti-government groups merged into the Southern Sudan Liberation Movement, which negotiated a peace agreement in 1972 after 500,000 had lost their lives. However, the peace agreement was shattered in 1983, when the president of Sudan declared the country to be an Islamic state and imposed traditional *shari'ah* law, including amputation for theft and public flogging for possession of alcohol. Accordingly, the civil war resumed, but with more ferocity than before. Some 200,000 women and children in the south were enslaved following raids from the north, and the south was on the verge of starvation. Negotiations for a peace treaty, which began as early as 1993, finally bore fruit in 2005. Under the peace agreement, monitored by a UN force, the south enjoyed regional autonomy until 2011, when a plebiscite was administered. Voters then overwhelmingly voted to create the new state of South Sudan, though border conflicts with Sudan have erupted. From 1983, the civil war is one of the most lethal internal conflicts since World War II, as 1.9 million died and 4 million were displaced.

In 2004, the first year of the Peace and Security Council's operation, AU authorized peacekeeping brigades on the part of five subregions (ECOWAS, SADC, ECCAS, COMESA, and CEN-SAD), organizations discussed below. The aim was to be able to mobilize troops in some parts of Africa if needed elsewhere. AU and the Council have had a full plate ever since. Because the UN takes such a long time to organize peacekeeping financing and troop recruitment on matters of great urgency, an AU standby force has been proposed but never authorized, so subregional forces have been encouraged.

An African Mission on the Sudan (AMIS) was sent in 2004 to monitor the ceasefire in the North–South civil war, and in 2005 AMIS II authorized some 7,000 monitoring troops for the conflict in Darfur. In both cases, AU did not take sides but simply documented truce violations and sought to provide a layer of protection to the refugees and villagers. However, in September 2005, the AU envoy to the Sudan condemned the government for re-painting Sudanese government military vehicles with AU colors and for violating the ceasefire. As a result, Khartoum has twice been denied AU's rotating chairmanship by the rest of the membership. In 2005, when the AU requested the UN to take over the operation, Sudan expressed a preference for AU troops over a UN or a NATO contingent out of fear that the latter would serve as an occupation force, even though UN forces were continuing to assist implementation of a peace agreement in South Sudan. The AU unit was extended to 2007, integrated into the UN force, and remained in Darfur as of 2013.

Indeed, AU had a very busy year in 2005. With civil war imminent in Togo, AU dispatched a special envoy to mediate between the parties in conflict. As a result, the coup leaders agreed to hold elections to reestablish constitutional rule, though election fraud may have occurred.

Also in 2005, a military coup took power in Mauritania. AU called for the "restoration of constitutional order" and suspended Mauritania's membership. Two years later, an election was held, membership was restored, but another coup occurred in 2008 and membership was suspended again. In 2009, elections were held, and Mauritania was back in the good graces of AU.

In 2005, two years after reports of serious human rights abuses, including replacing Caucasian agricultural landowners with locals without agricultural experience or training, thereby prompting thousands of starving Zimbabweans to flee to neighboring Botswana, AU took up the case of Zimbabwe, urging mediation to form a national unity government. The government in Harare, however, refused to cooperate with AU initiatives. Also in 2005, AU brokered an agreement to disarm an armed group in the Congo (Kinshasa).

In March 2007, an AU peacekeeping force arrived in Somalia, but neighboring Eritrea refused to cooperate. Two years later, AU asked the UN to impose sanctions on Eritrea for supporting Somali rebels, and sanctions were indeed voted by the UN Security Council in 2009. Eritrea then backed down.

In 2008, AU became involved in the Union of Comoros, a nation of several islands that has had about two dozen coups since independence in 1975. The pretext was that the self-proclaimed president of one of the islands refused to step down after elections in 2007. AU then sent a military force and restored constitutional order after he fled to Réunion, a French-controlled island colony, where he was arrested.

From 2008 to 2010, AU suspended Guinea after a coup. Suspension following the Niger coup in 2010 was restored in 2011. Unconstitutional government changes caused membership suspension for Madagascar in 2009, the Ivory Coast in 2010, and Guinea-Bissau in 2011, but no forces were sent.

In 2011, AU sought to mediate in the dispute between Libyan rebels and the government, opposing the no-fly zone proposal. NATO's intervention, including the no-fly zone and support for rebels precluded AU involvement.

In 2012, an AU force was deployed in Uganda to hunt for Joseph Kony and his Lord's Resistance Army. Also that year, the UN Security Council approved AU troop deployment to join Mali's army, to be trained by EU forces, in order to stop terrorist control of half the country. On the last day of 2012, the AU warned rebels to stop an armed revolt in the Central African Republic, and they agreed to peace talks on January 3, 2013.

Because of the AU structure of executive, legislature, and courts, the concept of a Union Government has been discussed. Although the idea has been studied, a United States of Africa is a long way off. The AU has close relations with other independent African organizations, including the African Commission on Human and Peoples' Rights, the African Committee of Experts on the Rights and Welfare of the Child, and various subregional organizations. They are discussed next.

• **African Commission on Human and Peoples' Rights**. The **African Charter on Human and Peoples' Rights** was signed in 1981 within the OAU framework. Although the Universal Declaration of Human Rights cryptically says that "everyone has duties to the community," the African Charter is unique in enumerating specific duties, such as the harmonious development of the family and the duty of individuals not to discriminate against one another, thereby recognizing the fundamentally communitarian nature of African society.

The Charter, ratified by all AU countries, went into force in 1986 to establish the **African Commission on Human and Peoples' Rights**, which has six functions:

o The education and information function is accomplished by promoting human rights awareness, such as by encouraging each country to set up human rights bodies.

o Institutional cooperation involves holding joint seminars with nongovernmental organizations; recent topics include refugees and contemporary forms of slavery.

o Regarding the complaint resolution function, the Commission has received more than 200 communications (complaints) from individuals, organizations, and member states, but tends to conciliate, lacking the authority to issue binding rulings.

o The quasi-legislative function is to set standards for legal principles to be adopted by member countries and to interpret the Charter on Human and Peoples' Rights in specific terms.

o Monitoring is carried out by asking member states to submit periodic reports on measures taken to implement the Charter.

○ The research function is to assign thematic issues to rapporteurs to make studies; current subjects under review are prison conditions, extrajudicial executions, and women's rights.

The Commission is located in Banjul, Gambia.

Similar to UN treaty-based committees described in Chapter 10, the African Charter on Human and Peoples' Rights requires self-compliance **reports** – initial reports two years after ratification or accession to the Charter, and two-year periodic reports thereafter. The Commission then **reviews** the reports and makes **concluding observations**. Thus far, 5 states have fully complied, but 12 have never submitted reports. Decisions of the Commission are based on the African Convention on Human and People's Rights. Some 59 fact-finding **state missions** have been conducted so far. Concluding observations on the Nigerian report for 2008–2010, for example, commended the country for promoting civil and political rights to ensure equal treatment of vulnerable groups, including the disabled and women, but urged more efforts to combat disease, illiteracy, and poverty.

Individuals may submit complaints, known as **communications**, based on Charter violations (and no other treaties). About 400 are now submitted each year. In recent years, **provisional measures** were declared in 6 cases, 6 resulted in **amicable settlements**, 74 were **decided on the merits** (ruled in favor of complainants), and the rest were either inadmissible or ran into procedural problems. In Malawi, for example, the Commission ruled in 1995 that a new democratic government was responsible to undo the wrongs committed by the previous government, notably the release of those imprisoned for up to 12 years without charges or trial, others sentenced to life imprisonment in faulty trials, and many others subjected to inhumane prison conditions.

Consistent with the Charter, the Commission has established subsidiary bodies on specific issues. The first, the Special Rapporteur on Prisons and Conditions of Detention, created in 1996, has undertaken 16 **country missions**. The remaining 14 focus on the death penalty; disabilities; economic, social, and cultural rights; freedom of expression and access to information; human rights defenders; HIV/ AIDS; indigenous populations; industrial safety; refugees, asylum seekers, internally displaced persons, migrants; torture; and women. Of the remaining 16 country missions, 14 were by the Working Group in Indigenous Populations/Communities in Africa, mostly to acquaint countries with procedures and strategies for promoting compliance.

In 1998, the AU Assembly adopted the **Protocol to the African Charter on Human and Peoples' Rights on the Establishment of an African Court on Human and Peoples' Rights**, establishing the African Court on Human and Peoples' Rights. Since the Protocol went into effect, in 2004, the Commission has had the additional responsibility of preparing cases for trial by the new court.

• **African Court on Human and Peoples' Rights**. Twenty-six countries thus far have ratified the protocol establishing the court.[10] The court, with 11 independent judges, started in Addis Ababa in 2006, and then moved in 2007 to headquarters in Arusha, Tanzania. By 2010, rules of procedure were harmonized with the Commission so that the court could begin operation.

Cases and **advisory opinions** may be referred to the court by five types of entities – the Commission, another African intergovernmental body, nongovernmental international organizations that have observer status with the Commission, by states parties to the Protocol, or by individuals in those states. Thus far, only five states have accepted jurisdiction – Burkina Faso, Ghana, Mali, Malawi, and Tanzania. Of the 24 **applications**, the court has ruled on 12 cases, though they were dismissed because they were filed against countries that have not accepted the court's jurisdiction. The first **public hearing** was in 2012, *Mkandawire v. Malawi*, a case in which a university lecturer claimed that he was improperly fired.

The court may **refer cases to the Commission**, order **provisional measures**, attempt an **amicable settlement**, or give **considerations on the merits**. The court's recommendation may include a request for **compensation** or reparations to those found to be victims of violations. The AU's Secretary-General is empowered to monitor whether the recommendation is honored. The court can invoke not only the Charter to provide a legal foundation but also can cite other human rights documents (Table 13.2).

TABLE *13.2* **HUMAN RIGHTS TREATIES PROMOTED BY THE AFRICAN UNION**

Adopted	Title	In force
1969	Convention Governing the Specific Aspects of Refugee Problems in Africa	1974
1976	Cultural Charter for Africa	1990
1977	Convention for the Elimination of Mercenaries in Africa	1985
1981	African Charter on Human and Peoples' Rights	1986
1998	• Protocol … on the Establishment of an African Court on Human and Peoples' Rights	2004
2003	• Protocol … on the Rights of Women in Africa	2005
2008	• Protocol on the Statute of the African Court of Justice and Human Rights	2012
1985	Agreement for the Establishment of the African Rehabilitation Institute	1991
1990	African Charter on the Rights and Welfare of the Child	1999
2000	Constitutive Treaty of the African Union	2001
2003	• Protocol on Amendments	
2002	Protocol Relating to the Establishment of the Peace and Security Council of the African Union	2003
2003	Protocol of the Court of Justice of the African Union	2009
2003	African Union Convention on Preventing and Combating Corruption	2003
2005	The African Union Non-Aggression and Common Defense Pact	2009
2006	African Youth Charter	2009
2006	Charter for African Cultural Renaissance	
2007	African Charter on Democracy, Elections and Governance	2012
2009	African Union Convention for the Protection and Assistance of Internally Displaced Persons in Africa (Kampala Convention)	2012
2011	African Charter on Democracy, Elections and Governance	2012

In March 2011, several Libyans complained to the commission, which in turn referred their complaints to the court. As a result, the court ordered, as provisional measures, that the government "must immediately refrain from any action that would cause loss of life or violate physical integrity of persons … ." Although Libya was ordered to report on compliance within 15 days, the request was ignored, and the bloody civil war continued.

• **African Committee of Experts on the Rights and Welfare of the Child.** In 1999, when the **African Charter on the Rights and Welfare of the Child** went into force, states were required to submit triennial **implementation reports** to the African Committee of Experts on the Rights and Welfare of the Child in Addis Ababa. The committee is a treaty-based organ separate from the AU. Among the Committee's current priorities is the elimination of polio from Africa. Forty-six African countries have ratified thus far.

The experts have focused on several thematic concerns. They are violence against children; education of children; juvenile justice; child participation; early childhood integrated development; child survival; orphans and other vulnerable children; family responsibilities and child responsibilities; registration of children; child abuse and exploitation; children in armed conflicts and natural disasters; and refugee and displaced children.

In 2005, the Committee undertook an **investigation mission** to Northern Uganda, where child soldier recruitment takes place. Of two **communications** received thus far, the one acted upon was filed on behalf of Nubians in Kenya, alleging mistreatment. The Committee found, in 2011, the complaint valid and made **recommendations** that all Nubians born in Kenya should be allowed citizenship and that they should be granted the right to education and health care on a nondiscriminatory basis.

• **Economic Community of West African States** (ECOWAS). In 1975, ECOWAS was established by the Treaty of Lagos primarily for economic cooperation. Revised in 1993, the Treaty of ECOWAS identifies 11 principles, among which are (1) "human and peoples' rights," (2) "economic and social justice and popular participation in development," and (3) "promotion and consolidation of a democratic system of governance … ." The secretariat, renamed the commission in 2005, is in Abuja, Nigeria. There are seven administrative units, including the **Human Development and Gender Department**, which operates programs on child protection, health, human trafficking, and labor laws, including social security.

In 1981, ECOWAS members signed a Protocol on Mutual Assistance in Defense, establishing an Allied Armed Force of the Community. In 1990, when the 14 members[11] agreed that ethnic conflicts inside West African countries were so endemic that an ECOWAS Cease-Fire Monitoring Group (ECOMOG) was needed as a standby force, ECOMOG was first sent to Liberia after a coup and stayed until free elections in 1998.

In 1991, member countries agreed on the **Declaration of Political Principles** to uphold democracies in the region. In 1994, ECOMOG was assigned to Sierra Leone and assisted in bringing about a ceasefire by 1999. ECOMOG also went to Guinea-Bissau to put down a rebellion in 1998 and to Sierra Leone in 1998–1999 for a ceasefire and free elections. The interventions were sometimes controversial, however, because Nigerians were the primary troops, and the interventions have tended to take sides, so Nigeria decided not to do so in the future.

In 1999, the **Protocol Relating to the Mechanism for Conflict Prevention, Management, Resolution, Peace-keeping and Security** established the Authority, the Mediation and Security Council, and the Executive Secretariat to assist ECOMOG. ECOMOG then went to Guinea in 2001.

Further, the **Protocol on Democracy and Good Governance** of 2001 provided comprehensive nondiscriminatory rules regarding elections, empowered ECOWAS to monitor elections, and urged countries to fulfill the basic needs of their people, including civilian control over the military, the right to education, children's rights, the development of culture, elimination of poverty, rights of corporations and trade unions, press freedom, the promotion of social dialog, and "laws that are in conformity with the provisions on human rights." The 2001 Protocol requires each country to report any human rights violation to the ECOWAS Executive Secretariat and permits ECOWAS, in turn, to impose sanctions on any country where there is a "massive violation of human rights."

ECOMOG returned to Sierra Leone in 2002. ECOWAS sent election observers to Togo in 2002 and to Guinea-Bissau in 2005. ECOWAS also brokered a truce between rival factions in Togo in 2005. On account of coups and election irregularities, some ECOWAS members have been suspended – Guinea in 2008, Niger in 2009, and Sierra Leone in 2010. In October 2012, ECOWAS agreed to send troops to help Mali combat terrorists that took over the northern half of the country and successfully asked the UN Security Council to approve, though French troops arrived in early 2013 before an ECOWAS force could be assembled.

In 1993, the **Community Court of Justice** was created by a protocol that was included in the Revised ECOWAS Treaty of the Community. The court began in 1996, when the agreement went into force. The court's jurisdiction is on interstate disputes over the Revised Treaty as well as general matters of international law, including human rights. The court can issue advisory opinions.

ECOWAS has also created several specialized agencies, including the **Gender Development Center**, and the **West African Health Organization**. In 2005, the ECOWAS **Committee on Women and Child's Rights** called for stiffer restrictions against small arms producers.

Only eight ECOWAS member countries (Benin, Burkina Faso, Guinea-Bissau, the Ivory Coast, Mali, Niger, Sénégal, Togo) have agreed to the West African Economic and Monetary Union. ECOWAS members Cape Verde, Gambia, Ghana, Guinea, Liberia, Nigeria, and Sierra Leone, remain outside the Union. However, the countries are further divided into currency areas, with former French colonies still retaining the franc, whereas former English-speaking colonies plan to adopt the ECOWAS common currency by 2015.

• **Economic Community of Central African States** (ECCAS). Although formed in 1983 as a successor to three earlier organizations, ECCAS was inactive from 1992 to 1999 because of the labyrinthine conflict involving Central African states that produced nearly three million deaths. Members merged from the Customs and Economic Union of Africa (Cameroon, Central African Republic, Chad, Gabon, Equatorial Guinea, Republic of Congo) with the Economic Community of the Great Lakes (Democratic Republic of the Congo, Burundi, Rwanda) plus

São Tomé and Príncipe. Rwanda suspended itself in 2001–2002 and left ECCAS in 1999 for COMESA (discussed below), whereupon Angola, which for a time fought on the opposite side of Rwanda, joined ECCAS.

The **Treaty Establishing the Economic Community of Central African States** primarily sets up a framework to improve economic and social development, leading to an eventual common market. However, Article 34 allows sanctions in the form of trade restrictions against any country in the interest of "the protection of human, animal or plant health or life or the protection of public morality," "the protection of national treasures of artistic or archaeological value," or "control of nuclear materials, radioactive products or any other equipment used in the development or exploitation of nuclear energy." Article 43 mandates cooperation in food production "to raise the standard of living of rural populations." Articles 60–62 pledge cooperation in cultural, educational, and social affairs.

In 1999, ECCAS members agreed to form the **Council for Peace and Security in Central Africa**, including an early-warning system and a multinational military force to handle conflicts in the region. The organization then participated in negotiations to end the war in the Democratic Republic of the Congo in 2000. In 2002, ECCAS agreed to set up the Network of Parliamentarians of Central Africa, the Defense and Security Commission, Multinational Force of Central Africa, and the Early Warning Mechanism of Central Africa. After mediating an end to the coup in São Tomé and Príncipe in 2003, ECCAS set up a monitoring unit. The military force was first deployed in 2005 to implement the peace agreement in the Congo.

In 2002, meanwhile, ECCAS launched the **Center for Human Rights and Democracy in Central Africa** at Yaoundé, Cameroon. In 2004, a declaration on gender equality was adopted by the ECCAS summit conference, and a meeting of agriculture ministers approved a program on food security.

In 2006, ECCAS monitored elections in the Democratic Republic of the Congo, Gabon, and São Tomé and Príncipe. In 2007 and 2008, ECCAS was on the scene during elections in Angola, Cameroon, and the Republic of Congo. In 2010, ECCAS decided to subcontract future election observation to a Johannesburg-based nongovernmental organization, the Electoral Institute for Sustainable Democracy in Africa. The same body is under contract with the AU and other African organizations.

- **Community of Sahel-Saharan States** (CEN-SAD). With the leadership of Muammar Gaddafi (1942–2011), six countries bordering the Sahara (Burkina Faso, Chad, Libya, Mali, Niger, Sudan) in 1998 formed an organization not only to promote economic integration but also to confer equal rights to citizens of one member country while living or working in another. At the summit the following year, the Central African Republic and Eritrea signed the Tripoli Treaty. Twenty more members joined by 2009,[12] some of which belong to other subregional bodies. The headquarters is in Tripoli.

One of the advisory organs, located in Bamako, Mali, is the **Economic, Social and Cultural Council**, which consists of four commissions, including the **Education, Cultural, Sciences, Information and Rural Development Commission**; the **Social Affairs, Health and Environment Commission**; and two commissions relating to the main purpose, an economic community. Health ministers met together in 1999 to forge important links.

The first effort, financed by Libya, was a regional food security program in light of the growing problem of desertification. In 2002, CEN-SAD sent election observers to Togo along with the AU and ECOWAS and offered to do so in later years.

Unrest in the Central African Republic prompted a CEN-SAD troop deployment to support the government from 2001 to 2003. But Libyan troops, then central to the unit, may be less available today for external operations.

Although economic goals are primary, since CEN-SAD seeks to be a building block for an African common market or free trade area, political stability was a particular priority during the Conference of Leaders and Heads of State meeting in 2009: Gaddafi sought to mediate regarding the conflict in Darfur that spilled from Sudan into Chad, the conflict between Eritrea and Ethiopia, and the Mali–Niger conflict. CEN-SAD dispatched an election observer mission to observe elections in unsettled Guinea-Bissau; expressed sympathy for child, elderly, and female victims of indiscriminate violence in Somalia; and urged Guinea and Mauritania to hold free and fair elections.

Despite the death of Gaddafi in 2011, the organization, sometimes called the Community of Sahelo, continues. CEN-SAD foreign ministers, meeting in 2012, contemplated reorganization and a refocus on terrorism.

- **Common Market for Eastern and Southern Africa** (COMESA). In 1994, primarily to expand a free trade area from a preferential trade area that 14 countries (Burundi, Comoros, Democratic Republic of the Congo, Djibouti, Ethiopia, Kenya, Madagascar, Malawi, Mauritius, Rwanda, Sudan, Swaziland, Zambia, Zimbabwe) set up in 1981, COMESA seeks cooperative economic development. Five current member countries joined later – Egypt (1999), Eritrea (1994), Libya (2005), Seychelles (2001), and South Sudan (2011). Although five additional countries signed the Treaty Establishing the Common Market for Eastern and Southern Africa in 1994 to join, they dropped out later to become members of other trade blocs – Angola (2007), Lesotho (1997), Mozambique (1997), Namibia (2004), and Tanzania (2000). The secretariat is in Lusaka, Zambia.

The treaty establishing COMESA established 12 technical committees, one of which is on **Labor, Human Resources and Social and Cultural Affairs**. Article 155 stresses the need to include women in business and development planning, a goal reiterated in 2002 by a formal **Declaration on the COMESA Gender Policy**. Created in Zimbabwe during 1993, the **Federation of National Associations of Women in Business in Common Market for Eastern and Southern Africa** is considered a COMESA body; all 19 COMESA countries are members.

In 2005, COMESA foreign ministers agreed to set up an African Standby Brigade. When the AU asked for troops to serve in Darfur, COMESA's force was able to respond. In 2011, the **COMESA Observer Mission** monitored the election in Zambia and, in 2012, the elections in Kenya and Zimbabwe.

Nine member states formed a free trade area (FTA) in 2000 (Djibouti, Egypt, Kenya, Madagascar, Malawi, Mauritius, Sudan, Zambia, Zimbabwe). Rwanda and Burundi joined the FTA in 2004, the Comoros and Libya in 2006. In 2008, COMESA agreed to an expanded free trade zone including members of two other African trade blocs, discussed below – the East African Community (EAC) and the Southern Africa Development Community (SADC).

- **East African Community** (EAC). Several economic antecedent organizations in the East African subregion were superseded when the treaty establishing the EAC was adopted in 1999 by Kenya, Tanzania, and Uganda. Burundi and Rwanda joined in 2007. According to the founding **Treaty for the Establishment of the East African Community**, cooperation is contemplated in "political, economic, social and cultural fields, research and technology, defence, security and legal and judicial affairs," including gender mainstreaming. The basic principles include "good governance including adherence to the principles of democracy, the rule of law, accountability, transparency, social justice, equal opportunities, gender equality, as well as the recognition, promotion and protection of human and peoples' rights." Although economic aspects dominate the agreement, the treaty has a provision for cooperation in matters of children, civil society, cultural activities, the disabled, education, the elderly, health, indigenous languages, poverty alleviation, and enhancing the role of women in development.

Headquartered in Arusha, Tanzania, EAC has established programs in culture, disabilities, health, human resource development, social welfare, and women in business. In 2004, EAC sent peacekeepers to Darfur. From 2005, annual joint exercises have been held by the military forces of EAC states in the context of the East African Community Memorandum of Understanding on Cooperation in Defense. EAC military efforts have dealt with piracy off the coast of Somalia, cutting in half the number of incidents in 2012.

Because of concern over the security of voting in Kenya in 2012, representatives from the East African Legislative Assembly and the EAC secretariat undertook a pre-election visit to make recommendations. As in the case of ECCAS, the Electoral Institute for Sustainable Democracy in Africa also took part. By the end of 2012, principles for election monitoring were adopted in draft form.

The primary goal is economic. Members have agreed to a customs union (in 2004) and a common market (in 2010). With the creation of the Community's **East African Court of Justice** and its **East African Legislative Assembly**, key institutions are in place for a contemplated East African political union. The court has jurisdiction over fundamental breaches under international law.

- **Southern African Development Community** (SADC). In 1980, the Southern African Development Co-ordination Conference (SADCC) was formed in part to reduce economic dependence on *apartheid* South Africa and to promote democracy, human rights, and the rule of law. The first goal of the original members (Angola, Botswana, Lesotho, Malawi, Mozambique, Swaziland, Tanzania, Zambia, Zimbabwe) was the dismantling of the system of racial separation practiced by the Pretoria government.

SADC, which superseded SADCC in 1992, now applies more broadly. The founding **Treaty of the South African Development Community** of 1992 identifies five major principles:

- "sovereign equality" of members
- "solidarity, peace, and security"
- "human rights, democracy, and the rule of law"
- "equity, balance, and mutual benefit"
- "peaceful settlement of disputes."

The Secretariat is in Garbonne, Botswana.

SADC began with the same SADCC countries plus Namibia, which became independent in 1990. South Africa joined upon holding its first post-*apartheid* election in 1994. Mauritius was admitted in 1995. Seychelles was a member from 1997 to 2004 but rejoined in 2008. Madagascar became a member in 2009 but was suspended because of a coup in 2009.

In 2003, the **Charter of the Fundamental Social Rights of SADC** was adopted. Among the rights specified are the following:

- Freedom of association and collective bargaining
- Equal treatment of men and women
- Protection of children, the disabled, and the elderly
- Improved living and working conditions
- A living wage and social security
- Occupational safety and worker training.

Six Cluster Committees are subsidiary to the SADC Council of Ministers. One consists of **Ministers Responsible for Social and Human Development and Special Programs**, which focuses on education, employment and gender, labor, and HIV/AIDS.

Several projects exist in the field of human resource development, including the establishment of labor, public health, and welfare standards. In 1997, the SADC **Declaration on Gender and Development** set a goal of at least 30 percent females in political and decision-making structures by 2005. Accordingly, the Secretariat set up a **Department of Strategic Planning, Gender and Development and Policy Harmonization** to promote gender mainstreaming within SADC programming.

In 1994, the organization agreed to establish a regional peacekeeping force. In 1995, the **Inter-State Defense and Security Committee** was established for that end. The SADC force was first deployed in 1998 to quell unrest in Lesotho after violence erupted over a disputed election. SADC sought to negotiate an end to the conflict in the Congo (Kinshasa) in 1998 and the Central African Republic in 1999, respectively, though diplomacy proved difficult. Multinational peacekeeping exercises have been held. In 2003, the Mutual Defense Pact was adopted to provide treaty guarantees, and in 2007 the SADC Brigade first went on parade at a ceremony in Zambia.

Another activity has been to send **Forum Observer Missions** to monitor elections in Zambia (2001), Zimbabwe (2002), and South Africa (2004). Despite criticism from the head of the SADC Parliamentary Forum regarding undemocratic practices in Zimbabwe's 2002 election, delegates to the 2003 SADC conference applauded President Robert Mugabe (1924–) of Zimbabwe, whose regime has been boycotted economically by the EU.

Five SADC member countries (Botswana, Lesotho, Namibia, South Africa, Swaziland) embarked on the SADC free trade area in 2000 with the goal of economic integration. All the other countries signed up later except Angola, Democratic Republic of the Congo, and Seychelles. In 2008, the SADC free trade area agreed to link with EAC and COMESA to form the African Free Trade Zone.

MULTICONTINENTAL ORGANIZATIONS

Several organizations headquartered in Europe have members outside the continent, notably the North Atlantic Treaty Organization (NATO) and the Organization for Economic Cooperation and Development (OECD).[13] With the Singapore secretariat, the Asia Pacific Economic Cooperation (APEC) organization is also multicontinental. Several intergovernmental organizations deal with the Antarctic. Two other organizations have brought three continents together:

•   **Non-Aligned Movement** (NAM). As the Cold War developed in Asia amid Western efforts in the 1950s to sign up countries to contain communist powers into the South-East Asia Collective Defense Treaty of 1954, India and Indonesia were appalled that their economic development needs were being ignored. Accordingly, they hosted a 29-nation conference in 1955 at Bandung, Indonesia, to launch a nonaligned movement, which then gave diplomatic support to many more countries seeking to avoid militarization throughout Asia and Africa. Regardless, the South-East Asia Treaty Organization emerged in 1955, seeking to protect Indochina from communist aggression. In 1961, the organization was formalized at a meeting in Belgrade. Today, some 120 countries claim NAM membership, which requires acceptance of the Bandung Principles:

  ○   Respect for fundamental human rights and for the purposes and principles of the UN Charter
  ○   Sovereignty and territorial integrity of all nations
  ○   Recognition of the movements for national independence
  ○   Recognition of the equality of all races and the equality of all nations, large and small
  ○   Nonintervention and noninterference in the internal affairs of another country
  ○   Right of each nation to defend itself singly or collectively
  ○   Refraining from acts or threats of aggression or the use of force against the territorial integrity or political independence of any country
  ○   Peaceful settlement of international disputes
  ○   Promotion of mutual interests and cooperation
  ○   Respect for justice and international obligations.

•   **BRICS.** The rapidly advancing economic powers of Brazil, Russia, India, and China found common interest in 2009, when their government leaders held a summit on their future in the world economy, dominated in their judgment by OECD. Reacting to the economic meltdown within OECD countries during 2008, their aim was to provide a more equitable world economic order. Known as the BRICS after the addition of South Africa in 2010, they have held annual summit meetings. In 2011, they formed the BRICS Forum, and BRICS finance ministers began to discuss an intergovernmental bank as an alternative to the World Bank Group to raise infrastructure investment funds. They are considering a capitalization either with equal shares for the five countries or shares proportional to the relative size of their economies, similar to the World Bank. In 2013, the BRICS Forum in Durban, South Africa, held a meeting with African countries to forge a cooperative spirit based on "democracy and equality" that would challenge the ossified World Bank as a source of infrastructure investment funds. Although China will be the dominant economic player within BRICS, policy making has been collegial.

CONCLUSION

Regional intergovernmental organizations outside Europe differ considerably in the scope of human rights activity, but the following important generalizations apply:

- Some African organizations actively pressure countries to improve human rights by using military means.
- Multi-purpose regional bodies are more effective than single-purpose organizations in regard to civil and political rights, while the opposite is the case for economic and social rights.
- Quiet diplomacy is more common among regional organizations than in the klieg lights of UN deliberations.
- Some regional human rights organizations have successfully prompted members to change their laws or to reverse their actions in order to conform to higher standards.
- Nevertheless, there is room for improvement in regional organizations, many of which need to go beyond mere verbal statements on the subject of human rights and the establishment of structures that lack operational functions.

For many years, some UN officials looked upon regional efforts as breakaway movements, somehow subversive to the world body. Meanwhile, many countries looked upon the UN as too distant from their concerns, so they established regional bodies in which there would be sufficient cultural affinity to operate in a manner more in keeping with national traditions. But from the 1980s, the UN recognized the value of regional organizations. Thus, regional organizations play an essential role in regard to international human rights today.

DISCUSSION TOPIC 13.1 WHICH PARTS OF THE DEVELOPING WORLD HAVE THE BEST AND WORST RECORDS IN DEALING WITH HUMAN RIGHTS?

Comparing Africa, the Americas, Asia, the Middle East, and the Pacific, which region has the best record on human rights? The worst? Why? What could be done to improve human rights in any or all regions outside Europe?

CHAPTER 14

New Dimensions and Challenges

Many dimensions of human rights have been discussed thus far, but not all. History and statistical evidence prove that mainstream groups get human rights on mainstream issues before anyone else. Indeed, as civil rights progress for ethnic and racial minorities occurred in the 1960s, the American Civil Liberties Union (ACLU) discovered that several types of persons had fallen through the cracks, excluded from enjoying the rights of free speech, free press, and the like. Such persons, who together constitute a numerical majority, were still hobbled by restrictions imposed by the dominant group in American society. Accordingly, ACLU began a series of publications under the title *The Rights of* — focusing on aliens, chronically and acutely ill persons, crime victims, the disabled, former offenders, gays and lesbians, hospital patients, military personnel, the poor, prisoners, refugees, single people, suspects, tribes and native peoples, women, and young people. A volume on the rights of adoptees is lacking, and other categories could doubtless be added. Currently, ACLU has discontinued the series, which is out of print. Although some issues on their list have been covered in the chapters above, others have not.

At least three issues are increasingly emerging as important aspects of international human rights that were long left at the margin during human rights discussions – the rights of gays, lesbians, bisexuals, and the transgendered; environmental rights; and even perhaps "animal rights," that is, the obligations of humans toward animals. Since the moral claims of today often become the rights of tomorrow, this chapter explores all three topics and concludes after a discussion on the efficacy of the rights-based approach.

GAY AND LESBIAN RIGHTS

In 2003, Sandra Day O'Connor (1930–), while US Supreme Court Justice, was asked what "the burning issue might be for the twenty-first century." Her response, which astonished many, was the effort to define the scope of gay rights, which she identified as "the first important civil rights struggle of the twenty-first century." That struggle began earlier, of course, but the chronicle of how gay rights have been recognized contemporaneously may be considered a paradigm, greatly accelerated in time and place, of the human rights movement itself.

Sexual activity among persons of the same gender has taken place for millennia, sometimes unremarkably, as when prosperous Athenian men sponsored the training of handsome young athletes for the original Olympic Games with an expectation that sexual favors might be exchanged. Although church records demonstrate that Christian religious leaders have sometimes blessed same-sex relationships,[1] those who engaged in such practices were persecuted during the Spanish Inquisition from 1478, though Leonardo da Vinci (1452–1519) and Michelangelo Buonarroti (1475–1564) are also remembered as men who enjoyed the company of younger men during the European Renaissance. Male concubines were a part of the royal courts in some Asian countries, a practice continued by some of the original peoples who left Asia to populate Polynesia. From ancient times, Hindu priests in India have performed same-sex rituals, and some still do today.

Taboos on sexual activity have also existed, especially when supported by religious authorities. Indeed, Jewish and Christian scriptures condemned men who dressed as women to be available as prostitutes at the temples of fertility religions, where married men presumably could overcome sexual dysfunctions and return to their wives with renewed virility. The debatable belief that such prohibitions apply to contemporary gays and lesbians has been a major source of persecution of sexual minorities.

Masculinized Jeanne d'Arc (1412–1431) was accepted by the French army as a leader in battling the English, whereupon the English placed a handsome bounty on her head. In 1430, she was captured by a Frenchman, turned over to a priest who was in the pay of the English, and then condemned to death. There is some unsubstantiated speculation that Jeanne was in fact a man (Jean d'Arc) dressed as a woman rather than the reverse.

Transgendered persons have sometimes played nonsexual roles in society, notably the effeminate Bugi men who dressed as women so that order could be maintained among the women left ashore while Bugi fishermen and pirates were at sea in Southeast Asian waters. The *Kamasutra* (300 BCE) classifies humans into three sexes and accepts attraction between persons of the same gender. In the performance of the plays of Shakespeare (1564–1616), men took the parts of women and then shed women's clothes to re-appear as men off stage.

In 1533, Henry VIII (1491–1509) promulgated the Buggery Law, which provided the death penalty for anal intercourse between two men or between a man and an animal. The term "bugger" was slang for what the English perceived as a practice among Bulgarians of demasculinizing men by raping them. Britain's 13 colonies in

North America adopted the same law, later known as the sodomy law, and Britain imposed its peculiar obsession in India and other colonies. Nevertheless, references to male prostitution and buggery as common phenomena are found in the writings of Michael Drayton (1563–1631) and Samuel Pepys (1633–1703).

The first work censored by the English government on grounds of "obscenity," *Sodom, or The Quintessence of Debauchery* (1684), by John Wilmot (1647–1680), dealt with sex between persons of the same gender. In 1698, Captain Edward Rigby was the first to be tried for sodomy; in his defense he claimed to be an eyewitness to same-sex lovemaking involving Peter the Great (1672–1725), and he evidently repeated a false rumor about the same conduct on the part of Louis XIV (1638–1715). Publicity about his trial throughout Europe encouraged police to engage in entrapment of men who frequented male brothels, parks, pubs, and similar meeting places. Although convicted, Rigby escaped to France without serving a sentence.

Meanwhile, women had liaisons with one another over the ages with hardly a negative comment until some unmarried women were identified as witches and burned at the stake. Sometimes underneath the pyre were effeminate men, who were burned before the flames reached the so-called witches (thus, the origin of the term "faggot"). The witch-hunting craze swept through Europe and North America from 1450–1750, though rumors about sexual proclivities were only one reason for the practice.

The right to have sex with adults of the same gender was not a part of the early development of the concept of human rights. In 1862, however, Karl Heinrich Ulrichs (1825–1895), declaring that he was a Uranian, provided legal and moral support to a man arrested for having sex with another man in Germany and continued to argue for decriminalization of sexual behavior among consenting adults; his books, however, were confiscated and banned. In 1869, Austrian writer Károly-Mária Kertbeny (1824–1882) coined the term "homosexual." Ulrichs and Kertbeny, thus, opened discussion on the subject as gay and lesbian subcultures became more visible in the cities that grew around the increasing numbers of factories of the Industrial Revolution.

The first use of the word "gay," to mean a male who enjoys the company of other males in a sociosexual sense, emerged in 1889. In the Cleveland Street scandal, a male prostitute in a London brothel described himself as "gay" while testifying in court to defend himself against prosecution under an 1885 British law banning prostitution and the procuring of sex by one male from another.

In 1891, Oscar Wilde (1854–1900) published *The Picture of Dorian Gray*, a novel that was condemned for its homoerotic theme. Although bisexual, shortly after his novel appeared, Wilde befriended 22-year old Lord Alfred Douglas (1870–1945), and they became lovers. Alfred's father, John Sholto Douglas (1844–1900), soon demanded that his son must end his "intimacy" with Wilde and engaged in a campaign against Wilde for his "indecency." In 1895, Wilde sued Douglas for libel but dropped the charges when Douglas threatened to bring to court young male witnesses who were prepared to testify that they had sex with him. Then Wilde was put on trial for sodomy by some of his former sex partners. Rather than fleeing England, as some expected, Wilde decided to appear in court, and he was convicted. He then served two years in prison, became a social outcast, and the publicity generated negative attitudes toward what was thereby revealed as a secret community of males who had social and sexual relations with one another.

The quest to recognize the right of adults to have sex with consenting same-sex partners gained some momentum when John Addington Symonds (1840–1893) published *A Problem in Modern Ethics* (1891). In 1897, Magnus Hirschfeld (1868–1935) set up a foundation in Berlin to promote greater understanding of the human sexual condition and to decriminalize sexual practices involving consenting males.

The first large-scale gay rights activism occurred in Berlin during the 1920s, and in 1924 the Chicago-based Society for Human Rights became the earliest known gay rights organization in the United States. However, the German gay rights movement ended when Nazis persecuted gays and sent them to concentration camps along with Jews and others.

During World War II, sexual liaisons formed among some American soldiers, many of whom stayed in the larger cities, notably London, New York, and San Francisco, before and after their discharge from the armed services in 1945. Those who were identifiably gays and lesbians increasingly appeared in public on their way to social occasions, such as "gay bars" and public parks, though gay pubs existed in England more than a half-century earlier.

In 1948, Alfred Kinsey (1894–1956) published *Sexual Behavior in the Human Male*, one finding of which was that homosexual behavior was a more common practice than previously thought, with 10 percent of the population engaging in sex with members of the same sex at least once in their lives. Since gays were closeted and unwelcome in the larger society, they were often subjected to blackmail and thought to be easily forced to engage in treasonous activity. In 1953, President Dwight Eisenhower (1890–1969) issued Executive Order 10450 barring gay men and lesbians from all federal jobs, and many state and local governments and private corporations did so as well. The Federal Bureau of Investigation began to compile information about activities of homosexuals so that they could be rejected if they ever applied for government employment.

Problems encountered by nonheterosexuals after World War II, thus, came to the fore at a time when the defeat of militarism and racism was inspiring democracies to advance human rights. Among the most common concerns of gays are protection from violence and freedom from discrimination, issues in common with minorities and women. In addition, nonheterosexuals sought a right to privacy so that they might associate together in public and engage in private sexual activity without fear of prosecution for criminal offenses.

The silence of traditional international law on the subject of sexual lifestyles has meant that progress began within particular countries as a spillover from generic concerns about human rights. Gays and lesbians have challenged various unfriendly laws, although political authorities have not responded uniformly.

In 1954, Reading University Vice Chancellor Sir John Wolfenden (1906–1985), whose son was gay, was asked to chair an investigation of British laws on homosexuality after several prosecutions of gays received wide publicity. The resulting Wolfenden Report of 1957, which did not condone homosexuality, said that homosexuality was not a psychiatric illness and should be decriminalized. The first positive response occurred in 1962, when Illinois became the first state in the United States to decriminalize private sex between consenting adults, male or female. Britain followed suit in 1967. In 1973, the American Psychiatric Association removed homosexuality from its list of diseases.

On July 4, 1965, some 40 gays and lesbians held a demonstration in front of the Liberty Bell at Independence Hall in Philadelphia, and soon the demonstrations expanded to New York and Washington, DC. In 1967, some 200 gays demonstrated on Sunset Boulevard in the Silverlake district of Los Angeles to protest police raids that occurred at two gay bars on New Year's Eve. In response to the 1967 demonstration, the Reverend Troy Perry (1940–) put an ad in a gay newspaper in Los Angeles during 1968, asking Christian gays to meet at his residence. He soon founded the Universal Fellowship of Metropolitan Community Churches (MCC), a denomination of 172 churches that now flourishes in 37 countries around the world and consecrates holy unions between gay and lesbian partners.

HISTORIC EVENT 14.1 THE STONEWALL RIOTS (1969)

After World War II, police throughout the United States were accustomed to disrupting gay bars by entering on the phony pretext of checking the identification of patrons so that they could fine the owners for serving alcohol to minors or knowingly serving liquor to gays. Police also entered public restrooms to entrap gays by exposing their genitals and arresting men who showed some interest. However, in 1966 the New York City police chief adopted a policy against entrapment as well as against bar shutdowns on the basis of the clientele. Nevertheless, on June 28, 1969, the police unexpectedly raided a Greenwich Village gay bar, Stonewall Inn, which was frequented by nonwhite drag queens. Usually, gays quietly left while such raids were conducted, but on that night the patrons objected, attacked police, and soon outnumbered them. Several gays were severely beaten. Demonstrations during two subsequent nights attracted "gay power" signs on the nearby buildings, and the activist gay liberation movement had been launched. Gay Pride marches began in several cities in 1970 and quickly spread throughout the world.

The Stonewall Riot of 1969 did more to launch the gay rights movement than any other event. In 1970, some 5,000 gays and lesbians participated in a Gay Pride march in New York, a practice that soon extended throughout the country and the world. Various progressive cities then began to outlaw discrimination based on sexual orientation, a bill was introduced in Congress to ban sexual orientation discrimination in 1974, and in 1975 the US Civil Service Commission rescinded the prohibition on employing homosexuals in most government jobs.

In 1978, the gay and lesbian rights movement went international with the founding in Brussels of the **International Lesbian and Gay Association** (ILGA). In contrast with developments in the United States, most initial ILGA members were women. ILGA tried to become a recognized nongovernmental organization with the UN Economic and Social Council and was accepted in 1993.

The sudden appearance of several deaths from rare conditions in 1981 among gay men in London, Los Angeles, and San Francisco was yet another significant event. While alternative explanations abounded for the disease, association with gays added a stigma to it, as well as to the practice of male homosexuality itself, despite later evidence of a serious epidemic among heterosexuals in Africa. There was uncertainty what to call the disease until the term Acquired Immune Deficiency Syndrome (AIDS) was coined in 1982. Some called for isolation of those with AIDS, anti-gay violence surged, and gay rights agitation demanded government support for medical research. The hysteria served notice that discrimination against gays needed to be addressed as a life-and-death concern.

After the culprit was determined in 1984 to be a virus, later called the human immunodeficiency virus (HIV), antibody screening blood tests began in 1985. That was the year when film star Rock Hudson (1925–1985) died from complications of HIV that had progressed to AIDS.

Since previously obtained blood transfusions could transmit the disease, those outside the gay community were at risk, too. In 1984, after teenage hemophiliac Ryan White (1971–1990) was diagnosed with terminal AIDS from a blood transfusion, parents and teachers in his hometown of Kokomo, Indiana, at first did not want him to return to school and then boycotted the school when he returned. Outrage over his mistreatment prompted Congress to pass the Ryan White Care Act four months after his death in 1990 in order to improve availability of care for low-income, uninsured, and underinsured victims of AIDS and their families.

Then, gay athletes Magic Johnson (1959–), in 1991, and Arthur Ashe, Jr (1943–1993), in 1992, held press conferences to urge more research. In 1994, a lesbian with asymptomatic HIV went for dental treatment but was refused service. When the case reached the US Supreme Court, *Bragdon v. Abbott* (524US524), the ruling was that the refusal violated the Americans with Disabilities Act of 1990. By then, the furor died down as, in 1995, the first medicines emerged to end the AIDS death sentence. HIV is now a chronic medical condition treated with a regimen of two or three daily pills, less bother than those with some forms of diabetes. But AIDS cases continue to occur where such medicines are unavailable, so funding to treat HIV in Africa is now a high priority of the World Health Organization. In 2012, testing revealed that one of the pills regularly taken by those with HIV may prove to be the equivalent of a vaccine, if taken daily.

The freedom to practice homosexual acts and live in communities with gays and lesbians in Argentina, Australia, Europe, and the United States has attracted persons from other parts of the world to live, visit, and work, sometimes under the watchful eyes of consular officials and other nationals from their own countries. Fearing prosecution for their preferences, they have sought legal recourse to remain in gay-friendly communities after expiration of their visas. Accordingly, the nongovernmental **International Gay and Lesbian Human Rights Commission** (IGLHRC) began as an asylum project in New York during 1990. Today, IGLHRC has broadened concerns to a full range of gender-related issues, including HIV/AIDS, with offices around the world.

In 1991, **Amnesty International** broadened its "prisoner of conscience" concept to include persecuted gays. After women from 25 countries testified before the **Global Tribunal on Violation of Women's Human Rights**, as organized by the Center for Women's Global Leadership, the first mention of "sexual rights" occurred during the **Vienna Conference on Human Rights** in 1993, though the issue was rape – the right to be free from sexual violence. The tribunal appeared again in 1995, before the World Conference on Women, which in turn accepted the concept of the "right to sexuality." **Human Rights Watch** began reporting on issues involving gays and lesbians in 1996 after *Romer v. Colorado*, when the US Supreme Court ruled that voters in Colorado could not adopt a constitutional amendment that would prohibit counties and cities from passing nondiscrimination laws involving gays and lesbians. The cities of Aspen, Boulder, and Denver had done so earlier.

Whereas some countries have granted more rights to gays and lesbians in recent years, the same governments often were merely dismantling barriers that they earlier had erected in the first place. Not all countries have used government to regulate morals, preferring to allow society to do so instead. From 2000, to seek membership in the EU, a state must respect sexual orientation rights, as established by a directive following adoption of the Maastricht Treaty and the evolving jurisprudence being established by European institutions (the *acquis communautaire*). Indeed, the EU established the **European Institute for Gender Equality** at Vilnius, Lithuania, in 2007 to collect information in order to make policy recommendations. Accordingly, Europe leads the world among countries that provide a variety of rights to gays, lesbians, bisexuals, and the transgendered (Table 14.1).

In 2006, to address issues regarding sexual orientation and gender identity, a meeting was held at Gadjah Maha University, in Jogjakarta, Indonesia, involving the International Committee of Jurists, the International Service for Human Rights, and international human rights legal experts from around the world The result was the adoption of the **Jogjakarta Principles**, consisting of the following provisions:

- Nondiscrimination, including sexual reassignment
- Right to personal security
- Economic, social, and cultural rights
- Freedom of association and expression
- Freedom of asylum and movement
- Rights of family life
- Rights of accountability and redress.

Notably lacking is the right to marry.

In response, various UN treaty-based committees (CAT, CEDAW, CRC, CECSR, HRC) began to review human rights compliance records based on the Jogjakarta Principles. The Committee on the Elimination of All Forms of Discrimination Against Women (CEDAW), for example, condemned Uganda in 2010 for passage in 2009 of the Anti-Homosexual Bill, for exclusion of gays and lesbians from Ugandan Equal Opportunities Commission reporting, and for violence following publication of a magazine headlined "Hang Them" that listed known gays and lesbians in the country. In 2012, when the Human Rights Committee

TABLE 14.1   RIGHTS OF GAYS, LESBIANS, BISEXUALS, AND THE TRANSGENDERED

Issue	Countries providing protections
Antidiscrimination constitutions/laws protecting gays, lesbians, bisexuals	Albania, Andorra, Argentina, Australia (5 states), Austria, Belgium, Bolivia, Bosnia and Herzegovina, Botswana, Brazil, Bulgaria, Canada, Chile, Costa Rica, Croatia, Cuba, Cyprus, Czech Republic, Denmark, Ecuador, El Salvador, Estonia, Finland, France, Georgia, Germany, Greece, Greenland, Guatemala, Guernsey, Honduras, Hungary, Iceland, Ireland, Isle of Man, Israel, Italy, Jersey, Kosovo, Latvia, Lithuania, Luxembourg, Macedonia, Malta, Mauritius, México, Moldova, Montenegro, Mozambique, Nepal, Netherlands, New Zealand, Nicaragua, Norway, Perú, Philippines (2 cities), Poland, Portugal, Romania, Serbia, Seychelles, Slovakia, Slovenia, South Africa, Spain, Sweden, Switzerland, Taiwan, United Kingdom, United States (21 states, 1 territory), Uruguay, Venezuela
Prohibition of hate crimes based on sexual orientation	Belgium, Chile, Croatia, Czech Republic, Iceland, Ireland, Liechtenstein, Luxembourg, México (1 state), Micronesia, Netherlands, Northern Marianas, Norway, Spain, Sweden, United Kingdom (England, Wales), United States, Uruguay
Civil unions/domestic partnerships recognized	Andorra, Argentina,[a] Australia (5 states),[a] Austria, Belgium, Brazil, Canada, Colombia, Croatia,[a] Czech Republic, Denmark, Ecuador, Finland, France, Germany, Greenland, Hungary, Iceland, Ireland, Isle of Man, Israel,[a] Jersey, Liechtenstein, Luxembourg, México (1 state), Netherlands, New Zealand, Norway, Poland, Portugal, Slovenia, South Africa,[a] Spain, Sweden, Switzerland, United Kingdom, United States (14 states, 1 territory), Uruguay, Venezuela (1 city)
Same-sex marriage laws/ court rulings	Argentina, Australia,[b] Belgium, Brazil (4 states), Canada, Colombia, Denmark, France, Iceland, México, Nepal, Netherlands, New Zealand, Norway, Portugal, South Africa, Spain, Sweden, United Kingdom, United States (13 states, 1 territory), Uruguay
Adoption by gay or lesbian partners	Andorra, Argentina, Australia (4 states), Belgium, Brazil, Cambodia, Canada, Denmark, Finland, Germany, Greece, Greenland, Guernsey, Iceland, Isle of Man, Israel, Italy, Jersey, Malta, México, Netherlands, New Zealand, Norway, Philippines, South Africa, Spain, Sweden, United Kingdom, United States (22 states, 2 territories), Uruguay
Transgender antidiscrimination laws of various sorts	Albania, Argentina, Australia, Austria, Belgium, Bolivia, Brazil, Canada, Chile, China, Croatia, Cyprus, Czech Republic, Denmark, Ecuador, Estonia, Finland, France, Germany, Guernsey, Hungary, Iceland, Israel, Italy, Japan, Jersey, Latvia, Lithuania, México, Montenegro, Nepal, Netherlands, New Zealand, Norway, Poland, Portugal, Romania, Serbia, South Africa, South Korea, Spain, Slovakia, Slovenia, Sweden, Taiwan, Turkey, United Kingdom, United States (13 states), Uruguay

[a] Common-law recognition.

[b] Allowed only if one partner has changed sex biologically.

Source: www.actwin.com/eatonohio/gay/world.htm; other news sources.

reviewed Turkey's human rights record, Ankara was asked not only to ban discrimination against gays, lesbians, bisexuals, and the transgendered but also to protect them from harassment and violence.

A proposed resolution, Sexual Orientation and Human Rights, was once presented at a meeting in 2003 of the predecessor to the current UNHRC, but strong opposition came from Islamic states. In 2008, the Organization of American States adopted a resolution recognizing the applicability of human rights protections to sexual orientation and gender identity. Then in 2011, HRC passed that resolution and commissioned a worldwide report on the situation of (the treaty-based Human Rights Committee) gays, lesbians, and the transgendered in relation to human rights. When the report was completed later that year, HRC decided to formally entertain complaints from gays, lesbians, bisexuals, and the transgendered within the scope of its regular complaint processing mechanism (see Chapter 10).

As rights have been gradually granted to gays and lesbians, many issues have come to the fore. Each topic requires separate comment, as discussed next.

Employment Nondiscrimination. Perhaps the earliest concern in the gay rights movement was to reverse barriers to employment. Because of social disapproval, many gays or lesbians have worked alongside others without disclosing their sexual identities. Those who found out might blackmail them, threatening to expose them to their employers, family, friends, or even their unaware spouses. The danger of blackmail kept many nonheterosexuals fearful of entering some jobs, including sensitive government positions, so members of the gay rights movement in the 1980s urged members to "come out of the closet" so that such discrimination, if present, could be addressed, and *Out Magazine* began publishing in 1982 to expose gays who even hid their identity by taking anti-gay positions in the political arena. But openly gay and lesbian workers, in turn, had to cope with harassment.

To be deprived of one's livelihood for a non-job-relevant reason, nevertheless, is clearly discrimination. The civil rights era of the 1950s sought to prohibit employment discrimination on the basis of race, and various laws to enforce such a ban were adopted in many countries. As new laws added sex (gender), age, handicapped status, and other conditions as protected classes, discrimination on the basis of sexual orientation would logically be next.

In 1982, Wisconsin became the first American state to pass a law banning employment discrimination based on sexual orientation. Although a federal law was first proposed in Congress in 1974, only in 1989 did a second state (Massachusetts) pass a similar law. France, in 1990, and the Netherlands, in 1991, passed the first nondiscrimination laws in Europe, and the practice swept through Europe during the 1990s, expanding coverage from public to private employers. Today, 67 countries or parts of countries ban employment discrimination based on sexual orientation or gender identity (Table 14.1). Only 21 states in the United States protect employment discrimination against gays and lesbians, but no such law has ever passed Congress. In 1998, by Executive Order 13087, President Bill Clinton (1946–) banned sexual orientation discrimination in most federal government jobs, but not for military service, where gays and lesbians could be discharged if "outed" for their sexual orientation. In 2000, the European Court of Human Rights ruled in *Lustig-Prean v. UK* and *Smith v. UK* that the European Convention for Human

Rights prohibited Britain from banning a gay person from enlisting in the country's military service. Congress repealed the ban on open admission of sexual orientation among members of the military in the Don't Ask Don't Tell Repeal Act of 2010.

Sexual Privacy. In *Dudgeon v. UK* (1981), *Norris v. Ireland* (1988), and *Modinos v. Cyprus* (1993), the European Court of Human Rights found that the right to privacy was violated by the criminalization of sexual acts between consenting adults. The HRC, which handles complaints filed on the basis of the International Covenant on Civil and Political Rights, ruled in *Toonen v. Australia* (1994), that the nondiscrimination and privacy rights provisions in the Covenant apply to sexual orientation, thereby decriminalizing the sodomy law of the State of Tasmania. In 1997, the same body condemned the death penalty for homosexuality imposed in Sudan. The US Supreme Court decriminalized adult consensual sex in 2003 in *Lawrence v. Texas* (539US558).[2] With the exception of Muslim countries, most governments permit consensual sexual acts today.[3]

In 1997, the European Commission of Human Rights struck down the unequal age of consent for homosexual and heterosexual acts in the United Kingdom in *Sutherland v. UK*; a similar ruling came from the European Court of Human Rights in *L & V v. Austria* (2003). Nevertheless, 7 countries still maintain age differentials (Colombia, Guatemala, Indonesia, Pakistan, Lesotho, Panamá, Swaziland), 5 countries (Bahrain, Bolivia, Oman, Qatar, Saudi Arabia) require at least one of the partners to be married, yet about 100 countries have no age requirement. There is no worldwide agreement on what constitutes an "adult" for purposes of sexual consent, though the youngest is 12 (México) and the oldest is 20 (Tunisia); age disparity between those involved is taken into consideration when the younger person claims rape.

Hate Crimes. As gays and lesbians became more visible to the larger society, the possibility of anti-gay violence increased, particularly among those trying to sublimate latent homosexual tendencies by proving their masculinity through inflicting violence on gays in schools or at gay establishments. Hate crime legislation, of course, has applied to ethnic and racial minorities, members of certain political parties, and even the disabled, so many governments have sought to include gender identity or sexual orientation within the scope of existing national laws, increasing penalties for violent offenders when they are motivated by prejudice. Some laws

---

▌COURT CASE 14.1 *NEW JERSEY V. RAVI* (2012)

Tyler Clementi (1991–2010) and Dharun Ravi (1992–), students at Rutgers University in New Jersey, shared the same room in the college dormitory. On September 19, 2010, Dharun Ravi viewed a webcam, taken without Tyler's knowledge, along with Molly Wei (1992–) in her room within the same dorm. The webcam showed Clementi kissing another man. On September 21, Ravi made a second webcam in which

Continued

Clementi engaged in sex with his friend. On both occasions Ravi posted the webcams on the Internet and urged his Twitter followers to view the scenes. On September 22, when Clementi found out that others were viewing his tryst, he went to the George Washington Bridge opposite New York City and jumped to his death. On September 28, following worldwide attention over the matter, both students were charged with invasion of privacy, bias intimidation, tampering with evidence, witness tampering, hindering prosecution, but not for a role in the suicide. Wei pled guilty, offering to testify against Ravi, and was sentenced in 2011 to 300 hours of community service, counseling, and classes on dealing with people of alternative lifestyles. In 2012, Ravi was found guilty and sentenced to 30 days in jail, 3 years probation, 300 hours of community service, a US$10,000 fine, and counseling on cyberbullying and alternate lifestyles. He was released after 20 days.

apply to hate speech, others to hate-motivated violence, but *New Jersey v. Ravi*, a court case in 2012, applied the law to sexual harassment.

In 2003, amid vivid memories of Nazi death camps, Belgium, Britain, and France were the first countries to ban hate-motivated violence based on sexual orientation. Within the United States, lynchings of African Americans by members of the Ku Klux Klan after the Civil War clearly constituted hate crimes. The first American state to ban sexual orientation violence was Alaska in 1982. Violence based on sexual orientation and gender identity was not banned at the federal level until the earlier hate crimes law of 1969 was superseded in 2009 by the **Matthew Shepard and James Byrd, Jr. Hate Crimes Prevention Act**, named after two persons (a gay and an African American) who were lynched in 1998. In 2012, the EU Council and Parliament issued a directive to ban hate crimes on the basis of sexual orientation, gender identity, and gender expression, so EU members had three years to adopt into law the provisions outlined in the **Directive of the European Parliament and of the Council Establishing Minimum Standards on the Rights, Support and Protection of Victims of Crime.**

An extreme hate crime is the extrajudicial execution of gays within Muslim countries. In 2010, UN efforts to denounce arbitrary, extrajudicial, and summary executions were included in a resolution adopted by the General Assembly's Third Committee but passed only when application to gays was removed at their insistence. In 2012, when the measure came up again, the United Arab Emirates, on behalf of the Organization of Islamic Cooperation, sought to strip "sexual orientation and gender identity" from the specific list of protected classes. Delegates from Brazil, Japan, South Africa, and the United States specifically spoke against the amendment, which was then defeated 108–1 with 65 abstentions.

Civil Unions. Many gays and lesbians seek to live with partners, but society has historically ignored various spousal rights for all but those with certificates of marriage. When patients with AIDS were hospitalized in the 1980s, they hoped to receive visits from their partners, only to be denied entry in some cases to patient rooms because they were not "immediate family members," even though some had undergone "holy unions" in MCC churches. Although the unstated pretext for denial may have been the early view that AIDS was a contagious disease and should therefore be quarantined, the refusal to allow one loving partner to comfort another demanded a remedy – some form of state recognition.

Governmental recognition of civil unions, domestic partnerships, or common-law partners of the same sex first emerged in 1982 within the Québec Province of Canada but did not spread to other Canadian provinces until the early 1990s. Meanwhile, Denmark took the lead in Europe, establishing a domestic partner registry in 1989, followed by Sweden in 1995, and then Hungary and Iceland in 1996. An American quasi-domestic partnership law in the United States was adopted during 1997 in Hawai'i as a ploy by the state legislature to discourage its Supreme Court from legalizing gay marriage. Called the Reciprocal Beneficiaries Act, the law envisaged a family unit in traditional Asian terms as consisting of a single elderly grandparent living with a single grandson or granddaughter, as the last child in the family is expected to provide filial care and is not supposed to marry if an elderly widow or widower would otherwise be left to live alone.

But in 1999, Vermont's Supreme Court ruled in *Baker v. State* (744A2d864) that same-sex couples could not be denied the same rights as opposite-sex couples, leaving the resolution of the issue to the state legislature, which then established civil unions in 2000. A civil union law did not pass in Hawai'i until 2011, by which time civil unions had been established in 14 American states[4] and all or parts of 38 countries, mostly in Europe (Table 14.1).

The main problem of civil unions is the lack of many protections afforded by marriage, such as survivor benefits. In *Young v. Australia* (2003) the HRC (under the International Covenant on Civil and Political Rights) ruled that Australia should not deny a government pension to the spouse of the deceased of a same-sex civil union, so the law was changed. Elsewhere, gay and lesbian couples may have to file court cases to challenge such restrictions. One estimate is that of approximately 1,000 benefits conferred on marriage partners, civil unions offer only 300. Civil partners cannot file joint income tax returns, have one partner change citizenship to the country of the other partner, be assured of hospital visitation rights, and cannot take sick leave to care for a partner.

Gay Marriage. The problems of civil unions can be overcome with marriage, a goal entirely unanticipated when the gay rights movement began. The origin of gay marriage can be traced back to 1921, when women's advocacy groups sought to adopt a constitutional amendment that would provide equal treatment for women and men on the same basis as the Fourteenth Amendment to the American Constitution, which guarantees racial equality before the law. A proposed Equal Rights Amendment (ERA) was adopted by Congress in 1972, subject to ratification by three-fourths of the states by 1982, but ERA failed to get support from the required 38 states. Meanwhile, several states voted to incorporate ERAs into their own constitutions. The significance of the state ERAs for gays and lesbians was not fully understood until 1990, when six persons went to the Department of Health in Honolulu to apply for marriage licenses at the suggestion of ACLU Legal Director and University of Hawai'i law school professor, Daniel Foley (1947–).

After being turned down because all three applications listed names of persons of the same gender, Foley filed a test case (*Baehr v. Lewin*) in state court in 1991. After an appeal from a lower court, which tried to dismiss the case, the Hawai'i Supreme Court ruled in 1993 that the state ERA prohibited the state from denying marriage licenses on the basis of gender (74Haw645;852P2d44) and remanded the case to the lower court for a remedy. However, the ruling sparked controversy: Congress passed the Defense of Marriage Act to ban the practice at the federal level in 1996, and during 1998 voters in the Aloha State adopted a constitutional amendment to allow the legislature to prohibit same-sex marriage, which was quickly passed. State after state then passed laws to ban same-sex marriage.

In 1994, the European Parliament asked the Commission of the European Community to recommend that member states stop the "barring of lesbians and homosexual couples from marriage or from an equivalent legal framework." In 2000, the Netherlands became the first to make same-sex marriage legal, and the European legalization snowball soon ran through Belgium, Portugal, Scandinavia (except Finland), and Spain as well as beyond to Argentina, Australia, Brazil, Canada, Colombia, México, Nepal, South Africa, and Uruguay (Table 14.1). However, in 2012, the European Court of Human Rights ruled in *Gas v. France* that gay marriage is not a right in international law that European countries are required to honor, leaving the matter to individual state laws.

In 2003, the Massachusetts Supreme Court ruled in *Goodrich v. Massachusetts* (798NE2d941) that the state legislature must resolve the issue, which it did that year by authorizing issuance of certificates of marriage to same-sex couples. The California State Legislature passed a gay marriage bill in 2005, but the law was vetoed by the governor. After the law passed again in 2008, a ballot referendum to reverse the law was adopted later that year after many gay marriages had been recognized. The resulting legal confusion went for resolution before the US Supreme Court, which in 2013 let California's same-sex marriages stand. Currently, gay marriages are legal in 13 American states and the District of Columbia.

However, various states in the United States have been alarmed that partners of gay marriages in one state might move to other states, forcing the latter to recognize their legal status. Accordingly, Congress passed the Defense of Marriage Act in 1996 to authorize such nonreciprocity, but the Supreme Court ruled in 2013 that married same-sex couples are entitled to full federal benefits.

The debate in the United States, in other words, is in constitutional terms rather than within the mainstream of international human rights jurisprudence. In several press conferences while president, George W. Bush (1946–) opposed recognition of gay marriage on the basis of cultural relativism, that is, because of a Christian tradition in the United States. His former Vice President, Dick Cheney (1941–), whose daughter is a lesbian, disagreed. Former President Jimmy Carter (1924–), whose home state of Georgia would not allow marriage between persons of difference races until the Supreme Court case *Loving v. Virginia* (388US1) in 1967, has a different idea, based on the fact that only late in human history (in the fourteenth century for England) did states issue pieces of paper called "certificates of marriage," especially as literacy spread beyond persons of noble rank. He has argued that governments

DISCUSSION TOPIC 14.1 SHOULD CIVIL MARRIAGE BE ABOLISHED OR IS THERE A RIGHT TO MARRY?

For some, the traditional expectation is that partners of opposite sexes (a man and a woman) who are deeply in love will seek recognition as a married couple and will then form a household and start a family. However, same-sex couples have lived together for centuries under many circumstances. If loving same-sex couples share expenses, eat together, engage in social activities together, share a bedroom, and adopt or bring up children from a previous opposite-sex marriage, should they be allowed legal recognition by means of a governmentally-issued certificate of marriage? Or should they instead be recognized as partners in a civil union? Alternatively, should governments now certify civil unions to all couples of marriage age, leaving the sacrament of marriage for churches to perform and to record, as in much of human history? Or is marriage a right that all governments must respect regardless of the gender of the partners?

should leave marriages to churches and instead grant civil unions to all couples who otherwise meet normal age requirements.

Adoption. Gays and lesbians have also encountered restrictions on the right to be parents or to adopt or take on foster children. The adoption could be jointly by a same-sex couple, adoption by one partner of a same-sex couple of the other's biological child, or adoption by a single gay or lesbian. Objections that such arrangements are unnatural often fail to consider the fact that many children grow up in single-parent families where one spouse is dead, missing, or lives alone due to a divorce, whereas gay and lesbian couples maintain loving relationships that are important for healthy upbringing.

In 1993, Rhode Island became the first state to allow adoption by same-sex couples. The District of Columbia (1995) and New Jersey (1998) followed. By 2012, Guam and 20 more American states granted the right of adoption to either civil union partners or married couples of the same gender.

In 1994, the European Parliament asked the Commission of the European Community to recommend member states to stop "any restriction on the right of lesbians and homosexuals to be parents or to adopt or foster children." But no European country did so until 2001, when the Netherlands became the first to permit adoptions for same-sex partners. In 1999, the European Court of Human Rights ruled that an individual's gender should not be a factor in determining child custody in *Salgueiro Da Silva Mouta v. Portugal*. The case involved a man who lived with a man after divorcing his wife and sought custody of a child from the marriage. Today, adoptions involving same-sex couples are allowed in all or part of Australia, Cambodia, Canada, 18 European countries, Israel, four Latin American countries, New Zealand, Philippines, South Africa, and the United States (Table 14.1). The ruling in *Gas v. France* (2012), mentioned above, denied the right of adoption to a lesbian couple; they had hoped that the increasing European recognition of gay marriage would trump French law.

An individual gay or lesbian may adopt in nine countries where partner adoption is not allowed (Colombia, Costa Rica, Estonia, French Guiana, Ireland, Latvia, Poland, Portugal, Slovenia). Step-parent (one partner adopts the child of the other) and foster parent adoption is also available wherever same-sex partners can do so. Two-thirds of couples who adopt are lesbians.

Transgendered Rights. Gays and lesbians dominated the early movement but soon realized that they were leaving out a very vulnerable type of person who often attended MCC churches and for whom sexual identity classification was still not established. Accordingly, in about 1988, the term LGBT arose to describe the entire group of persons seeking rights – lesbians, gays, bisexuals, and the transgendered. The latter are persons whose presumed emotional or physical characteristics do not match their biological characteristics.

Some transgendered seek to become transsexuals through operations to change that biology to conform to their appearance, but others prefer to stay just as they are. The transgendered, a term referring generically to all such persons, may have sex with men, women, or nobody. A cross-dresser or transvestite, on the other hand, dresses as a member of one sex while biologically has organs of the other sex. Androgyne, bigender, drag kings and queens, and genderqueer are other terms to describe individuals who do not fit conventional categories. Socially, transgendered feel most comfortable with gays and lesbians, but legally they have been in limbo. Vice President Joe Biden (1942–), going beyond Sandra Day O'Connor's earlier statement, said in 2012 that transgendered discrimination is "the civil rights issue of our time."

In 1977, Champaign, Illinois, was the first jurisdiction to afford some protection to the transgendered, applying the city's antidiscrimination law on the basis of sex in employment, housing, and public accommodations to explicitly cover the transgendered. Minnesota and New Mexico in 1993 became the first states to do so. Today, 13 American states and 108 localities have some protection for gender identity or expression.

In 1989, the European Parliament passed a resolution banning discrimination against transsexuals. In 1996, the European Court of Human Rights ruled in *P v. S and Cornwall County Council* that an individual could not be fired for undergoing gender reassignment.

For the transgendered, discrimination can also occur in education, employment, housing, public accommodations, and even the right to marry. Other issues involve name changes, changes of gender on birth certificates, and the right to surgery for organ changes. Some laws that cover sexual orientation explicitly cover gender

COURT CASE 14.2 *X, Y AND Z V. UNITED KINGDOM* (1997)

Should a birth certificate of a child born from artificial insemination of the mother show the mother's partner, a female-to-male transsexual, as the father of the child? That question arose in Britain when Z (the child born of the female Y) was born.

Continued

X (the female-to-male transsexual) asked to be designated the father of Z. Under British law, however, the request was denied because such a transsexual would still be considered a female, and indeed X and Y could not marry. When the case was appealed to the European Court of Human Rights, the court held that the relationship of X with Y was legally a "family" under the European Convention for the Protection of Human Rights and Fundamental Freedoms (24EHRR143) because the couple had been living together for 18 years without objection in Britain and were both exercising responsibility to care for the child, but that there was no common standard within the European Union to decide whether Britain acted contrary to the Convention.

identity or expression, but some do not. Forty-nine countries recognize some form of protection for the transgendered, albeit very limited. In 2012, Argentina became the only country to recognize the right of gender reassignment without imposing any regulations.

In 1997, the European Court of Human Rights brought the issue to the fore in *X, Y and Z v. UK*, ruling that a transgendered male partnered with a female for 18 years did constitute a "family," but not for purposes of state benefits. But in 2002, when Britain was asked to change the gender on legal documents of a person who changed sex through an operation, the court, in *Goodwin v. UK*, ruled in favor of the plaintiff, arguing that everyone has a right to privacy and to employment, pensions, and social security. *Goodwin* reversed *Rees v. UK* (1987).

To sum up, LGBT issues are going through conventional channels to become recognized in a variety of states. As late as 2012, for example, the HRC ruled in *Fedotova v. Russia*, involving women who held a public sign "Homosexuality is normal," that the law in some Russian provinces banning "gay propaganda" was a violation of the fundamental right of free expression. Moscow's defiant response was to consider extending the ban throughout the country.

There is no international treaty on LGBT rights, even within Europe. But on Human Rights Day December 10, 2012, UN Secretary-General Ban Ki-Moon said, "Lesbian, gay bisexual and transgender people are entitled to the same rights as everyone else. They too are born free and equal. I stand shoulder-to-shoulder with them in their struggle for human rights."

ENVIRONMENTAL RIGHTS

Humans have long believed that they have a right to exploit their environment in order to survive. At the same time, urban civilizations have sought to keep their cities and roads free from garbage and their water supplies free from contamination. With wide acceptance of the principle of economic self-interest and the advent of the Industrial Revolution, however, urban filth became a byproduct of economic growth, a phenomenon known as the **tragedy of the commons** because individuals benefit from discarding small quantities of what they do not need without realizing the consequences of their collective behavior. Efforts to set aside pristine environments into national parks in the late nineteenth century were among the first to recognize the value of the natural environment, which can be regarded as the common heritage of all humans, but today the effort to save the wilderness has been lost by most accounts.

The premise for a discussion of environmental rights within a book on human rights, thus, is because of the basic human right to life and health. Pollution in the air, on the land, and across the seas chronically threatens human life, sometimes even fatally. Measures taken to bolster the environment also much take into account the fact that overexploitation of environmental resources, such as overfishing, may endanger the supply of food and other commodities necessary for daily living on the planet.

After World War II, London and Los Angeles became particularly notable for a mixture of fog and smoke known as smog. During 1952, such a thick layer of smog began to collect over London that by December hospitals were overcrowded with patients suffering from respiratory problems. An estimated 12,000 died up to the end of February 1953 because of complications from what became known as "killer smog," while I and my fellow Angelenos suffered eye and respiratory discomfort.

In 1959, as I drove east from smoggy Los Angeles to attend Yale University, I noticed a strange pigmentation in a body of water flowing through downtown Cleveland into Lake Erie: the bright orange color was unquestionably an example of eerie industrial pollution. In 1962, biologist Rachel Carson (1907–1964) published *Silent Spring*. Her argument, that nature was dying because of DDT and other pesticides, stunned the world. Indeed, *The New York Times* referred to her book as a twentieth century version of *The Rights of Man*. Later that year, London's killer smog claimed another 106 lives.

In 1969, John McConnell (1915–2012) proposed an Earth Day at the 1969 National UNESCO Conference in San Francisco. Shortly thereafter, his proposal was accepted by San Francisco City and County, which proclaimed the first Earth Day. In the same year, Congress voted to establish the Environmental Protection Agency. The concept of a worldwide Earth Day quickly gained support, and the March equinox is now marked each year by the tolling of the United Nations Peace Bell. McConnell went on to form the Earth Society Foundation in 1976, and issued such documents as *Earth Rights* (1974), *Earth Charter* (1979), and an *Earth Magna Carta* (1995).

Today, the global warming from environmental pollution is likely to cause such catastrophic climate changes that the health of the planet may be in jeopardy. Although many environmental concerns may be categorized as human health issues, planetary health has become a major concern for the first time in recent years. Meanwhile, many industrial producers are reluctant to spend additional amounts in order to stop profitable practices that destroy natural resources, and politicians derive more campaign financing from industry than from environmentalists.

In short, the political will to cope with pressing environmental issues is stymied by alternative perspectives regarding the environment. At least four coexist today:

- **Econocentrism.** Economic growth should be maximized with no concern for environmental consequences except when there are direct adverse economic consequences. For less affluent countries, the right to development trumps environmental concerns.

- **Utilitarianism.** There should be a balance, such that the costs of minimizing pollution will not be so excessive that jobs and economies will be jeopardized. Under the label **sustainable development**, intergovernmental banks as well as intergovernmental aid agencies appear to tilt toward industry rather than providing a compromise that would save the environment from disaster.

- **Anthropocentrism.** The health and survival of humans prevails over all other values, including animal and ecological survival. Although the onset of disaster from global warming is impossible to predict, anthropocentrics insist on immediate action to stop the effects of impending environmental disaster on humans.

- **Ecocentrism.** Environmental damage should be prevented, stopped, and reversed so that the planet can return to as pristine a condition as possible. Forests and wilderness areas should be restored for the sake of the planet.

In part because of a lack of consensus on the appropriate strategy, the concept of environmental rights has only gained substance through incremental treaties and court actions that deal with two basic issues – **damage** and **prevention**. Agreements to prevent environmental damage, whether ongoing or anticipated, have been

TABLE 14.2 **EARLY INTERNATIONAL ENVIRONMENTAL AGREEMENTS**[a]

Date	Agreement
1900	Convention for the Protection of Wild Animals, Birds and Fish in Africa
1900	Convention Between the Riverine States of the Rhine Respecting Regulations Governing the Transport of Corrosive and Poisonous Substances
1902	Convention for the Protection of Birds Useful to Agriculture
1911	Treaty for the Preservation and Protection of Fur Seals
1911	Convention Between the United States of America, the United Kingdom of Great Britain and Northern Ireland, and Russia, for the Preservation and Protection of Fur Seals
1921	Convention Concerning the Use of White Lead in Painting
1923	Convention for the Preservation of the Halibut Fishery of the Northern Pacific Ocean
1927	Agreement on Development of the Fishing Resources of the Southern Coast of the Caspian Sea
1931	International Agreement for the Regulation of Whaling
1933	Convention on Preservation of Fauna and Flora in Their Natural State
1937	International Agreement for the Regulation of Whaling
1940	Convention on Nature Protection and Wildlife Preservation in the Western Hemisphere

[a] Excludes bilateral agreements.

difficult to gain adoption. Although there are many environmental concerns, the discussion below primarily focuses on the pollution of air, land, and water.

The earliest efforts to deal with environmental issues on an international basis occurred in Europe and North America (Table 14.2). Although the Final Act of the Congress of Vienna of 1815 set up the Central Commission for the Navigation of the Rhine, and in 1856 the Treaty of Paris established the European Commission of the Danube, both commissions dealt with disputes concerning the principle of free navigation, not the health of the waterways. A half-century of Rhenish cooperation led to the **Convention Between the Riverine States of the Rhine Respecting Regulations Governing the Transport of Corrosive and Poisonous Substances** of 1900, the first treaty dealing with pollution.

Friendly relations between Canada and the United States facilitated the further development of international environmental law. In 1909, the **Treaty Between the United States and Great Britain Relating to Boundary Waters Between the United States and Canada** provided that water "shall not be polluted on either side to the injury of health or property on the other." An International Joint Commission was established in case of future disputes.

COURT CASE 14.3 THE TRAIL SMELTER ARBITRATIONS (1931, 1938, 1941)

In 1927, residents of Washington State complained to the state and federal governments that sulfur dioxide emissions in the form of smoke from a Canadian copper smelting company in Trail, British Columbia, were causing environmental damage to crops and forests as prevailing winds swept through the Columbia River Valley. The two countries then referred the matter to the US–Canadian International Joint Commission, originally set up in 1909 to arbitrate water disputes between the two countries. In 1931, the Commission ruled that farmers should be compensated US$350,000 and, without specifying how, that sulfur dioxide emissions should be reduced. The farmers rejected the settlement, so in 1935 the two countries adopted the Convention for Settlement of Difficulties Arising from Operation of Smelter at Trail and set up an arbitral panel. Although the smelter company then agreed to compensate local farmers US$350,000 for all damages before January 1, 1932, the offer was turned down by local residents, farmers, and the Washington State government. Because pollution continued, an arbitral tribunal was set up. In 1938, the arbitrators preliminarily awarded US$78,000 in damages for two burns causing visible damage in 1934 and 1936. The tribunal's final decision in 1941 granted an additional US$78,000 to the farmers. The case was the first to cover cross-border environmental damage. In all, Canada paid to the United States approximately US$420,000 so that

Continued

the American government could compensate farmers whose crops were adversely affected. Although the company resisted reducing sulfur dioxide emissions, as required by the 1941 arbitration, they adopted emission standards only after they learned that sulfur dioxide could be recycled to make fertilizer

After World War I, the newly established International Labor Organization recognized the health risks of paints containing lead. As a result, the **Convention Concerning the Use of White Lead in Painting** emerged in 1921.

Before 1931, there was no international legal precedent to resolve a dispute between Canada and the United States regarding air pollution emanating from the city of Trail in British Columbia. Accordingly, new principles had to be developed. The joint commission established in the 1909 treaty was then constituted as an arbitration tribunal, which ruled that pollution moving from one country to another was a form of criminal **trespass**, and the consequence of pollution was determined to be a **nuisance** subject to compensation. In other words, the "polluter pays" principle was first enunciated.

In 1992, the United Nations Conference on Environment and Development, known popularly as the Earth Summit, was held in Río de Janeiro. The first of the 26 principles in the resulting **Río Declaration on Environment and Development** states: "Human beings are at the center of concerns for sustainable development. They are entitled to a healthy and productive life in harmony with nature." The Declaration, however, avoided the use of the word "right." The conference adopted **Agenda 21**, a 900-page action plan with 109 recommendations for protecting global resources, which urged accountability for all new development projects, including environmental impact statements. Perhaps the most important outcome was the creation that year of the UN Environmental Program (UNEP), which undertook to deal with water pollution, nuclear pollution, air and land pollution, and conservation efforts.

Water Pollution. After World War II, the use of large oil tankers from the Middle East to Europe, the Americas, and Asia prompted concern about the possibility of oil spilling into the ocean, particularly after the *Torrey Canyon* disaster in 1967. Accordingly, in 1954, the **International Convention for the Prevention of Pollution of the Sea by Oil** (OILPOL) was adopted. Agreements on Lake Constance, the North Sea, and the Mosel and Rhine rivers followed (Table 14.3). However, ship operators made little effort to comply. The **Convention on the High Seas**, though principally adopted to provide rules for international commerce, also had a provision banning pollution.

The Intergovernmental Maritime Consultative Organization (IMCO), which began operation on a treaty basis in 1958, originally had a primary mandate over navigation in international waters. But in 1969, IMCO shifted focus to pollution with the adoption of the **Convention Relating to Intervention on the High Seas in Cases of Oil Pollution Casualties**, which empowered ships to act in case of

TABLE 14.3 MAJOR CONTEMPORARY INTERNATIONAL AGREEMENTS DEALING WITH WATER POLLUTION

Date	Agreement	In force
1954	International Convention for the Prevention of Pollution in the Sea by Oil (OILPOL)[a]	1958
1958	Convention on the High Seas	1962
1960	Convention on the Protection of Lake Constance Against Pollution	1961
1961	Protocol Concerning the Establishment of an International Commission to Protect the Mosel Against Pollution	1962
1963	Agreement on the International Commission for the Protection of the Rhine Against Pollution	1965
1969	Convention Relating to Intervention on the High Seas in Cases of Oil Pollution Casualties	1957
1969	• Protocol Relating to Intervention on the High Seas in Cases of Marine Pollution by Substances Other than Oil	1983
1969	Agreement for Cooperation in Dealing with Pollution of the North Sea by Oil	1969
1969	International Convention on Civil Liability for Oil Pollution Damage[a]	1975
1971	International Convention on the Establishment of an International Fund for Compensation to Oil Pollution Damage[a]	1978
1972	International Convention for the Prevention of Marine Pollution by Dumping of Waste and Other Matter (London Convention)[a]	1975
1973	International Convention for the Prevention of Pollution from Ships (MARPOL)[a]	1983
1973	Convention on Fishing and Conservation of the Living Resources in the Baltic Sea	1974
1973	Protocol Relating to Intervention on the High Seas in Cases of Marine Pollution by Substances Other than Oil	1983
1974	Convention for the Prevention of Marine Pollution from Land-Based Sources	1978
1976	Convention on the Protection of the Rhine Against Pollution from Chlorides	
1976	Agreement for the Protection of the Rhine Against Chemical Pollution	
1976	Convention for the Protection of the Mediterranean Sea Against Pollution[a]	1978
1978	Kuwait Regional Convention for Co-operation on the Protection of the Marine Environment from Pollution[a]	1979
1981	Agreement on Regional Cooperation in Combating Pollution of the South-East Pacific by Hydrocarbons or Other Harmful Substances in Case of Emergency[a]	1986
1982	Regional Convention for the Conservation of the Red Sea and the Gulf of Aden Environment	1985
1982	• Protocol Concerning Regional Co-Operation in Combating Pollution by Oil and Other Harmful Substances in Cases of Emergency	1985
1982	United Nations Convention on the Law of the Sea (UNCLOS)	1984
1983	Agreement for Cooperation in Dealing with Pollution of the North Sea by Oil and Other Harmful Substances (Bonn Agreement)[a]	1989

Continued

TABLE 14.3 (CONTINUED)

Date	Agreement	In force
1983	Protocol Concerning Co-operation in Combating Oil Spills in the Wider Caribbean Region[b]	1986
1985	Protocol Concerning Co-operation in Combating Marine Pollution in Cases of Emergency in the Eastern African Region	1996
1986	Protocol Concerning Co-operation in Combating Pollution Emergencies in the South Pacific Region[a]	1990
1986	Protocol for the Prevention of Pollution of the South Pacific Region by Dumping	1990
1989	Basel Convention on the Control of Transboundary Movements of Hazardous Wastes and Their Disposal[a]	1992
1989	Agreement for Cooperation in Dealing with Pollution of the North Sea by Oil	1989
1989	Convention on Civil Liability for Damage Caused during Carriage of Dangerous Goods by Road, Rail, and Inland Navigation Vessels	
1990	International Convention on Oil Pollution Preparedness, Response and Cooperation	1995
1992	Convention on the Protection of the Black Sea Against Pollution[a]	1994
1992	Convention on the Transboundary Effects of Industrial Accidents	2000
2003	• Protocol on Civil Liability and Compensation for Damage Caused by the Transboundary Effects of Industrial Accidents on Transboundary Waters	
1992	Convention on the Protection and Use of Transboundary Watercourses and International Lakes	1996
1999	• Protocol on Water and Health	2005
1993	Convention on Civil Liability for Damage Resulting from Activities Dangerous to the Environment	
1996	International Convention on Liability and Compensation for Damage in Connection with the Carriage of Hazardous and Noxious Substances by Sea	
2000	• Protocol on Preparedness, Response and Co-operation to Pollution Incidents by Hazardous and Noxious Substances	2007
1997	Convention on the Law of the Non-Navigable Uses of International Watercourses	
1998	CoE Convention on the Protection of the Environment Through Criminal Law	
1999	Convention on the Protection of the Rhine[c]	2003
1999	Protocol Concerning Pollution from Land-Based Sources and Activities to the Convention for the Protection and Development of the Marine Environment of the Wider Caribbean Region	
2000	European Agreement Concerning the International Carriage of Dangerous Goods by Inland Waterways	2008
2001	International Convention on Civil Liability for Bunker Oil Pollution Damage	2008
2001	International Convention on the Control of Harmful Anti-Fouling Systems on Ships	2008
2007	International Convention on the Removal of Wrecks	

Continued

TABLE 14.3 (CONTINUED)

Date	Agreement	In force
2008	United Nations Convention on Contracts for the International Carriage of Goods Wholly or Partly by Sea (Rotterdam Rules)	

[a] Amended or revised later, sometimes by protocols.
[b] Supersedes the earlier (1969) agreement.
[c] Replaces the Agreement on the International Commission for the Protection of the Rhine Against Pollution of 1963.

actual or possible oil spillage. The 1969 treaty was later augmented by treaties on dumping.

Since OILPOL had little effect, IMCO sponsored the **International Convention for the Prevention of Pollution from Ships** (MARPOL) in 1973, but once again there was resistance, and the treaty was not immediately ratified. However, after the *Amoco Cadiz* spilled 270,000 tons of petroleum in 1978, the treaty was ratified in 1983; annexes dealing with garbage and sewage followed in 1988 and 2003, respectively.

IMCO, later renamed International Maritime Organization (IMO), has fathered more treaties relating to pollution than any other organization. After MARPOL, agreements were drawn up regarding the Baltic Sea, Black Sea, Caribbean, East Africa, Gulf of Aden, the Mediterranean, North Sea, Persian Gulf, Red Sea, Rhine River, and the Southeast and South Pacific. Liability formulas from dumping and compensation were also codified into treaties.

The European Union's **Amsterdam Treaty** of 1997 specifically states that environmental protection should be on the basis of the polluter pay principle. In 2001, the EU adopted the Clean Air for Europe Program as a coordinated effort involving scientific information, legislative proposals, and cost-effective methods for compliance.

Two important enforcement treaties were adopted in Europe during 1998. The Council of Europe adopted the **Convention on the Protection of the Environment Through Criminal Law**, which identifies any pollution of the air, land, or sea as a crime, and empowers those damaged thereby to find a remedy through courts where the damages occur or have affected. Possible remedies include compensation, imprisonment, property confiscation, and reinstatement of the environment. However, the treaty has not gone into effect. The UN Economic Commission for Europe also sponsored the **Convention on Access to Information, Public Participation in Decision-Making and Access to Justice in Environmental Matters**, which not only provided freedom-of-information rights but also specifically acknowledged an obligation to future generations.

In 2010, the nearly bankrupt South Pacific state of Nauru, eager to attain financial solvency, considered the possibility of sponsoring an international firm to prospect the ocean floor within territorial waters but feared that in so doing liability would be assumed that might bankrupt the country in the event of resulting pollution or damage to the ocean. Accordingly, Nauru e-mailed the International

TABLE 14.4 **TREATIES DEALING WITH NUCLEAR ACCIDENTS, NUCLEAR POLLUTION, AND RADIOACTIVE WASTE**

Adopted	Agreement	In force
1957	Treaty Establishing the European Atomic Energy Community[a]	1958
1960	Convention on Third Party Liability in the Field of Nuclear Energy (Paris Convention)	1968
1963	• Convention Supplementary to the Paris Convention on Third Party Liability in the Field of Nuclear Energy (Brussels Convention)	1968
1988	• Joint Protocol Relating to the Application of the Vienna Convention and the Paris Convention	1992
1997	• Convention on Supplementary Compensation for Nuclear Damage	2003
1963	Vienna Convention on Civil Liability for Nuclear Damage	1977
1988	• Joint Protocol Relating to the Application of the Vienna Convention and the Paris Convention	1992
1997	• Protocol to Amend the Vienna Convention on Civil Liability for Nuclear Damage	2003
1997	• Convention on Supplementary Compensation for Nuclear Damage	2003
1963	Treaty Banning Nuclear Weapon Tests in the Atmosphere, in Outer Space and Under Water (Partial Test Ban Treaty)	1963
1971	Treaty on the Prohibition of the Emplacement of Nuclear Weapons and Other Weapons of Mass Destruction on the Sea Bed and the Ocean Floor and in the Subsoil Thereof	1972
1971	Convention Relating to Civil Liability in the Field of Maritime Carriage of Nuclear Material	1975
1977	Guidelines for Nuclear Transfers (London Guidelines)[b]	
1979	Convention on the Physical Protection of Nuclear Material	1987
1986	Convention on Early Notification of a Nuclear Accident	1986
1986	Convention on Assistance in the Case of a Nuclear Accident or Radiological Emergency	1987
1989	Protocol for the Protection of the South-East Pacific Against Radioactive Contamination	1995
1990	Code of Practice on the International Transboundary Movement of Radioactive Waste	1990
1994	Convention on Nuclear Safety	1996
1995	Convention to Ban the Importation into Forum Island Countries of Hazardous and Radio Active Waste and to Control the Transboundary Movement of Hazardous Waste Within the South Pacific Region	2001
1996	Comprehensive Test Ban Treaty	
1997	Joint Convention on the Safety of Spent Fuel Management and on the Safety of Radioactive Waste Management	2001
1998	Convention on the Protection of the Environment Through Criminal Law	

Continued

TABLE 14.4 (CONTINUED)

Date	Agreement	In force
2004	Code of Conduct on the Safety and Security of Radioactive Sources and the Supplementary Guidance on the Import and Export of Radioactive Sources	
2006	Code of Conduct on the Safety of Nuclear Reactors	

[a] Amended in 2009.

[b] Amended in 1993.

Tribunal on the Law of the Sea (ITLOS), which had been created in 1982, asking for an **advisory opinion**. The case, known as *Responsibilities and Obligations of States Sponsoring Persons and Entities with Respect to Activities in the Area*, provides the most definitive statement on the subject. The opinion, issued in 2011, indicated that Nauru's responsibility, as sponsor for the exploration, was to exercise "due diligence" by applying a precautionary approach and the "best environmental practices," that is, make preparations in case of emergencies and liability for pollution damage, and to conduct environmental impact assessments. As a developing country, ITLOS stated that Nauru thus would need technical assistance to meet the "due diligence" obligation. Active efforts to exercise "due diligence," based on Nauru's law and administrative enforcement regulations, would serve to absolve Nauru from liability for irresponsible actions of the contracting company. The liability would continue even after completion of exploration, since unexpected occurrences might later be evident on account of the disturbance created within the ocean.

Nuclear Pollution. In the 1950s, while the Cold War frightened the world with the prospect of mutual annihilation, nuclear weapons testing in Nevada and Siberia began without full knowledge of the adverse consequences. However, so much radioactive rain from Siberia landed in the Pacific Northwest and in Northern California, while I was studying at Stanford in 1957, that agricultural crops were deemed unfit for human and animal consumption, so I joined the outcry for a ban on atmospheric nuclear tests. That year the **Treaty Establishing the Atomic Energy Commission** was adopted, and the partial test ban treaty – the **Treaty Banning Nuclear Weapon Tests in the Atmosphere, in Outer Space and Under Water** – was adopted in 1963.

Dangers of nuclear pollution have been well recognized in international treaties (Table 14.4), particularly after the disaster at the nuclear power plant in Chernobyl, Ukraine, during 1986. Some countries have gone beyond by forming regional denuclearization pacts in Africa, the Antarctic, Caribbean, Central Asia, Latin America, Mongolia, the South Atlantic, the South Pacific, and Southeast Asia (Table 7.8). But the **Comprehensive Test Ban Treaty** of 1976 has lacked sufficient ratifications to go into effect (as well as the Convention on the Protection of the Environment Through Criminal Law of 1998).

In 2001, the International Tribunal for the Law of the Sea deliberated on the case of *Ireland v. UK* (2001), which involved British transportation of radioactive materials in the Irish Sea to a nuclear power plant in England. After Britain suspended shipments of radioactive materials in response to Ireland's request for **provisional**

TABLE 14.5 **MAJOR CONTEMPORARY AGREEMENTS DEALING WITH AIR AND LAND POLLUTION**

Adopted	Agreement	In force
1957	European Agreement Concerning the International Carriage of Dangerous Goods by Road (ADR)	1968
1967	Phyto-Sanitary Convention for Africa	1967
1968	European Agreement on the Restriction of the Use of Certain Detergents in Washing and Cleaning Products	1971
1971	Convention Concerning Protection Against Hazards of Poisoning Arising from Benzene	1973
1977	Convention Concerning the Protection of Workers Against Occupational Hazards in the Working Environment due to Air Pollution, Noise and Vibration	1979
1979	Convention on Long-Range Transboundary Air Pollution[a]	1983
1985	Vienna Convention for the Protection of the Ozone Layer	1988
1987	• Montréal Protocol on Substances That Deplete the Ozone Layer[a]	1989
1986	Single European Act	1987
1989	Convention on the Control of Transboundary Movements of Hazardous Wastes and Their Disposal[a]	1992
1999	• Protocol on Liability and Compensation for Damage Resulting from Transboundary Movements of Hazardous Wastes	
1989	Convention on Civil Liability for Damage Caused During Carriage of Dangerous Goods by Road, Rail and Inland Navigation Vessels	
1991	Convention on the Ban of the Import into Africa and the Control of Transboundary Movement and Management of Hazardous Wastes Within Africa (Bamako Convention)[a]	1998
1991	Convention on Environmental Impact Assessment in a Transboundary Context[a]	1997
1992	[Central American] Regional Agreement on Transboundary Movements of Hazardous Wastes	1995
1992	Framework Convention on Climate Change	1994
1997	• Kyoto Protocol	2005
1992	Convention on the Transboundary Effects of Industrial Accidents	2000
1993	Convention on Civil Liability for Damage Resulting from Activities Dangerous to the Environment	
1993	North American Agreement on Environmental Cooperation	1994
1993	Convention Concerning the Prevention of Major Industrial Accidents	1997
1994	Agreement on the Application of Sanitary and Phytosanitary Measures	1995
1994	Energy Charter Protocol on Energy Efficiency and Related Environmental Aspects	1998
1997	Amsterdam Treaty	1999
1998	CoE Convention on the Protection of Environment Through Criminal Law	
1998	Rotterdam Convention On the Prior Informed Consent Procedure for Certain Hazardous Chemicals and Pesticides in International Trade[a]	2004

Continued

TABLE *14.5* (CONTINUED)

Adopted	Agreement	In force
2001	Stockholm Convention on Persistent Organic Pollutants	2004
2002	ASEAN Agreement on Transboundary Haze Pollution	2002
2003	Kiev Protocol on Pollutant Release and Transfer Registers[a]	2009
2009	Statute of the International Renewable Energy Agency	

[a] Amended or revised, sometimes by protocols.

measures from ITLOS, the tribunal ruled that the two countries should establish cooperative arrangements to ensure that no mishaps would occur in the future.

Air and Land Pollution. The *Trail Smelter* case was the first international dispute to deal with pollution of the land coming through the air. Smog-choked industrial cities after World War II fuelled the demand for clear air apart from problems on land (Table 14.5).

The first major agreement was the **Convention on Long-Range Transboundary Air Pollution** of 1979, an effort of the UN Economic Commission for Europe. Nine subsequent protocols have identified deadlines for reducing various airborne chemicals by specific percentages, including fluxes, heavy metals, nitrous oxides, ozone, sulfur, and toxic organic pesticides.

HISTORIC EVENT 14.2 THE BHOPAL INDUSTRIAL ACCIDENT (1984)

In 1984, 40 tons of chemicals leaked from the Union Carbide pesticide plant in Bhopal, India, resulting ultimately in some 22,000 deaths and 550,000 injuries. An investigation later concluded that Union Carbide was liable because alarm and safety systems had been scaled back to reduce costs. Two years later, an Indian court subpoenaed Warren Anderson (1921–), the head of the company, for questioning. Although promised that he would not be arrested, Indian authorities placed him in custody upon arrival in the country. Anderson posted bail, returned to the United States, and has refused to return to India. In 1986, Union Carbide, sued in an American court, offered a settlement, whereupon the court transferred jurisdiction to India. In 1989, the Indian government accepted an out-of-court settlement with Union Carbide of US$470 million for the victims. However, the company abandoned the plant without cleaning up the toxic chemicals, so the poisons remain to haunt the people, and about one person per day dies from the exposure. In 1992, Anderson was declared a fugitive by an Indian court for failing to appear as a defendant charged with manslaughter. In 2001, Dow Chemical Company bought Union Carbide, which hoped thereby to escape liability, but the Indian court then added Dow to the lawsuit and asked the US government to extradite Anderson, a

Continued

request that Washington has refused. In June 2010, seven former employees of the Union Carbide subsidiary, all Indian nationals, were convicted of causing death by negligence and sentenced to two years imprisonment and fined about US$2,000, but they were later released. Litigation seeking damages for personal injury, medical monitoring, property damage, and injunctive relief to clean up the drinking water for residents near Bhopal failed in *Sahu v. Union Carbide* during 2012, but the case was dismissed on appeal.

Efforts to reduce air pollution continued in the 1980s, particularly after the leaking of chemicals from a plant in Bhopal, India, during 1984. In 1985, after a hole in the ozone layer of the Antarctic had been discovered, the **Vienna Convention for the Protection of the Ozone Layer** was adopted as a framework agreement while provisions of the **Montréal Protocol on Substances That Deplete the Ozone Layer** were developed. The protocol, adopted in 1987, then banned most known causes of ozone depletion, especially chlorofluorocarbons, and set a compliance deadline of 2000. The two agreements, sponsored by the UNEP, were the first efforts to control global pollutants. The ozone layer is expected to be repaired by 2025 as a result.

In 1986, the **Single European Act** empowered the European Community to act on environmental and natural-resources issues. In 1993, the European Union established the European Environmental Agency, with a secretariat at Copenhagen, to facilitate data collection so that over 200 environmental protection directives, mostly regarding air and water pollution and waste disposal, could be enforced. The agency, with expanded powers under the **Amsterdam Treaty** of 1997, has suggested many new environmental standards. Similar agreements were adopted for Africa and Central America. Several treaties dealing with aid and land pollution have also focused on hazardous chemicals.

A case involving air and land pollution dating from 1988 reached the European Commission, which referred the case to the European Court of Human Rights as its first case on environmental pollution. In *Lopez Ostra v. Spain* (1994), the plaintiff complained that for three years a licensed waste-treatment plant emitted polluting fumes, pestilential and irritant smells, and repetitive noise that prompted his family to move because of adverse health to a family member. The court ruled that Spain had violated the European Convention for Human Rights because, apart from health considerations, the plant adversely affected the family's "private and family life." A similar ruling emerged in *Guerra et al. v. Italy* (1998).

Meanwhile, evidence that world temperatures were increasing had appeared to some scientists during the mid-1980s. Accordingly, UNEP and the World Meteorological Organization, another UN Specialized Agency, set up an Intergovernmental Panel on Climate Change (IPCC) in 1988 to evaluate scientific evidence about possible environmental and socioeconomic risks of climate change trends caused by human activity and to determine what could be done to mitigate the effects. The first reports in 1990 and 1992 were startling, reporting a 41 percent increase in carbon dioxide since the beginning of the Industrial Revolution, resulting in an increase in the planet temperature by 1.5 degrees Fahrenheit since 1950. They predicted a meltdown of frozen ice masses that would cause spring floods, a rise in sea levels, and such an acidification and cooling of the warm currents in the Atlantic and Pacific that there would be an increase in catastrophic storms as well as drought on account of soil erosion worldwide. The cause was identified as increased infrared radiation caused by the burning of fossil fuels, particularly coal and petroleum. The main socioeconomic impact was that food production would drop as crops died before harvest because of high temperatures during cultivation, and millions of animal species would become extinct because of ecosystem changes and acidifying oceans. The analogy of a greenhouse was offered as an explanation: The planet was getting hotter because CO_2 and other gases (methane, nitrous oxide, ozone, water vapor) were trapped in the atmosphere with vegetation, particularly forests, unable fully to absorb the CO_2 being depleted by the higher temperatures. The consensus has developed that the changes are largely irreversible but mitigable.

In 1992, the **Framework Convention on Climate Change** was adopted with a pledge to decrease greenhouse gases. Specific protocols were expected to follow. The **North American Agreement on Environmental Cooperation** of 1993 appeared to address the issue but left enforcement to the three states (Canada, México, United States).

A follow-up conference met in 1997. After evaluating IPCC reports, delegates adopted the **Kyoto Protocol** to the Framework Convention in 1997. Under the protocol, which went into effect in 2005, three dozen industrialized countries agreed to reduce gas emissions an average of 5.2 percent for 2008–2012, relative to their annual emissions in 1990 or some other base year. The method for reducing emissions was left to individual states. Industrial enterprises would have to pay for the cost of retrofitting facilities unless governments picked up the enormous cost, but neither was eager to fulfill the Kyoto pledge.

A clever feature in the Kyoto Protocol is the **Clean Development Mechanism**, which supports energy projects in developing countries that produce electricity through alternatives, such as hydropower projects, that serve to reduce carbon dioxide emissions. Sometimes known by the name "cap and trade," the mechanism encourages developed countries to made reductions by trading one ton of CO_2 produced in excess of the 1990 level for a project in a developing country that will save an equivalent amount of carbon dioxide.

Climate change already had an adverse effect on the South Pacific island nation of Tuvalu. In 2002, the first of 11,000 citizens began an evacuation from their nine coral atolls to New Zealand, since the country is gradually becoming inundated as the ocean floor rises. Similar developments are occurring in Kiribati and along shorelines of other South Pacific island states as well as the Maldives in the Indian Ocean. An estimated 200–240 million inhabitants living along coastlines around the world will be forced to move as their habitats are overwhelmed by a sea level increase by 7 inches or more by 2050. Where will they go?

Since methane from animal excrement in open pits accounts for about 7 percent of the CO_2 in the atmosphere, an Irish firm with UN funding installed a biomass project in Villegrán, México, during 2005. One of many Clean Development

Mechanism projects consistent with the Kyoto Protocol, the biomass facility not only produces electric power but also eliminates the stench from pig excrement that formerly bothered local residents.

After the Kyoto Protocol went into force in 1994, more IPCC reports appeared in 1995, 2001, 2007, and another is due in 2014. In 2008, the intergovernmental committee of the Framework Convention set the maximum allowable warming at an increase of no more than 3.6° Fahrenheit. By 2012, they agreed that the goal appeared unattainable, as there was a 3 percent increase in emissions during 2011 alone.

Although 150 countries have ratified the Kyoto Protocol, coalburning Australia and the United States refused to do so, and developing countries were not required to implement provisions until 2012, when the treaty expired for developed countries. The United States, then the largest polluter of CO_2 emissions, signed the Protocol but the Senate did not ratify the agreement. Senators from states contributing the most CO_2, representing polluting industries, even began to deny the claims of climate change. Thus, progress did not occur as planned. Although many countries agreed voluntarily to continue to reduce greenhouse gases at a conference in 2009, the Protocol lapsed in 2012, by which time China had become the world's worst polluter of greenhouse gases. Nevertheless, the US Environmental Protection Agency launched a Green Power Partnership in which some 24 cities in the United States have adopted "green power" as the sole basis for municipal utilities, and businesses and colleges have been encouraged to do likewise. The State of Hawai'i declared that 70 percent of electric sources would be from renewable energy by 2030.

Proactive efforts to cope with climate change led to two agreements. The **Energy Charter Protocol on Energy Efficiency and Related Environmental Aspects** of 1994 requires countries to minimize pollution by making energy production more efficient. An Energy Charter Conference, with 51 members mostly from industrial countries, provides a forum for exchange on information on making energy production more efficient. In 2009, the **Statute of the International Renewable Energy Agency** was adopted as a separate intergovernmental organization, headquartered in Abu Dhabi, to promote the use of alternative energy sources. The agency currently has 105 member countries, including not only industrial countries but also many African countries. An Innovation Technology Center is located in Bonn, Germany, where the statute was signed. The budget for 2012 was US$28.4 million, hardly enough for the task at hand, and the treaty has not yet entered into force.

With the lapse of the Kyoto Protocol in 2012, there is no international treaty to protect the planet from global warming. American courts have consistently argued that there is no clear basis for asserting environmental rights under international law. Meanwhile, evidence of global warming suggests a doomsday scenario in which much of the earth will be flooded, and the rest will turn into desert, making planet earth largely uninhabitable. A major need is to find a way to stop the continual increase in temperature before a tipping point is reached.

DISCUSSION TOPIC 14.2 HOW CAN COUNTRIES BE PERSUADED TO STOP GLOBAL WARMING?

Developed countries are responsible for a very large percentage of greenhouse gas emissions today, and such developing countries as India are catching up. Meanwhile, less developed countries seek prosperity by utilizing energy sources that pollute, but they may not be able to bear the high cost of environmental measures to stop pollution. Island nations in the Indian and Pacific oceans, meanwhile, are experiencing rising sea levels that have already destroyed agriculture and habitable land and may inundate their countries in the future. Currently, Palau wants the International Court of Justice to issue an advisory opinion that countries failing to take effective measures to stop their own pollution are committing a breach of the most fundamental Westphalian principle of international law – engaging in transboundary harm. Is a legal opinion the best way to stop global warming? What are the alternatives?

The urgency of acting to save civilization provides solemn responsibilities to the human race.

CONSERVATION

The opening up of the wilderness of what became the coast-to-coast United States of America was initially seen in commercial terms, with no concern for the native peoples of North America. After the American Civil War, NGOs became involved in conservation efforts. In 1876, after the Civil War, astronomer/physicist, Edward Charles Pickering (1846–1919), formed the **Appalachian Mountain Club**, at first to conserve, explore, and promote outdoor recreation in the White Mountains of New Hampshire. The club grew along the Appalachian range down the east coast. In 1886, the **Audubon Society** was founded in the United States with particular interest in keeping the environment safe for birds. On the Pacific coast, naturalist John Muir (1838–1914) formed the **Sierra Club** on similar lines in 1892 with the goals of establishing natural parks in Alaska and Yosemite Valley as well as saving the redwoods from over-logging. In 1903, Muir escorted President Theodore Roosevelt (1858–1919) through Yosemite, and the president championed the national park system as a way to preserve the natural environment for its own sake.

The commercial interest in the dangers of overhunting prompted agreements in the 1890s and the first half of the twentieth century to limit catches of birds, fishes, fur seals, whales, and wild animals.[5] Those concerns continue to the present.

After World War II, more IGOs blossomed. In 1948, the **International Union for Conservation of Nature** was formed in France to bring governments, scientists, and NGOs together to "influence, encourage and assist societies throughout the world to conserve nature and to ensure that any use of natural resources is equitable and ecologically sustainable." The world's oldest and largest global environmental network, the Union encompasses more than 1,000 government and NGO member organizations and almost 11,000 volunteer scientists in more than 160 countries.

In 1961, the World Wildlife Fund (WWF) was established in New York "to halt and reverse the destruction of our environment." Under the new name, **World Wide Fund for Nature** (but still as WWF), the organization's focus on climate change and endangered species has attracted some five million supporters in over 100 countries, and is noted for a logo with the giant panda. Many other NGOs have pressured governments to respect nature.

Rachel Carson's *Silent Spring* (1962) not only urged a ban on DDT but also expressed a deep concern for measures that would isolate and protect the natural environment from commercial exploitation. But serious concern about conservation was not taken up for three decades.

Then, in 1992, a major international effort to deal with global environmental issues finally came when the United Nations sponsored the Conference on the Environment and Development at Stockholm. One key provision of the **Stockholm Declaration on the Human Environment** stated, "Man has a fundamental right to freedom, equality and adequate conditions of life, in an environment of a quality that permits a life of dignity and well-being …." The principles of nuisance and trespass from the *Trail Smelter* case were recognized in the declaration. The concept of sustainable development was also endorsed at the conference as a compromise, namely, that the goal of substantially increasing living standards of the impoverished was to occur in an environmentally sustainable manner.

A meeting of Experts on Human Rights and the Environment at the United Nations in 1994 produced a Draft Declaration of Principles on Human Rights and the Environment, stating that everyone has "the right to a secure, healthy and ecologically sound environment." Once again, there was a reluctance to state environmental issues in terms of rights, and the draft statement was never issued. That same year, President Bill Clinton (1946–) coined a new term, **environmental justice**, within Executive Order 12898, entitled Federal Actions to Address Environmental Justice in Minority Populations and Low-Income Populations, which recognizes that environmental problems are often dumped into communities with the least political power.

In 1997, UNESCO issued **the Declaration on the Responsibilities of the Present Generation Towards Future Generations**. After a general provision that the present generation should feel obligated to ensure that the needs of future generations would be met, the Declaration identified 10 basic needs. One was to ensure that ecosystems would not be irreversibly damaged. A second was that "present generations should preserve for future generations natural resources necessary for sustaining human life and for its development."

The **Millennium Declaration**, issued by the United Nations in 2000, provided eight major goals to be achieved by 2010. One of the goals, sustainable development, mandated the reversal of the loss of environmental resources without sacrificing economic development.

In 2002, at the World Summit on Sustainable Development, a **Plan of Action** was adopted that took note of "the possible relationship between environment and human rights, including the right to development." The statement went on to endorse "good governance" (public participation and government responsiveness) as central to the task of development alongside the need for a clean and healthy environment.

Concern over conservation of the world's natural resources has led to three types of international agreements:

- Protection of forests and plants
- Protection of coastal, riparian, and oceanic ecosystems
- Protection of species, including birds, fish, and mammals.

However, many agreements have tilted more in the direction of commercial motivations rather than toward the future of the planet.

Conservation of Forests and Plants. The earliest plant conservation agreement, the **Convention on Preservation of Fauna and Flora in Their Natural State** of 1933, set the tone for later agreements. But as the world population grew dramatically after World War II, pests were destroying crops at an alarming rate. The Food and Agriculture Organization of the UN (FAO) then sponsored the **International Plant Protection Convention** of 1951, a milestone in focusing on the problem of how plants can be damaged by pests, though the clear subtext was plant preservation. Subsequent plant protection agreements were developed for Antarctica, Europe, the Mediterranean, the Near East, the Pacific, and Southeast Asia as well as for new hybrids (Table 14.6). One particular pest, the locust, prompted special treaties for Africa. But one pest treatment was DDT, which the WHO had approved to eradicate malaria. The sun and absence of rain have been a pest too, causing desertification in Africa, which has also been addressed by international treaties (Table 14.6).

In 1970, President Richard Nixon (1913–1994) urged the UN to act on a proposal by former President Lyndon Johnson (1908–1973) in 1965 for a World Heritage Trust to protect the environment in special areas around the world. In response, in 1972 UNESCO sponsored the adoption of the **Convention Concerning the Protection of World Cultural and Natural Heritage**, which established the World Heritage Committee to identify World Heritage Sites around the world. Currently, there are 644 cultural, 162 natural, and 24 mixed cultural/natural World Heritage Sites in 138 countries. Three examples of natural World Heritage Sites are Kew Gardens in London, the Galápagos Islands, and the rice terraces of Bauaue, Philippines. In 1998, the Heritage Committee asked Australia to stop uranium mining near Kakadu Park, which was listed as a World Heritage Site, or the site would be listed as "in danger."

Subsequently, UNEP and other organizations sponsored international environmental agreements that fluctuated from retail to wholesale approaches. Regional agreements were adopted for Africa, the Alps, the Amazon, Benelux countries, Central America, Central Asia, Scandinavia, Southeast Asia, and the South Pacific (Table 14.6).

As always, nongovernmental organizations had to lead the way. In 1987, a nongovernmental initiative, **Rainforest Alliance** (RA), was founded to curtail the wanton felling of trees and damaging of ecosystems by promoting sustainable agriculture and forestry. In 1989, RA founded **SmartWood**, a forestry product certification system. RA joined in 1994 with similar groups in five countries to form the **Sustainable**

TABLE *14.6* CONTEMPORARY CONSERVATION TREATIES ON FORESTS AND PLANTS

Adopted	Treaty	In force
1951	International Plant Protection Convention	1952
1951	Convention for the Establishment of the European and Mediterranean Plant Protection Organization	1953
1956	Plant Protection Agreement for the South East Asia and Pacific Region	1956
1959	Concerning Cooperation in the Quarantine of Plants and Their Protection Against Pests and Diseases	1960
1959	The Antarctic Treaty[a]	1964
1964	• Agreed Measures for the Conservation of Antarctic Flora and Fauna	1978
1991	• Protocol to the Antarctic Treaty on Environmental Protection	1998
1961	International Convention for the Protection of New Varieties of Plants	1968
1965	Agreement for the Establishment of a Commission for Controlling the Desert Locust in the Central Region	
1972	Stockholm Declaration on the Human Environment	
1972	Convention Concerning the Protection of the World Cultural and Natural Heritage	1975
1973	Convention for International Trade in Endangered Species of Wild Fauna and Flora (CITES)	1975
1974	Nordic Convention on the Protection of the Environment	1976
1978	Treaty for Amazonian Cooperation	1980
1982	Convention on Biological Diversity	1993
2000	• Cartagena Protocol	2003
1982	World Charter for Nature	
1982	Benelux Convention on Nature Conservation and Landscape Protection	1983
1983	International Tropical Timber Agreement	1985
1985	ASEAN Agreement on the Conservation of Nature and Natural Resources	1985
1986	Convention for the Protection of the Natural Resources and Environment of the South Pacific Region	1990
1991	Convention on Environmental Impact Assessment in a Transboundary Context	1997
2003	• Protocol on the Assessment of the Environmental Impact of Strategic Decisions	2010
1991	Convention Concerning the Protection of the Alps (Alpine Convention)	
1994	• Protocol on the Implementation of the Alpine Convention of 1991 Relating to Spatial Planning and Sustainable Development	1995
1994	• Protocol ... Relating to the Conservation of Nature and the Countryside[b]	
1994	• Protocol ... in the Field of Mountain Farming	
1996	• Protocol ... Relating to Mountain Forests	
1998	• Protocol ... in the Field of Soil Conservation	
2000	• Protocol ... in the Field of Transport	
2000	• Protocol ... Relating to the Conservation of Nature and the Countryside	
1992	Río Declaration on Environment and Development	
1992	Convention on Biological Diversity	1993
2000	• Cartagena Protocol on Biological Diversity	2003

Continued

TABLE 14.6 (CONTINUED)

Adopted	Treaty	In force
1992	Statement of Principles for Global Consensus on the Management, Conservation and Sustainable Development of All Types of Forests	
1992	Convention for the Conservation of the Biodiversity and the Protection of Wilderness Areas in Central America	1994
1992	Constitution of the Joint Authority for the Study and Development of the Nubian Sandstone Aquifer	1992
1993	Agreement on the Establishment of a Near East Plant Protection Organization	2009
1993	[Central American] Regional Convention for the Management and Conservation of the Natural Forest Ecosystems and the Development of Forest Plantations	1999
1994	UN Convention to Combat Desertification in those Countries Experiencing Serious Drought and/or Desertification	1996
1994	International Tropical Timber Agreement	1997
1994	Lusaka Agreement on Cooperative Enforcement Operations Directed at Illegal Trade in Wild Flora and Fauna	1996
1994	United Nations Convention to Combat Desertification in Those Countries Experiencing Serious Drought and/or Desertification, Particularly in Africa	1996
1995	Formalization of the Organization of the Fishing and Agricultural Sector of the Central American Isthmus (Act of San Salvador)	
1995	Protocol Concerning Specially Protected Areas and Biological Diversity in the Mediterranean (SPA and Biodiversity Protocol)	1999
2000	Agreement for the Establishment of a Commission for Controlling the Desert Locust in the Western Region	
2001	International Treaty on Plant Genetic Resources for Food and Agriculture	2004
2003	Framework Convention on the Protection and Sustainable Development of the Carpathians	2006
2011	• Protocol on Sustainable Forest Management	
2004	Agreement on the Establishment of the Global Crop Diversity Trust	2004
2005	Treaty on the Conservation and Sustainable Development of the Forest Ecosystems of Central Africa	
2006	Framework Convention for the Protection of the Environment for Sustainable Development in Central Asia	
2006	International Tropical Timber Agreement	2007

[a] Amended or revised, sometimes by protocols.

[b] The omitted words are "on the Implementation of the Alpine Convention of 1991."

Agricultural Network (SAN), which has certified more than 80,000 farms accounting for 1.8 million hectares of bananas, citrus products, cocoa, coffee, cut flowers, ferns, pineapples, timber, and other products as ecologically sound within 36 countries. Currently, SAN is linked to organizations in 10 Central and South American countries. RA provides SAN's secretariat in New York. Most certification criteria focus on conservation (ecosystem, water, wildlife) and agricultural management (crop, soil, and waste management), but community development and fair labor standards for workers are also involved, thereby overlapping with Fair Trade standards (see Chapter 6). RA certification deals primarily with ecological and scientific elements, while the Fair Trade movement focuses on uplifting farmers from poverty. RA's first major success came in 1994, when a Chiquita Banana plantation received the first RA certification. In the next decade, Dole Corporation spent US$20 million to gain RA certification for all its banana plantations. RA also promotes ecotourism.

One of the outcomes of the Stockholm Conference of 1992 was a nonbinding **Statement of Principles for Global Consensus on the Management, Conservation and Sustainable Development of All Types of Forests.** The object was to limit logging in rainforests because developing countries feared that their forests would be internationalized. Forest preservation agreements now exist for the Africa, the Alps, the Carpathian Mountains, and Central America as well as agreements to preserve timber from overharvesting (Table 14.6).

Major progress, also in 1992, was the adoption of the **Convention on Biological Diversity.** The agreement not only focuses on the need to preserve biological species before they become extinct but also deals with the regulation of biotechnology, as the fear is that genetically modified organisms (GMOs) will cannibalize existing species, resulting in a loss of species.

The **Cartagena Protocol** of 2000 to the Biological Diversity Convention establishes procedures for countries to follow when they import modified organisms. Today, 61 countries, including all of Europe, have some form of mandatory labels on genetically engineered foods. In 2012, a ballot proposition in California to require such labeling failed because the industry, particularly tomato growers, outspent proponents with deceptive ads, while the anti-GMO campaign was pitched at a philosophical level, failing to point out such facts as GMO tomatoes are injected with an Arctic fish enzyme to promote shelf life.

Conservation of Coastal, Riparian, and Oceanic Resources. Cooperation among countries along the Danube and Rhine occasioned agreements in the nineteenth century. In the twentieth century, the same imperative has resulted in agreements regarding coastal (African), riparian (Amazon, Baltic and Black Seas, Caspian Sea, Central Asia, Chad, Danube, Elbe, Lake Tanganyika, Mekong, Meuse, Niger, Okavango, Red Sea, Scheldt, Senegal, Zambezi), and oceanic (Atlantic, Bengal Bay, Gulf of Aden, Caribbean, Mediterranean, Pacific) regions as well as the continental shelf (Table 14.7).

The most generic agreement regarding the high seas is the **United Nations Convention on the Law of the Sea** of 1982, which was designed to settle disputes overfishing and continental shelf mining by assigning a uniform exclusive economic zone of 200 miles adjacent to all countries with oceanic coastlines. The International Tribunal for the Law of the Sea, as discussed above, was set up to handle disputes regarding protection of the marine environment as the "common heritage of mankind" through arbitration. In 1984, when the Convention received sufficient ratifications to go into force, the International Seabed Authority was established at Kingston, Jamaica, and ITLOS at Hamburg. In 2003, when Malaysia

TABLE 14.7   CONTEMPORARY COASTAL, RIPARIAN, AND OCEANIC CONSERVATION TREATIES

Adopted	Treaty	In force
1947	Canberra Agreement [for the South Pacific Commission]	1948
1948	Convention Concerning the Regime of Navigation on the Danube[a]	1949
1958	Convention Concerning Fishing in the Waters of the Danube	1958
1958	Convention on the Continental Shelf	1964
1959	Convention Concerning Fishing in the Black Sea	1960
1964	Agreement Concerning the Niger River Commission and the Navigation and Transport on the River Niger	1966
1964	Convention and Statute Relating to the Development of the Chad Basin	
1964	Convention for the International Council for the Exploration of the Sea	1968
1971	Convention on Wetlands of International Importance Especially as Waterfowl Habitat[a]	1975
1972	Agreement Establishing the Lake Chad Basin Commission Development Fund	
1972	Convention Concerning the Status of the Senegal River, and Convention Establishing the Senegal River Development Organization	1972
1973	Agreement Revising the Agreement Concerning the Niger River Commission and the Navigation and Transport on the River Niger of 25 November 1964	1973
1974	Convention for the Protection of the Marine Environment of the Baltic Sea Area[a]	1980
1974	Convention on the Protection of the Environment Between Denmark, Finland, Norway and Sweden	1975
1976	Convention for the Protection of the Marine Environment and Coastal Region of the Mediterranean Sea (Barcelona Convention)	1978
1978	Treaty for Amazonian Cooperation	1980
1980	Convention Creating the Niger Basin Authority	1982
1981	Convention for Co-operation in the Protection and Development of the Marine and Coastal Environment of the West and Central African Region	1984
1981	Convention for the Protection of the Marine Environment and Coastal Area of the South-East Pacific[a]	1986
1982	Protocol Concerning Mediterranean Specially Protected Areas (SPA Protocol)	1986
1982	Regional Convention for the Conservation of the Red Sea and the Gulf of Aden	1985
1983	Convention for the Protection and Development of the Marine Environment of the Wider Caribbean (Cartagena Convention)[a]	1986
1985	Convention for the Protection, Management and Development of the Marine and Coastal Environment of the Eastern African Region (Nairobi Convention)[a]	1996
2010	• Amended Nairobi Convention for the Protection, Management and Development of the Marine and Coastal Environment of the Western Indian Ocean	

Continued

Table 14.7 (Continued)

Adopted	Treaty	In force
1986	Convention for the Protection of the Natural Resources and Environment of the South Pacific Region	1990
1987	Agreement on the Action Plan for the Environmentally Sound Management of the Common Zambezi River System	1987
1990	Convention for a North Pacific Marine Science Organization	1992
1990	Convention Between the Federal Republic of Germany and the Czech and Slovak Federal Republic and the European Economic Community on the International Commission for the Protection of the Elbe	1991
1992	Convention on the Protection and Use of Transboundary Watercourses and International Lakes[a]	1996
1992	Convention for the Protection of the Marine Environment of the North-East Atlantic (OSPAR Convention)	1998
1993	Agreement Establishing the South Pacific Regional Environment Program	1995
1993	Agreement to Promote Compliance with International Conservation and Management Measures by Fishing Vessels on the High Seas	2003
1994	Convention on Cooperation for the Protection and Sustainable Use of the Danube	1998
1994	Treaty for the International Commission for the Protection of the Meuse and Scheldt Rivers	1995
1994	Agreement on the Protection of the River Meuse	1995
1994	Agreement on the Protection of the River Scheldt	1995
1994	Agreement Between the Governments of the Republic of Angola, the Republic of Botswana, and the Republic of Namibia on the Establishment of a Permanent Okavango River Basin Water Commission	1994
1995	Agreement on the Cooperation for Sustainable Development of the Mekong River Basin	1995
1995	Protocol on Shared Watercourse Systems in the Southern African Development Community Region[a]	1998
1998	Convention on the Protection of the Rhine	1999
2002	Convention for Cooperation in the Protection and Sustainable Development of the Marine and Coastal Environment of the Northeast Pacific	
2003	Convention on the Sustainable Management of Lake Tanganyika	2005
2003	Framework Convention for the Protection of the Marine Environment of the Caspian Sea	2006
2003	Bay of Bengal Program Inter-Governmental Organization Agreement	2003
2006	Framework Convention for the Protection of the Environment for Sustainable Development in Central Asia	
2008	Niger Basin Water Charter	

Continued

TABLE 14.7 **(CONTINUED)**

Adopted	Treaty	In force
2009	Agreement Recognizing the International Legal Personality of the Partnerships in Environmental Management for the Seas of East Asia	2009
2009	Agreement on the Central Asian and Caucasus Regional Fisheries and Aquaculture Commission	

[a] Amended or revised, sometimes by protocols.

filed a case against Singapore regarding the latter's plans to reclaim land that might adversely affect Malaysia's navigation, coastal deposition, and deteriorating ecohydraulic and water quality conditions, ITLOS ruled that Singapore should abandon its plan because of potential damage to the marine environment.

In the age of free trade under the WTO, corporations have gradually bought sources of fresh drinking water around the world, even with the encouragement in Europe by the European Union, and then have sold water at high prices. Implicit in the Stockholm Declaration of 1992 was that there is a **right to water** for human consumption. The **Convention on the Law of the Non-Navigational Uses of International Watercourses** of 1992 and the **Protocol on Shared Watercourse Systems in the Southern African Development Community Region** of 1995 were designed to compete with efforts of transnational corporations to buy up sources of fresh water. Target 10 of the later Millennium Goals mandates the "reductions by half [of] the proportion of people without sustainable access to safe drinking water and basic sanitation" by 2015, though by 2010 some 1.2 billion persons still had no access to fresh water and 2.6 billion lacked adequate sanitation. The right to water is addressed in at least two treaties (Convention on the Elimination of All Forms of Discrimination Against Women; Convention on the Rights of the Child). Recently, several countries have included the right to water in their constitutions – Ecuador (1998), Uganda (1995), Gambia, South Africa, and Zambia (1996), Ethiopia (1998), Uruguay (2004), Kenya and Nicaragua (2005), and Democratic Republic of the Congo (2006). In 2010, the UN General Assembly and Human Rights Council declared that there is a basic right to water and sanitation.

Conservation of Fisheries and Cetaceans. In 1923, the **Convention for the Preservation of the Halibut Fishery of the North Pacific**, and in 1927 the **Agreement on Development of the Fishing Resources of the Southern Coast of the Caspian Sea** were the first international agreements aimed at conserving fish stocks.

But efforts to cope with the whale population stole the show. The **International Convention for the Regulation of Whaling** of 1931 between Britain, Germany, and Norway, totally prohibited killing right whales, though there was an exemption for aboriginal groups that used traditional harvesting methods. The **International Agreement for the Regulation of Whaling** of 1937 expanded coverage to all gray whales as well as smaller blue, fin, humpback, and sperm whales, but no purpose was stated in either treaty other than regulation. By the time of the latter treaty, 10 countries had ratified. Specific protocols in 1938, 1944, 1945, and 1946 extended coverage.

TABLE 14.8 **CONTEMPORARY CONSERVATION TREATIES ON FISHERIES AND CETACEANS**

Adopted	Treaty	In force
1946	Convention for the Regulation of the Meshes of Fishing Nets and Size Limits of Fish	1953
1946	International Convention for the Regulation of Whaling[a]	1948
1948	Agreement for the Establishment of the Asia-Pacific Fishery Commission	1948
1949	International Convention for the Northwest Atlantic Fisheries	1950
1949	Convention for the Establishment of an Inter-American Tropical Tuna Commission	1950
1952	International Convention for the High Seas Fisheries of the North Pacific Ocean[a]	1953
1952	Agreement Concerning Measures for the Protection of the Stocks of Deep-Sea Prawns (*Pandalus borealis*), European Lobsters (*Homarus vulgaris*), Norway Lobsters (*Nephrops norvegicus*) and Crabs (*Cancer pagurus*)	1959
1953	Convention for the Preservation of the Halibut Fishery of the Northern Pacific Ocean and Bering Sea	1953
1979	• Protocol Amending the Convention	1980
1958	North-East Atlantic Fisheries Convention	1959
1958	Convention on Fishing and Conservation of the Living Resources of the High Seas[a]	1966
1959	Convention Concerning Fishing in the Black Sea	1960
1962	Agreement Concerning Cooperation in Marine Fishing	1962
1966	International Convention for the Conservation of Atlantic Tuna[a]	1969
1967	Agreement Establishing the Southeast Asian Fisheries Development Center	1967
1978	Convention on Future Multilateral Cooperation in the Northwest Atlantic Fisheries	1979
1978	Convention on Future Multilateral Cooperation in North-East Atlantic Fisheries	1982
1979	South Pacific Forum Fisheries Agency Convention	1979
1980	Convention on Future Multilateral Cooperation in Northeast Atlantic Fisheries	1982
1982	Constitutional Agreement of the Latin American Organization for Fisheries Development	1984
1982	Convention for the Conservation of Salmon in the North Atlantic Ocean	1983
1982	Nauru Agreement Concerning Cooperation in the Management of Fisheries of Common Interest	1982
1984	Convention Concerning the Regional Development of Fisheries in the Gulf of Guinea	1991
1985	Convention Establishing the Subregional Fisheries Commission	
1987	Multilateral Treaty on Fisheries Between Certain Governments of the Pacific Island States and the Government of the United States of America[a]	1987

Continued

TABLE 14.8 (CONTINUED)

Adopted	Treaty	In force
1987	Fisheries Treaty Between the Pacific Island Parties and the United States of America	1988
1989	Convention for the Prohibition of Fishing with Long Driftnets in the South Pacific[a]	1989
1992	Niue Treaty on Cooperation in Fisheries Surveillance and Law Enforcement in the South Pacific Region	1993
1992	Convention for the Conservation of Anadromous Stocks in the North Pacific Ocean	1993
1992	Agreement on the Conservation of Small Cetaceans of the Baltic and North Seas	1994
1993	Commission for the Conservation of South Bluefin Tuna	1994
1993	Agreement for the Establishment of the Indian Ocean Tuna Commission	1996
1995	Agreement for the Implementation of the Provisions of the UN Convention on the Law of the Sea of 10 December 1982 Relating to the Conservation and Management of Straddling Fish Stocks and Highly Migratory Fish Stocks	2001
1994	Convention on the Conservation and Management of Pollock Resources in the Central Bering Sea Area	1995
1994	Convention for the Establishment of the Lake Victoria Fishing Organization	1996
1995	Formalization of the Organization of the Fishing and Agricultural Sector of the Central American Isthmus (Act of San Salvador)	2001
1995	UN Fish Stocks Agreement	
1996	Agreement on the Conservation of Cetaceans of the Black Sea, Mediterranean Sea and Contiguous Atlantic Area	2001
1999	Agreement for the Establishment of the Regional Commission for Fisheries [Persian Gulf]	2001
2000	Convention for the Conservation and Management of Highly Migratory Fish Stocks in the Western and Central Pacific Ocean (WCPF Convention)	2004
2000	Framework Agreement for the Conservation of Living Marine Resources on the High Seas of the South Pacific	
2001	Convention on the Conservation and Management of Fishery Resources in the South-East Atlantic	2003
2002	Agreement Establishing the Caribbean Regional Fisheries Mechanism	2002
2006	Southern Indian Ocean Fisheries Agreement	2012
2007	Convention for the Establishment of the Fishery Committee for the West Central Gulf of Guinea	
2009	Convention on the Conservation and Management of High Seas Fishery Resources in the South Pacific Ocean	2012
2009	Agreement on the Central Asian and Caucasus Regional Fisheries and Aquaculture Commission	

[a] Amended or revised, sometimes by protocols.

The **International Convention for the Regulation of Whaling** of 1946, which for the first time explicitly stated the objective as "to protect all species of whales from further over-fishing," established the **International Whaling Commission** to enforce terms of the agreement. Amendments to the 1946 convention have been adopted annually, depending mostly upon market conditions, so the countries involved have continued to view the agreement in commercial terms with at least lip service to conservation.

FAO has sponsored dozens of fisheries treaties over the years (Table 14.8). Some focus on specific regions, covering all the oceans and many inland lakes, rivers, and seas. Others deal with particular species of fish (halibut, pollock, salmon, tuna) or crustaceans (crabs, lobsters, prawns). Some coastal, riparian, and oceanic resource management treaties (Table 14.7) are also oriented to fishing stocks but have wider concerns.

Despite the **Convention for the Regulation of the Meshes of Fishing Nets and Size Limits of Fish** of 1946, there was an outcry in the South Pacific during the 1980s over fishnets of 200 miles in length that trapped and killed dolphins, porpoises, and turtles. In response, the **Convention for the Prohibition of Fishing with Long Driftnets in the South Pacific** was adopted in 1989.

In 1991, the United States decided to ban the import of tuna caught by driftnets because dolphins were trapped and discarded. México, under the General Agreement of Tariffs and Trade (GATT), then complained that the import restriction was a violation of GATT rules. In 1993, when Norway resumed whale hunting, the United States also threatened a boycott of all Norwegian products, so Oslo also complained to GATT. In response to both complaints, a GATT panel in Geneva ruled that import bans were unacceptable nontariff barriers to trade, ignoring the "moral exception." Although GATT had no way to enforce the ruling, Washington backed down on the Norwegian ban but continued to stop importing Mexican tuna. In 1995, when the WTO went into effect to supersede GATT, México complained again. WTO then ruled that the United States must either rescind its ban and compensate México, or the rest of the world could retaliate by imposing restrictions on some American imports. Washington's response was to place a "dolphin safe" warning label on imported tuna. When México filed another complaint with WTO in 2003 on the basis that the label served as a nontariff trade barrier, Washington dropped the use of the warning label. Although WTO began negotiations in 2002 for an agreement that would take animal protection considerations into account, and a draft text was completed in 2005, the matter is still being debated within WTO.

In 1999, the ITLOS received a case from Australia and New Zealand, which charged Japan with overfishing bluefin tuna. Preliminarily, ITLOS ruled against Japan, issuing provisional measures that Tokyo must abide by maximum catch requirements while awaiting an arbitral decision, and compensate Canberra and Wellington for litigation costs. In 2000, however, the arbitral panel found no jurisdictional basis to rule on the matter and reversed the provisional measures. In a word, ITLOS was considerably weakened.

In January 2013, the European Parliament adopted in a vote of 502 to 137 a sweeping reform to protect endangered fish stocks, responding to pressure from Greenpeace, WWF, as well as high-profile celebrity chefs and other environmental groups. Subject to approval by the 27 European governments, the Common Fisheries Policy would stop overfishing, which applies to an estimated three-quarters of the species, especially Atlantic bluefin tuna, cod, and sole. The new policy would limit fish catches to no more than each species could reproduce; in other words, sustainability would become the new principle guiding the fish industry, with a target date of stock recovery by 2020.

Conservation of Birds, Amphibious and Land Mammals. Nearly half of the earliest environmental agreements dealt with the preservation of birds and mammals (Table 14.2), especially amphibious fur seals. The **Convention on Preservation of Fauna and Flora in Their Natural State** of 1933 and the **Convention on Nature Protection and Wildlife Preservation in the Western Hemisphere** of 1940 were clearly conservation minded.

After World War II, several agreements related to birds and wild animals in general, but others had specific species in mind (polar bears, seals, vicuña, waterfowl). Regional treaties were drawn up for the Amazon, Antarctica, the Baltic, North Sea, and the South Pacific (Table 14.9).

In 1982, the **World Charter for Nature** stated two premises:

- "Every form of life is unique, warranting respect regardless of its worth to man, and, to accord other organisms such recognition, man must be guided by a moral code of action"
- "Man can alter nature and exhaust natural resources by his action or its consequences and, therefore, must fully recognize the urgency of maintaining the stability and quality of nature and of conserving natural resources."

And then went on to declare that the

- "genetic viability on the earth shall not be compromised; the population levels of all life forms, wild and domesticated, must be at least sufficient for their survival, and to this end necessary habitat shall be safeguarded."

Thereafter, agreements were adopted for the Benelux countries, the Alps, the Black Sea, the Caribbean, East and Southern Africa, the Mediterranean, and the Wadden Sea. Species evoking particular interest were albatrosses, bats, petrels, and seals.

The **Lusaka Agreement on Cooperative Enforcement Operations Directed at Illegal Trade in Wild Flora and Fauna** of 1994 sought to combat destructive commercial efforts. However, agreements that aim to preserve species from depletion or extinction raise a fundamental question: is commercial exploitation the real reason? If commercial motives are not the reason, are conservation treaties merely for the amusement of humans? Or do animals themselves have basic rights, unstated in current international treaties, which humans are now recognizing without saying so?

ANIMAL RIGHTS

Animal conservation treaties originally had commercial motives in mind, but the situation today has reversed: Animals are being viewed from a much more humane perspective. Environmental rights treaties, whether on land or sea, are increasingly embedded with conceptions of animal rights. Although concern for the rights of

TABLE 14.9   CONTEMPORARY CONSERVATION TREATIES ON BIRDS, AMPHIBIOUS, AND LAND MAMMALS

Adopted	Treaty	In force
1950	International Convention for the Protection of Birds	1963
1957	Interim Convention on Conservation of North Pacific Fur Seals	1957
1959	The Antarctic Treaty[a]	1964
1964	• Agreed Measures for the Conservation of Antarctic Flora and Fauna	1978
1972	• Convention for the Conservation of Antarctic Seals	1982
1976	• Convention on the Conservation of Antarctic Marine Living Resources	1982
1968	African Convention on the Conservation of Nature and Natural Resources[a]	1969
1969	Convention for the Conservation and Management of the Vicuña	1969
1970	Benelux Convention Concerning Hunting and the Protection of Birds	1972
1971	Convention on Wetlands of International Importance Especially as .Waterfowl Habitat[a]	1975
1972	Convention Concerning the Protection of the World Cultural and Natural Heritage	1975
1973	Agreement on the Conservation of Polar Bears	1976
1973	Convention for International Trade in Endangered Species of Wild Fauna and Flora (CITES)	1975
1976	Convention on Conservation of Nature in the South Pacific	1990
1978	Treaty for Amazonian Cooperation	1980
1979	Convention for the Conservation and Management of the Vicuña	1983
1979	Convention on the Conservation of Migratory Species of Wild Animals (CMS)	1983
1979	Convention on the Conservation of European Wildlife and Natural Habitats	1982
1982	Convention on Biological Diversity	1993
2000	• Cartagena Protocol	2003
1982	World Charter for Nature	
1982	Benelux Convention on Nature Conservation and Landscape Protection	1983
1983	Convention for the Protection and Development of the Marine Environment of the Wider Caribbean (Cartagena Convention)[a]	1986
1990	• Protocol Concerning Specially Protected Areas and Wildlife	2000
1985	Protocol Concerning Protected Areas and Wild Fauna and Flora in the Eastern African Region	1996
1985	ASEAN Agreement on the Conservation of Nature and Natural Resources	1985
1990	Agreement on the Conservation of Seals in the Wadden Sea	1991
1991	Agreement on the Conservation of Populations of Bats in Europe	1994
1994	Lusaka Agreement on Cooperative Enforcement Operations Directed at Illegal Trade in Wild Flora and Fauna	1996
1994	Protocol to the Convention Concerning the Protection of the Alps Relating to the Conservation of Nature and the Countryside[a]	
1995	Agreement on the Conservation of African-Eurasian Migratory Waterbirds	1999
1999	Protocol on Wildlife Conservation and Law Enforcement of the Southern African Development Community	
2001	Agreement on the Conservation of Albatrosses and Petrels	2004

[a] Amended or revised, sometimes by protocols.

animals might be considered irrelevant in a book on human rights, in fact the term "animal rights" refers to human conduct vis-à-vis animals and thus regulates how humans behave in situations where the consequences of their actions usually cannot be challenged by the victims.

Animal rights have been largely ignored historically because humans probably would not have assumed dominion on the planet without first winning a contest for supremacy. During snowbound winters in prehistoric times, there were no vegetables to harvest but plenty of animals to kill and eat. Today, humans have no such logistical problems in obtaining protein-rich food, so the custom of eating animals may be anachronistic. Similarly, cotton and synthetic fabrics have replaced the need for animal skins as the basis for clothing.

Analytically, theologian Andrew Linzey (1952–) helps to explain the case for animal rights by suggesting three practices that are touchstones for determining views toward animal rights:

•   **Battery Hen Production**. About nine billion hens currently lay eggs in the United States in small cages, five confined to a cage of wire mesh the size of a sheet of 9"×11" looseleaf notebook paper, eating a diet of dry mash along with antibiotics to prevent disease. They stay encaged for about one year, whereupon they go to the slaughterhouse, are hung upside down, pre-stunned with an electric shock, have their throats cut electronically, and are then put into scalding water to make their feathers fall off. Male chicks live only three days; afterward, they are gassed, suffocated, or fed through chopping machines.

•   **Deer Hunting with Hounds**. In England for five centuries until declared illegal in 2004, from April to October, deer of both sexes, including pregnant females, have been chased by hounds for three to four hours to weaken and exhaust them. Although the hounds sometimes catch them, and deer are occasionally shot by hunters in the fields, most are caught in the riverbeds and shot dead.

•   **Animal Experimentation**. There is a creature called the "oncomouse," which is patented in Europe and the United States. The animal is a normal mouse that is genetically altered to develop cancer. In Europe, the patent extends to all non-human mammals, so the oncopig, oncochicken, and oncosheep are also possible. After experimentation is completed on oncomice, medical science next conducts experiments on primates, that is, chimps and monkeys. Universities and medical labs currently have committees to determine whether animal experimentations (or experiments upon humans) are legally and scientifically justifiable, but oncomice pass the test every time. The Animal Protection Institute estimates that 27 million animals are used in education, research, and testing each year and feels that "replacement techniques" could reduce the number to 2.7 million.

The question to consider is whether any of the three practices might violate animal rights. Linzey offers several theories, some already considered in Chapter 2, to place the debate in perspective.

Humanocentrism. Animals have no moral status, and humans have no obligations to animals, according to such thinkers as Aristotle (384–322 BCE), Thomas Aquinas (1227–1274), and René Descartes (1596–1650). Aquinas has a twofold justification:

- Animals are intended for man's use according to biblical and natural law.
- Animals are not rational beings and thus lack a soul.

In the mid-nineteenth century, for example, Pope Pius IX (1792–1878) cited humanocentrist doctrine by forbidding the opening of an animal protection office in Rome. Cruelty to animals is wrong, according to humanocentrism, not because animal rights are infringed but because cruelty makes humans into beasts, and thus the habit of cruelty will inevitably carry over to humans. But there is nothing in humanocentrism to stop hen battery production or deer hunting. Although oncomice might be considered to alter the order of creation, experimentation is justified for the benefit of humans.

Contractualism. A second theory argues that rights are conferred only on those who enter into contracts. Since animals cannot make contracts, the argument goes, they have no rights. Social contract theorists, from Thomas Hobbes (1588–1679) to John Locke (1632–1704) to Jean-Jacques Rousseau (1712–1778) to contemporary philosopher John Rawls (1921–2002), thus have no place for animal rights in their conceptions of rights. Once again, humans determine the moral rules of the game and load the dice against animals, just as males have been thinking up various justifications to deny rights to females, the poor, and down the list of groups that historically have not enjoyed their full rights because they were not writing the rules. Under contractualism, battery production, deer hunting, and animal experimentation will continue regardless of how much animals suffer.

Humanitarianism. Anglican priests Arthur Broome (17??–1837) and Humphrey Primatt (1736–1779) believed that humans should prevent unnecessary cruelty and promote kindness while exercising benevolence or philanthropy toward others. They specifically grounded their views on their Christian faith and equated cruelty with atheism and heresy. However, humanitarianism only opposes unnecessary cruelty. Humanitarianism would stop deer hunting, mitigate the suffering of hens, stop the slaughter of male chicks, but animal experimentation would continue.

Utilitarianism. According to philosophy professor Peter Singer (1946–), any being that has feeling or consciousness is entitled to equal rights, so he draws the line at mollusks (clams, oysters, and the like). However, rights are considered from a utilitarian perspective, such that more suffering on the part of a few animals is justified if thousands will experience less suffering as a result. Jeremy Bentham (1748–1832), indeed, was an advocate of extending some rights to animals. Utilitarianism would stop deer hunting and possibly hen battery production, but experimentation on animals would continue.

Rights Theory. Philosophy professor Tom Regan (1938–) and others rely on three premises:

- Animals are ends in themselves and should not be regarded as means to human ends.
- All animals have inherent value and therefore have rights.
- Animals have equal rights with humans.

One variant of rights theory is theological, arguing that God created animals separately from humans for their own sake. Hen battery production, deer hunting, and animal experimentation are wrong because animals have not consented. However, rights theory is a theory of what should not be done to animals, providing no imperative to do something positive for animals.

Generosity Theory. Animals should not only be respected, according to Andrew Linzey, but they should also be given greater consideration. The weak, according to his Christian view, should have moral priority. Humans should not only have dominion over nature, but also should care for the creatures of God. The higher creatures should sacrifice for the lower, not the reverse. Generosity theory stresses affirmative action for animals, just as parents give special care to dependent infants: because they are innocent and so easily abused, they should be protected. The biblical Noah, perhaps, was the earliest practitioner of generosity theory.

Vegetarianism. In Buddhism and Hinduism, animals, even cockroaches, are considered sacred. Some vegetarians drink milk but do not eat cows and other animals; others, known as **vegans**, are fully vegetarian. Even the killing of insects is unacceptable. Why? According to the theory of reincarnation, all creatures are equal, and the insect that someone might kill could have been their grandparent. Of course, some vegetarians may choose to avoid meat for health reasons rather than any concern for the rights of animals. Plato (427–347 BCE) and Michel de Montaigne (1533–1592) are among the various philosophers who are claimed to have been exponents of vegetarianism.

Animal Rights Movement. Similar to movements in pursuit of human rights, the quest to establish animal rights has been spearheaded by books and nongovernmental organizations. Primatt, for example, wrote the first coherent statement on the need to respect animal rights in his *Dissertation on the Duty of Mercy and the Sin of Cruelty to Brute Animals* (1776). In 1796, philosopher John Lawrence (1753–1839) published *A Philosophical and Practical Treatise on Horses, and on the Moral Duties of Man Towards the Brute Creation*. And in 1824, Broome formed the Society for the Prevention of Cruelty to Animals (SPCA). In *The Rights of Man* (1792), American revolutionary Thomas Paine (1737–1809) also raised animal rights issues. Social reformer Henry Salt's *Animals' Rights: Considered in Relation to Social Progress* (1905) was the next major treatise on the subject.

In 1875, British suffragette Frances Power Cobbe (1822–1904) founded several anti-vivisection societies in protest of animal experimentation. Nearly a half-century later, Stephen Coleridge (1854–1936), longtime president of the British National Anti-Vivisection Society, proposed an Animals' Charter to the League of Nations, which was further developed into *An Animals' Bill of Rights* by Geoffrey Hodson (1886–1983), president of the Council of Combined Animal Welfare Organizations of New Zealand. In 1924, columnist André Géraud (1882–1974) produced *A Declaration of Animal Rights*. An intergovernmental organization on animal health, the Office International des Epizooties (since 2003 the World Organization for Animal Health), was launched in 1924 and now has 178 member countries. In 1926, Florence Barkers drafted the International Animals Charter. But momentum stopped during World War II.

After the war, retired Presbyterian minister W. J. Piggott published an *Appeal for the International Animals' Charter* in 1953, and he presented his appeal as a revised International Animals' Charter to a World Congress of Animal Welfare Societies in London in 1954. From 1953 to 1956, more preliminary charters were drawn up by the World Federation for Animal Protection Associations. The title "Humane Society," for an organization originally founded in Amsterdam during 1767 to rescue shipwrecked sailors, was adopted in 1954 by the Humane Society of the United States, which claims to be the world's largest organization to protect animals. Currently, the Humane Society of the United States claims that 7,000 farms and 100 producers (Foster Farms) are "American Human Society certified."

In 1968, the Animal Protection Institute (API), which now promotes itself as Born Free USA, was founded to publicize what it called the "animal welfare movement" by public events. API recommends several ways to reduce cruelty in animal experimentation, such as computer simulation and in-vitro techniques.

In 1969, the International Fund for Animal Welfare (IFAW) was founded with the objective of stopping foxhunting, the trade in ivory tusks, and whalehunting. Although originally formed to protest nuclear weapons tests, Greenpeace emerged in 1972 with a reputation for direct action advocacy to protest environmental destruction. A few members of Greenpeace founded Project Ahab to protest commercial whaling, and in 1975 got world attention by trying to interpose a Greenpeace vessel between a whale and a Soviet vessel. Otherwise, Greenpeace focuses on nuclear power, toxic waste, and similar environmental issues.

HISTORIC EVENT 14.3 GREENPEACE STOPS A SOVIET WHALING SHIP (1975)

In 1975, with a Soviet fishing fleet of 13 ships reportedly harvesting whales in the North Pacific, the nongovernmental organization Greenpeace chartered the *Phyllis Cormack* at Vancouver and sailed toward the whale hunters. Upon arrival in the area, Greenpeace saw one of the Soviet vessels in pursuit of a whale and proceeded to place Zodiac inflatables between the harpoon ship and the whale. The image of a harpoon being fired over the Greenpeace crew, caught on a video camera, was later broadcast on television, thereby dramatizing the lengths to which whalers are often prepared to go. Subsequently, Greenpeace established itself as a major activist nongovernmental organization and has pursued Japanese whaling ships.

Following Greenpeace's example, API assisted IFAW by filming the clubbing of baby harp seals in Eastern Canada in 1981. As a result, many European countries banned the import of the seals in 1983. Animal Liberation Front (ALF), a leaderless direct action organization founded in 1976, has been accused of being a terrorist organization for inflicting economic damage to protect those who profit from the exploitation and misery of animals. ALF also liberates animals from laboratories and other allegedly inhumane places of captivity. Four years later, in 1980, People for the Ethical Treatment of Animals (PETA) was founded to lobby for the humane treatment of animals on factory farms, in laboratories, in the clothing trade, and in the entertainment industry in February 2013, an American appeals court ruled that Sea Shepherd was a terrorist organization for ramming ships, hurling glass containers of acid, dragging metal-reinforced ropes in the water to damage propellers and rudders, launching smoke bombs and flares with hooks, and pointing high-powered lasers at Japanese ships seeking to harvest whales in Australian waters within the Antarctic.

In 1977, the International League of Animal Rights and Affiliated National Leagues, during the International Meeting on Animal Rights in London, adopted a *Universal Declaration of Animal Rights*, which was presented in 1978 in the main hall of the UNESCO House in Paris.

In 1988, the Committee for the Convention for the Protection of Animals, a coalition of two animal rights organizations, proposed an **International Convention for the Protection of Animals** to consolidate all existing animal rights concerns into one document, including transportation of animals, methods of taking wildlife, care of exhibited wildlife, and protection from cruel treatment. But the proposal languishes, too sweeping for consideration by countries more protective of their sovereignty than of their animals.

In 2000, the World Society for the Protection of Animals drafted the **Universal Declaration on Animal Welfare** (UDAW), which in turn has been accepted by the American Society for the Prevention of Cruelty to Animals, Compassion in World Farming, the Humane Society of the United States, and the Royal Society for the Prevention of Cruelty to Animals. Thereafter, the movement has sought the worldwide intergovernmental adoption of UDAW.

In recent years, there has been some practical success. In 2000, McDonald's Corporation became the first company to ask egg producers to comply with guidelines for the humane treatment of hens – providing at least 72 square inches per hen, adequate food and water, and a ban on trimming beaks. In the same year, McDonald's decided to purchase meat only from suppliers that guarantee a minimum standard of humane treatment of livestock. Burger King soon followed. Chipotle Mexican Grill, which has operated restaurants in Britain, Canada, and the United States from 1993, advertised in 2000 that all its pork is humanely raised. In 2006, Whole Foods Market, a grocery chain of 440 stores in Britain, Canada, and the United States that began in 1980, decided to label beef, chicken, and pork with the label "animal compassionate" to indicate that they have been raised in a humane manner before slaughter. Smaller grocery retailers now use "cage free," "certified humane," "free farm," and "free range" labels. Some upscale restaurants now make similar claims to patrons. Although the cost of the newly labeled produce is higher, many consumers not only do not mind but also testify that the food tastes better.

Legal Advances. Britain's **Act to Prevent the Cruel and Improper Treatment of Cattle** of 1822, the first law adopted by a country on the subject, was generalized by the **Protection of Animals Act** of 1911. Many countries now have legislation about

TABLE 14.10 **EUROPEAN CONVENTIONS ON DOMESTICATED ANIMALS**

Adopted	Treaty	Protection	In force
1968	European Convention for the Protection of Animals During International Transport	Mishandling	1971
1979	• Additional Protocol to the European Convention for the Protection of Animals During International Transport		1989
1976	European Convention for the Protection of Animals Kept for Farming Purposes	Against suffering in animal husbandry	1978
1992	• Protocol of Amendment to the European Convention for the Protection of Animals Kept for Farming Purposes	Updated to include biotechnology	
1979	European Convention for the Protection of Animals for Slaughter	Humane slaughtering	1982
1986	European Convention for the Protection of Vertebrate Animals Used for Experimental and other Scientific Purposes	Humane experimental methods	1991
1987	European Convention for the Protection of Pet Animals	Ban on extinct animals as pets; humane treatment of pets	1992
1997	Treaty of Amsterdam	Humane treatment in agriculture, experimentation, transport	1999
1997	• Protocol on Animal Welfare		1999
1998	CoE Convention on the Protection of Environment Through Criminal Law	Criminalizes harm to animals	

animal cruelty and endangered species, but international agreements were very limited in scope at first (Table 14.2).

Fish are the subjects of the earliest recorded international treaties that deal with animals: A treaty between France and Great Britain in 1867 was the first, followed by similar agreements concerning fishing in the Rhine River and in the North Sea. After agreements between Britain and the United States on fur seals in the late nineteenth century, the **Convention for the Protection of Wild Animals, Birds and Fish in Africa** of 1900 was the first multilateral treaty on the subject. However, the earliest agreements dealt with the rights of commercial exploitation more than the rights of animals (Table 14.2).

Insofar as international law has been interested in protecting species from extinction, such as birds, fish, fur seals, and whales, the concept of animal rights was addressed only as a subtext. The goal of saving species from extinction prompted two other treaties. The **Convention on Preservation of Fauna and Flora in Their Natural State** of 1933 focused on Africa, and the **Convention on Nature Protection and Wild Life Preservation** of 1940 applied to the Americas.

In the 1957 **Treaty of Rome**, which launched the European Economic Community, one provision stated that animal welfare was a goal. But no specific form of welfare was authorized, and no right was stated.

The **Antarctic Treaty** of 1959 opened the door for more specific conservation agreements. Subsequent agreements protected Antarctic flora and fauna (1964), seals (1972), and other marine living resources (1976).

Animal research is responsible for the development of medicines and vaccines that have saved millions of human lives from deformities, pain, and premature death. For that reason, the US Congress defined "animal" in the **Animal Welfare Act** of 1966 to exclude birds, mice, and rats, which together account for 90 percent of all laboratory animals. "Warm-blooded animals," such as farm animals and pets, are protected by the law.

Then, from 1968, the Council of Europe (CoE) began to adopt agreements banning human maltreatment of animals, mostly those used in farming and as pets (Table 14.10). A treaty dealing with transportation of animals has provisions on the space, ventilation and hygiene, transportation means, food and water, loading and unloading of animals, and veterinary assistance for the international transport of animals. Farm animals are protected against maltreatment in their care, feeding, housing, machinery used with them, and slaughtering, which are in turn subject to CoE inspection. A recent protocol to the treaty updates coverage to reflect newer methods, especially biotechnology. CoE's treaty on experimentation urges countries to conduct animal experimentation only when absolutely necessary and establishes conditions that must be met in those cases; in particular, animal suffering is prohibited.

In 1972, meanwhile, French animal rights advocate Georges Heuses submitted a **Universal Declaration of Animal Rights** to UNESCO, asking for its adoption. The following year, the Declaration was adopted in France by the National Council for the Protection of Animals.

UNEP has forged several significant agreements. In 1973, the **Convention for International Trade in Endangered Species of Wild Fauna and Flora** (CITES) was adopted, classifying animals into three categories:

- Those threatened with extinction
- Those possibly threatened with extinction
- Those overexploited.

Appendices to CITES list specific animal and plant species, which can expand as the treaty's governing body considers new information. International trade in all three categories is regulated by import and export licenses. UNEP serves as the secretariat for CITES. In 2013, Canada was able to defeat a ban on polar bear hunting within CITES.

Efforts to adopt a more general international animal rights agreement continued. In 1979, UNEP efforts resulted in the **Convention on the Conservation of Migratory Species of Wild Animals** (CMS), which operates in a manner similar to CITES. The focus is on efforts to conserve subspecies of such animals as antelopes, bats, cranes, deer, and turtles. Under the CMS framework, agreements on specific species for particular geographic subregions have been adopted for Antarctic marine animals, Wadden Sea seals, European bats, Euro-African waterbirds, European-Mediterranean dolphins, porpoises, and albatrosses.

After Greenpeace brought worldwide attention to the problem of excessive whale slaughtering in 1975, the whaling treaty was amended to abolish the aboriginal exception in 1977. In 1982, the International Whaling Commission adopted a moratorium, effective 1986, on commercial whaling to enable whales to regain their numbers after more than a century of watching their numbers decline from 250,000 blue whales in the nineteenth century to about 1,000. However, a loophole was left for "scientific whaling," that is, killing of unlimited numbers of whales for scientific research. Although Iceland and Japan then engaged in "scientific whaling," Norway rejected the moratorium. In 2006, after intense lobbying by Japan to allow secret ballots, the vote to rescind the ban was 33–32, but the Commission can only rescind the moratorium with an affirmative vote by 75 percent of the 70 members of the commission. Japan then lavished foreign aid on microstates in the South Pacific in order to increase votes for its position, but the ban remains in effect. Nevertheless, Iceland resumed commercial whaling. Although an unprecedented sighting of a gray whale off the coast of Israel on May 10, 2010, brought comfort to those seeking to preserve cetaceans from extinction, some 2,000 whales are still slaughtered each year.

Back in 1986, the **Single European Act** opened the door for further action. The European Union began to adopt regulations similar to those of CoE. In 1992, when the Treaty on European Union was signed at Maastricht, the **Declaration on the Protection of Animals** was annexed. The **Treaty of Amsterdam** of 1997 introduced a significant change: for the first time, animals were referred to as sentient beings – able to feel pain and suffering. EU policies relating to agricultural, internal market, research, and transport were required "to pay full regard to the welfare requirements of animals."

Based on evidence that zoo animals are maltreated, a Council Directive in 1999 established a licensing and inspection system. The Lisbon Treaty of 2009 reiterated the Amsterdam Treaty language.

In 2003, delegates from 19 governments at the Manila Conference on Animal Welfare agreed that captive animals should be guaranteed the basic **Five Freedoms and Three R's**:

- Freedom from hunger, thirst, and malnutrition
- Freedom from fear and distress
- Freedom from physical and thermal discomfort
- Freedom from pain, injury, and disease
- Freedom to express normal patterns of behavior
- Reduction in numbers of animals
- Refinement of experimental methods
- Replacement of animals with non-animal techniques.

The conference also agreed upon the text of UDAW, as proposed by the World Society for the Protection of Animals three years earlier. The conference then urged the UN General Assembly to adopt UDAW as a preliminary step for a comprehensive treaty.

An intergovernmental steering committee was formed in 2005 by Costa Rica, the Czech Republic, India, Kenya, and the Philippines to gain support for UDAW. As a result, more countries have indicated agreement. The latest version of the draft emerged in 2011. The UN General Assembly, however, has not reviewed any of the draft agreements or the European texts, and no generic animal rights treaty has been adopted to date.

DISCUSSION TOPIC 14.3 DO ANIMALS HAVE RIGHTS ON A PAR WITH HUMANS?

Apart from the desire to preserve animals for commercial and ecological reasons, do animals have rights of their own? Why not let some species become extinct? Should the concept of animal rights be considered a subset of environmental or even human rights? What are the ethical implications of the cloning of animals?

In 2007, transport ships killed four blue whales en route to the ports of Los Angeles and Long Beach, and in 2010 five whales were struck by ships off the coast of Central and Northern California. As a result, the US Coast Guard and the National Oceanic Atmospheric Administration petitioned the International Maritime Organization (IMO), a UN Specialized Agency responsible for safety in navigation, to shift global shipping lanes to ports in San Francisco Bay as well as to the Los Angeles/Long Beach destinations. In 2012, IMO agreed. The change was headlined "to help protect whales."

Despite efforts to save polar bears and whales, animal rights advocates never urge special considerations for bears, beavers, coyotes, feral cats, foxes, geese, raccoons, vultures, or white-tailed deer, which have exponentially increased in population throughout the United States, abandoning the wild to invade major cities that have crept toward the woods, even killing unattended children in the daytime and eating roofs and vegetation during the night. Baboons, similarly, are in aggressive pursuit of food in Capetown, South Africa. While residents of Los Angeles have been eager to provide animal corridors for deer whose habitats have been interrupted by urban sprawl, deer come out of the woods of Michigan and elsewhere, producing some 3,000 annual collisions with automobiles, sometimes killing all those inside. Whereas the Humane Society may be eager to extend protection of abused domestic cats to feral cats, they are opposed by the Audubon Society's interest in preserving songbirds. The case for animal rights, in other words, may have produced a serious backlash.

In summary, the focus on animal rights gets to the root of the issue of rights. Is not the campaign to advance human rights in reality an effort to protect those who are weak, powerless, and capable of being abused? If humans have rights because of the need to protect against abuse, so may animals. However, since animals cannot assert their rights, any discussion about animal rights is really about human responsibilities. One reason for inclusion of the topic in a book about human rights is to emphasize that rights cannot protect anyone without a corresponding sense of obligations. The same argument applies to the environment, where a failure to take human responsibilities seriously may have the consequence of jeopardizing all life.

PROBLEMS OF THE RIGHTS-BASED APPROACH

The incremental problem-oriented approach to international human rights by governments and international organizations presented in the present volume stands in contrast with the more philosophical rights-based approach. Although many treaties can identify specific problems and establish institutional mechanisms for dealing with each problem, they often make generic statements that allow some latitude for interpretation. Accordingly, some scholars argue that a rights-based discourse is not capable of advancing the goals sought by the human rights project. There are at least 10 important arguments and counterarguments.

- **Individualism**. One point is that the major threat to liberty and freedom today is not from governments but instead by corporate entities and individuals in the private sector. For example, prejudiced people massively continue to discriminate socially despite laws to the contrary; they simply do not accept rights for anyone but themselves. Corporations often respect profits more than rights and thereby marginalize workers, even entire countries. Because the human rights project primarily focuses on what governments should or should not do, the major arena in which violations occur is often ignored.

The counterargument is that governments are major violators of rights but can also protect human rights, so a rights-based discourse keeps the pressure on governments to limit abuses in the private and public sectors. In the United States, for example, the Equal Employment Opportunity Commission, whose members are appointed by the president, is independent of all three branches of government; the Commission's jurisdiction covers both private and public employment discrimination.

DISCUSSION TOPIC 14.4 HAS THE GLOBAL COMMUNITY EVER OVERRIDDEN STATE SOVEREIGNTY IN THE NAME OF HUMAN RIGHTS?

A basic principle of the Westphalian nation-state system is that every country is free to determine its own laws and practices without interference from other countries.

Continued

Some claim that the UN Charter and subsequent treaties have brought about a post-Westphalian world. Does that mean that the basic principle of self-determination has been breached? If so, cite examples.

- **Sovereignty**. The concept of state sovereignty protects governments from accountability for violating human rights. "Sovereign" states demand immunity from pressure from other countries under international law. Appealing to tyrants with a rights-based discourse is thus futile. Military action alone seems appropriate to enforce regime change, yet there is insufficient will throughout the world to turn every state that seriously violates human rights into a UN trusteeship on a pathway to democracy.

On the contrary, military action occasionally has been used to stop massive human rights violations, though on a priority basis. The principles of humanitarian intervention and responsibility to protect in international law can be applied if there is international or regional consensus. Yet sovereign states are adopting and implementing human rights principles short of war because they appeal to populations that want governments accountable.

- **Ambiguity**. Another argument is that rights-based discourse is vague and indeterminate. A politician who engages in malicious namecalling of another politician can be sued in Britain or Singapore but not in the United States, so the identification of rights is ultimately arbitrary and inconsistent from country to country. Since rights-based thinking does not provide a uniform guide concerning what are the basic or derivative rights, those who want to promote human rights must step outside rights-based discourse to determine what conduct is or is not acceptable.

But lack of uniformity in recognizing human rights violations serves as a challenge for world leaders to urge improvements. The people in various countries can humble governments to increase their respect for human rights by pointing to practices in other countries. Amnesty International, the United Nations Development Program, and other organizations publish annual reports that compare most countries in the world on a set of human rights parameters, and treaty-based international organizations, as described in Chapter 10, goad compliance in very specific terms.

- **Lip Service**. A related objection is that the human rights agenda pretends to be universal, and many countries sign human rights treaties, but they often ignore them, either in principle or in practice. Not all governments have ratified human rights treaties, and compliance varies among those that have ratified. In other words, human rights are similar to New Year's resolutions that are never fulfilled. Politicians use the rhetoric of human rights to look good in public but ignore them to stay in power.

However, the European Union and the United States base foreign aid allocations in part on human rights records. Although human rights are declared as universal, implementation will differ from country to country, depending upon historical traditions and cultural values. Countries are required to file reports on implementation to the treaty-based organizations created to monitor compliance with human rights treaties, and the record clearly shows that progress does occur.

- **Political Naïveté**. Freedom is granted by struggles rather than appeals to the concept of "rights." Power does not yield unless confronted by mobilizations of the oppressed, as in the case of the civil rights movements in South Africa and the United States. Most progress toward bringing all groups into the mainstream has been through the political process rather than through exhortation or litigation based on rights.

The answer is that human rights movements, including the American civil rights struggle of the 1960s, led to legislative reforms, but implementation of the new legal norms must rely ultimately on voluntary compliance, which is easier to achieve when justified in moral terms by legal principles. Court action, now imbedded in the global human rights culture, is needed only for those who are recalcitrant violators. Among more than 80 percent of the countries of the world that have ratified basic human rights instruments, empirical evidence proves that human rights improve after countries ratify the basic treaties because political parties out of power campaign effectively to implement human rights standards, thus embarrassing governments in power and appealing to citizens to vote against them.

- **Overly Litigious**. Turning the previous objection upside down, some argue that a focus on rights produces unnecessary legal conflict. In a discourse full of talk about "rights," the smoker insists that there is a right to smoke, whereas others claim the right to clean, fresh air free from such toxic chemicals as the ingredients in cigarettes. Clashes over where rights begin or end, in this view, are posed in the rhetoric of individualism and legal norms rather than in conversations to determine just public policy. Some opponents of rights-based discourse fear that resolution of such conflicts will result in the imperialistic determination of which rights have priority over others. They prefer a more deliberative and legislative problem-oriented cost-benefit approach that will bring about consensus, taking cultural, economic, and political perspectives into account.

But those who abhor increased conflict generated by invoking the concept of human rights appear to look at the trees rather than the forest – at petty conflicts rather than the generic quest for a just society. Human rights norms are invoked to resolve conflicts, leading to political compromise. Compared to the political process, courts have played a secondary role, as their decisions are followed most enthusiastically only when public opinion agrees.

- **Cultural Insensitivity**. The "Asian values" thesis accuses rights-based discourse of a fundamental contradiction: The Western conception of human rights wants the individual protected from government, but government should have the discretion to protect society from unbridled individualism in order to guarantee harmony and stability. China and some other Asian countries have asserted that human rights priorities of the West are simply inapplicable to its Confucian culture.

In answer to the "Asian values" approach, the human rights approach points out that government protection of society from dysfunctional individualism leaves government as the sole arbiter of what is dangerous to society. If governments do their job properly, they must utilize a theory of rights to determine when individuals act dangerously; if governments fail to protect society, then they are either incompetent or tyrannical, and Confucianism advises people of the right to overthrow rulers whose injustices can only be identified by a rights-based critique. The "Asian values" thesis, after all, is a cynical method by certain governments to deny basic rights to individuals in order to maintain iron rule in the exaggerated fear that simmering discontent will ultimately bring about their downfall. In other words, those who rely on an "Asian values" exception to the universalism of human rights engage in a self-fulfilling prophesy about their own precarious hold on power. Their astute citizens transparently recognize that "Asian values" are a phony basis for old-fashioned repression. Respect for human rights instead brings legitimacy and therefore stability.

• **Estoppel.** A country that has its human rights record criticized as violating international law by another country, which otherwise engages in commercial and diplomatic contact, has the option of filing suit in the ICJ, asking for an order of provisional measure that would prohibit such criticism under the principle of estoppel. "Estoppel" is a legal principle that claims in court are not allowed to contradict practices previously accepted by acquiescence. Were such an order issued, Asian, Muslim, and other states might withdraw from human rights treaties, arguing that human rights requirements are no longer universal, contrary to the International Covenant on Civil and Political Rights.

The objection to the "estoppel" argument is that the concept applies only to legal proceedings as a procedural way for a judge to stop a litigant from talking nonsense. Human rights are constitutional matters designed to benefit both individuals and the larger society. Obscure rules of evidence used in court cannot barter away generic freedoms based on constitutional principles.

• **Ignorance and Reticence.** Most people do not know what their rights are, and they are reluctant to assert rights that they may know they have. The argument is that enjoyment of rights requires an assertiveness that most people lack, concerned as they are with daily living. Denials of human rights seldom generate complaints for redress because administrative and legal remedies are a daunting, even fearful experience. As a result, those who are more assertive take advantage, leaving much of the passive population in a country as second-class citizens. Instead of a rights-based framework, the argument is that rights should be translated into specific entitlements, such as mandatory voting.

The counterargument is that human rights education should be a part of the human rights package in any country. Human rights bodies generally practice affirmative action in the form of outreach publicity in various forums.

• **Terrorism.** The concern over international terrorism in the twenty-first century has provoked a willingness on the part of nervous leaders and populations to sacrifice some civil rights. The claim is that greater security is preferable to a strictly rights-based discourse that would permit terrorists to take advantage of freedoms previously taken for granted.

Those who object to burdensome restrictions on human rights in the quest to prevent every possible terrorist act in the future point to several facts. One is that the attack on 9/11 occurred because airport officials ignored precautions already in place that should have barred entry to airplanes to persons already on a no-fly list. Second, terrorists have been clever enough to find ways to defeat existing precautions but not to elude the watchful eyes of air marshals and ordinary passengers.

Third, the almost unlimited American "right to bear arms," unknown in other countries, has been responsible for more deaths from domestic terrorist attacks than those who died on 9/11.

The debate over rights under the threat of terrorism, nevertheless, poses the question about how to achieve a proper balance between liberty and security. As long as such debates about international human rights continue, the struggle to make governments and humans accountable for decent treatment will endure.

CONCLUSION

Many cynics pooh-pooh the influence of human rights in the world today. The present volume clearly refutes their skepticism by identifying significant advances over the years.

For example, the present volume demonstrates that human rights debates are raging within time-honored religious traditions (Chapter 2). Historical social movements that brought about major human rights advances are even stronger today (Chapter 3). Nongovernmental organizations are now the most relentless source of challenge to violators of civil and political rights as well as a vital resource that actively works to overcome deprivations of economic, social, and cultural rights (Chapter 4). Ruthless dictators have been forced to step down by people's power movements and now truth commissions have enabled countries to go beyond a dark past (Chapter 5). Hundreds of businesses have adopted codes of conduct, pledging to accept no products made by child labor, prison labor, or under substandard working conditions, while the Fair Trade movement has brought substantial benefits to small-scale farmers in developing countries (Chapter 6). The law of warfare has expanded to include crimes against humanity, a development that has prompted the world community to treat systematic human rights violations in one country as problems of global concern (Chapter 7). Empirical research has identified a pragmatic strategy for improving human rights, stressing carrots rather than sticks (Chapter 8). The framework for multilateral action has borne fruit in countless situations, both inside and outside the United Nations (Chapters 9–10). Individual countries and regional organizations have used diplomatic, legal, economic, and military means to stop human rights abuses in ways unimagined in previous periods of world history (Chapters 11–13). There has even been progress in the development of rights for sexual minorities, environmental rights, and animal rights (Chapter 14). Many examples of human rights progress have been identified in the present volume, which has amply demonstrated that intellectual debates about whether to pursue human rights issues have been superseded by direct action from the streets, the courts, the legislatures, the executives, and even armies around the world that are in a position to engage in responsibility-to-protect missions.

Victor Hugo once said, "Nothing can stop an idea whose time has come." Although the path has been stony, the upward trend over the centuries suggests that the future is even brighter. On the world stage, the subject of human rights has gone beyond the era of debate and promise to the era of accountability and action.

GLOSSARY

9/11	date in 2001 when terrorists seized control of airplanes in the United States, resulting in the destruction of the World Trade Center towers in New York, a portion of the Pentagon building outside Washington, DC, and an airplane crash in rural Pennsylvania with no survivors
absolute right	legally enforceable right to take some action or to refrain from acting at the sole discretion of the person having the right
acquis	obligations of membership (primarily in the European Union)
act-of-state doctrine	immunity of a government official from prosecution for official acts
admissibility	a complaint that falls within a court's jurisdiction
advisory opinion	a nonbinding court ruling to provide guidance
affirmative action	a procedure for diversifying an employer's workforce based on the ethnic/racial/sex workforce in the geographic area from which the employer recruits
amnesty	a waiver of culpability for a crime
anthropocentrism	the view that the health and survival of humans prevails over animal and ecological survival
anticipatory self-defense	the use of force by a government which expects that another government is about to attack
apartheid	racial segregation (in South Africa)
application	a formal complaint to an international body
arbitration	judicial settlement by an independent third party
assimilationism	a belief that minority peoples should conform to the customs and language of the mainstream group
award	a settlement for a plaintiff who prevails
bill of attainder	a law convicting a person of a crime without a trial
binding ruling	court decision that parties agree in advance to accept
boycott	refusal to deal with goods or services of a company or country
buffer stock	a commodity stockpiled for emergencies
burka	full body covering for females
cap and trade	arrangement in which a high carbon-emitting entity pairs with a low carbon-emitting entity to achieve a low average to meet a target
cartel	a group of businesses or governments who uniformly fix prices far above the cost of production

caste system	a socioeconomic arrangement in which certain ancestral groups are assigned to particular jobs
Caux Principles	corporate codes of conduct based on human dignity and the common good
Ceres Principles	environmentally sound corporate practices
chivalry principle	in case of war, no harming of civilians
civil liberties	freedom from unwarranted governmental interference, as stated in a Bill of Rights
civil rights	claims of protection from discrimination
civil society	social and political organizations outside government in which people freely participate
claim-rights	obligations of individuals toward others
code of conduct	a set of just operating principles (for corporations)
command responsibility	culpability of superior officers for war crimes violations by subordinates
communitarian globalization	the process of forging common world norms
communitarianism	the view that individual rights should be limited to achieve social order; use of interpersonal cooperative arrangements rather than government programs
compensatory financing	loan terms adjusted to the likely long-term return on the investment
concessional rate	an interest rate on a loan below the world market rate for a longer term than average
constitutional rights	freedoms stated in the basic law of a country
constructive engagement	unpublicized diplomatic efforts of one country to urge another country to change a policy
contentious case	a formal complaint against a party
contractualism	the view that rights only exist when agreed in legal documents by all affected parties
corporate imperialism	control of the politics of Third World countries by giant corporations, often allowing unsafe working conditions and exploitation of workers
correlation	a statistical association between variables
cosmopolitanism	the view that all individuals are members of the planet and enjoy equal rights wherever they live
crimes against humanity	inhumane acts committed against members of a civilian population, or persecutions on political, racial or religious grounds
crimes against peace	planning, preparation, initiation or waging of a war of aggression, or conspiracy to do so
criminal law	statutes that define offenses against government laws
cultural rights	claims to respect a group's longstanding customs, language, and/or religion
curvilinearity	a statistical relationship in which two variables are positively related up to an asymptote and then are inversely related
democide	acts committed by a government that massively kills members of its own population
democracy	rule by the people through elections
democratic rights	claims to have government decisions made by the people, as in elections
deportation	expulsion of a foreigner from a country

deregulation, economic	reduction in governmental economic restrictions
derogation, right of	the claim of a government to be able to ignore certain legal obligations during an emergency
developmentalism	the view that economic and social rights are superior and prior to civil and political rights
diplomacy	respectful interactions between countries through ambassadors and other public officials or groups
diplomacy, coercive	use of threats of force by one country to gain concessions from another country
diplomacy, public	publicized interactions between countries conducted by ambassadors and other officials
diplomacy, quiet	unpublicized interactions between countries conducted by ambassadors and other officials
direct effect, doctrine of	the principle of applying rights stated in a treaty immediately to individuals that have to be enforced by member governments
direct trade	trade from primary producer to retail company without intervention from import–export companies
discrimination principle	in case of war, avoidance of civilian targets
displaced person	an imperiled individual who has fled from a home residence to avoid mortal danger
divestment	selling off stocks of companies that condone unpalatable practices
drone	unmanned aerial vehicle
duty bearers	individuals or governments obligated to respect the rights of others
early-warning procedure	a measure adopted so that an ongoing problem will not escalate out of control
ecocentrism	the view that the environment should be maintained in a pristine state
econocentrism	the view that economic growth should be maximized, avoiding only adverse economic consequences to the environment
economic liberalization	a policy of encouraging privatization, deregulation, and free trade
economic migrant	persons who leave a home country to work abroad
economic rights	claims to engage in remunerative activity under humane conditions
elitism	the view that those born superior should rule
emancipation	lifting legal restrictions on a person or group so that they can enjoy rights accorded to the mainstream
embargo	ban on exports and/or imports from a company or country
environmental justice	the practice of not polluting in poor neighborhoods
environmental sustainability	agricultural production without adverse impacts on ecosystems or humans
equality of states	the legal view that all governments are equal under international law
estoppel	a legal doctrine that bars a litigant from denying a fact that has already been established
ethnic cleansing	systematic extermination of members of one ethnic group that lives in the same territory as another; euphemism for genocide
ethnocide	denial of a people's right to enjoy, develop, and transmit its own culture
ex aequo et bono	general principles of justice and fairness
ex post facto law	a statute that criminalizes something in the past

exceptional report	a compliance report requested before the standard due date
exhaustion of local remedies	the principle that world courts do not try cases until national courts have first had a chance to do so
export promotion	an economic policy of encouraging local industries to compete internationally
extradition	procedure by which one government, after formally requested by a second government, physically transmits an individual charged with or convicted of a crime to the second government
extrajudicial execution	death carried out on an accused person without trial
extraordinary rendition	procedure, upon locating a person accused of a crime, of transmitting that person to a secret location
extraterritorial jurisdiction	a country's claim to have the authority to try persons who have committed offenses abroad
fair labor	workers with freedom of association, safe working conditions, and a living wage
fair price	an economic charge reasonably close to the cost of production
fair trade	purchases from small-scale farmers who provide humane working conditions for workers
First World	industrial democracies
Fourth World	indigenous peoples
free agency	the right of a worker to resign and obtain employment in a competing athletic team
free market environmentalism	allowing corporations to establish environmental regulations instead of the government
free trade	international commerce without governmental restrictions
Freudianism	the view that human behavior is conditioned by base instincts
friendly settlement	mutual agreement by complainer and complainant, as negotiated by a third party
frozen assets	disallowed transactions from a bank account
frustration-aggression theory	the view that violence occurs in response to trauma
functionalism	the view that cooperative human behavior results from a conditioning based on past positive experiences
gay rights	claims of persons who prefer relations with same-sex friends to enjoy the benefits accruing to those who bond with members of the opposite sex
gender equity	equal treatment of males and females; equal rights for the sexes
general measure	a settlement when a state found in violation of an international treaty changes its laws to conform to the treaty
generalized system of preferences	a tariff reduction schedule granted by rich countries to poor countries
generosity theory	the view that the strong should protect the rights of the weak
genocide	acts committed with intent to destroy, in whole or in part, a national, ethnical, racial, or religious group
global governance	decision making by transnational actors to resolve international problems in which compliance is voluntary but in the interests of those involved

globalism	the view that a single world economy, polity, and society should be promoted
globalization	the process of forging a single world economy, polity, and society
good governance	a government that operates accountably, democratically, and effectively, by the rule of law and without corruption
good offices	a form of third-party intervention in a conflict in which a neutral country transmits messages
group conflict theory	the view that politics can be explained by a struggle among competing, usually ethnic, groups
group rights	claims of subordinate groups to enjoy the same privileges as the mainstream group
habeas corpus, writ of	the right of a detained individual to appear in court in order to ascertain or challenge grounds for detention
hard law	legal requirements that are designed to be enforced effectively by use of a penalty for noncompliance
headquarters doctrine	a legal claim that subordinates are not culpable for following orders
herrenfolk democracy	rule of and by the people of the dominant group, while others are denied political rights
hierarchical relationship	an empirical pattern in which the attainment of some conditions serve as preconditions to attaining other conditions
horizontal enforcement	pressure by governments and groups in the form of protests, threats, and economic sanctions to secure compliance with international norms
human rights	the claim of individuals to enjoy a minimally restrictive yet optimal quality of life with liberty, equal justice before law, and an opportunity to fulfill basic cultural, economic, and social needs
human rights commission	a body set up to receive complaints about human rights violations that then investigates the complaints and passes judgment
human rights infrastructure	the existence of advocacy groups, government institutions, and legal norms favorable to human rights
human trafficking	transporting persons to conditions of forced labor
humanitarian intervention	action of one government on the territory of another country to rescue seriously imperiled groups of individuals
humanitarianism	the view that humans are obligated to promote kindness toward animals as well as humans
humanity principle	in case of war, treating civilians and prisoners with respect
humanocentrism	the view that humans have no obligations toward animals except to avoid cruelty
illiberal democracy	a polity that respects the political right of voting but restricts civil rights, such as the right to freely assemble and exchange information
imminent jeopardy	severe use of force, anticipated without delay
immunities	exemptions from legal requirements
import substitution	an economic policy of erecting trade barriers so that a country can develop local industries and keep out foreign competition
impunity	exemption from liability for wrongdoing
indemnity	a sum recovered by the victor from a war aggressor

individual measure	a settlement that a wrongdoer provides to a victim
informal citizen	an individual living in a country illegally who enjoys benefits of citizenship
informational globalization	dissemination of information around the world
intergovernmental organization	an institution whose members are governments
interim measure	temporary action or inaction to avoid irreparable harm while a dispute is under consideration
internally displaced person	an imperiled individual who has fled a home residence to avoid danger by living elsewhere inside the homeland
international custom	practices conventionally observed by states in relation to other states
international law	legal requirements applied primarily to conduct between states
international law, hard	international law that is enforced by a penalty
international law, soft	international law that lacks a penalty
internationalized court	a domestic tribunal set up in cooperation with and staffed in part by judges from another country or international organization
inverse relationship	a statistical relationship in which an increase in one variable correlates with a decrease in another variable or vice versa
irredentism	advocacy of uniting peoples living in different states yet with similar cultural traditions into a single state
jus ad bellum	an international law principle that war can be waged legitimately in defense, to recover losses, to stop a gross injustice, and in last resort
jus cogens	an international law principle that certain state practices cannot be derogated
jus in bello	an international law principle that legitimate means of warfare include avoidance of harm to civilian targets and of disproportionate destruction
just authority	a government or international body legitimately empowered by a treaty to take action
just cause	a legitimate pretext for righting a wrong through war
just intervention	legitimate military action by one government in the territory of another country to stop severe human rights violations
just peace	after war ends, actions of the victor to maintain order, repair economic damages, prosecute human rights violations, and transfer sovereignty to the country being occupied
just satisfaction	an acceptable settlement for a prevailing complainant
just war	an armed conflict launched for honorable reasons and conducted in an honorable manner
last resort	an international law principle that war can only be legitimately launched after all peaceful methods for resolving a serious conflict have failed
last-in-line principle	the legal custom of interpreting later legal agreements to supersede earlier agreements
lawfare	the use of lawsuits to win political victories
legal rights	freedoms from government misconduct, as established in law
letter of marque and reprisal	a written authorization by a government for a person outside government to use force to respond to an unfriendly act abroad

liberal democracy	a form of government in which the majority rules, provided that minority rights are respected and there is freedom of assembly and information
libertarianism	opposition to unwarranted government restrictions; minimal government
liberties	actions exempt from unwarranted government regulation
lustration	purge of government officials associated with a discredited regime
lynching	seizure and execution of a person by an unofficial mob
MacBride Principles	rules used in Northern Ireland to ensure nondiscriminatory trade
mainstream group	a country's dominant ethnolinguistic or religious group
mandate	a territory that the League of Nations entrusted to a government to promote self-government
market economy	commercial transactions where prices are determined by supply and demand, not by governments
mass society	a social system lacking political groups independent of government control
Médecins Sans Frontières	Doctors Without Borders
military necessity	a legal justification for using force in response to aggression
military occupation	rule imposed by a victor on a defeated country
minority rights	the claim of subgroups of a population to be treated the same as members of the mainstream
minority treaty	an international agreement to protect a nonmainstream group inside a country
mistrial	a courtroom trial that has been terminated prior to its normal conclusion
mixed arbitral tribunal	an arbitration court with members from several countries
mobilization, political	the process of raising consciousness of likeminded individuals to redress grievances
mobilization of shame	a campaign to use public opinion in order to embarrass those engaging in misconduct
moral rights	claims of just treatment based on ethical principles
Moscow mechanism	the use of independent experts to resolve human rights complaints, using on-site visits
most-favored-nation principle	according the same trade conditions to one country that are granted to the country that enjoys the most generous conditions
multidimensionality	a statistical relationship in which interrelated variables form separate empirical clusters
nation-state	government for a country inhabited primarily by members of a specific ancestral or cultural group
natural law	self-evident principles justified by God or by nature
natural rights	freedoms that governments must respect that existed before humans established governments
negative liberty	limits to adverse human behavior
negative rights	claims to prohibitions of government action
neutrality	a government's impartiality toward a foreign war
new international economic order	a proposed restructuring of the world economy to benefit poor countries
no-fly zone	airspace that a country is prohibited from using

noblesse oblige	benevolent, honorable behavior of the nobility toward those of lower rank
non-application procedure	refusal to act on a formal request
nongovernmental organization	a group composed of persons outside government
noninterference principle	the international law view that a government has no jurisdiction over how another government treats its own people inside its own homeland
normal trade relations	commerce between states without special restrictions
notification principle	an international requirement for a government to make a public statement before using force abroad
nuisance	a legal term describing something annoying to individuals
ozone	a form of oxygen (O_3) that absorbs ultraviolet rays so that they cannot reach the earth's surface
pacta sunt servanda	the practice of following legal precedent
peacekeeping	monitoring and promoting a peace agreement
people power	mass demonstrations that seek to force governments to make changes
persona non grata	an unwelcome diplomat
petition	a citizen's request to have a government redress a grievance
plebiscite	an election by residents of a territory to choose under which state they prefer to be governed
political rights	claims to participate in politics without restrictions
population exchange	movement of minorities in two countries to live in ethnic homelands in the other country
positive liberty	power to act autonomously
positive rights	claims to have government improve the well-being of the people
positivism	a theory of knowledge that rejects metaphysics
positivism, legal	the view that rights and obligations only exist when stated by governments in law
power elite	economic leaders who command political power
powers	legal capabilities
precautionary measure	immediate action to ward off a perilous situation
preclusion	action taken when there is no alternative response
preemptive war	armed aggression by one government to stop imminent, severe aggression by another
preventive procedure	measure taken to avoid a perilous situation
primacy principle	exclusive jurisdiction of a court over certain offenses
privateer	a private shipowner authorized by a government to harass and seize enemy ships
privatization	selling government corporations to private hands
privilege	a power reserved to those who qualify
prize of war	tangible property, such as an enemy ship, that is seized during armed inter-state conflict
proactive action	measures taken to encourage positive behavior

procedural rights	claims that government must follow standard practices and processes
pro forma trial	a judicial proceeding that observes forms of a trial though guilt has already been determined
program rights	obligations of governments to meet certain goals over time, such as extending schooling to all
proportionality	condign response of one state to actions of another state
protocol, treaty	a supplementary agreement to a treaty
provisional measure	action ordered by a court before a ruling to forestall irreparable harm
punitive action	retaliatory measure
qualified right	a right that can be limited, especially when the rights of others are jeopardized
quasi-trusteeship	a territory that the UN administers temporarily until a new government is legitimized by an election
quid pro quo	a condition that must be met by one party to gain a favor from another party
rationalism	the philosophy that bases principles on reason, not experience
realism	the ideology that government actions should be based on the expectation that powerful states will dominate weak states
realpolitik	actions by governments to maintain power relative to other states
rebus sic stantibus	a doctrine that a fundamental change in the assumptions of a legal agreement serves to void the agreement
refugee	an imperiled person who flees the homeland to seek sanctuary in a second country
region, international	a small, contiguously geographic area of the world
relativism	the view that universal moral absolutes do not exist
reprisal	a measured punitive reaction short of war by one government in response to an unfriendly act by another government
reprisal, private	reaction short of war by an individual who has been authorized by a government to respond to an unfriendly act by another government
reservation, treaty	statement made by a government that expresses exceptions or interpretations of provisions of a treaty while being ratified
responsibilities	obligations of individuals to respect rights of others
restorative justice	efforts to return to normal human rights observance after a period of many violations, ideally to heal an earlier conflict
retorsion	a measured peaceful but negative response by one government to an unfriendly act by another government
retributive justice	the outcome of a proceeding that brings violators of human rights to trial
right	a claim to exercise certain conduct or to enjoy certain benefits without unnecessary restrictions
right to life	a claim to enjoy subsistence (food, clothing, shelter)
right to peace	a claim to have conflicts resolved nonviolently
right to water	a claim that governments must ensure clean water for all
rights theory	the view that all should be treated as free and equal based on established norms and principles

sanction	a penalty imposed for disapproved conduct
scepticism	a philosophy that distrusts all claims to knowledge
Second World	non-market socialist countries
security rights	claims to freedom from violations of the human person
self-determination	ability of peoples to govern themselves
self-executing treaty	an international agreement containing implementation procedures
serfdom	the practice of forcing peasants to work on lands owned by feudal lords
shari'ah	Islamic law
show trial	a highly publicized trial aimed at frightening the public into compliance
social constructionism	the view that elites determine truth for those living in societies
social contract	the primordial agreement between individuals and governments to secure a stable social order
Social Darwinism	the view that only superior humans are worthy of survival in the process of human history
social democracy	a form of government in which the majority rules, minority rights are respected, and government protects those suffering economic misfortunes
social market capitalism	a nonsocialist welfare state
social rights	claims on governments to provide well-being to those living in its borders
soft law	legal requirements that lack enforcement capabilities
sovereign	the source of power in a state
sovereign immunity	exemption of a government leader from prosecution for official acts
sovereignty	the exclusive power of governments to rule within the borders of their countries
stages of growth	a series of distinct thresholds for progress
standard setting	specification of norms and principles
state immunity doctrine	the international law practice of exempting top government officials from prosecution for official acts
state secrets doctrine	the principle that courts cannot try cases in which national security secrets might be revealed
statism	the view that the only legitimate units of international politics are nation-states
structural violence	deprivation by the rich of food and shelter to the poor
subjective awareness	a legal principle that a superior who aids and abets a subordinate's war crimes is also culpable
substantive rights	claims on governments to respect specific freedoms
suffragettes	women who sought the right to vote through dramatic civil action
Sullivan Principles	fair labor practices designed to end *apartheid*
summit conference	a formal meeting involving heads of governments
supranational organization	an international body that can require government members to change national laws and practices under penalty of sanctions
sustainable development	economic growth that observes environmentally sound practices and enables future generations to satisfy basic human needs
technical assistance	use of expert training to learn how to use new technology
terrorism	the use of violence and threats of violence to make political statements

third-party complaint	an allegation that one country or person is violating the rights of another but brought by neither party
Third World	developing countries
traditionalism	respect for customs of the past
tragedy of the commons	minor, uncoordinated individual acts that produce a collective wrong
transgender	a person whose apparent physical characteristics do not match biological characteristics
transitional justice	establishment of a new human rights regime that follows one that severely violated human rights
transnationalism	advocacy of cooperation across national boundaries
transsexual	a person who changes biologically into a person of the opposite sex
transvestite	a person whose clothing resembles a sex opposite of the person's biological organs
treaty	a legal agreement that goes into effect when ratified by governments
trespass	an unlawful entry on land owned by another
trusteeship	a territory that the UN entrusted to a government in order to promote self-government in the territory
truth commission	a body that gathers evidence to establish facts about culpability but does not necessarily prosecute
unidimensionality	a statistical relationship in which variables are so highly interrelated that there are no correlational subclusters
universal jurisdiction	legal competence claimed by states to prosecute criminals regardless of where the crime took place
urgent procedure	measures taken to stop a serious, massive, or persistent pattern of misconduct
utilitarianism	a belief that what is good is what gives pleasure and avoids pain to the greatest number of persons
vegan	a person who consumes no animal products
vegetarianism	the view that humans should not consume animals
vertical enforcement	use of military action to enforce norms
vicarious liability	culpability of a superior for not stopping war crimes violations known to be committed by subordinates
Vienna mechanism	procedure used by one government member of the OSCE to complain about another
visit in *loco*	on-site visit
waiver	exception
war	a state of armed hostility between sovereign nations or governments
war crimes	violations of the laws or customs of armed state aggression
white slavery	forced prostitution
white torture	extreme painful procedure that produces no visible marks afterward
yellow dog contract	an employment contract in which management prohibits workers from joining a union

REFERENCES AND FURTHER READING

CHAPTER 1: Introduction

Anonymous (2003). *How Should Human Rights Be Defined?* San Diego, CA: Greenhaven Press.

Bartelson, Jens (2010). "The Social Construction of Globality," *International Political Sociology*, 4 (3): 219–35.

Beitz, Charles (2003). "What Human Rights Means," *Daedalus*, 132 (1): 36–46.

Berlin, Isaiah (1958). *Two Concepts of Liberty*. Oxford, UK: Clarendon Press.

Bøås, Morton, and Kevin C. Dunn (2007). *African Guerrillas: Raging against the Machine*. Boulder, CO: Rienner.

Boli-Bennett, John (1981). "Human Rights or State Expansion? Cross-National Definitions of Constitutional Rights, 1870–1970." In Ved P. Nanda, James R. Scarritt, and George W. Shepherd, Jr (eds), *Global Human Rights: Public Policies, Comparative Measures, and NGO Strategies*. Boulder, CO: Westview: Chapter 11.

Brown, Seyom (2000). *Human Rights in World Politics*. New York: Longman.

Charvey, John, and Elisa Kacznska-Nay (2008). *The Liberal Project and Human Rights: The Theory and Practice of a New World Order*. New York: Cambridge University Press.

Chowdhury, Arjun (2010). "'The Giver or the Recipient?' The Peculiar Ownership of Human Rights," *International Political Sociology*, 5 (1): 36–51.

Claude, Richard Pierre, and Burns H. Weston (eds) (1989). *Human Rights in the World Community: Issues and Action*. Philadelphia: University of Pennsylvania Press.

Colburn, Theo, Dianne Dumanoski, and John Peterson Myers (1996). *Our Stolen Future: Are We Threatening our Fertility, Intelligence, and Survival?: A Scientific Detective Story*. New York: Dutton.

Condé, H. Victor (2004). *A Handbook of International Human Rights Terminology*. 2nd edn. Lincoln: University of Nebraska Press.

Constant, Benjamin ([1814] 1988). *Political Writings*. Cambridge, UK: Cambridge University Press.

Cranston, Maurice (1983). "Are There Any Human Rights?," *Daedalus*, 112 (Fall): 1–17.

Donnelly, Jack (1989). *Universal Human Rights in Theory and Practice*. Ithaca, NY: Cornell University Press.

Donnelly, Jack (2013). *International Human Rights*. 4th edn. Boulder, CO: Westview: especially Chapters 1–3.

Donnelly, Jack, and Rhoda E. Howard (1988). "Assessing National Human Rights Performance: A Theoretical Framework," *Human Rights Quarterly*, 10 (May): 214–48.

Doyle, Michael W. (2011). "International Ethics and the Responsibility to Protect," *International Studies Review*, 13 (1): 72–84.

Dworkin, Ronald (1978). *Taking Rights Seriously*. London: Duckworth.

Edmundson, William A. (2004). *An Introduction to Rights*. New York: Cambridge University Press.

Egendorf, Laura K. (ed) (2003). *Human Rights: Opposing Viewpoints*. San Diego, CA: Greenhaven Press.

Estévez, Ariadna (2011). "Human Rights in Contemporary Political Sociology: The Primacy of Social Subjects," *Human Rights Quarterly*, 33 (4): 1142–62.

Finnis, John (1980). *Natural Law and Natural Rights*. Oxford: Clarendon.

Fleiner, Thomas (1999). *What Are Human Rights?* Sydney: Federation Press.

Forsythe, David P. (1991). *The Internationalization of Human Rights*. Lexington, MA: Lexington Books.

Forsythe, David P. (2009). *The Encyclopedia of Human Rights*. New York: Oxford University Press.

Forsythe, David P. (2012). *Human Rights in International Relations*. 3rd edn. Cambridge, UK: Cambridge University Press.

Freeman, Michael (2002). *Human Rights: An Interdisciplinary Approach*. Cambridge, MA: Polity.

Galtung, Johan (1994). *Human Rights in Another Key*. Cambridge, UK: Polity Press.

Gewirth, Alan (1978). *Reason and Morality*. Chicago, IL: Chicago University Press.

Gewirth, Alan (1982). *Human Rights: Essays on Justification and Applications*. Chicago, IL: University of Chicago Press.

Gibson, John (1996). *Dictionary of International Human Rights Law*. Lanham, MD: Scarecrow Press.

Haas, Michael (1994). *Improving Human Rights*. Westport, CT: Praeger.

Hanski, Raija, and Markku Suksi (eds) (1999). *An Introduction to the International Protection of Human Rights: A Textbook*. 2nd edn. Turku, Finland: Åbo Akademi University.

Harvard Human Rights Journal (1988–).

Headley, John M. (2008). *The Europeanization of the World: On the Origins of Human Rights and Democracy*. Princeton, NJ: Princeton University Press.

Hohfeld, Wesley N. ([1919] 2001). *Fundamental Legal Conceptions as Applied in Judicial Reasoning*. Burlington, VT: Ashgate.

Human Rights Law Journal (1980–).

Human Rights Law Review (2001–).

Human Rights Quarterly (1979–).

Human Rights Review (2000–).

Ingram, James D. (2008). "What Is a 'Right to Have Rights'? Three Images of the Politics of Human Rights," *American Political Science Review*, 102 (4): 401–16.

Jones, Peter (1994). *Rights*. Basingstoke, UK: Macmillan.

Journal of Human Rights (2002–).

Jütersonke, Oliver (2010). *Morgenthau, Law and Realism*. Cambridge, UK: Cambridge University Press.

Kayaoglu, Turan (2010). "Westphalian Eurocentrism in International Relations Theory," *International Studies Review*, 12 (2): 193–217.

Langley, Winston (comp) (1999). *Encyclopedia of Human Rights Issues Since 1945*. Westport, CT: Greenwood Press.

Lawson, Edward (comp) (1996). *Encyclopedia of Human Rights*. 2nd edn. Washington, DC: Taylor & Francis.

Mackie, J. L. (1977). *Ethics: Inventing Right and Wrong*. Harmondsworth, UK: Penguin.

Marshall, Thomas H. (1964). *Class, Citizenship, and Social Development*. Garden City, NY: Doubleday.

Morris, Lydia (2005). *Rights: Sociological Perspectives*. New York: Routledge.

Moyn, Samuel (2010). *The Last Utopia: Human Rights in History*. Cambridge, MA: Belknap Press.

Muskie, Edmund S. (1980). "The Foreign Policy of Human Rights," *Department of State Bulletin*, 80 (December): 7–9.

Nickel, James (1987). *Making Sense of Human Rights: Philosophical Reflections on the Universal Declaration of Human Rights*. Berkeley: University of California Press.

Nowak, Manfred, and Teresa Swinehart (eds) (1989). *Human Rights in Developing Countries: 1989 Yearbook*. Arlington, VA: Engel.

O'Byrne, Darren J. (2003). *Human Rights: An Introduction*. New York: Longman.

Robertson, A. H., and J. G. Merrils (1996). *Human Rights in the World: An Introduction to the Study of the International Protection of Human Rights*. 4th edn. New York: St Martin's Press.

Robertson, David (2004). *A Dictionary of Human Rights*. 2nd edn. London: Europa Publications.

Romano, David (2006). *The Kurdish Nationalist Movement: Opportunity, Mobilization, and Identity*. New York: Cambridge University Press.

Schwelb, Egon (1964). *Human Rights and the International Community*. Chicago, IL: Quadrangle Books.

Shue, Henry (1980). *Basic Rights: Subsistence, Affluence, and US Foreign Policy*. Princeton, NJ: Princeton University Press.

Shute, Stephen, and Susan Hurley (eds) (1993). *On Human Rights: The Oxford Amnesty Lectures*. New York: Basic Books.

Smith, Rhona K. M. (2005). *Textbook on International Human Rights*. 2nd edn. Oxford, UK: Oxford University Press.

Sreenivasan, Gopal (2005). "A Hybrid Theory of Claim-Rights," *Oxford Journal of Legal Studies*, 25 (2): 257–74.

Sriran, Chandra Lakha, Olga Martin-Ortega, and Johanna Herman (2010). *War, Conflict and Human Rights: Theory and Practice*. New York: Routledge.

Stanislawski, Bartosz H. (ed) (2008). "Para-States, Quasi-States, and Black Spots: Perhaps Not States, But Not 'Ungoverned Territories' Either," *International Studies Review*, 10 (2): 366–96.

Steiner, Henry J., and Philip Alston (eds) (2000). *International Human Rights in Context: Law, Politics, Morals: Text and Materials*. 2nd edn. New York: Oxford University Press.

Tai, Hung-Chao (1985). "Human Rights in Taiwan: Convergence of the Two Political Cultures." In James C. Hsiung (ed), *Human Rights in an East Asian Perspective*. New York: Paragon House.

United Nations Development Program (1992–). *Human Development Report*. New York: Oxford University Press.

Van Ness, Peter (ed) (1999). *Debating Human Rights: Critical Essays from the United States and Asia*. New York: Routledge.

Vance, Cyrus R. (1977). "Law Day Address on Human Rights Policy." In Donald P. Kommers and Gilburt D. Loescher (eds), *Human Rights and American Foreign Policy*. Notre Dame, IN: University of Notre Dame Press: 309–15.

Vašák, Karel (ed) (1982). *The International Dimensions of Human Rights*. Westport, CT: Greenwood.

Vincent, R. J. (1986). *Human Rights and International Relations*. Cambridge, UK: Cambridge University Press.

Waldron, Jeremy (ed) (1984). *Theories of Rights*. Oxford, UK: Oxford University Press.

Zakaria, Fareed (1997). "The Rise of Illiberal Democracy," *Foreign Affairs*, 76 (6): 22–43.

CHAPTER 2: The Philosophical Basis for Human Rights

Ahmad, Ilyas (1965). *Sovereignty Islamic and Modern: Conception of Sovereignty in Islam*. Karachi: The Allies Book Corporation.

Al-Sadr, Muhammad B. (1980). *Islam and Schools of Economics*. Karachi: Islamic Seminary Pakistan.

An-Na'im, Abdullah Ahmed (1990). *Toward an Islamic Reformation: Civil Liberties, Human Rights, and International Law*. Syracuse, NY: Syracuse University Press.

Arberry, A. J. (1995). *Aspects of Islamic Civilization as Depicted in the Original Texts*. Westport, CT: Greenwood Press.

Armstrong, Karen (2006). *The Great Transformation: The Beginning of Our Religious Traditions*. New York: Knopf.

Aslan, Reza (2005). *No God But God: The Origins, Evolution, and Future of Islam*. New York: Random House.

Avonius, Leena, and Damien Kingsbury (eds) (2008). *Human Rights in Asia: A Reassessment of the Asian Values Debate*. New York: Palgrave Macmillan.

Bauer, Joanne R., and Daniel A. Bell (eds) (1999). *The East Asian Challenge for Human Rights*. Cambridge, UK: Cambridge University Press.

Bellah, Robert N., and Hans Joas (eds) (2012) *The Axial Age and Its Consequences*. Cambridge, MA: Belknap Press.

Berdal, Aral (2004). "The Idea of Human Rights as Perceived in the Ottoman Empire," *Human Rights Quarterly*, 26 (May): 454–82.

Berger, Peter, and Thomas Luckmann (1967). *The Social Construction of Reality: A Treatise in the Sociology of Knowledge*. New York: Anchor.

Berryman, Phillip (1987). *Liberation Theology: Essential Facts about the Revolutionary Movement in Latin America – and Beyond*. Philadelphia, PA: Temple University Press.

Bigongiari, Dino (ed) (1953). *The Political Ideas of St Thomas Aquinas*. New York: Hafner.

Bloom, Irene, J., Paul Martin, and Wayne L. Proudfoot (eds) (1996). *Religious Diversity and Human Rights*. New York: Columbia University Press.

Boswell, J. (1994). *Same-Sex Unions in Premodern Europe*. New York, Toronto: Vintage Books.

Bourdieu, Pierre (2000). *The Social Structures of the Economy*. Malden, MA: Polity.

Bowersock, G. W. (2013). "A Different Turning Point for Mankind?," *New York Review of Books*, May 9.

Bryce, James (1961). *The Holy Roman Empire*. New York: Schocken.

Buchanan, Allan (2004). *Justice, Legitimacy, and Self-Determination: Moral Foundations for International Law*. New York: Oxford University Press.

Bull, Hedley, Benedict Kingsbury, and Adam Roberts (eds) (1992). *Hugo Grotius and International Relations*. New York: Oxford University Press.

Burston, W. H. (1973). *James Mill on Philosophy and Education*. London: Athlone Press.

Calvar, Georg (1999). *Kant and the Theory and Practice of International Right*. Cambridge, UK: Cambridge University Press.

Cohler, Anne (1988). *Montesquieu's Comparative Politics and the Spirit of American Constitutionalism*. Lawrence, KS: University Press of Kansas.

Cohn, Haim H. (1989). *Human Rights in the Bible and Talmud*. Tel-Aviv: MOD Books.

Cox, Richard H. (1982). *Locke on War and Peace*. Washington, DC: University Press of America.

Crowe, Ian (ed) (2004). *An Imaginative Whig: Reassessing the Life and Thought of Edmund Burke*. Columbia, MO: University of Missouri Press.

Dalacoura, Katerina (2003). *Islam, Liberalism, and Human Rights*. 2nd edn. London: Taurus.

Dalai Lama (1975). *The Buddhism of Tibet and the Key to the Middle Way*. New York: Harper & Row.

Darwin, Charles ([1871] 1998). *The Descent of Man*. Amherst, NY: Prometheus Books.

Davidson, Herbert A. (2005). *Moses Maimonides: The Man and His Works*. New York: Oxford University Press.

de Bary, William T. (1998). *Asian Values and Human Rights: A Confucian Communitarian Perspective*. Cambridge, MA: Harvard University Press.

Donnelly, Jack (1989). *Universal Human Rights in Theory and Practice*. Ithaca, NY: Cornell University Press.

Donnelly, Jack (1999). "The Social Construction of Human Rights." In Tim Dunne and Nicholas J. Wheeler (eds), *Human Rights in Global Politics*. Cambridge, UK: Cambridge University Press: 71–109.

Donnelly, Jack (2007). "The West and Economic Rights." In Shareen Hertel and Lanse Minkler (eds), *Economic Rights: Conceptual, Measurement, and Policy Issues*. Cambridge, UK: Cambridge University Press.

Donnelly, Jack (2013). *International Human Rights*. 4th edn. Boulder, CO: Westview.

Douzinas, Costas (2006). *The End of Human Rights: Critical Legal Thought at the Turn of the Century*. Portland, OR: Hart Publishing.

Durr, Clifford (1981). *Jesus as a Free Speech Victim: Trial by Terror 2000 Years Ago*. New York: Basic Pamphlets.

El Guindi, F. (1995). "Hijab." In J. L. Espisito (ed), *The Oxford Encyclopedia of the Modern Islamic World*. New York: Oxford University Press: 2: 108–11.

Etzioni, Amitai (1995). *Rights and the Common Good: The Communitarian Perspective*. New York: St Martin's Press.

Etzioni, Amitai (2006). "A Neo-Communitarian Approach to International Relations," *Human Rights Review*, 7 (4): 69–80.

Falk, Richard A. (1981). *Human Rights and State Sovereignty*. New York: Holmes & Meier.

Falk, Richard A. (2001). *Religion and Humane Global Governance*. New York: Palgrave Macmillan.

Ferrara, Alessandro (2003). "Two Notions for Humanity and the Judgment Argument for Human Rights," *Political Theory*, 31 (3): 392–420.

Finnis, John (1980). *Natural Law and Natural Rights*. New York: Oxford University Press.

Fonte, John (2004). "Democracy's Trojan House," *Institute of Public Affairs Review*, 56 (December): 3–6.

Forsythe, David P. (2012). *Human Rights in International Relations*. 3rd edn. New York: Cambridge University Press.

Foucault, Michel (1977). *Discipline and Punish: The Birth of the Prison*. New York: Pantheon Books.

Franklin, Julian H. (1963). *Jean Bodin and the Sixteenth-Century Revolution in the Methodology of Law and History*. New York: Columbia University Press.

Freeman, Michael D. A. (2004). "The Problem of Secularism in Human Rights Theory," *Human Rights Quarterly*, 26 (May): 375–400.

Freud, Sigmund (1930). *Civilization and Its Discontents*. London: Hogarth Press.

Freyburg-Inan, Annette, Ewan Harrison, and Patrick James (eds) (2009). *Rethinking Realism in International Relations: Variations on a Realist Theme*. Baltimore, MD: Johns Hopkins University Press.

Fukuyama, Francis (2001). "Natural Rights and Human History," *The National Interest*, 64 (Summer): 19–30.

Fukuyama, Francis (2002). *The End of History and the Last Man*. New York: Free Press.

Fukuyama, Francis (2011). *The Origins of Political Order: From Prehuman Times to the French Revolution*. New York: Farrar, Straus and Giroux.

Galtung, Johan (1992). *The Way Is the Goal: Gandhi Today*. Ahmenabad, India: Gujarat Vidyapith.

Galtung, Johan (1993). *Buddhism: A Quest for Unity and Peace*. Ratmalana, Sri Lanka: Sarvodaya.

Galtung, Johan, and Anders Wirak (1976). *Human Needs, Human Rights, and the Theory of Development*. Oslo: University of Oslo.

Gandhi, Mahatma (1948). *The Gospel of Selfless Action*. Ahmedabad, India: Navajivan Publishing House.

Gearon, Liam (ed) (2000). *Human Rights and Religion: A Reader*. Brighton, UK: Sussex Academic Press.

George, Robert P. (2001). *In Defense of Natural Law*. New York: Oxford University Press.

Goldie, Mark (1999). *The Reception of Locke's Politics*. Brookfield, VT: Pickering & Chatto.

Goodell, Edward (1994). *The Noble Philosopher: Condorcet and the Enlightenment*. Buffalo, NY: Prometheus Books.

Goodman, Lenn E. (1998). *Judaism, Human Rights, and Human Values*. New York: Oxford University Press.

Gopnik, Adam (2005). "Voltaire's Garden: The Philosopher as a Campaigner for Human Rights," *The New Yorker*, 81 (March 7): 74.

Habermas, Jürgen (2005). *Time of Transitions*. Oxford, UK: Blackwell Publishing.

Harrison, Ross (2003). *Hobbes, Locke, and Confusion's Empire: An Examination of Seventeenth-Century Political Philosophy*. New York: Cambridge University Press.

Hastrup, K. (ed) (2001). *Legal Cultures and Human Rights: The Challenge of Diversity*. The Hague: Kluwer Law International.

Hayden, Patrick (2001). *The Philosophy of Human Rights*. St Paul, MN: Paragon House.

Hendricks, Obery M. (2006). *The Politics of Jesus: Rediscovering the True Revolutionary Nature of the Teachings of Jesus and How They Have Been Corrupted*. New York: Doubleday.

Hindu Human Rights Group (2001). *Charter on Hindu International Human Rights*. Available at: http://www.hinduhumanrights.org.

Hobbes, Thomas ([1651] 2010). *Leviathan*. New Haven, CT: Yale University Press.

Hoffmann, Stanley, and David Fidler (eds) (1991). *Rousseau on International Relations*. New York: Oxford University Press.

Hofstadter, Richard (1944). *Social Darwinism in American Thought*. Boston: Beacon.

Human Rights and the World's Major Religions (2005). Various editors, 5 Volumes. New York: Praeger.

Huntington, Samuel P. (1968). *Political Order in Changing Societies*. New Haven, CT: Yale University Press.

Huntington, Samuel P. (1996). *The Clash of Civilizations and the Remaking of World Order*. New York: Simon & Schuster.

Ishay, Micheline R. (ed) (1997). *The Human Rights Reader: Major Political Essays, Speeches, and Documents from the Bible to the Present*. New York: Routledge.

Jacobsen, Michael, and Ole Brunn (eds) (2000). *Human Rights and Asian Values: Contesting National Identities and Cultural Representations in Asia*. Richmond, VA: Curzon.

Jaspers, Karl (1953). *The Origin and Goal of History*. New York: Routledge.

Kendall, Willmore (1941). *John Locke and the Doctrine of Majority-Rule*. Urbana, IL: University of Illinois Press.

Kolakowski, Leszek. (1983). "Marxism and Human Rights," *Daedalus*, 112 (Fall): 81–92.

Kolakowski, Leszek (2006). *Main Currents of Marxism*. 3 Vols. New York: Norton.

Kraynak, Robert P. (2001). *Christian Faith and Modern Democracy: God and Politics in the Fallen World*. Notre Dame, IN: University of Notre Dame Press.

Kuran, Timur (2004). *Islam and Mammon: Critical Perspectives on the Economic Agenda of Islamism*. Princeton, NJ: Princeton University Press.

Langlois, Anthony J. (2001). *The Politics of Justice and Human Rights: Southeast Asia and Universalist Theory*. New York: Cambridge University Press.

Lebow, Richard Ned (2003). *The Tragic Vision of Politics: Ethics, Interests, and Orders*. Cambridge, UK: Cambridge University Press.

Lee Kuan Yew (2000). "America's New Agenda." In *From Third World to First: The Singapore Story, 1965–2000*. Singapore: Straits Times Press: Chapter 30.

Levinson, David (ed) (2003). *The Wilson Chronology of Human Rights: A Record of the Human Striving for Freedom from Ancient Times to the Present*. Bronx, NY: Wilson.

Long, Douglas G. (1977). *Bentham on Liberty: Bentham's Idea of Liberty in Relation to His Utilitarianism*. Toronto: University of Toronto Press.

Lyons, Gene (1994). *Rights, Welfare, and Mill's Moral Theory*. New York: Oxford University Press.

MacIntyre, Alasdair (1981). *After Virtue: A Study in Moral Theory*. Notre Dame, IN: University of Notre Dame Press.

Madison, James, Alexander Hamilton, and John Jay ([1787–1789] 2004). *The Federalist Papers*. New York: Pocket Books.

Marcuse, Herbert (1941). *Reason and Revolution: Hegel and the Rise of Social Theory*. New York: Oxford University Press.

Martin, Wayne M. (1997). *Idealism and Objectivity: Understanding Fichte's Jena Project*. Stanford, CA: Stanford University Press.

Marx, Karl ([1875] 1947). *Critique of the Gotha Program*. Moscow: Foreign Languages Publishing House.

Mayer, Ann E. (1991). *Islam and Human Rights: Tradition and Politics*. Boulder, CO: Westview.

McDonough, Sheila (1984). *Muslim Ethics and Modernity: A Comparative Study of the Ethical Thought of Sayyid Ahmad Khan and Mawlana Mawdudi*. Waterloo, Ont.: Wilfred Laurier University Press.

Mencken, H. L. ([1907] 1973). *The Philosophy of Friedrich Nietzsche*. Folcroft, PA: Folcroft Library Editions.

Mill, Harriet Taylor, and John Stuart Mill ([1859] 1983). *Enfranchisement of Women by Harriet Taylor Mill and The Subjection of Women by John Stuart Mill*. London: Virago.

Morgan, Robert J. (1988). *James Madison on the Constitution and the Bill of Rights*. New York: Greenwood Press.

Morgenthau, Hans J. (1948). *Politics Among Nations: The Struggle for Power and Peace*. 1st edn. New York: Knopf.

Moussalli, Ahmad S. (2001). *The Islamic Quest for Democracy, Pluralism, and Human Rights*. Gainesville, FL: University Press of Florida.

Nardin, Terry, and David R. Mapel (eds) (1992). *Traditions of International Ethics*. New York: Cambridge University Press.

Nye, Joseph S., Jr (2004). *Soft Power: The Means to Success in World Politics*. New York: Public Affairs.

Orfield, G., and C. Lee (2006). *Racial Transformation and the Changing Nature of Segregation*. Cambridge, MA: The Civil Rights Project, Harvard University.

Paine, Thomas (1792). *The Rights of Man*. London: Symonds.

Parekh, Serena (2007). "Resisting 'Dull and Torpid' Ascent: Returning to the Debate over the Foundations of Human Rights," *Human Rights Quarterly*, 29 (3): 754–78.

Parekh, Serena (2008). *Hannah Arendt and the Challenge of Modernity: A Phenomenology of Human Rights*. New York: Routledge.

Parfit, Derek (2001). *On What Matters*. New York: Oxford University Press.

Perera, L. P. (1991). *Buddhism and Human Rights: A Buddhist Commentary on the Universal Declaration of Human Rights*. Colombo, Sri Lanka: Karunaratne & Sons.

Pickering, Mary (2012). *Auguste Comte: An Intellectual Biography*, 3 vols. New York: Cambridge University Press.

Rasmussen, Douglas, and J. Den Uyl (1991). *Liberty and Nature: An Aristotelian Defense of Liberal Order*. La Salle, IL: Open Court.

Rawls, John (1971). *A Theory of Justice*. Cambridge, MA: Harvard University Press.

Rawls, John (1996). *Political Liberalism*. New York: Columbia University Press.

Rawls, John (1999). *The Law of Peoples*. Cambridge, UK: Cambridge University Press.

Renteln, Alison D. (1990). *International Human Rights: Universalism Versus Relativism*. London: SAGE Publications.

Rouner, Leroy S. (ed) (1988). *Human Rights and the World's Religions*. Notre Dame, IN: University of Notre Dame Press.

Rumble, Wilfred E. (1985). *The Thought of John Austin: Jurisprudence, Colonial Reform, and the British Constitution*. London: Athlone Press.

Ryan, Alan (2012). *A History of Political Thought*, 2 vols. New York: Liveright.

Searle, John (1995). *The Construction of Social Reality*. New York: Free Press.

Sen, Amartya (1997). "Human Rights and Asian Values: What Lee Kuan Yew and Le Peng Don't Understand About Asia," *The New Republic*, 217 (July 14): 33–40.

Sen, Amartya (2004). "Elements of a Theory of Human Rights," *Philosophy and Public Affairs*, 27 (Fall): 315–56.

Sharma, Arvind (2004). *Hinduism and Human Rights: A Conceptual Approach*. New York: Oxford University Press.

Sheldon, Garrett W. (1991). *The Political Philosophy of Thomas Jefferson*. Baltimore, MD: Johns Hopkins University Press.

Shestack, Jerome J. (1998). "The Philosophic Foundations of Human Rights," *Human Rights Quarterly*, 20 (2): 201–34.

Singer, Beth J. (1999). *Pragmatism, Rights, and Democracy*. New York: Fordham University Press.

Smith, Steven (1989). *Hegel's Critique of Liberalism: Rights in Context*. Chicago, IL: University of Chicago Press.

Spencer, Herbert (1864). *Social Statics*. New York: Appleton.

Strawson, John (1997). "A Western Question to the Middle East: 'Is There a Human Rights Discourse in Islam?'," *Arab Studies Quarterly*, 19 (Winter): 31–58.

Sumner, W. G. (1883). *What Social Classes Owe to Each Other*. New York: Harper.

Swidler, Arlene (ed) (1982). *Human Rights in Religious Traditions*. New York: Pilgrims Press.

Tuck, Richard (1979). *Natural Rights Theories*. Cambridge, UK: Cambridge University Press.

Tuck, Richard (1989). *Hobbes*. New York: Oxford University Press.

Waldron, Jeremy (ed) (1987). "Nonsense upon Stilts." In *Bentham, Burke and Marx on the Rights of Man*. London: Methuen.

Walker, Thomas C. (2008). "Two Faces of Liberalism: Kant, Paine, and the Question of Intervention," *International Studies Quarterly*, 52 (3): 449–68.

Waltz, Susan (2004). "Universal Human Rights: The Contribution of Muslim States," *Human Rights Quarterly*, 26 (November): 799–844.

Waltzer, Michael (1994). *Thick and Thin: Moral Argument at Home and Abroad*. Notre Dame, IN: University of Notre Dame Press.

Watkins, Frederick M. (ed) (1953). *Jean-Jacques Rousseau: Political Writings; Containing the Social Contract, Considerations on the Government of Poland, and Part I of the Constitutional Project for Corsica*. New York: Nelson.

Wedgwood, C. V. (1938). *The Thirty Years War*. London: Cape.

Weinert, Matthew S. (2007). "Bridging the Human Rights–Sovereignty Divide: Theoretical Foundations of a Democratic Sovereignty," *Human Rights Review*, 8 (2): 5–32.

Wernick, Andrew (2001). *Auguste Comte and the Religion of Humanity: The Post-Theistic Program of French Social Theory*. Cambridge: University of Cambridge Press.

Wood, Neal (1991). *Cicero's Social and Political Thought*. Berkeley, CA: University of California Press.

Woods, Jeanne M. (2003). "Rights as Slogans: A Theory of Human Rights Based on African Humanism," *Black Law Journal*, 17 (1): 52–66.

Yogi, Maharishi M. (1963). *The Science of Being and Art of Living*. New York: Allied Publishers.

CHAPTER 3: The Historical Basis for Human Rights

Amar, Akhil R. (2005). *America's Constitution: A Biography*. New York: Random House.

Barone, Michael (2007). *Our First Revolution: The Remarkable British Upheaval That Inspired America's Founding*. New York: Crown.

Best, Geoffrey (1999). "Peace Conferences and the Century of Total War: The 1899 Hague Conference and What Came After," *International Affairs*, 55 (3): 619–34.

Carlyle, Thomas ([1839] 1885). *Chartism*. New York: Lovell.

Clarkson, Thomas (1787). *A Summary View of the Slave Trade and of the Probable Consequences of Its Abolition*. London: Phillips.

Coplin, William D., and Martin J. Rochester (1972). "The Permanent Court of International Justice, The International Court of Justice, The League of Nations, and the United Nations: A Comparative Empirical Survey," *American Political Science Review*, 66 (2): 529–50.

Dawes, James (2009). "Human Rights in Literary Studies," *Human Rights Quarterly*, 31 (2): 394–409.

Delbanco, Andrew (2012). *The Abolitionist Imagination*. Cambridge, MA: Harvard University Press.

Dunant, Henri ([1862] 1939). *A Memory of Solferino*. Washington, DC: American National Red Cross.

Eubanks, Rodney (1971). "International Arbitration in the Political Sphere," *Arbitration Journal*, 26 (3): 129–46.

Fairbanks, Charles H., Jr (1982). "The British Campaign Against the Slave Trade: An Example of Successful Human Rights Policy." In F. E. Baumann (ed), *Human Rights and American Foreign Policy*. Gambier, OH: Public Affairs Conference Center, Kenyon College: 87–135.

Falk, Richard A. (1981). *Human Rights and State Sovereignty*. Teaneck, NJ: Holmes & Meier.

Ferrell, Robert H. (1952). *Peace in Their Time: The Origins of the Kellogg–Briand Pact*. Hamden, CT: Archon.

Figes, Orlando (2011). *The Crimean War: A History*. Dallas, TX: Metropolitan.

Foner, Philip (1975). *History of the Labor Movement in the United States*. New York: International Publishers.

Fox-Decent, Evan, and Evan J. Criddle (2012). "Human Rights Emergence and the Rule of Law," *Human Rights Quarterly*, 34 (1): 39–87.

Goldenberg, David M. (2006). *The Curse of Ham: Race and Slavery in Early Judaism, Christianity, and Islam*. Princeton, NJ: Princeton University Press.

Haas, Michael (1992). *Polity and Society: Philosophical Underpinnings of Social Science Paradigms*. Westport, CT: Praeger.

Halpern, Rick, and Enrico Dal Lago (eds) (2002). *Slavery and Emancipation*. Malden, MA: Blackwell.

Herzl, Theodore ([1896] 1917). *A Jewish State: An Attempt at a Modern Solution of the Jewish Question*. 3rd edn. New York, Federation of American Zionists.

Heyrick, Elizabeth (1825). *Immediate, not Gradual Abolition, or, An Inquiry into the Shortest, Safest, and Most Effectual Means of Getting Rid of West Indian Slavery*. New York: Seaman.

Hochschild, Adam (2005). *Bury the Chains: Prophets and Rebels in the Fight to Free an Empire's Slaves*. Boston: Houghton Mifflin.

Hudson, Manley O. (1944). *International Tribunals, Past and Future*. Washington, DC: Carnegie Endowment for International Peace and Brookings Institution.

Hunt, Lynn (2008). *Inventing Human Rights: A History*. New York: Norton.

Ishay, Micheline R. (2008). *The History of Human Rights: From Ancient Times to the Globalization Era*. 2nd edn. Berkeley: University of California Press.

Jennings, Judi (1997). *The Business of Abolishing the British Slave Trade, 1783–1807*. Portland, OR: Frank Cass.

Lauren, Paul Gordon (2011). *The Evolution of International Human Rights: Visions Seen*. 2nd edn. Philadelphia, PA: University of Pennsylvania Press.

Lenin, Vladimir Ilich ([1914] 1935). "The War and Russian Social-Democracy." In J. Fineberg (ed), *Selected Works*. New York: International Publishers: 5: 123–30.

Leo XIII ([1891] 1940). *Rerum Novarum, Encyclical Letter of Pope Leo XIII on the Condition of Labor*. New York: Paulist Press.

Levinson, David (ed) (2003). *The Wilson Chronology of Human Rights: A Record of the Human Striving for Freedom from Ancient Times to the Present 2003*. New York: H. W. Wilson.

MacMunn, George Fletcher (1938). *Slavery Through the Ages*. London: Nicholson & Watson.

Mair, Lucy Philip (1928). *The Protection of Minorities: The Working and Scope of the Minorities Treaties Under the League of Nations*. London: Christophers.

Mair, Lucy Philip (1929). *Human Welfare and the League*. 5th edn. London: League of Nations Union.

Margalith, Aaron Morris (1930). *The International Mandates: A Historical, Descriptive, and Analytical Study of the Theory and Principles of the Mandates System*. Baltimore: Johns Hopkins Press.

Marx, Karl, and Friedrich Engels ([1848] 1948). *Manifesto of the Communist Party*. Moscow: Foreign Languages Publishing House.

Meyer, Carl Ludwig Wilhelm (1923). *Memorandum on the Origin, Status, and Achievements of the Hague Tribunal and of the Permanent Court of International Justice*. Washington, DC: Library of Congress.

Mill, Harriet Taylor, and John Stuart Mill ([1859] 1983). *Enfranchisement of Women by Harriet Taylor Mill and The Subjection of Women by John Stuart Mill*. London: Virago.

Miller, David Hunter (1928). *The Peace Pact of Paris: A Study of the Briand–Kellogg Treaty*. New York: Putnam's Sons.

Moorehead, Caroline (1999). *Dunant's Dream: War, Switzerland, and the History of the Red Cross*. New York: Carroll & Graf.

Northedge, F. S. (1986). *The League of Nations: Its Life and Times 1920–1946*. Leicester, UK: Leicester University Press.

Nussbaum, Martha (2012). *The New Religious Intolerance: Overcoming the Politics of Fear in an Anxious Age*. Cambridge, MA: Belknap Press.

Owen, Robert ([1831] 1991). *A New View of Society*. New York: Woodstock Books.

Reynolds, Davis S. (2010). *Mightier Than the Sword: Uncle Tom's Cabin and the Battle for America*. New York: Norton.

Schindler, Dietrich, and Jiří Toman (comps) (2004). *The Laws of Armed Conflicts: A Collection of Conventions, Resolutions, and Other Documents*. Boston: Martinus Nihjoff.

Scott, J. B. (1909). *The Hague Peace Conferences of 1899 and 1907*. Baltimore, MD: Johns Hopkins Press.

Scott, S. P. (ed) (1932). *The Civil Law, Including the Twelve Tables, the Institutes of Gaius, the Rules of Ulpian, the Opinions of Paulus, the Enactments of Justinian, and the Constitutions of Leo*. Cincinnati, OH: Central Trust Company.

Sen, Amartya (2005). *The Argumentative Indian: Writings on Indian History, Culture and Identity*. New York: Farrar, Straus & Giroux.

Sewell, Samuel ([1700] 1969). *The Selling of Joseph: A Memorial*. Amherst, MA: University of Massachusetts Press.

Sharp, Granville ([1774] 1971). *A Declaration of the People's Natural Right to a Share in the Legislature; Which is the Fundamental Principle of the British Constitution of State*. New York: Da Capo Press.

Stowe, Harriet Beecher ([1852] 2005). *Uncle Tom's Cabin*. West Berlin, NJ: Townsend Press.

Szabo, Imre (1982). "Historical Foundations of Human Rights and Subsequent Developments." In K. Vašák and P. Alston (eds), *The International Dimensions of Human Rights*. Westport, CT: Greenwood: 1, 11–42.

Walters, Francis P. (1952). *A History of the League of Nations*. New York: Oxford University Press.

Wambaugh, Sarah (1933). *Plebiscites Since the World War*. Washington, DC: Carnegie Endowment for International Peace.

Wells, H. G. (1933). *The Shape of Things to Come*. New York: Macmillan.

Wesley, John (1744). *Thoughts upon Slavery*. London: Hawes.

Wollstonecraft, Mary ([1792] 1845). *A Vindication of the Rights of Woman, With Strictures on Political and Moral Subjects*. New York: Vale.

CHAPTER 4: The Contemporary Basis for Human Rights

Agha, Hussein, and Robert Malley (2011). "The Arab Counterrevolution," *New York Review of Books*, 58 (14): 42–44.

Agha, Hussein, and Robert Malley (2012). "This Is Not a Revolution," *New York Review of Books*, 59 (17): 71–73.

Albert, Peter J., and Ronald Hoffman (1990). *We Shall Overcome: Martin Luther King, Jr, and the Black Freedom Struggle*. New York: Pantheon Books.

Alfredsson, Gudmundur, and Ashbjørn Eide (eds) (1999). *The University Declaration of Human Rights: A Common Standard of Achievement*. Boston: Nijhoff.

Alston, Philip (ed) (2005). *Non-State Actors and Human Rights*. New York: Oxford University Press.

Baker, Gideon (2005). "Saving Global Civil Society with Rights." In Gideon Baker and David Chandler (eds), *Global Civil Society: Contested Futures*. New York: Routledge: 114–29.

Barnett, Michael, and Thomas G. Weiss (eds) (2008). *Humanitarianism in Question: Politics, Power, Ethics.* New York: Cornell University Press.

Barnett, Thomas (2011). *Empire of Humanity: A History of Humanitarianism.* Ithaca, NY: Cornell University Press.

Bereffi, Gary, Ronnie García-Johnson, and Erika Sasser (2001). "The NGO-Industrial Complex," *Foreign Policy,* 125 (July/August): 556–65.

Boyd, K. Lee (2004). "Universal Jurisdiction and Structural Reasonableness," *Texas International Law Journal,* 90 (Fall): 1–58.

Brysk, Alison (ed) (2002). *Globalization and Human Rights.* Berkeley: University of California Press.

Brysk, Alison (2009). *Global Good Samaritans: Human Rights as Foreign Policy.* New York: Oxford University Press.

Buchanan, Tom (2002). "'The Truth Will Set You Free': The Making of Amnesty International," *Journal of Contemporary History,* 37 (4): 575–97.

Burgenthal, Thomas, Dinah Shelton, and David P. Stewart (2002). *International Human Rights in a Nutshell.* 3rd edn. St Paul, MN: West Group.

Burke, Roland (2011). *Decolonization and the Evolution of International Human Rights.* Philadelphia: University of Philadelphia Press.

Busby, Joshua W. (2010). *Moral Movements and Foreign Policy.* Cambridge, UK: Cambridge University Press.

Carter, Jimmy (1995). *Keeping Faith: Memoirs of a President.* Fayetteville, AK: University of Arkansas Press.

Chayes, Abraham, and Antonia Chandler Chayes (1995). *The New Sovereignty: Compliance with International Regulatory Agreements.* Cambridge, MA: Harvard University Press.

Clifford, Bob (ed) (2009). *The International Strategy for New Human Rights.* Philadelphia: University of Pennsylvania Press.

Coicaud, Jean-Marc, Michael W. Doyle, and Anne-Marie Gardner (eds) (2003). *The Globalization of Human Rights.* New York: United Nations University Press.

Davis, David R., Amanda Murdie, and Cory Garnett Steinmetz (2012). "'Makers and Shakers': Human Rights INGOs and Public Opinion," *Human Rights Quarterly,* 34 (1): 199–224.

Drinan, Robert F. (2001). *The Mobilization of Shame: A World View of Human Rights.* New Haven, CT: Yale University Press.

Falk, Richard A. (1995). *On Human Governance: Toward a New Global Politics.* University Park, PA: Pennsylvania State University Press.

Falk, Richard A. (1999). *Predatory Globalization: A Critique.* Malden, MA: Polity Press.

Findley, Michael G., and Joseph K. Young (2011). "Terrorism, Democracy and Credible Commitments," *International Studies Quarterly,* 55 (2): 357–78.

Forsythe, David (2005). *The Humanitarians: The International Committee of the Red Cross.* New York: Cambridge University Press.

Freeman, Will (2010). "The Accuracy of China's 'Mass Incidents'," *Financial Times,* March 2.

Glendon, Mary Ann (2001). *A World Made New: Eleanor Roosevelt and the Universal Declaration of Human Rights.* New York: Random House.

Goodhand, Jonathan (2006). *Aiding Peace? The Role of NGOs in Armed Conflict.* Boulder, CO: Rienner.

Goodhart, Michael (2009). *Human Rights: Politics and Practice.* New York: Oxford University Press.

Gray, Robert C., and Stanley I. Michalak (eds) (1984). *American Foreign Policy Since Détente.* New York: Harper & Row.

Gready, Paul (ed) (2004). *Fighting for Human Rights.* New York: Routledge.

Harris, Whitney R. (1999). *Tyranny on Trial: The Trial of the Major German War Criminals at the End of World War II at Nuremberg, Germany, 1945–1946.* Dallas, TX: Southern Methodist University Press.

Heins, Volker (2008). *Nongovernmental Organizations in International Society: Struggles over Recognition.* New York: Palgrave Macmillan.

Ignatieff, Michael (2012). "The Man Who Shaped History," *New York Review of Books,* 59 (15): 31–3.

Jacobs, Steven L. (ed) (1992). *Raphael Lemkin's Thoughts on Nazi Genocide: Not Guilty?* Lewiston, ME: Mellen Press.

Jones, Jackie, Anna Grear, Rachel Ann Fenton, and Kim Stevenson (eds) (2011). *Gender, Sexualities and Law.* New York: Routledge.

Kaufman, Burton I. (1993). *The Presidency of James Earl Carter, Jr.* Lawrence, KS: University of Kansas Press.

Keck, Margaret E., and Kathryn Sikkink (1998). *Activists Beyond Borders: Advocacy Networks in International Politics.* Ithaca, NY: Cornell University Press.

Keenan, Joseph B., and Brendan Francis Brown (1950). *Crimes Against International Law.* Washington, DC: Public Affairs Press.

Khagram, Sanjeev, James V. Riker, and Kathryn Sikkink (eds) (2002). *Restructuring World Politics: Transnational Social Movements, Networks, and Norms.* Minneapolis: University of Minnesota Press.

Kirkup, Alex, and Tony Evans (2009). "The Myth of Western Opposition to Economic, Social, and Cultural Rights? A Reply to Whelan and Donnelly," *Human Rights Quarterly,* 31 (1): 221–38.

Korey, William (1998). *NGOs and the Universal Declaration of Human Rights: A Curious Grapevine.* New York: Palgrave Macmillan.

Kuper, Leo (1981). *South Africa: Human Rights and Genocide.* Bloomington: Indiana University Press.

Lauren, Paul Gordon (1998). *The Evolution of International Human Rights.* Philadelphia: University of Pennsylvania Press.

Lelyveld, Joseph (2011). *Great Soul: Mahatma Gandhi and His Struggle with India.* New York: Knopf.

Lincoln, C. Eric (ed) (1970). *Martin Luther King, Jr: A Profile.* New York: Hill & Wang.

Link, Perry (2011). "How China Fears the Middle East Revolutions," *New York Review of Books,* 58 (5): 21–24.

Lipstadt, Deborah (1993). *Denying the Holocaust: The Growing Assault on Truth and Memory.* New York: Plume.

Longerich, Peter (2011). *Holocaust: The Nazi Persecution and Murder of the Jews.* New York: Oxford University Press.

Mayall, James, and Gene M. Lyons (2003). *International Human Rights in the 21st Century: Protecting the Rights of Groups.* Lanham, MD: Rowman & Littlefield.

Mertus, Julie A. (2009). *Human Rights Matters: Local Politics and National Human Rights Institutions.* Stanford, CA: Stanford University Press.

Miéville, China (2006). *Between Equal Rights: A Marxist Theory of International Law.* Chicago, IL: Haymarket Books.

Minear, Richard H. (1971). *Victors' Justice: The Tokyo War Crimes Trial.* Princeton, NJ: Princeton University.

Mintoma, Glenn Tatsuya (2008). "Civil Society and Human Rights: The Commission to Study the Organization of Peace and the Origins of the UN Human Rights Regime," *Human Rights Quarterly,* 30 (3): 607–30.

Morsink, Johannes (1999). *The Universal Declaration of Human Rights: Origins, Drafting, and Intent.* Philadelphia: University of Pennsylvania Press.

Neier, Aryeh (2003). *Taking Liberties: Four Decades in the Struggle for Rights.* New York: Public Affairs Press.

Neier, Aryeh (2012). *The International Human Rights Movement: A History.* Princeton, NJ: Princeton University Press.

Nelson, Paul J., and Ellen Dorsey (2008). *New Rights Advocacy: Changing Strategies of Development and Human Rights NGOs.* Washington, DC: Georgetown University Press.

Nurser, John (2005). *For All Peoples and All Nations.* Washington, DC: Georgetown University Press.

O'Donovan, Katherine, and Gerry R. Rubin (eds) (2002). *Human Rights and Legal History.* New York: Oxford University Press.

Parker, Peter, and Joyce Mokhesi-Parker (1998). *In the Shadow of Sharpeville: Apartheid and Criminal Justice.* New York: New York University Press.

Posner, Eric (2009). *The Perils of Global Legalism.* Chicago, IL: University of Chicago Press.

Power, Jonathan (2001). *Like Water on Stone: The Story of Amnesty International.* Boston: Northeastern University Press.

Quataert, Jean H. (2009). *Advocating Dignity: Human Rights Mobilizations in Global Politics.* Philadelphia: University of Pennsylvania Press.

Quirk, Joel (2011). *The Anti-Slavery Project: From the Slave Trade to Human Trafficking.* Philadelphia: University of Pennsylvania Press.

Risse, Thomas, Stephen C. Ropp, and Kathryn Sikkink (eds) (1999). *The Power of Human Rights: International Norms and Domestic Change.* New York: Cambridge University Press.

Roberts, Adam, and Timothy Garton Ash (eds) (2009). *Civil Resistance and Power Politics: The Experience of Non-Violent Action from Gandhi to the Present*. New York: Oxford University Press.

Roosevelt, Eleanor (1992). *The Autobiography of Eleanor Roosevelt*. New York: Da Capo Press.

Rummel, R. J. (1994). *Death by Government*. New Brunswick, NJ: Transaction Publishers.

Schmidt, Sebastian (2011). "To Order the Minds of Scholars: The Discourse of the Peace of Westphalia in International Relations Literature," *International Studies Quarterly*, 53 (3): 601–24.

Smith, Jackie (2008). *Social Movements for Global Democracy*. Baltimore, MD: Johns Hopkins University Press.

Smith, Jackie, and Ron Pagnucco (1998). "Globalizing Human Rights: The Work of Transnational Human Rights NGOs in the 1990s," *Human Rights Quarterly*, 20 (2): 378–412.

Soros, George (2011). "My Philanthropy," *New York Review of Books*, 58 (11): 12, 14, 16.

Stammers, Neil (2009). *Human Rights and Social Movements*. New York: Pluto Press.

Stannard, David (1992). *American Holocaust*. New York: Oxford University Press.

Steger, Manfred B., and Erin K. Wilson (2012). "Anti-Globalization or Alter-Globalization? Mapping the Political Ideology of the Global Justice Movement," *International Studies Quarterly*, 56 (3): 439–54.

Storey, Robert G. (1968). *The Final Judgment? Pearl Harbor to Nuremberg*. San Antonio, TX: Naylor.

Taylor, Telford (1970). *Nuremberg and Vietnam: An American Tragedy*. Chicago: Quadrangle.

Taylor, Telford (1992). *Anatomy of the Nuremberg Trials: A Personal Memoir*. Boston: Back Bay Books.

Thomas, Daniel C. (2005). "Human Rights Ideas, the Demise of Communism, and the End of the Cold War," *Journal of Cold War Studies*, 7 (Spring): 110–41.

Tomuschat, Christian, and Jean-Marc Thouvenin (eds) (2006). *The Fundamental Rules of the International Legal Order: Jus Cogens and Obligations Erga Omnes*. Boston: Nijhoff.

Tsutsui, Kiyoteru, and Christine Min Wotipka (2004). "Global Civil Society and the International Human Rights Movement: Citizen Participation in Human Rights International Nongovernmental Organizations," *Social Forces*, 83 (2): 587–620.

United States Department of State (1975–). *Country Reports on Human Rights Practices*. Washington, DC: Government Printing Office, annual.

Urquhart, Brian (1989). *Decolonization and World Peace*. Austin: University of Texas Press.

Urquhart, Brian (2000). "Mrs Roosevelt's Revolution," *New York Review of Books*, 46 (7): 32–4.

Van Tuijl, Peter (1999). "NGOs and Human Rights: Sources of Justice and Democracy," *Journal of International Affairs*, 53 (2): 493–512.

Weeranantry, C. G. (2004). *Universalizing International Law*. New York: Nijhoff.

Welch, Claude E., Jr, and Ashley F. Watkins (2011). "Extending Enforcement: The Coalition for the International Criminal Court," *Human Rights Quarterly*, 33 (4): 927–1031.

Willetts, Peter (2011). *Non-Governmental Organizations in World Politics. The Construction of Global Governance*. New York: Routledge.

CHAPTER 5: Civil and Political Rights and Crimes Against Humanity

Addis, Aneno (2009). "Imagining the International Community: The Constitutive Dimension of Universal Jurisdiction," *Human Rights Quarterly*, 31 (1): 129–62.

Alston, Wilton D., and Walter E. Black (2008). "Reparations Once Again," *Human Rights Review*, 9 (3): 379–92.

Appiah, Kwame Anthony, and Martin Bunzl (eds) (2007). *Buying Freedom: The Ethics and Economics of Slave Redemption*. Princeton, NJ: Princeton University Press.

Associated Press (2012). "UK Court Rules Abu Hamza Can Be Extradited to US," *Seattle Times*, October 5.

Bair, Johann (2006). *The International Covenant on Civil and Political Rights and Its (First) Optional Protocol: A Short Commentary Based on Views, General Comments, and Concluding Observations by the Human Rights Committee*. New York: Lang.

Bales, Kevin (1999). *Disposable People: New Slavery in the Global Economy*. Berkeley: University of California Press.

Bales, Kevin (ed) (2005). *Understanding Global Slavery: A Reader*. Berkeley, CA: University of California Press.

Bales, Kevin (2007). *Ending Slavery: How We Free Today's Slaves*. Berkeley: University of California Press.

BBC (2012). "Mau Mau Uprising: Kenyans Win UK Torture Ruling." Available at: www.bbc.co.uk/news/uk-19843719, October 5.

Beigbeder, Yves (1994). *International Monitoring of Plebiscites, Referenda and National Elections: Self-Determination and Transition to Democracy*. Boston: Nijhoff.

Benhabib, Seyla (2004). *The Rights of Others: Aliens, Residents, and Citizens*. New York: Cambridge University Press.

Blum, William (1998). *Killing Hope: US Military and CIA Interventions Since World War II*. Buffalo, NY: Black Rose Books.

Bradford, William (2005). "Beyond Reparations: Justice as Indigenism," *Human Rights Review*, 6 (3): 5–79.

Brahm, Eric (2004). "Truth Commissions." Available at: www.beyondintractibility.org/m/truth_commissions.jsp/.

Brahm, Eric (2007). "Uncovering the Truth: Examining Truth Commission Success and Impact," *International Studies Perspectives*, 8 (1): 16–25.

Braithwaite, John (2002). *Law Versus Justice: From Adversarialism to Communitarianism*. New York: Oxford University Press.

Bronkhorst, Daan (1995). *Truth and Reconciliation: Obstacles and Opportunities for Human Rights*. Amsterdam: Amnesty International Dutch Section.

Brysk, Alison, and Gershon Shafir (eds) (2004). *People out of Place: Globalization, Human Rights, and the Citizenship Gap*. New York: Routledge.

Cabrera, Luis (2010). *The Practice of Global Citizenship*. New York: Cambridge University Press.

Carlson, Scott N., and Gregory Gisvold (2003). *Practical Guide to the International Covenant on Civil and Political Rights*. Ardsley, NY: Transnational Publishers.

Chauvin, Sebastien, and Blanca Garcés-Macarenas (2012). "Beyond Informal Citizenship: The New Moral Economic of Migrant Illegality," *International Political Sociology*, 6 (3): 241–59.

Connell, John (2008). *The International Migration of Health Workers: A Global Health System?* New York: Routledge.

Conte, Alex, Scott Davidson, and Richard Burchill (2004). *Defining Civil and Political Rights: The Jurisprudence of the United Nations Human Rights Committee*. Burlington, VT: Ashgate.

Davis, Howard (2009). *Human Rights Law Directions*. 2nd edn. New York: Oxford University Press.

Debrix, François, and Alexander D. Barder (2009). "Nothing to Fear But Fear: Governmentality and the Biopolitical Production of Terror," *International Political Sociology*, 3 (4): 398–413.

Drache, Daniel (2008). *Defiant Publics: The Unprecedented Reach of the Global Citizen*. Cambridge, UK: Polity Press.

Earnest, David C. (2008). *Old Nation, New Voters: Nationalism, Transnationalism, and Democracy in the Era of Global Migration*. Albany: State University of New York Press.

Fletcher, Laurel E., and Harvey E. Weinstein, with James Rowan (2009). "Context, Timing and the Dynamics of Transitional Justice: A Historical Perspective," *Human Rights Quarterly*, 31 (1): 163–220.

Fortina, Virginia Page, and Reyco Huang (2012). "Democratization after Civil War: A Brush-Clearing Exercise," *International Studies Quarterly*, 56 (4): 801–8.

Fortman, Bas de Gaay (2011). "Minority Rights: A Major Misconception?," *Human Rights Quarterly*, 33 (2): 65–303.

Foster, Steve (2008). *Human Rights and Civil Liberties*. 2nd edn. New York: Pearson.

Franck, Thomas M. (2001). "Are Human Rights Universal?," *Foreign Affairs*, 80 (1): 191–204.

Freeman, Mark (2009). *Necessary Evils: Amnesties and the Search for Justice*. New York: Cambridge University Press.

Goldsmith, Jack L., and Posner, Eric A. (2005). *The Limits of International Law*. New York: Oxford University Press.

Goldston, James A. (2010). "The Struggle for Roma Rights: Arguments That Have Worked," *Human Rights Quarterly*, 32 (2): 311–25.

Gordenker, Leon (1987). *Refugees in International Politics*. New York: Columbia University Press.

Greenhill, Kelly M. (2010). *Weapons of Mass Migration*. Ithaca, NY: Cornell University Press.

Hansen, Thomas B., and Finn Stepputat (eds) (2005). *Citizens, Migrants, and States in the Post-Colonial World*. Princeton, NJ: Princeton University Press.

Hathaway, James C. (2005). *The Rights of Refugees under International Law*. New York: Cambridge University Press.

Hayner, Priscilla B. (1994). "Fifteen Truth Commissions – 1974 to 1994: A Comparative Study," *Human Rights Quarterly*, 16 (4): 597–655.

Hayner, Priscilla B. (2001). *Unspeakable Truths: Facing the Challenge of Truth Commissions*. New York: Routledge.

Hertel, Shareen (2006). *Unexpected Power: Conflict and Change among Transnational Activists*. Ithaca, NY: Cornell University Press.

Higgins, Peter (2008). "Open Borders and the Right to Immigration," *Human Rights Review*, 9 (4): 525–35.

Holder, Cindy (2005). "Self-Determination as a Universal Human Right," *Human Rights Review*, 7 (4): 5–18.

Huysmans, Jef (2006). *The Politics of Insecurity: Fear, Migration, and Asylum in the EU*. New York: Routledge.

Jojarth, Christine (2009). *Crime, War, and Global Trafficking: Designing International Cooperation*. New York: Cambridge University Press.

Juss, Satvinder Singh (2006). *International Migration and Global Justice*. Farnham, UK: Ashgate.

Kara, Siddharth (2009). *Sex Trafficking: Inside the Business of Modern Day Slavery*. New York: Columbia University Press.

Kausikan, Bilahari (1997). "Asian Versus 'Universal' Human Rights," *The Responsive Community*, 7 (3): 9–21.

Keith, Linda Camp (1999). "The United Nations Covenant on Civil and Political Rights: Does It Make a Difference in Human Rights Behavior?," *Journal of Peace Research*, 38 (1): 95–118.

Kim, Hunjoon, and Kathryn Sikkink (2010). "Explaining the Deterrent Effect of Human Rights Prosecutions for Transitional Countries," *International Studies Quarterly*, 54 (4): 939–63.

Leach, Susan Llewellyn (2004). "Slavery Is Not Dead, Just Less Recognizable," *Christian Science Monitor*, September 1.

Leebaw, Bronwyn Anne (2009). "The Irreconcilable Goals of Transitional Justice," *Human Rights Quarterly*, 30 (1): 95–118.

Lemarchand, René (ed) (2011). *Forgotten Genocides: Oblivion, Denial, and Memory*. Philadelphia: University of Pennsylvania Press.

Lipscomb, Leigh Ashley (2010). "Beyond the Truth: Can Reparations Move Peace and Justice Forward in Timor-Leste?," *Asia Pacific Issues*, 93 (March): 12 pp.

Margarrell, Lisa, and Joya Wesley (2008). *Learning from Greensboro: Truth and Reconciliation in the United States*. Philadelphia: University of Pennsylvania Press.

Marinova, Nadejda K., and Patrick James (2012). "The Tragedy of Human Trafficking: Competing Theories and European Evidence," *Foreign Policy Analysis*, 8 (3): 231–54.

May, Larry (2010). *Genocide: A Normative Account*. New York: Cambridge University Press.

Mazzei, Julie M. (2011). "Finding Shame in Truth: The Importance of Public Engagement in Truth Commissions," *Human Rights Quarterly*, 33 (2): 431–52.

Meernik, James D., Angela Nichols, and Kimi L. King (2010). "The Impact of International Tribunals and Domestic Trials on Peace and Human Rights after Civil War," *International Studies Perspectives*, 11 (4): 309–34.

Mégret, Frédéric (2009). "The Disabilities Convention: Human Rights of Persons with Disabilities as Disability Rights?," *Human Rights Quarterly*, 30 (2): 494–516.

Meijer, Martha (ed) (2001). *Dealing with Human Rights: Asian and Western Views on the Value of Human Rights*. Bloomfield, CT: Kumarian Press.

Moravcsik, Andrew (2000). "The Origins of Human Rights Regimes," *International Organization*, 54 (Spring): 217–52.

Mungazi, Dickson A. (1989). *The Struggle for Social Change in Southern Africa: Visions of Liberty*. New York: Crane Russak.

Nalepa, Monika (2010). *Skeletons in the Closet: Transitional Justice in Post-Communist Europe*. New York: Cambridge University Press.

Neier, Aryeh (1997). "Asia's Unacceptable Double Standard," *The Responsive Community*, 7 (3): 22–30.

Nowak, Manfred (1993). *UN Covenant on Civil and Political Rights: CCPR Commentary*. Arlington, VA: Engel.

Paige, Arthur (2009). "How 'Transitions' Reshaped Human Rights: A Conceptual History of Transitional Justice," *Human Rights Quarterly*, 31 (2): 321–36.

Parsons, Craig A., and Timothy M. Smeeding (eds) (2006). *Immigration and the Transformation of Europe*. Cambridge, UK: Cambridge University Press.

Pécoud, Anthoine, and Paul De Guchteneire (2007). *Migration without Borders: Essays on the Free Movement of Peoples*. Paris: UNESCO.

Phuong, Catherine (2005). *The International Protection of Internally Displaced Persons*. New York: Cambridge University Press.

Plender, Richard (1988). *International Migration Law*. 2nd edn. Boston: Nijhoff.

Ragazzi, Francesco (2009). "Governing Diasporas," *International Political Sociology*, 3 (4): 378–97.

Reichel, Philip (2005). *Handbook of Transnational Crime and Justice*. Thousand Oaks, CA: SAGE Publications.

Rejali, Darius (2007). *Torture and Democracy*. Princeton, NJ: Princeton University Press.

Robertson, Geoffrey (1999). *Crimes Against Humanity: The Struggle for Global Justice*. London: Allen Lane.

Roht-Arriaza, Naomi (ed) (1995). *Impunity and Human Rights in International Law and Practice*. New York: Oxford University Press.

Rosenblatt, Adam (2010). "International Forensic Investigations and the Human Rights of the Dead," *Human Rights Quarterly*, 32 (4): 921–50.

Sadat, Leila Nadya (ed) (2011). *Forging a Convention for Crimes Against Humanity*. New York: Cambridge University Press.

Shelley, Louise (2010). *Human Trafficking: A Global Perspective*. New York: Cambridge University Press.

Simmons, Beth (2009). *Mobilizing for Human Rights: International Law in Domestic Politics*. New York: Cambridge University Press.

Smolensky, Kirsten Rabe (2009). "Rights of the Dead," *Arizona Legal Studies Discussion Paper No. 06-27*. Tucson: University of Arizona, College of Law.

Soysal, Yasemin Nuhoğlu (1994). *Limits of Citizenship: Migrants and Postnational Membership in Europe*. Chicago: University of Chicago Press.

Starr, Sonja (2007). "Extraordinary Crimes at Ordinary Times: International Justice Beyond Crisis Situations," *Northwestern University Law Review*, 101 (3): 1257–314.

Talbott, William (2005). *Which Rights Should Be Universal?* New York: Oxford University Press.

Theofilopoulou, Anna (2006). *The United Nations and Western Sahara: A Never-Ending Affair*. Special Report 166. Washington, DC: US Institute of Peace.

Waldron, Jeremy (2012). *The Harm in Hate Speech*. Cambridge, MA: Harvard University Press.

Welch, Claude E. (2009). "Defining Contemporary Forms of Slavery: Updating a Venerable NGO," *Human Rights Quarterly*, 31 (1): 70–128.

CHAPTER 6: Economic, Social, and Cultural Rights

Acemoglu, Daron, and James A. Robinson (2012). *Why Nations Fail: The Origins of Power, Prosperity, and Poverty*. New York: Crown.

Addo, Michael K. (ed) (1999). *Human Rights Standards and the Responsibility of Transnational Corporations*. Boston: Kluwer.

Anaya, S. James, and Claudio Grossman (2002). "The Case of Awas Tingni v. Nicaragua: A New Step in the International Law of Indigenous Peoples," *Arizona Journal of International and Comparative Law*, 19 (1): 1–15.

An-Na'im, Abdullahi Ahmed (ed) (1992). *Human Rights in Cross-Cultural Perspectives: A Quest for Consensus*. Philadelphia: University of Pennsylvania Press.

Appiah, Kwame Anthony (2006). "Whose Culture Is It?," *New York Review of Books*, 53 (February 9): 38–42.

Bales, Kevin (1999). *Disposable People: New Slavery in the Global Economy*. Berkeley: University of California Press.

Bayulgen, Oksan (2008). "Muhammad Yunus, Grameen Bank and the Nobel Peace Prize: What Political Science Can Contribute to and Learn from the Study of Microcredit," *International Studies Review*, 10 (3): 525–47.

BBC (2012). "Bolivia Returns Stolen Money to Peru." Available at: www.bbc.co.uk, November 6.

Bernhagen, Patrick, and Neil J. Mitchell (2010). "The Private Promotion of Public Goods: Corporate Commitments and the United Nations Global Compact," *International Studies Quarterly*, 54 (4): 1175–87.

Bhagwati, Jagdish N. (ed) (1977). *The New International Economic Order: The North–South Debate*. Cambridge, MA: MIT Press.

Brecher, Jeremy, John Brown Childs, and Jill Cutler (eds) (1993). *Global Visions: Beyond the New World Order*. Boston: South End Press.

Brecher, Jeremy, Tim Costello, and Brendan Smith (2000). *Globalization from Below: The Power of Solidarity*. Boston: South End Press.

Chapman, Audrey R., and Benjamin Carbonetti (2011). "Human Rights Protections for Vulnerable and Disadvantaged Groups: The Contributions of the UN Covenant on Economic Social and Cultural Rights," *Human Rights Quarterly*, 33 (3): 682–732.

Chigara, Ben (2007). "Late comers to the ILO and the Authorship and Ownership of the International Labour Code," *Human Rights Quarterly*, 29 (3): 706–26.

Cobo, José Martínez (1986). *The Study of the Problem of Discrimination Against Indigenous Populations*. UN Document E/CN.4/Sub.2/1986/7. New York: United Nations.

Cohen, Daniel (2006). *Globalization and Its Enemies*. Cambridge, MA: MIT Press.

Cowan, Jane K., Marie-Bénédicte Dembour, and Richard A. Wilson (eds) (2001). *Culture and Rights: Anthropological Perspectives*. New York: Cambridge University Press.

Darrow, Mac, and Amparo Tomás (2005). "Power, Capture, and Conflict: A Call for Human Rights Accountability in Development Cooperation," *Human Rights Quarterly*, 27 (2): 461–540.

De Schutter, Olivier (2011). "The Right of Everyone to Enjoy the Benefits of Scientific Progress and the Right to Food: From Conflict to Complementarity," *Human Rights Quarterly*, 33 (2): 304–50.

Dimitris, Stevis, and Terry Boswell (2008). *Globalization and Labor: Democratizing Global Governance*. Lanham, MD: Rowman & Littlefield.

Dorgan, Byron L. (2006). *Take This Job and Ship It: How Corporate Greed and Brain-Dead Politics Are Selling out America*. New York: St Martin's Press.

Eakin, Hugh (2011). "What Went Wrong at the Getty?," *New York Review of Books*, 58 (11): 27–9.

Easterly, William (2006). *The White Man's Burden: Why the West's Efforts to Aid the Rest Have Done So Much Ill and So Little Good*. New York: Penguin.

Edsall, Robert M. (2006). *Rescuing Da Vinci: Recovering Europe's Art from Hitler and the Nazis*. Dallas, TX: Laurel.

Ehrlich, Sean D. (2010). "The Fair Trade Challenge to Embedded Liberalism," *International Studies Quarterly*, 54 (4): 1013–33.

Eide, Ashbørn, Catarina Krause, and Allan Rosas (eds) (2001). *Economic, Social, and Cultural Rights: A Textbook*. 2nd edn. Boston: Nijhoff.

Elliott, Kimberly Ann, and Richard B. Freeman (2003). *Can Labor Standards Improve Under Globalization?* Washington, DC: Institute for International Economics.

Felch, Jason, and Ralph Frammolino (2011). *Chasing Aphrodites: The Hunt for Looted Antiquities at the World's Richest Museum*. Boston: Houghton Mifflin Harcourt.

Felice, William F. (2003). *The Global New Deal: Economic and Social Human Rights in World Politics*. Lanham, MD: Rowman & Littlefield.

Fenwick, Colin, and Tonia Novitz (eds) (2010). *Human Rights at Work: Perspectives on Law and Regulation*. Oxford, UK: Hart Publishing.

Freeman, Marsha A. (1999). "International Institutions and Gendered Justice," *Journal of International Affairs*, 53 (Spring): 513–32.

Friedman, Thomas (2006). *The World Is Flat: A Brief History of the Twenty-First Century*. New York: Farrar, Straus & Giroux.

Fukuda-Parr, Sakiko (2011). "Theory and Policy in International Development: Human Development and Capability Approach and the Millennium Development Goals," *International Studies Review*, 13 (1): 122–32.

Galtung, Johan (1964). "A Structural Theory of Aggression," *Journal of Peace Research*, 1 (2): 95–119.

Ganji, Manouchehr (1975). *The Realization of Economic, Social and Cultural Rights: Problems, Policies, Progress*. New York: United Nations.

Gordon, Joy (2010). *Invisible War: The United States and the Iraq Sanctions*. Cambridge, MA: Harvard University Press.

Gosselin, Abigail (2007). "Global Poverty and Responsibility: Identifying the Duty-Bearers of Human Rights," *Human Rights Review*, 8 (1): 35–52.

Hoard-Hassmann, Rhoda E. (2010). *Can Globalization Promote Human Rights?* Harrisburg: Pennsylvania State University Press.

Hodgson, Dorothy L. (2002). "Introduction: Comparative Perspectives on the Indigenous Rights Movement in Africa and the Americas," *American Anthropologist*, 104 (4): 1037–51.

Holtmaat, Rikki, and Jonneke Nabel (2011). *Women's Human Rights and Culture: From Deadlock to Dialogue*. Cambridge, UK: Intersentia.

Howard, Bradley Red (2003). *Indigenous Peoples and the State: The Struggle for Native Rights*. DeKalb: Northern Illinois University Press.

Howell, Jude, and Jeremy Lind (2009). *Counter-Terrorism, Aid, and Civil Society: Before and after the War on Terror*. New York: Palgrave Macmillan.

Hughes, Barry B., and Mohammad T. Irfan (2007). "Assessing Strategies for Reducing Poverty," *International Studies Review*, 9 (4): 690–710.

Hunt, Paul (1996). *Reclaiming Social Rights: International and Comparative Perspectives*. Brookfield, VT: Dartmouth.

Ibhawoh, Bonny (2011). "The Right to Development: The Politics and Polemics of Power and Resistance," *Human Rights Quarterly*, 33 (1): 76–104.

International Labour Office (1991). *Still So Far to Go: Child Labour in the World Today*. Geneva: ILO.

Jerbi, Scott (2009). "Business and Human Rights at the UN: What Might Happen Next?," *Human Rights Quarterly*, 31 (2): 299–320.

Kay, Tamara (2011). *NAFTA and the Politics of Labor Transnationalism*. Cambridge, UK: Cambridge University Press.

Kinley, David (2009). *Civilizing Globalization: Human Rights and the Global Economy*. Cambridge, UK: Cambridge University Press.

Kuruvilla, Shyama, Flavia Bustreo, Paul Hunt, Amarjit Singh, Eric Friedman, Thiago Luchesi, Stefan Germann, Kim Terje Loraas, Alicia Ely Yamin, Ximena Andion, Julio Frenk, and other members of the Working Group on the MDGs and Human Rights for the UN Secretary-General's Global Strategy for Women's and Children's Health (2012). "The Millennium Development Goals and Human Rights: Realizing Shared Commitments," *Human Rights Quarterly*, 34 (1): 141–77.

Lâm, Maivân (2004). "Remembering the Country of Their Birth: Indigenous Peoples and Territoriality," *Journal of International Affairs*, 57 (2): 129–52.

Leane, Geoffrey W. G. (2011). "Rights of Ethnic Minorities in Liberal Democracies: Has France Gone Too Far in Banning Muslim Women from Wearing the Burka?," *Human Rights Quarterly*, 33 (4): 1032–61.

Leary, Virginia (1994). "The Right to Health in International Human Rights Law," *Health and Human Rights*, 1 (1): 24–56.

Lee, Daniel E., and Elizabeth J. Lee (2010). *Human Rights and the Ethics of Globalization*. New York: Cambridge University Press.

Lenzerini, Federico (ed) (2008). *Reparations for Indigenous Peoples: International and Comparative Perspectives*. New York: Oxford University Press.

Levine, Ruth (2004). *Millions Saved: Proven Successes in Global Health*. Washington, DC: Center for Global Development.

Marshall, Jill (2008). "Conditions for Freedom? European Human Rights Law and the Islamic Headscarf Debate," *Human Rights Quarterly*, 30 (3): 631–54.

Meier, Benjamin Mason, and Ashley M. Fox (2008). "Development as Health: Employing the Collective Right to Development to Achieve the Goals of the Individual Right to Health," *Human Rights Quarterly*, 30 (2): 259–355.

Merryman, John Henry (1986). "Two Ways of Thinking about Cultural Property," *American Journal of International Law*, 80 (October): 831–53.

Minkler, Lanse (2009). "Economic Rights and Political Decision Making," *Human Rights Quarterly*, 31 (2): 368–93.

Moghadam, Valentine M. (2005). *Globalizing Women: Transnational Feminist Networks*. Baltimore, MD: The Johns Hopkins University Press.

Mosley, Layna (2011). *Labor Rights and Multinational Production*. New York: Cambridge University Press.

Moulin, Carolina, and Peter Nyers (2007). "'We Live in a Country of UNHCR' – Refugee Protests and Global Political Society," *International Political Sociology*, 1 (4): 356–72.

Muehlebach, Andrea (2001). "'Making Place' at the United Nations: Indigenous Cultural Politics at the UN Working Group on Indigenous Populations," *Cultural Anthropology*, 16 (3): 415–50.

Murphy, Craig (1984). *Emergence of the NIEO Ideology*. Boulder, CO: Westview.

Nicholas, Lynn H. (1994). *The Rape of Europa: The Fate of Europe's Treasures in the Third Reich and the Second World War*. New York: Knopf.

Niezen, Ronald (2003). *The Origins of Indigenism: Human Rights and the Politics of Identity*. Berkeley: University of California Press.

Peksen, Dursun (2011). "Economic Sanctions and Human Security: The Public Health Effect of Economic Sanctions," *Foreign Policy Analysis*, 7 (3): 237–52.

Plomer, Aurora (2005). *The Law and Ethics of Medical Research: International Bioethics and Human Rights*. Singapore: Cavendish.

Pogge, Thomas (2002). *World Poverty and Human Rights: Cosmopolitan Responsibilities and Reforms*. Malden, MA: Polity.

Pollis, Adamantia, and Peter Schwab (eds) (1979). *Human Rights: Cultural and Ideological Perspectives*. New York: Praeger.

Robinson, Mary (2004). "Advancing Economic, Social and Cultural Rights: The Way Forward," *Human Rights Quarterly*, 26 (4): 866–72.

Rodgers, Gerry, Eddy Lee, Lee Swepston, and Jasmine Var Daele (2009). *The International Labour Organization and the Quest for Social Justice, 1919–2000*. Ithaca, NY: Cornell University Press.

Rodrick, Dani (1999). *The New Global Economy and the Developing Countries*. Washington, DC: Overseas Development Council.

Roht-Arviaza, Naomi (1999). "Institutions of International Justice," *Journal of International Affairs*, 52 (Spring): 473–91.

Ross, Susan Deller (2008). *Women's Human Rights: The International and Comparative Law Casebook*. Philadelphia: University of Pennsylvania Press.

Rothstein, Robert L. (1979). *Global Bargaining: UNCTAD and the Quest for a New International Economic Order*. Princeton, NJ: Princeton University Press.

Sachs, Jeffrey D. (2006). *The End of Poverty: Economic Possibilities for Our Time*. New York: Penguin.

Sarkin, Jeremy, and Mark Koenig (2011). "Developing the Right to Work: Intersecting and Dialoguing Human Rights and Economic Policy," *Human Rights Quarterly*, 33 (1): 1–42.

Scheppele, Lim Lane (2004). "A Realpolitik Defense of Social Rights," *Texas Law Review*, 82 (4): 727–68.

Scruggs, Lyle, Sharon Hertel, Samuel J. Best, and Christopher Jeffords (2011). "Information, Choice, and Political Consumption: Human Rights in the Checkout Lane," *Human Rights Quarterly*, 33 (4): 1092–121.

Sen, Amartya (1981). *Poverty and Famines: An Essay on Entitlement and Deprivation*. New York: Oxford University Press.

Sen, Amartya (1999). *Development as Freedom*. New York: Oxford University Press.

Spar, Debora L. (1988). "The Spotlight and the Bottom Line," *Foreign Affairs*, 77 (2): 7–12.

Springer, Jane (1997). *Listen to Us: The World's Working Children*. Toronto: Groundwood.

Wallace, Scott (2011). *The Unconquered: In Search of the Amazon's Last Uncontacted Tribes*. New York: Crown Publishers.

Whelan, Daniel J. (2007). "The West, Economic and Social Rights, and the Global Human Rights Regime: Setting the Record Straight," *Human Rights Quarterly*, 29 (4): 908–49.

Wilkinson, Richard, and Kate Pickett (2010). *The Spirit Level: Why Greater Equality Makes Societies Stronger*. New York: Bloomsbury Press.

Wilmer, Franke (1993). *The Indigenous Voice in World Politics*. London: SAGE Publications.

Winston, Morton (2002). "NGO Strategies for Promoting Corporate Social Responsibility," *Ethics & International Affairs*, 16 (1): 71–88.

Woods, Jeanne M., and Hope Lewis (2005). *Human Rights and the Global Marketplace: Economic, Social and Cultural Dimensions*. Ardsley, NY: Transaction Publishers.

Xanthaki, Alexandra (2010). "Multiculturalism and International Law: Discussing Universal Standards," *Human Rights Quarterly*, 32 (1): 21–48.

Yamin, Alicia Ely (2005). "The Right to Health under International Law and Its Relevance to the United States," *American Journal of Public Health*, 95 (7): 1156–61.

CHAPTER 7: Crimes Against Peace and War Crimes

Annan, Kofi (2005). *In Larger Freedom: Towards Development, Security and Human Rights for All*. New York: United Nations Office of Information.

Annan, Kofi (2010). *Early Warning, Assessment and the Responsibility to Protect*. New York: United Nations Office of Information.

Annan, Kofi (2011). *The Role of Regional and Subregional Arrangements in Implementing the Responsibility to Protect*. United Nations Office of Information.

Annan, Kofi (2012). *Interventions: A Life in War and Peace*. New York: Penguin.

Arai-Takahashi, Yutaka (2009). *The Law of Occupation: Continuity and Change of International Humanitarian Law and Its Interaction with Human Rights Law*. Leiden: Brill.

Badescu, Cristina G., and Thomas G. Weiss (2010). "Misrepresenting R2P and Advancing Norms: An Alternative Spiral?," *International Studies Perspectives*, 11 (4): 354–74.

Ban, Ki-Moon (2009). *Implementing the Responsibility to Protect: Report of the Secretary-General*. New York: United Nations, January 12 (A/63/677).

Ban, Ki-Moon (2010). *Early Warning, Assessment and the Responsibility to Protect: Report of the Secretary-General*. New York: United Nations, July 14 (A/64/864).

Ban, Ki-Moon (2011). *The Role of Regional and Subregional Arrangements in Implementing the Responsibility to Protect: Report of the Secretary-General*. New York: United Nations, June 27 (A/65/877–S/2011/393).

Bassiouni, M. Cherif (2003). *Introduction to International Criminal Law*. Ardsley, NY: Transnational Publishers.

Bellamy, Alex (2009). "Realizing the Responsibility to Protect," *International Studies Perspectives*, 10 (2): 111–28.

Benvenisti, Eyal (1993). *The International Law of Occupation*. Princeton, NJ: Princeton University Press.

Boutros-Ghali, Boutros (2006). *Uniting Against Terrorism: Recommendations for a Global Counter-Terrorism Strategy; Report of the Secretary-General*. New York: United Nations, April 27 A/60/825.

Boyd, K. Lee (2004). "Universal Jurisdiction and Structural Reasonableness," *Texas International Law Journal*, 90 (Fall): 1–58.

Brecher, Jeremy, Jill Cutler, and Brendan Smith (eds) (2005). *In the Name of Democracy: American War Crimes in Iraq and Beyond*. New York: Metropolitan Books.

Byers, Michael (2005). *War Law: Understanding International Law and Armed Conflict*. New York: Grove Press.

Chang, Iris (1997). *The Rape of Nanking: The Forgotten Holocaust of World War II*. New York: Penguin.

Charles, J. Daryl (2005). *Between Pacifism and Jihad: Just War and Christian Tradition*. Downers Grove, IL: InterVarsity Press.

Chatterjee, Deen, and Don E. Scheid (eds) (2003). *Ethics and Foreign Intervention*. Cambridge, UK: Cambridge University Press.

Chomsky, Noam (2006). *Failed States: The Abuse of Power and the Assault on Democracy*. London: Hamish Hamilton.

Cigar, Norman (2009). *Al-Qa'ida's Doctrine for Insurgency*. Washington, DC: Potomac Books.

Cohen, David B., and John W. Wells (eds) (2004). *American National Security and Civil Liberties in an Era of Terrorism*. New York: Palgrave Macmillan.

Cohen, Esther R. (1985). *Human Rights in the Israeli-Occupied Territories, 1967–1982*. Manchester, UK: Manchester University Press.

Cole, David (2006). "Why the Court Said No," *New York Review of Books*, 53 (August 10): 41–3.

Cole, David (2011). "Killing Our Citizens Without Trial," *New York Review of Books*, 58 (18): 27–8.

Cole, David (2012). "Obama and Terror: The Hovering Questions," *New York Review of Books*, 59 (12): 32–34.

Cronin, Bruce (2007). "The Tension between Sovereignty and Intervention in the Prevention of Genocide," *Human Rights Review*, 8 (4): 293–305.

Deibert, Ronald J., and Rafal Rohozinski (2010). "Rethinking Security: Policies and Paradoxes of Cyberspace Security," *International Political Sociology*, 4 (1): 15–32.

de Waal, Alex (1998). "US War Crimes in Somalia," *New Left Review*, 30 (February 28): 131–44.

Doyle, Michael W. (2011). "International Ethics and the Responsibility to Protect," *International Studies Review*, 13 (1): 72–84.

European Parliament (2006). *Draft Report on the Alleged Use of European Countries by the CIA for the Transportation and Illegal Detention of Prisoners*. Available at: www.europarl.europa.eu/compar1/tempcom/tdip/default_en.pdf.

Evangelista, Matthew (2008). *Law, Ethics, and the War on Terror*. Malden, MA: Polity Press.

Evans, Gareth (2008). *The Responsibility to Protect: Ending Mass Atrocity Crimes Once and For All*. Washington, DC: Brookings.

Falk, Richard A. (1986). "Forty Years After the Nuremberg and Tokyo Tribunals: The Impact of the War Crimes Trials on International and National Law," *Proceedings, Eightieth Annual Meeting*, American Society of International Law: 65–7.

Falk, Richard A., Gabriel Kolko, and Robert J. Lifton (eds) (1971). *Crimes of War: A Legal, Political-Documentary, and Psychological Inquiry into the Responsibility of Leaders, Citizens, and Soldiers for Criminal Acts in Wars*. New York: Random House.

Fein, Helen (1993). *Genocide: A Sociological Perspective*. London: SAGE Publications.

Ferrell, Robert H. ([1952] 1968). *Peace in Their Time: The Origins of the Kellogg–Briand Pact*. Hamden, CT: Archon Books.

Freedland, Jonathan (2012). "An Exclusive Corner of Hebron," *New York Review of Books*, 59 (3): 21–3.

Gates, Scott, and Simon Reich (2010). *Child Soldiers in the Age of Fractured States*. Pittsburg, PA: University of Pittsburgh Press.

Glanville, Luke (2011). "Ellery Stowell and the Enduring Dilemma of Humanitarian Intervention," *International Studies Review*, 13 (2): 241–58.

Glueck, Sheldon (1944). *War Criminals, Their Prosecution and Punishment*. New York: Knopf.

Gould, Benjamin J., and Liora Lazarus (eds) (2007). *Security and Human Rights*. Oxford, UK: Hart.

Greenberg, Karen J., and Joshua L. Dratel (eds) (2005). *The Torture Papers: The Road to Abu Ghraib*. New York: Cambridge University Press.

Gross, Michael L. (2010). *Moral Dilemmas of Modern War: Torture, Assassination, and Blackmail in an Age of Asymmetric Conflict*. New York: Cambridge University Press.

Grotius, Hugo ([1609] 2001). *The Freedom of the Seas, or, The Right Which Belongs to the Dutch to Take Part in the East Indian Trade*. Union, NJ: Lawbook Exchange.

Grotius, Hugo ([1625] 1948). *De Jure Belli ac Pacis*. The Hague: Nijhoff.

Haas, Michael (2009). *George W. Bush, War Criminal? The Bush Administration's Liability for 269 War Crimes*. Santa Barbara, CA: Praeger.

Haas, Michael (2010). *America's War Crimes Quagmire: From Bush to Obama*. Los Angeles: Publishinghouse for Scholars.

Haas, Michael, and David Cole (2012). "Obama and Terror," *New York Review of Books*, 59 (14): 98–9.

Harris, Robert, and Jeremy Paxman (2002). *A Higher Form of Killing: The Secret History of Chemical and Biological Warfare*. New York: Random House.

Heineman, Elizabeth D. (2011). *Sexual Violence in Conflict Zones: From the Ancient World to the Era of Human Rights*. Philadelphia: University of Pennsylvania Press.

Holzgrefe, J. L., and Robert O. Keohane (eds) (2003). *Humanitarian Intervention: Ethical, Legal, and Political Dilemmas*. New York: Cambridge University Press.

Hudson, Kimberly A. (2009). *Justice, Intervention, and Force in International Relations: Reassessing Just War Theory in the 21st Century*. New York: Routledge.

International Commission on Intervention and State Sovereignty (2001). *The Responsibility to Protect*. Ottawa: International Development Research Centre.

Jones, Seth, and Martin C. Libicki (2008). *How Terrorist Groups End: Lessons for Countering al Qa'ida*. Santa Monica, CA: Rand Corporation.

Keene, Edward (2002). *Beyond the Anarchical Society: Grotius, Colonialism and Order in World Politics*. New York: Cambridge University Press.

Kelly, Michael J. (2003). "Time Warp to 1945: Resurrection of the Reprisal and Anticipatory Self-Defense Doctrines in International Law," *Journal of Transnational Law and Policy*, 13 (1): 1–39.

Kennedy, David (2004). *The Dark Sides of Virtue: Reassessing International Humanitarianism*. Princeton, NJ: Princeton University Press.

Klintworth, Gary (1989). *Vietnam's Intervention in Cambodia in International Law*. Canberra: Australian Government Publishing Service.

Kuper, Leo (1981). *Genocide: Its Political Use in the Twentieth Century*. New Haven, CT: Yale University Press.

Kuperman, Alan J. (2008). "The Moral Hazard of Humanitarian Intervention: Lessons from the Balkans," *International Studies Quarterly*, 52 (1): 49–80.

Lang, Anthony F., Jr (ed) (2003). *Just Intervention*. Washington, DC: Georgetown University Press.

Lang, Anthony F., Jr, and Amanda Russell Beattie (eds) (2009). *War, Terror and Terrorism: Rethinking the Rules of International Security*. New York: Routledge.

Lelyveld, Joseph (2007). "No Exit," *New York Review of Books*, 54 (February 15): 12–17.

Lifton, Robert J. (1986). *The Nazi Doctors: Medical Killing and the Psychology of Genocide*. New York: Basic Books.

Maguire, Peter (2000). *Law and War: An American Story*. New York: Columbia University Press.

Malešević, Siniša (2008). "The Sociology of New Wars? Assessing the Causes and Objectives of Contemporary Violent Conflicts," *International Political Sociology*, 2 (2): 97–112.

Margulies, Joseph (2006). *Guantánamo and the Abuse of Presidential Power*. New York: Simon & Schuster.

Marrus, Michael R. (1997). *The Nuremberg War Crimes Trial 1945–1946: A Documentary History*. Boston: Bedford Books.

Meisels, Tamar (2008). *The Trouble with Terror: Liberty, Security, and the Response to Terrorism*. New York: Cambridge University Press.

Mendelsohn, Barak (2009). *Combating Jihadism: American Hegemony and Interstate Cooperation in the War on Terrorism*. Chicago, IL: University of Chicago Press.

Meron, Theodore (2000). "The Humanization of International Humanitarian Law," *American Journal of International Law*, 94 (April): 239–78.

Miles, Stephen H. (2006). *Oath Betrayed: Torture, Medical Complicity, and the War on Terror*. New York: Random House.

Moore, John Bassett (1906). *A Digest of International Law*. Washington, DC: Government Printing Office.

Morris, Benny (1999). *Righteous Victims: A History of the Zionist–Arab Conflict, 1881–1999*. New York: Knopf.

Murdie, Amanda M., and David R. Davis (2010). "Problematic Potential: The Human Rights Consequences of Peacekeeping Interventions in Civil Wars," *Human Rights Quarterly*, 32 (1): 49–72.

Murphy, Sean D. (1996). *Humanitarian Intervention: The United Nations in an Evolving World Order*. Philadelphia: University of Pennsylvania Press.

Neff, Stephen C. (2005). *War and the Law of Nations: A General History*. New York: Cambridge University Press.

Neier, Aryeh (1998). *War Crimes: Brutality, Genocide, Terror, and the Struggle for Justice*. New York: Times Books.

Neier, Aryeh (2012). *The International Human Rights Movement: A History*. Princeton, NJ: Princeton University Press.

O'Hanlon, Michael E. (2003). *Expanding Global Military Capacity for Humanitarian Intervention*. Washington, DC: Brookings Institution.

Oppenheim, Lassa (1991). *International Law: A Treatise*. 9th edn. New York: Longmans, Green.

Osiel, Mark (2009). *The End of Reciprocity: Terror, Torture, and the Law of War*. New York: Cambridge University Press.

Parker, Tom (2011). "Redressing the Balance: How Human Rights Defenders Can Use Victim Narratives to Confront the Violence of Armed Groups," *Human Rights Quarterly*, 33 (4): 1122–41.

Pelton, Robert (2006). *Licensed to Kill: Hired Guns in the War on Terror*. New York: Crown.

Pham, Phuong N., Patrick Vinck, and Eric Stover (2009). "The Lord's Resistance Army and Forced Conscription in Northern Uganda," *Human Rights Quarterly*, 30 (2): 404–11.

Power, Samantha (2002). *"A Problem from Hell": America and the Age of Genocide*. New York: Basic Books.

Preston, Thomas (2007). *From Lambs to Lions: Future Security Relationships in a World of Biological and Nuclear Weapons*. Lanham, MD: Rowman & Littlefield.

Prunier, Gérard (1995). *The Rwanda Crisis: History of a Genocide*. New York: Columbia University Press.

Prunier, Gérard (2005). *Darfur: The Ambiguous Genocide*. Ithaca, NY: Cornell University Press.

Ramsbotham, Oliver, and Tom Woodson (1996). *Humanitarian Intervention in Contemporary Conflict: A Reconceptualization*. Cambridge, MA: Polity Press.

Ratner, Steven R., and Jason S. Abrams (2001). *Accountability for Human Rights Atrocities in International Law: Beyond the Nuremberg Legacy*. 2nd edn. New York: Oxford University Press.

Rauchhaus, Robert W. (2009). "Principal-Agent Problems in Humanitarian Intervention: Moral Hazards, Adverse Selection, and the Commitment Dilemma," *International Studies Quarterly*, 53 (40): 871–84.

Rees, Laurence (2002). *Horror in the East: Japan and the Atrocities of World War II*. Cambridge, MA: Da Capo Press.

Reno, William (2011). *Warfare in Independent Africa*. New York: Cambridge University Press.

Rieff, David (2005). *At the Point of a Gun: Democratic Dreams and Armed Intervention*. New York: Simon & Schuster.

Rieffer-Flanagan, Barbara Ann (2009). "Is Neutral Humanitarianism Dead? Red Cross Neutrality: Walking the Tightrope of Neutral Humanitarianism," *Human Rights Quarterly*, 31 (4): 888–915.

Robertson, Geoffrey (1999). *Crimes Against Humanity: The Struggle for Global Justice*. London: Allen Lane.

Rogers, A. V. P. (2004). "Humanitarian Intervention and International Law," *Harvard Journal of Law and Public Policy*, 27 (Summer): 725–36.

Roht-Arriaza, Naomi (ed) (1995). *Impunity and Human Rights in International Law and Practice*. New York: Oxford University Press.

Rupérez, Javier (2005). "The Role of the United Nations in the Fight Against Terrorism: A Provisional Balance," *Perceptions*, 10 (Summer): 41–8.

Scahill, Jeremy (2007). *Blackwater: The Rise of the World's Most Powerful Mercenary Army*. New York: Nation Books.

Schindler, Dietrich, and Jiří Toman (eds) (2004). *The Laws of Armed Conflicts: A Collection of Conventions, Resolutions, and Other Documents*. Boston: Nihjoff.

Schumacher, Colonel Gerald (2006). *A Bloody Business: America's War Zone Contractors and the Occupation of Iraq*. St Paul, MN: Zenith Press.

Segev, Tom (1973). *The Seventh Million: The Israelis and the Holocaust*. New York: Hill & Wang.

Shawcross, William (2011). *Justice and the Enemy: Nuremberg, 9/11, and the Trial of Khalid Sheikh Mohammed*. New York: Public Affairs.

Simons, Lewis M. (2006). "Genocide and the Science of Proof," *National Geographic*, 209 (1): 28–35.

Singer, J. David (2007). "Nuclear Proliferation and the Geocultural Divide: The March of Folly," *International Studies Review*, 9 (4): 663–72.

Singer, Peter W. (2005). *Children at War*. New York: Pantheon.

Singer, Peter W. (2009). *Wired for War: The Robotics Revolution and Conflict in the Twenty-First Century*. New York: Penguin.

Starr, Sonja (2007). "Extraordinary Crimes at Ordinary Times: International Justice Beyond Crisis Situations," *Northwestern University Law Review*, 101 (3): 1257–314.

Stearns, Jason K. (2011). *Dancing in the Glory of Monsters: The Collapse of the Congo and the Great War of Africa*. New York: PublicAffairs.

Stowell, Ellery (1921). *Intervention in International Law*. Washington, DC: Bryne.

Terry, Fiona (2002). *Condemned to Repeat? The Paradox of Humanitarian Action*. Ithaca, NY: Cornell University Press.

Totani, Yuma (2006). *The Tokyo War Crimes Trials: The Pursuit of Justice in the Wake of World War II*. Cambridge, MA: Harvard University Press.

Tunç, Hakan (2009). "Preemption in the Bush Doctrine: A Reappraisal," *Foreign Policy Analysis*, 5 (1): 1–16

Turner, Bryan S. (2006). *Vulnerability and Human Rights*. University Park: Pennsylvania State University Press.

United Nations Secretary-General, High-Level Panel on Threats, Challenges and Change (2004). *A More Secure World: Our Shared Responsibility*. London: The Stationery Office.

Vreeland, Hamilton, Jr ([1917] 1986). *Hugo Grotius: The Father of the Modern Science of International Law*. Little, CO: Rothman.

Wagnusson, Charlotte, Maria Hellman, and Arita Holmberg (2010). "The Centrality of Non-Traditional Groups for Security in the Globalized Era: The Case of Children," *International Political Sociology*, 4 (1): 1–14.

Walzer, Michael (2000). *Just and Unjust Wars: A Moral Argument with Historical Illustrations*. 3rd edn. New York: Basic Books.

Weiss, Thomas G., and Cindy Collins (2000). *Humanitarian Challenges and Intervention*. 2nd edn. Boulder, CO: Westview.

Wells, H. G. (1919). *The Idea of the League of Nations*. Boston: Atlantic Monthly Press.

Wessells, Michael (2006). *Child Soldiers: From Violence to Protection*. Cambridge, MA: Harvard University Press.

Wheeler, Nicholas J. (2001). *Saving Strangers: Humanitarian Intervention in International Society*. New York: Oxford University Press.

Williams, Robert E., Jr, and Dan Caldwell (2006). "Jus Post Bellum: Just War Theory and the Principles of Just Peace," *International Studies Perspectives*, 7 (4): 309–20.

Wilson, Page (2009). *Aggression, Crime and International Security: Political and Legal Dimensions of International Relations*. New York: Routledge.

Wypijewski, JoAnn (2006). "Conduct Unbecoming," *Mother Jones*, 24 (1): 26–7.

Yoo, John (2005). *The Powers of War and Peace: The Constitution and Foreign Affairs After 9/11*. Chicago: University of Chicago Press.

CHAPTER 8: Quantitative and Theoretical Dimensions

Abouharb, M. Rodwan, and Cingranelli, David L. (2008). *Human Rights and Structural Adjustment*. New York: Cambridge University Press.

Abrams, Burton A., and Kenneth A. Lewis (1993). "Human Rights and the Distribution of US Foreign Aid," *Public Choice*, 77 (4): 815–21.

Adelman, Irma, and Cynthia Taft Morris (1967). *Society, Politics, and Economic Development: A Quantitative Approach*. Baltimore, MD: Johns Hopkins University Press.

Adeola, Francis O. (1996). "Military Expenditures, Health, and Education: Bedfellows or Antagonists in Third World Development?," *Armed Forces and Society*, 22 (3): 441–67.

Alesina, Alberto, and David Dollar (2000). "Who Gives Foreign Aid to Whom and Why?," *Journal of Economic Growth*, 5 (1): 33–63.

Alston, Philip (2000). "Using Indicators for Human Rights Accountability." In UN Development Program, *Human Development Report*. New York: Oxford University Press: Chapter 5.

Amnesty International (1962–). *Report*. London: Amnesty International, annual.

Apodaca, Clair (2001). "Global Economic Patterns and Personal Integrity Rights after the Cold War," *International Studies Quarterly*, 45 (4): 587–602.

Apodaca, Clair, and Michael Stohl (1999). "United States Human Rights Policy and Foreign Assistance," *International Studies Quarterly*, 43 (1): 185–98.

Arat, Zehra F. (1991). *Democracy and Human Rights in Developing Countries*. Boulder, CO: Lynne Rienner.

Banks, Arthur S. (1971). *Cross-Polity Time-Series Data*. Cambridge: MIT Press.

Banks, Arthur S. (1979). *Cross-National Time Series Data Archive*. Binghamton: Center for Social Analysis, State University of New York.

Banks, Arthur S., and Robert B. Textor. (comps) (1963). *A Cross-Polity Survey*. Cambridge, MA: MIT Press.

Banks, David L. (1985). "Patterns of Oppression: A Statistical Analysis of Human Rights," *American Statistical Association, Proceedings of the Social Statistics Section*, 62: 154–62.

Banks, David L. (1986). "The Analysis of Human Rights Data Over Time," *Human Rights Quarterly*, 8 (December): 654–80.

Banks, David L. (1992). "New Patterns of Oppression: An Updated Analysis of Human Rights Data." In T. B. Jabine and R. P. Claude (eds), *Human Rights and Statistics: Getting the Record Straight*. Philadelphia: University of Pennsylvania Press: Chapter 14.

Barsh, Russel L. (1993). "Measuring Human Rights: Problems of Methodology and Purpose," *Human Rights Quarterly*, 15 (February): 87–121.

Bentley, Arthur F. (1908). *Process of Government: A Study of Social Pressures*. New Brunswick, NJ: Transaction Books.

Blanton, Robert G., and Shannon Lindsey Blanton (2012). "Rights, Institutions, and Foreign Direct Investment: An Empirical Assessment," *Foreign Policy Analysis*, 8 (4): 431–51.

Blanton, Shannon Lindsey (1994). "Impact of Human Rights on US Foreign Assistance to Latin America," *International Interactions*, 19 (4): 339–58.

Blanton, Shannon Lindsey (1999). "Instruments of Security or Tools of Repression? Arms Imports and Human Rights Conditions in Developing Countries," *Journal of Peace Research*, 36 (2): 233–44.

Blanton, Shannon Lindsey, and Robert G. Blanton (2009). "A Sectoral Analysis of Human Rights and FDI: Does Industry Type Matter?," *International Studies Quarterly*, 53 (2): 469–93.

Blasi, Gerald J., and David L. Cingranelli (1996). "Do Constitutions and Institutions Protect Human Rights?" In David L. Cingranelli (ed), *Human Rights and Developing Countries*. Greenwich, CT: JAI Press: 223–37.

Blondel, Jean (1969). *An Introduction of Comparative Government*. New York: Praeger.

Boli-Bennett, John (1981). "Human Rights or State Expansion? Cross-National Definitions of Constitutional Rights, 1870–1970." In Ved P. Nanda, James R. Scarritt, and George W. Shepherd, Jr (eds), *Global Human Rights: Public Policies, Comparative Measures, and NGO Strategies*. Boulder, CO: Westview: Chapter 11.

Bollen, Kenneth A. (1979). "Political Democracy and the Timing of Development," *American Sociological Review*, 44 (August): 572–87.

Bollen, Kenneth A. (1980). "Issues in the Comparative Measurement of Political Democracy," *American Sociological Review*, 45 (June): 370–90.

Bollen, Kenneth A. (1983). "World System Position, Dependency, and Democracy: The Cross-National Evidence," *American Sociological Review*, 45 (June): 468–79.

Bollen, Kenneth A. (1986). "Political Rights and Political Liberties in Nations: An Evaluation of Human Rights Measures, 1950 to 1984," *Human Rights Quarterly*, 8 (December): 567–91.

Bollen, Kenneth A. (1992). "Political Rights and Political Liberties in Nations: An Evaluation of Human Rights Measures, 1950 to 1984." In Thomas B. Jabine and Richard P. Claude (eds), *Human Rights and Statistics: Getting the Record Straight*. Philadelphia: University of Pennsylvania Press: Chapter 7.

Bollen, Kenneth A. (1993). "Liberal Democracy: Validity and Method Factors in Cross-National Measures," *American Journal of Political Science*, 37 (4): 1207–30.

Bollen, Kenneth A., and Burke D. Grandjean (1981). "The Dimension(s) of Democracy: Further Issues in the Measurement and Effects of Political Democracy," *American Sociological Review*, 46 (October): 651–59.

Bollen, Kenneth, and Robert W. Jackman (1989). "Democracy, Stability, and Dichotomies," *American Sociological Review*, 54 (August): 612–20.

Booysen, Frederik (2002). "An Overview and Evaluation of Composite Indices of Development," *Social Indicators Research*, 59 (2): 115–51.

Boswell, Terry, and William J. Dixon (1990). "Dependency and Rebellion: A Cross-National Analysis," *American Sociological Review*, 55 (August): 540–59.

Bueno de Mesquita, Bruce, Alastair Smith, Randall M. Siverson, and Morrow, James D. (2003). *The Logic of Political Survival*. Cambridge, MA: MIT Press.

Bueno de Mesquita, Bruce, Feryal Marie Cherif, George W. Downs, and Alastair Smith (2005). "Thinking Inside the Box: A Closer Look at Democracy and Human Rights," *International Studies Quarterly*, 49 (September): 439–57.

Byers, Michael (2006). *War Law: Understanding International Law and Armed Conflict*. New York: Grove Press.

Cain, Michael, Richard P. Claude, and Thomas B. Jabine (1992). "A Guide to Human Rights Data Sources." In T. B. Jabine and R. P. Claude (eds), *Human Rights and Statistics: Getting the Record Straight*. Philadelphia: University of Pennsylvania Press: Chapter 15.

Caprioli, Mary, and Peter F. Trumbore (2006). "Human Rights Rogues in Interstate Disputes, 1980–2001," *Human Rights Quarterly*, 43 (2): 131–45.

Carey, Sabine, and Steven C. Poe (eds) (2004). *Understanding Human Rights Violations: New Systematic Studies*. Burlington, VT: Ashgate.

Carleton, David, and Michael Stohl (1985). "The Foreign Policy of Human Rights: Rhetoric and Reality from Jimmy Carter to Ronald Reagan," *Human Rights Quarterly*, 7 (May): 205–29.

Carleton, David, and Michael Stohl (1987). "The Role of Human Rights in US Foreign Assistance Policy: A Critique and Reappraisal," *American Journal of Political Science*, 31 (4): 1002–18.

Carmichael, Stokely [later, Kwame Ture], and Charles V. Hamilton (1967). *Black Power*. New York: Random House.

Charny, Israel W. (1982). *How Can We Commit the Unthinkable? Genocide, the Human Cancer*. Boulder, CO: Westview.

Chayes, Abram, and Antonia Chandler Chayes (1993). "On Compliance," *International Organization*, 47 (2): 175–205.

Choi, Seung-Whan, and Yiagadeesen Samy (2008). "Reexamining the Effect of Democratic Institutions on Inflows of Foreign Direct Investment in Developing Countries," *Foreign Policy Analysis*, 4 (2): 83–103.

Chomsky, Noam (1991). *Deterring Democracy*. New York: Hill & Wang.

Cingranelli, David L., and Thomas E. Pasquarello (1985). "Human Rights Practices and the Distribution of US Foreign Aid to Latin American Countries," *American Journal of Political Science*, 29 (August): 539–63.

Cingranelli, David L., and David I. Richards (1999a). "Measuring the Level, Pattern, and Sequence of Government Respect for Physical Integrity Rights," *International Studies Quarterly*, 43 (2): 407–17.

Cingranelli, David. L., and David I. Richards (1999b). "Respect for Human Rights after the End of the Cold War," *Journal of Peace Research*, 36 (5): 511–34.

Cingranelli, David L., and David I. Richards (2010). "The Cingranelli and Richards (CIRI) Human Rights Data Project," *Human Rights Quarterly*, 32 (2): 401–24.

Cingranelli, David L., and Kevin N. Wright (1988). "Correlates of Due Process." In David L. Cingranelli (ed), *Human Rights: Theory and Measurement*. New York: St Martin's Press: Chapter 9.

Cohn, Norman (1967). *Warrant for Genocide: The Myth of Jewish World-Conspiracy and the Protocols of the Elders of Zion*. New York: Harper & Row.

Cohn, Norman (1970). *The Pursuit of the Millennium: Revolutionary Millenarians and Mystical Anarchists of the Middle Ages*. New York: Oxford University Press.

Cohn, Norman (1977). *Europe's Inner Demons: An Enquiry Inspired by the Great Witch-Hunt*. New York: Meridian.

Cole, Wade M. (2005). "Sovereignty Relinquished? Explaining Commitment to the International Human Rights Covenants, 1966–1999," *American Sociological Review*, 70 (3): 472–95.

Conway, Henderson (1982). "Military Regimes and Rights in Developing Countries," *Human Rights Quarterly*, 4 (1): 110–23.

Crotty, Patricia McGee, and Harold Jacobs (1996). "Women's Rights: Legislating Equality." In David L. Cingranelli (ed), *Human Rights and Developing Countries*. Greenwich, CT: JAI Press: 31–42.

Cutright, Phillips (1963). "National Political Development: Its Measurement and Social Correlates," *American Sociological Review*, 28 (April): 253–64.

Cutright, Phillips (1965). "Political Structure, Economic Development, and National Social Security Programs," *American Journal of Sociology*, 70 (March): 537–50.

Cutright, Phillips (1967a). "Inequality: A Cross-National Analysis," *American Sociological Review*, 32 (August): 562–78.

Cutright, Phillips (1967b). "Income Redistribution: A Cross-National Analysis," *Social Forces*, 46 (December): 180–90.

Cutright, Phillips, and James A. Wiley (1969). "Modernization and Political Representation, 1927–1966," *Studies in Comparative International Development*, 5 (2): 23–44.

Dahl, Robert A. (1971). *Polyarchy: Participation and Opposition*. New Haven, CT: Yale University Press.

Davenport, Christian (1988). "Liberalizing Event or Lethal Episode? An Empirical Assessment of How National Elections Affect the Suppression of Political and Civil Liberties," *Social Science Quarterly*, 79 (2): 321–40.

Davenport, Christian (1995). "Multi-Dimensional Threat Perception and State Repression," *American Journal of Political Science*, 39 (3): 685–713.

Davenport, Christian (1996). "Constitutional Promises and Repressive Reality," *Journal of Politics*, 58 (3): 627–54.

Davenport, Christian, and David A. Armstrong II (2004). "Democracy and Violation of Human Rights: A Statistical Analysis from 1976 to 1996," *American Journal of Political Science,* 48 (3): 538–54.

de Mesquita, Bruce, Feryal Marie Chief, George W. Downs, and Alastair Smith (2005). "Thinking Inside the Box: A Closer Look at Democracy and Human Rights," *International Studies Quarterly*, 49 (3): 439–57.

De Soysa, Indra and Paul Midford (2012). "Enter the Dragon! An Empirical Analysis of Chinese Versus US Arms Transfers to Autocrats and Violators of Human Rights, 1989–2006," *International Studies Quarterly*, 56 (4): 843–56.

Derian, Patricia (1979). "Human Rights in American Foreign Policy," *Notre Dame Lawyer*, 55 (December): 264–80.

Dixon, William J. (1984). "Trade Concentration, Economic Growth, and the Provision of Basic Human Needs," *Social Science Quarterly*, 65 (September): 761–74.

Donnelly, Jack (1989). *Universal Human Rights in Theory and Practice*. Ithaca, NY: Cornell University Press.

Donnelly, Jack, and Rhoda E. Howard (1988). "Assessing National Human Rights Performance: A Theoretical Framework," *Human Rights Quarterly*, 10 (May): 214–48.

Drury, A. Cooper, and Yitan Li (2006). "US Economic Sanction Threats Against China: Failing to Leverage Better Human Rights," *Foreign Policy Analysis*, 2 (4): 307–24.

Duff, Ernest A., and John F. McCamant (1976). *Violence and Repression in Latin America*. New York: Free Press.

Duvall, Raymond D., and Michael Stohl (1988). "Governance by Terror." In Michael Stohl (ed), *The Politics of Terrorism*. 3rd edn. New York: Dekker: Chapter 7.

Enterline, Andrew J., and J. Michael Grieg (2008). "Against All Odds? The History of Imposed Democracy and the Future of Iraq and Afghanistan," *Foreign Policy Analysis*, 4 (4): 321–48.

Escribà-Folch, Abel, and Joseph Wright (2010). "Dealing with Tyranny: International Sanctions and the Survival of Authoritarian Rulers," *International Studies Quarterly*, 54 (2): 335–59.

Feierabend, Ivo K., and Rosalind L. Feierabend (1971). "The Relationship of Systemic Frustration, Political Coercion, International Tension and Political Instability: A Cross-National Analysis." In J. V. Gillespie and B. A. Nesvold (eds), *Macro-Quantitative Analysis: Conflict, Development, and Democratization*. Beverly Hills, CA: SAGE Publications: Chapter 19.

Fein, Helen (1993). *Genocide: A Sociological Perspective*. Newbury Park, CA: SAGE Publications.

Feng, Yi (2001). "Political Freedom, Political Instability, and Policy Uncertainty: A Study of Political Institutions and Private Investment in Developing Countries," *International Studies Quarterly*, 45 (2): 271–94.

Fitzgibbon, Russell H. (1956). "A Statistical Evaluation of Latin American Democracy," *Western Political Quarterly*, 9 (September): 607–19.

Fitzgibbon, Russell H., and Kenneth F. Johnson (1961). "Measurement of Latin American Political Change," *American Political Science Review*, 55 (September): 515–26.

Flanigan, William, and Edwin Fogelman (1971). "Patterns of Democratic Development: An Historical Comparative Analysis." In J. V. Gillespie and B. A. Nesvold (eds), *Macro-Quantitative Analysis: Conflict, Development, and Democratization*. Beverly Hills, CA: SAGE Publications: Chapter 21.

Foweraker, Joe, and Todd Landman (1997). *Citizenship Rights and Social Movements: A Comparative and Statistical Analysis*. New York: Oxford University Press.

Foweraker, Joe, and Todd Landman (1999). "Individual Rights and Social Movements: A Comparative and Statistical Inquiry," *British Journal of Political Science*, 29 (2): 291–322.

Frakt, Phyllis M. (1977). "Democracy, Political Activity, Economic Development, and Governmental Responsiveness: The Case of Labor Policy," *Comparative Political Studies*, 10 (July): 177–212.

Franck, Thomas M. (1995). *Fairness in International Law and Institutions*. New York: Oxford University Press.

Frank, André Gunder (1967). *Capitalism and Development in Latin America: Historical Studies of Chile and Brazil*. New York: Monthly Review Press.

Franklin, James C. (1997). "IMF Conditionality, Threat Perception and Political Repression," *Comparative Political Studies*, 30 (5): 576–606.

Franklin, James C. (2008). "Shame on You: The Impact of Human Rights Criticism on Political Repression in Latin America," *International Studies Quarterly*, 52 (1): 187–211.

Freedom House (1978–). *Freedom in the World: Political Rights & Civil Liberties*. Lanham, MD: Freedom House, annual.

Freud, Sigmund (1930). *Civilization and Its Discontents*. London: Hogarth.

Frey, R. Scott, and Ali Al-Roumi (1999). Political Democracy and the Physical Quality of Life: The Cross-National Evidence," *Social Indicators Research*, 47 (1): 73–97.

Friedman, Milton (1988). "A Statistical Note on the Gastil Survey of Freedom." In R. D. Gastil (ed), *Freedom in the World*. Lanham, MD: Freedom House: 183–7.

Gartner, Scott Sigmund, and Patrick M. Regan (1996). "Threat and Repression," *Journal of Peace Research*, 33 (3): 273–87.

Gastil, Raymond D. (1972). "Comparative Survey of Freedom," *Freedom at Issue*, 14: 4.

Gibney, Mark, and Matthew Dalton (1996). "The Political Terror Scale." In David L. Cingranelli (ed), *Human Rights and Developing Countries*. Greenwich, CT: JAI Press: 73–84.

Goldstein, Robert J. (1986). "The Limitations of Using Quantitative Data in Studying Human Rights Abuses," *Human Rights Quarterly*, 8 (November): 607–27.

Green, Maria (2001). "What We Talk about When We Talk about Indicators: Current Approaches to Human Rights Measurement," *Human Rights Quarterly*, 23 (4): 1062–97.

Greenhill, Brian (2010). "The Company You Keep: International Socialization and the Diffusion of Human Rights Norms," *International Studies Quarterly*, 54 (1): 127–45.

Gupta, Dipak K., Albert J. Jongman, and Alex P. Schmid (1994). "Creating a Composite Index for Assessing Country Performance in the Field of Human Rights: Proposal for a New Methodology," *Human Rights Quarterly*, 16 (1): 131–62.

Gurr, Ted Robert (1966). *New Error-Compensated Measures for Comparing Nations: Some Correlates of Civil Violence*. Princeton, NJ: Center of International Studies, Princeton University.

Gurr, Ted Robert (1970). *Why Men Rebel*. Princeton, NJ: Princeton University Press.

Gurr, Ted Robert (1986). "The Political Origins of State Violence and Terror: A Theoretical Analysis." In Michael Stohl and George A. Lopez (eds), *Government Violence and Repression: An Agenda for Research*. Westport, CT: Greenwood: 45–71.

Gurr, Ted Robert (1988). "War, Revolution, and the Growth of the Coercive State," *Comparative Political Studies*, 21 (April): 45–65.

Gurr, Ted Robert (1993). *Minorities at Risk: A Global View of Ethnopolitical Conflicts*. Washington, DC: US Institute of Peace.

Gurr, Ted Robert, and Erika B. K. Gurr (1983). "Group Discrimination and Potential Separatism in 1960 and 1975." In C. L. Taylor and D. Jodice (eds), *World Handbook of Political and Social Indicators*. 3rd edn. New Haven, CT: Yale University Press: 1, 50–7, 66–75.

Haas, Ernst B. (1958). *The Uniting of Europe: Political, Social, and Economic Forces, 1950–1957*. Stanford, CA: Stanford University Press.

Haas, Ernst B. (1964). *Beyond the Nation State: Functionalism and International Organization*. Stanford, CA: Stanford University Press.

Haas, Ernst B. (1970). *Human Rights and International Action*. Stanford, CA: Stanford University Press.

Haas, Ernst B. (1990). *When Knowledge is Power: Three Models of Change in International Organizations*. Berkeley: University of California Press.

Haas, Michael (1992). *Polity and Society: Philosophical Underpinnings of Social Science Paradigms*. Westport, CT: Praeger.

Haas, Michael (1994). *Improving Human Rights*. Westport, CT: Praeger.

Haas, Michael (1996). "Empirical Dimensions of Human Rights." In David L. Cingranelli (ed), *Human Rights and Developing Countries*. Greenwich, CT: JAI Press: 43–72.

Haas, Michael (2007). "From Human Rights Numbercrunching to Human Rights Theory." Paper archive of the International Studies Association annual convention website.

Hadenius, Axel (1992). *Democracy and Development*. New York: Cambridge University Press.

Hafner-Burton, Emilie M. (2005a). "Right or Robust? The Sensitive Nature of Repression to Globalization," *Journal of Peace Research*, 42 (6): 679–98.

Hafner-Burton, Emilie M. (2005b). "Trading Human Rights: How Preferential Trade Agreements Influence Government Repression," *International Organization*, 59 (30): 593–629.

Hafner-Burton, Emilie M., and Kiyoteru Tsutsui (2005). "Human Rights in a Globalizing World: The Paradox of Empty Promises," *American Journal of Sociology*, 110 (March): 1373–412.

Harff, Barbara (1986). "Genocide as State Terrorism." In Michael Stohl and George Lopez (eds), *Government Violence and Repression: An Agenda for Research*. Westport, CT: Greenwood: Chapter 6.

Harff, Barbara, and Ted Robert Gurr (1988). "Toward an Empirical Theory of Genocides and Politicides: Identification and Measurement of Cases Since 1945," *International Studies Quarterly*, 32 (3): 359–71.

Harvey, David (2005). *A Brief History of Neoliberalism*. New York: Oxford University Press.

Hathaway, Oona (2002). "Do Treaties Make a Difference? Human Rights Treaties and the Problem of Compliance," *Yale Law Journal*, 111 (8): 1935–2042.

Henderson, Conway W. (1982). "Military Regimes and Rights in Developing Countries," *Human Rights Quarterly*, 4 (1): 110–23.

Henderson, Conway W. (1991). "Conditions Affecting the Use of Political Repression," *Journal of Conflict Resolution*, 35 (1): 120–42.

Henderson, Conway W. (1993). "Population Pressures and Political Repression," *Social Science Quarterly*, 74 (2): 322–37.

Hertel, Shareen (2006). "Why Bother? Measuring Economic Rights: The Research Agenda," *International Studies Perspectives*, 7 (August): 215–30.

Hewitt, Christopher (1977). "The Effect of Political Democracy and Social Democracy on Equality in Industrial Societies," *American Sociological Review*, 42 (June): 450–64.

Hibbs, Douglas A., Jr (1973). *Mass Political Violence: A Cross-National Causal Analysis*. New York: Wiley.

Hicks, Alexander (1988). "Social Democracy, Corporatism and Economic Growth," *Journal of Politics*, 50 (August): 677–704.

Hoffenbert, Richard I., and David Louis Cingranelli (1996). "Democratic Institutions and Respect for Human Rights." In David L. Cingranelli (ed), *Human Rights and Developing Countries*. Greenwich, CT: JAI Press: 145–59.

Hofrenning, Daniel J. B. (1990). "Human Rights and Foreign Aid: A Comparison of the Reagan and Carter Administrations," *American Politics Quarterly*, 18 (4): 514–26.

Horowitz, Irving L. (1976). *Genocide: State Power and Mass Murder*. New Brunswick, NJ: Transaction. [The third edition in 1980 was retitled *Taking Lives*.]

Howard, Rhoda E. (1990). "Monitoring Human Rights: Problems of Consistency," *Ethics & International Affairs*, 4: 33–51.

Human Rights First (2003). *Holding the Line: A Critique of the Department of State's Annual Reports (for 2002) on Human Rights Practices*. Available at: www.humanrightsfirst.org/pubs/descriptions/holdingtheline.pdf.

Humana, Charles (1983). *World Human Rights Guide*. 1st edn. New York: Pica Press.

Humana, Charles (1987). *World Human Rights Guide*. 2nd edn. New York: Pan Books.

Humana, Charles (1992). *World Human Rights Guide*. 3rd edn. New York: Oxford University Press.

Huntington, Samuel P. (1968). *Political Order in Changing Societies*. New Haven, CT: Yale University Press.

Innes, Judith E. (1992). "Human Rights Reporting as a Policy Tool: An Examination of the State Department Country Reports." In T. B. Jabine and R. P. Claude (eds), *Human Rights and Statistics: Getting the Record Straight*. Philadelphia: University of Pennsylvania Press: Chapter 9.

International Association for Official Statistics (2000). Conference on Statistics, Development and Human Rights, Montreaux. Available at: www.iaos2000.admin.ch.

Jackman, Robert W. (1975). *Politics and Social Equality: A Comparative Analysis*. New York: Wiley.

Johnson, M. Glen (1988). "Human Rights in Divergent Conceptual Settings: How Do Ideas Influence Policy Choices?" In David L. Cingranelli (ed), *Human Rights: Theory and Measurement*. New York: St Martin's Press: Chapter 2.

Keith, Linda Camp (2002). "Constitutional Provisions for Individual Human Rights (1977–1996): Are They More than Mere 'Window Dressing'?," *Political Research Quarterly*, 55 (1): 111–43.

Keith, Linda Camp, and Ato Ogundele (2007). "Legal Systems and Constitutionalism in Sub-Saharan Africa: An Empirical Examination of Colonial Influences on Human Rights," *Human Rights Quarterly*, 29 (4): 1066–97.

Keith, Linda Camp, and Steven C. Poe (2000). "The United States, the IMF, and Human Rights: A Policy-Relevant Approach." In David P. Forsythe (ed), *The United States and Human Rights: Looking Inward and Outward*. Lincoln: University of Nebraska Press: 273–99.

Keith, Linda Camp, and Steven C. Poe (2004). "Are Constitutional State of Emergency Clauses Effective? An Empirical Explanation," *Human Rights Quarterly*, 26 (4): 1071–97.

Kerr, Clark, John T. Dunlop, Frederick H. Harbison, and Charles A. Myers (1964). *Industrialism and the Industrial State*. New York: Oxford University Press.

Koh, Harold Hongju (1997). "Why Do Nations Obey International Law?," *Yale Law Journal*, 106 (8): 2599–659.

Kolakowski, Leszek (1983). "Marxism and Human Rights," *Daedalus*, 112 (Fall): 81–92.

Kornhauser, William (1959). *The Politics of Mass Society*. Glencoe, IL: Free Press.

Krain, Matthew (2012). "*J'accuse!* Does Naming and Shaming Perpetrators Reduce the Severity of Genocides or Politicides?," *International Studies Quarterly*, 56 (3): 574–89.

Kuper, Leo (1981). *Genocide: Its Political Use in the Twentieth Century*. New Haven, CT: Yale University Press.

Lai, Brian (2003). "Examining the Goals of US Foreign Assistance in the Post-Cold War Period, 1991–96," *Journal of Peace Research*, 40 (1): 103–28.

Landman, Todd (2005). *Protecting Human Rights: A Comparative Study*. Washington, DC: Georgetown University Press.

Landman, Todd, and Marco Larizza (2009). "Inequality and Human Rights: Who Controls What, When, and How," *International Studies Quarterly*, 53 (3): 715–36.

Lawyers Committee for International Human Rights (1982). *A Critique of the Department of State's Country Reports on Human Rights Practices for 1981*. New York: Lawyers Committee for International Human Rights.

Lawyers Committee for International Human Rights (2003). *Holding the Line: A Critique of the US Department of State's Annual Reports on Human Rights Practices for 2002*. New York: Lawyer's Committee for Human Rights.

Lebovic, James H. (1988). "National Interests and US Foreign Aid: The Carter and Reagan Years," *Journal of Peace Research*, 25 (2): 115–33.

Lee, Hsien Long (1987). *When the Press Misinforms*. Singapore: Information Division, Ministry of Commerce & Industry.

Lenin, Vladimir I. ([1917] 1964). *Imperialism: The Highest Stage of Capitalism*. Peking: People's Publishing House.

Lenski, Gerhard (1966). *Power and Privilege: A Theory of Social Stratification*. New York: McGraw-Hill.

Lerner, Daniel (1958). *The Passing of Traditional Society: Modernizing the Middle East*. New York: Free Press.

Li, Quan, and Rafael Reuveny (2009). *Democracy and Economic Openness in the International System: Complex Transformations*. New York: Cambridge University Press.

Lifton, Robert J. (1986). *The Nazi Doctors: Medical Killing and the Psychology of Genocide*. New York: Basic Books.

Lindberg, Staffan I. (2006). *Democracy and Elections in Africa*. Baltimore, MD: Johns Hopkins University Press.

Lindblom, Charles E. (1977). *Politics and Markets: The World's Political Economic Systems*. New York: Basic Books.

Lipset, Seymour Martin (1959). "Some Social Requisites of Democracy: Economic Development and Political Legitimacy," *American Political Science Review*, 53 (March): 69–105.

Lizhi, Fang (1990). "The Chinese Amnesia," *New York Review of Books*, 37 (October 27): 30–31.

Locke, John ([1688] 1967). *Second Treatise of Government*. Cambridge, UK: Cambridge University Press.

London, Bruce, and Bruce A. Williams (1988). "Multinational Corporate Penetration, Protest, and Basic Needs Provision in Non-Core Nations: A Cross-National Analysis," *Social Forces*, 66 (3): 747–73.

Lopez, George A., and Michael Stohl (1992). "Problems of Concept and Measurement in the Study of Human Rights." In Thomas B. Jabine and Richard P. Claude (eds), *Human Rights and Statistics: Getting the Record Straight*. Philadelphia: University of Pennsylvania Press: Chapter 8.

Lowenstein, Ralph L. (1967). *Measuring World Press Freedom as a Political Indicator*. Columbia, MO: PhD dissertation, University of Missouri.

Marcuse, Herbert (1955). *Eros and Civilization: A Philosophical Inquiry into Freud*. Boston: Beacon.

Marshall, Monty, and Keith Jaggers (2000). *Polity IV: Political Regime Characteristics and Transitions, 1800–1999*. College Park, MD: Integrate Network for Societal Conflict. [The data are updated from time to time.]

Marx, Karl, and Friedrich Engels (1848). *Manifesto of the Communist Party*. Reprinted in Robert C. Tucker (ed), *The Marx–Engels Reader*. New York: Norton: 331–62.

Mazian, Florence (1990). *Why Genocide? The Armenian and Jewish Experiences in Perspective*. Ames: Iowa State University Press.

McCamant, John F. (1981). "A Critique of Present Measures of 'Human Rights Development' and an Alternative." in Ved P. Nanda, James R. Scarritt, and George W. Shepherd, Jr (eds), *Global Human Rights: Public Policies, Comparative Measures, and NGO Strategies*. Boulder, CO: Westview: Chapter 9.

McCann, James A., and Mark Gibney (1996). "An Overview of Political Terror in the Developing World, 1980–1991." In David L. Cingranelli (ed), *Human Rights and Developing Countries*. Greenwich, CT: JAI Press: 15–27.

McCormick, James, and Neal Mitchell (1997). "Human Rights Violations, Umbrella Concepts, and Empirical Analysis," *World Politics*, 49 (4): 510–25.

McCrone, David J., and Charles F. Cnudde (1967). "Toward a Communications Theory of Democratic Political Development," *American Political Science Review*, 61 (March): 72–9.

McGann, Anthony, and Wayne Sandholtz (2012). "Patterns of Death Penalty Abolition, 1960–2000: Domestic and Alliance Formation," *International Studies Quarterly*, 56 (2): 275–89.

McKinley, R. D., and R. Little (1979). "The US AID Relationship: A Test of the Recipient Need and Donor Interest Models," *Political Studies*, 27 (2): 236–50.

McNitt, Andrew D. (1988). "Some Thoughts on the Systematic Measurement of the Abuse of Human Rights." In David L. Cingranelli (ed), *Human Rights: Theory and Measurement*. New York: St Martin's Press: Chapter 8.

Meernik, James, Eric L. Krueger, and Steven C. Poe (1998). "Testing Models of US Foreign Policy: Foreign Aid During and After the Cold War," *Journal of Politics*, 60 (1): 63–85.

Melander, Erik (2005). "Political Gender Equality and State Human Rights Abuses," *Journal of Peace Research*, 42 (2): 149–66.

Meyer, William H. (1996). "Human Rights and MNCs: Theory Versus Quantitative Analysis," *Human Rights Quarterly*, 18 (2): 368–97.

Michels, Roberto (1915). *Political Parties*. New York: Collier.

Mills, C. Wright (1956). *The Power Elite*. New York: Oxford University Press.

Milner, Wesley T. (2002). "Economic Globalization and Rights." In Alison Brysk (ed), *Globalization and Human Rights*. Berkeley: University of California Press: Chapter 4.

Milner, Wesley, Steven C. Poe, and David Leblang (1999). "Security Rights, Subsistence Rights, and Liberties: A Theoretical Survey of the Empirical Landscape," *Human Rights Quarterly*, 21 (2): 403–43.

Minkler, Lanse, and Shawna Sweeney (2011). "On the Indivisibility and Interdependence of Basic Rights in Developing Countries," *Human Rights Quarterly*, 33 (2): 351–96.

Mitchell, Christopher, Michael Stohl, David Carleton, and George A. Lopez (1986). "State Terrorism: Issues of Concept and Measurement." In Michael Stohl and George A. Lopez (eds), *Government Violence and Repression: An Agenda for Research*. Westport, CT: Greenwood: Chapter 1.

Mitchell, Neil J., and James M. McCormick (1988). "Economic and Political Explanations of Human Rights Violations," *World Politics*, 40 (4): 476–98.

Mitrany, David (1943). *A Working Peace System: An Argument for the Functional Development of International Organization*. New York: Oxford University Press.

Moaddel, Mansoor (1994). "Political Conflict in the World Economy: A Cross-National Analysis of Modernization and World-System Theories," *American Sociological Review*, 59 (April): 276–303.

Moon, Bruce E., and William J. Dixon (1985). "Politics, the State, and Basic Human Needs: A Cross-National Study," *American Journal of Political Science*, 29 (4): 661–94.

Moon, Bruce E., and William J. Dixon (1992). "Basic Needs and Growth–Welfare Trade-Offs," *International Studies Quarterly*, 36 (2): 191–212.

Moravcsik, Andrew (2000). "The Origin of Human Rights Regimes: Democratic Delegation in Postwar Europe," *International Organization*, 54 (4): 217–52.

Morgenthau, Hans J. (1979). *Human Rights and Foreign Policy*. New York: Council on Foreign Relations.

Morris, Morris D. (1979). *Measuring Conditions of the World's Poor: The Physical Quality of Life Index*. New York: Pergamon.

Mosca, Gaetano ([1896] 1939). *The Ruling Class*. New York: McGraw-Hill.

Muller, Edward N. (1988). "Democracy, Economic Development, and Income Inequality," *American Sociological Review*, 53 (February): 50–68.

Murdie, Amanda M., and David R. Davis (2012). "Shaming and Blaming: Using Events Data to Assess the Impact of Human Rights INGOs," *International Studies Quarterly*, 56 (1): 1–16.

Myrdal, Gunnar (1957). *Economic Theory and Under-Developed Regions*. London: Duckworth.

Nesvold, Betty A. (1969). "Scalogram Analysis of Political Violence," *Comparative Political Studies*, 2 (July): 172–94.

Neubauer, Deane E. (1967). "Some Conditions of Democracy," *American Political Science Review*, 41 (December): 1002–9.

Neumayer, Eric (2003a). "Do Human Rights Matter in Bilateral Aid Allocation? A Quantitative Analysis of 21 Donor Countries," *Social Science Quarterly*, 84 (3): 650–66.

Neumayer, Eric (2003b). "Is Respect for Human Rights Rewarded? An Analysis of Total Bilateral and Multilateral Aid Flows," *Human Rights Quarterly*, 25 (2): 510–27.

Neumayer, Eric (2005). "Do International Human Rights Treaties Improve Respect for Human Rights?," *Journal of Conflict Resolution*, 49 (6): 925–53.

Nickel, James W. (2008). "Rethinking Indivisibility: Towards a Theory of Supporting Relations Between Human Rights," *Human Rights Quarterly*, 30 (4): 984–1001.

Nincic, Miroslav (2006). "The Logic of Positive Engagement: Dealing with Renegade Regimes," *International Studies Perspectives*, 7 (4): 321–41.

Nixon, Raymond B. (1960). "Factors Related to Freedom in National Press Systems," *Journalism Quarterly*, 37 (Winter): 13–28.

Nixon, Raymond B. (1965). "Freedom in the World's Press: A Fresh Appraisal with New Data," *Journalism Quarterly*, 42 (Winter): 3–5,118–19.

Nye, Joseph S., Jr (2004). *Soft Power: The Means to Success in World Politics*. New York: Public Affairs Press.

Ogwang, Tomson (1997). "The Choice of Principal Variables for Computing the Physical Quality of Life Index," *Journal of Economic and Social Measurement*," 23 (3): 213–22.

Organski, A. F. K. (1965). *The Stages of Political Development*. New York: Knopf.

Pareto, Vilfredo ([1916] 1935). *The Mind and Society*. New York: Harcourt, Brace.

Park, Han S. (1987). "Correlates of Human Rights," *Human Rights Quarterly*, 9 (3): 405–13.

Pasquarello, Thomas E. (1986). "Human Rights and US Bilateral Aid Allocations to Africa." In David L. Cingranelli (ed), *Human Rights: Theory and Measurement*. New York: St Martin's Press: Chapter 14.

Payaslian, Simon (1996). "Human Rights and US Bilateral Assistance to Developing Countries: The Bush Administration, 1989–1990." In David L. Cingranelli (ed), *Human Rights and Developing Countries*. Greenwich, CT: JAI Press: 163–81.

Piazza, James A., and James Igoe Walsh (2009). "Transnational Terror and Human Rights," *International Studies Quarterly*, 53 (1): 125–48.

Poe, Steven C. (1991a). "Human Rights and the Allocation of US Military Assistance," *Journal of Peace Research*, 28 (2): 205–16.

Poe, Steven C. (1991b). "U.S. Economic Aid Allocation: The Quest for Cumulation," *International Interactions*, 16 (4): 295–316.

Poe, Steven C. (1992). "Human Rights and the Allocation of US Military Aid Allocation under Ronald Reagan and Jimmy Carter," *American Journal of Political Science*, 36 (1): 146–67.

Poe, Steven C., and Rangsima Sirirangsi (1992). "Human Rights and US Economic Aid to Africa," *International Interactions*, 18 (4): 309–22.

Poe, Steven C., and Rangsima Sirirangsi (1994). "Human Rights and US Economic Aid During the Reagan Years," *Social Science Quarterly*, 75 (3): 494–509.

Poe, Steven C., and Neal Tate (1994). "Repression of Human Rights to Personal Integrity in the 1980s: A Global Analysis," *American Political Science Review*, 88 (4): 476–98.

Poe, Steven C., and James Meernik (1995). "US Military Aid in the 1980s: A Global Analysis," *Journal of Peace Research*, 32 (4): 399–411.

Poe, Steven C., Deirdre Wendel-Blunt, and Karl Ho (1997). "Global Patterns in the Achievement of Women's Human Rights to Equality," *Human Rights Quarterly*, 19 (4): 813–35.

Poe, Steven C., Neal Tate, and Linda Camp Keith (1999). "Repression of the Human Right to Personal Integrity Revisited: A Global Cross-National Study Covering the Years 1976–1993," *International Studies Quarterly*, 43 (2): 291–313.

Poe, Steven C., Sabine C. Carey, and Tanya C. Vazquez (2001). "How Are These Pictures Different? A Quantitative Comparison of the US State Department and Amnesty International Human Rights Reports, 1976–1995," *Human Rights Quarterly*, 23 (3): 650–77.

Poe, Steven C., Suzanne Pilatovsky, Brian Miller, and Ayo Ogundele (1994). "Human Rights and US Foreign Aid Revisited: The Latin American Region," *Human Rights Quarterly*, 16 (3): 539–58.

Population Crisis Committee (1987). *The International Human Suffering Index*. Washington, DC: Population Crisis Committee.

Population Crisis Committee (1992). *The International Human Suffering Index*. Washington, DC: Population Crisis Committee.

Pourgerami, Abbas (1992). "Authoritarian Versus Nonauthoritarian Approaches to Economic Development: Update and Additional Evidence," *Public Choice*, 74 (3): 365–77.

Powell, Emilia Justyna, and Jeffrey K. Staton (2009). "Domestic Judicial Institutions and Human Rights Treaty Violation," *International Studies Quarterly*, 53 (1): 149–74.

Pritchard, Kathleen (1988). "Comparative Human Rights: Promise and Practice." In David L. Cingranelli (ed), *Human Rights: Theory and Measurement*. New York: St Martin's Press: Chapter 8.

Pritchard, Kathleen (1989). "Human Rights and Development." In David P. Forsythe (ed), *Human Rights and Development: International Views*. New York: St Martin's Press: Chapter 19.

Raworth, Kate (2001). "Measuring Human Rights," *Ethics and International Affairs*, 15 (1): 111–32.

Regan, Patrick M. (1995). "US Economic Aid and Political Repression," *Political Research Quarterly*, 48 (3): 613–28.

Richards, David L. (1999). "Perilous Proxy: Human Rights and the Presence of National Elections," *Social Science Quarterly*, 80 (4): 648–65.

Richards, David L., Ronald D. Gelleny, and David H. Sacko (2001). "Money with a Mean Streak? Foreign Economic Penetration and Government Respect for Human Rights in Developing Countries." *International Studies Quarterly*, 45 (2): 219–39.

Rosh, Robert M. (1986). "Militarization, Human Rights and Basic Needs in the Third World." In David. L. Cingranelli (ed), *Human Rights: Theory and Measurement*. New York: St Martin's Press: Chapter 11.

Rubin, Barnett R., and Paula R. Newberg (1980). "Statistical Analysis for Implementing Human Rights Policy." In Paula R. Newberg (ed), *The Politics of Human Rights*. New York: New York University Press: 268–84.

Rubison, Richard (1976). "The World-Economy and the Distribution of Income Within States: A Cross-National Study," *American Sociological Review*, 41 (August): 639–59.

Ruggie, John G. (ed) (1993). *Multilateralism Matters: The Theory and Praxis of an Institutional Form*. New York: Columbia University Press.

Rummel, R. J. (1972). *The Dimensions of Nations*. Beverly Hills: SAGE Publications.

Rummel, R. J. (1983). "Libertarianism and International Violence," *Journal of Conflict Resolution*, 27 (1): 27–71.

Russett, Bruce N., Hayward R. Alker, Karl W. Deutsch, and Harold D. Lasswell (1964). *World Handbook of Political and Social Indicators*. 1st edn. New Haven, CT: Yale University Press.

Rustow, Dankwart A. (1967). *World of Nations: Problems of Political Modernization*. Washington, DC: Brookings.

Samuelson, Douglas A., and Herbert F. Spirer (1992). "Use of Incomplete and Distorted Data in Inference about Human Rights Violations." In Thomas B. Jabine and Richard P. Claude (eds), *Human Rights and Statistics: Getting the Record Straight*. Philadelphia: University of Pennsylvania Press: Chapter 3.

Schoultz, Lars (1981a). "US Foreign Policy and Human Rights Violations in Latin America," *Comparative Politics*, 13 (January): 149–70.

Schoultz, Lars (1981b). "US Policy Toward Human Rights in Latin America: A Comparative Analysis of Two Administrations." In Ved P. Nanda, James R. Scarritt, and George W. Shepherd, Jr (eds), *Global Human Rights: Public Policies, Comparative Measures, and NGO Strategies*. Boulder, CO: Westview: Chapter 6.

Scoble, Harry M., and Laurie S. Wiseberg (1981). "Problems of Comparative Research on Human Rights." In Ved P. Nanda, James R. Scarritt, and George W. Shepherd, Jr (eds), *Global Human Rights: Public Policies, Comparative Measures, and NGO Strategies*. Boulder, CO: Westview: 147–71.

Scott, James W., and Carie A. Steele (2011). "Sponsoring Democracy: The United States and Democracy Aid to the Developing World, 1988–2001," *International Studies Quarterly*, 55 (1): 47–69.

Singer, J. David (1961). "The Level-of-Analysis Problem in International Relations," *World Politics*, 14 (1): 77–92.

Sivard, Ruth Leger (1975–). *World Military and Social Expenditures*. Washington, DC: World Priorities, annual.

Smith, Adam ([1776] 1937). *An Inquiry into the Nature and Causes of the Wealth of Nations*. New York: Modern Library.

Smith, Arthur K., Jr (1969). "Socio-Economic Development and Political Democracy: A Causal Analysis," *American Journal of Political Science*, 13 (February): 95–125.

Sorens, Jason, and William Ruger (2012). "Does Foreign Investment Really Reduce Repression?," *International Studies Quarterly*, 56 (2): 427–36.

Spalding, Nancy L. (1988). "Democracy and Human Rights in the Third World." In David L. Cingranelli (ed), *Human Rights: Theory and Measurement*. New York: St Martin's Press: Chapter 10.

Spalding, Nancy L. (1996). "Structural Adjustment Policies and Economic Human Rights in Africa." In David L. Cingranelli (ed), *Human Rights and Developing Countries*. Greenwich, CT: JAI Press: 193–210.

Spirer, Herbert F. (1990). "Violations of Human Rights – How Many? The Statistical Problems of Measuring Such Infractions Are Tough, But Statistical Science Is Equal to It," *American Journal of Economics and Sociology*, 49 (2): 199–210.

Staats, Joseph L., and Glen Biglaiser (2012). "Foreign Direct Investment in Latin America: The Importance of Judicial Strength and Rule of Law," *International Studies Quarterly*, 56 (1): 193–202.

Stack, Steven (1978). "International Political Organization and the World Economy of Income Inequality," *American Sociological Review*, 43 (April): 271–92.

Staub, Ervin (1989). *The Roots of Evil: The Psychological and Cultural Origins of Genocide and Other Forms of Group Violence*. Cambridge, UK: Cambridge University Press.

Stohl, Michael (1986). "The Superpowers and International Terrorism." In Michael Stohl and George A. Lopez (eds), *Government Violence and Repression*. New York: Greenwood: Chapter 8.

Stohl, Michael, David Carleton, and Steven E. Johnson (1984). "Human Rights and US Foreign Assistance from Nixon to Carter," *Journal of Peace Research*, 21 (3): 215–26.

Stohl, Michael, D. Carleton, George A. Lopez, and Stephen Samuels (1986). "State Violations of Human Rights: Issues and Problems of Measurement," *Human Rights Quarterly*, 8 (November): 592–606.

Strouse, James C., and Richard P. Claude (eds) (1976). *Comparative Human Rights*. Baltimore, MD: Johns Hopkins University Press.

Svensson, Jakob (1999). "Aid, Growth and Democracy," *Economics and Politics*, 11 (3): 275–97.

Taylor, Charles Lewis, and Michael C. Hudson (1972). *World Handbook of Political and Social Indicators*. 2nd edn. New Haven, CT: Yale University Press.

Taylor, Charles Lewis, and David A. Jodice (eds) (1983). *World Handbook of Political and Social Indicators*. 3rd edn. New Haven, CT: Yale University Press.

Thomas, Oskar N. T., and James Ron (2007). "Do Human Rights Violations Cause Internal Conflict?," *Human Rights Quarterly*, 29 (3): 674–705.

Tilly, Charles (1978). *From Mobilization to Revolution*. Reading, MA: Addison-Wesley.

Tilly, Charles (2007). *Democracy*. New York: Cambridge University Press.

Timberlake, Michael, and Kirk R. Williams (1984). "Dependence, Political Exclusion, and Government Repression: Some Cross-National Evidence," *American Sociological Review*, 49 (1): 141–6.

Tomaševski, Katarina (1992). "A Critique of the UNDP Political Freedom Index 1991." In Bard-Anders Andreassen and Theresa Swinehart (eds), *Human Rights in Developing Countries Yearbook 1991*. Oslo: Scandinavian University Press: 3–24.

Tomaševski, Katarina (1997). *Between Sanctions and Elections: Aid Donors and Their Human Rights Performance.* Washington, DC: Pinter.

Travis, Rick (1995). "US Security Assistance Policy and Democracy: A Look at the 1980s," *Journal of Developing Areas*, 29 (4): 541–62.

Trumbull, William N., and Howard J. Wall (1994). "Estimating Aid-Allocation Criteria with Panel Data," *Economic Journal*, 104 (July): 876–82.

Tsutsui, Kiyoteru, and Christine Min Wotipka (2004). "Global Civil Society and the International Human Rights Movement: Citizen Participation in Human Rights International Nongovernmental Organizations," *Social Forces*, 83 (2): 587–620.

United Nations Development Program (1990–). *Human Development Report.* New York: Oxford University Press, annual.

United Nations Statistical Office (1948–). *Demographic Yearbook.* New York: United Nations, annual.

United Nations Statistical Office (1948–). *Statistical Yearbook.* New York: United Nations, annual.

United States Department of Health and Human Services (1958–). *Social Security Programs Throughout the World.* Washington, DC: Social Security Administration Research Report series, biennial.

United States, Department of State (1975–). *Country Reports on Human Rights Practices.* Washington, DC: Government Printing Office, annual.

United States, Department of State (1999–). *Annual Report to Congress on International Religious Freedom.* Washington, DC: Government Printing Office, annual.

Valverde, Gilbert A. (1999). "Democracy, Human Rights, and Development Assistance for Education: The USAID and World Bank in Latin America and the Caribbean," *Economic Development and Cultural Change*, 47 (2): 401–18.

Van Den Berghe, Pierre L. (1981). *The Ethnic Phenomenon.* New York: Elsevier.

Vanhanen, Tatu (2000). "A New Dataset for Measuring Democracy, 1810–1998," *Journal of Peace Research*, 37 (2): 251–65.

Vorhies, Frank, and Fred Glahe (1988). "Liberty and Social Progress: A Geographical Examination." In *Freedom in the World*. Lanham, MD: Freedom House: 189–201.

Walker, Scott, and Steven C. Poe (2002). "Does Cultural Diversity Affect Countries' Respect for Human Rights?," *Human Rights Quarterly*, 24 (1): 237–63.

Watchirs, Helen (2002). "Review of Methodologies Measuring Human Rights Implementation," *Journal of Law, Medicine & Ethics*, 30 (4): 716–34.

Weber, Max (1913). *The Theory of Social and Economic Organization.* Glencoe, IL: Free Press.

Weber, Max ([1918] 1979). *Economy and Society: An Outline of Interpretive Sociology.* Berkeley: University of California Press.

Weede, Erich (1980). "Beyond Misspecification in Sociological Analyses of Income Inequality," *American Sociological Review*, 45 (June): 497–501.

Weiner, Myron (1987). "Empirical Democratic Theory." In Myron Weiner and Ergun Ozbudun (eds), *Competitive Elections in Developing Countries*. Durham, NC: Duke University Press: Chapter 1.

Weisberg, Laurie S., and Harry M. Scoble (1981). "Problems of Comparative Research on Human Rights." In Ved P. Nanda, James R. Scarritt, and George W. Shepherd, Jr (eds), *Global Human Rights: Public Policies, Comparative Measures, and NGO Strategies*. Boulder, CO: Westview: Chapter 10.

Welling, Judith V. (2008). "International Indicators and Economic, Social, and Cultural Rights," *Human Rights Quarterly*, 30 (4): 933–58.

Whitten-Woodring, Jennifer (2009). "Watchdog or Lapdog? Media Freedom, Regime Type, and Government Respect for Human Rights," *International Studies Quarterly*, 53 (3): 595–625.

Wolpin, Miles (1986). "State Terrorism and Repression in the Third World: Parameters and Prospects." In Michael Stohl and George A. Lopez (eds), *Government Violence and Repression*. New York: Greenwood: Chapter 5.

Wood, Reed M. (2008). "'A Hand upon the Throat of the Nation': Economic Sanctions and State Repression, 1976–2001," *International Studies Quarterly*, 52 (3): 489–513.

Wood, Reed M., and Mark Gibney (2010). "The Political Terror Scale (PTS): A Re-Introduction and Comparison to CIRI," *Human Rights Quarterly*, 32 (2): 367–400.

Zanger, Sabine C. (2000). "A Global Analysis of the Effect of Regime Change on Life Integrity Violations, 1977–1993," *Journal of Peace Research*, 37 (2): 213–33.

Ziegenhagen, Eduard A. (1986). *The Regulation of Political Conflict*. New York: Praeger.

Ziegler, Harmon (1988). "The Interrelationships of Freedom, Equality, and Development." In *Freedom in the World*. Lanham, MD: Freedom House: 203–28.

Zvobgo, Eddison J. M. (1979). "A Third World View." In Donald P. Kommers and Gilburt D. Loescher (eds), *Human Rights and American Foreign Policy*. Notre Dame, IN: University of Notre Dame Press: Chapter 5.

▌CHAPTER 9: United Nations Charter-Based Organizations

Abouharb, M. Rodwan, and David L. Cingranelli (2006). "The Human Rights Effects of World Bank Structural Adjustment, 1981–2000," *International Studies Quarterly*, 50 (June): 233–62.

Alexander, Michael (1999). "Refugee Status Determination Conducted by UNHCR," *International Journal of Refugee Law*, 11 (April): 251–88.

Alfredsson, Gudmundur, and Rolf Ring (eds) (2000). *The Inspection Panel of the World Bank: A Different Complaints Procedure*. Leiden, Netherlands: Brill.

Annan, Kofi (2005). *In Larger Freedom: Towards Development, Security and Human Rights for All*. New York: United Nations, Department of Information.

Annan, Kofi (2012). *Intervention: A Life in War and Peace*. New York: Penguin.

Arnove, Anthony (ed) (2002). *Iraq under Siege: The Deadly Impact of Sanctions and War*. 2nd edn. Boston: South End Press.

Bain, William (2003). *Between Anarchy and Society: Trusteeship and the Obligations of Power*. New York: Oxford University Press.

Bauhr, Monika, and Naghmed Nasirtousi (2012). "How Do International Organizations Promote Quality of Government? Contestation, Integration, and the Limits of IO Power," *International Studies Review*, 14 (4): 541–66.

Bellamy, Carol (ed) (2004). *The State of the World's Children 2005: Childhood under Threat*. United Nations: UNICEF.

Bellamy, Carol (2005). *Mental Health, Human Rights and Legislation*. United Nations: UNICEF.

Bent, Jacqueline (2012). "Ambiguity and Uncertainty in International Organizations: A History of Debating IMB Conditionality," *International Studies Quarterly*, 56 (4): 674–88.

Blustein, Paul (2001). *The Chastening: Inside the Crisis That Rocked the Global Financial System and Humbled the IMF*. New York: Public Affairs Press.

Bond, Patrick (2004). "Should the World Bank and the IMF Be 'Fixed' or 'Nixed'? Reformist Posturing and Popular Resistance," *Capitalism, Nature, Socialism*, 15 (June): 85–105.

Boserup, Ester (1970). *Women's Role in Economic Development*. New York: St Martin's Press.

Boutros-Ghali, Boutros (1992). "An Agenda for Peace: Preventive Diplomacy, Peacemaking and Peace-Keeping." *Report of the Secretary-General Pursuant to the Statement Adopted by the Summit Meeting of the Security Council on January 31, 1992*. A/47/277 - S/24111, June 17.

Boutros-Ghali, Boutros (1995). *An Agenda for Development*. New York: Office of Public Information, United Nations.

Brysk, Alison, and Gershon Shafir (eds) (2004). *People out of Place: Globalization, Human Rights, and the Citizenship Gap*. New York: Routledge.

Buergenthal, Thomas, and Judith V. Torney (1976). *International Human Rights and International Education*. New York: US National Commission for UNESCO.

Caplan, Richard (2005). *International Governance of War-Torn Territories: Rule and Reconstruction*. New York: Oxford University Press.

Carson, Rachel (1962). *Silent Spring*. Boston: Houghton Mifflin.

Clapp, Jennifer, and Doris Fuchs (eds) (2009). *Corporate Power in Global Agrifood Governance*. Cambridge, MA: MIT Press.

Clark, Dana L. (2002). "The World Bank and Human Rights," *Harvard Human Rights Journal*, 15 (Spring): 205–26.

Cohen, Daniel (2006). *Globalization and Its Enemies*. Cambridge, MA: MIT Press.

Cohen, Roberta, and Francis M. Deep (1998). "Exodus Within Borders: The Uprooted Who Left Home," *Foreign Affairs*, 77 (4): 12–16.

Colclough, Christopher (2005). "Rights, Goals and Targets: How Do Those for Education Add Up?," *Journal of International Development*, 27 (1): 101–11.

Conte, Alex, Scott Davidson, and Richard Burchill (2004). *Defining Civil and Political Rights: The Jurisprudence of the United Nations Human Rights Committee*. Burlington, VT Ashgate.

Cooper, Andrew P., and John J. Kirton (eds) (2009). *Innovation in Global Health Governance*. Burlington, VT: Ashgate.

Cortright, David, and George A. Lopez (2000). *The Sanctions Decade: Assessing UN Strategies in the 1990s*. Boulder, CO: Lynne Rienner.

Dallaire, Roméo (2004). *Shake Hands with the Devil: The Failure of Humanity in Rwanda*. New York: Carroll & Graf.

Daniel, Donald C. F., and Bradd C. Hayes (eds) (1995). *Beyond Traditional Peacekeeping*. New York: St Martin's Press.

Darrow, Mac (2003). *Between Light and Shadow: The World Bank, the International Monetary Fund and International Human Rights Law*. Portland, OR: Hart-Oxford.

De Feyter, Koen (2004). "The International Financial Institutions and Human Rights: Law and Practice," *Human Rights Review*, 6 (10): 59–90.

Dennis, Michael J. (2003). "Human Rights in 2002: The Annual Sessions of the UN Commission on Human Rights and the Economic and Social Council," *American Journal of International Law*, 97 (April): 364–86.

Flood, Patrick James (1998). *The Effectiveness of UN Human Rights Institutions*. Westport, CT: Praeger.

Forsythe, David (2012). "The UN Security Council and Response to Atrocities: International Criminal Law and the P-5," *Human Rights Quarterly*, 34 (3): 840–63.

Green, Nick (2004). "Stonewalling Justice," *Harvard International Review*, 26 (Summer): 34–7.

Haas, Ernst B. (1964). *Beyond the Nation State: Functionalism and International Organization*. Stanford, CA: Stanford University Press.

Haas, Ernst B. (1970). *Human Rights and International Action: The Case of Freedom of Association*. Stanford, CA: Stanford University Press.

Haas, Peter (1992). "Epistemic Communities and International Policy Coordination," *International Organization*, 45(1): 1–35.

Henkin, Louis (1996). *The Age of Rights*. New York: Columbia University Press.

Horta, Korinna (2002). "Rhetoric and Reality: Human Rights and the World Bank," *Harvard Human Rights Journal*, 15 (Spring): 227–44.

Hüfner, Klaus (1998). *How to File Complaints on Human Rights Violations: A Manual for Individuals and NGOs*. Bonn: UNESCO National Commission for Germany.

Ignatieff, Michael (2003). *Empire Lite: Nation-Building in Bosnia, Kosovo and Afghanistan*. London: Vintage.

International Labour Organization (2005). *Rules of the Game: A Brief Introduction to International Labour Standards*. Geneva: International Labour Office.

Joyner, Christopher C. (1999). "The United Nations and Democracy," *Global Governance*, 5 (July–September): 333–57.

Kaufman, Daniel, Aart Kraay, and Pablo Zoido-Lobaton (1999). *Governance Matters*. Washington, DC: World Bank, Policy Research Working Paper 2196 (October).

Kille, Kent (2006). *From Manager to Visionary: The Secretary-General of the United Nations*. New York: Palgrave Macmillan.

Kuczynski, Pedro-Pablo, and John Williamson (eds) (2003). *After the Washington Consensus: Restarting Growth and Reform in Latin America*. Washington, DC: Institute for International Economics.

Lauren, Paul Gordon (2007). "'To Preserve and Build on Its Achievements and to Redress Its Shortcomings': The Journey from the Commission on Human Rights to the Human Rights Council," *Human Rights Review*, 29 (2): 307–45.

Levovic, James H., and Eric Voeten (2006). "The Politics of Shame: The Condemnation of Country Human Rights Practices in the UNCHR," *International Studies Quarterly*, 56 (4): 861–88.

Marquette, Heather (2001). "Corruption, Democracy and the World Bank," *Crime, Law and Social Change*, 36 (4): 395–407.

Mattioli, Maria C., and V. K. Sapovadia (2004). "Laws of Labor," *Harvard International Review*, 26 (Summer): 60–4.

Möller, Jakob T, and Alfred de Zayes (2009). *The United Nations Human Rights Committee Case Law, 1977–2008: A Handbook*. Arlington, VA: Engel.

Oestreich, Joel E. (2004). "The Human Rights Responsibilities of the World Bank," *Global Social Policy*, 4 (1): 55–76.

Ogata, Sadako N. (2005). *The Turbulent Decade: Confronting the Refugee Crises of the 1990s*. New York: Norton.

Ogata, Sadako N., and Barbara John (1996). *The Right of Asylum Must Be Strongly Upheld*. Berlin: Free University of Berlin.

Payer, Cheryl (1974). *The Debt Trap: The IMF and the Third World*. Harmondsworth, UK: Penguin Books.

Payer, Cheryl (1982). *The World Bank: A Critical Analysis*. New York: Monthly Review Press.

Perkins, John (2004). *Confessions of an Economic Hit Man*. San Francisco, CA: Berrett-Koehler Publishers.

Pogge, Thomas (2003). *World Poverty and Human Rights: Cosmopolitan Responsibilities and Reforms*. Oxford, UK: Polity Press.

Ramcharan, Bertrand G. (2002). *The United Nations High Commissioner for Human Rights: The Challenges of International Protection*. New York: Nijhoff.

Roberts, Alisdair (2004). "A Partial Revolution: The Diplomatic Ethos and Transparency in Intergovernmental Organizations," *Public Administrative Review*, 64 (July/August): 410–14.

Salomon, Margot E., Arne Tostensen, and Wouter Vandenhole (eds) (2007). *Casting the Net Wider: Human Rights, Development and New Duty-Bearers*. Oxford, UK: Intersentia Press.

Seybolt, Taylor B. (2009). "Harmonizing the Humanitarian Aid Network: Adaptive Change in a Complex System," *International Studies Quarterly*, 53 (4): 1027–50.

Shawcross, William (2001). *Deliver Us from Evil: Peacekeepers, Warlords, and a World of Endless Conflict*. New York: Simon & Schuster.

Shelton, Dinah (2005). *Remedies in International Human Rights Law*. 2nd edn. New York: Oxford University Press.

Skogly, Sigrun (2000). *The Human Rights Obligations of the World Bank and the IMF*. London: Cavendish.

Stiglitz, Joseph E. (2002). *Globalization and Its Discontents*. New York: Norton.

Subedi, Surya P. (2011). "Protection of Human Rights Through the Mechanism of UN Special Rapporteurs," *Human Rights Quarterly*, 33 (1): 128–47.

Szasz, Paul C. (2002). "The Security Council Starts Legislating," *American Journal of International Law*, 96 (October): 901–5.

Teretta, Meredith (2012). "'We Had Been Fooled into Thinking That the UN Watches over the Entire World': Human Rights, UN Trust Territories, and African Decolonization," *Human Rights Quarterly*, 34 (2): 329–60.

Thakur, Ramesh, and Thomas G. Weiss (2009). "United Nations 'Policy': An Argument with Three Illustrations," *International Studies Perspectives*, 10 (1): 18–35.

Tolley, Howard, Jr (1987). *The UN Commission on Human Rights*. Boulder, CO: Westview.

Tomaševski, Katarina (1997). *Between Sanctions and Elections: Aid Donors and Their Human Rights Performance*. Washington, DC: Pinter.

van Genugten, Willem J. M., and Gerald A. de Groot (eds) (1999). *United Nations Sanctions: Effectiveness and Effects, Especially in the Field of Human Rights: A Multi-Disciplinary Approach*. Antwerp: Intersentia.

Wallensteen, Peter, and Carina Staibano (2005). *International Sanctions: Between Words and Wars in the Global System*. New York: Cass.

Weissbrodt, David, and Rose Farley (1994). "The UNESCO Human Rights Procedure: An Evaluation," *Human Rights Quarterly*, 14 (2): 391–414.

Wilde, Ralph (2001). "From Danzig to East Timor and Beyond: The Role of International Territorial Administration," *European Journal of International Law*, 95 (July): 583–606.

Wilde, Ralph (2008). *International Territorial Administration: How Trusteeship and the Civilizing Mission Never Went Away*. New York: Oxford University Press.

Williams, Sope (2002). "The International Human Rights Obligations of the World Bank and the International Monetary Fund," *Journal of Financial Regulation and Compliance*, 10 (2): 195–9.

Winslow, Anne (ed) (1995). *Women, Politics, and the United Nations*. Westport, CT: Greenwood.

Woods, Ngaire (2006). *The Globalizers: The IMF, the World Bank, and Their Borrowers*. Ithaca, NY: Cornell University Press.

World Bank (2003). *Accountability at the World Bank: The Inspection Panel 10 Years On*. Washington, DC: World Bank.

Zhang, Ruosi (2004). "Food Security: Food Trade Regime and Food Aid Regime," *Journal of International Economic Law*, 7 (3): 565–84.

Zinn, Howard (2003). *A People's History of the United States*. New York: HarperCollins.

CHAPTER 10: Treaty-Based Global International Organizations

Addo, Michael (2010). "Practice of United Nations Human Rights Treaty Bodies in the Reconciliation of Cultural Diversity with Universal Respect for Human Rights," *Human Rights Quarterly*, 32 (6): 601–64.

Attanasio, John B. (1995–1996). "Rapporteur's Overview and Conclusion: Of Sovereignty, Globalization, and Courts," *New York University Journal of International Law and Politics*, 28 (1): 1–33.

Barria, Lilian A., and Steven D. Roper (2005). "Providing Justice and Reconciliation: The Criminal Tribunals for Sierra Leone and Cambodia," *Human Rights Review*, 7 (10): 5–26.

Bass, Gary J. (2000). *Stay the Hand of Vengeance: The Politics of War Crimes Tribunals*. Princeton, NJ: Princeton University Press.

Bayefsky, Anne F. (ed) (2000). *The UN Human Rights Treaty System in the 21st Century*. Boston: Kluwer Law International.

Bedjaoui, Mohammed (1995–1996). "The Reception by National Courts of Decisions of International Tribunals," *New York University Journal of International Law and Politics*, 28 (1): 45–64.

Boucher, David (2009). *The Limits of Ethics in International Relations: Natural Law, Natural Rights and Human Rights in Transition*. New York: Oxford University Press.

Butler, Israel de Jesús (2004). "A Comparative Analysis of Individual Petitions in Regional and Global Human Rights Protection Mechanisms," *University of Queensland Law Journal*, 23 (1): 22–53.

Chapman, Audrey R., and Benjamin Carbonetti (2011). "Human Rights Protections for Vulnerable and Disadvantaged Groups: The Contributions of the UN Covenant on Economic Social and Cultural Rights," *Human Rights Quarterly*, 33 (3): 682–732.

Charnovitz, Steve (1994). "The World Trade Organization and Social Issues," *Journal of World Trade*, 28 (5): 17–33.

Cryer, Robert (2005). *Prosecuting International Crimes: Selectivity and the International Criminal Law Regime*. New York: Cambridge University Press.

Dougherty, Beth (2004). "Victims' Justice, Victors' Justice: Iraq's Flawed Tribunal," *Middle East Policy*, 11 (2): 61–74.

Drumbl, Mark A. (2007). *Atrocity, Punishment, and International Law*. New York: Cambridge University Press.

El-Baradei, Mohammed (2011). *The Age of Deception: Nuclear Diplomacy in Treacherous Times*. New York: Metropolitan.

Evatt, Elizabeth (2002). "Finding a Voice for Women's Rights: The Early Years of CEDAW," *George Washington International Law Review*, 34 (3): 515–53.

Gow, James (2003). *The Serbian Project and Its Adversaries: A Strategy of War Crimes*. London: Hurst.

Haas, Michael (2009). *George W. Bush, War Criminal? The Bush Administration's Liability for 269 War Crimes*. Santa Barbara: Praeger.

Hertel, Shareen (2005). "Strategic Bargaining and Protest at the WTO Third Ministerial Meeting," *Human Rights Review*, 6 (3): 102–17.

Heyns, Christof, and Frans Viljoen (eds) (2002). *The Impact of the United Nations Human Rights Treaties at the Domestic Level*. Boston: Kluwer Law International.

Keith, Linda Camp (1999). "The United Nations International Covenant on Civil and Political Rights: Does It Make a Difference in Human Rights Behavior?," *Journal of Peace Research*, 36 (1): 95–118.

Kelly, Tobias (2009). "The UN Committee Against Torture: Human Rights Monitoring and the Legal Recognition of Cruelty," *Human Rights Quarterly*, 31 (3): 777–800.

Kirsche, Philippe (2004). "The Role and Functions of the International Criminal Court," *World Affairs Journal*, 16 (1): 111–18.

Klinghoffer, Arthur Jay, and Judith Apter (2002). *International Citizen's Tribunals: Mobilizing Public Opinion to Advance Human Rights*. New York: Palgrave Macmillan.

López-Hurtado, Carlos (2002). "Social Labelling and WTO Law," *Journal of International Economic Law*, 5 (3): 719–46.

Lutz, Ellen L., and Caitlin Reiger (eds) (2009). *Prosecuting Heads of State*. New York: Cambridge University Press.

McNeil, Desmond, and Asunción Lena St Clair (2009). *Global Poverty, Ethics and Human Rights: The Role of Multilateral Organizations*. New York: Routledge.

Nowak, Manfred, and Elizabeth McArthur (2008). *The United Nations Convention Against Torture: A Commentary*. New York: Oxford University Press.

Oosterveld, Valerie (2009). "Special Court for Sierra Leone's Consideration of Gender-Based Violence: Contribution to Transitional Justice?," *Human Rights Review*, 10 (1): 73–98.

Orentlicher, Diane F. (2010). *That Some Guilty Be Punished? The Impact of ICTY in Bosnia*. New York: Open Society Justice Initiative.

Petersmann, Ernst-Ulrich (2003). "Human Rights and the Law of the World Trade Organization," *Journal of World Trade*, 37 (2): 241–81.

Roach, Steven C. (2006). *Politicizing the International Criminal Court: The Convergence of Politics, Ethics, and Law*. Lanham, MD: Rowman & Littlefield.

Roach, Steven C. (ed) (2009). *Governance, Order and the International Criminal Court: Between Realpolitik and a Cosmopolitan Court*. Oxford, UK: Oxford University Press.

Rodley, Nigel S. (2003). "United Nations Human Rights Treaty Bodies and Special Procedures of the Commission on Human Rights: Complimentarily or Competition?," *Human Rights Quarterly*, 25 (4): 882–908.

Roth, Kenneth (1998). "The Court the US Doesn't Want," *New York Review of Books*, 45 (18): 45–7.

Sands, Philippe (ed) (2003). *Pluralizing International Criminal Justice from Nuremberg to The Hague: The Future of International Criminal Justice*. Cambridge, UK: Cambridge University Press.

Schabas, William A. (2004). *An Introduction to the International Criminal Court*. New York: Cambridge University Press.

Sivakumaran, S. (2004). "The Rights of Migrant Workers One Year On: Transformation or Consolidation?," *Georgetown Journal of International Law*, 36 (Fall): 113–53.

Slaughter, Anne-Marie (2000). "Judicial Globalization," *Virginia Journal of International Law*, 40 (4): 1103–24.

Stein, Michael Ashley, and Janet E. Lord (2010). "Monitoring the Convention on the Rights of Persons with Disabilities: Innovations, Lost Opportunity, and Future Potential," *Human Rights Quarterly*, 33 (30): 689–728.

Subotić, Jelena (2009). *Hijacked Justice: Dealing with Past in the Balkans*. Ithaca, NY: Cornell University Press.

Un, Kheang, and Judy Ledgerwood (2010). "Is the Trial of 'Duch' a Catalyst for Change in Cambodia's Courts?," *Asia Pacific Issues*, 95 (June): 12 pp.

Welch, Claude E., Jr, and Ashley F. Watkins (2011). "Extending Enforcement: The Coalition for the International Criminal Court," *Human Rights Quarterly*, 33 (4): 927–1031.

Wilson, Page (2009). *Aggression, Crime and International Security: Moral, Political, and Legal Dimension of International Relations*. New York: Routledge.

Zoglin, Katie (2005). "The Future of War Crimes Prosecution in the Former Yugoslavia: Accountability or Junk Justice?," *Human Rights Quarterly*, 25 (1): 41–77.

▌ CHAPTER 11: American Approaches to International Human Rights

Anker, Deborah E. (1999). *The Law of Asylum in the United States.* 3rd edn. Boston, MA: Refugee Law Center.

Anziska, Seth (2012). "A Preventable Massacre," *New York Herald Tribune*, September 16.

Apodaca, Clair (2006). *Understanding US Human Rights Policy: A Paradoxical Legacy.* New York: Routledge.

Askari, Hossein G. (2003). *Case Studies of US Economic Sanctions: The Chinese, Cuban, and Iranian Experience.* Westport, CT: Praeger.

Barkan, Elazar (2000). *The Guilt of Nations: Restitution and Negotiating Historical Injustices.* New York: Norton.

Bazyler, Michael J. (2003). *Holocaust Justice: The Battle for Restitution in America's Courts.* New York: New York University Press.

Bluhm, William (2002). *Rogue State: A Guide to the World's Only Superpower.* London: Zed Books.

Burgermann, Susan (2004). "First Do No Harm: US Foreign Policy and Respect for Human Rights in El Salvador and Guatemala." In Debra Liang-Fenton (ed), *Implementing US Human Rights Policy.* Washington, DC: US Institute of Peace Press: 267–98.

Chatterjee, Deen K., and Don E. Scheid (eds) (2003). *Ethics and Foreign Intervention.* Cambridge, UK: Cambridge University Press.

Chung, Ellen Y. (2002). "A Double-Edged Sword: Reconciling the United States' International Obligations under the Convention Against Torture," *Emory Law Journal*, 51 (Winter): 355–78.

Cutrone, Ellen A., and Benjamin O. Fordham (2011). "Commerce and Imagination: The Sources of Concern about International Human Rights in the US Congress," *International Studies Quarterly*, 54 (3): 633–55.

Danner, Mark (2004). *Torture and Truth: America, Abu Ghraib, and the War on Terror.* New York: New York Review Books.

de Grazia, Victoria (2006). *Irresistible Empire: America's Advance Through Twentieth-Century Europe.* Cambridge, MA: Belknap.

Diven, Polly (2006). "A Coincidence of Interests: The Hyperpluralism of US Food Aid Policy," *Foreign Policy Analysis*, 2 (2006): 307–24.

Dobson, Alan P. (2002). *US Economic Statecraft for Survival, 1933–1991: Of Sanctions, Embargoes, and Economic Warfare.* New York: Routledge.

Drury, A. Cooper, and Yitan Li (2006). "US Economic Sanction Threats Against China: Failing to Leverage Better Human Rights," *Foreign Policy Analysis*, 2 (October): 307–24.

Early, Bryan R. (2011). "Unmasking the Black Knights: Sanctions Busters and Their Effects on the Success of Economic Sanctions," *Foreign Policy Analysis*, 7 (4): 381–402.

EarthRights International (2004). *In Our Court: ATCA, Sosa, and the Triumph of Human Rights.* Washington, DC: EarthRights International.

Eizenstat, Stuart E. (2003). *Imperfect Justice: Looted Assets, Slave Labor, and the Unfinished Business of World War II.* New York: Public Affairs.

Etzioni, Amitai (1962). *The Hard Way to Peace: A New Strategy.* New York: Collier.

Farer, Tom (2008). "Un-Just War Against Terrorism and the Struggle to Appropriate Human Rights," *Human Rights Quarterly*, 30 (2): 356–403.

Fielding, Alex (2008). "Yahoo? Reining in the Wild West with the Alien Tort Claims Act," *Human Rights Review*, 9 (4): 513–23.

Fry, Earl H. (1998). *The Expanding Role of State and Local Governments in U.S. Foreign Affairs.* New York: Council on Foreign Relations.

George, Alexander L., David K. Hall, and William E. Simons (1971). *The Limits of Coercive Diplomacy: Laos, Cuba, Vietnam.* Boston: Little Brown.

Guay, Terrence (2000). "Local Government and Global Politics: The Implications of Massachusetts' 'Burma Law'," *Political Science Quarterly*, 113 (Fall): 353–76.

Haas, Michael (2009). *George W. Bush, War Criminal? The Bush Administration's Liability for 269 War Crimes.* Westport, CT: Praeger.

Haas, Michael (2010). *America's War Crimes Quagmire, from Bush to Obama.* Los Angeles: Publishinghouse for Scholars.

Hawkins, Darren (2003). "Universal Jurisdiction for Human Rights: From Legal Principle to Limited Reality," *Global Governance*, 9 (3): 347–65.

Hertzke, Allen D. (2000). "Defending the Faiths," *The National Interest*, 61 (Fall): 74–81.

Hufbauer, Gary C., Jeffrey J. Schott, and Kimberly A. Elliott (1990). *Economic Sanctions Reconsidered: History and Current Policy*. 3rd edn. Washington, DC: Institute for International Economics.

Ignatieff, Michael (2004). *The Lesser Evil: Political Ethics in an Age of Terror*. Princeton, NJ: Princeton University Press.

Kim, Moonhawk (2012). "Ex Ante Due Diligence: Formation of PTAs and Protection of Labor Rights," *International Studies Quarterly*, 56 (4): 704–19.

Klare, Michael T., Cynthia Arnson, Delia Miller, and Daniel Volman (1981). *Supplying Repression: US Support for Authoritarian Regimes Abroad*. Washington, DC: Institute for Policy Studies.

Lelyveld, Joseph (2007). "No Exit," *New York Review of Books*, 54 (February 15): 12–17.

Levi, Werner (2004). "International Statecraft." In Michael Haas (ed), *International Systems*. San Francisco: Chandler.

Liste, Philip (2008). "Articulating the Nexus of Politics and Law: War in Iraq and the Practice within Two Legal Systems," *International Political Sociology*, 2 (1): 38–55.

Murphy, Sean D. (1999). "US Involvement in Claims by Victims of the German Holocaust or Their Heirs," *American Journal of International Law*, 93 (October): 883–92.

O'Connor, Sandra Day (1995–1996). Federalism of Free Nations," *New York University Journal of International Law and Politics*, 28 (1): 35–43.

Posner, Eric (2009). *The Perils of Global Legalism*. Chicago, IL: University of Chicago Press.

Power, Samantha (2002). *"A Problem from Hell": America in the Age of Genocide*. New York: Basic Books.

Romano, Cesare P. R. (ed) (2009). *The Sword and the Scales: The United States and International Courts and Tribunals*. New York: Cambridge University Press.

Roth, Kenneth (2004). "The Fight Against Terrorism: The Bush Administration's Dangerous Neglect of Human Rights." In Thomas G. Weiss, Margaret E. Crahan, and John Goering (eds), *Wars on Terrorism and Iraq: Human Rights, Unilateralism and US Foreign Policy*. London: Routledge: 113–31.

Rubenzer, Trevor, and Steven B. Redd (2010). "Ethnic Minority Groups and US Foreign Policy: Examining Congressional Decision Making and Economic Sanctions," *International Studies Quarterly*, 54 (3): 755–77.

Scott, James M., and Carie A. Steele (2011). "Sponsoring Democracy: The United States and Democracy Aid to the Developing World, 1988–2001," *International Studies Quarterly*, 55 (1): 47–69.

Slaughter, Anne-Marie, and David Bosco (2000). "Plaintiff's Diplomacy," *Foreign Affairs*, 79 (5): 102–16.

Steinhardt, Ralph G., and Anthony A. D'Amato (eds) (1999). *The Alien Tort Claims Act: An Analytical Anthology*. Ardsley, NY: Transnational Publishers.

Stephens, Beth (2002). "Translating Filartiga: A Comparative and International Law Analysis of Domestic Remedies For International Human Rights Violations," *Yale Journal of International Law*, 27 (1): 1–57.

Tarnoff, Curt, and Larry Nowels (2005). *Foreign Aid: An Introductory Overview of US Programs and Policy*. Washington, DC: Congressional Research Service.

Tomaševski, Katarina (1997). *Between Sanctions and Elections: Aid Donors and Their Human Rights Performance*. Washington, DC: Pinter.

Townley, Stephen (2006). "Kilburn v. Libya: Cause for Alarm?," *Yale Law Journal*, 115 (5): 1177–85.

United States, Nazi War Criminal Records Interagency Working Group (1999). *Implementation of the Nazi War Crimes Disclosure Act: An Interim Report to Congress*. Washington, DC: The National Archives.

Vázquez, Carlos Manuel (1995). "The Four Doctrines of Self-Executing Treaties," *American Journal of International Law*, 89 (4): 695.

Warde, Ibrahim (2007). *The Price of Fear: The Truth Behind the Financial War on Terror*. Berkeley: University of California Press.

White, Richard Alan (2004). *Breaking Silence: The Case That Changed the Face of Human Rights*. Washington, DC: Georgetown University Press.

Woodward, Bob (2004). *Plan of Attack*. New York: Simon & Schuster.

Zinn, Howard (2003). *A People's History of the United States*. New York: HarperCollins.

CHAPTER 12: European Approaches to International Human Rights

Alston, Philip (ed) (1999). *The EU and Human Rights*. New York: Oxford University Press.

Archer, Clive, and Stephen Maxwell (eds) (1980). *The Nordic Model: Studies in Public Policy Innovation*. Farnborough, UK: Gower.

Azimov, Anvar (2005). "OSCE at the Crossroads," *International Affairs* (Moscow), 51 (2): 57–66.

Bajaj, Monisha (2011). "Human Rights Education: Ideology, Location, and Approaches," *Human Rights Quarterly*, 33 (2): 481–508.

Bernhard, Stefan (2011). "Beyond Constructivism: The Political Sociology of an EU Policy Field," *International Political Sociology*, 5 (4): 426–45.

Boyle, Kevin (ed) (2008). *New Institutions for Human Rights Protection*. New York: Oxford University Press.

Christiansen, T., and E. Kirchner (eds) (2000). *Committee Governance in the European Union*. Manchester, UK: Manchester University Press.

Christou, Theodorea A., and Juan Pablo Raymond (eds) (2005). *European Court of Human Rights: Remedies and Execution of Judgments*. London: British Institute of International and Comparative Law.

Cichowsky, Rachel A. (2007). *The European Court and Civil Society: Litigation, Mobilization and Governance*. Cambridge, UK: Cambridge University Press.

Clauwaert, Stefan (ed) (1998). *Fundamental Social Rights in the European Union: Comparative Tables and Documents*. Brussels: European Trade Union Institute.

Coombes, David L. (1979). *The Future of the European Parliament*. London: Policy Studies Institute.

Costa, Jean-Paul (2003). "The European Court of Human Rights and Its Recent Case Law," *Texas International Law Journal*, 38 (3): 455–67.

Crawford, Oliver (1970). *Done This Day: The European Idea in Action*. London: Hart-Davis.

Donkerly, Craig G. (2004). "Considering Security Amidst Strategic Change: The OSCE Experience," *Middle East Policy*, 11 (Fall): 131–8.

Ellert, Robert B. (1963). *NATO "Fair Trial" Safeguards: Precursor to an International Bill of Procedural Rights*. The Hague: Nijhoff.

European Movement (1949). *European Movement and the Council of Europe*. With Forewords by W. S. Churchill and P.-H. Spaak. New York: Hutchinson.

European Union, Council (2000–). *Annual Report on Human Rights*. Luxembourg: Office for Official Publications of the European Communities.

Gilbert, Geoff (1996). "The Council of Europe and Minority Rights," *Human Rights Quarterly*, 18 (February): 160–89.

Gilbert, Geoff (2002). "The Burgeoning Minority Rights Jurisprudence of the European Court of Human Rights," *Human Rights Quarterly*, 24 (3): 736–80.

Greer, Scott (2008). "What's Wrong with the European Convention on Human Rights?," *Human Rights Quarterly*, 30 (3): 680–703.

Haas, Ernst B. ([1958] 2004). *The Uniting of Europe: Political, Social, and Economic Forces, 1950–1957*. Notre Dame, IN: University of Notre Dame Press.

Haas, Ernst B. (1960). *Consensus Formation in the Council of Europe*. Berkeley: University of California Press.

Harris, Seth R. (2000). "Asian Human Rights: Forming a Regional Covenant," *Asian-Pacific Law & Policy Journal*, 1 (June): 1–22.

Heyns, Christof (2002). *Human Rights Law in Africa*, Vol. 4. Amsterdam: Brill.

Hix, Simon, Abdul G. Noury, and Gérard Roland (2007). *Democratic Politics in the European Parliament*. Cambridge, UK: Cambridge University Press.

Hopmann, P. Terrence (2003). "Managing Conflict in Post-Cold War Eurasia: The Rise of the OSCE in Europe's Security 'Architecture'," *International Politics*, 40 (1): 75–100.

Johnstone, Ian (2003). "The Rule of the UN Secretary-General: The Power of Persuasion Based on Law," *Global Governance*, 9 (October–December): 441–58.

Jordan, Pamela A. (2003). "Does Membership Have Its Privileges? Entrance into the Council of Europe and Compliance with Human Rights Norms," *Human Rights Quarterly*, 25 (August): 660–91.

Katsumata, Hiro (2004). "Why Is ASEAN Diplomacy Changing from 'Non-Interference' to 'Open and Frank Discussions'?," *Asian Survey*, 44 (2): 237–54.

Kechichian, Joseph A. (1994). *Security Efforts in the Arab World: A Brief Examination of Four Regional Organizations*. Santa Monica, CA: Rand Corporation.

Knaus, Gerald, and Marcus Cox (2005). "The 'Helsinki Movement' in Southeastern Europe," *Journal of Democracy*, 16 (January): 39–53.

Knodt, Michèle, and Sebastian Princen (eds) (2003). *Understanding the European Union's External Relations*. London: Routledge.

Lindfeldt, Mats (2007). *Fundamental Rights in the European Union: Towards Higher Law of the Land? A Study of the Status of Fundamental Rights in a Broader Constitutional Setting*. Abo, Finland: Akademi University Press.

Mahncke, Dieter, Wyn Rees, and Wayne C. Thompson (2004). *Redefining Transatlantic Security Relations: The Challenge of Change*. Manchester, UK: Manchester University Press.

Maksoud, Clovis (1995). "Diminished Sovereignty, Enhanced Sovereignty: United Nations–Arab League Relations at 50," *Middle East Journal*, 49 (Autumn): 582–94.

Manby, Bronwen (2004). "The African Union, NEPAD, and Human Rights: The Missing Agenda," *Human Rights Quarterly*, 26 (November): 983–1027.

Marshall, Jill (2008). "Conditions for Freedom? European Human Rights Law and the Islamic Headscarf Debate," *Human Rights Quarterly*, 30 (3): 631–54.

Melby, Karl (ed) (2000). *The Nordic Model of Marriage and the Welfare State*. Copenhagen: Nordic Council.

Mohan, Giles, Bob Milward, and Alfred B. Zack-Williams (eds) (2000). *Structural Adjustment: Theory, Practice and Impacts*. New York: Routledge.

Moir, Lindsay (2003). "Law and the Inter-American Human Rights System," *Human Rights Quarterly*, 25 (1): 182–212.

Nicoladis, Kalypso (2004). "'We the Peoples of Europe …'," *Foreign Affairs*, 83 (November–December): 97–110.

Norton-Taylor, Richard (2012). "CIA 'Tortured and Sodomised' Terror Suspect, Human Rights Court Rules," *Guardian*, December 13.

O'Flaherty, Michael (2004). "Sierra Leone's Peace Process: The Role of the Human Rights Community," *Human Rights Quarterly*, 26 (February): 29–62.

Organization for Security and Cooperation in Europe (1998). *Combating Torture and Other Cruel, Inhuman or Degrading Treatment or Punishment: The Role of the OSCE*. Warsaw: Organization for Security and Cooperation in Europe, Office for Democratic Institutions & Human Rights.

Packer, Corrine A. A., and Donald Rukare (2002). "The New African Union and Its Constitutive Act," *American Journal of International Law*, 46 (2): 365–79.

Pastor, Robert (1987). *Condemned to Repetition: The United States and Nicaragua*. Princeton, NJ: Princeton University Press.

Patel, Preeri, and Paolo Tripodi (2001). "The Challenge of Peacekeeping in Africa," *Contemporary Review*, 279 (March): 144–50.

Peers, Steve, and Angela Ward (eds) (2004). *The European Union Charter of Fundamental Rights*. Portland, OR: Hart.

Petersmann, Ernst-Ulrich (2002). "Time for a United Nations 'Global Compact' for Integrating Human Rights into the Law of Worldwide Organizations: Lessons from European Integration," *European Journal of International Law*, 13 (3): 621–50.

Reid, T. R. (2004). *The United States of Europe: The New Superpower and the End of American Supremacy*. New York: Penguin.

Ress, Georg (2005). "The Effect of Decisions and Judgments of the European Court of Human Rights in the Domestic Legal Order," *Texas International Law Journal*, 40 (3): 359–82.

Robertson, A. H. (1961). *The Council of Europe: Its Structure, Functions and Achievements*. With a Foreword by Guy Mollet. 2nd edn. New York: Praeger.

Sabatello, Maya (2011). "Advancing Family Rights Through Science: A Proposal for an Alternative Framework," *Human Rights Quarterly*, 23 (1): 43–75.

Sabel, Jonathan Zeitlin (ed) (2010). *Experimentalist Governance in the European Union: Toward a New Architecture.* Oxford, UK: Oxford University Press.

Schubert, Carlos Bohigas, and Hans Martens (2005). *The Nordic Model: Recipe for Success?* Brussels: European Policy Center.

Tallberg, Jonas (2006). *Leadership and Negotiation in the European Union.* Cambridge, UK: Cambridge University Press.

Tang, James T. H. (ed) (1995). *Human Rights and International Relations in the Asia-Pacific Region.* New York: St Martin's Press.

Tennberg, Monica (1998). *The Arctic Council: A Study in Governmentality.* Rovaniemi, Finland: University of Lapland Press.

Thies, Wallace J. (2009). *Why NATO Endures.* New York: Cambridge University Press.

Tomaševski, Katarina (1997). *Between Sanctions and Elections: Aid Donors and Their Human Rights Performance.* Washington, DC: Pinter.

Tömmel, Ingeborg, and Amy Verdun (eds) (2009). *Innovative Governance in the European Union: The Politics of Multilevel Policymaking.* Boulder, CO: Rienner.

Voelen, Erik (2008). "The Impartiality of International Judges: Evidence from the European Court of Human Rights," *American Political Science Review*, 102 (4): 417–33.

Westlake, Martin (1999). *The Council of the European Union.* London: Catermill.

Williams, Andrew J. (2004). *EU Human Rights Policies: A Study in Irony.* New York: Oxford University Press.

CHAPTER 13: Developing Country Approaches to International Human Rights

Acharya, Amitav (2011). "Engagement and Entrapment? Scholarship and Policymaking on Asian Regionalism," *International Studies Review*, 13 (1): 18–23.

Adebajo, Adakeye (2002). *Building Peace in West Africa: Liberia, Sierra Leone, and Guinea-Bissau.* Boulder, CO: Rienner.

Al Attar, Mohsen, and Rosalie Miller (2010). "Towards an Emancipatory International Law: The Bolivian Reconstruction," *Third World Quarterly*, 31 (3): 347–63.

Bach, Daniel (ed) (1999). *Regionalization in Africa: Integration and Disintegration.* Bloomington: Indiana University Press.

Bösl, Anton, and Joseph Diescho (2009). *Human Rights in Africa: Legal Perspectives on Their Protection and Promotion.* New York: Macmillan.

Boyle, Kevin (ed) (2008). *New Institutions for Human Rights Protection.* New York: Oxford University Press.

Buergenthal, Thomas, and Dinah Shelton (1995). *Protecting Human Rights in the Americas: Cases and Material.* Kehl, VA: Engel Publisher.

Burgorgue-Larsen, Laurence, and Amaya Ubeda de Torres (2011). *The Inter-American Court of Human Rights: Case Law and Commentary.* Oxford, UK: Oxford University Press.

Byrnes, Andrew C., Andrea Durbach, and Catherine Renshaw (2008). "Joining the Club: The Asia Pacific Forum of National Human Rights Institutions, the Paris Principles, and the Advancement of the Human Rights Protection of the Region," *Australian Journal of Human Rights*, 14 (1): 63–89.

Ciorciari, John D. (2012). "ASEAN Intergovernmental Commission on Human Rights," *Human Rights Quarterly*, 34 (3): 695–724.

Crone, Donald (1993). "Does Hegemony Matter? The Reorganization of the Pacific Political Economy," *World Politics*, 45 (4): 501–25.

Dash, Kishore C. (2008). *Regionalism in South Asia: Negotiating Cooperation, Institutional Structures.* New York: Routledge.

Davidson, Scott (1997). *The Inter-American Human Rights System.* Brookfield, VT: Ashgate.

Doebbler, Curtis Francis (2002). "Reading the African Charter on Human and Peoples' Rights," *Texas International Law Journal*, 37 (1): 227–30.

Domínguez, Francisco, and Marcos Guedes de Oliveira (eds) (2004). *Mercosur: Between Integration and Democracy*. New York: Oxford University Press.

Duffield, John (2001). "Why Is There No APTO? Why Is There No OSCASP? Asia-Pacific Security Institutions in Comparative Perspective," *Contemporary Security Policy*, 22 (2): 69–95.

Evans, Malcolm D., and Rachel Murray (eds) (2008). *The African Charter on Human and Peoples' Rights: The System in Practice 1986–2006*. 2nd edn. New York: Cambridge University Press.

Fawcett, Louise, and Andrew Hurrell (eds) (1995). *Regionalism in World Politics: Regional Organization and International Order*. New York: Oxford University Press.

Fiss, Owen (2009). "Within Reach of the State: Prosecuting Atrocities in Africa," *Human Rights Quarterly*, 31 (1): 59–69.

Flint, Julie, and Alex de Waal (2005). *Darfur: A Short History of a Long War*. London: Zed Books.

Goldman, Robert K. (2009). "History and Action: The Inter-American Human Rights System and the Role of the Inter-American Commission on Human Rights," *Human Rights Quarterly*, 31 (4): 839–55.

Grieco, Joseph M. (1999). "Realism and Regionalism: American Power and German and Japanese Institutional Strategies During and After the Cold War." In Ethan B. Kapstein and Michael Mastandono (eds), *Unipolar Politics: Realism and State Strategies after the Cold War*. New York: Columbia University Press: 107–31.

Grossman, Claudio (2012). "Challenges to Freedom of Expression within the Inter-American System: A Jurisprudential Analysis," *Human Rights Quarterly*, 34 (2): 361–403.

Guicherd, Catherine (2007). *The AU in Sudan: Lessons for the African Standby Force*, New York: International Peace Academy.

Haas, Michael (1989a). *The Asian Way to Peace: A Story of Regional Cooperation*. New York: Praeger.

Haas, Michael (1989b). *The Pacific Way: Regional Cooperation in the South Pacific*. New York: Praeger.

Haas, Michael (2013). *Asian and Pacific Regional Cooperation: Turning Zones of Conflict into Arenas of Peace*. New York: Palgrave Macmillan.

Harris, David J., and Stephen Livingstone (eds) (1998). *The Inter-American System of Human Rights*. New York: Oxford University Press.

Kahler, Miles (2000). "Legalization Strategy: The Asia-Pacific Case," *International Quarterly*, 54 (3): 549–71.

Katzenstein, Peter (1997). "Introduction: Asian Regionalism in Comparative Perspective." In Peter Katzenstein and Takeshi Shirashi (eds), *Network Power: Japan and Asia*. Ithaca, NY: Cornell University Press: 1–46.

Killander, Magnus (2008). "The African Peer Review Mechanism and Human Rights: The First Review and the Way Forward," *Human Rights Quarterly*, 30 (1): 41–75.

Lee Yoong Yoong (ed) (2011). *ASEAN Matters! Reflecting on the Association of Southeast Asian Nations*. Singapore: World Scientific Publishing Company.

MacDonald, Robert W. (1965). *The League of Arab States: A Study in Regional Organization*. Princeton, NJ: Princeton University Press.

Murray, Rachel (2004). *Human Rights in Africa: From the OAU to the African Union*. New York: Cambridge University Press.

Mutua, Makau (ed) (2009). *Human Rights NGOs in East Africa: Political and Normative Tensions*. Philadelphia: University of Pennsylvania Press.

Nischalke, Tobias (2002). "Does ASEAN Measure Up?: Post-Cold War Diplomacy and the Idea of Regional Community," *Pacific Review*, 15 (1): 89–117.

Nye, Joseph S., Jr (ed) (1968). *International Regionalism: Readings*. Boston: Little, Brown.

Oosthuizen, Gabriël (2006). *The Southern African Development Community: The Organisation, Its History, Policies and Prospects*. Midrand, South Africa: Institute for Global Dialogue.

Ravenhill, John (2001). *APEC and the Construction of Pacific Rim Regionalism*. New York: Cambridge University Press.

Ravenhill, John (2002). "A Three Bloc World? The New East Asian Regionalism," *International Relations of the Asia-Pacific*, 2 (2): 167–95.

Rubio-Marín, Ruth, and Clara Sandoval (2011). "Engendering the Reparations Jurisprudence of the Inter-American Court of Human Rights: The Promise of the Cotton Fields Judgment," *Human Rights Quarterly*, 33 (4): 1062–91.

Ryan, Curtis R. (1998). "Jordan and the Rise and Fall of the Arab Cooperation Council," *Middle East Journal*, 52 (Summer): 386–401.

Salafi, Ali (1989). *The League of Arab States: Role and Objectives*. Washington, DC: Arab Information Center.

Shelton, Dinah (2008). *Regional Protection of Human Rights*. New York: Oxford University Press.

Tinto, Mónica Feria (2007). "Justiciability of Economic, Social, and Cultural Rights in the Inter-American System of Protection of Human Rights: Beyond Traditional Paradigms and Notions," *Human Rights Review*, 29 (2): 431–59.

White, Lucie E., and Jeremy Perelman (eds) (2011). *Stones of Hope: How African Activists Reclaim Human Rights to Challenge Global Poverty*. Stanford, CA: Stanford University Press.

Zachariah, George (2004). "Regional Framework for State Reconstruction in the Democratic Republic of the Congo," *Journal of International Affairs*, 58 (Fall): 215–36.

CHAPTER 14: New Dimensions and Challenges

The Advocate (2006). "Death by Sodomy," *The Advocate*, (September) 12: 25.

Andonova, Liliana G., Michele Betsill, and Hariet Bulkeley (2009). "Transnational Climate Governance," *Global Environment Politics*, 9 (2): 52–73.

Angle, Stephen C. (2008). "Human Rights and Harmony," *Human Rights Quarterly*, 30 (1): 71–94.

Bakker, Karen (2010). *Privatizing Water: Governance Failure and the World's Urban Water Crisis*. Ithaca, NY: Cornell University Press.

Baldwin, Belinda (2006). "L.A., 1/1/67: The Black Cat Riots," *Gay & Lesbian Review*, 13 (2): 28–30.

Bauer, Joanne (ed) (2006). *Forging Environmentalism: Justice, Livelihood, and Contested Environments*. New York: Sharpe.

Berg, Charles, and Allen Clifford (1958). *The Problem of Homosexuality*. New York: Citadel Press.

Betsill, Michele, and Elisabeth Corell (eds) (2008). *NGO Diplomacy: The Influence of Nongovernmental Organizations in International Environmental Negotiations*. Cambridge, MA: MIT Press.

Bierman, Frank, and Bernd Siebenhuner (eds) (2009). *Managers of Global Change: The Influence of International Environmental Bureaucracies*. Cambridge, MA: MIT Press.

Biswas, Asit, Eglal Rached, and Cecilia Tortajada (eds) (2008). *Water as a Human Right for the Middle East and North Africa*. London: Routledge.

Blanco, Elena, and Jona Razzaque (2009). "Ecosystem Services and Human Well-Being in a Globalized World: Assessing the Role of Law," *Human Rights Quarterly*, 31 (30): 692–720.

Boswell, John (1994). *Same-Sex Unions in Premodern Europe*. New York: Villard.

Boyle, Alan. E., and David Freestone (1999). *International Law and Sustainable Development: Past Achievements and Future Challenges*. New York: Oxford University Press.

Breitmeier, Helmut, Arild Underdal, and Oran R. Young (2011). "The Effectiveness of International Environmental Regimes: Comparing and Contrasting Findings from Quantitative Research," *International Studies Review*, 13 (4): 579–605.

Broome, Arthur (1824). *Prospectus of the SPCA*. Vol. 2. London: SPCA Records.

Brown, Weiss, Edith Jacobson, and Harold Jacobson (1998). *Engaging Countries: Strengthening Compliance with International Environmental Accords*. Cambridge, MA: MIT Press.

Burkett, Maxine (2011). "In Search of Refuge: Pacific Islands, Climate-Induced Migration, and the Legal Frontier," *Asia Pacific Issues*, 98 (January): 8 pp.

Carson, Rachel (1962). *Silent Spring*. Boston: Houghton Mifflin.

Chapouthier, Georges, and Jean-Claude Nouët (eds) (1998). *The Universal Declaration of Animal Rights: Comments and Intentions*. Paris: Ligue Française des Droits de l'Animal.

Clapp, Jennifer, and Doris Fuchs (eds) (2009). *Corporate Power in Global Agrifood Governance*. Cambridge, MA: MIT Press.

Conca, Ken (2006). *Governing Water: Contentious Transnational Politics and Global Institution Building*. Cambridge, MA: MIT Press.

Cruikshank, Margaret (1992). *The Gay and Lesbian Liberation Movement.* New York: Routledge.

Currah, Paisley, Richard M. Juang, and Shannon Price Minter (eds) (2006). *Transgender Rights.* Minneapolis: University of Minnesota Press.

Dauvergne, Peter (1997). *Shadows in the Forest: Japan and the Politics of Timber in Southeast Asia.* Cambridge, MA: MIT Press.

Delmas, Magali, and Oran R. Young (eds) (2009). *Governance for the Environment: New Perspectives.* New York: Cambridge University Press.

Dembour, Marie-Bénédite (2010). "What Are Human Rights? Four Schools of Thought," *Human Rights Quarterly*, 32 (1): 1–20.

DeSombre, Elizabeth R. (2006). *Global Environmental Institutions.* New York: Taylor and Francis.

Dombrowsky, Daniel A. (1984). *The Philosophy of Vegetarianism.* Amherst, MA: University of Massachusetts Press.

Donnelly, Jack (2007). "The Relative Universality of Human Rights," *Human Rights Quarterly*, 29 (2): 281–306.

Engel, Stephen M. (2001). *The Unfinished Revolution: Social Movement Theory and the Gay and Lesbian Movement.* New York: Cambridge University Press.

Evans, Tony (1998). *Human Rights Fifty Years On: A Reappraisal.* Manchester, UK: Manchester University Press.

Falk, Richard A. (1974). "Ecocide, Genocide, and the Nuremberg Tradition of Individual Responsibility." In Virginia Held, Sidney Morgenbesser, and Thomas Nagel (eds), *Philosophy, Morality, and International Affairs.* New York: Oxford University Press: 123–37.

Falk, Richard A. (1984). "Environmental Disruption by Military Means and International Law." In A. H. Westing (ed), *Environmental Warfare: A Technical, Legal, and Policy Appraisal.* Philadelphia, PA: Taylor & Francis: 33–51.

Fields, A. Belden (2003). *Rethinking Human Rights for the New Millennium.* New York: Palgrave Macmillan.

Flannery, Tim (2012). "On the Minds of the Whales," *New York Review of Books*, 59 (2): 34–36.

Francione, Gary L. (2000). *Introduction to Animal Rights: Your Child or the Dog?* Philadelphia, PA: Temple University Press.

Géraud, André (1924). *A Declaration of Animal Rights.* Essay appeared as selection in other's books.

Gehring, Thomas, and Isabel Plocher (2009). "Making an Administrative Trustee Agent Accountable: Reason-Based Decision Making within the Kyoto Protocol's Clean Development Mechanism," *International Studies Quarterly*, 53 (3): 669–93.

Gillis, Justin, and John M. Broder (2012). "With Carbon Dioxide Emissions at Record High, Worries on How to Slow Warming," *New York Times*, December 2.

Godlovitch, Stanley, Roslind Godlovitch, and John Harris (eds) (1971). *Animals, Men and Morals: An Enquiry into the Maltreatment of Non-Humans.* New York: Taplinger.

Haas, Peter, Robert O. Keohane, and Marc A. Levy (eds) (1993). *Institutions of the Earth: Sources of Effective International Environmental Protection.* Cambridge, MA: MIT Press.

Hardin, Garett (1968). "The Tragedy of the Commons," *Science*, 162 (3859): 1243–48.

Hayward, Tim (2005). *Constitutional Environmental Rights.* Oxford, UK: Oxford University Press.

Hegarty, Angela, and Siobhan Leonard (eds) (1999). *Human Rights: An Agenda for the 21st Century.* London: Cavendish.

Helminiak, Daniel A. (1994). *What the Bible Really Says About Homosexuality.* San Francisco, CA: Alamo Square Press.

Hill, Barry E., Steve Wolfson, and Nicholas Targ (2004). "Human Rights and the Environment: A Synopsis and Some Predictions," *Georgetown International Environmental Law Review*, 16 (3): 359–404.

Hiskes, Richard (1994). "Environmental Human Rights and Intergenerational Justice," *Human Rights Review*, 7 (3): 81–95.

Hoffmann, Matthew J. (2005). *Ozone Depletion and Climate Change: Constructing a Global Response.* Albany, NY: SUNY Press.

Howard-Hassmann, Rhoda E. (2012). "Human Security: Undermining Human Rights?," *Human Rights Quarterly*, 34 (1): 88–112.

Ignatieff, Michael (1999). "Human Rights: The Midlife Crisis," *New York Review of Books*, 46 (9): 58–62.

Kausikan, Bilahari (1997). "Asian Versus 'Universal' Human Rights," *The Responsive Community*, 7 (3): 9–21.

Kennedy, Sean (2006). "Jimmy Carter," *The Advocate,* January 17: 6.

Kibel, Paul S. (1999). *The Earth on Trial: Environmental Law on the International Stage*. New York: Routledge.

Kinsey, Alfred C., Wardell B. Pomeroy, and Clyde E. Martin (1948). *Sexual Behavior in the Human Male*. Philadelphia, PA: Saunders.

Klare, Karl E. (1991). "Legal Theory and Democratic Reconstruction: Reflections on 1989," *University of British Columbia Law Review*, 25 (1): 69–103.

Kravchenko, Svilana, and John E. Bonine (2008). *Human Rights and the Environment: Cases, Law and Policy*. Durham, NC: Carolina Academic Press.

Lau, Holning (2004). "Sexual Orientation: Testing the Universality of International Human Rights Law," *University of Chicago Law Review*, 71 (4): 1689–720.

Laudan, Larry (1994). *The Book of Risks*. New York: Wiley.

Laures, Robert Anthony, and Ronald Edward Zupko (1996). *Straws in the Wind: Medieval Urban Environmental Law: The Case of Northern Italy*. Boulder, CO: Westview.

Lawrence, John (1796). *A Philosophical and Practical Treatise on Horses, and on the Moral Duties of Man Towards the Brute Creation*. London: Symonds.

Leahy, Michael, and Dan Cohn-Sherbok (eds) (1996). *The Liberation Debate: Rights at Issue*. New York: Routledge.

Levak, Brian P. (1995). *The Witch Hunt in Early Modern Europe*. 2nd edn. New York: Longman.

Linzey, Andrew (1976). *Animal Rights: A Christian Assessment*. London: SCM Press.

Linzey, Andrew (1996). "For Animal Rights." In M. Leahy and D. Cohn-Sherbok (eds), *The Liberation Debate: Rights at Issue*. New York: Routledge.

Liotard, Kartika, and Steven P. McGiffen (2009). *Poisoned Spring; The EU and Water Privatisation*. London: Pluto Press.

Lipschutz, Ronnie D. (2004). *Global Environmental Politics: Power, Perspectives, and Practice*. Washington, DC: CQ Press.

Lytle, Mark Hamilton (2007). *The Gentle Subversive: Rachel Carson, Silent Spring, and the Rise of the Environmental Movement*. New York: Oxford University Press.

Madders, Kevin J. (1981). "Trail Smelter Arbitration." In Rudolf Bernhardt (ed), *Encyclopedia of Public International Law*. New York: North-Holland Publishing Company: 276–80.

Marotta, Toby (2006). "What Made Stonewall Different?," *Gay & Lesbian Review*, 13 (2): 33–5.

Mauzy, Diane K. (1997). "The Human Rights and 'Asian Values' Debate in Southeast Asia: Trying to Clarify the Key Issues," *Pacific Review*, 10 (2): 210–36.

McKibben, Bill (2006). *The End of Nature*. New York: Random House.

McNeill, J. R. (2000). *Something New Under the Sun: An Environmental History of the Twentieth-Century World*. New York: Norton.

Meijer, Martha (ed) (2001). *Dealing with Human Rights: Asian and Western Views on the Value of Human Rights*. Bloomfield, CT: Kumarian Press.

Merrett, Stephen (1997). *Introduction to the Economics of Water Resources: An International Perspective*. London: University College, London.

Mertus, Julie (2007). "The Rejection of Human Rights Framings: The Case of LGBT Advocacy in the US," *Human Rights Quarterly*, 29 (4): 1036–64.

Meyer, Stephen M. (2007). *The End of the Wild*. Cambridge, MA: MIT Press.

Mihr, Anja, and Hans Peter Schmitz (2007). "Combating Apathy with Education: Developing Strategies for Sustainable Global Human Rights Protection," *Human Rights Quarterly*, 29 (4): 908–49.

Miller, Marian A. L. (1995). *The Third World in Global Environmental Politics*. Boulder, CO: Lynne Reiner.

Mitchell, Ronald B. (2009). *International Politics and the Environment*. Los Angeles: SAGE Publications.

Neier, Aryeh (1997). "Asia's Unacceptable Double Standard," *The Responsive Community*, 7 (3): 22–30.

Oreskes, Naomi, and Erik M. Cowway (2013). "The Collapse of Western Civilization: A View from the Future," *Daedalus*, 142 (1): 40–58

Osiatyński, Wikton (2009). *Human Rights and Their Limits*. New York: Cambridge University Press.

Paarlberg, Robert (2010). *Food Politics: What Everyone Needs to Know*. New York: Oxford University Press.

Paine, Thomas (1792). *The Rights of Man*. London: Symonds.

Parson, Edward A. (2003). *Protecting the Ozone Layer: Science and Strategy*. New York: Oxford University Press.

Piggott, W. J. (1953). *Appeal for the International Animals' Charter*. Published in India.

Potsdam Institute for Climate Impact Research and Climate Analytics (2012). *Turn Down the Heat: Why a 4°C Warmer World Must Be Avoided*. Washington, DC: World Bank.

Price, Richard (1997). *The Genealogy of the Chemical Weapons Taboo*. Ithaca, NY: Cornell University Press.

Primatt, Humphrey (1776). *Dissertation on the Duty of Mercy and the Sin of Cruelty to Brute Animals*. Edinburgh: Constable.

Rawls, John (1972). *A Theory of Justice*. Oxford, UK: Oxford University Press.

Rawls, John (1999). *The Law of Peoples*. Cambridge, MA: Harvard University Press.

Regan, Tom (1983). *The Case for Animal Rights*. Berkeley: University of California Press.

Regan, Tom (2003). *Animal Rights, Human Wrongs: An Introduction to Moral Philosophy*. New York: Rowman & Littlefield.

Regan, Tom (2004). *Empty Cages: Facing the Challenge of Human Rights*. New York: Rowman & Littlefield.

Renteln, Alison Dundes (1990). *International Human Rights: Universalism Versus Relativism*. London: SAGE Publications.

Ross, Susan Deller (1983). *Rights of Women: The Basic ACLU Guide to a Woman's Rights*. 3rd edn. New York: American Civil Liberties Union.

Ryder, Richard D. (1989). *Animal Liberation: Changing Attitudes Toward Specieism*. Oxford, UK: Blackwell.

Salt, Henry (1905). *Animals' Rights: Considered in Relation to Social Progress*. London: Macmillan.

Sands, Philippe (ed) (1994). *Greening International Law*. New York: New Press.

Schlager, Edella, and William Blomquist (2008). *Embracing Watershed Politics*. Boulder: University of Colorado Press.

Shrader-Frechette, Kristin (2000). "Flawed Attacks on Contemporary Human Rights: Laudan, Sunstein, and the Cost-Benefit State," *Human Rights Review*, 7 (1): 92–110.

Shrader-Frechette, Kristin (2007) *Taking Action, Saving Lives: Our Duties to Protect Environmental and Public Health*. New York: Oxford University Press.

Silber, Gregory K., Anbelia S. M. Vanderlaan, Ana Tejedor Arceredillo, Lindy Johnson, Christopher T. Taggart, Moira W. Brown, Shannon Bettridge, and Ricardo Sagarminaga (2012). "The Role of the International Maritime Organization in Reducing Vessel Threat to Whales: Process, Options, Action and Effectiveness," *Marine Policy*, 35 (6): 1221–33.

Singer, Peter (1975). *Animal Liberation*. Wellingborough, UK: Thorsons.

Souder, William (2012). *On a Farther Shore: The Life and Legacy of Rachel Carson*. New York: Crown.

Steinbruner, John D., Paul C. Stern, and Jo L. Husbands (eds) (2012). *Climate and Social Stress: Implications for Security Analysis*. Washington, DC: National Research Council.

Sterba, Jim (2012). *Nature Wars: The Incredible Story of How Wildlife Comebacks Turned Backyards into Battlegrounds*. New York: Crown.

Stone, Christopher D. (1993). *The Gnat Is Older than Man: Global Environment and Human Agenda*. Princeton, NJ: Princeton University Press.

Stone, Richard (2002). "Counting the Cost of London's Killer Smog," *Science*, 298 (December 13): 2106–7.

Strand, Jonathan R., and John P. Tumen (2012). "Foreign Aid and Voting Behavior in an International Organization: The Case of Japan and the International Whaling Commission," *Foreign Policy Analysis*, 8 (4): 409–30.

Sunstein, Cass R. (1995). "Rights and Their Critics," *Notre Dame Law Review*, 70 (4): 727–68.

Sunstein, Cass R. (2002). *Risk and Reason*. New York: Cambridge University Press.

Tahmindjis, Phillip, and Helmut Graupner (eds) (2005). *Sexuality and Human Rights: A Global Overview*. Binghamton, NY: Haworth Press.

Turner, Brian S. (2006). *Vulnerability and Human Rights*. University Park: Pennsylvania State University Press.

Vanita, Ruth (2006). *Love's Rite: Same-Sex Marriage in India and the West*. New York: Palgrave Macmillan.

Wapner, Paul (1996). *Environmental Activism and World Civic Politics*. Albany, NY: State University of New York Press.

Weiss, Edith (ed) (1992). *Environmental Change and International Law: New Challenges and Dimensions*. Tokyo: United Nations University Press.

Weiss, Kenneth R. (2012). "A Move to Help Protect Whales," *Los Angeles Times*, December 28.

Weston, Burns H. (2012). "The Theoretical Foundations of Intergenerational and Ecological Justice: An Overview," *Human Rights Quarterly*, 34 (10): 251–66.

Wilmer, Franke (1993). *The Indigenous Voice in World Politics*. London: SAGE Publications.

Wolfenden, Sir John (1957). *Report of the Departmental Committee on Homosexual Offences and Prostitution*. London: Her Majesty's Stationery Office.

Wolgast, Elizabeth (1987). "Wrong Rights," *Hypatia*, 2 (1): 25–43.

Woodiwiss, Anthony (2003). *Making Human Rights Work Globally*. London: Glasshouse Press.

Yokota, Yozo (1999). "International Justice and the Global Environment," *Journal of International Affairs*, 52 (Spring): 583–98.

Young, Oran R. (ed) (1999). *The Effectiveness of International Environmental Regimes: Causal Connections and Behavioral Mechanisms*. Cambridge, MA: MIT Press.

NOTES

CHAPTER 2: The Philosophical Basis for Human Rights

1 Ezekiel 16:49, Isaiah 1:10, and Jeremiah 23:14 explicitly identify the "sin of Sodom" as inhospitality, though many authorities prefer to sexualize the story to refer exclusively to anal intercourse.

2 The historian J. Boswell, *Same-Sex Unions in Premodern Europe* (1994), has uncovered early church records of male–male unions blessed by Catholic priests. The topic of same-sex marriage is discussed in more detail within Chapter 14.

3 Aquinas was influenced by Al-Farabi and relied on the commentary of Aristotle by the Spanish-born Islamic philosophy scholar, Ibn Rushd, also known as Averroës (1126–1198). However, when Europeans feared the advance of Muslim invaders into France and Spain, cooperation with the Islamic world stopped, and both were embroiled in issues of internal security and warfare. Accordingly, the opportunity for continued ecumenical human rights progress was missed. Political scientist Jack Donnelly (2007:40) disputes the claims made by Mawdudi, pointing out for example that a "right to justice" cannot be logically inferred from the Qur'an's requirement that rulers must establish justice.

4 Although laws requiring school segregation were struck down in 1954 by the Supreme Court ruling in *Brown v. Board of Education* (347US483), statistical evidence demonstrates as much de facto segregation today as in 1954, according to G. Orfield and C. Lee, *Racial Transformation and the Changing Nature of Segregation* (2006). In 1981, federal financial assistance to assist desegregation was abolished. In *Missouri v. Jenkins* (495US33), the Supreme Court allowed the Kansas City school district to stop expensive but ineffectual efforts at desegregation, a precedent that affects other school districts.

CHAPTER 3: The Historical Basis for Human Rights

1 The Second Amendment's statement about the right of citizens to "bear arms," that is, to own such weapons as pistols and assault weapons, is not generally recognized as a human right under international law.

2 At diplomatic conferences, the five countries did authorize Austrian troops to go to Spain in 1820 and French troops to Italy in 1822 in order to stop democratic uprisings. However, Britain supported neither Austria's military intervention in Italy in 1821 nor France's intervention in Spain in 1823. France opted out from 1830. Nevertheless, the Concert did support the independence of Greece in 1830 and Belgium in 1831.

3 There was no organized effort to end serfdom, the practice of requiring peasants to work land owned by feudal lords. When feudalism ended, serfs were emancipated. England did so in the 1550s. France abolished serfdom in 1789, and most of the rest of Europe during the first half of the early nineteenth century. Russia's emancipation of serfs was in 1861. The latest country to abolish serfdom was Bhutan in 1956.

4 Except for matters of race discrimination, the Fourteenth Amendment had very little civil rights applicability until a 1925 case, *Gitlow v. New York* (268US652), in which the Supreme Court for the first time ruled that the Fourteenth Amendment required state governments to abide by a provision in the Bill of Rights,

specifically the First Amendment guarantee of freedom of speech. Subsequently, other provisions of the Bill of Rights have been ruled in various court cases to apply to the states.

5   The former Ottoman territories became Class "A" mandates: Britain governed Iraq and Palestine; France controlled Syria, which included the future independent Lebanon. Class "B" mandates were former German colonies in Africa: Ruanda-Urundi (Belgium); Tanganyika (Britain); Cameroon and Togoland were split into British and French administrations. Most Class "C" mandates were in the Pacific: New Guinea and Nauru were assigned to Britain but governed by Australia; German Samoa was assigned to Britain but governed by New Zealand; and Japan had the mandate over Micronesia, the Northern Marianas, and Palau. Namibia, a Class "C" mandate, was assigned to South Africa.

6   According to the Treaty of Versailles, the highly industrialized Saar was governed by the League of Nations for 15 years, during which its coalfields were ceded to France. When a plebiscite was held in 1935, more than 90 percent of the population voted to accept German sovereignty, whereupon the Jewish population applied for refugee status.

7   The Rhineland, a territory along the Rhine River between France and Germany, was occupied by Allied forces at the end of the war. Demilitarized under the terms of the Treaty of Versailles to provide a buffer between the two countries, the area was divided into three occupation zones. Forces were to be withdrawn at five-year intervals until 1935. But, as a good-will gesture to the German government, they all left in 1930. In 1936, German troops rode in on bicycles to take control during a weekend. By Monday, when British and French officials might have launched a response to the blatant violation of the treaty, the occupation was a fait accompli.

8   South Africa refused to allow the UN to take over monitoring of its South West Africa mandate until 1988. Namibia, the former South West Africa, became independent after a UN-organized transition in 1990.

CHAPTER 4: The Contemporary Basis for Human Rights

1   The term "genocide" has been applied to the 1.5 million Armenians killed by the Turks during 1915–1917, the seven million who died from forced famines in the Soviet Union from 1932–1933, Japan's massacre of 300,000 Chinese in Nanking during 1937–1938, the 1.5 million Cambodians who died from disease, execution, exhaustion, and starvation from 1975–1978, the one million Tutsis slaughtered by the Hutus of Rwanda in 1994, and to the death of tens of millions Native Americans from disease and massacres during the expansion into the New World. Indeed, Hitler made reference to the Armenian and American exterminations as precedents for his own ethnic cleansing. However, several observers insist that there has been only one Holocaust, the Jewish Holocaust by the Nazis, whereas the rest are either *genocides* (intentional and systematic exterminations of entire ethnic, linguistic, or religious groups) or the more comprehensive *democides* (mass murders, including genocides, for any other reason).

2   Charges were initially brought against Admiral Karl Dönitz (1891–1980) for waging unrestricted submarine war in violation of the London Naval Agreement of 1930. However, when Fleet Admiral Chester Nimitz (1885–1966) admitted that he authorized similar offences, charges were dropped. Dönitz was instead convicted of waging aggressive war, that is, of committing a crime against peace, and of the war crime of sinking neutral ships without warning.

3   During America's intervention in the Vietnamese Civil War, the most famous court martial convened to try soldiers for murdering innocent civilian Vietnamese involved Lieutenant William Calley, Jr (1943–), who in 1971 received a life sentence for directing the massacre in 1968 of at least twenty-two persons at My Lai, although the conviction was overturned in 1974 by a civilian court, citing pretrial publicity prejudicial to a fair trial. In the same year, he was pardoned by President Richard Nixon (1913–1994) and paroled. Whereas at least 36 American soldiers were convicted and disciplined for human rights violations in Vietnam, 18 American soldiers had been found guilty of human rights violations in Afghanistan and Iraq by the end of 2006 out of 64 charged, including 10 officers.

4   See www.polfilms.com.

CHAPTER 5: Civil and Political Rights and Crimes Against Humanity

1 See Simmons (2009), whose extensive study contradicts previous research by Keith (1999).
2 The East Timor and Guatemala bodies are described below. Haïti's National Truth and Justice Commission investigated human rights abuses from 1991–1994, when the democratically elected government of Jean-Bertrand Aristide (1953–) was overthrown by a military coup that was reportedly financed by the CIA. Aristide was restored to power in 2001 but deposed by another military coup in 2004. The Truth and Reconciliation Commission of Sierra Leone, organized with assistance from the Office of the UN Commissioner for Human Rights, investigated war crimes committed in a civil war from 1991–2002 in which there were some 75,000 deaths, 20,000 victims of mutilation, and 2 million displaced; an estimated 5,400 children were forced into combat, or were victims of forced labor or sexual slavery, and many women were raped.
3 Another nongovernmental truth and reconciliation commission was set up within Greensboro, North Carolina, in 2004. Although remembered as the Southern city where some 400 students took turns sitting at a lunch counter until it was desegregated in 1960, the reason for the commission was a massacre in 1979, when members of the American Nazi Party and the Ku Klux Klan opened fire on a biracial "Death to the Klan" demonstration in which police were allowed to go off duty at a prearranged time before the shooting. When the carnage stopped, at least 4 were dead and 10 were wounded. All-white juries acquitted six defendants, a widow won a civil damage suit, but the incident was quickly suppressed. Unlike official truth commissions, the impetus for nongovernmental efforts is usually not a shift in political power. The sponsors are private citizens operating without public funds seeking to discredit those who engaged in misdeeds outside the judicial system.
4 See Smolensky (2009).

CHAPTER 6: Economic, Social, and Cultural Rights

1 Among current members of FLA are Adidas-Salomon, Asics, Eddie Bauer, GEAR for Sports, Gildan Activewear, Liz Claiborne, New Era Cap, Nordstrom, Nike, Outdoor Cap, Patagonia, Phillips-Van Heusen, Puma, Reebok, Top of the World, and Zephyr Graf-X.

CHAPTER 7: Crimes Against Peace and War Crimes

1 However, millions of Armenians died during that Turkish war of independence. Pasha was renamed Atatürk by the Turkish parliament in 1934.
2 A list of 269 specific war crimes, breaking each of the four major categories into subcategories, is found in Haas (2009). Whereas six crimes were identified under the rubric "aggression," the study found 36 types of crimes regarding the military conduct of war, 175 violations of the rights of prisoners of war, and 52 deviations from the rules governing military occupations.
3 The situations occasioning General Assembly actions are as follows: the Anglo–French–Israeli invasion of Suez (1956), Hungary (1956), the Middle East (1958, 1967), Congo (1960), Afghanistan (1980), Palestine (1980, 1983), Namibia (1981), and Israeli actions in occupied East Jerusalem and the rest of the occupied Palestinian Territory (1982, 1997, 1999, 2000, 2001, 2002). In 2003, during a General Assembly debate, several countries called upon the American-led invasion of Iraq to cease, but no vote was taken.
4 The UN sent a military force to the Ivory Coast, which was embroiled in civil war after an election in 2011. South Sudan, which voted to secede from Sudan, was under attack from the latter.

CHAPTER 8: Quantitative and Theoretical Dimensions

1 Amnesty International's judgment is based on the following: (1) The United States is the largest exporter of military weapons. (2) Recipients of American military weapons, often through military aid, are countries that engage in gross human rights abuses (genocide, torture, etc.). (3) American allies in the Third World have engaged in serious human rights abuse over the years (Argentina, Colombia, Indonesia, Liberia, etc.). (4) More recently, the United States has refused to abide by the Geneva Conventions, instead engaging in such practices as indefinite detention and torture.

2 See Neubauer (1967).

3 A tabulation of more than one hundred statistical studies can be found in M. Haas (2007).

CHAPTER 9: United Nations Charter-Based Organizations

1 The Territory of Hawai'i was on the agenda of the General Assembly's Committee on Non-Self-Governing Territories up to 1959, when voters chose to accept American statehood. The Kingdom of Hawai'i was annexed by the United States in 1898 without a plebiscite; President Grover Cleveland (1837–1908) stated that annexation was contrary to international law, and a return to the monarchy was the platform of the winning party in Hawai'i's first post-annexation election in 1900, the closest equivalent to a plebiscite. But that party was defeated in 1902 and went out of existence.

2 The Special Committee is still active and now focuses attention on American Samoa, Anguilla, Bermuda, British Virgin Islands, Cayman Islands, the Falkland or Malvinas Islands, Gibraltar, Guam, Montserrat, New Caledonia, Pitcairn, St Helena, Tokelau, the Turks and Caicos Islands, United States Virgin Islands, and Western Sahara. In 2007, Puerto Rico asked the UN to monitor its status, but in 2012 the territory voted in favor of statehood.

3 Among nongovernmental organizations that work with UNHCR, the most prominent are the International Committee of the Red Cross, the International Federation of Red Cross and Red Crescent Societies, and the International Organization for Migration.

4 Other UN Specialized Agencies include the International Civil Aviation Organization, International Maritime Organization, International Telecommunications Union, UN Environmental Fund, UN Population Fund, Universal Postal Union, World Intellectual Property Organization, and the World Meteorological Organization.

5 The Bantustan enclave of Lesotho also withdrew from 1971–1980 because a complaint was lodged over unfair treatment of a trade union.

6 The eight are Britain, Canada, France, Germany, Italy, Japan, Russia, and the United States.

7 The treaties are as follows: Convention Against Illicit Traffic in Narcotic Drugs and Psychotropic Substances, Single Convention on Narcotic Drugs, and the Convention on Psychotropic Substances.

CHAPTER 10: Treaty-Based Global International Organizations

1 The Iraq Special Tribunal was set up by the provisional Iraqi National Congress to try Saddam Hussein (1937–2006) and 12 other members of the Ba'ath Party. Iran and Kuwait sought in vain to bring Iraqi war crimes to the attention of the same court. In 2006, Saddam Hussein was found guilty, sentenced to death, and executed. Although Amnesty International and Human Rights Watch faulted the proceedings for failing to observe established international procedures, and human rights groups in Europe and elsewhere objected to the death penalty sentence, many international law experts believe that the verdict was appropriate. In 2005, the court was retitled the Supreme Iraq Criminal Court.

▍ CHAPTER 11: American Approaches to International Human Rights

1 Federalism is one reason why the United States has failed to ratify international human rights treaties. Members of the Senate, the body that ratifies treaties, come from the 50 states. From the founding of the United States, each state has jealously guarded its own prerogatives from encroachment by the national government. For example, the constitutional right to free speech was first applied only to actions of the national government; states were not covered until the Supreme Court ruling in *Gitlow v. New York* (268US652) in 1925. Thus, states often view obligations under international law as further encroachments on their authority. Senators often attach reservations to the treaties, thereby watering down the obligations stated in the text. Some states permit the death penalty and thus their senators will not subscribe to the Optional Protocol of the International Covenant on Civil and Political Rights that bans the death penalty and the International Convention on the Rights of the Child because of restrictions on abortion for minors in various states. An excellent example of the American reluctance to ratify human rights treaties is the International Convention on the Prevention and Punishment of the Crime of Genocide, which was adopted in 1948 and went into force without American ratification in 1951. On his first day in the Senate in 1957, Senator William Proxmire (1915–2005) of Wisconsin spoke to urge his colleagues to ratify the Genocide Convention. Indeed, he spoke on the subject every single day when the Senate was in session for 29 years until 1986, when his colleagues finally gave in. Similarly, the Torture Convention was ratified in 1994 only after a flurry of domestic court cases on the subject. At the same time, the United States is not necessarily violating international law by not ratifying human rights treaties. Washington has thus stayed outside much of the recent developments in international human rights law.
2 In 1946, Congress passed the Federal Tort Claims Act to provide remedies to American citizens about misconduct by American government officials but specifically exempted claims of aliens from the scope of the law.
3 Another case, *Kar v. Rumsfeld*, a lawsuit regarding the arbitrary detention and later torture of an American filmmaker by the US military while visiting Iraq, was mentioned in the first edition of the present volume. The case, which did not involve ATCA, was also dismissed.
4 The Peterson Institute for International Economics has detailed chronologies of all American sanctions on its website (www.piie.com/publications/papers/sanctions).
5 See Haas (2009: Chapter 4).
6 See Haas (2009: Chapter 5).

▍ CHAPTER 12: European Approaches to International Human Rights

1 When Marshall Plan aid ended by 1952, OEEC languished until 1961, when a new body, the Organization for Economic Co-operation and Development (OECD), was established with membership from the major industrial countries. There are now 34 members of OECD, including several non-European countries – Australia, Canada, Chile, Israel, Japan, New Zealand, South Korea, Turkey, and the United States. OECD produces many macroeconomic analyses and assists developing countries.
2 EFTA currently has four members. The original members, Norway and Switzerland, were reluctant to have their economies subjected to regulations from a supranational entity. Two members joined later – Iceland in 1970 and Liechtenstein in 1991. When EFTA began, members signed bilateral agreements with EU countries. In 1992, EFTA and EU sponsored the formation of the European Economic Area (EEA) so that EFTA members could enjoy the benefits of EU membership without joining. EEA currently has 28 members; Switzerland, a member of EFTA, opted out of EEA, but signed bilateral agreements with EU countries. The EEA mandate is for the free movement of goods, persons, services, and capital. The EFTA Surveillance Authority and the EFTA Court parallel the work of the EU's European Commission and European Court of Justice, respectively. They act in accordance with the Agreement Between the EFTA States on the Establishment of a Surveillance Authority and a Court of Justice of 1992. The only court action relating to human rights, filed in 1994, concerned the issue of legal aid; the court dismissed the case for lack of jurisdiction. The founding Convention Establishing the European Free Trade Association, of 1960, has no provision

relating to human rights. The annex to the convention, adopted in 2001, provides for the free movement of persons from one member country to another, thereby generalizing an earlier protocol between Lichtenstein and Switzerland on the subject.

3   In 1954, when Germany and Italy ratified the Brussels treaty, the organization was renamed the **Western European Union** (WEU), with a headquarters in London. In 1960, WEU transferred its cultural and economic activities to the Council of Europe. In 1984, WEU was reactivated; some saw the organization as a possible military arm of the European Union, but the decision to do so was not finalized until 1991. In 1992, the WEU agreed in principle to form humanitarian, rescue, peacekeeping, and peacemaking missions, including combat forces in crisis management. In 1993 the headquarters moved to Brussels in preparation for eventual absorption into EU. In 1996, the Council of the European Union asked WEU to assist the EU's humanitarian operations involving displaced persons and refugees and displaced persons in the Great Lakes region in Africa. WEU–EU cooperation resulted in evacuation operations, supported African peacekeeping efforts, and engaged in mine clearance. In 1999, NATO, as well as WEU Secretary-General Javier Solana, was named EU Secretary-General, thereby smoothing the way for the European Union to incorporate most of WEU's remaining military and nonmilitary functions in 2000.

4   Also during 1996, the United States sought to organize countries in the Balkan region within the Southeast European Cooperative Initiative by providing a vehicle for technical assistance. The Initiative is not related to other Southeast European or Balkan organizations.

5   Members are Austria, Canada, Council of Europe, Council of Europe Development Bank, Czech Republic, Denmark, European Bank for Reconstruction and Development, European Investment Bank, European Union, Finland, France, Germany, Greece, Hungary, International Organization for Migration, Ireland, Italy, Latvia, Macedonia, Moldova, North Atlantic Treaty Organization, Norway, Organization for Economic Co-operation and Development, Organization for Security and Co-operation in Europe, Poland, Romania, South East European Co-operative Initiative, Spain, Sweden, Switzerland, Turkey, United Kingdom, United Nations, UN Economic Commission for Europe, UN Development Program, the United States, and the World Bank.

CHAPTER 13: Developing Country Approaches to International Human Rights

1   Some developed countries are located within Third World regions – namely, Australia, Israel, Japan, New Zealand, and South Korea.

2   The initial members were Argentina, Bolivia, Brazil, Chile, Colombia, Costa Rica, Cuba, Dominican Republic, Ecuador, El Salvador, Guatemala, Haïti, Honduras, México, Nicaragua, Panamá, Paraguay, Perú, United States, Uruguay, and Venezuela. Later members to join are Barbados, Trinidad and Tobago (1967), Jamaica (1969), Grenada (1975), Suriname (1977), Dominica, St Lucia (1979), Antigua and Barbuda, St Vincent and the Grenadines (1981), Bahamas (1982), St Kitts and Nevis (1984), Canada (1990), Belize, Guyana (1991). Those joining in 2013 are Aruba, Bonaire, Curaçao, Saba, Sint Eustatius, and Sint Maarten.

3   The initial members were Egypt, Iraq, Lebanon, Jordan (Transjordan in 1945), Saudi Arabia, Syria, and Yemen. Newer members joined in the following years: Algeria (1962), Bahrain (1971), Comoros (1993), Djibouti (1977), Kuwait (1961), Libya (1953), Mauritania (1973), Morocco (1958), Oman (1971), Palestine (1974), Qatar (1971), Somalia (1974), South Yemen (1967–1990), Sudan (1956), Tunisia (1958), and United Arab Emirates (1971).

4   Surviving SEAMCED organizations are identified in Haas (1989a: Ch 6; 2013).

5   See Haas (1989a; 2013).

6   Australia, Brunei, Canada, Chile, China, Hong Kong, Indonesia, Japan, Malaysia, México, New Zealand, Papua New Guinea, Perú, Philippines, Russia, Singapore, South Korea, Taiwan, Thailand, United States, and Vietnam.

7   See Haas (1989b; 2013). In 1988, the South Pacific Organizations Coordinating Committee was formed to coordinate about a dozen of the more important bodies. In 1999, the name was changed to the Council of Regional Organizations in the Pacific.

8   The island members are *American Samoa*, Cook Islands, Federated States of Micronesia, Fiji, *French Polynesia*, *Guam*, Kiribati, Marshall Islands, Nauru, *New Caledonia*, Niue, *Northern Mariana Islands*, Palau, Papua New Guinea, *Pitcairn*, Samoa, Solomon Islands, *Tokelau*, Tonga, Tuvalu, Vanuatu, and *Wallis and Futuna*. Those in italics are not independent.

9   Members consist of the 14 nonitalicized island states enumerated in the previous footnote plus Australia and New Zealand.

10 Algeria, Burkina Faso, Burundi, Comoros, Congo, Gabon, Gambia, Ghana, the Ivory Coast, Kenya, Libya, Lesotho, Mali, Malawi, Mozambique, Mauritania, Mauritius, Nigeria, Niger, Rwanda, South Africa, Sénégal, Tanzania, Togo, Tunisia, and Uganda.

11 Current members are listed in the text below. Mauritania withdrew in 2000.

12 Benin (2002), Cape Verde (2009), Comoros (2007), Djibouti (2000), Egypt (2001), Gambia (2000), Ghana (2005), Guinea (2007), Guinea-Bissau (2004), the Ivory Coast (2004), Kenya (2008), Liberia (2004), Morocco (2001), Nigeria (2001), Sénégal (2000), Sierra Leone (2005), São Tomé and Príncipe (2008), Somalia (2001), Togo (2002), Tunisia (2001). Mauritania joined in 2008 but withdrew in 2012.

13 For more information about OECD, see Chapter 12, note 1. Another relevant organization is the (formerly British) Commonwealth of Nations.

CHAPTER 14: New Dimensions and Challenges

1   See Boswell, *Same-Sex Unions in Premodern Europe* (1994) for more details. Some criticisms of his scholarship have emerged in recent years.

2   Ironically, the decision was a dramatic reversal of the 1986 court ruling in *Bowers v. Hardwick* (478US186), in which the pivotal opinion by Justice O'Connor had argued that states should enforce their own laws on the subject without federal interference. Much had happened in the intervening 17 years to change her mind.

3   In the first edition of *International Human Rights: A Comprehensive Introduction*, Table 14.1 had a section listing countries that no longer criminalize adult consensual sex. By the time of the second edition, such a table would have listed almost every country in the world except for Muslim-majority states.

4   The states are almost identically those with voting majorities for recent Democratic presidential candidates.

5   Bilateral treaties between Britain (on behalf of Canada) and the United States in 1891 and 1892 limited fur seal catches in the Bering Sea.

INDEX